# Digital Transformation and Internationalization Strategies in Organizations

Orkun Yildiz
*Izmir Democracy University, Turkey*

IGI Global
PUBLISHER of TIMELY KNOWLEDGE

A volume in the Advances in Business Strategy and Competitive Advantage (ABSCA) Book Series

Published in the United States of America by
IGI Global
Business Science Reference (an imprint of IGI Global)
701 E. Chocolate Avenue
Hershey PA, USA 17033
Tel: 717-533-8845
Fax: 717-533-8661
E-mail: cust@igi-global.com
Web site: http://www.igi-global.com



Library of Congress Cataloging-in-Publication Data

Names: Yildiz, Orkun, DATE- editor.
Title: Digital transformation and internationalization strategies in organizations / Orkun Yildiz, editor.
Description: Hershey, PA : Information Science Reference, 2021. | Includes bibliographical references and index. | Summary: "This book covers a wide range of issues and topics related to digital transformation and internationalization strategies on institutional governance such as employment, quality management, system design and control, education and language policies, business and law models for the organizations"-- Provided by publisher.
Identifiers: LCCN 2021017725 (print) | LCCN 2021017726 (ebook) | ISBN 9781799881698 (hardcover) | ISBN 9781799881704 (paperback) | ISBN 9781799881711 (ebook)
Subjects: LCSH: Organizational learning. | Digital media. | Globalization.
Classification: LCC HD58.82 .D535 2021 (print) | LCC HD58.82 (ebook) | DDC 658.05--dc23
LC record available at https://lccn.loc.gov/2021017725
LC ebook record available at https://lccn.loc.gov/2021017726

This book is published in the IGI Global book series Advances in Business Strategy and Competitive Advantage (ABSCA) (ISSN: 2327-3429; eISSN: 2327-3437)

British Cataloguing in Publication Data
A Cataloguing in Publication record for this book is available from the British Library.



For electronic access to this publication, please contact: eresources@igi-global.com.

# Advances in Business Strategy and Competitive Advantage (ABSCA) Book Series

Patricia Ordóñez de Pablos
Universidad de Oviedo, Spain

ISSN:2327-3429
EISSN:2327-3437

## Mission

Business entities are constantly seeking new ways through which to gain advantage over their competitors and strengthen their position within the business environment. With competition at an all-time high due to technological advancements allowing for competition on a global scale, firms continue to seek new ways through which to improve and strengthen their business processes, procedures, and profitability.

The **Advances in Business Strategy and Competitive Advantage (ABSCA) Book Series** is a timely series responding to the high demand for state-of-the-art research on how business strategies are created, implemented and re-designed to meet the demands of globalized competitive markets. With a focus on local and global challenges, business opportunities and the needs of society, the **ABSCA** encourages scientific discourse on doing business and managing information technologies for the creation of sustainable competitive advantage.

## Coverage

- Balanced Scorecard
- Economies of Scale
- Entrepreneurship & Innovation
- Differentiation Strategy
- Tacit Knowledge
- Competitive Strategy
- Ethics and Business Strategy
- Co-operative Strategies
- Strategic Management
- Strategic Alliances

IGI Global is currently accepting manuscripts for publication within this series. To submit a proposal for a volume in this series, please contact our Acquisition Editors at Acquisitions@igi-global.com or visit: http://www.igi-global.com/publish/.

The Advances in Business Strategy and Competitive Advantage (ABSCA) Book Series (ISSN 2327-3429) is published by IGI Global, 701 E. Chocolate Avenue, Hershey, PA 17033-1240, USA, www.igi-global.com. This series is composed of titles available for purchase individually; each title is edited to be contextually exclusive from any other title within the series. For pricing and ordering information please visit http://www.igi-global.com/book-series/advances-business-strategy-competitive-advantage/73672. Postmaster: Send all address changes to above address. 

## Titles in this Series

***For a list of additional titles in this series, please visit: http://www.igi-global.com/book-series/advances-business-strategy-competitive-advantage/73672***

***Analyzing the Relationship Between Corporate Governance, CSR, and Sustainability***
Muddassar Sarfraz (Hohai University, China) and Syed Ghulam Meran Shah (Southwestern University of Finance & Economics, China)
Business Science Reference • © 2022 • 315pp • H/C (ISBN: 9781799842347) • US $215.00

***Leadership and Followership in an Organizational Change Context***
Sajjad Nawaz Khan (Iqra University, Pakistan)
Business Science Reference • © 2022 • 361pp • H/C (ISBN: 9781799828075) • US $225.00

***Emerging Ecosystem-Centric Business Models for Sustainable Value Creation***
Xenia Ziouvelou (National Centre for Scientific Research "Demokritos", Greece & University of Southampton, UK) and Frank McGroarty (University of Southampton, UK)
Business Science Reference • © 2022 • 237pp • H/C (ISBN: 9781799848431) • US $195.00

***Impact of Disruptive Technologies on the Sharing Economy***
Ford Lumban Gaol (Bina Nusantara University, Jakarta, Indonesia) Natalia Filimonova (Vladimir State University, Russia) and Chandan Acharya (College of Staten Island, City University of New York, USA)
Business Science Reference • © 2021 • 269pp • H/C (ISBN: 9781799803614) • US $245.00

***Global Corporate Social Responsibility Initiatives for Reluctant Businesses***
Syed Abdul Rehman Khan (School of Management and Engineering, Xuzhou University of Technology, Xuzhou, China & Department of Business Administration, ILMA University, Karachi, Pakistan & Beijing Key Laboratory of Urban Spatial Engineering, Beijing, China) Zhang Yu (Chang'an University, China) Mirela Panait (Petroleum-Gas University of Ploiesti, Romania & Institute of National Economy, Bucharest, Romania) Laeeq Razzak Janjua (Poznan University of Economics and Business, Poland) and Adeel Shah (Institute of Business Management, Pakistan)
Business Science Reference • © 2021 • 280pp • H/C (ISBN: 9781799839880) • US $195.00

***Impacts and Implications for the Sports Industry in the Post-COVID-19 Era***
Armand Faganel (University of Primorska, Slovenia) Igor Rižnar (University of Primorska, Slovenia) and Arne Baruca (Texas A&M University San Antonio, USA)
Business Science Reference • © 2021 • 304pp • H/C (ISBN: 9781799867807) • US $215.00

***Computational Thinking for Problem Solving and Managerial Mindset Training***
Luisa Dall'Acqua (University of Bologna, Italy & LS TCO, Italy)
Business Science Reference • © 2021 • 293pp • H/C (ISBN: 9781799871262) • US $225.00

IGI Global
PUBLISHER of TIMELY KNOWLEDGE

701 East Chocolate Avenue, Hershey, PA 17033, USA
Tel: 717-533-8845 x100 • Fax: 717-533-8661
E-Mail: cust@igi-global.com • www.igi-global.com

# Editorial Advisory Board

# Table of Contents

# Detailed Table of Contents



There has been a strong relationship between digitalism and the future of jobs. Reports by OECD and WEF examined the jobs in the coming decades, and the findings show that there is a completely new order in the professions that we are not familiar with. In addition, how the impacts of artificial intelligence (AI), machine learning, data science, and robotics have affected labour, the market is analyzed. The findings in the reports clearly would affect the careers of the next generations. With the post-pandemic developments and the rapid advancement of technology in many areas worldwide, digitalization has gained significant momentum. This situation manifested itself in professions and workforce. However, it is obvious that in the coming years, with digitalization, many occupational groups and accordingly, differences in skills will be seen. While some occupational groups disappear completely, it is seen that some new occupational groups will emerge and, some will transform.



As culturally responsive, social-emotional learning (SEL) competencies continue being essential skills in a 21st century workforce, both university and industry will continue placing greater focus on effective training for students and employees to strengthen workforce readiness. The following chapter introduces one example of how Polish Fulbright scholars prepared for a U.S. assignment through a digital training program, taken before participants departed their home country, as a way to support post arrival integration, safety, and success in the U.S. Compared to the control group, research findings from this phenomenological research study indicated that the four-week training program supported increases in self-awareness and self-management skills, social skills and cultural awareness, English communication skills, academic and professional readiness skills, and responsible decision-making skills in the treatment group. This study contributes one new strategy to strengthen internationalization efforts, global leadership skills, and cross-cultural relations.

poverty and hunger. In this chapter, the authors focus on introducing relevant technology-enabled services that will ensure economic sustainability, enhance food security through data-driven decision making by various stakeholders like farmers,agri-business and agri-tech start-ups, farmpreneurs, government, agronomists, and IT suppliers. The analyzed information will be used as a vantage by farmers to select precision farming practices to aid productivity to empower personnel to provide timely assistance and industries to implement real-time monitoring using sensors and devices. The chapter will help formulate concepts, methods, practices, benefits, and introducing several case scenarios to effectively propagate the service mode of farming that will imbibe pay-as-you go model ensuring cost optimization and operational ease.

**Chapter 6**
Cloud Computing Service Provider Business Model Success Characteristics .................................. 124
*Ignitia Motjolopane, North West University, South Africa*
*Tshinakaho Relebogile Seaba, Tshwane University of Technology, South Africa*

In a digital arena, information technology services provision is shifting to a cloud computing ecosystem. Cloud computing is an enabler for digital transformation with cloud computing service providers central to the digital transformation of both companies and higher education. As cloud computing service providers play the role of an 'architect' for companies as supply chain is digitised and in supporting higher education institutions striving to deliver user-focused services in the face of increasing competition, an understanding of successful characteristics of cloud computing service provider business models is of main interest for providers and may also be of value for companies and higher education institutions when selecting cloud computing service providers. Despite the importance of cloud computing service providers' business models, information systems literature has provided limited analysis on the characteristics of successful business models. As such, the chapter aims to contribute to the emerging research on characteristics of successful business models.

**Section 3**
**Digitalization and Internationalization Policies**

**Chapter 7**
Inequalities in Access to and Outcomes of Higher Education in Africa ........................................... 150
*Roy Alexander Carr-Hill, Institute of Education, University College London, UK*

There have been very few studies of the socio-economic background and outcomes for students in Africa because of the lack of data. This chapter draws on an institute which has information about their parental background and subsequent careers collected from surveys. In terms of access, the combination of parents not having more than primary education, renting and not owning land identified less than 1% of students whilst the percentage of entrants reporting that their parents had a post-secondary qualification is considerably higher (around 57%) than the norm at the time the parents would have been studying (around 7%). These students were upper middle class. In terms of outcomes, both current students and alumni say that the curriculum only partly fits their employment needs, but 85% of alumni would recommend AIMS to other students. In general, employers are satisfied with AIMS interns, but the percentage of AIMS graduates who are unemployed has risen from 2% in 2011 to 29% in 2016. Finally, rather than contributing to Africa, over one-third of graduates since 2012 are in the West.

student application process is discussed. This chapter involves different application methods used in universities and some enhanced processes. This chapter is to be a guide for effectively conducting the process of international student applications in universities using information technologies and how to perform integration with educational practices.



This chapter addresses the internationalization process from the standpoint of international accreditations. More precisely, it explores whether in Slovenia their implementation is affected primarily by globalization or regionalization of (quality assurance in) higher education. Initially, it discusses globalization and regionalization from the standpoint of internationalization and Europeanization of higher education. Then, it overviews the main international (professional) accreditors, which are relevant for Slovenian higher education (institutions). In the continuation, it outlines the internationalization of Slovenian quality assurance system at the national level, whilst afterwards, it concentrates in more detail on the analysis of institutional (internationalization) strategies and official websites of Slovenian higher education institutions with respect to international accreditations. In conclusion, it highlights that having more international accreditations does not necessarily mean more internationalization of (Slovenian) higher education.



The internationalisation of higher education has become increasingly important for many higher education institutions (HEIs) globally. To recruit national and international students, HEIs must invest in effective digital marketing and recruitment strategies. This study investigated the development of a strategic university of choice model that can assist universities in the recruitment of international students. A survey was completed by 306 international students studying at a South African university. The factors identified in this study included academic programme and quality, visa requirements, country/city attractiveness, lectures in English, costs, student life, safety and security, university location, university reputation, and assistance from the international office. The strategic university of choice model could assist university marketing personnel to develop a focused, targeted, and cost-effective digital marketing and recruitment strategy to recruit international students.

# Preface

Thanks to globalization, access to internet connectivity and other information communication technologies developments has become easier. Thus, digitalization has gained increased significance in governments and private sector services in the last decades. Furthermore, digital services have been in steady demand as a result of the increasing population.

Due to the rapidly increasing demand for digital services, there has been a drastic change in the business and service fundamental processes and models in many different sectors. Hence, many institutions have been trying to diversify their service provisions to increase their sales and market share. Moreover, each department's organizational mission and vision statements and strategic plans depend on this competitive vision of digitalization. Digital transformation is considered a fundamental tool for many institutions to achieve their goals. However, these institutions could realize digital transformation successfully if their organizations have sufficient business process management skills and organizational maturity level. On the other hand, digital transformation is not adequate for being a global market player for the institutions. Because these institutions could have the potential to meet standards and sell their products and services worldwide if they effective strategic design and management systems. Consequently, companies and governmental authorities may need to track digital developments in real life and seize cooperation opportunities with other institutions since concepts such as competitiveness, cooperation, and internationalization seem to be highly intertwined. As such, this edited book aims to include examples of scholarly work that focus on digital transformation and internationalization perspectives about the system and management of organizations. For instance, higher education institutions may have a high reputation and international success due to highly qualified education services, research-based activities, university-industry collaboration-based activities, and internationalization strategies. Furthermore, after the outbreak of the COVID-19 pandemic, it has become nearly impossible to carry out all these activities face to face. In other words, it has become compulsory for institutions to use digitalization to maintain or improve their success. If organizations cannot complete their digital transformation processes, millions of stakeholders may be deprived of business, service, research activities and institutional contributions to the economy and society may not be provided. Consequently, digital transformation processes have increased enormously in all sectors particularly in the pandemic process. This edited book targets at covering a wide range of issues and topics, including but not limited to digital transformation and internationalization strategies on institutional governance such as employment, quality management, system design/control, education and language policies, business, and legal issues in organizations.

This edited book aims to present an overview of digital transformation and internationalization in several domains ranging from education to farming, from commerce to governance in different geographical contexts. The book intends to shed light on both theory and practice in various fields. Hence, considering the scope and variety of the issues dealt with in this edited book, I believe that the book has excellent potential for providing practical implications and guidance to policymakers, decision-makers, practising managers in business, industry, government, and academics, graduate and undergraduate students focusing on ICTs in any given domain. The book incorporates various business process management, information and communication technologies adoption perspectives. It draws on a wide range of scholarly disciplines, such as agriculture, cognitive psychology, communication, computer science, decision sciences, education, management information systems, marketing, operations management, social psychology, strategic management, to name a few. To be more specific, the book aims to address issues that include as seen below:

- How can digital transformation affect future jobs?
- How can different digital marketing concepts and strategies be adopted by major global companies?
- How can the digital transformation process for electronic document management systems be managed?
- How can e-learning systems influence and improve student perceptions and learning?
- How can industry 4.0 affect a sustainable agriculture ecosystem?
- How can cloud computing services affect business model success characteristics?
- What are the factors that may impact the inequalities in access to and outcomes of higher education in Africa?
- What are internationalization and language policies for higher educations?
- What are internationalization quality assurance and accreditation systems?

The book is a cooperation between the editor, authors, and reviewers. Although the book mainly features empirical studies investigating digital transformation and internationalization in a given domain, it also includes a few theoretical accounts that provide detailed information and insights about digital transformation and internationalization. The contributors to this edited book can be characterized as a blend of scholarly insight and practical experience. Each contributor has contributed to this edited book based on their research efforts and practices in their respective fields and contexts.

The book contains three sections and 12 chapters revealing experiences and research practices of authors in Albania, Czechia, Germany, India, Nigeria, Qatar, Slovenia, the Republic of South Africa, the Republic of Turkey, the United Kingdom, and the United States of America. A brief description of each section and chapter has been provided as follows.

## Chapter 1: Digitalism and Jobs of the Future

In this chapter, Dr. Gamze Sart and Dr. Orkun Yildiz presented a new approach to the relationship between digitalism and the future of jobs. Dr. Sart and Dr. Yildiz reviewed the reports such as OECD and WEF that examined the jobs in the coming decades. The detailed information presented in this chapter revealed the effects of digitalism on the current jobs in the different fields. In addition, how Artificial Intelligence, Machine Learning, Data Science, and Robotics have affected the labour market is analyzed. Moreover, the chapter provided the report results for the researchers who aim to investigate the relationship between jobs and digitalism, which could affect the careers of the next generations.

## Chapter 2: Bridging Academic and Industry Skills via Digital Collaboration – Training for International Assignment

In this chapter, Dr. Madden-Dent describes a research study that examined how culturally responsive social-emotional competency development influenced international relocation and integration experiences for Polish Fulbright Scholars preparing to travel to the United States. This chapter highlights a partnership between universities and industry to provide digital professional development through early, evidence-based training that increases successful post-arrival adjustment into new societal and organizational cultures. Moreover, the chapter shares common challenges associated with unsuccessful integration preparation. Information in this chapter reveals the outcomes of the study and how effective hybrid professional development can better prepare global citizens to work, study, and live abroad safely and more effectively.

## Chapter 3: The Role of Digital Marketing in Achieving Sustainable Competitive Advantage

In this chapter, Ms. Denga, Dr. Vajjhala, and Dr. Rakshit presented the role of digital marketing in assisting companies to achieve sustainable competitive advantage. The outbreak of the Covid-19 pandemic has put an end to companies' sales and business growth predictions, and digital marketing is no exception. Ms. Denga, Dr. Vajjhala, and Dr. Rakshit focus on understanding digital marketing concepts and how firms can achieve a competitive edge using various examples. This chapter reviewed the different digital marketing concepts and strategies adopted by major global companies.

## Chapter 4: Digital Transformation Process in Selection and Implementation of Electronic Document Management System

In this chapter, Dr. Leyla Ozgur Polat examined the digital transformation to e-DMS process in a real university in detail. Dr. Ozgur Polat visualised the steps required to manage the process with workflow charts and determined the criteria that should be considered in selecting e-DMS applications. The selection process is assessed together with the indeterminacy in real life from a university. The process is executed by weighting the selected criteria with the Fuzzy AHP approach and selecting the most proper software. This chapter also includes the numerical data that would help other institutions in designing their systems. Also, environmental benefits calculated as well as the number of documents created formally was given in the chapter.

## Chapter 5: Farming as a Service (FAAS) for Sustainable Agricultural Ecosystem in India – Design of an Innovative Farm Management System 4.0

In this chapter, Dr. Chandrani Singh, Dr. Sunil Khilari, and Prof. Archana Nair presented scientific insights on Farming-As-A-Service (FaaS) and focused on introducing relevant technology-enabled services that would ensure economic sustainability, enhance food security through data-driven decision making by various stakeholders of agriculture. The stakeholders comprise farmers, agri-businesses and agri-tech startups, farm entrepreneurs, government and non-government agencies, equipment suppliers, agronomists, IT suppliers and vendors. As per the authors' view, the analyzed information can be used as a vantage by the farmers and others to select precision farming practices to aid productivity, invest personnel to provide appropriate assistance and implement real-time monitoring using the industries the sensors and devices. This is considered highly pertinent in a country where the primary source of occupation is Agriculture. Dr. Chandrani Singh, Dr. Sunil Khilari, and Prof. Archana Nair have in their study reviewed four different aspects of Farming Services, namely Food-as-a-Service (FaaS), Agriculture Drone-as-a-Service (ADaaS), Equipment-as-a-Service (EaaS), and Agriculture Robot-as-a-Service (ARaaS). Through numerous cases, concepts, methods, and practices, they have effectively tried to propagate the service mode of farming that imbibes the pay-as-you-go model, ensuring cost optimization and operational ease. In addition, the chapter also sets the base for researchers who aim to carry on critical and analytical studies to investigate the effect of ICTs on farming systems.

## Chapter 6: Cloud Computing Service Provider Business Model Success Characteristics

In this chapter, Dr. Motjolopane and Dr. Seaba explain how information technology services providers are shifting to a cloud computing ecosystem in a digital arena. Cloud computing is an enabler for digital transformation, with cloud computing service providers central to the digital transformation of both companies and higher education. As cloud computing service providers play the role of an 'architect' for companies as the supply chain is digitized and in supporting higher education institutions striving to deliver user-focused services in the face of increasing competition. Therefore, understanding the successful characteristics of cloud computing service provider's business models is of main interest for providers and may also be of value for companies and higher education institutions when selecting cloud computing service providers. Despite the importance of cloud computing service providers' business models, information systems literature has provided limited analysis on the characteristics of successful business models. As such, the chapter aims to contribute to the emerging research on characteristics of successful business models.

## Chapter 7: Inequalities in Access to and Outcomes of Higher Education in Africa

In this chapter, Dr. Roy Alexander Carr-Hill provides information to draws on an Institute which has information about their parental background and subsequent careers collected from surveys from Africa. In terms of access, the combination of parents not having more than primary education, renting, and not owning land identified less than 1% of students; whilst the percentage of entrants reporting that their parents had a post-Secondary qualification is considerably higher (around 57%) than the norm at the time the parents would have been studying (around 7%). These students were upper-middle class. In terms of outcomes, both current students and alumni say that the curriculum only partly fits their employment needs; but 85% of alumni would recommend AIMS to other students. In general, employers are satisfied with AIMS interns, but the percentage of unemployed AIMS graduates has risen from 2% in 2011 to 29% in 2016. Finally, rather than contributing to Africa, over one-third of graduates since 2012 are in the West.

## Chapter 8: Internationalization Policies and Strategies From the Comparative Standpoint of Student Mobility in Slovenian and Turkish Higher Education

In this chapter, Dr. Maruša Hauptman Komotar and Dr. Tugba Elif Toprak-Yildiz explored the development and implementation of internationalization policies, strategies, and practices from the standpoint of student mobility. They focused on Slovenia and Turkey, which usually do not make part of comparative research in this field. Initially, they investigated student mobility in national and institutional internationalization policies, strategies, and practices of each selected country case. On this basis, they continued with the comparative evaluation of key similarities and differences between Slovenia and Turkey in this field. In conclusion, they argued that future design and implementation of internationalization policies, strategies, and practices in the field of student mobility should consider the increasingly relevant role of ICT and its impact on physical and virtual forms of student mobility within diverse (non-European higher education contexts.

## Chapter 9: Internationalisation and Language Policy in European Higher Education – The Case of Austria and the Czech Republic

This chapter is entitled "Internationalisation and Language Policy in European Higher Education: The Case of Austria and the Czech Republic", Dr. Tugba Elif Toprak-Yildiz discusses possible links between internationalisation and language policy. Dr. Toprak-Yildiz examines the meso-level language policy of two European countries, Austria and the Czech Republic, which have established formal and comprehensive higher education internationalisation strategy frameworks. Dr. Toprak-Yildiz mainly focuses on the language component of language management in higher education internationalisation strategies of Austria and the Czech Republic by considering relationships between internationalisation, multilingualism, and English-medium instruction.

## Chapter 10: Integration of International Students With Education Processes Through Information Systems

In this chapter, Dr. Omer Gulec and Dr. Leyla Ozgur Polat discussed digital transformation and integration in educational activities through the international student application process. Dr. Gulec and Dr. Ozgur Polat analyzed different application methods for international students used in universities and suggested a guide for effectively conducting international student applications in universities using information technologies. Moreover, the chapter provided an efficient information technology for selection and placement systems of international students to be used in universities.

## Chapter 11: Internationalizing Quality Assurance Systems With International Accreditations in Slovenian Higher Education – Globalization and Regionalization Influences

In this chapter, Dr. Maruša Hauptman Komotar presented explorative information on the implementation of international accreditations in Slovenian higher education from the perspective of globalization and regionalization of quality assurance systems in higher education. Initially, Dr. Hauptman Komotar examined complex relationships between globalization and regionalization and their links with internationalization and the Europeanization of higher education. Next, she overviewed the leading international (i.e., global and regional) accreditors in Slovenia and discussed the achievement of international (professional) accreditations in the internationalisation framework of national and institutional quality assurance systems in the selected country case. The chapter provided a better understanding of the effects of globalization and regionalization on the extent of internationalization through international accreditations. It offered valuable insights for those interested in applying for international accreditations or investigating this topic in other (less-researched) higher education settings.

## Chapter 12: A Strategic Model to Promote University of Choice Decisions Among International Students

In this chapter, Dr Jooste and Professors Cullen and Calitz investigated the development of a strategic university of the choice model that can assist universities in recruiting international students. The study identified the factors that influenced a student's choice of university. Based on the criteria used in related international research, an empirical study was conducted amongst 306 international students studying at a South African university. The questionnaire was operationalized from literature, and Exploratory Factor Analysis was conducted to identify the minimum possible factors and items per factor. The factors identified in the study included academic program and quality, visa requirements, country/city attractiveness, lectures in English, costs, student life, safety and security, university location, university reputation and assistance from the International Office. The chapter proposes a strategic university of choice model for the recruitment of international students by universities. The model can be used by university marketing personnel to develop focused, targeted, and cost-effective marketing and recruitment strategies to recruit a diverse international student body.

# Section 1
# Digitalization and Transformation

# Chapter 1
# Digitalism and Jobs of the Future

**Gamze Sart**
*Istanbul Üniversitesi-Cerrahpaşa, Turkey*

**Orkun Yildiz**
https://orcid.org/0000-0002-6773-5859
*Izmir Democracy University, Turkey*

## ABSTRACT

*There has been a strong relationship between digitalism and the future of jobs. Reports by OECD and WEF examined the jobs in the coming decades, and the findings show that there is a completely new order in the professions that we are not familiar with. In addition, how the impacts of artificial intelligence (AI), machine learning, data science, and robotics have affected labour, the market is analyzed. The findings in the reports clearly would affect the careers of the next generations. With the post-pandemic developments and the rapid advancement of technology in many areas worldwide, digitalization has gained significant momentum. This situation manifested itself in professions and workforce. However, it is obvious that in the coming years, with digitalization, many occupational groups and accordingly, differences in skills will be seen. While some occupational groups disappear completely, it is seen that some new occupational groups will emerge and, some will transform.*

## INTRODUCTION

Today's world is becoming even more digital with the emergence of the Covid-19 epidemic. Rapid technological developments draw attention in the new age called Industry 4.0 before the epidemic. The First Industrial Revolution was about the use of water and steam power to mechanize production. In the Second Industrial Revolution, we see the mass production that began with electric power. The Third Industrial Revolution follows it. During this time, electronics and information technology have been used to automate the means of production.

DOI: 10.4018/978-1-7998-8169-8.ch001

On the other hand, the Fourth Industrial Revolution takes the automation used today to a higher level and uses technology to perform the tasks done by humans. Thus, the undeniable presence of technology is seen in every field from biology to production, from logistics to education. The Fourth Industrial Revolution is different. First of all, people can constantly produce new information. People can realize the connection with each other without any limitation due to internet and mobile devices, which has required processing, storage and image capacities because of technological advances by the fourth industrial revolution. At the same time, thanks to the developing technology, the relationship between the form of production and the elements of its processes have also been changing (Sun, 2018).

Third and last, the Fourth Industrial Revolution will give rise to a new economy form, the "sharing economy." As a result, new technologies are being heard of globally, such as intelligent machines, the Internet of Things, and Neuralink, which aims to implant wireless computer chips into the brain to cure neurological diseases. Following the COVID-19 pandemic, countries' economies are moving towards technology and automation, too. However, with the digitalization that came with industry 4.0, humanity will face an unprecedented revolution in the era of computers, Artificial Intelligence (AI) and robots, and radical changes will occur in every field. Labour and occupations are among the elements that this change will transform.

## EFFECTS OF DIGITALIZATION ON LABOUR

The development of technology will result in breakthrough innovations in many areas, from business to industry and from education to business sectors and work styles. It requires a new vision for all of humanity. The Fourth Industrial Revolution and digitalization will impact employment and its consequences that will influence all industries. Many vocations will be lost simultaneously while new job requirements will emerge because developments in information and communication technologies impact the execution process of jobs in many different sectors. More importantly, Adams-Prassl et al. (2020) have critically pointed out that less-educated workers, including most women, are more affected by this new crisis. Thus, individuals and organizations will have been naturally affected by robotic automation and digitalization in business processes management in the coming decades (Yildiz et al., 2021).

In 2017, researchers from Oxford University published a highly referenced study. According to Frey and Osborne (2017), an article covers a discussed topic about the possibility of transformation based on computerization for various vocations. The following are the top 30 out of approximately 700 occupations that are most at risk. Namely, it is claimed that robotic automation and digital transformation will be significant in many sectors in the future, as seen below (Frey & Osborne, 2017; Sun, 2018):

1. Telemarketers
2. Title examiners, abstractors, and searchers
3. Hand sewers
4. Mathematical technicians
5. Insurance underwriters
6. Watch repairers
7. Cargo and freight agents
8. Tax preparers
9. Photographic process workers and processing machine operators

10. New accounts clerks
11. Library technicians
12. Data entry keyers
13. Timing device assemblers and adjusters
14. Insurance claims and policy processing clerks
15. Brokerage clerks
16. Order clerks
17. Loan officers
18. Insurance appraisers, auto damage assessors
19. Umpires, referees, and other sports officials
20. Tellers
21. Etchers and engravers
22. Packaging and filling machine operators and tenders
23. Procurement clerks
24. Shipping, receiving, and traffic clerks
25. Metal and plastic milling and planing machine setters, operators, and tenders
26. Credit analysts
27. Parts salespersons
28. Claims adjusters, examiners, and investigators
29. Drivers/sales workers
30. Radio operators.

On the other hand, Frey & Osborne (2017) and Sun (2018) claimed that many different jobs might be affected minimally or not by the 4.0 industrial revolution and digitalization due to the nature of the business process. According to Frey and Osborne (2017) and Sun (2018), the following list shows the top 30 safest jobs which are not expected to perform a computer-based transformation in current technological developments:

1. Recreational therapists
2. First-line supervisors of mechanics, installers, and repairers
3. Emergency management directors
4. Mental health and substance abuse social workers
5. Audiologists
6. Occupational therapists
7. Orthotists and prosthetists
8. Healthcare social workers
9. Oral and maxillofacial surgeons
10. First-line supervisors of firefighting and prevention workers
11. Dietitians and nutritionists
12. Lodging managers
13. Choreographers
14. Sales engineers
15. Physicians and surgeons
16. First-line supervisors of transportation and material-moving machine and vehicle operators

17. Instructional coordinators
18. Psychologists, mental health positions
19. First-line supervisors of police and detectives
20. Dentists
21. Elementary school teachers, except special education
22. Medical scientists, except epidemiologists
23. Education administrators in elementary and secondary schools
24. Podiatrists
25. Clinical, counselling, and school psychologists
26. Mental health counsellors
27. Fabric and apparel patternmakers
28. Set and exhibit designers
29. Human resource managers
30. Recreation workers

As understood from the list above, robotic automation and digitalization have revolutionary effects on the processes and features of jobs. As a result of this situation, it is an expected result that the relationship between work and employees will become very different due to technological developments. Thereby, to fulfil contemporary corporate goals and customer demands, the central of business process management is shifting from general audience to individual attention. Companies can individually discover the characteristics and needs of their customers. Then, these companies can establish close one-to-one relationships with these customers. Of course, for this process to be carried out successfully, both the organization and each employee in the company must be adapted to digitalization or robotic automation in business processes (Yildiz, 2021b). At this point, the human-centred approach should be an essential framework to benefit technologies and recover investments for organizations. Otherwise, in the future, governance and private institutions may face increasing challenges as well as opportunities. In addition, digitalization allows collecting, transforming, and analyzing big data in societal issues for public governance. Particularly those involving social inequality and unemployment should be well researched and recognized. Governments, legislators, international organizations, regulators, corporate groupings, universities, and civil societies should collaborate to manage robust emerging technologies, limit risks, and share future goals.

On the other hand, a growing number of publications featuring digitalization highlights its increasing significance, and the process now has a severe and undeniable place in the literature. Because digitalization is one of the main factors to construct a new dimension to shape society and business. The employee characteristics expected by the industry have evolved to a much different dimension compared to previous periods. People can respond to the needs in a fast-developing and one-to-one customer relationship with flexible, agile and digital skills. These people have become ideally sought the employees by today's companies (Yildiz, 2021b; Yildiz et al., 2021). Günay et al. (2021) argue that higher education institutions should adopt a further education and training mission and concept to meet new digital age needs. The relationship between the higher education institutions having 3. mission and industries is a fundamental requirement for managers, scientific researchers and industry representatives. There are many academic studies, including supportive cases on a new framework of higher education and their relations with industry in the literature (Atiku, 2021; Haliloğlu, 2021; Keynes, 2010; Singh, 2021; Windisch et al., 2021; Yildiz, 2021a). In the centre of digitalization and robotic automation, studies on institutional transformation and restructuring for education are carried out. Nevertheless, an important question needs to be answered: How will technological changes impact the meaning of work and leisure?

Advances in technology during the past century did not cause unemployment. On the contrary, they provided new job opportunities and created new and innovative products. The future development of the workforce will depend on the balance that can be struck between traditional work practices and employees' free time and the extent to which workers may choose between them. From an economic perspective, technological progress means that fewer workers are required to produce desired outputs.

The concept of work has developed through generations and has a philosophical, sociological, verifiable, and judicial point of view. Work has always had negative connotations. In ancient Greece, it was related to subjugation, while not working implied opportunities. Work attained an elevated status following the adoption by the Protestant church of the "protestant hard-working ethic," which portrayed work and its related actions as being fundamental to the satisfaction of the people and a method for the integration of society (Weber & Kalberg, 2013).

With the advent of industrialization, the concept of work made a significant impact in the public arena, and views and attitudes toward it have changed over the years. During the 1990s, sociologists anticipated the "end of work," although, since the 2000s, the pattern has reverted to the fundamental premise of work ensuring a social order (Méda & Vendramin, 2013). Several external factors lend significance to work; individuals need to work to protect their mental health and social inclusivity, individual flexibility, and independence that makes these factors easier.

In the Western world, the perception of work is typified by moderately safe business that guarantees pay and social insurance. The compromise between work and relaxation is viewed.

Regularly as an issue, but this is not the case in developing nations. In developing countries, business is characterized by weak and casual enterprises, poor social security, and long hours spent working in low-skilled jobs, disproportionally by women. However, the concept of work remains vague. There is a danger of death at work. According to Pega et al. (2021), 745,000 people died that in 2020 from overwork. In this result, the primary causes of death were stroke and heart disease. Globally, nations are at various degrees of advancement and limitations in their plans for the future. A few nations are at the cutting edge of development and innovation, while others are attempting to get up to speed. Those at the forefront lead the conversation around the eventual fate of work. However, fundamentally, the degree to which improvement may be achieved must be considered. From an African nation's perspective, getting up to speed with the technological innovations of the developed world is associated with a significant level of learning at a considerable expense (Pega et al., 2021). It appears incomprehensible that Western bodies begin developing inclusive innovation when they have previously demonstrated an inclination to control it. The significance of the Western model remains, in part, undisputed. Nevertheless, product innovations from agriculturally dependent nations face barriers in the West, such as utilization, adjusting for an aged population, and dumping electronic waste. This issue should be explored in a global context.

With advances in technology, the future of work will face structural changes. Among other innovations, the computerized economy, artificial brainpower, robotization, and 3D printing will fundamentally change businesses and workplaces, and, thus, the kinds of occupations required by economies will be reimagined. There is a component of fear, which is expected in any state of vulnerability, yet these improvements will also provide opportunities to create more (and possibly better) roles. As demonstrated through past industrial upheavals, the facts confirm that following initial disruptions, innovative change has resulted in a higher quality of work without fundamentally diminishing the range of occupations. The current modern unrest, driven by digital transformation, presents the opportunity to create more and better positions. Even though the experience may offer a positive reference point, people are motivated to accept that this technological transformation might be unique. For instance, the speed of progress is quicker, offering just brief periods for pre-emptive action and an opportune response.

As computerization plays a role in most occupations, jobs that involve repetitive actions and the work conducted in those positions will be lost. These losses will include traditionally recognized positions and middle-class occupations, interestingly (considering previous redundancy circumstances). Work that is hard to mechanize will require the highest quality human input, such as complex undertakings that demand an undeniable level of intellectual ability and inventiveness. Certain businesses may disappear because of specific advancements (for example, 3D printing), where the whole production chain might be redesigned.

The changes resulting from automation will create a demand for certain types of jobs, qualifications, and skills. According to the advantages people have over machines, the occupational structure of the global economy will also change. As machines permeate all occupations, jobs of the future will involve working with machines or computers. Set of strategic, proactive, catalytic, and capacity-building activities, research, development, and support for new technologies will continue and progress. Enhanced productivity will lead to increased leisure time, thereby boosting the demand for services in the entertainment sector.

Additionally, there will be a rapid expansion of jobs in the nursing sector. However, eventually, mechanization will allow the performance of related tasks without any emotional support or social interaction. Thereby, the impact of innovation and technology on the business world varies from country to country. In other words, Acemoglu and Restrepo (2020) have mentioned that countries' investment in new technology, including the education quality, changes from one country to another. The capital investment in production automation technologies is not only enough to have production quality without qualified workers. Also, the quality of work may not necessarily be improved due to technological changes.

Furthermore, human labour will always be competitive through the acceptance of low salaries. In turn, this highlights the challenges facing developing countries and their ability to remain competitive in a global economy. Productivity, innovation, and competitiveness depend on high-level science, technology, engineering, and mathematics (STEM) skills, rare in less-developed nations (European Commission, 2014).

## Greater Productivity

Future work will be set apart by more obvious disparities both inside and between nations. Gains in usefulness will be overwhelmed by entrepreneurs who will profit from future efficiency. There will be a decline in pay, and if capital remains in possession of the few, disparities will increase dramatically. Market influence, a component that conveys abundance in the public arena, may not guarantee appropriate daily working environments. Reallocation bodes well, and governments can play an essential role in tackling the development of disparity.

Innovation has brought the world to a defining moment; it is in a progression phase, and commonly accepted reallocation strategies are fundamental to accomplishing simple change. Decreasing disparity ought to be the fundamental goal of every future approach. The world should pause and reflect on the sort of future that it desires for its citizens, and strategic conversations should be guided by a variety of new information and experimental research. Subsequent approaches could be based on rights, focus on the agreement, and expand on worldwide fortitude and administration, while social equity and human prosperity should be at the heart of the core values.

Several policy tools can be used for reorganizing productivity gains, all of which give governments and multilateral organizations a prominent role. They include a secured basic salary for all in the robot tax, which is described as the obligation to pay taxes. In this concept, companies replace employees with automated workers who are asked to pay a tax or engage in internal corporate profit sharing. Traditional political tools and systems remain as crucial as ever. This includes wage-setting mechanisms, labour market supervision, collective bargaining, social dialogue, and social protection. Profit-sharing or worker ownership plans may also be effective solutions to redistribute profit in productivity. The profit-sharing plan avoids competition between labour and capital and can benefit both workers and employers. These plans are standard in some countries, such as South Africa and France, and provide an opportunity for trade unions to strengthen their part in discussing future work.

Technological changes will disrupt the labour market and will create a demand for new types of jobs. As a result, these changes and the required skills will change education expectations. Compared with career-oriented education, liberal arts education is in higher demand. It may be necessary to develop measures to incentivize workers to upgrade their skills and acquire advanced proficiencies, especially in emerging economies. Additionally, it may be necessary to provide specific incentives for people in the most challenging positions to relearn skills and adjust to new jobs, as they did between 1940 and 1960. Thereby, universities and technical/professional institutions should follow the technology constantly.

However, this concerns the controversy over education providers providing students with broad or limited skills. It may mean providing educational services that allow students to move on to general rather than vocational education, thereby lack of specialization and incompetence.

Thus, in the medium term, students will change careers or even disappear from them altogether. General education (such as liberal arts) enables students to master flexible skills and remain relevant in the ever-changing job market. Therefore, there must be strong communication between education providers, employers, trade unions, and government agencies to ensure that the skills provided are consistent with the requirements of employers. In this sense, STEM skills and vocational training can help meet future needs and provide better places for innovation.

There are significant differences in young human resources regarding gender, income level, educational opportunities, skills, and location. Some young people can accept globalization and new technologies, while others cannot take advantage of the increased opportunities. Also, it is essential to note that the job expectations of the younger generation may differ from those of previous generations. Today, the norm is to accept several short-term jobs, such as voluntary or unpaid jobs, or internships, all of which are subject to limited social protection.

In addressing the growing mismatch between youth employability and labour supply and demand reduction, education that includes lifelong learning methods is considered a good strategy. It can solve the problem of adapting to the rapidly changing business world, where people can switch jobs and accept short-term employment. In addition, everyone should develop soft skills, such as communication and networking.

Internships can enhance a young person's employability and assist their transition to the labour market. However, unpaid internships have become a problematic issue because they violate the principle of equal pay for equal work.

Other measures for making better connections during the transition to work include vocational training and apprenticeships, which can provide access to the labour market and guarantee training instead of regular employment. However, the quality of learning is crucial, and some people believe that vocational training still has a certain stigma compared with university qualifications. Policymakers need to understand the challenges are faced by young people in the labour market, and their voices must be heard and amplified. It should begin with the understanding that young people are the future driving force of governments, economies, and societies. Rising inequality remains one of the most significant issues.

Considering the new realities in the world of work, it is also necessary to address youth representation in trade union movements because more young people will find themselves in a typical form of employment or informal work. Other issues include reforming the current educational system by expanding the social protection system to cover everyone, addressing population growth, tackling international migration, and addressing climate change within the current global political context. The need to protect young people is of the utmost importance; they are a particularly relevant group because they represent the future of work.

## Work and Production Organization

How the rapid changes in work and the organization of production will affect existing employment patterns, and employee-employer relationships are additional issues that must be addressed. In recent decades, there has been a fundamental change in work organisation, leading to a disjointed workplace that allows companies to cut their production costs drastically. Outsourcing, franchising, and third-party management are some examples of this type of structural transformation in production.

This shift in working was facilitated by information and computing technology (ICTs). The prior result of division into functions, such as tasks that previously were managed internally, is that companies can exercise control without being responsible for suppliers or working conditions within suppliers' networks in different locations. Large companies with well-known brands delegate responsibility for their employees to an increasingly complex and fluid network of suppliers and franchisees. This can lead to unclear definitions of safety responsibilities and gaps in coordination. A considerable challenge is how to redistribute political power to re-manage the organization of both work and production. A critical issue that needs to be addressed in this context is the re-adjustment of the control and accountability of the global supply chain (GSC). Regulatory frameworks and laws need to be reviewed to fulfil their obligations to workers while retaining the positive aspects of globalization. This can be achieved by centralizing and realigning the responsibilities of commercial enterprises or by decentralizing control and responsibilities and transferring power to local governments. Some attempts have been made to improve the role of intermediaries, such as in Indonesia or Latin American countries. Similar examples can be found outside of cooperative medical systems (such as cooperatives), which should receive political support because of difficulties in implementation. Both the centralization and decentralization options are enormous challenges that require the support of governments.

This strategy must be tailored to specific supply chains because the characteristics of GSCs vary across departments and regions. For example, in the agri-food and mining sectors, the main problem is controlling primary resources. In contrast, in the automotive and electronic industries, exercising control depends on the location of the resource, its ownership, and the nature of the competitive market. Therefore, there is no one-size-fits-all strategy.

The second issue in transferring employment to a third party is that labour laws and social protection are established at the national level. Therefore, workers with different economic circumstances and working conditions will be at odds with their supply chain's employment terms and conditions. Therefore, the possibility of creating new forms of responsibility should be considered while incorporating the different actors and their various levels of control. The best option is to combine centralized/

decentralized and private/public enforcement. In this regard, it has been suggested that the International Labour Organization (ILO) can play a vital role in ensuring the effectiveness of law enforcement. The transfer of employment to a third party will also lead to a lack of protection for workers (self-employed, independent, and casual), and the appropriate provision of this is a matter of social protection. The debate continues are about that concrete actions have been taken to formalize the economy, and while it is recognized that some steps have been taken, more needs to be done.

In this case, controversy has arisen over the provision of social protection for these workers. Supporters of an extension of social protection to self-employed and casual workers believe that these workforces face more unstable labour market conditions and greater occupational and safety risks. Furthermore, their exclusion would stimulate the hiring of personnel through these informal arrangements. Others believe that self-employed workers voluntarily choose to be self-employed and do not require collective social security agreements. Discussions on atypical, self-employed, and casual forms of work have also raised questions about the tripartite structure as a related model. The general opinion is that there is no need to change it.

Although some aspects of traditional forms of employment still exist in new versions—the dynamics of control and dependence between employers and employees have not disappeared—it is necessary to develop a series of new job types. All aspects of these relationships should be considered. Trade unions must rethink traditional bargaining paradigms and develop new forms of collective bargaining in which they can negotiate with the workplace rather than with specific employers or departments. There is a requirement for a coordinated approach between unions to cope with changes in the global labour market.

United unions are believed to have greater bargaining power with multinational companies and better empower those who lack influence. Furthermore, more significant effort should be made to transfer some of the benefits of globalization from companies to workers. There are many historical examples of this. In the Netherlands, unions negotiated part-time contracts with employers that included equal treatment and access to the preconditions of the social security system. Many vital experiments are underway to integrate these changes into the system, and some emerging organizations are striving to devise effective methods to realize this. Determining the appropriate mechanism is the main issue for supervising a GSC is that it crosses national borders and multiple systems of supervision. Rules alone are not enough, and compliance measures are essential. In GSCs, some suppliers simultaneously deliver goods to multiple companies, and pressure on these suppliers may impact many brands, resulting in adverse consequences for the entire system.

Consumers can also play an essential role in promoting fair working conditions for all, including the self-employed. Consumer demand for fair trade products will pressure companies and pave the way for sustainable working conditions. Additionally, a combined effort by different participants would help to achieve this. For example, the Fair Apparel Foundation works with brands, factories, unions, and non-governmental organizations to demonstrate how coordination can effectively promote change in working conditions within supply chains. Additionally, to ensure that products are produced to specified fair standards, numerous national certificates could be replaced by a single international certificate, a set of certification rules, and an agency responsible for inspection and certification. It has been observed that the need for an international framework agreement seems more urgent in a world where capital is highly mobile and crosses national borders while labour remains within those boundaries.

Some tangible steps have been taken to improve working conditions, but some aspects of globalization still need to be addressed to create decent working conditions for all. In this sense, international organizations can play a crucial role in responding to globalization by promoting internationally recognized standards and instruments. ILO strategies are related to realizing better working conditions in the globalized labour market, while new technologies will continue to transform the workplace. The ILO strives to ensure that all forms of work are appropriately recognized; however, governments must ensure that ILO instruments are translated into their respective national laws and practices to be fully effective.

## Governance of Work

The debate on the governance of work focuses on two key issues: First, how does society respond to the erosion of established frameworks, norms, and institutions that regulate work? Second, is there a requirement for a new management structure to organize businesses effectively?

It is essential to realize that the world of work has no predetermined future, and there are multiple options, some of which may be more effective than others. For a discussion about the future, it is necessary to reflect on labour relations from a historical perspective, especially concerning the 1944 Philadelphia Declaration of the International Labour Organization titled "Work is not a Commodity," the principle expressed in the preamble of this document. Moreover, to consider the opinions of others. In Karl Polanyi's book of the same year, The Great Change, work is considered a fictitious commodity. This premise helps to explain the three stages of labour relations. The first stage occurred in the 19th century when industrialization expanded in some countries with the commercialization of work. The second event occurred in the 20th century when the commodity status of labour was regulated to limit the influence of market forces. The third manifestation is underway under current deregulations, in which increasingly clear market rules constrain work.

In this case, the main challenge facing the employment relationship is how to reduce the impact of commoditization. It is necessary to examine whether a new mechanism is needed or whether the old system that linked work, consumption and social welfare can be recovered. What will happen if the traditional employment relationship disappears? Despite the trend toward deregulation, old methods still have the potential to be revitalized. For example, labour inspectorates have been reformed to play new roles, such as in Latin America. Methods can be adapted to a form of regulatory acupuncture, which is a strategy to select critical areas in which pressure can be applied, as in GSCs. Simultaneously, if work is treated as a commodity, after Polanyi, society will experience a reverse movement, which can take different forms. In this sense, the culmination of current global populism can be analyzed in the context of a Polanyi response. Additionally, it must be remembered that the world is diverse, and changes never occur in isolation. Although the in-formalization of work may be a problem in some parts of the world, in other places, more than 50% of workers are self-employed or unpaid family workers, most of whom are in unstable jobs. In the clothing industry (as in GSCs), people are sometimes forced to become domestic workers without the protection of any labour regulations. Although they are counted as self-employed, their family members contribute $4,444 (US -2020) to production as unpaid domestic workers, although they are neither counted nor protected. Therefore, in the absence of a regulatory system, it is necessary to establish an appropriate regulatory framework.

A national funding system needs to be established that goes beyond the employment relationship and ensures protection for all workers. Citizens' income could be a solution, but there are doubts about whether it would be economically affordable, socially just, or politically feasible. Despite these reservations, it is essential to recognize that this option provides a way to address the commodification of labour and the weakening of market power. Another option is to establish a rights-based system, but this raises questions over who defines the rights and how they are defined and interpreted. Some may be sceptical of this idea because, as observed by the European Court of Justice, it can be seen as giving too much power to judges. However, it must be recognized that it should be possible to include people outside of employment relationships in the scope of social protection.

In the past decade, rights-based social protection methods have made some progress. There is no other way but to formalize the informal economy, although it will be difficult. When atypical forms of employment become the norm, the framework for managing such employment must be reimagined. There are some innovative initiatives on private governance, such as the recently passed French legislation that requires large employers to report human rights due diligence in their GSCs. Similarly, during the Brazilian carnivals, temporary workers who signed very short-term service contracts were given guarantees through the negotiation of commercial contracts. In this case, semi-legal methods were used instead of formal procedures.

In addition, it is necessary to re-evaluate the limitations of private governance, such as corporate social responsibility and codes of conduct, to see how it complements rather than replaces public governance. However, it is essential to realize that the so-called standard employment relationship only accounts for 29% of the workforce. In addition, there are significant challenges related to the discussion of informality, social change, automation, the gig economy, and demographic/immigration changes. New employment forms, like the sharing economy, pose challenges to the definition of employers because of the provision of jobs and services across borders, the difficulty in monitoring and controlling them. It is not easy to foresee how the situation will develop because there is not enough comparative data to understand the new processes occurring.

The expectation that governments should do more does not mean that regulatory bureaucracy should increase. Instead, they should regulate acupuncture, which is a strategy for selecting critical areas in which pressure can be applied, such as GSCs. From a governance perspective, governmental actors, including judges, labour inspectors, health institutions, and safety research institutions, can serve as bridges with other actors to build innovative solutions.

Additionally, there should be an improvement in supervision, in which various contractual states coexist and create friction among workers, which effects on the relationship between workers and companies. Individualization has emerged to undermine the governance of the world of work. Under current conditions, the issues are first, whether it is still possible to organize social dialogue, social peace, and provide occupational safety and health protection as before, and second, to determine how these institutions should develop to meet the challenges of new workplaces.

The social partners such as employment services and labour policy have agreed that all changes should be made within dialogue and representation. In social dialogue, it is necessary to expand representation to include multinational companies and informal or unregulated workers. At the same time, employers must be clearly defined and must not disappear behind intermediaries. Additionally, trade unions must adapt to the new challenges and not rely on their achievements to date. There may be other new forms of organization that will benefit workers and employers and make dialogue more democratic. These initiatives are already in progress, such as self-employed individuals organizing around specific industries or young people expressing their concerns and wishes via social media. The digital economy may help organize and reach workers, but it is equally essential that leading companies conduct dialogue with the ILO. Considering national conditions, it is also essential to replicate the European model of social dialogue in developing nations.

Furthermore, there needs to be more thought on how society can be made more inclusive. Employment is viewed in a broader context with a more cohesive approach to social dialogue. A framework must be developed to create a process that allows participants to negotiate and consider specific issues in different departments.

Trade unions are developing new negotiation methods, and there is evidence of closer cooperation with civil society. For example, the Bangladesh fire and construction safety agreement reached after the Rana Plaza tragedy is a binding agreement that includes two global unions and more than 2,000 brands, including the world's largest clothing company and the Bangladeshi unions. The Accord on Fire and Building Safety in this country was signed on May 15th, 2013. The agreement requires brands to inspect and fix occupational health and safety risks, which affect more than two million workers. In the United States, healthcare is traditionally linked to employment, so new forms of atypical employment pose a challenge to the existing system. It is necessary to change the previous paradigm and give more consideration to the social unit.

Shifting the relationship between employers and employees to a stronger relationship between citizens and their countries will also help people to move from the world of traditional employment to the broader world of work. It is essential to rethink universal healthcare for all workers, not just those in traditional jobs. However, the complexity of dismantling institutions and creating new ones cannot be ignored, and careful decisions must be made on what to cancel and what to keep or recreate.

The future of work must be inspired by considerations of human nature, social justice, and peace. Although the subject is broad and complex, it is essential to discuss the future of work, society, and the economic possibilities of future generations. A truly global perspective on the future of work is required that addresses the needs and realities of all member states rather than skewing discussions toward one specific region or another. So far, this paper has discussed paradigm shifts, the move to a new way of thinking about work, and what can be seen as a new organization or category of work. Next, this thinking must be transformed into tangible results.

## DIGITALIZATION AND JOBS OF THE FUTURE

Not only Economic Co-operation and Development (OECD) but also the World Economic Forum (WEF) has emphasized that how technology and the innovations derived from it will alter the parameters of the business world (Commonwealth Secretariat, 2020). World Economic Forum (2021) states that in 2030, society will face a world with different dynamics to the current one, and humanity will be reshaped. "We need to embrace innovation, not only in the development of new technologies but also in how we do things. This includes new business models (platforms and ecosystems, marketplaces, digital commons), public and private collaborations, and incentives to ensure solutions are applied to solving our greatest social and environmental problems" (World Economic Forum, 2021). The OECD and the WEF analyzed the new world's jobs, professions, and workforce through their reports. This section examines reports on the future world by both organizations.

First, the OECD's report is discussed, which was issued by the organization's secretary-general. The OECD's directorate developed it for science, technology, and innovation under the strategic guidance of the secretary general's chief adviser and Sherpa to the G7, Gabriela Ramos (Organisation for Economic Co-operation and Development, 2017). OECD (2018) presented that the Preparation for Future Work report for the G7 Ministers of Employment and Innovation ministerial conference on employment, which took place in Montreal, Canada, from March 27 to 28, 2018. Preparing for jobs of the future was declared as the main issue. The views expressed and the arguments used in this report do not necessarily reflect the official opinions of the OECD or the G7 member countries (Organisation for Economic Co-operation and Development, 2017). In addition, the Preparation for Future Work focused on the impact of digital transformation on employment and productivity. It planned to reference the G7 development ecclesiastical discussion at the 2018 G7 advancement and business clerical gathering titled "Preparation for Future Work" (OECD, 2018). It supplemented on future work prepared by the OECD to facilitate the gathering of the G7 work ministers, which considered how strategies and practices intended for the 20th-century universe of work could be changed to guarantee fairness and value and to provide remunerating. G7 countries are transitioning to a digital economy and society. Compared with some notable declarations, this digital transformation is not new and has progressed for nearly half a century. The impact of ICTs has led to significant structural changes and improvements in productivity, and many businesses in the G7 countries have reaped these rewards (OECD, 2018). The main difference from the previous era of digital transformation is that three dividing lines have pushed this issue to the top of the agendas of the G7, G20, the OECD, and many other international fora.

The first dividing line extends connectivity to almost all businesses in the G7 countries. Currently, 95% of these businesses already have high-speed internet connections. Although the intensity of digitization varies from sector to sector (OECD, 2017), companies in all sectors of the economy are now affected by a digital transformation that expands their reach and offers potential benefits.

The second is the rise of always-connected smartphones, followed by the era of universal connectivity and ubiquitous computing. In June 2017, Japan led the G7 and the OECD countries with 157 mobile broadband users per 100 inhabitants as more devices are connected to the IoT (OECD, 2018).

Third, these devices combined with many of the services that feed into the web generate vast amounts of information. For example, in the well-connected Nordic countries, between 2014 and 2016, the monthly data flow per mobile subscriber grew by 60% in Sweden, 180% in Denmark, and 185% in Finland, where the common monthly usage is around 11 gigabytes (OECD, 2018). These flows are somewhat lower in the G7 countries, but they are also growing, too. Further growth is predicted as connected devices. We can find those devices as an example in automated vehicles.

The combination of data and the steady increase in computing power have led to the emergence of data-driven innovations. Online and network activities generate big data, which feeds machine learning and facilitates AI. Consequently, this leads to advances in intelligent machines (robotics, automated vehicles, etc.), and the discovery of new scientific techniques may spur further innovations. The expansion of the amount, variety, and velocity of knowledge and the ability to analyze and use it is a significant departure from the past and marks the emergence of a replacement factor in production that augments traditional capital and labour while retaining its unique properties (OECD, 2018).

Robert Gordon, who is a macroeconomist, has a pessimistic view. He has a particular interest in unemployment, inflation, and both the long-run and cyclical aspects of labour productivity. According to his research, he alleges that the recent slowdown may be a permanent phenomenon (Gordon, 2012). Gordon says future economic progress will encounter some obstacles. Those obstacles may be demography, education, inequality, globalization, the environment, and debt. On the other hand, Brynjolfsson and McAfee (2014) have a more optimistic view. They argue that the underlying rate of technological progress has not slowed, and the IT revolution will still dramatically transform frontier economies (OECD, 2018).

On the other hand, since the 1950s, there has been a slowdown in productivity growth. Long-term trends show this landscape. This was a time of remarkable growth. Following World War II (OECD, 2015), there was significant scope for catching up and for rebuilding the G7 countries. Between 1972 to 1995, productivity growth remained high in most G7 countries (OECD, 2018). The reason was the continuation of the convergence process.

Furthermore, from 1995 to 2004, an acceleration in productivity growth has occurred in the U.S.A. It was principally due to gains from the roll-out of ICT technologies. Thereby, it failed to materialize to the same degree in other G7 countries. Their productivity growth stalled considerably compared with previous periods. Productivity growth has been hindered in all G7 countries due to a mixture of cyclical and structural factors from the early-to-mid-2000s (OECD, 2018). In addition, the potential impacts on the productivity of the continued digital transformation must be considered within the context of this long-term slowdown. However, exact causes for today's productivity paradox remain challenging to unravel, and numerous factors are likely to contribute to it.

OECD (2018) has stated that the first factor in the report is that the digital transformation has limited development to date causes the distribution level of digital technologies across the global economy. Many businesses have access to broadband networks, the utilization of more advanced digital tools and applications within firms still differs significantly between countries. For instance, in 2016, only 16% to 17% of firms in France and Germany used cloud computing compared with 45% in Japan (OECD, 2017). Furthermore, there are essential differences between firms within countries, with small-medium enterprises lagging. Similar to the other periods of rapid technological change; initially, advanced technologies are adopted only by some leading firms (OECD, 2018). It is only later that they spread to other companies, who adopt the technologies to grow new business models and reduce costs.

As a result, there is a significant gap in automation between leading and typical firms. OECD research has shown that in both manufacturing and services, the leading global companies have continued to perform strongly since the economic downturn compared with most other firms, which have not experienced much productivity growth (OECD, 2015). Especially in ICT services sector, this is different.

Second, digital transformation needs more than technology. The essential complementary investments that firms must make in skills, organizational changes, process innovations, new systems, and new business models (Haskel & Westlake, 2017; OECD, 2019). These complementary investments can be challenging for many firms, such as the size, complexity etc. (Brynjolfsson et al., 2019).

Third, the limited impacts of digital technologies on productivity are associated with the slow pace of structural change and resource reallocation in OECD countries. For example, old non-viable firms create problems in this issue. Those are the businesses older than ten years having negative profits over a minimum of two consecutive years. Also, those firms have been increasing in many OECD countries, particularly since the 2007/08 financial crisis (OECD, 2018). Compared with successful old firms and younger businesses, their productivity has been falling rapidly (Berlingieri et al., 2017; McGowan et al., 2017). It has occurred amid a slowdown in regulatory reform that impedes market competition (OECD, 2017).

As we told, digital transformation needs more than technology; other factors than technological change are currently driving significant change within the G7. In some G7 countries, notably Japan and Germany, ageing populations with already significant impacts can have severe repercussions for the growth of the labour force, the expansion of pension obligations, and various other key policies. Simultaneously, because the economies of G7 countries have strengthened, several are now starting to experience labour shortages, such as specific technical occupations, including data scientists (OECD, 2018). Furthermore, the recent financial crisis has been overcome to a large extent. This crisis has left the world economy with a range of long-term challenges like the burden of high public and personal debt. Shifts within the global economy, especially the growth of emerging economies, also affect G7 countries, such as changing world competitiveness patterns and their effect on jobs (OECD, 2018). The OECD supposes that in 2014, between 14% and 42% of jobs in businesses in G7 countries were sustained by foreign demand (OECD, 2017). Additionally, different significant trends, like temperature changes and the growing demand for water, energy, and food, affect the global economy. These will endorse economic structural changes, including the expansion of specific industries and, consequently, the decline of others (OECD, 2018).

The Future of Jobs report, prepared biennially by the WEF, was presented in October 2020. Unlike previous reports, the future of jobs considered the COVID-19 pandemic, affected the entire world since the beginning of 2020, among its variables. The report includes in-depth analyses of 15 industrial sectors and 26 developed/developing countries. Its goal was to address the disruptions due to the pandemic, the contextualized cycles over a more extended economic period, and the outlook for jobs and occupations emerging through the adoption of technologies over the next five years.

The World Economic Forum (WEF) (2020) presented a report. This report has tracked the introduction of longer-term labour in the last five years, identified the potential scale of worker displacement due to technological automation and augmentation, and devised effective strategies to empower job transitions from decaying to newly developed jobs. At the core of the report is the job survey, which is a tool that assesses the short- and long-term trends and impacts of technology on labour markets. According to the WEF report in 2020, New technologies quickly entered the field of use among the businesses surveyed. Cloud computing, big data, and e-commerce remains priorities and follow a trend established in previous years (World Economic Forum, 2020b). After all, it is significantly more interested in encryption, reflecting the new vulnerabilities of the digital age, along with a significant increase in the number of firms expecting to adopt non-humanoid robots and computing. Both technologies are becoming a mainstay of labour among many industries (World Economic Forum, 2020b).

On the other hand, according to the WEF (2020) shared a report on the future jobs, AI is the most popular sector amid the digital information and communication, financial services, healthcare, and transportation industries. Furthermore, Big data, the IoT, and non-humanoid robotics are experiencing a strong uptake in the mining and metal industries. It should be emphasized that the government and public sectors are particularly interested in encryption (World Economic Forum, 2020b). Therefore, new technologies drive future growth among industries and increase the demand for new roles and skillsets. However, such positive effects are offset by workforce disruptions. Many researchers reveal that the use of new technology will impact jobs by displacing some human tasks into the realm of machine labour. The extent of disruption will vary, depending on the occupations and skillsets involved (World Economic Forum, 2020b).

However, the reapportionment of current tasks between humans and machines is already in a working process. One of the central findings of the long-term outlook for jobs in the 2018 report is that by 2025, the typical, estimated work time will be equal for both humans and machines. Algorithms and machines are focused primarily on knowledge processing and retrieval, administrative tasks, and a few aspects of traditional labour. There are features expected from the human labour force to maintain their competitive power. These include the following: qualities managing, advising, decision-making, reasoning, communicating, and interacting.

World Economic Forum's (2020b) the future of jobs survey also reveals similarities among industries when examining increasingly strategic and redundant job roles in its 2020 version. Like the 2018 survey, wanted job positions are data analysts and scientists, AI and machine-learning specialists, robotics engineers, software and application developers, and digital transformation specialists. Still, process automation specialists, information security analysts, and IoT specialists are newly emerging as well as automation and the resurgence of cybersecurity risks are in-demand job titles from employers.

New and emerging professions created with the development of technology are a natural result of the adoption of new technologies and the increasing demand for new products and services. This process brings the demand for jobs in the green economy, roles at the forefront of the data/AI economy, and new positions in engineering, cloud computing, and product development. Furthermore, the emerging professions highlight the continuing importance of human interaction in the new economy through care, marketing, sales, and content production positions. Due to constraints related to data availability, the following analysis does not include jobs in the care or green sectors.

By analyzing career changes, it becomes apparent that some of these jobs of tomorrow present more significant opportunities for workers looking to switch to an entirely new job, and thus, they present more options for reimagining professional trajectories (Ratcheva et al., 2020).

At the same time, other emerging professions remain more fully bounded. Only 19% and 26% of job transitions into the engineering and people/culture sectors, respectively, come from outside the job family in which those roles currently exist. In contrast, 72% of data and AI-bound transitions originate from a different job family, while 68% transition into emerging sales jobs (Ratcheva et al., 2020). Here there is one more significant issue. It is about the set of distinctive job families, but the diversity of those source job families varies by emerging profession. While emerging roles in product development draw professionals from a range of job families, those attracted to emerging roles in the people and culture job clusters typically transition from the human resources job family. The emerging cloud computing job cluster is populated primarily by professionals transitioning from IT and engineering.

Finally, several jobs may present significant opportunities for entering professions that require a significant change in skills profile. It can be observed that transitions into the people and culture and engineering sectors have typically involved similar high skillsets. At the same time, the marketing and content development sectors have revealed a similarity in low skills. Across the emerging professions outlined in The Future of Jobs, transitions into data and AI allow for an enormous variation in the skills profiles between source and destination job titles.

According to the report, the newer emerging professions present more opportunities to break into these frontier fields such as data, AI, product development, and cloud computing. Such transitions do not require a complete skill match between the source and destination occupations (World Economic Forum, 2020a). It is a new process that needs emerging jobs together with appropriate reskilling and upskilling.

In the absence of available talent, According to WEF (2020a) report in labour market evolution forecast in 2020-2025, on average, employers provide access to reskilling and upskilling to 62% of their workforce and that by 2025, they will expand that provision to a further 11% of their workforce. Also, it is only 42% of employees taking up employer-supported reskilling and upskilling opportunities. However, as in the research exhibited by Sart (2014), the talent-based assessment helps any person be more involved in the current and prospective needs of the different industries by becoming more aware of his/her skills and talents, capabilities, and goals. Furthermore, the World Economic Forum (2020a) report identifies the highest skills and skill groups that employers see as increasing in prominence up to 2025. Moreover, according to Sart (2014), it has clarified that people in these groups have been critical thinking, analysis, and problem-solving groups, which have topped the agenda with year-on-year consistency. Skills in self-management, which include active learning, resilience, stress tolerance, and flexibility, are wanted features. Additionally, the information obtained through metrics partnerships with

LinkedIn and Coursera allows the types of special skills required for the roles of tomorrow to be traced with unprecedented granularity (Zahidi, 2020).

According to World Economic Forum (2020a), an in-depth look at the state of skills is that formal upskilling appears to be more closely focused on the use of technology and skills, while emotional intelligence skills are less frequently targeted in the provision of formal reskilling. "For workers, governments, and economies across the globe, growth is increasingly predicated on skills. While COVID-19 disrupted education systems and jobs worldwide, the transition to online learning ensured people could learn skills to adapt and rebuild their careers. Workforce development leaders will play a critical role in ensuring these systems can be extended and sustained moving forward" (Coursera, 2021a). According to data from Coursera (2021), the main target areas of workforce recovery programs, employer-led reskilling and upskilling activities are confirmed through findings in the report analysis. Innovation and disruptive technologies need new skills and new workers in today's economy. It is estimated that about 85 million jobs may be displaced by 2025. Technical and managerial skills in strategy and leadership will be in high demand over the next five years (Coursera, 2021b).

## CONCLUSION

The future of work must be inspired by considerations of human nature, social justice, and peace. Although the subject is both broad and complex, it is critical to discuss the future of work, society, and the economic possibilities of future generations. It is essential to develop a truly global perspective on the future of work that addresses the needs and realities of all member states rather than weighting discussions toward one specific region or another. This study has discussed paradigm shifts, the development of novel ways of thinking about work, and creating a new work organization or categories of employment. In the context of a rapidly changing, complex, and uncertain economic and societal environment, decision-makers must plan strategically for future skills requirements.

Global predictions are not wrong to say that people are on a future trajectory that pushes the limits of human imagination in terms of technology and digitalization. At this point, the jobs and skills required for these occupations are changing according to the era's requirements. Despite the disappearance of many professions, technology will drive the emergence of new ones. However, these new professions will require new skills. While robots or AI will do some of the work, humans will need to manage and direct these technologies. As a result, the future will be shaped by the drivers of digitalization. These changes will provide the world with a fresh set of dynamics that will affect both jobs and skills, although there are deficiencies in knowing what the new technologies will bring in terms of appropriate skills. Otherwise, there is a reality that usability tools based on artificial intelligence and software skills are essential talents for workers in different sectors soon in future.

## REFERENCES

Acemoglu, D., & Restrepo, P. (2017). *Robots and Jobs: Evidence from US Labor Markets*. NBER Working Paper No. 23285. National Bureau of Economic Research.

Adams-Prassl, A., Boneva, T., Rauh, C., & Golin, M. (2020). Inequality in the Impact of the Coronavirus Shock: Evidence from Real-Time Surveys. IZA DP No. 13183, IZA Institute of Labor Economics.

Atiku, S. O. (2021). Human Capacity Building Through University-Industry Collaboration. In *University-Industry Collaboration Strategies in the Digital Era* (pp. 321–336). IGI Global.

Berlingieri, G., Blanchenay, P., Calligaris, S., & Criscuolo, C. (2017). Firm-level productivity differences: Insights from the OECD's multiprod project. *International Productivity Monitor*, *32*, 97–115.

Brynjolfsson, E., & McAfee, A. (2014). *The Second Machine Age: Work, Progress, and Prosperity in a Time of Brilliant Technologies*. WW Norton & Company.

Brynjolfsson, E., Rock, D., & Syverson, C. (2019). *1. Artificial Intelligence and the Modern Productivity Paradox: A Clash of Expectations and Statistics*. University of Chicago Press.

Commonwealth Secretariat. (2020). *Commonwealth FinTech Toolkit Helping Governments to Leverage Financial Innovation.* https://www.thecommonwealth.io/wp- content/uploads/2020/10/Commonwealth-Fintech-Toolkit.pdf

Coursera. (2021a). *Global Skills Index Report*. https://www.coursera.org/skills-reports/global

Coursera. (2021b). *Transform your workforce with the skills of the future*. https://www.coursera.org/skills-reports/global

European Commission. (2014). *Assessing the Implications of Climate Change Adaptation on Employment in the EU* [Final Report & Annexes]. https://ec.europa.eu/clima/sites/clima/files/adaptation/what/docs/climate_change_employment_eu_en.pdf

Frey, C. B., & Osborne, M. A., (2017). The Future of Employment: How Susceptible are Jobs to Computerisation? *Technological Forecasting and Social Change*, *114*, 254–280.

Gordon, R. (2012). *Is U.S. Economic Growth Over? Faltering Innovation Confronts the Six Headwinds*. Available from: https://www.nber.org/papers/w18315

Günay, D., Asunakutlu, T., & Yildiz, O. (2021). *University-industry Collaboration Strategies in the Digital Era*. IGI Global.

Haliloğlu, E. Y. (2021). Efficiency Assessment of University-Industry Collaboration. In *University-Industry Collaboration Strategies in the Digital Era* (pp. 155–175). IGI Global.

Haskel, J., & Westlake, S. (2017). *Capitalism Without Capital: The Rise of the Intangible Economy*. Princeton University Press. doi:10.2307/j.ctvc77hhj

Keynes, J. M. (2010). Economic Possibilities for our Grandchildren. In *Essays in Persuasion* (pp. 321–332). Palgrave Macmillan. doi:10.1007/978-1-349-59072-8_25

McGowan, M. A., Andrews, D., & Millot, V. (2017). *The Walking Dead: Zombie Firms and Productivity Performance in OECD Countries*. OECD Economics Department Working Papers, No. 1372.

Méda, D., & Vendramin, P. (2013). *Réinventer le Travail*. PUF. doi:10.3917/puf.meda.2013.01

OECD. (2015a). *The Future of Productivity*. OECD Publishing. doi:10.1787/9789264248533-en

OECD. (2017a). *OECD Science, Technology, and Industry Scoreboard 2017: The Digital Transformation.* OECD Publishing. doi:10.1787/9789264268821-en

OECD (2017b). *OECD Economic Outlook.* OECD Publishing. doi:10.1787/eco_outlook-v2017-2-en

OECD. (2018). *Broadband Portal database.* Available from: www.oecd.org/sti/broadband/oecdbroadbandportal.htm

OECD. (2019). *Productivity Growth in the Digital Age.* https://www.oecd.org/going- digital/productivity-growth-in-the-digital-age.pdf

OECD. (2018). *Transformative technologies and jobs of the future. Background report for the Canadian G7 Innovation Ministers' Meeting.* https://www.oecd.org/innovation/transformative-technologies-and-jobs-of-the-future.pdf

OECD Publishing. https://www.oecd-ilibrary.org/docserver/9789264279179- en.pdf?expires=1632734967&id=id&accname=ocid43023557&checksum=FE8146CB4D1EF B6A1FB3CC236D85F05F

Organization for Economic Co-operation and Development. (2017). International productivity monitor: CSLS-OECD special issue from the first OECD global forum on productivity.

Pega, F., Náfrádi, B., Momen, N. C., Ujita, Y., Streicher, K. N., Prüss-Üstün, A. M., Descatha, A., Driscoll, T., Fischer, F. M., Godderis, L., Kiiver, H. M., Li, J., Magnusson Hanson, L. L., Rugulies, R., Sørensen, K., & Woodruff, T. J. (2021). Global, regional, and national burdens of ischemic heart disease and stroke attributable to exposure to long working hours for 194 countries, 2000–2016: A systematic analysis from the WHO/ILO Joint Estimates of the Work-related Burden of Disease and Injury. *Environment International, 154*, 106595. https://doi.org/10.1016/j.envint.2021.106595

Ratcheva, V., Leopold, T. A., & Zahidi, S. (2020). *Jobs of Tomorrow: Mapping Opportunity in the New Economy.* World Economic Forum.

Singh, M. K. M. (2021). A Synergized Education 4.0 Ecosystem Sustainably Aligned With Industry 4.0. In University-Industry Collaboration Strategies in the Digital Era (pp. 283– 299). IGI Global.

Sun, M. (2018). *The Impacts of the Fourth Industrial Revolution on Jobs and the Future of the Third Sector.*

*University-Industry Collaboration Strategies in the Digital Era*, 1–21.

Weber, M. (1990). *The Protestant Ethic* (Vol. G). Allen and Unwin Ltd.

Windisch, L., Schwinn, A., & Faix, W. G. (2021). Leadership. Personality. Education: The Innovation-Promoting Triad in University-Industry Collaboration–Real-World Projects Foster Students' Innovative Capability. *University-Industry Collaboration Strategies in the Digital Era*, 337–365.

World Economic Form. (2021). *2030Vision—Partnering together to scale technologies for the global goals.* 2030Vision. https://www.weforum.org/projects/frontier-2030

World Economic Forum. (2020a). *Forecasts for Labour Market Evolution in 2020-2025* (The Future of Jobs Report 2020). World Economic Forum Geneva. http://www3.weforum.org/docs/WEF_Future_of_Jobs_2020.pdf

World Economic Forum. (2020b). *The Future of Jobs Report 2020*. World Economic Forum Geneva. http://www3.weforum.org/docs/WEF_Future_of_Jobs_2020.pdf

Yildiz, O. (2021a). Changing Paradigms in the Digital Age and Entrepreneurial Universities.

Yildiz, O. (2021b). *Recent Developments in Individual and Organizational Adoption of ICTs*. IGI Global. http://doi:10.4018/978-1-7998-3045-0

Yildiz, O., Ersoy, A. S., & Yıldırım, İ. S. (2021). The Impact of Information and Communication Systems on Organizations. In *Recent Developments in Individual and Organizational Adoption of ICTs* (pp. 1–25). IGI Global.

Zahidi, S. (2020). *The Jobs of Tomorrow*. International Monetary Fund. https://www.imf.org/external/pubs/ft/fandd/2020/12/WEF-future-of-jobs-report-2020- zahidi.htm

# Chapter 2
# Bridging Academic and Industry Skills via Digital Collaboration:
## Training for International Assignment

**Tara Madden-Dent**
*Sierra Nevada University, USA*

## ABSTRACT

*As culturally responsive, social-emotional learning (SEL) competencies continue being essential skills in a 21st century workforce, both university and industry will continue placing greater focus on effective training for students and employees to strengthen workforce readiness. The following chapter introduces one example of how Polish Fulbright scholars prepared for a U.S. assignment through a digital training program, taken before participants departed their home country, as a way to support post arrival integration, safety, and success in the U.S. Compared to the control group, research findings from this phenomenological research study indicated that the four-week training program supported increases in self-awareness and self-management skills, social skills and cultural awareness, English communication skills, academic and professional readiness skills, and responsible decision-making skills in the treatment group. This study contributes one new strategy to strengthen internationalization efforts, global leadership skills, and cross-cultural relations.*

## INTRODUCTION

Global markets are dependent upon an educated workforce equipped with cross-cultural and social emotional learning skills (SEL) to navigate in-person and digital interactions with people from diverse backgrounds. In the U.S., culturally-responsive SEL skills are competencies sought after by employers (Cunningham & Villasenor, 2016; Fitzgerald & Sigelman, 2018; Future of Jobs Report, 2020; Job Outlook, 2016; Maldonado, 2019; National Association of Colleges & Employers, 2019; Yoder, et al., 2020) and have been increasingly in demand over the last several decades (Deming, 2017). The five SEL competencies (Self-Awareness, Self-Management, Social Awareness, Relationship Skills, Responsible Decision-Making Skills), are acquired through a lifelong process to which all people learn and apply

DOI: 10.4018/978-1-7998-8169-8.ch002

culturally responsive, "knowledge, skills, and attitudes to develop healthy identities, manage emotions and achieve personal and collective goals, feel and show empathy for others, establish and maintain supportive relationships, and make responsible and caring decisions" (CASEL, 2020).

*While employers value all skill sets, there is a greater demand for socio-emotional skills and higher-order cognitive skills than for basic cognitive or technical skills. These results are robust across region, industry, occupation, and education level. Employers perceive that the greatest skills gaps are in socio-emotional and higher-order cognitive skills. (Cunningham & Villasenor, 2016, p. 1).*

According to the National Association of Colleges and Employers (2019), there are eight competencies associated with career readiness (Critical Thinking/Problem Solving; Oral/Written Communication; Teamwork/Collaboration; Digital Technology; Leadership; Professionalism/Work Ethic; Career Management; Global/Intercultural Fluency), all of which require SEL skills. Universities in the U.S. and abroad act as a workforce pipeline, fostering these essential skills in its student body and through on-going professional development. By bridging university and industry collaboration, the partnership can better develop systems of innovative training that align current workforce needs with curriculum to ensure graduates develop skills that employers need in job candidates. One way that U.S. universities and industry can partner to foster these skills is through international professional development opportunities to visiting scholars. These cultural exchange programs provide academic and professional opportunities to strengthen global citizen skillsets that empower individuals to navigate indicate matrixes of human interactions.

Visiting international students and scholars have often encountered cross-cultural challenges and acculturation distress during U.S. work and study assignments. Although research demonstrates that cross-cultural training helps mitigate negative integration experiences (Deardorff, 2004; Kegel, 2009; Madden-Dent, 2014; Madden-Dent & Laden, 2016; Sherry, Bhat, Beaver, & Ling, 2004; Pitts, 2009), most U.S. institutions of higher education address these integration issues only after students and scholars arrive on campus via post arrival orientations (Madden-Dent, Wood, & Roskina, 2019). The post arrival time period is often too late to prepare international students and scholars with the knowledge and skills necessary for a safe and successful integration.

To address earlier preparation training during the pre-departure phase, the following chapter introduces an example of university and industry collaboration that conducted a phenomenological research study examining how a socio-cultural training program for Polish Fulbright Scholars influenced international integration and mission achievement. The following chapter will introduce the research findings around integration experiences of Polish Fulbright Scholars, who either completed a pre-departure class on U.S. cultural, linguistic, academic, and professional integration strategies or received their Fulbright Commission's standard international student services.

The findings help illuminate pre-departure preparation influences on post-arrival adjustment and integration into U.S. academic and cultural systems. This chapter also contributes to a better understanding of international student challenges related to pre-departure anxieties, communication barriers, socialization challenges, personal safety and health concerns, transportation, and student engagement. Results from the study indicated that the Treatment Group experienced increases in self-awareness and social awareness, cross-cultural communication and relationship skills, professional and academic skills, and self-management and responsible decision-making skills compared to the Control Group. This study contributes a new understanding of how universities and professional industries can strengthen international programs, global leadership skills, and cross-cultural relations through better understanding of people from different backgrounds.

This article is organized to achieve two objectives. The first objective is to provide a new understanding of one pre-departure culturally-responsive SEL online training and how it contributed to the participants' post arrival integration experiences. The second objective is to provide Polish Fulbright Scholar recommendations on how higher education and industry can improve integration experiences during overseas study and work assignments. This article will conclude with a discussion of implications for practice and future research directions.

## BACKGROUND

University graduates, today more than ever before, must demonstrate proficiencies beyond academic capacities that include culturally-responsive social emotional learning (SEL) competencies allowing them to navigate diverse relationships with people from different backgrounds, advance through dynamic work and study environments, and succeed in complex globalized economies. In 2016, the state of Nevada's Governor's Office of Economic Development (GOED), recognized this need and began encouraging university – industry collaboration on a global scale to help support the development of a culturally competent workforce that diversifies cross-sector partnerships and stimulate micro and macro economies.

Through State support, the Nevada Governor's office funded an American delegation of U.S. university and professional representatives to visit Warsaw, Poland in the fall of 2016 with the mission of expanding foreign university and business partnerships. While abroad, Sierra Nevada University was introduced to the Fulbright Commission in Warsaw, Poland. The two organizations identified common goals around bridging university and industry partnerships, specifically to encourage culturally-responsive SEL skills in professional scholars preparing to relocate to the U.S. for work and study. The Fulbright Scholars Program, which sponsors international scholar exchanges in all areas of endeavor, including the sciences, business, academe, public service, government, and the arts to increase mutual understanding between people from around the world.

*Today, Fulbright is the most widely recognized and prestigious international exchange program in the world, supported for more than half a century by the American people through an annual appropriation from the U.S. Congress and by the people of partner nations. The program—working with universities, schools, binational Fulbright commissions, government agencies, nongovernmental organizations and the private sector—actively seeks out individuals of achievement and potential who represent the full diversity of their respective societies and selects nominees through open, merit-based competitions (Fulbright Scholar Program, 2020).*

The Fulbright Scholarship Program is an example of how universities and industry collaborate to advance global connections between countries and cultures. For the purpose of this chapter, the term Fulbright Scholar is understood to be a professional learner, one who studies, teaches, and researches in the U.S. for one-year on a non-immigrant, temporary visa. This cross-sector partnership generated this chapter's current study to examine how a training on this goal could influence post-arrival integration experiences in the U.S.

## Review of the Literature

The field of social emotional learning emerged nearly thirty years ago and has provided basic and applied research (Cantor et al., 2018; Jones & Kahn, 2017; Madden-Dent, 2021; Osher et al., 2018; Durlak et al., 2011; Taylor et al., 2017). When implemented with fidelity, SEL applications have contributed to more equitable and safe environments for youth and adults (Jagers, Rivas-Drake, & Williams, 2019). Developed by the Collaborative for Academic, Social, and Emotional Learning (CASEL), the term SEL refers to the lifelong process through which all people learn and apply culturally responsive, "knowledge, skills, and attitudes to develop healthy identities, manage emotions and achieve personal and collective goals, feel and show empathy for others, establish and maintain supportive relationships, and make responsible and caring decisions" (2020).

According to the CASEL, SEL encompasses five competencies: Self-Awareness; Self-Management; Social Awareness; Relationship Skills; Responsible Decision-Making. All of these skills are as predictive of academic and career achievement as is IQ (Almlund, Duckworth, Heckman., & Kautz. 2011). The competencies are illustrated and described below.

*Figure 1.*

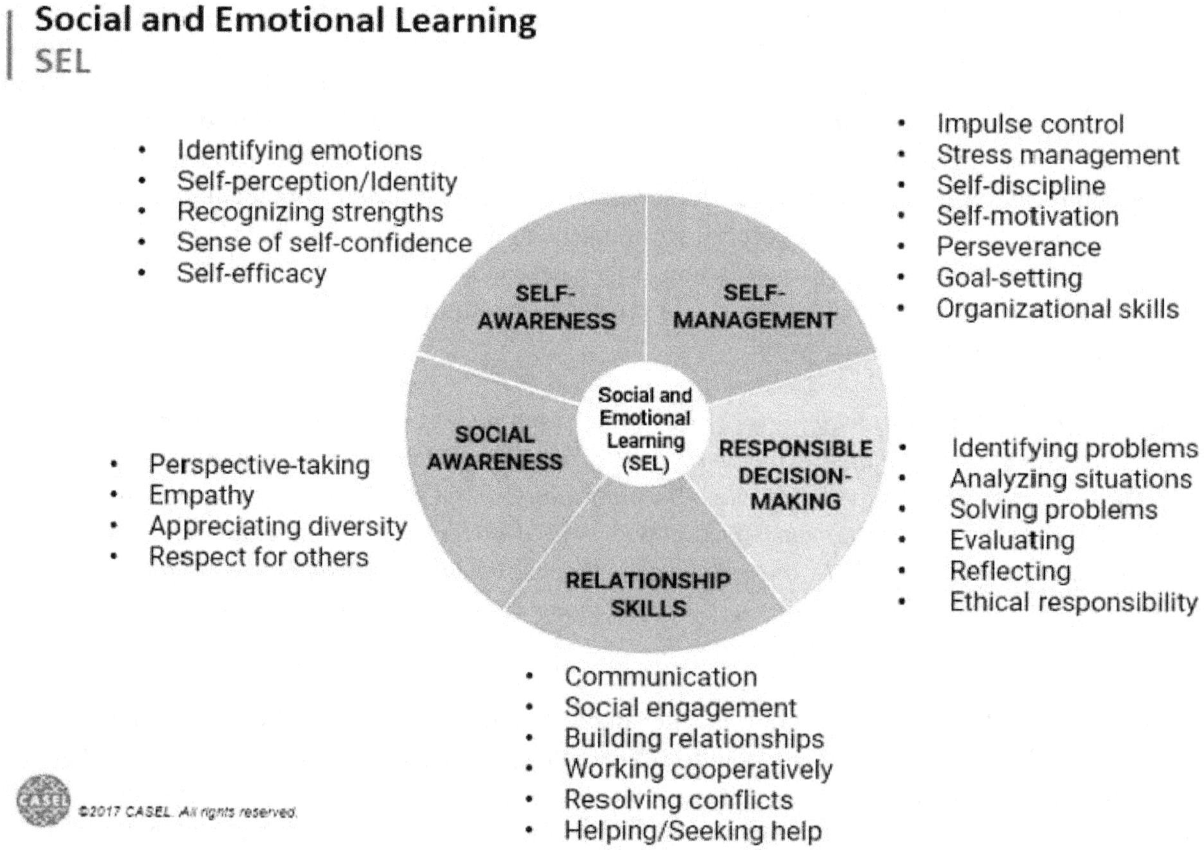

The interconnected relationship between SEL practices and academics, referred to as SEAD practices (Social, Emotional, and Academic Development), aims to reinforce equitable and human-centered environments (Aspen Institute, 2019). When implemented with fidelity, SEAD is linked with increased cultural competencies, linguistic skills, and academic success (Madden-Dent, 2016; Kerr & Madden-Dent, 2019), decreases in unhealthy behaviors, mental health issues, and school drop-out rates (Kautz, Heckman, Diris, Bas ter Weel, & Borghans, 2014), increases of 11-14% point gains in grades and test scores and more equitable learning environments (Durlak, Weissberg, Dymnicki, Taylor, & Schellinger, 2011; Taylor, Oberle, Durlak, & Weissberg, 2017). Research also indicates that SEAD implementation in academia returns a range from $11 to $104.90 for every dollar invested (Belfield, Bowden, Klapp, Levin, Shand, & Zander, 2015; Swain-Bradway, Lindstrom Johnson, Bradshaw, & McIntosh, 2017), which is not including significant cost saving from long-term benefits over the lifespan for the individual and society (Jones, Greenberg, & Crowley, 2015), including decreases in substance abuse and drug use (Klapp, Belfield, Bowden, Levin, Shand, & Zander, 2017).

Of critical note, it is important that equitable and culturally-responsive SEL competence training be inclusive to the values and preferences of all. We humans use SEL skills as a platform to express ourselves and this is why SEL skills and behaviors can look so different for each person as they are founded on the individual's culture; a set of socially transmitted ways of thinking, feeling, interacting, and communicating through shared value in traditions and customs distinguishing members of one organization from another (Hofstede, 1994; Kluckhohn, 1951; Lustig & Koester, 2003; Wohl, 2012). Culturally-responsiveness training refers to the process of developing awareness of the significance of our others' backgrounds including cultural and historical contexts, and then intentionally integrating their cultural orientations and values into equitable curriculum that recognizes individual differences as assets. Intentional culturally-responsive SEAD training has been found to assist the academic and personal success of traditionally marginalized populations in higher education's international student communities (Madden-Dent, 2014).

In U.S. higher education system hosted more than 1,095,299 international students in the 2018/2019 academic year, an 0.05% increase from the previous year (IIE, 2019), and by 2025, more than 8 million students are projected to be studying outside their home country (Chow, Gutierrez, Baumgartner, & Sato, 2009). In addition to international students helping increase campus diversification (Sahin, 2008; Ward, 2001), they contribute more than $45 Billion dollars to the U.S. economy and for every seven international students, three U.S. jobs are created (NAFSA, 2018). This influx in multinational representation adds value to higher educational systems while simultaneously stimulating the complex matrix of cultural interactions, insisting upon the need for culturally-responsive SEL training to guide safe and respectful environments aligned with campus policies and host country laws.

During integration into the U.S. academic system, international students can experience negative integration distress and additional acculturation challenges compared to domestic students as they face unfamiliar host country laws and policies, academic systems, communication and interaction styles, foreign cuisine, healthcare, transportation, weather, and environmental variables (Akhtar & Kroner-Hewig, 2015; Berry, 2006; Elturki, Liu, Hjeltness, & Hellmann, 2019; Hansen, Sheyderman, McNamara, & Grace, 2018; Leong, Mallinckrodt, & Kralj,1990; Madden-Dent & Laden; 2016; Mori, 2000). Weng, Cheong, and Cheong (2010) stated that, "Poor academic performance is often indicative of difficulties in adjusting to university environment and makes dropout more likely" (p. 337). With no previous knowledge of or experience with western academic systems or culture, international students often times discover differences in U.S. learning environments through unwanted experimental methods which can result in more than distress. Beyond these acculturation challenges acting counterproductive to academic pursuits (Weng, Cheong, & Cheong, 2010), it has also been found to negatively impact international students' sociocultural adjustment (Ward & Kennedy, 1994), health and psychological well-being, (Sandhu & Asrabadi, 1994; Shadowen, Williamson, Guerra, Ammigan, & Drexler, 2019; Tochkov, Levine, & Sanaka, 2010; Yoon, Lee, & Goh, 2008), communication (Shah, 1991), and persistence (Gardner, 2007).

Compounding the acculturation challenges, international students have traditionally avoided using campus support services such as counseling to address challenges (Poyrazli, Kavanaugh, Baker, & Al-Timimi, 2004; Yeh & Inose, 2003). If challenges are left unresolved, conflict can negatively impact academic success, socialization, language development, professional development, and psychological well-being (Benjamin, Earnest, Gruenewald, & Arthur, 2007; Hechanova-Alampay, Beehr, Christiansen, & Van Horn, 2002; Madden-Dent, 2014; Sandhu &

Asrabadi, 1994; Smith & Khawaja, 2011; Swagler & Ellis, 2003; Wang, 2004; Weng, Cheong, & Cheong, 2010; Zhou, Frey, & Bang, 2011).

Like with the example of homesickness, which has been found to be a predictive variable of poor cross-cultural adjustment (Ying & Liese, 1994), students and professionals can address cultural adjustment issues if their interpersonal expectations and their actual experiences are better aligned (Kegel, 2009). Integration challenges can be better managed with more accurate adaptation practices to local norms and expectations (Sullivan & Kashubeck-West, 2015). With a better understanding of host country culture through intentional culturally-responsive SEL training, individuals can develop more accurate expectations of integration related issues and may develop more accurate methods for coping with host country norms (Pitts, 2009).

Although research indicates that culturally-responsive training increases awareness and management skills for better cross-cultural transition and adjustment (Dekaney, 2008; Neill, 2008; Madden-Dent & Laden, 2016; Madden-Dent, 2021; Pitts, 2009; Sanchez, Spector, & Cooper, 2000; Selmer, 2001; Shim & Paprock, 2002; Ying & Liese, 1990; Zhu, 2008), increases intercultural communication and understanding (Atlay, 2005; Samovar, Porter, & McDaniel, 2011; Shemshadsara, 2012), strengthens intercultural sensitivity (Altshuler, Sussman, & Kachur, 2003; Madden-Dent, Jackson, & Cason, 2021), increases relational empathy in host cultures (Neill, 2008; Zhu, 2008), increases in self-awareness of personal cultural preferences and styles (Kerr & Madden-Dent, 2019; Kristjansdottir, 2003), and supports cross-cultural adaptation processes (Chen, 2000; Dekaney, 2008), most U.S. colleges and universities provide international students and scholars integration training only after they arrive in the U.S. (Madden-Dent, Wood, & Roskina. 2019). Furthermore, many institutions often provide underdeveloped, inconsistent, and/or optional cultural training services (Hser, 2005). This is problematic for international students seeking early and effective strategies to relocate safely and integrate quickly.

This gap in research and practice around the impacts of pre-departure culturally-responsive SEL training on post arrival integration is addressed in this chapter's study. A goal of this chapter is to introduce one method that universities and industry can prepare international scholars with U.S. cultural, social, emotional, academic, and professional skills to increase integration safety and mission achievement.

## RESEARCH METHOD

In an effort to investigate how a culturally responsive SEL training, provided during the pre-departure phase, could influence post arrival integration experiences of Polish Fulbright Scholars, a phenomenological approach was selected for this study. The study included a narrative research inquiry relying on spoken and written accounts related to cross-cultural experiences before and during the first few months in the U.S. Qualitative data sources (Written reflections; Interviews), and two descriptive data sources (Cultural Intelligence Scale (CQS) assessment; Intercultural Effectiveness Scale (IES) assessment), were used in partnership, creating a triangulated body of data for collective analysis.

## Participants

With assistance from the Fulbright Commission in Warsaw, Poland, purposive sampling was used to select volunteer participants with the following criteria: those who originated from Poland, who had never had prior experience in the U.S., and who spoke English as a second language. There was a total of fourteen participants who held graduate and post-doctorate standings and were preparing for a one-year study and work assignment in the U.S. Of the fourteen, six were male and eight were female with ages ranging between 24 to 38. All participants' home cities were located throughout Poland and English was their second language. The 2017 fall semester was the participants' first time working and studying in the U.S. The participants' assignment locations placed in destinations across the U.S.

There were two groups of participants (Treatment Group; Control Group), and all completed a one-day orientation in Warsaw, Poland as a required standard training activity prior to U.S. departure. The Treatment Group (n = 7), received an additional treatment, an intensive four-week SEAD training program consisting of online curriculum, two in-person orientation workshops (hosted in Poland), and three post-arrival student surveys in the U.S. The second group of participants was the Control Group (n = 7). These participants only received Fulbright's standard 1-day orientation prior to departing to the U.S. Of note, these participants also committed to completing three post-arrival surveys during their first semester in the U.S.

## The Study

Although all participants were required to complete Fulbright's one-day pre-departure orientation in Warsaw, Poland, only the Treatment Group received an additional 29-day culturally-responsive SEL training. The training was offered by Fulbright's partnering U.S. institution of higher education, Sierra Nevada University (SNU), a private liberal arts college located in Incline Village, Nevada, USA. The 29-day training was held online with the exception of two, one-day in-person workshops hosted in Warsaw, Poland. The first workshop was completed on the first day of training, and the second workshop was completed on the last day of the training.

Applying a culturally responsive SEL framework, the training intervention was designed to aid in the development of more accurate expectations of contemporary U.S. life and work, in addition to post-arrival integration management skills. Students learned about U.S. classroom dynamics and study skills, student responsibilities and ethical academic practices, classroom etiquette, APA formatting, cultural integration strategies, intercultural communication, and professional development skills. The Treatment Group examined their own cultural orientations and values (Self-Awareness) before comparing/contrasting those to U.S. cultural norms (Social Awareness), ways to appropriately bridge cultural and linguistic differences with U.S. peers and colleagues (Relationship Skills), methods to manage stressful phases of cross-cultural adaptation during international relocation and post arrival integration (Self-Management

Skills), and how to set and achieve professional and academic goals while in the U.S. (Responsible Decision-Making Skills).

Several types of instructional methods were used for this online training including lecture videos, audio podcasts, small group discussions, readings, student reflections, validated instruments, and a final written action plan. During the 29-day training, the Fulbright Scholars completed 20 homework assignments, 20 online quizzes, virtual one-on-one office hour meetings with the U.S. professor. Throughout their training, scholars worked on a written assignment entitled, "My Action Plan", where they described what they learned in this class and how they planned to use their new knowledge and skills to better integrate, transition, and adjust into U.S. academic, cultural, and workforce systems.

## Data Sources

Ten sources of data were used in this study: Participant interviews, written reflections, Cultural Intelligence Scale (CQS), Intercultural Effectiveness Scale (IES), GlobeSmart Profile (GSP), three online post-arrival surveys, training artifacts, and a course evaluation.

### Participant Interviews

Treatment Group participants completed one open-ended, semi-structured student interview via Skype. The interview was conducted during the first week of the pre-departure training to collect participants' perceptions on international relocation challenges and what their preparation plans were. The 45-60-minute interviews elicited information relevant to experiences that international scholars had regarded as important and how they made meaning about their experiences. This interview collected participants' narratives regarding their perception of culture and how they believed culture may impact their overall international goals.

### Written Reflections

The second data source was collected from on-going reflections. During the 4-week training, Treatment Group participants completed weekly written reflections responding to a series of question prompts about culture, social emotional learning, and how culture influenced sense-of-self, relationships, academics, social interactions and communication styles, and professional development. In these reflections, participants shared how they defined culture and how culture shaped their beliefs and worldviews. Participants shared their knowledge of U.S. culture, their concerns, and ways to manage or cope with those concerns in the U.S. Participants also wrote about a variety of culturally related topics including, but not limited to, how they interpret culture and how it impacted their development, how their cultural styles differ from U.S. cultural styles, how they prefer to interact with others and why.

### Cultural Intelligence Scale (CQS) Assessment

The Cultural Intelligence Scale (CQS) is designed by the Cultural Intelligence Center and is a valid and reliable measure of a person's ability to navigate effectively in diverse conditions. The CQS Assessments measure, "An individual's capability for working and relating across cultures" (Cultural Intelligence Center, 2018). Participants complete the CQS assessment online before receiving a personalized report that identifies strengths and developmental opportunities for functioning effectively in multicultural settings. The report helps the student interpret how they scored in four CQ Capabilities: CQ Drive, CQ Knowledge, CQ Action, and CQ Strategy. The feedback report was used to guide participants through the process of creating a personal Development Plan. The CQS has a strong internal reliability exceeding Cronbach's alpha of .70 and has been researched and published in more than seventy academic journals (Cultural Intelligence Center, 2018a).

Both Treatment and Control Group completed the Cultural Intelligence Scale (CQS). The Treatment Group completed the CQS twice; one pre-assessment and one post-assessment to identify changes in their CQ levels. The Control Group completed the CQS once since they did not receive a treatment.

## Intercultural Effectiveness Scale (IES)

Both the Treatment and Control Group completed the Intercultural Effectiveness Scale (IES), an online assessment designed by Aperian Global to measure competencies essential for effective interaction with people from different cultures. The IES is a 52-item Likert scale survey available in seven languages (English, French, German, Spanish (Latin American), Chinese, Japanese, and Arabic). The IES assessment examines the following three dimensions of cultural competence:

- Continuous Learning: Does one learn effectively? What is one's interest in people from other cultures and in self-understanding?
- Interpersonal Engagement: Does one develop and maintain relationships well? What is one's interest in developing relationships with people who are different from us?
- Hardiness: Ability to manage one's thoughts and emotions effectively in challenging situations.

Cultural competency was measured on a Likert scale of 1 (low) to 7 (high) for Continuous Learning, Interpersonal Engagement, Hardiness and Overall Cultural Effectiveness.

The Treatment Group completed the IES twice, once at the training's start date (pre-assessment), and again at the training's conclusion (post-assessment), to identify changes in IES levels. The pre-and post-course assessments provide an objective assessment of the impact that the pre-departure course may have had on their cultural competence. The Control Group completed the IES once since they did not receive a treatment. Individual feedback reports are provided to participants after each survey. Reports include a 24-page feedback report including information about their IES score, a personalized action plan for improvement, explanations of scores and typical profiles, definitions of the dimensions and strategies for development, strategies to develop intercultural capacities, and additional support resources.

## GlobeSmart Profile (GSP)

The GlobeSmart Profile (GSP), designed by Aperian Global, was used to support reflection on how cultural preferences and how those preferences influenced communication and relationships. The 40-question survey was available in 13 languages, including Arabic, Chinese, Danish, Dutch, English, French, German, Japanese, Korean, Portuguese, Russian, Spanish, and Thai. The survey included five key cultural dimensions rooted in Hofstede's model that can likely manifest themselves in campus and workplace contexts. The dimensions include: Independent – Interdependent; Egalitarianism – Status; Risk – Certainty; Direct – Indirect; and Task – Relationship. The GSP provided a user-friendly Poland

and U.S. comparison report for cultural dimensions. The report illustrated where participants' cultural preferences ranged along a dimension spectrum and provided suggestions for overcoming cultural gaps with those who have different cultural preferences. The Treatment Group participants used the GSP report throughout their 4-week training in partnership with other lessons, reflection assignments, and office hour discussions.

### Online Surveys

Both Treatment and Control Groups completed three online surveys, one each month, for three months after arriving to the U.S. These post arrival surveys inquired about relocation and adjustment experiences, what they wished they had known before arriving to the States, what they would have wanted in the pre-departure training program if they had the foresight, and what they recommend future preparatory programs provide to scholars prior to relocating to the U.S. Participants responded to questions about culture, cultural knowledge, cultural preparation, cross-cultural transition and adjustment experiences. The surveys identified student perceptions of their pre-departure experience, its impact on their cross-cultural awareness and preparation, and what students thought about cross-cultural preparation. All participants completed the online surveys via Survey Monkey. There were two versions of the survey, one for the Treatment Group that referenced the pre-departure treatment, and a second version for the Control Group that referenced Fulbright's standard 1-day pre-departure orientation.

### Training Artifacts

An array of training documents was collectively analyzed in conjunction with all data sources. These documents included the U.S. professor's notes from training activities and office hour meetings, homework assignments, quizzes, a course evaluation, assessments, and email correspondences. These sources were analyzed together to help create a triangulated body of data for collective analysis.

### Course Evaluation and Self-Assessment

When concluding the 29-day pre-departure training, participants were asked to complete a 50-question survey about their experience in the training program and their perception of it on their own culturally-responsive SEL skills and readiness for their U.S. assignment. The Fulbright Scholarship Program helped facilitate the surveys in-person at their office in Warsaw, Poland.

## RESULTS

Two research findings are addressed in this chapter. The first pertains to how a culturally-responsive SEL training, conducted during the pre-departure phase with Polish Fulbright Scholars, contributed to the participants' post-arrival integration experiences, socio-cultural knowledge, and SEL skills. The second research finding provides recommendations from Polish Fulbright Scholars on how to improve international visitors through support services within pre-departure and post-arrival adjustment phases.

## A Pre-Departure Culturally-Responsive SEL Training

Treatment Group participants indicated that the training was helpful to prepare them develop more accurate expectations of what they actually experienced in the U.S. through the study of cultural norms, professional and academic etiquette, and cross-cultural integration strategies. One Treatment Group participant shared, "The pre-departure training helped me to clarify my doubts and concerns that I had before I came to the U.S.". Another participant shared, "Knowing that people from the U.S. tend to not establish relationships with their coworkers, it helps me set expectations and not get disappointed when someone is only focused on his or her work." One participant similarly reflected, "Before I have the chance to talk with Americans, the professor and pre-departure class were good examples and training before my relocation." One participant shared. The following participant's statement echoes this point in her statement, "Even though, some aspects of U.S. culture may seem obvious, it is always worth trying to understand it better and learn more about our own expectations and needs." Lastly, the following participant's written homework reflection demonstrates one way that he applied knowledge gained from the training into his integration expectations and action plan:

*My GOAL is to communicate more freely and naturally when I am speaking with the other people in English. Challenges associated with achieving my goal include:*

Communication barrier related with my insufficient English proficiency;
Fear that someone may find me as a not prepared for this kind of conversation;
Fear that I will not be able to find common themes with another person coming from another culture;
Fear of being misunderstand because the cultural differences and different communication styles.

*Strategies I will use to overcome the challenges so that I may achieve the goal:*

Using a "small talks" to break the ice at the beginning of the conversation;
Remembering the openness and high communicativeness of people in the United States;
Remembering about non-verbal communication during the conversation;
Awareness of cultural differences between myself and the people from the US (distance, unformal style of communication).

The Treatment Group's data demonstrated an ability to apply their gained culturally-responsive SEL knowledge and skills to bridge cultural gaps after arrival in the U.S. These participants expressed that their gained cultural knowledge aided with understanding the U.S. culture. This is demonstrated in the following participant's statement who had identified having an in-direct communication style preference, "I don't take personally every remark. People here are usually very direct and sometimes they say something point-blank." Another participant recognized from the training that course syllabi were different in the U.S. compared to in Poland universities. During one of the training office hours, he worked with the U.S. professor to restructure the syllabi that he was designing to teach in the U.S. The following participant's written reflection demonstrates one way that he applied the knowledge gained during the training into meaningful ways during his integration experience:

*I really appreciate the opportunity to learn more about the U.S. culture with your program! It really helped me in my first weeks here. First of all, I was noticing very quickly all the interpersonal differences that were explained during the course. For example, handshakes, larger personal space (especially when two persons talk with each other, or in a queue), small talks, the expectation to introduce myself with the references to my background and my motivation to come to the U.S. Besides that, I really notice punctuality and its importance for the U.S. Americans. Following agenda, and replying to emails are also noticeable for me. Until now I am struggling a little bit with making friends with the U.S. Americans. I have met a lot of people so far, but I get along most with those U.S. Americans who have traveled before or are curious about my culture. However, it is a minority of people who I have met. Since I am an only international student in my Department, it is pretty challenging to establish a relationship with my classmates.*

Through the online surveys, written reflections, homework assignments, one-on-one office hour meeting notes, in-person workshop observation notes, the "My Action Plan" assignment, the CQS, the IES, and the GlobeSmart Profile, Treatment Group participants indicated that the pre-departure training had helped them during their post-arrival integration experience. This data was represented in the following student-reported themes which emerged from the data: Increased language and communication skills; Increased U.S. networking skills; Increased U.S. cultural knowledge; Increased confidence to travel to the USA; Increased U.S. professional skills; Increased knowledge and confidence around integration strategies; Increased U.S. academic readiness skills; Increased confidence to speak with U.S. natives. Furthermore, according to the two Treatment Group IES assessment scores (pre and post), Treatment Group participants' IES scores increased for all categories: Continuous Learning (5.00 to 6.00); Interpersonal Engagement (4.80 to 5.00); Hardiness (3.60 to 4.40); and Overall Cultural Competency (4.40 to 5.60).

The Control Group's data was analyzed and the following themes emerged from the data:

Had consistent difficulty with understanding why they were experiencing intercultural communication conflict after arriving in the U.S.

Expressed having more surprises and challenges with U.S. nuances such as socialization and transportation issues.

Shared feelings of being unsafe and homesick more often than the Treatment Group.

Shared being unfamiliar with U.S. laws and policies, university rules, and legal processes related to housing and banking.

Indicated that friends were their main source of support and information.

Control Group quotes from post-arrival surveys that support these themes:

*"The first week was the hardest one. It was not the first time when I moved abroad, but this time the administration part was really difficult... Everything takes forever!"*

*"I am here around 3 weeks and still I am not completely done with all the documents, banking and another registration stuff."*

*"Formalities! The way how the U.S. takes care about it (work, banking etc.) is too challenging for some European people here."*

*"In Chicago I don't feel very safe, even in Hyde Park."*

*"It is very hard to build friendship to US people; friendships - hard to establish."*

*"I am adjusting to the culture of "unofficial", that is something different than in my home country. I guess that in classrooms this facilitates the contact with students, but on the other hand it may impact on the respect towards the professor."*

*"I am not sure if I am addressing everyone properly, though."*

*"My challenges are making friends, meeting people, hanging out with people from other nations."*

*"I am afraid that I take care about my health less because of the speed of work in which I'm involved here."*

*"It is still hard to build relationships here among other people - the best way is to keep with other polish people."*

*"I don't feel that building relationships/friendships are possible here without being completely fluent in English and culture. It has an impact on me. Also, I spend lot of time in close polish society which is little unhealthy - closed societies are always unhealthy at some point."*

## International Students' Recommendations for U.S. Higher Education

The Polish scholar participants provided one main recommendation to improve the international program. The recommendation included that international scholars explicitly study integration strategies through culturally-responsive SEL training prior to departing for the U.S. Participants recommended that the training explicitly teach cultural, academic, and professional norms, host country law and policies, transportation systems, and financial strategies for cost effective integration. The following Treatment Group statements demonstrate this theme:

*"I recommend taking it for everyone who is curious about other cultures! Thank you for sharing that with me!"*

*"I definitely recommend this course, especially for people who aren't aware of intercultural differences or for those who have never been overseas before."*

Statements from the Control Group reflected this theme in the following statements:

*"I wish I had known more about U.S. culture, life styles, people, communication, transportation, laws, and banking before arriving in the U.S."*

*"I am here around 3 weeks and still I am not completely done with all the documents, banking and another registration stuff."*

*"Formalities! The way how the U.S. takes care about it (work, banking etc.) is too challenging for some European people here."*

*"I think it would have been nice if I had a preparation training program before coming here."*

*"I am not sure if I am addressing everyone properly, though."*

*"More information about the educational system: who is senior, sophomore etc... Also transferring from Polish to the U.S. educational system has been challenging. Training would help get familiar with all the policies, regulations etc."*

## RESEARCH IMPLICATIONS FOR PRACTICE

This study's research findings suggest that the Treatment Group gained knowledge, confidence, and skills from the pre-departure training that increased first semester success, health, safety, academic and professional development, and overall satisfaction. This study's findings advance current research showing that cultural training increases cultural knowledge, awareness, and sensitivity (Altshuler, Sussman, & Kachur, 2003; Black & Mendenhall, 1990; Kristjansdottir, 2003; Pieter Van Oudenhoven & Van der Zee, 2002; Zhu, 2008). This study contributes further evidence supporting literature that early and intentional examination of self and cultural awareness during the pre-departure stage leads to greater cultural competencies and cross-cultural integration skills. Based on this study, implications for practice encourage U.S. higher education institutions and business industries to provide pre-departure training around culturally-responsive SEL competencies to increase integration success abroad for international students, scholars, and expatriates.

## FUTURE RESEARCH DIRECTIONS

Building on this study's findings, future research is encouraged to explore how preparation training and coursework for students and employees, prior to their international departure, influences integration experiences and mission achievement. There is a need for future research to investigate how a similar pre-departure training program can be expanded into a cultural bridge training program that provides on-going support throughout the first year in a hosting country. It would be helpful for the field, if future research replicated a similar study as in this chapter with longitudinal data for international student performance and retention rates of both Treatment and Control Groups. This next step in research is a way to assess long-term relationships between pre-departure training and post-arrival successes (e.g., Language development; Academic achievement; Professional achievement). Future studies may also want to consider examining specific participant demographics (e.g., Countries of origin; Undergraduate Students; Families with dependents). Finally, future research may consider including how early, pre-departure training such as the one introduced in this study, can influence the post arrival integration experiences of accompanying family members who are traveling internationally with the student, scholar, or professional.

## CONCLUSION

This chapter provided an introduction to how one university and industry partnership provided an innovative pre-departure culturally-responsive Social Emotional Learning training intervention. This study described its phenomenological approach collecting Polish Fulbright Scholars' perspectives about how training for U.S. work and study had influenced their integration experience. The research findings contribute to the understanding of how explicit culturally-responsive Social Emotional education supports increases in self-awareness, social awareness, self-management, relationship skills, and responsible decision-making skills. As research continues to demonstrate the effectiveness of pre-departure training to facilitate safer and more efficient integration into international work and study environments, a greater emphasis will be placed on accessible digital training and resources.

## REFERENCES

Akhtar, M., & Kröner-Herwig, B. (2015). Acculturative stress among international students in context of socio-demographic variables and coping styles. *Current Psychology, 34*, 803–815. doi:10.1007/s12144-015-9303-4

Altay, I. F. (2005). Developing Cultural Awareness. *Journal of Language and Linguistic Studies., 2*, 171–182.

Altshuler, L., Sussman, N. M., & Kachur, E. (2003). Assessing changes in intercultural sensitivity among physician trainees using the intercultural development inventory. *International Journal of Intercultural Relations, 27*(4), 387–401. doi:10.1016/S0147-1767(03)00029-4

Aspen Institute. (2019). *What is Social, Emotional, and Academic Development?* Retrieved at https://www.aspeninstitute.org/publications/pursuing-social-and-emotional-development-through-a-racial-equity-lens-a-call-to-action/

Balcazar, F. E., Suarez-Balcazar, Y., & Taylor-Ritzler, T. (2009). Cultural competence: Development of a conceptual framework. *Disability and Rehabilitation, 31*(14), 1153–1160. doi:10.1080/09638280902773752 PMID:19802931

Belfield, B., & Klapp, L. (2015). The economic value of social and emotional learning. New York, NY: Center for Benefit-Cost Studies in Education: Teachers College, Columbia University.

Benjamin, M., Earnest, K., Gruenewald, D., & Arthur, G. (2007). The first few weeks of the first year. *New Directions for Student Services, 2007*(117), 13–24. doi:10.1002s.229

Berry, J. W. (2003). Conceptual approaches to acculturation. In K. M. Chun., P. Balls-Organista, & G. Marin (Eds.), Acculturation: Advances in theory, measurement, and applied research (pp. 17-38). Washington, DC: American Psychological Association. doi:10.1037/10472-004

Berry, J. W. (2006). *Stress perspectives on acculturation. The Cambridge Handbook of Acculturation Psychology*. University Press.

Black, J. S., & Mendenhall, M. E. (1990). Cross-Cultural effectiveness: A review and theoretical framework for future research. *Academy of Management Review*, *15*(1), 113–136. doi:10.5465/amr.1990.11591834

Chen, C. P. (1999). Common stressors among international college students: Research and counseling implications. *Journal of College Counseling*, *2*(1), 49–65. doi:10.1002/j.2161-1882.1999.tb00142.x

Chen, Z. (2000). International students' preparation for and adaptation to the American higher education system: A study of cross-cultural communication. *World Communication*, *29*(2), 25–48.

Collaborative for Academic, Social, and Emotional Learning (CASEL). (2017). *Making the Case for SEL* (PowerPoint). Retrieved at https://docs.google.com/presentation/d/1Tb9WundNcsURexo2RTvVGVIVlzD_q9i6Vv4jcNtqZjI/edit#slide=id.p4

Cultural Intelligence Center. (2018). *CQ Assessment*. Retrieved at https://culturalq.com/products-services/assessments/cq-assessments/

Cultural Intelligence Center. (2018a). *Academic Construct Validity*. Retrieved at https://culturalq.com/wp-content/uploads/2018/01/Academic-Construct-Validity_v.1.18.pdf

Cunningham, W., & Villasenor, P. (2016). Employer voices, employer demands, and implications for public skills development policy. Washington, DC: World Bank; Cary, NC: Oxford University Press. doi:10.1093/wbro/lkv019

Deardorff, D. K. (2004). *The identification and assessment of intercultural competence as a student outcome of internationalization at institutions of higher education in the United States*. Dissertation: North Carolina State University. Retrieved from https://repository.lib.ncsu.edu/ir/bitstream/1840.16/5733/1/etd.pdf

Dekaney, E. M. (2008). Students' pre-departure expectations and post-sojourn observations in a short-term international program abroad on the culture, music, and art of Brazil. *International Education*, *37*(2), 17–29.

Elturki, E., Liu, Y., Hjeltness, J., & Hellmann, K. (2019). Needs, expectations, and experiences of international students in pathway program in the united states. *Journal of International Students*, *9*(1), 192–210. doi:10.32674/jis.v9i1.274

Fitzgerald, B. K., & Sigelman, M. (2018). *The new foundational skills of the digital economy: Developing the professionals of the future*. Burning Glass Technologies. Retrieved from www.burning-glass.com

Fulbright Scholar Program. (2018). *About Fulbright*. Retrieved from https://www.cies.org/about-us/about-senator-j-william-fulbright

Fulbright Scholars Program. (2020). *About Fulbright*. Retrieved from https://www.cies.org/about-us/about-senator-j-william-fulbright

Future of Jobs Report. (2020). *World Economic Forum*. Retrieved from https://www.weforum.org/agenda/2020/10/top-10-work-skills-of-tomorrow-how-long-it-takes-to-learn-them/

Gardner, S. K. (2007). I heard it through the grapevine: Doctoral student socialization in chemistry and history. *Higher Education*, *54*(5), 723–740. doi:10.100710734-006-9020-x

Hansen, H. R., Shneyderman, Y., McNamara, G. S., & Grace, L. (2018). Assessing acculturative stress of international students at a U.S. community college. *Journal of International Students*, *8*, 215–232. doi:10.32674/jis.v8i1.161

Hechanova-Alampay, R., Beehr, T. A., Christiansen, N. D., & Van Horn, R. K. (2002). Adjustment and strain among domestic and international student sojourners: A longitudinal study. *School Psychology International*, *23*(4), 458–474. doi:10.1177/0143034302234007

Hofstede, G. (2001). *Cultural consequences. Comparing values, behaviors, institutions, and organizations across nations* (2nd ed.). Sage.

Hser, M. (2005). Campus internationalization: A study of American universities' internationalization efforts. *International Education*, *35*(1), 35–48.

Institute of International Education. (2019). *Open Doors 2019: Fast facts: United States*. Institute of International Education. Retrieved from https://www.iie.org/Research-and-Publications/Open-Doors/Data/Fast-Facts

Jagers, R. J., Rivas-Drake, D., & Williams, B. (2019). Transformative Social and Emotional Learning (SEL): Toward SEL in service of educational equity and excellence. *Educational Psychologist*, *54*(3), 162–184. doi:10.1080/00461520.2019.1623032

Jones, D., Crowley, D. M., & Greenberg, M. T. (2017). *Improving social emotional skills in childhood enhances long-term well-being and economic outcomes*. Edna Bennet Pierce Prevention Research Center, Pennsylvania State University.

Jones, S., & Khan, J. (2017). *The evidence base for how we learn: Supporting students' social, emotional, and academic development*. Aspen Institute. Retrieved from http://nationathope.org/wp-content/uploads/final_cds-evidence-base.pdf

Kautz, Diris, Bas ter Weel, & Borghans. (2014). Fostering and measuring skills: Improving cognitive and non-cognitive skills to promote lifetime success. Paris, France: Organization for Economic Cooperation and Development.

Kegel, K. (2009). Homesickness in international college students. In G. R. Walz, J. C. Bleuer, & R. K. Yep (Eds.), *Compelling counseling interventions: VISTAS 2009* (pp. 67–76). American Counseling Association.

Kerr, D. B., & Madden-Dent, T. (2019). Cultural Transition and Adjustment of International East Asian Undergraduate Students. In S. E. Brock & P. J. McAliney (Eds.), *Discourses on Business Education at the College Level: On the Boundaries of Content and Praxis*. Touro University Press Books. doi:10.1515/9781644691205-009

Kim, B. S. K., & Abreu, J. M. (2001). Acculturation measurement: Theory, current instruments, and future directions. In J. G. Ponterotto, J. M. Casa, L. A. Suzuki, & C. M. Alexander (Eds.), *Handbook of multicultural counseling*. Sage.

Kim, Y. Y. (2001). *Becoming intercultural: An integrative theory of communication and cross-cultural adaptation*. Sage.

Klapp, A., Bowden, B., Belfield, C., Levin, H., Shand, R., & Zander, S. (2017). A benefit-cost analysis of a long-term intervention on social and emotional learning in compulsory school. *The International Journal of Emotional Education*, (9), 3–19.

Kluckhohn, C. (1951). *The study of culture. The Policy Sciences*. Stanford University Press.

Kristjansdottir, E. S. (2003). *Invisibility dreaded and desired: Phenomenological inquiry of sojourners' cross-cultural adaptation* (Dissertation). Arizona State University, UMI Dissertations Publishing.

Leong, F. T. L., & Chou, E. L. (1996). Counseling international students. In P. Pedersen (Ed.), *Counseling across cultures* (4th ed., pp. 210–242). Sage.

Leong, F. T. L., Mallinckrodt, B., & Kralj, M. M. (1990). Cross-cultural variations in stress and adjustment among Asian and Caucasian graduate students. *Journal of Multicultural Counseling and Development*, *18*(1), 19–28. doi:10.1002/j.2161-1912.1990.tb00433.x

Lustig, M. W., & Koester, J. (2003). *Intercultural competence: Interpersonal communication across cultures* (4th ed.). Pearson Education, Inc.

Luu, V. (2016). *The 10 skills you'll need by 2020 (And beyond)*. CareerFAQS. Retrieved from https://www.careerfaqs.com.au/news/news-and-views/the-10-skills-you-ll-need-by-2020-and-beyond

Madden-Dent, T. (2014). *A phenomenological study of cultural transition and adjustment of Asian undergraduate international students using different cross-cultural treatments. ProQuest*. UMI Dissertations Publishing.

Madden-Dent, T. (2021). Advancing equity through culturally responsive social-emotional education: Addressing international student integration. In *Advances in Motivation and Achievement. Motivating the SEL Field Forward Through Equity*. Emerald Publishing Limited. Retrieved at https://www.emerald.com/insight/publication/issn/0749-7423 doi:10.1108/S0749-7423202221

Madden-Dent, T., Jackson, I., & Cason, J. (2021). Culturally-responsive social emotional academic development. In *Leading Schools with Social Emotional Academic Development (SEAD)*. IGI Global Publication. Retrieved at https://www.igi-global.com/book/leading-schools-social-emotional-academic/256645

Madden-Dent, T., & Laden, R. (2016). *Pre-departure cultural preparation for international students. In Global Perspectives and Local Challenges Surrounding International Student Mobility*. IGI Global Publication.

Madden-Dent, T., Wood, D., & Roskina, K. (2019). A Survey of International Student Services at 200 U.S. Universities and Colleges. *Journal of International Students, 9*(4), 346-362. Retrieved at https://www.ojed.org/index.php/jis/article/view/346/830

Maldonado, C. (2019). *Integrating workforce development practices in higher education*. Workforce Development Center, University of Nevada.

Medina-López-Portillo, A. (2004). Intercultural learning assessment: The link between program duration and the development of intercultural sensitivity. *Frontiers: The Interdisciplinary Journal of Study Abroad*, *X*(1), 179–199. doi:10.36366/frontiers.v10i1.141

Mori, S. C. (2000). Addressing the mental health concerns of international students. *Journal of Counseling and Development, 78*(2), 137–144. doi:10.1002/j.1556-6676.2000.tb02571.x

NAFSA. (2013). *The economic benefits of international students to the U.S. economy for the 2012-2013 academic year: A statistical analysis.* NAFSA: Association of International Educators annual Economic Impact Statement. Retrieved from https://www.iie.org/Research-and-Publications/Open-Doors/Data/Economic-Impact-of-International-Students

NAFSA. (2018). *Economic benefits of international students.* Association of International Educators. Retrieved at https://www.nafsa.org/isev/reports/state?state=NV&year=2018

National Association of Colleges and Employers. (2019). *Career readiness for the new college graduate: A definition of competencies* (revised). Retrieved from https://www.naceweb.org/career-readiness/competencies/career-readiness-defined/

National Network of Business and Industry Associations. (2014). *Common employability skills: A foundation for success in the workplace: The skills all employees need, no matter where they work.* National Network of Business and Industry Associations. Retrieved at http://businessroundtable.org/sites/default/files/Common%20Employability_asingle_fm.pdf

Neill, J. (2008). *The expatriate venture: What role does cross-cultural training play and what theories guide research in the field?* Schmidt Labor Research Center Seminar Research Series. University of Rhode Island.

Outlook, J. (2016). *The attributes employers want to see on new college graduates' resumes.* National Association of Colleges and Employers. Retrieved from https://www.naceweb.org/career-development/trends-and-predictions/job-outlook-2016-attributes-employers-want-to-see-on-new-college-graduates-resumes/

Pieter Van Oudenhoven, J., & Van der Zee, K. I. (2002). Predicting multicultural effectiveness of international students: The Multicultural Personality Questionnaire. *International Journal of Intercultural Relations, 26*(6), 679–694. doi:10.1016/S0147-1767(02)00041-X

Pilhofer, K. (2010). *Cultural knowledge: An ethical deconstruction of the concept as a foundation for respect for cultural differences from a post-colonial and Levinasian perspective.* Copenhagen Business School. Retrieved from http://studenttheses.cbs.dk/bitstream/handle/10417/1677/katharina_pilhofer.pdf?sequence=1

Pitts, M. J. (2009). Identity and the role of expectations, stress, and talk in short-term student sojourner adjustment: An application of the integrative theory of communication and cross-cultural adaptation. *International Journal of Intercultural Relations, 33*(6), 450–462. doi:10.1016/j.ijintrel.2009.07.002

Poyrazli, S., Kavanaugh, P. R., Baker, A., & Al-Timimi, N. (2004). Social support and demographic correlates of acculturative stress in international students. *Journal of College Counseling, 7*(1), 73–82. doi:10.1002/j.2161-1882.2004.tb00261.x

Rew, L., Becker, H., Cookston, J., Khosropour, S., & Martinez, S. (2003). Measuring cultural awareness in nursing students. *The Journal of Nursing Education, 42*(6), 248–257. doi:10.3928/0148-4834-20030601-07 PMID:12814215

Rose, J., & Smith, K. (2020). *Embedding culturally responsive practices in Tier I. Center on PBIS*. Positive Behavioral Interventions & Supports. Retrieved at www.pbis.org

Sahin, M. (2008). Cross-cultural experience in preservice teacher education. *Teaching and Teacher Education*, *24*(7), 1777–1790. doi:10.1016/j.tate.2008.02.006

Samovar, L. A., Porter, R. E., & McDaniel, E. R. (2011). *Intercultural communication: A reader* (13th ed.). Wadsworth, Cengage Learning.

Sanchez, J. I., Spector, P. E., & Cooper, C. L. (2000). Adapting to a boundaryless world: A developmental expatriate model. *The Academy of Management Executive*, *14*(2), 96–106. doi:10.5465/ame.2000.3819309

Sandhu, D., & Asrabadi, B. (1994). Development of an acculturative stress scale for international students: Preliminary findings. *Psychological Reports*, *75*(1), 435–448. doi:10.2466/pr0.1994.75.1.435 PMID:7809315

Selmer, J. (2001). Coping and adjustment of Western expatriate managers in Hong Kong. *Scandinavian Journal of Management*, *17*(2), 167–185. doi:10.1016/S0956-5221(99)00040-8

Sewell, W. H., & Davidson, O. M. (1956). The adjustment of Scandinavian students. *The Journal of Social Issues*, *12*(1), 9–19. doi:10.1111/j.1540-4560.1956.tb00351.x

Shadowen, N. L., Williamson, A. A., Guerra, N. G., Ammigan, R., & Drexler, M. L. (2019). Prevalence and correlates of depressive symptoms among international students: Implications for university support offices. *Journal of International Students*, *9*, 129–148.

Shah, H. (1991). Communication and cross-cultural adaptation patterns among Asian Indians. *International Journal of Intercultural Relations*, *15*, 311–321.

Shemshadsara, Z. G. (2012). Developing cultural awareness in foreign language teaching. *English Language Teaching*, *5*(3), 95–99.

Sherry, C., Bhat, R., Beaver, B., & Ling, A. (2004). Students as customer: The expectations and perceptions of local and international students. In *Transforming Knowledge into Wisdom. Proceedings of the 27th HERDSA Annual Conference*. Retrieved from https://www.herdsa.org.au/wp-content/uploads/conference/2004/papers/sherry.pdf

Shim, I., & Paprock, K. E. (2002). A study focusing on American expatriates' learning in host countries. *International Journal of Training and Development*, *6*(1), 13–24. doi:10.1111/1468-2419.00146

Smith, R. A., & Khawaja, N. G. (2011). A review of the acculturation experiences of international students. *International Journal of Intercultural Relations*, *35*(6), 699–713. doi:10.1016/j.ijintrel.2011.08.004

Spradley, J. P. (1980). *Participant observation*. Harcourt Brace Jovanovich College Publishers.

Sullivan, C., & Kashubeck-West, S. (2015). The interplay of international students' acculturative stress, social support, and acculturation modes. *Journal of International Students*, *5*(1), 1–11. doi:10.32674/jis.v5i1.438

Swagler, M. A., & Ellis, M. V. (2003). Crossing the distance: Adjustment of Taiwanese graduate students in the United States. *Journal of Counseling Psychology*, *50*(4), 420–437. doi:10.1037/0022-0167.50.4.420

Swain-Bradway, J., Lindstrom Johnson, S., Bradshaw, C., & McIntosh, K. (2017). *What are the economic costs of implementing SWPBIS in comparison to the benefits from reducing suspensions?* Technical Brief from Center for Positive Behavioral Interventions and Supports. https://assets-global.website-files.com/5d3725188825e071f1670246/5d76c00cb9339d5f3f267ee7_economiccostsswpbis.pdf

Tochkov, K., Levine, L., & Sanaka, A. (2010). Variation in the prediction of cross-cultural adjustment by Asian-Indian students in the United States. *College Student Journal*, *44*(3), 677–689.

Traiandis, H. C., Brislin, R., & Hui, C. H. (1988). Cross-cultural training across the individualism-collectivism divide. *International Journal of Intercultural Relations*, *12*(3), 269–289. doi:10.1016/0147-1767(88)90019-3

Training Management Corporation©. (2020). *Cultural Orientations Indicator®*. Retrieved from http://www.tmcorp.com

Trompenaars, F. (1993). *Riding the waves of culture: Understanding cultural diversity in business.* Economist Books.

Vande Berg, M., Connor-Linton, J., & Paige, R. M. (2009). The Georgetown Consortium Project: Interventions for Student Learning Abroad. *Frontiers: The Interdisciplinary Journal of Study Abroad*, *18*(1), 1–75. doi:10.36366/frontiers.v18i1.251

Wang, Y. (2004). Pursuing cross-cultural graduate education: A multifaceted investigation. *International Education,* 52-75.

Ward, C. (2001). *The impact of international students on domestic student and host institutions.* New Zealand Ministry of Education. Retrieved from https://www.educationcounts.govt.nz/publications/international/the_impact_of_international_students_on_domestic_students_and_host_institutions

Ward, C., & Kennedy, C. (1994). Acculturation strategies, psychological adjustment, and sociocultural competence during cross-cultural transitions. *International Journal of Intercultural Relations*, *18*(3), 329–343. doi:10.1016/0147-1767(94)90036-1

Wehling, S. (2008). Cross-cultural competency through service-learning. *Journal of Community Practice*, *16*(3), 293–315. doi:10.1080/10705420802255080

Weng, F., Cheong, F., & Cheong, C. (2010). The combined effect of self-efficacy and academic integration on higher education students studying IT majors in Taiwan. *Education and Information Technologies*, *15*(4), 333–353. doi:10.100710639-009-9115-y

Wohl, A. F. (2012). *Citizenship and social activism: A mixed method case study to understand cultural competence in students of a service-learning based course* (Thesis). North Dakota State University.

Wong, C. K., & Blissett, S. (2007). Assessing performance in the area of cultural competence: An analysis of reflective writing. *Journal, Physical Therapy Education*, *21*(1), 40–47. doi:10.1097/00001416-200701000-00006

Yeh, C. J., & Inose, M. (2003). International students' reported English fluency, social support satisfaction, and social connectedness as predictors of acculturative stress. *Counselling Psychology Quarterly*, *16*(1), 15–28. doi:10.1080/0951507031000114058

Ying, Y., & Liese, L. H. (1990). Initial adaptation of Taiwan foreign students to the United States: The impact of prearrival variables. *American Journal of Community Psychology, 18*(6), 825–845. doi:10.1007/BF00938066

Ying, Y., & Liese, L. H. (1991). Emotional well-being of Taiwan students in the U.S: An examination of pre-to post-arrival differential. *International Journal of Intercultural Relations, 15*(3), 345–366. doi:10.1016/0147-1767(91)90007-4

Ying, Y., & Liese, L. H. (1994). Initial adjustment of Taiwanese students to the United States: The impact of post arrival variables. *Journal of Cross-Cultural Psychology, 25*(4), 466–477. doi:10.1177/0022022194254003

Yoder, N., Atwell, M. N., Godek, D., Dusenbury, L., Bridgeland, J. M., & Weissberg, R. (2020). *Preparing youth for the workforce of tomorrow: Cultivating the social and emotional skills employers demand.* CASEL Publication. Retrieved at https://casel.org/collaborative-state-initiative/

Yoon, E., Lee, R. M., & Goh, M. (2008). Acculturation, social connectedness, and subjective wellbeing. *Cultural Diversity & Ethnic Minority Psychology, 14*(3), 246–255. doi:10.1037/1099-9809.14.3.246 PMID:18624589

Zhou, Y., Frey, C., & Bang, H. (2011). Understanding of international graduate students' academic adaptation to a U.S. graduate school. *International Education, 41*(1), 76–94.

Zhu, Y. (2008). From cultural adaptation to cross-cultural discursive competence. *Discourse & Communication, 2*(2), 185–204. doi:10.1177/1750481307088483

## KEY TERMS AND DEFINITIONS

**Acculturation:** The process of changes over time to an individual's behavior, values, knowledge, and cultural identity as a result of contact between cultural groups and experiencing a stress-adaptation-growth cycle as they adapt to a new culture (Berry, 2003, 2006; B.S.K. Kim & Abreu, 2001; & Y.Y. Kim, 2001).

**Control Group:** This study's international participants who received no additional intervention other than Fulbright's standard international student orientation and services.

**Cross-Cultural Adaptation:** An acculturation process of dynamic unfolding of the natural human tendency to struggle for an internal equilibrium in the face of often adversarial environmental conditions impacted by multiple simultaneous forces influencing the communicative interface between the individual and the host environment impacting changes in behavioral, cognitive, and emotional norms and underlying assumptions (Y. Y. Kim, 2001).

**Cross-Cultural Competence:** The ability to compare and contrast two cultural groups including culture-specific concepts.

**Cultural Awareness:** A means toward gradually increasing a person's power, energy and freedom of choice in a multicultural world (Pederson, 1998) by developing inner senses of the equality of cultures, increasing an understanding of the individual's culture, other people's cultures, and a positive interest in how cultures are similar, interconnected, and differ (Tomlinson, 2001) through "increasing a person's intentional and purposive decision making ability by accounting for the many ways that culture influences different perceptions of the same situation" (Altay 2005, p. 171).

**Cultural Competence:** The multifaceted, evolving capacity to interact and communicate with others having different cultural backgrounds (Balcazar, Suarex-Balcazar, & Taylor-Ritzler, 2009; IHEAC, 2008; Wehling, 2008).

**Cultural Knowledge:** The awareness and sensitivity to existing cultural preferences, values, and behaviors interpreted by an individual that generates cross-cultural competencies aiming to decrease transitional emotional discomfort while increasing respect for other cultures (Hall, 1955, 1959, 1966, 1973; Hofstede, 1980; Pilhofer, 2010; Spradley, 1980; Trompenaars, 1993). For the purpose of this study, cultural knowledge will include participants' understanding and interpretation of "culture" (see definition above).

**Cultural Responsiveness:** The process of developing awareness of the significance of our others' backgrounds including cultural and historical contexts and then intentionally integrating their cultural orientations and values into systems (modified from Rose & Smith, 2020).

**Cultural Sensitivity:** The degree of an individual's psychological ability to deal with cultural differences (Medina-López-Portillo, 2004); and to value and respect these cultural differences (Rew, Becker, Cookston, Khosropour, & Martinez, 2003).

**Culture:** Sets of socially transmitted ways of thinking, feeling, interacting, and communicating through shared value in traditions and customs distinguishing members of one organization from another (Hofstede, 1994; Kluckhohn, 1951; Lustig & Koester, 2003; Wohl, 2012).

**International Student:** Anyone studying in the U.S. on a non-immigrant, temporary visa that allows for academic coursework. These students include both degree and non-degree students (IIE, 2013).

**Social, Emotional, Academic Development:** Social, Emotional, and Academic Development (SEAD) is the interconnected relationship between academics and social emotional learning skills that reinforce equitable and human-centered educational environments (Aspen Institute, 2019).

**Social Emotional Learning:** A lifelong process through which all people acquire and effectively apply culturally responsive, "knowledge, skills, and attitudes to develop healthy identities, manage emotions and achieve personal and collective goals, feel and show empathy for others, establish and maintain supportive relationships, and make responsible and caring decisions" (CASEL, 2020).

**Treatment Group:** This study's international participants who received the four-week online predeparture academic and cultural integration preparation class treatment.

# Chapter 3
# The Role of Digital Marketing in Achieving Sustainable Competitive Advantage

**Edna Mngusughun Denga**
*American University of Nigeria, Nigeria*

**Narasimha Rao Vajjhala**
https://orcid.org/0000-0002-8260-2392
*University of New York Tirana, Albania*

**Sandip Rakshit**
*American University of Nigeria, Nigeria*

## ABSTRACT

*Digital marketing is a growing trend day by day, with internet marketing concepts becoming a powerful medium for digital marketing and electronic devices such as cell phones, digital billboards, tablets and laptops, portable game devices, and many gadgets that help in digital marketing. In this chapter, the role of digital marketing in assisting companies to achieve a sustainable competitive advantage was analyzed. The outbreak of the COVID-19 pandemic has put an end to companies' sales and business growth predictions, and digital marketing is no exception. Digital marketing will be at the forefront as many marketers might be looking for creative ways to sell online, reduce lead costs, increase click-through rates and conversion rates, and seek out what's new in digital marketing. This chapter focuses on understanding digital marketing concepts and how firms can achieve a competitive edge using various examples. This chapter reviews the different digital marketing concepts and strategies adopted by major global companies.*

DOI: 10.4018/978-1-7998-8169-8.ch003

## INTRODUCTION

Digital marketing utilizes the internet and online-based digital technologies such as desktop computers, mobile phones, and other digital media and platforms to promote products and services. Some marketing experts consider digital marketing a whole different challenge, involving a new approach to consumers and new ways of understanding how customers to act compared to conventional marketing. Digital marketing focuses on a particular segment of the consumer audience and is interactive. Digital marketing is on the rise and involves search results ads, email ads, and promotional tweets – anything that integrates customer feedback marketing or a two-way connection between the company and the customer (Cluley, Green, & Owen, 2020). Digital marketing grew increasingly sophisticated in the 2000s and 2010s, as the explosion of devices capable of accessing digital media led to rapid expansion. With social media innovations in the 2000s, such as LinkedIn, Facebook, YouTube, and Twitter, consumers have become increasingly dependent on digital electronics in their everyday lives. Consequently, consumers anticipated consistent user experience through multiple platforms to search for product details. The evolving customer behavior has increased the diversification of marketing technologies.

In digital marketing, advertisers are commonly referred to as sources, whereas target ad representatives are commonly referred to as receivers. Sources often concentrate on precise, well-defined receivers (Yongvongphaiboon & Chantamas, 2021; Zahay, 2021). Digital marketing tools such as search engine optimization (SEO), search engine marketing (SEM), content marketing, content marketing, content automation, campaign marketing, and data-driven marketing, to mention a few (Sinha, Healey, & Sengupta, 2020). It also refers to non-Internet outlets that include digital media, such as short message services (SMS), multimedia messaging service (MMS), call back and on-hold smartphone ring tones, e-books, etc (Janice & Frank, 2021). Internet marketing is distinct from digital marketing. Internet marketing is an advertisement that is exclusively on the Internet. In contrast, digital marketing may occur via mobile devices, a subway network, a video game, or a smartphone app. A key digital marketing goal is to engage consumers and encourage them to connect with the brand through digital media service and delivery (Bartholomew, 2018). This is done by constructing digital media to involve some form of end-user intervention to access or obtain the inspiration behind the development of such media.

## BACKGROUND

The growth of digital marketing is indistinguishable from the development of technology. One of the first main events occurred in 1971 when Ray Tomlinson sent the first email, and his innovation set up a network to allow people to send and receive files through various machines. However, the far more noticeable era as the beginning of Digital Marketing was in 1990, when the Archie search engine was developed as an index for FTP sites (Sinha et al., 2020). In the 1980s, computers' storage capacity was high enough to hold large quantities of customer information. Companies began preferring online strategies, such as database marketing, rather than small list brokers. These databases enabled companies to monitor customer information more efficiently, thereby reforming the interaction between buyer and seller. The manual method, however, was not as effective (Chaisit, Pansuwan, & Isaranontakul, 2020).

Digital Marketing was first coined in the 1990s with the advent of the server/client architecture and the popularity of personal computers; customer Relationship Management (CRM) applications became a central factor in marketing technology. Intense competition compelled vendors to provide more resources in their apps. Marketers were also able to own large online consumer data through CRM software after the Internet's advent. Companies could update consumer demand data and obtain the priorities of their experience. This contributed to the first clickable banner ad going live in 1994, which was AT&T's "You Will" campaign, and within four months of its going live, 44% of all the people who saw it clicked on the ad (Du, Malik, Koh, & Theocharous, 2018). In the 2000s, with a growing number of Internet users and the birth of an iPhone, consumers first started looking for goods and making choices about their needs online instead of contacting a salesperson who created a new challenge for its marketing department. A survey conducted in the United Kingdom in 2000 found that most retailers had not registered their domain addresses. These challenges inspired marketers to find new ways to incorporate emerging technologies into business growth. Marketing Automation is the mechanism by which software is used to automate traditional marketing processes (Bonardi, 2021; Wertenbroch, 2021). Marketing automation has helped businesses segment consumers, initiate multi-channel marketing strategies, and provide customized knowledge. However, the speed of its adaptability to consumer devices has not been high enough.

## Digital Marketing Channels

Digital Marketing Channels are Internet-based systems that can generate, accelerate and distribute product value from manufacturer to customer terminal via digital networks. Several digital marketing platforms support digital marketing. One of the advertiser's key goals is to find channels that result in optimum two-way contact and a better overall ROI for the brand. Digital marketing channels are tools that companies use to reach target customers with knowledge about their brand, product, or service. Using these platforms helps companies to assist consumers with any concerns or challenges. There are a lot of options when it comes to online marketing platforms. They all have their pros and cons, and each of them is suitable for different goals.

## Search Engine Optimization (SEO)

This technique increases website traffic efficiency and quantity to a website or web page from search engines. SEO is targeted at unpaid traffic rather than direct or paid traffic (Samuel, Subbaiyan, Balusamy, Doraikannan, & Gandomi, 2021). Unpaid traffic can originate from various searches, including image search, video search, academic search, news search, and industry-specific vertical search engines. SEO is introduced as an Internet marketing tactic because it can attract more traffic from the search engine when the websites are ranked higher on the search engine results list (SERP). These visitors can then eventually be converted to a consumer.

## Content Marketing

A marketing approach focused on producing, publishing, and delivering content to a specific online audience. Content marketing attracts prospects and turns prospects into consumers through the creation and sharing of useful free content (Angel Wong An & Rashad, 2015). Content marketing helps marketers develop sustainable brand loyalty, offers useful knowledge to customers, and generates a desire to buy goods from the future. This relatively new method of marketing does not include direct sales. Instead, it creates confidence and a connection with the audience. It uses blog posts, e-books and whitepapers, infographics, and online brochures.

## Pay-Per-Click (PPC)

PPC is an internet promotional mechanism used to direct traffic to websites where the advertiser pays the publisher (usually the search engine, website owner, or network of websites) (Dinev, Hu, & Yayla, 2008). Marketers set up PPC campaigns on Google, Bing, Linked In, Twitter, Pinterest, or Facebook and display their advertising to users searching for a product or service-related keywords. PPC campaigns may segment users based on their demographic characteristics (such as age or gender) or even target their specific interests or venue. Google Ads and Facebook Ads are the most common PPC channels.

## Email Marketing

Companies use email marketing as a form of communicating with their audiences. Email is usually used to endorse content, discounts, and activities and refer people to the company's website. Email marketing is also one of the most powerful channels of digital marketing (Ángel José Lorente, Ángel Hernández, & Julián Chaparro, 2021). Many people associate email marketing with spam email notifications, but that's not what email marketing is all about. Email marketing is the way to contact your future buyers or people who are interested in your brand. Many digital marketers use all other digital marketing platforms to add leads to their email lists and then, via email marketing, create customer acquisition entries to turn those leads into customers.

## Inbound Marketing and Video Marketing

Inbound marketing is a strategy used to attract consumers to goods and services through content marketing, social media marketing, search engine optimization, and branding. Inbound marketing increases customer service and builds loyalty by providing future customers with an appreciation for corporate-funded newsletters, blogs, and entries on various social media sites (Liu, Wei Shi, Teixeira, & Wedel, 2018). YouTube seems to have become the second largest search engine, and a lot of users are turning to YouTube before they make a purchasing decision, learn something, read a review, or relax. Many video marketing sites, including Facebook Images, Instagram, and even TikTok, can be used to run a video marketing campaign. Companies are most effective in combining video with SEO, content marketing, and wider social media marketing strategies.

## Affiliate Marketing

Affiliate marketing is among the earliest marketing methods, and the Internet has given new life to this old standby (Mariussen, 2011). With affiliate marketing, influencers endorse other people's goods and get a fee whenever a sale is made, or a lead is made. Many well-known corporations like Amazon have affiliate schemes that cost millions of dollars a month to websites that sell their goods. One common way is online product parties, where a host invites a few people to an online product sale event. The host is an associate and stimulates interest in the commodity. They act as a go-between for marketing and selling. All the business has to do is sit back and make a profit. Although part of the benefit goes to the affiliate, the organization earns a lot of free marketing. The affiliate will post articles and advertisements for the brand.

## Social Media and Website Marketing

This uses social media channels and websites for advertising goods or services. While e-marketing and digital marketing are still prevalent in research, social media marketing is becoming increasingly popular in practice and research (Appel, Grewal, Hadi, & Stephen, 2020). Most social media sites have built-in data analytics tools that allow companies to monitor ad campaigns' development, effectiveness, and interaction. The website is the focal point of all digital marketing activities. A very influential channel when used alone but also a platform required to run several online marketing campaigns. The website should reflect a brand, product, and service simply and memorably. It should be fast, mobile-friendly, and easy to use.

# DISCUSSION

## Sustainable Competitive Advantage through Digital Marketing

Michael Porter (1980) defined competitive advantage as "the ability gained through attributes and resources to perform at a higher level than others in the same industry or market (O'Shaughnessy, 1996). The study of this advantage has generated a deep interest in research due to contextual issues involving superior performance levels. Competitive advantage is instituting value-creating strategies not being accomplished concurrently by a new or potential competitor. A competitive advantage is a leverage a business has over its industry rivals. Competitive advantage can be achieved by providing excellent and greater value to the customer: Promotional goods or services with lower prices or superior quality, stimulating end-users and market segments that identify such distinct products or services. This is the rationale why customers choose one specific good or service instead of another.

Porter (1985) also explained that a company must create clear goal strategies and operations to build sustainable competitive advantage (O'Shaughnessy, 1996). The organizational culture and beliefs of employees must be aligned with those objectives. He further surveyed firms to determine the three key ways businesses can gain competitive advantage:

1. Cost leadership
2. Differentiation
3. Focus

Cost leadership is the expertise of a firm to manufacture a product or service at a lower price than other rivals (Takeaki, 2017). This they do by consistently upgrading operational efficiency. Companies achieve a competitive advantage when they produce the same quality product but sell it for a lesser price than their major competitors. This then provides consumers with a price value. Lower prices would result in higher prices, as firms still make a fair profit on all goods or services sold. Companies that do not make a massive profit should seek a lower cost base like labor, supplies, and facilities. This provides businesses with lower production costs than their competitors, thus adding value to consumers by transferring cost benefits. Firms also rely on economics of scale to attain efficiency. Economics of scale is generated with the decrease in the cost of goods and services due to increased production.

A differential advantage is achieved when the goods or services of a company are distinct from those of its rivals. Such products or services are appealing enough to distinguish them from their rivals. Businesses would require good research development and design thinking to generate new ideas. These changes in products or services could involve the provision of high quality to customers. When customers see a good or service as unique from others, they will be willing to pay more to enjoy such benefits. There are two significant types of differentiation strategies a firm can execute (Takeaki, 2017).

(a) Broad differentiation: This consists of building or creating a distinct brand in some way from its rivals. it should be relevant to the market and attract a wide variety of consumers
(b) Focused differentiation strategy: This strategy enables firms to provide unique characteristics to a product or service and satisfy the niche or narrow market conditions. A business trying to implement this should design incredibly distinct goods or services that generate enhanced values for its consumers.

*Figure 1. Building blocks of competitive advantage*

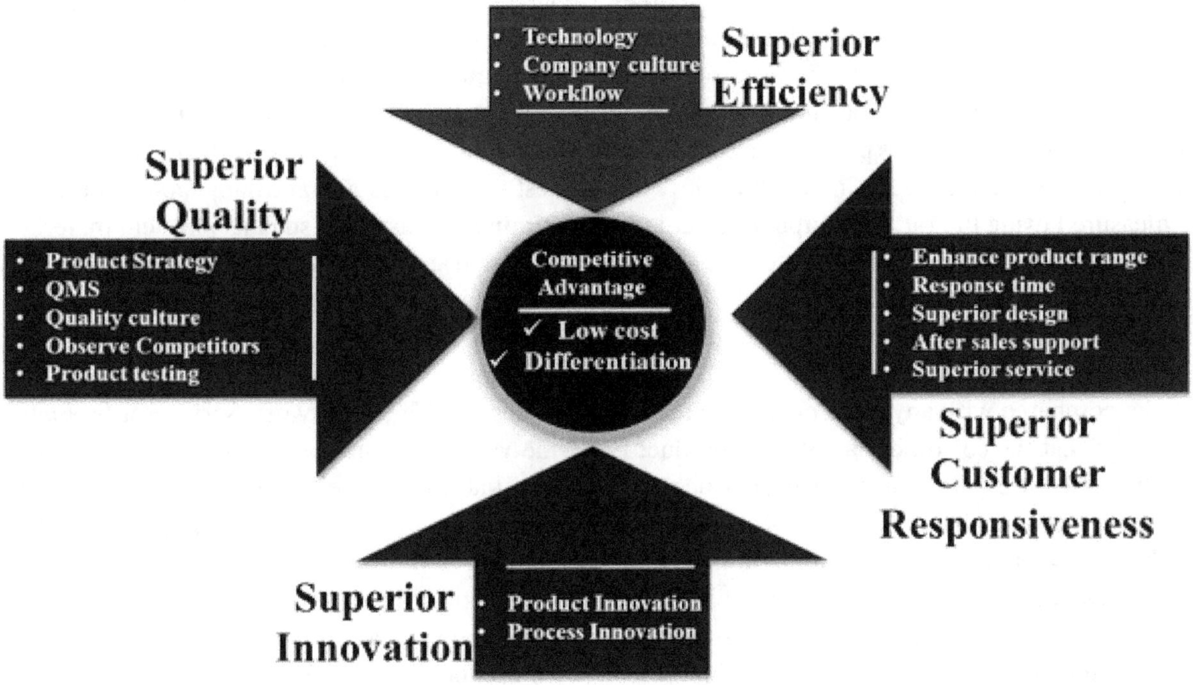


Focus strategy is best to get companies to target a few intended audiences instead of targeting everybody (Dombrowski, Krenkel, & Wullbrandt, 2018). Smaller firms mostly use the approach because they do not have the necessary resources or capacity to reach everybody. Businesses that use this approach concentrate on the customers' needs and offer goods and services to enhance their everyday lives. Firms also encourage customers to provide feedback for their products or services. The following steps are used in building a focus strategy.

i. Conduct a SWOT analysis
ii. Use five forces analysis to understand market competition
iii. Compare SWOT analysis to five forces analysis
iv. Determine the goals and target markets of the strategy
v. Verify alignment of strategic and organization priorities.

There are four generic building blocks of competitive advantage that businesses can embrace, irrespective of industry or the products and services they offer: Efficiency, Quality, Innovation, and Customer responsiveness (Dombrowski et al., 2018). Those factors enable such companies to develop and maintain a competitive edge. Each factor results from how the diverse value-chain activities are implemented inside an organization to achieve superior efficiency, superior quality, superior innovation, and superior customer responsiveness to differentiate its product offerings and thus provide added value to its customers and lower its cost base.

Superior efficiency is viewed from the standpoint of producers in the industry. This is one of the primary sources of competitive advantage since it empowers firms to boost employees' productivity and capital, thus decreasing their cost base (Dombrowski et al., 2018; O'Shaughnessy, 1996). Efficiency is a significant decline in the rate of wasted resources used to manufacture a specified number of goods or services known as outputs (Losha, Strang, & Vajjhala, 2017; Vajjhala, 2015; Vajjhala & Strang, 2014). Business is a procedure for the conversion of inputs into outputs. Inputs are the essential factors of production, like material, labor, time, equipment, capital, and technical expertise. Outputs, on the other hand, are goods and services produced by a firm. Efficiency indicates a maximum performance level that utilizes the lowest number of inputs to achieve the highest output. It is a quantifiable concept that can be measured using the ratio of output to total input. It eliminates wastages, such as physical materials, energy, and time, while attaining the desired output. Firms can use workflow, technology, and company culture to improve their efficiency (Losha et al., 2017; Vajjhala & Strang, 2018).

Quality is generally perceived as exceptional product characteristics and superior dependability. Quality is viewed as a critical instrument for the essential attributes of any product or service that enables it to be compared with any good or service in the same category. The quality of a service or product is the belief that the customer has of it. A product is a wide variety of multiple attributes, which entails the shape, features, alternatives, performance, durability, reliability, shape, style, and design. Superior quality of a product happens when its attributes are customers perceive it as having a higher value than attributes of a product sold by competitors.

Build a Product strategy. To stand out in an ocean of uncountable new products, companies need to develop and implement a magnificent product strategy. Formulating a product from the ground up is challenging but not impossible with the right ideas—each product strategy specifics the product details and its vision. The strategy outlines point such as the customers, the market, rivals, and business objectives. This strategy provides a clear direction from the development to the launch of a product.

Implement a quality management system. Although it is essential to visualize, formulate and generate a roadmap for the product, such moves alone will not, by default, ascertain the quality of the product. Quality Management System (QMS) is a collection of internal policies that establish how well a business creates and delivers its products or services. The implementation of QMS enables a company to audit its processes together with a certification body. The system contains principles that support develop a product for its launches, such as customer emphasis leadership, research, and proof-based decision-making.

Inculcate quality in the company's culture. Executing a QMS is essential but cannot translate to automatic compliance. These quality principles implemented need to be solidly anchored across the entire organization. All the employees must unanimously agree on what constitutes a quality product. To many, it is a low-cost product, whereas, for others, it is a state-of-the-art solution. Irrespective of what is agreed on, management teams must frequently promote the idea.

Study competitors. Observing competitors is an essential step in the development of a product. What are they doing that you are not (and vice versa) doing? How are their products functioning? What is working for them and why? Addressing these questions will place you in a more significant position to contend with similar companies in the industry.

Perform product testing. It is vital to assess and test a product before it is launched. The possibilities are firms might need to make corrections, add new features and modify usability so that the product meets the desires and requirements of end-users. Testing a product can be done through beta testing and how consumers respond to it through market testing. Beta testing assists in satisfying the pledged user experience and ensuring that all product elements, including quality, perform as originally intended. Product testing demonstrates how a product functions in the actual life versus the performance in a controlled setting. Products could be tested for functionality, support, and marketing to evaluate customer affirmation and improve product quality appropriately.

There are two main types of innovation: process innovation and process innovation (Labella-Fernández, Serrano-Arcos, & Payán-Sánchez, 2021). Process innovation is the introduction of new technology or technique to carry out activities that enable an organization to remain competitive and successful in meeting the needs of its customers. Process innovation enables a company to create more value by significantly reducing production costs. For example, Nike's lean production system helped strengthen employee performance, offering Nike a cost-based competitive edge. Product innovation is defined as introducing new products, changes in the design of existing products, or new components and materials in the production of established products. Product innovation generates value by developing new products and improving existing products, which customers perceive as having superior value. This allows companies to charge higher prices. In the long run, product and process innovation will certainly lead to an essential building block in creating sustainable advantages for any company. Furthermore, competition among firms is seen as a process focused on innovation in both products and processes.

When a company does an outstanding task than other competing companies in recognizing and satisfying customer wants, needs, and desires, it has competitive advantages termed superior customer responsiveness. In a 2002 "Business Strategy Review" article, Sean Meehan and Charlie Dawson describe customer responsiveness as being precise and insightful in offering customers what they need want or not aware they want and conducting it quite swiftly than anybody else. Customer responsiveness enables a company to personalize its products and services, enhance response time, superior design, and superior after-sales service, and provide outstanding service. Enhancing the company's product range's efficiency is compatible with attaining customer responsiveness as the recently designed products can possess attributes that may not be available in current products. Furthermore, the desire to create custom products and services to the distinctive requirements of specific customer groups is yet another aspect that may contribute to this edge. Customers might then attribute more significance to the products thereby, creating a competitive advantage based on differentiation.

Response time is a component of customer responsiveness that has attracted increasing attention in recent times; it refers to the length of time it takes for goods to be supplied or for services to be rendered (Appel et al., 2020; Yongvongphaiboon & Chantamas, 2021; Zahay, 2021). After-sales service is any assistance offered to the customer after the acquisition of a good or service. Firms use after-sales support as a business strategy, as it usually results in relatively high consumer satisfaction, brand loyalty, and even word-of-mouth marketing. Superior service Superior customer service is best defined as being above and beyond the customer's expectations during every interaction. To accomplish this objective, recognize what consumers require by conducting market research and survey. For example, suppose you own an online coupon clothes shop. In that case, you may discover that customers dislike having to wait for a shop assistant to receive validation from a manager when they make an unexpected request. To fix this, one can empower sales reps to make on-the-spot management decisions as long as it aims to keep a customer: a satisfied client is a repeat customer.

A sustainable competitive advantage is a business asset, resource, process, or ability that is difficult to replicate or purchase and offers a long-term advantage over competitors (Dombrowski et al., 2018; O'Shaughnessy, 1996; Takeaki, 2017). By creating a sustainable competitive advantage (SCA) that retains customers' loyalty to a brand while still attracting far more consumers towards its services and products, a business is thriving in today's highly competitive environment. Sustainability is concerned about whether or not it is easy for rivals to erase a business's competitive advantage. We live in a digital age, which means that they need to succeed in digital marketing no matter a firm's line of business, provide online customer service, and develop mobile-friendly websites and apps. Without these, such companies will struggle to get an advantage over their competitors (Strang, Bitrus, & Vajjhala, 2019). A typical example is Amazon, a champion of online marketing and thus totally dominates the online sector while operating in highly competitive markets.

## SOLUTIONS AND RECOMMENDATIONS

The role of digital marketing is significant, and the authors recommend how to leverage the power of top-notch digital marketing solutions and offer a few ways to build a sustainable competitive advantage in digital marketing:

*Figure 2. Digital marketing sustainable model for gaining competitive advantage*

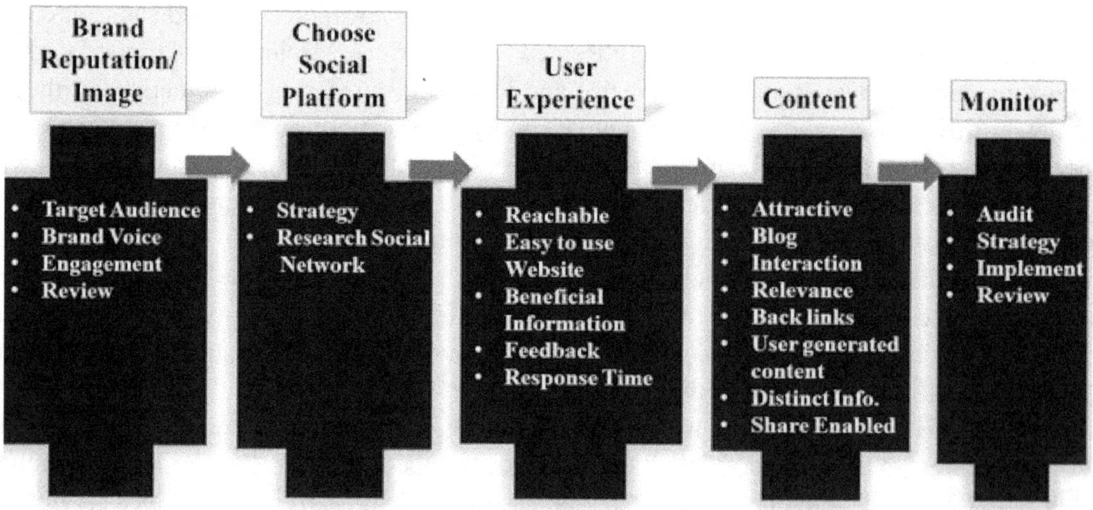

## Brand Reputation/Image

Brand reputation is a continuous process that requires a clear vision, a top-notch digital marketing course of action, and fast and efficient strategy implementation (Adi, 2021). Brand reputation is developed using various techniques and is sustained, integrating it with incredible quality at a reasonable price. A company that creates an extraordinary reputation and credibility will successfully rest assured that its customers will attach to it for several years. Here is how to do it

Audience. It is essential for a company, as a brand, to know who its target audience is and how best to get a message across to them. In addition, the objectives and efforts of digital marketing must be made clear. Identifying potential customers and their desired behavior patterns helps to enhance the content of the message. It further succors the image and reputation of the brand.

Brand tone. The manner a company convey their message and interact with their consumers is referred to as brand tone. When implemented correctly, it makes it relatively easy for customers to recognize spontaneously, genuinely love the company's offering. So much so that no matter what the competitor has to say, they want to hear from you.

Engagement. A company needs to be perceived as an authority in its target market, signifying that they know what they're doing. To create and maintain a strong brand reputation, a company must come across as a problem-solver – one with a willingness to share expertise to assist its customers and, in turn, enjoy a sustained competitive advantage.

And here are just a few ways to go about it:

- Develop valuable content through blog articles, videos, among others.
- Engage with customers on social media.
- Have a live social media session and respond to questions from the audience.
- Sustain a social media community to enable people to socialize with one another and you as well.

Reviews. People are increasingly turning to Google to find out more about products or services they're interested in. Next, they read reviews people have left for such a particular product or service. This is why companies must continue making efforts to manage reputations and get online reviews by requesting customers and offering incentives.

## Choose a Social Platform

In recent times, social media channels are overpowering the Web. A business must be present on almost all kinds of social media platforms or face a tough time in the marketplace to establish a dominant presence. And instead of wanting to govern on popular and widely platforms like Facebook, it is advisable to get on a novel and upcoming media that others have not become involved in so far. It appears ridiculous to opt for a platform people are not very active on. But it can yield returns when it starts to get famous.

Social media is essential to get a business message across in a very effective way and to establish a close-knit online community. Everybody enjoys being part of a group, otherwise known as an online community. When customers choose brands that offer them that, in addition to a fantastic service or product, they will stick to it for a long time, precisely what firms seek to accomplish.

To formulate a strategy properly, a firm can ask questions such as:

- What is the age range of my targeted audience? And which social media platforms are they almost sure to use?
- How can messages be clearly expressed? By creating detailed notes using Facebook or Instagram for image-based narration?
- Can my consumers catch pace with the dynamic patterns that other platform like Snapchat is offering?

Recognizing the intended audience, goals, and message is a midway journey towards an effective digital marketing strategy. After which, the firm can explore the different social networks: the demographic groups they attract, and whether the content format matches the voice and image of the brand.

## User- Experience

Providing outstanding efficient customer service is a must if businesses must experience sustained competitive advantage. The experience that users have with a brand today plays a crucial role in the relationship that they will have with a firm in the future, which further indicates that the customer will be committed to the brand until the very end. This is the kind of sustained competitive advantage that a company requires.

- Easy to use the website. When operating an e-commerce business, building a fantastic website is indispensable as firms need not compromise consumers' web experience. But rather develop and sustain an easy-to-use, top-notch website with loading speed time, brand new design, and captivating yet straightforward content, along with other things, such that users that land on your site to get details or read a blog article should not have a terrible experience.
- Easily reachable. Firms seeking a competitive edge ought to be reached with a single click. Customers must be able to instantly contact a customer service representative and not spend eternity on the Internet searching for a means of contacting you. And it's getting pretty easy through social media channels – given that you have people working on them during business hours.
- Beneficial information. Add more value to the content in the form of valuable information so that what you end up sharing will be advantageous to the users who utilize it. Otherwise, you will waste their time, and they will remember that for a long time.
- Response time. We are living in an age of quick results. People hardly like to wait any longer. And it is truer once they get in touch with a brand with a request or a complaint. To have an excellent brand experience and become committed, long-term customers, it is essential to attend to them speedily and not keep them waiting. Not on social media in particular!
- Feedback. Requesting customers to provide input shows them how much you care about what they want. This is a simple and effective way to build a loyal consumer base as you follow thoroughly as possible the plan and do not entirely disregard their suggestions. In addition, be constantly aware of their changing needs, or risk them turning to competitors when their needs are unmet. Those two reasons are the best ways to build a sustainable competitive advantage.

## Content

Businesses require a great deal of content to create a powerful brand image and market themselves skilfully on social media platforms. Great content empowers them to develop an embodiment, a narrative that people remember for decades to come. This translates automatically to a competitive edge over all rivals, as you will be the first to go to their imaginations when they think of products or services in the industry. To enjoy a sustainable competitive advantage, generate unique content, adds value, and is hard to duplicate.
Here are a few things that could be featured in a content marketing strategy:

- Develop content that captures and retains attention instantly because it is worth recalling. Use taglines and slogans to create such catchy content for all social media channels.
- Keep a useful up-to-date blog as you desire to be perceived as a niche expert even while disseminating information that creates value to your audience/users.
- Gain popularity with interactive posts on social media that might be in the form of posts asking questions, requesting viewpoints, or playing games.
- Seek is always relevant as it is easy to divert attention from what the audience is searching for, thereby leaving them with only one option; switch to other competing brands.
- Concentrate on user-generated content like reviews on your channels. Media platforms Such as Instagram are perfect for enabling easy sharing of content shared by end-users.
- Acquire authority backlink profile to your content. This solidifies your validity since a reliable site considers your content to be outstanding enough to link to it directly.
- Produce shared content that allows potential users to view such content, and this can only occur when immediate audiences share content with their communities.
- Instead of re-writing certain existing content for products sold on different platforms, consider making improvements by posting distinct information such as instructions for use and professional comments.

## Monitor

In digital marketing, efforts are meaningless if success is not adequately monitored, even though it might seem to be on the appropriate path. Digital marketing analytics is necessary to gain a comprehensive picture. Digital marketing solutions vary widely from one business to another in different ways; however, there is a flow that cannot be overlooked. Digital marketing audits can be carried out to investigate where one stands at the moment. A strategy can then be developed to address these research results and achieve the set objectives effectively. Execute the strategic plan and evaluate the strategy regularly, distinctively, with a thorough digital marketing report. This enables a firm to know which techniques produce the desired results and focus more on the areas not yielding the required outcome. All the components discussed above may seem hard to achieve, but that is precisely why all these factors offer a sustainable competitive advantage. Investing resources and implementing a long-term digital marketing strategy enables one to achieve a leadership role that can take decades for rivals' companies to catch up. A primary objective is carrying out activities uniquely and distinctively better than other competing companies, which is the key! Conducting business, the same way as others makes you become just another niche company: subsequently neglected, forgotten, and incapable of leveraging on maximum potential. Digital marketing, when used effectively, enables a firm to stand out from the rest and gain an edge that no rival can successfully match or replicate for the foreseeable future.

## Amazon Digital Marketing Case Study

Amazon is an American multinational corporation concentrating on cloud computing, digital streaming, e-commerce, and artificial intelligence. The secret to Amazon's success is an extremely efficient digital marketing strategy. It has been a customer-centric company for the last 26 years and has promised to maintain that position for the long term. Amazon is an undisputed leader of how digital marketing is an unquestionably brilliant strategy in this emerging technological globe.

*"Earth's most customer-centric company"*

This has been Amazon's motto since 1994, which clearly shows that they were determined to provide services where customers can find anything they want online. To a certain extent, they sought to present their customers with a fair price that was possible and convenient. Amazon's founder Jeff Bezos has often stressed the value of a more customer-focused business than other factors such as product-focused or competitor-focused.
Amazon's marketing strategy focuses on the proceeding four key elements.

- It is utilizing customer-friendly platforms. The technology giant seems to have a sophisticated interface that incorporates customized suggestions and recent search history, among many others.
- They are providing a wide selection of products. The world's largest Internet retailer in revenue delivers tens of millions of product lines. The range of products offered on Amazon.com comes from third-party vendors.
- They are effortlessly adjusting from small to large. This e-commerce and cloud computing corporation have experience and expertise in adjusting from small to large. This component plays a significant role in discovering innovative business segments.
- To date, the technology company has made full utilization of affiliate products and resources to add value to the lower part line of the business.

Amazon's marketing strategy is centered on the following principles:

- Amazon's marketing information sharing mix incorporates print and media advertising, sales promotions, happenings and experiences, public relations, and direct marketing. In particular, the company focuses on print and media advertising and sales promotion components of marketing channels of communication.
- Amazon segmentation target marketing and positioning policies are linked to the targeting of the broadest customer segment. The general merchandise company does this by applying multi-segment, dynamic, and anticipatory positioning tactics.
- Amazon's unique sales proposition merges the largest range of products and services made available at competitive rates, quick shipping, and outstanding customer service. The e-commerce company places such distinct sales initiatives at the heart of its promotional communications messages.

- Amazon's marketing 7ps focuses mainly on product and place aspects of the marketing mix. Its product range is the broadest between online and offline retailers. In addition, the company is able to offer its quality products at affordable prices due to the huge cost reductions obtained from the online on the online nature of its business operational activities.

Amazon has implemented various Digital marketing strategies that have given them an edge over competitors, such as

1. Innovation and Technology: Amazon has attained various achievements in the technology world, subsequently leading the way in the digital marketing world, Utilizing artificial intelligence, computer vision, and machine learning. For example, Amazon Prime is a premium monthly subscription that offers fast and free delivery compared to regular Amazon service and offers unlimited streaming of TV shows and movies.

    1. Customer's Review: Amazon's customer review program has become one of the pillars of digital marketing services. In exploring the Amazon website, the user comes across feed-back, both before and after purchase. Review services are now very popular and have been made accessible via different websites; Amazon has provided a blueprint for businesses on how to develop a model which will be successful. Amazon also offers group engagement by encouraging customers to vote with the "Helpful" option on the importance and usefulness of the feedback left by other customers. Customers may also ask a direct question about the product.
    2. Interaction with Customers: These days, every e-commerce company informs customers of the confirmation of their order, the estimation of the delivery date, the shipment, and the notification of deliveries that every company did not provide years ago. Most notably, Amazon was setting up templates for other e-commerce firms back then.
    3. Free Shipping and Discounts: The free shipping approach helps to maximize the consumer purchase cap. If there's a condition attached, the customer will try to meet that amount by increasing the basket size to prevent extra charges. Eventually, this is a very beneficial deal for them. Amazon offers several discounts on different products, and such discount is impossible in offline stores, so more consumers are motivated to shop offline.
    4. Creative Digital marketing campaigns: An entire creative idea is the integrated and holistic "Key Concept" that encapsulates the audience's interest, shapes their emotional reaction, and motivates them to act immediately. It is a core theme that can be used across several campaigns, calls for intervention, channels of communication, and target audience. The creative concept is encompassed in the caption, the new slogan as well as pictorial. Successful creative ideas are unique, unforgettable, unifying, and significant. Email, Social Media, Google AdWords are channels used in digital marketing campaigns.

## CONCLUSION

By investing capital in and executing a long-term digital marketing strategy, a company can maintain a leadership role that might take years for rivals to catch up and obtain a sustainable competitive advantage.

To sum up, digital marketing has a promising future for the long-term survival of goods or services in the new technology market with all its pros and cons. Amazon has been the standard-bearer on how digital marketing can be an utterly ideal strategy in this evolving technology environment. Competition is very high in the 21st century. Thus, companies need to continuously innovate and build services or goods that can make life simpler for consumers. Digital marketing will be at the forefront as many marketers might be looking for creative ways to sell online, reduce lead costs, increase click-through rates and conversion rates, and seek out what's new in digital marketing. This chapter presented an understanding of digital marketing concepts and how firms can achieve a competitive edge using various examples. This chapter reviewed the different digital marketing concepts and strategies adopted by major global companies.

## REFERENCES

Adi, S. (2021). Psychological Effect of Brand Image and Brand Reputation on Sustainable Firm Performance in Indonesian Logistic Companies. *Ilkogretim Online*, *20*(4), 820–831. doi:10.17051/ilkonline.2021.04.89

Ángel José Lorente, P., Ángel Hernández, G., & Julián Chaparro, P. (2021). Modelling e-mail marketing effectiveness – An approach based on the theory of hierarchy-of-effects. *Management Letters. Cuadernos de Gestión*, *21*(1), 19–27. doi:10.5295/cdg.191094ah

Angel Wong An, K., & Rashad, Y. (2015). The Review of Content Marketing as a New Trend in Marketing Practices. *International Journal of Management, Accounting & Economics*, *2*(9), 1055–1064.

Appel, G., Grewal, L., Hadi, R., & Stephen, A. T. (2020). The future of social media in marketing. *Journal of the Academy of Marketing Science*, *48*(1), 79–95. doi:10.100711747-019-00695-1 PMID:32431463

Bartholomew, K. W. (2018). Digital marketing teaching strategies with google analytics and related tools: Tutorial presentation. *Journal of Computing Sciences in Colleges*, *34*(2), 56–57.

Bonardi, E. (2021). Marketing automation: The next generation of applications for real estate. *Journal of Property Management*, *86*(1), 20–21.

Chaisit, J., Pansuwan, L., & Isaranontakul, P. (2020). The Development of Digital Marketing Strategies and Distribution Channels for Community Products Using E-Commerce in The Lower Northern Region of Thailand. *Proceedings of the 2020 International Conference on Management of e-Commerce and e-Government*. 10.1145/3409891.3409903

Cluley, R., Green, W., & Owen, R. (2020). The changing role of the marketing researcher in the age of digital technology: Practitioner perspectives on the digitization of marketing research. *International Journal of Market Research*, *62*(1), 27–42. doi:10.1177/1470785319865129

Dinev, T., Hu, Q., & Yayla, A. (2008). Is There an On-line Advertisers' Dilemma? A Study of Click Fraud in the Pay-Per-Click Model. *International Journal of Electronic Commerce*, *13*(2), 29–59. doi:10.2753/JEC1086-4415130202

Dombrowski, U., Krenkel, P., & Wullbrandt, J. (2018). Strategic Positioning of Production within the Generic Competitive Strategies. *Procedia CIRP*, *72*, 1196–1201. doi:10.1016/j.procir.2018.03.007

Du, F., Malik, S., Koh, E., & Theocharous, G. (2018). *Interactive Campaign Planning for Marketing Analysts*. Paper presented at the Extended Abstracts of the 2018 CHI Conference on Human Factors in Computing Systems, Montreal, Canada. 10.1145/3170427.3188531

Janice, J. N.-C., & Frank, L.-C. (2021). Marketing communication objectives through digital content marketing on social media. *Fórum Empresarial*, 57-82. doi:10.33801/fe.v25i1.18514

Labella-Fernández, A., Serrano-Arcos, M. M., & Payán-Sánchez, B. (2021). Firm Growth as a Driver of Sustainable Product Innovation: Mediation and Moderation Analysis. Evidence from Manufacturing Firms. *International Journal of Environmental Research and Public Health*, *18*(5), 2588. Advance online publication. doi:10.3390/ijerph18052588 PMID:33807696

Liu, X., Wei Shi, S., Teixeira, T., & Wedel, M. (2018). Video Content Marketing: The Making of Clips. *Journal of Marketing*, *82*(4), 86–101. doi:10.1509/jm.16.0048

Losha, F., Strang, K. D., & Vajjhala, R. (2017). Assessing the risk of leveraging technology in small businesses entering the European Union. *International Journal of Risk and Contingency Management*, *6*(4), 99–122. doi:10.4018/IJRCM.2017100104

Mariussen, A. (2011). Rethinking Marketing Performance Measurement: Justification and Operationalisation of an Alternative Approach to Affiliate Marketing Performance Measurement in Tourism. *Ereview of Tourism Research*, *9*(3), 65–87.

O'Shaughnessy, N. J. (1996). Michael Porter's 'Competitive Advantage' revisited. *Management Decision, 34*(6), 12.

Samuel, P., Subbaiyan, S., Balusamy, B., Doraikannan, S., & Gandomi, A. H. (2021). A Technical Survey on Intelligent Optimization Grouping Algorithms for Finite State Automata in Deep Packet Inspection. *Archives of Computational Methods in Engineering*, *28*(3), 1371–1396. doi:10.100711831-020-09419-z

Sinha, M., Healey, J., & Sengupta, T. (2020). *Designing with AI for Digital Marketing*. Paper Presented at the Adjunct Publication of the 28th ACM Conference on User Modeling, Adaptation and Personalization, Genoa, Italy. 10.1145/3386392.3397600

Strang, K. D., Bitrus, S. N., & Vajjhala, N. R. (2019). Factors impacting farm management decision making software adoption. *International Journal of Sustainable Agricultural Management and Informatics*, *5*(1), 15–24.

Takeaki, W. (2017). Capability-based cost leadership strategy of Japanese firms. *Annals of Business Administrative Science*, *17*(1), 1–10. doi:10.7880/abas.0171018a

Vajjhala, N. R. (2015). Constructivist Grounded Theory Applied to a Culture Study. In K. D. Strang (Ed.), *Palgrave Handbook of Research Design in Business and Management* (pp. 447–464). Palgrave Macmillan. doi:10.1057/9781137484956_23

Vajjhala, N. R., & Strang, K. D. (2014). Collaboration strategies for a transition economy: Measuring culture in Albania. *International Journal of Cross Cultural Management*, *21*(1), 78–103. doi:10.1108/CCM-02-2013-0023

Vajjhala, N. R., & Strang, K. D. (2018). Sociotechnical challenges of transition economy SMEs during EU integration. In A. M. Dima (Ed.), *Doing Business in Europe - Economic Integration Processes, Policies, and the Business Environment* (pp. 295–313). Springer. doi:10.1007/978-3-319-72239-9_14

Wertenbroch, K. (2021). Marketing Automation: Marketing Utopia or Marketing Dystopia? *NIM Marketing Intelligence Review*, *13*(1), 18–23. doi:10.2478/nimmir-2021-0003

YongvongphaiboonP.ChantamasM. (2021). Influence of digital marketing communication and performance effectiveness between b2b companies and clients in Thailand. *Influencia de comunicacion del marketing digital y la eficacia del rendimiento entre empresas b2b y clientes en Tailandia, 26*, 171-182. doi:10.5281/zenodo.4678872

Zahay, D. (2021). Advancing research in digital and social media marketing. *Journal of Marketing Theory and Practice*, *29*(1), 125–139. doi:10.1080/10696679.2021.1882865

# Section 2
# Digitalization in Business Processes

# Chapter 4
# Digital Transformation Process in Selection and Implementation of an Electronic Document Management System

**Leyla Özgür Polat**
https://orcid.org/0000-0002-5143-359X
*Pamukkale University, Turkey*

## ABSTRACT

*An electronic document management system (e-DMS) is an information system that allows creating, distributing, filing, storing, searching, destroying, and archiving documents concerning certain criteria and standards as a critical part of every digital transformation. It is known that correspondence processes in public institutions such as universities are time-consuming activities that increase workload and bureaucracy. Therefore, it is a critical issue to select and implement the suitable e-DMS software which systematically supports institutions in managing the documents they produce in their work processes. This chapter provides decision support to the institutional managers for selecting proper software, the preparation process before the application, transformation stages, and the environmental benefits after the implementation of the system are shown with their workflows through an actual application in a university. Digital transformation of the system provides both environmental and social benefits for institutions beside its material benefits such as time and labour.*

## INTRODUCTION

Digitization refers to the internal optimization of processes such as work automation, paper minimization and results in cost reductions. Digital transformation requires different comprehensive actions that need to be taken by organizations to face new digital technologies (Yildiz et al., 2021). Whatever of the organizational or operational scope is every organization needs to manage documents to execute and sustain its operational processes (van der Voet et al., 2004). Their collection, storage, management, and archive

DOI: 10.4018/978-1-7998-8169-8.ch004

are significant cost for organisations if those documents are especially in the paper form. According to Armenia et al. (2021) "The dematerialization of documents is a key aspect in the digital transformation of an organization as it allows improving internal processes, structures, and working practices through the application of digital technology, hence improving internal efficiency, effectiveness, rationalization, simplification, and other reformulated goals". The digital transformation implies a deep change in many areas inside the public institutions, both on a technical perspective and from the tools needed to reach all the actions, up to the following redefinition of a Document Management System (Bruno de & George Leal, 2021; Casalino et al., 2017). Therefore, document transactions should be conducted with Electronic DMS (e-DMS), an information system that allows creating, distributing, filing, storing, searching, destroying, and archiving documents with respect to certain criteria and standards. It is a known fact that correspondence processes in the public institutions such as universities are time-consuming activities that increase the workload and bureaucracy. In this scope, e-DMS is an indispensable system in the digitalization and effectiveness of universities (Çubukçu & Aktürk, 2020). Therefore, it is a critical issue to select and implement the suitable e-DMS software which systematically supports institutions in managing the documents they produce in their work processes. In today's age of information, with all the important developments in Information Technologies (IT) sector, many public institutions have switched to e-DMS applications allowing creation, distribution, filing and storage of documents so that both internal and external correspondences are executed more effectively and more quickly in the electronic environment as a result of policies for transformation to e-Government. More of an imperative rather than a choice for the states of the world in the 21st century, e-Government is amongst the most important items in the present agenda of reformation of the public sector (Annttiroiko, 2008). Beside the laws and legislations, usage of e-DMS has become a necessity for institutions to benefit from the advantages of electronic environment such as reducing direct and indirect costs in public expenditures (Michael & Maximilian, 2014; Zantout & Marir, 1999). As a result of these developments in public institutions, it has become a necessity that universities switch to e-DMS applications accordingly. Thus, many universities have reached the stage of deploying the most suitable e-DMS application as per the criteria they have determined. Therefore, a selection process should be performed among the software that meets all rules, laws, and legislations. The problem which was considered in this chapter is to prevent time and material losses that occur due to the steps taken in order to improve the effectiveness of e-DMS software selection and transformation process for public institutions and organizations, particularly universities.

Selecting e-DMS software is considered as a decision making problem with more than one criterion and alternatives are available in a more qualitative and objective way (Andersen, 2001). Multi-criteria decision-making techniques such as AHP (Analytical Hierarchy Process), Fuzzy AHP, TOPSIS (Technic for Order Preference by Similarity to Ideal Solution) and ELECTRE (Elimination and Choice Expressing Reality) are usually used for such problems (Mardani et al., 2015). The uncertainties in the solution of this problem are due to the fact that people make decisions through linguistic expressions rather than scientific techniques. Thus, it is possible to offer solutions using fuzzy logic approaches. In this chapter, the Fuzzy AHP method was selected amongst the multi-criteria decision-making techniques due to the fact that the criteria were determined together by the participants with common scoring for the preparation of the matrix. It is difficult for the decision-makers to decide on the same score and fuzzy numbers may reflect people's assessments better than the real values. The Fuzzy AHP approach was first applied by Yager (1978). Today, it is frequently used for resolving the ambiguities of personal views of the decision-makers in multi-criteria decision-making problems. There are various studies where the

Fuzzy AHP approach is used for selecting the best choice amongst alternatives (Başlıgil, 2005; Cebeci, 2009; Mardani et al., 2015; Yaldır & Özgür Polat, 2016).

When the relevant literature is examined, it can be observed that the studies on e-DMS applications have gained momentum especially in the last two decades (Doverton, 2001). These are usually studies where increase in major productivity and performance are shown by applying new technology to documents and document processing (Sprague Jr, 1995); reasons for adopting e-DMS applications and the benefits to be derived accordingly (Bélanger & Carter, 2008; Irani et al., 2008; Knowles, 1995); ontologies for reorganizing e-DMS in public administration (Klischewski, 2003, 2006); the need to design e-DMS that carefully map their features to target organizations and user groups (Ginsburg & Kambil, 1999; Rui, 2006); analyses of how e-DMS was deployed and how the case organisation was transformed and the findings are mapped against the normative literature (Jones, 2012). There are also studies on how e-DMS and their metadata should be on the design and integration of the system to the institution (Bernotas et al., 2005; Cordella & Iannacci, 2010; Gilani et al., 2009; Harris et al., 1997). Recently, Goran et al. (2017) aim to identify the benefits of an approach in which DMSs are based on a formal and explicit document model, primarily in terms of facilitating domain-specific customization. It has been observed that many survey-based studies in recent years are aimed at examination of readiness statuses of users for the usage of e-DMS (Chan & Pan, 2008; Hung et al., 2009; Kaaki et al., 2013).

On the other hand, the studies related to e-DMS applications executed in universities are very limited. Kong et al. (2002) designed and developed an XML based document management system for the universities. Özdemirci (2007) presented general definitions and relevant laws and legislations on document management and archiving for Turkish universities. Sánchez-Martinez et al. (2008) presented interoperability processes of e-DMS inside the University of Murcia and its relationship with other organizations. Gilani et al. (2009) examined fundamental characteristics required to implement e-DMS in the university environment. The authors argued that simply converting paper-based activities to digital will not succeed an efficient e-DMS system. Instead, it is required to address complete model and its influencing factors at once. Costoiu et al. (2009) provided information on transforming old documents to electronic form with the implementation of an optical character recognition system for the University Politehnica of Bucharest. Külcü et al. (2013) presented the similarities and differences of the practices along with consistency and interoperability problems of e-DMS systems in Turkish universities.

Besides, there are limited studies on selecting e-DMS applications. Knowles (1995) intended to help potential users of e-DMS in determining the route to take in implementing a system. Dornberg and Lohmüller (2013) and Heinicke et al. (2015) were interested in measuring the usability of e-DMS which can be limitedly used in evaluation of the systems. Nijman (2011) developed a tool for e-DMS vendors to design and implement the required document management system effectively. Önaçan et al. (2012) have performed a study on the roadmap to be followed in the construction of e-DMS applications in institutions. Paramonova (2016) presented an e-DMS classification framework according to character of the functions of a system, data storage topology, used working technologies, scope, degree of adjustment, scale of introduction, character of the document management structure, level of the served management system, character of the development of a system, degree of accessibility and degree of the coverage of processes (end use). Kiplie et al. (2018) examined efficient system development steps of e-DMS and offered following steps: planning, system analysis, system design, system development, system testing and integration and system maintenance. Ismael and Okumus (2017) researched e-DMS system requirements, developed a desktop-based application and implemented it successfully in a university department. These studies highlight some important issues, many of which are often overlooked. Moreover, according to the authors' knowledge, the studies published in the literature so far do not provide adequate information on how a suitable e-DMS software is selected and the transformation process is managed in universities. Therefore, in this study, the selection and transformation process are simultaneously considered for the first time in order to fill this gap in the literature with a real study application in a Turkish university, which constitutes the main contribution of this study.

The remaining parts of this chapter are organised as follows: First, the design of the transformation process to e-DMS are described. The transformation process to e-DMS covers information on the general procedure of processes such as the preliminary preparation process that is performed before the transformation process, determination of board members, and the determination of criteria to be considered during the selection of e-DMS. Also, the appropriate flow of e-DMS after the selection is described in detail. Then, the stages performed are described via case study and the criteria are weighted with the Fuzzy AHP approach, and the suitable software is selected amongst alternatives. The current status after the application, number of users in the system, server properties and the number of documents generated per year and the environmental benefits obtained through the system using real data are detailed. Finally, the results and discussions of the study are given.

## E-DMS TRANSFORMATION PROCESS

After making the decision to switch to e-DMS application, it is important that the stages of preliminary preparation, selection of the software, and transformation process are managed respectively and effectively. It is essential that upper management should provide support to the process and create an institutional awareness for all staff to prevent any resistance in early stages. Also, it is another important aspect to express why a switch to e-DMS is made and what benefits it will provide to the institution. This is explained to the staff in considerate detail. All steps required in the transformation process are explained in the following sections, respectively.

### Preliminary Preparation

The developments in the digital era requires comprehensive revaluations in managerial processes at universities (Yildiz, 2021). One of these fundamental revaluations is e-DMS transformation. In the beginning of this transformation, preliminary preparation process should be executed by the Clerk's Office or Department of Document Management and Archive under the leadership of the Secretary General of the university. Preparation and announcement of formal communication codes for current and newly established departments are executed in the preliminary preparation process. This process also includes editing of correspondence rules determined by laws and legislations as per the institution and informing the relevant departments. Determination of limits of authorisation of the relevant titles in the documents such as the directive for signature authorizations are included in this process. Staff should be provided with well training through the process beside the standard file plan, document destruction and storage plan in order to complete the stages of preliminary preparation process successfully. Preliminary preparation process is shown in detail in Figure 1.

Preliminary preparation process is executed in order to make formal correspondences in all public institutions and organizations due to the relevant laws and legislations even if the decision for a transformation to e-DMS process is not made.

*Figure 1. Preliminary preparation process*

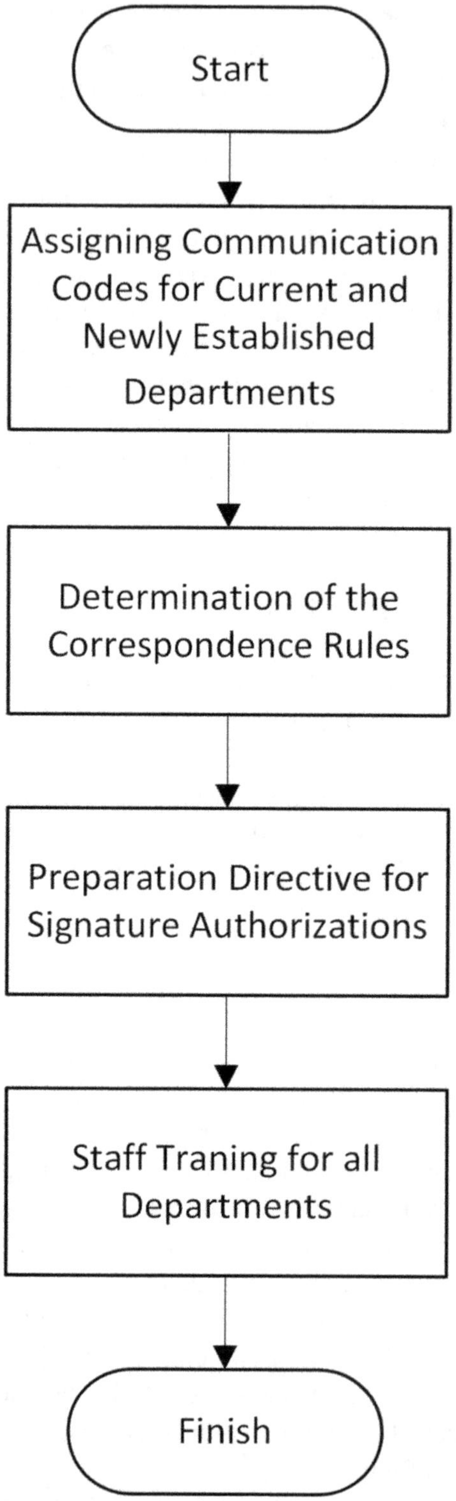

Directly following the preliminary preparation process, an authorized official board is established to ensure that all decisions are taken officially, and the institution apply these decisions accordingly. Care should be taken in the selection of board members for the sake of rapid and effective progress of the process. Therefore, the board have members who are directly effective in the process and members from upper management. In order to show what titles, the board members will have, the board members in the university where the application was performed has been explained in Determination of Board Members Section.

## Selection of Proper E-DMS Software

The effectiveness of selection of proper software process will prevent the losses both in terms of time and costs that may occur in the later stages. Therefore, the software to be selected should conform to the institution itself and meet all the required laws and legislations. Thus, waste of capital stock such as time wasted for the application of improper software in the institution, staffs labour losses, and software purchasing costs etc. should be prevented. The decision process is selecting among the alternatives as per some goal or criteria. It is essential to make the decision as per scientific criteria in order to make better decisions in the process of deciding the proper software. Selection of e-DMS software was made by a scientific approach using multi-criteria decision-making techniques as they are usually used in the selection of integrated systems such as corporate resource planning software. General representation of the e-DMS software selection process is shown in Figure 2.

The most important issue on the proper software selection process is the creation of a proper technical specification and determination of the priorities in the criteria scoring in accordance with the institution after determining the criteria. Therefore, in this study, the general criteria that may be used in all public institutions and organizations such as cost, reliability, integration, management, flexibility, support and service, ease of operation and access, and ease of archiving and reporting have been determined with the help of different users and experts from the universities. The literature related to selection of appropriate software (i.e. (Başlıgil, 2005; Cebeci, 2009; Mardani et al., 2015)) and user acceptance studies on the e-DMS (i.e. (Chan & Pan, 2008; Hung et al., 2009; Kaaki et al., 2013)) are also reviewed in the determination of the criteria. Criterion for conforming the laws and legislations is not included in the selection criteria as alternative software is always selected among the vendors conforming such criteria. Accordingly, criteria are given and explained as follows:

*A1. Cost:* Expresses system infrastructure and purchasing costs beside the maintenance and updates.

*A2. Reliability:* Determining the attitude against the system where both the operation of the system and the safety of users' access to the system are expected to be in high standard. Therefore, providing system and document access authorisations, taking a record of these authorisations, and establishing a good technical infrastructure against external and internal threats will improve users' trust against the system.

*A3. Integration and Management:* As a result of ensuring integration of available software with e-DMS application in the institution will accelerate the operation and reduce the dependence on the vendor and the system administrators. Ensuring integration, especially with systems where staff assignments, department and title changes, leaves and task assignments are executed such as the staff information system etc. should provide easiness in adding or removing users to/from the system automatically, in updating the information and in deputy operations. The fact that system management is performed by the institution is also an important element as it will reduce the dependence on the vendor. Therefore, interfaces which will ensure that all arrangements and workflows on the system are performed easily are required for the management of the system.

*Figure 2. General representation of proper e-DMS software selection process*

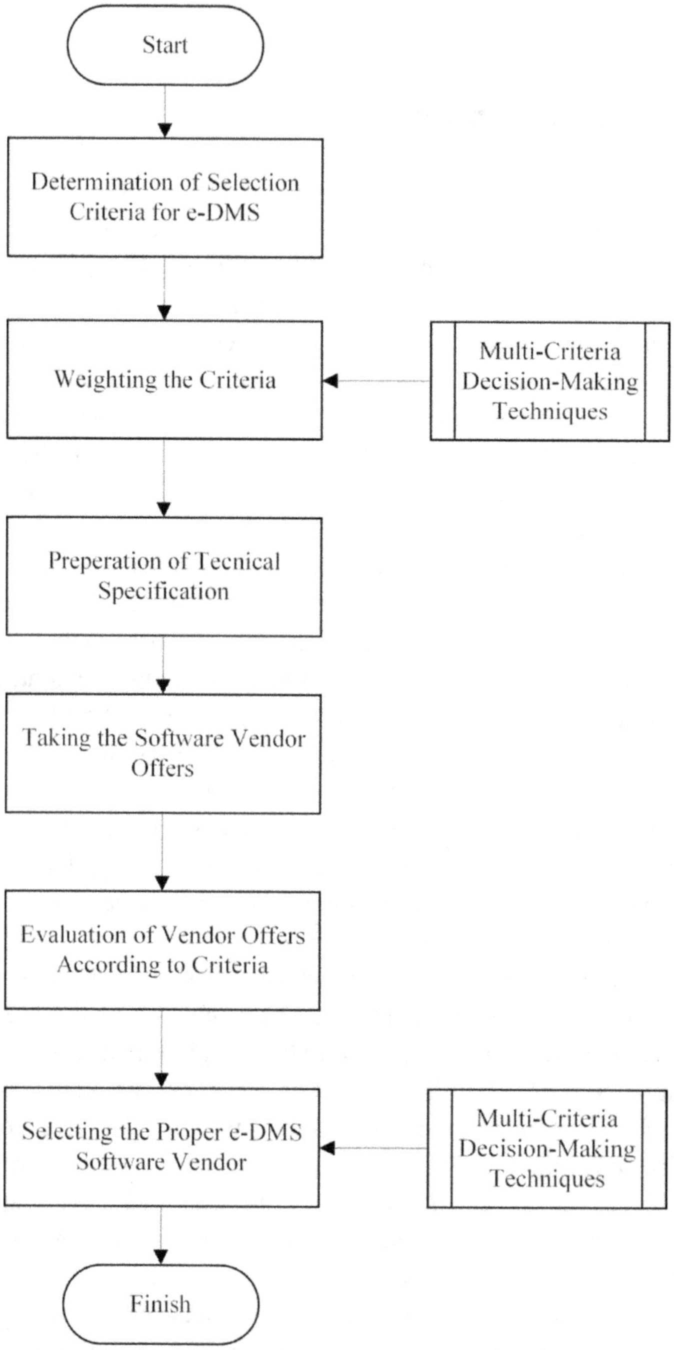

*A4. Flexibility:* System should be flexible against new arrangements. As laws and legislations may change in accordance with the conditions of current day, system should also keep up with this change in a rapid way. Moreover, menu designs should be customisable by the users, in other words, menu designs with a flexible structure are more desirable for the users in using the system.

*A5. Support and Service:* It is important that the vendor provides support together with the solution method in a short period of time in case of any fault until the system is rendered operational and afterwards. These include training support, security support, maintenance support, update support and receiving help from the relevant persons against system errors and opinion requests.

*A6. Ease of Operation and Access:* To ensure that users can produce documents quickly, submit them for initials and signature, write a response to incoming document, distribute them, and include the external correspondences to the system, interface designs and menus should be available and error messages should be understandable. Also, access to the system, user manuals and searched documents should be quick and easy.

*A7. Ease of Archiving and Reporting:* According to the relevant laws and legislations, document archiving and destruction processes should also be easily performed in the system. Additionally, it should be possible to access the statistical data beside transactions on the document and the reports that may be obtained easily and quickly.

After the determination of criteria, the most important criterion should be selected by weighting the criteria as per the expectations of the institution itself. Thus, the selected criterion and the priority of the alternative with higher criterion score on the selection decision should be determined. After weighting the criteria, purchasing process should be executed by the relevant department. On the latter stages, offers should be taken from the vendors as per the purchasing requirements, and vendor alternatives that comply with laws and legislations and technical specification should be determined. During this process, each weighted criterion should be scored in order to determine the superiority of vendor alternatives to each other. Scoring may be transformed to a single decision by using a method such as the weighted average method which enables taking the personal opinion of each decision-maker or by having them determine a common score. After scoring, weights of criteria and scores of alternatives for each criterion are then multiplied and thus the alternative which is superior according to the criterion with higher weight is brought forward.

## Application Process

There are various aspects to be considered in the latter stages after making the decision for the vendor that the e-DMS application will be implemented. In this context, steps to be followed are shown in Figure 3. In this figure, the process includes two more sub-processes, namely Preliminary Preparation and Selection of Proper Software that have been explained in Preliminary Preparation and Selection of Proper E-DMS Software Sections. Since the preliminary preparation is an essential process, it may be performed before the decision of switching to e-DMS application, or after determination of the board members in the institutions which have been late in performing the required work in this subject. Yet, it is recommended that the preliminary preparation stages should be completed in priority on a proper process. After the preliminary preparation, determination of board members and selection of proper software steps explained above, department analysis studies should be performed in order to examine the general operation of the departments and correspondence styles and different correspondence forms they use.

*Figure 3. General representation of transformation process to e-DMS*

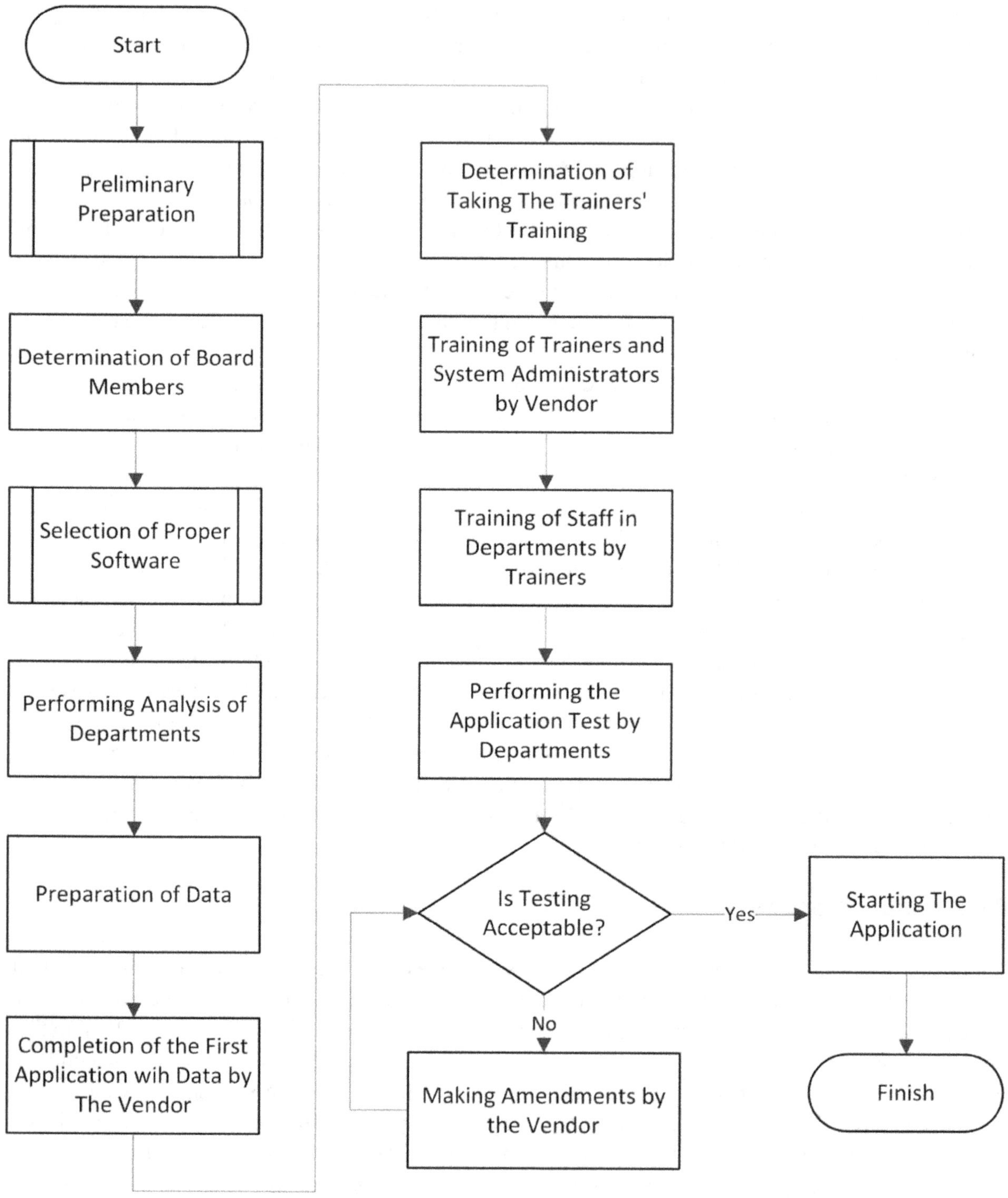

After the completion of analysis work within the process, correspondence templates and workflows needed to be produced. This information should be prepared with the participation of vendor representatives if possible, and recorded in writing, in order to confirm the validity of the flows and templates created in the application. After the preparation of workflows and correspondence templates, the departments in the institution, information on the users who will be using the system and authorisation and role groups based on titles should be determined. The information on the format of these data should be provided by the vendor, and the institution's part is to determine which departments, titles and users are registered in the system and prepare the lists accordingly. The task for uploading the lists to the system and to ensure that the system is operational at the current condition is the responsibility of the vendor.

After these processes, the trainings stage may start. The test stage may also get longer or shorter depending on how much the staff and upper management of the institution adopts the process. To make this stage shorter, the preliminary preparation process should be executed effectively. While the test stage may be performed at a pilot department, it may also be performed at whole institutions at the same time. It may be recommended to start the test at whole institutions in order to obtain different views as all departments have a different method of operation. The process will be completed when the application starts after completion of the test operation by informing the vendor about the deficiencies. However, the essential issue here is to ensure that the documents are created and distributed only through the system, in order to terminate manual documenting completely; consequently, the whole institution should be informed and rendered obligatory by an official board decision.

## E-DMS TRANSFORMATION PROCESS

Application procedures held in the cover of this study are performed a university in Turkey. Infrastructure work for e-DMS applications has been started in the Higher Education Council of Turkey in January 2012, and internal e-DMS applications have been launched in June 2013, and the first digitally signed document was created. As a result of these developments in the Higher Education Council of Turkey, it has become a necessity that the universities switch to e-DMS applications accordingly. The university performs all of its official correspondences via e-DMS since April 2013. Real application stages that are designed in the requirements phase and the general flow of actions as described above are dealt in this section.

### Preliminary Preparation Studies

Within the cover of the study, preparation of communication codes, correspondence rules, signature authorisations and required training operations that are included in the preliminary preparation process for the university are executed as described in Preliminary Preparation Section. These operations, which are included in the preliminary preparation process, were executed by the Department of Information Technology in cooperation with the board members and the departments where these board members are assigned. However, these operations were executed after the selection of board members and after deciding the software.

## Determination of Board Members

Members of the board have been selected from the following 14 titles to ensure that all decisions are made in unity and the institution applies the decisions for the comprehensive application of the process in the university:

*Vice Rector:* Acts as the chairman of the board and authorised signatory in communicating of all decisions taken through the rectorate. This post is very effective in accelerating the process and preventing the resistance of staff as an authority representing the upper management.

*General Secretary:* Acts as the chairman in meetings and owns the process when Vice Rector is absent.

*Chief Clerk:* The person who is in charge of document management and knows the process best.

*Legal Counsellor:* The person who is knowledgeable about the legal consequences of the process and what needs be performed in legal terms.

*Head of Human Resources Department:* Responsible for staff operations and for determination of the users in the following integration stage.

*Unit Manager in the Human Resources Department:* Assigned by the head of human resources department to share information through the process.

*Head of Information Technologies Department:* Acts as an interface between the university and the vendor in charge.

*Unit Manager in the Information Technologies Department:* Assigned by the head of information technology department to provide support in execution of the process and to share information.

*Internal Auditor:* Performs the assessments on behalf of the university throughout the whole process.

*Hospital Manager:* Responsible for the operations in the hospital which affiliated with the university.

*Clerk:* Responsible for arranging meetings and keep updated with official documents to share throughout the whole process.

*Faculty Secretary:* Responsible for the operations in academic units.

*Institutional Data Assessment Centre Expert:* Responsible for sharing information within the context of sense of quality.

*IT Expert:* Assigned as the coordinator of the whole process.

The most essential duty of these board members is to hold meetings when required and thus to ensure that decisions for executing the e-DMS process are taken and confirmed with the whole university in written form so that the relevant decisions are applied. Also, the board is required to make a decision in the selection process of the proper software.

## Selection of e-DMS Software with Fuzzy AHP Approach

Criteria were determined and scored through brain-storming method to obtain the opinions of stakeholders including upper management and relevant departments of the university with common scoring for the preparation of the matrix. It is difficult for the decision-makers to decide on the same score. AHP as a common method of multi-criteria decision making may be applied in such cases for the evaluation of criteria and alternatives that involve uncertain data. AHP is used to capture the expert's knowledge in general but cannot reflect the human thinking and preferences. Fuzzy set theory is used resembling human reasoning in its use of approximate information and uncertainty to generate decisions. Fuzzy AHP which has been used for many types of decision-making problem including software supplier selection problems for enterprises and institutions (Ho et al., 2010; Kahraman et al., 2003; Şen et al.,

2009). Hence, a fuzzy extension of AHP method was selected to evaluate the sustainable criteria to list the alternatives to solve the hierarchical fuzzy problems as human preferences.

*Table 1. Triangular fuzzy numbers conversion scale (Cheng, 1999)*

| Intensity of importance | Definition | Triangular Fuzzy Numbers | Inverse of Triangular Fuzzy Numbers |
|---|---|---|---|
| 1 | Equal importance | (1,1,1) | (1/1,1/1,1/1) |
| 2 | Intermediate values | (1,2,3) | (1/3,1/2,1/1) |
| 3 | Moderate importance of one over another | (2,3,4) | (1/4,1/3,1/2) |
| 4 | Intermediate values | (3,4,5) | (1/5,1/4,1/3) |
| 5 | Strong importance of one over another | (4,5,6) | (1/6,1/5,1/4) |
| 6 | Intermediate values | (5,6,7) | (1/7,1/6,1/5) |
| 7 | Very strong importance of one over another | (6,7,8) | (1/8,1/7,1/6) |
| 8 | Intermediate values | (7,8,9) | (1/9,1/8,1/7) |
| 9 | Extreme importance of one over another | (8,9,9) | (1/9,1/9,1/8) |

*Table 2. The pair-wise comparison matrix of selection criteria with fuzzy numbers*

| | A1 | A2 | A3 | A4 | A5 | A6 | A7 |
|---|---|---|---|---|---|---|---|
| **A1** | $\tilde{1}$ | $(\tilde{7})^{-1}$ | $(\tilde{6})^{-1}$ | $(\tilde{2})^{-1}$ | $(\tilde{4})^{-1}$ | $(\tilde{4})^{-1}$ | $(\tilde{6})^{-1}$ |
| **A2** | $\tilde{7}$ | $\tilde{1}$ | $\tilde{2}$ | $\tilde{5}$ | $\tilde{4}$ | $\tilde{3}$ | $\tilde{2}$ |
| **A3** | $\tilde{6}$ | $(\tilde{2})^{-1}$ | $\tilde{1}$ | $\tilde{3}$ | $\tilde{3}$ | $\tilde{2}$ | $\tilde{1}$ |
| **A4** | $\tilde{2}$ | $(\tilde{5})^{-1}$ | $(\tilde{3})^{-1}$ | $\tilde{1}$ | $(\tilde{3})^{-1}$ | $(\tilde{2})^{-1}$ | $(\tilde{5})^{-1}$ |
| **A5** | $\tilde{4}$ | $(\tilde{4})^{-1}$ | $(\tilde{3})^{-1}$ | $\tilde{3}$ | $\tilde{1}$ | $\tilde{2}$ | $(\tilde{4})^{-1}$ |
| **A6** | $\tilde{4}$ | $(\tilde{3})^{-1}$ | $(\tilde{2})^{-1}$ | $\tilde{2}$ | $(\tilde{2})^{-1}$ | $\tilde{1}$ | $(\tilde{4})^{-1}$ |
| **A7** | $\tilde{6}$ | $(\tilde{2})^{-1}$ | $(\tilde{1})^{-1}$ | $\tilde{5}$ | $\tilde{4}$ | $\tilde{4}$ | $\tilde{1}$ |

Within the cover of this study, criteria described in Application Process Section. were used for determination of proper e-DMS software. After the determination of the criteria, a paired comparison matrix is used to express the superiority of these criteria to each other numerically in order to determine their priorities. Triangular and trapezoidal fuzzy numbers are usually preferred for paired comparisons in the Fuzzy AHP approach. Thus, triangular fuzzy numbers were used in this study. Triangular membership functions were first defined and used by Van Laarhoven and Pedrycz (1983), and they are frequently used. Table 1 contains triangular fuzzy number conversion table.

Criteria in Table 2, which were scored similarly to the AHP method, are converted to triangular fuzzy numbers with the help of conversion scale given in Table 1.

After preparing the paired comparison matrix, a consistency analysis is performed in order to examine the logical and mathematical relationships of the priorities to each other. Acceptable upper limit for consistency ratio is 0.10. If this ratio is higher than 0.10, the decision-makers should review their comparisons.

Extended Analysis Method (EAM) is used in many of the decision-making problems where the Fuzzy AHP method is used. Therefore, in practice, decision-makers have assessed the criteria via conventional AHP first, then the assessments were transformed to fuzzy data and the problem was solved with the EAM. It may not be possible to calculate the consistency in some cases as in the EAM proposed by Chang (1996). This is because weights of some criteria are calculated as zero in the total weight vector as a result of the Fuzzy AHP operation, and in this case, the result may become indefinite in the calculation of consistency index as dividing a number by zero is indefinite. As per the EAM, steps of the Fuzzy AHP approach are followed in order. The steps are as follows:

*Step 1:* As per the EAM, synthesis values should be calculated first in the first stage. The following formulation is used for the calculation:

$$S_i = \sum_{j=1}^{m} M_{gi}^{j} \left[ \sum_{i=1}^{n} \sum_{j=1}^{m} M_{gi}^{j} \right]^{-1} \tag{1}$$

Synthesis values calculated accordingly are as follows:

$S_{A1}$ (0.019, 0.028, 0.048), $S_{A2}$ (0.160, 0.271, 0.450), $S_{A3}$ (0.109, 0.187, 0.315),

$S_{A4}$ (0.028, 0.052, 0.097), $S_{A5}$ (0.068, 0.122, 0.212), $S_{A6}$ (0.054, 0.097, 0.177) and

$S_{A7}$ (0.154, 0.243, 0.390).

*Step 2:* On the second step of the method, fuzzy numbers are compared using the following equality and thus, the priority values of the decision elements in the hierarchy are determined. These values are shown in Table 3.

Consider two triangular fuzzy numbers $M_1$ and $M_2$, $\widetilde{M_1} = (l_1, m_1, u_1)$ and $\widetilde{M_2} = (l_2, m_2, u_2)$.

$$V\left(\widetilde{M_2} \geq \widetilde{M_1}\right) = hgt\left(\widetilde{M_1} \cap \widetilde{M_2}\right) = \mu_{M_2}(d) = \begin{cases} 1 & if \rightarrow m_2 \geq m_1 \\ 0 & if \rightarrow l_1 \geq u_2 \\ \dfrac{l_1 - u_2}{(m_2 - u_2) - (m_1 - l_1)} & otherwise \end{cases} \quad (2)$$

*Table 3. Priority values of selection criteria*

| | | | |
|---|---|---|---|
| V(A1≥A2)=0<br>V(A1≥A3)=0<br>V(A1≥A4)=0.464<br>V(A1≥A5)=0<br>V(A1≥A6)=0<br>V(A1≥A7)=0 | V(A2≥A1)=1<br>V(A2≥A3)=1<br>V(A2≥A4)=1<br>V(A2≥A5)=1<br>V(A2≥A6)=1<br>V(A2≥A7)=1 | V(A3≥A1)=1<br>V(A3≥A2)=0.646<br>V(A3≥A4)=1<br>V(A3≥A5)=1<br>V(A3≥A6)=1<br>V(A3≥A7)=0.740 | V(A4≥A1)=1<br>V(A4≥A2)=0<br>V(A4≥A3)=0<br>V(A4≥A5)=0.294<br>V(A4≥A6)=0.487<br>V(A4≥A7)=0 |
| V(A5≥A1)=1<br>V(A5≥A2)=0.261<br>V(A5≥A3)=0.616<br>V(A5≥A4)=1<br>V(A5≥A6)=1<br>V(A5≥A7)=0.327 | V(A6≥A1)=1<br>V(A6≥A2)=0.092<br>V(A6≥A3)=0.432<br>V(A6≥A4)=1<br>V(A6≥A5)=0.811<br>V(A6≥A7)=0.139 | V(A7≥A1)=1<br>V(A7≥A2)=0.891<br>V(A7≥A3)=1<br>V(A7≥A4)=1<br>V(A7≥A5)=1<br>V(A7≥A6)=1 | |

*Step 3:* At the third step, i.e. obtaining of the priority values, the smallest value, d'($A_i$), of each decision element is selected amongst the values obtained by the comparison of fuzzy number pairs.

| | | | |
|---|---|---|---|
| d'(A1)=0 | d'(A2)=1 | d'(A3)=0.646 | d'(A4)=0 |
| d'(A5)=0.261 | d'(A6)=0.092 | d'(A7)=0.891 | |

Priority values obtained by the calculation creates the vector W'=(0, 1, 0.646, 0, 0.261, 0.092, 0.891).

*Step 4:* After the last step, i.e. normalisation, weight vector is transformed to non-fuzzy numbers. In the normalisation procedure, values of W' matrix are individually divided by the sum of matrix.

As a result, criteria weights are obtained as W'=(0, 0,346, 0.224, 0, 0.090, 0.032, 0.308). As per result obtained, the most significant criterion is *A2 (Reliability),* and second most significant criterion is *A7 (Ease of Archiving and Reporting)*. Here, the criteria *A1 (Cost)* and *A4 (Flexibility)* are not considered as their coefficient is 0.

After calculating the weights of the criteria, pre-meetings should be held with alternative vendors and their offers are taken. In the later months of 2012, when this work was announced, only three vendors that have contacted the university and they all have managed to be short listed as they all met the technical specifications. Vendors are named as A, B and C for ethical reasons. As a consequence of the determination of the weights of the criteria, decision for selecting the vendor may be taken by various multi-criteria decision-making techniques. Comparison matrix of alternatives for each criterion is given in Table 4 with the triangular fuzzy number transformation.

*Table 4. The pair-wise comparison matrix of alternatives according to selection criteria*

| | | Fuzzy Number | | | Triangular Fuzzy Numbers | | |
|---|---|---|---|---|---|---|---|
| | | **A** | **B** | **C** | **A** | **B** | **C** |
| **Criteria A2** | **A** | $\tilde{1}$ | $\tilde{5}$ | $\tilde{3}$ | (1,1,1) | (4,5,6) | (2,3,4) |
| | **B** | $(\tilde{5})^{-1}$ | $\tilde{1}$ | $(\tilde{4})^{-1}$ | (1/6,1/5,1/4) | (1,1,1) | (1/5,1/4,1/3) |
| | **C** | $(\tilde{3})^{-1}$ | $\tilde{4}$ | $\tilde{1}$ | (1/4,1/3,1/2) | (3,4,5) | (1,1,1) |
| **Criteria A3** | **A** | $\tilde{1}$ | $\tilde{6}$ | $\tilde{3}$ | (1,1,1) | (5,6,7) | (2,3,4) |
| | **B** | $(\tilde{6})^{-1}$ | $\tilde{1}$ | $(\tilde{5})^{-1}$ | (1/7,1/6,1/5) | (1,1,1) | (1/6,1/5,1/4) |
| | **C** | $(\tilde{3})^{-1}$ | $\tilde{5}$ | $\tilde{1}$ | (1/4,1/3,1/2) | (4,5,6) | (1,1,1) |
| **Criteria A5** | **A** | $\tilde{1}$ | $\tilde{4}$ | $\tilde{2}$ | (1,1,1) | (3,4,5) | (1,2,3) |
| | **B** | $(\tilde{4})^{-1}$ | $\tilde{1}$ | $(\tilde{3})^{-1}$ | (1/5,1/4,1/3) | (1,1,1) | (1/4,1/3,1/2) |
| | **C** | $(\tilde{2})^{-1}$ | $\tilde{3}$ | $\tilde{1}$ | (1/3,1/2,1/1) | (2,3,4) | (1,1,1) |
| **Criteria A6** | **A** | $\tilde{1}$ | $\tilde{2}$ | $(\tilde{3})^{-1}$ | (1,1,1) | (1,2,3) | (1/4,1/3,1/2) |
| | **B** | $(\tilde{2})^{-1}$ | $\tilde{1}$ | $(\tilde{4})^{-1}$ | (1/3,1/2,1/1) | (1,1,1) | (1/5,1/4,1/3) |
| | **C** | $\tilde{3}$ | $\tilde{4}$ | $\tilde{1}$ | (2,3,4) | (3,4,5) | (1,1,1) |
| **Criteria A7** | **A** | $\tilde{1}$ | $(\tilde{4})^{-1}$ | $(\tilde{2})^{-1}$ | (1,1,1) | (1/5,1/4,1/3) | (1/3,1/2,1/1) |
| | **B** | $\tilde{4}$ | $\tilde{1}$ | $\tilde{2}$ | (3,4,5) | (1,1,1) | (1,2,3) |
| | **C** | $\tilde{2}$ | $(\tilde{2})^{-1}$ | $\tilde{1}$ | (1,2,3) | (1/3,1/2,1/1) | (1,1,1) |

Paired precedence coefficients of alternatives for criteria A2, A3, A5, A6 and A7 are calculated in the same way as the weight coefficients. Accordingly, precedence coefficients of the vendors were calculated as W=(0.661, 0, 0.339) for criterion A2, W=(0.719, 0, 0.281) for criterion A3, W=(0.616, 0, 0.384) for criterion A5, W=(0.816, 0, 0.184) for criterion A6 and W=(0, 0.678, 0.322) for criterion A7.

As a result, weighted values are calculated by the multiplication of precedence coefficients and the weight coefficients of the criteria and total values of each alternative are compared and the vendor with the highest score is preferred. These values are shown in Table 5.

*Table 5. Comparison results of alternatives with fuzzy AHP*

| Criteria | Weight of Criteria (W) | A | B | C | W*A | W*B | W*C |
|---|---|---|---|---|---|---|---|
| A2 | 0.346 | 0.661 | 0 | 0.339 | 0.229 | 0 | 0.117 |
| A3 | 0.224 | 0.719 | 0 | 0.281 | 0.161 | 0 | 0.063 |
| A5 | 0.090 | 0.616 | 0 | 0.384 | 0.055 | 0 | 0.035 |
| A6 | 0.032 | 0.816 | 0 | 0.184 | 0.026 | 0 | 0.006 |
| A7 | 0.308 | 0 | 0.678 | 0.322 | 0 | 0.209 | 0.099 |
| Total | | | | | **0.471** | **0.209** | **0.320** |

When the Table 5 is examined, it can be seen that vendor A has the highest score. As it can be seen in these calculations, e-DMS software of vendor A was chosen as the most suitable software by the university. This is due to it being the best option in terms of integration, reliability, and support and service were offered by vendor A. More vendors, who have progressed in these fields, have also entered the market recently. Therefore, it has become more vital that this process is executed effectively.

## Software Implementation

After the decision was made for the proper software for the operations in the university, vendor staff and the university coordinator visited all academic and administrative departments and performed an analysis work in order to collect information on the correspondences in the departments and the operations of the departments. Analysis work took about two weeks. With this analysis work, the vendor had taken the university as a base for the general operations and used this information for other universities. The next stage is to prepare the departments, titles and users list and submit this list to the vendor; and then this information will be included in the system. Board members were included in making decisions such as which titles will be available in the system, whether the vendor staff are included in the system etc. and in the generation of such lists. Vendor staff was included in the system with official letter under the responsibility of department managers due to legal considerations. Also, persons who would receive and transfer a document in internal correspondences were authorised with the title of "Department Document Officer" with an official letter again.

When the users in the system are defined and the vendor has tested whether the system is operational, the staff who would be trained to become a trainer or system administrator should be appointed. The task for the staff who received a trainer's training is to train other staff in the department. The staff who will receive a trainer's training are specified to be at least two persons beside the authorised persons in the relevant departments such as department head, faculty secretary etc. The whole staff is included in the training in some administrative departments such as Clerk's Office. Accordingly, 193 staff have received training in the cover of Trainers' Training Programme. The system administrator training has also been given by the vendor to the specified staff. 328 people were trained in the cover of retraining of the trainers and the second stage trainings that should be held for one week. The system was opened for testing by the departments within this period and until April 2013, and time required for removing the deficiencies in the system has been provided. As a final step, the whole university has been rendered so that correspondences are written and received by e-DMS only in official correspondences with the board decision as of the beginning of April 2013. At the end of April 2013, 289 more people were trained again with the participation of the staff in the departments in order to discuss the execution and deficiencies of the process after the operation of the system, and support was taken from the vendor against different conditions that were encountered and offers for solutions of these problems were provided.

## RESULTS

This section provides the number of users, features of the available server, number of documents created annually, and the environmental benefits obtained with the application of the system through numerical data.

Although there are 3641 personnel in total, 2217 of which are academic and 1424 are administrative, in the e-DMS application of the university as of March 2021, there are 6631 active users with the addition of 2021 contractual staff. Most users have additional titles in more than one department. There are also 5019 personnel who have been rendered passive either when they have left the university or when their additional tasks have ended. Current database and application server features of the system are shown in Table 6. These data are included in the study with the numbers of staff and documents per year so that institutions that are going to switch to e-DMS application may have an opinion about the server features. These servers may be supplied with different features and capacities by comparing the number of staff, annual document circulation with the numbers of the public institutions and organisations themselves.

*Table 6. Server features*

| | Application Server | Database Server |
|---|---|---|
| Processor Feature | E5-4650v2 2.6Ghz | E5-4650v2 2.6Ghz |
| Number of Processor (Std/Max) | 8 | 8 |
| Hard Disk Capacity and Type | 2 TB /SCSI | 500GB /SCSI |
| Server Type | Virtual Server | Virtual Server |
| Memory Capacity | 8GB | 32GB |

Number of documents produced through the system between April 2013 and March 2021 are shown in Figure 4.

Also, the indication of the report about the environmental effects by the number of pages included in the system is shown in Figure 5. Data in the figure are given in pages, not in documents, as there may be more than one page in a document with its attachments. Data are taken from the system as of March 2021. The university has saved 2651 trees, prevented use of 748 tonnes of $CO_2$ gas and 53 tonnes of waste and unnecessary of use of 13201 litres of water by using e-DMS application in total.

As a result, the biggest difficulties in the transformation process were the fact that training was not given enough consideration, that the staff did not want to change their habits and that the subject was not known enough. Therefore, it is very important in the effectiveness of the transformation process that the preliminary preparation process is managed thoroughly.

*Figure 4. Number of documents produced according to years*

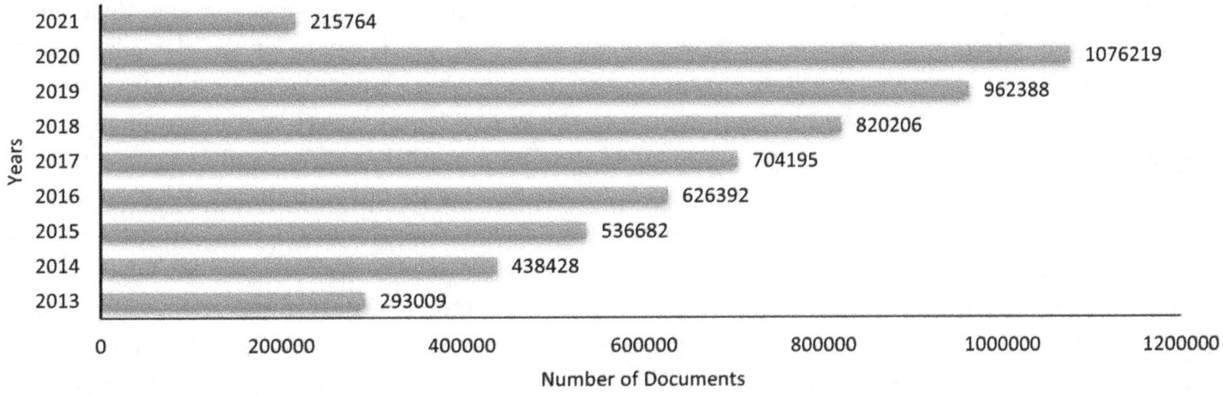


*Figure 5. Environmental benefits with e-DMS*

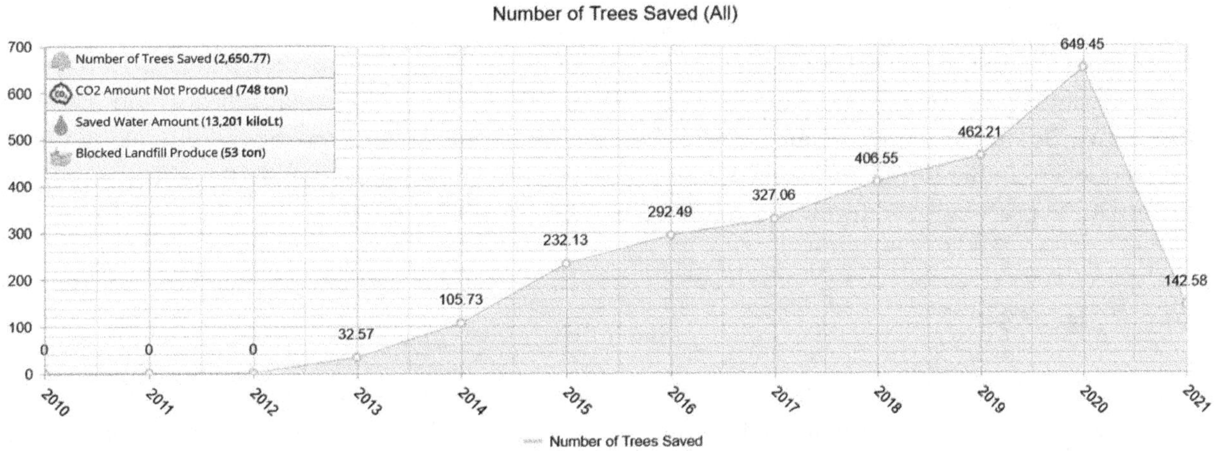


## CONCLUSION

The change towards document dematerialization in the way of the digital transformation requires a step-by-step process and the need for inner adaptation. It is a very complex revaluation that involves the assessment of many important phases: redesigning some processes of the document life cycle, reorganizing the management, processing, and storage(Armenia et al., 2021).

This chapter provides guidance by describing what the public institutions and organisations such as universities may encounter and should pay attention in selecting a proper e-DMS software and the transformation process via a real application. Within this context, many public institutions and organisations have called or even visited personally to get benefit from the experience and information obtained during these processes. The university continues to provide mentoring service to many universities in the context of selection and digital transformation process of e-DMS.

Within the cover of the chapter, digital transformation to e-DMS process in a real university has been examined step-by-step and the work performed has been described in detail. Steps required to manage the process are visualised by workflow charts, thus the comprehensibility of the study is intentionally increased. Leading on from this, criteria that should be considered in the selection of e-DMS application are determined and the selection process is assessed together with the indeterminacy in real life and the process is executed as weighting of the selected criteria with Fuzzy AHP approach and the selection of the most proper software. As a result of the calculations vendor A obtained the highest score amongst the alternatives. Accordingly, the most significant criterion for the university was determined as the criterion of A2-Reliability. As it also stated by Ismael and Okumus (2017), these results may vary as the evaluation of decision-makers depend on the structure and preferences of institutions. When selecting e-DMS, it is also important to comprise the criterion such as the character of the functions of a system (Paramonova, 2016).

This chapter also includes the numerical data such as the number of staff in the system after commissioning and number of documents created per year and server data that would help other institutions in designing their systems. Also, environmental benefits calculated as well as the number of documents created formally was given within the cover of the chapter.

As a result, it would be possible to execute the e-DMS transformation process effectively and start the process with minimum problems by taking effective decisions. Moreover, transformation to system will provide both environmental and social benefits for the institutions beside its material benefits such as time and labour. A promising step in the development of e-DMS is user adaptation and personalization to the individual characteristics (Obukhov et al., 2020). Machine learning approaches would increase the system's flexibility by personalizing it to the user's individual characteristics to provide the best user experience. In the future, different studies might be performed for describing the effectiveness of transformation processes and levels of perception and satisfaction of the staff.

## REFERENCES


Andersen, T. J. (2001). Information technology, strategic decision making approaches and organizational performance in different industrial settings. *The Journal of Strategic Information Systems, 10*(2), 101–119. doi:10.1016/S0963-8687(01)00043-9

Annttiroiko, A.-V. (2008). A brief introduction to the field of e-government. *Electronic Government: Concepts, Methodologies, Tools, and Applications, 1.*

Armenia, S., Casalino, N., Gnan, L., & Flamini, G. (2021). A systems approach to the digital transformation of public administration. *Prospettive In Organizzazıone, 14*, 1–20.

Başlıgil, H. (2005). The fuzzy analytic hierarchy process for software selection problems. *Sigma, 2005/3*(3), 24-33.

Bélanger, F., & Carter, L. (2008). Trust and risk in e-government adoption. *The Journal of Strategic Information Systems, 17*(2), 165–176. doi:10.1016/j.jsis.2007.12.002

Bernotas, M., Laurutis, R., & Slotkienė, A. (2005). Issues on forming metadata of editorial system's document management. *Information Technology and Control, 34*(4).

Bruno de, L., & George Leal, J. (2021). Digital Transformation for Businesses: Adapt or Die! Reflections on How to Rethink Your Business in the Digital Transformation Context. In A. Pedro Fernandes, P. Cláudio Roberto Magalhães, & J. George Leal (Eds.), Handbook of Research on Digital Transformation and Challenges to Data Security and Privacy (pp. 252-268). IGI Global. doi:10.4018/978-1-7998-4201-9.ch015

Casalino, N., Rubichi, V., Gasparri, C., & Pizzolo, G. (2017). Organization of Processes Digitization and E-Invoicing Services for an Effective Digital Transformation of Public Sector. *DigitCult–Scientific Journal on Digital Cultures*, *2*(1), 53–62.

Cebeci, U. (2009). Fuzzy AHP-based decision support system for selecting ERP systems in textile industry by using balanced scorecard. *Expert Systems with Applications*, *36*(5), 8900–8909. doi:10.1016/j.eswa.2008.11.046

Chan, C. M. L., & Pan, S. L. (2008). User engagement in e-government systems implementation: A comparative case study of two Singaporean e-government initiatives. *The Journal of Strategic Information Systems*, *17*(2), 124–139. doi:10.1016/j.jsis.2007.12.003

Chang, D.-Y. (1996). Applications of the extent analysis method on fuzzy AHP. *European Journal of Operational Research*, *95*(3), 649–655. doi:10.1016/0377-2217(95)00300-2

Cheng, C.-H. (1999). Evaluating weapon systems using ranking fuzzy numbers. *Fuzzy Sets and Systems*, *107*(1), 25–35. doi:10.1016/S0165-0114(97)00348-5

Cordella, A., & Iannacci, F. (2010). Information systems in the public sector: The e-Government enactment framework. *The Journal of Strategic Information Systems*, *19*(1), 52–66. doi:10.1016/j.jsis.2010.01.001

Costoiu, M., Isopescu, R., Plesu, V., Arsene, I., Alesincu, S., & Iancu, P. (2009). New developments for electronic document management in University Politehnica of Bucharest. *Source: PRES*, *9*, 309–314.

Çubukçu, C., & Aktürk, C. (2020). Digital transformation to university 4.0: A roadmap. *Uludağ University Journal of The Faculty of Engineering*, *25*(3), 1391–1408. doi:10.17482/uumfd.702617

Dornberg, J. H., & Lohmüller, L. (2013). *Optimizing the selection process of document-management systems International Conference on Advanced ICT*, Hainan, China.

Doverton, D. C. V. (2001). Techniques of document management: A review of text retrieval and related technologies. *The Journal of Documentation*, *57*(2), 192–217. doi:10.1108/EUM0000000007082

Gilani, S. M. M., Ahmed, J., & Abbas, M. A. (2009). Electronic document management: A paperless university model. *Computer Science and Information Technology, 2009. ICCSIT 2009. 2nd IEEE International Conference on.*

Ginsburg, M., & Kambil, A. (1999). Annotate: A web-based knowledge management support system for document collections. *Systems Sciences, 1999. HICSS-32. Proceedings of the 32nd Annual Hawaii International Conference on.*

Goran, S., Igor, C.-F., Stevan, G., Goran, S., Milan, S., & Miroslav, Z. (2017). Multilayer document model for semantic document management services. *The Journal of Documentation*, *73*(5), 803–824. doi:10.1108/JD-07-2016-0095

Harris, S., Owen, J., Bloor, M., & Hogg, I. (1997). Engineering document management strategy: Analysis of requirements, choice of direction and system implementation. *Proceedings of the Institution of Mechanical Engineers. Part B, Journal of Engineering Manufacture, 211*(5), 385–405. doi:10.1243/0954405971516365

Heinicke, A., Bröhl, C., Dokas, I., Walbaum, K., Bützler, J., & Schlick, C. (2015). Development of usability-criteria for the selection process of document management systems. In J. Abascal, S. Barbosa, M. Fetter, T. Gross, P. Palanque, & M. Winckler (Eds.), *Human-Computer Interaction – INTERACT 2015* (Vol. 9299, pp. 514–517). Springer International Publishing. doi:10.1007/978-3-319-22723-8_51

Ho, W., Xu, X., & Dey, P. K. (2010). Multi-criteria decision making approaches for supplier evaluation and selection: A literature review. *European Journal of Operational Research, 202*(1), 16–24. doi:10.1016/j.ejor.2009.05.009

Hung, S.-Y., Tang, K.-Z., Chang, C.-M., & Ke, C.-D. (2009). User acceptance of intergovernmental services: An example of electronic document management system. *Government Information Quarterly, 26*(2), 387–397. doi:10.1016/j.giq.2008.07.003

Irani, Z., Love, P. E. D., & Jones, S. (2008). Learning lessons from evaluating eGovernment: Reflective case experiences that support transformational government. *The Journal of Strategic Information Systems, 17*(2), 155–164. doi:10.1016/j.jsis.2007.12.005

Ismael, A., & Okumus, I. (2017). Design and Implementation of an Electronic Document Management System. *Mehmet Akif Ersoy Üniversitesi Uygulamalı Bilimler Dergisi, 1*(1), 9–17. doi:10.31200/makuubd.321093

Jones, S. (2012). eGovernment document management system: A case analysis of risk and reward. *International Journal of Information Management, 32*(4), 396–400. doi:10.1016/j.ijinfomgt.2012.04.002

Kaaki, F., Rayner, C., & Alshamrani, M. (2013). Female users' acceptance of the electronic document management system (EDMS). *Modelling Symposium (EMS), 2013 European.*

Kahraman, C., Cebeci, U., & Ulukan, Z. (2003). Multi-criteria supplier selection using fuzzy AHP. *Logistics Information Management, 16*(6), 382–394. doi:10.1108/09576050310503367

Kiplie, F. H., Yatin, S. F. M., Angutim, M., Hanani, N., & Hamid, A. (2018). System development for document management system. *International Journal of Academic Research in Business & Social Sciences, 8*(9). Advance online publication. doi:10.6007/IJARBSS/v8-i9/4652

Klischewski, R. (2003). Towards an ontology for e-document management in public administration-the case of Schleswig-Holstein. *System Sciences, 2003. Proceedings of the 36th Annual Hawaii International Conference on.*

Klischewski, R. (2006). Ontologies for e-document management in public administration. *Business Process Management Journal, 12*(1), 34–47. doi:10.1108/14637150610643742

Knowles, R. (1995). Electronic document management systems: How to select and implement the right documentation management system for your organisation. *The Electronic Library, 13*(6), 527–532. doi:10.1108/eb045423

Kong, B.-Y., Hwang, B.-K., & Cho, S.-H. (2002). Design and development of XML document management system for Cyber University. *Journal of Digital Contents Society*, *3*(1), 37–46.

Külcü, Ö., Çakmak, T., & Özel, N. (2013). Kurumsal bilgi sistemleri içerisinde belge yönetimi: Türkiye'deki kamu üniversitelerinde gerçekleştirilen uygulamalara yönelik bir durum analizi. *Information World/Bilgi Dunyasi*, *14*(2).

Mardani, A., Jusoh, A., & Zavadskas, E. K. (2015). Fuzzy multiple criteria decision-making techniques and applications–Two decades review from 1994 to 2014. *Expert Systems with Applications*, *42*(8), 4126–4148. doi:10.1016/j.eswa.2015.01.003

Michael, L., & Maximilian, H. (2014). Introduction of electronic documents: How business process simulation can help. *Business Process Management Journal*, *20*(6), 950–970. doi:10.1108/BPMJ-05-2013-0062

Nijman, A. (2011). A proposal and selection of a document management system for staatsolie suriname. Delft University of Technology.

Obukhov, A., Krasnyanskiy, M., & Nikolyukin, M. (2020). Algorithm of adaptation of electronic document management system based on machine learning technology. *Progress in Artificial Intelligence*, *9*(4), 287–303. doi:10.100713748-020-00214-2

Önaçan, M. B. K., Medeni, T. D., & Özkanlı, Ö. (2012). Elektronik belge yönetim sistemi (EBYS)'nin faydaları ve kurum bünyesinde EBYS yapılandırmaya yönelik bir yol haritası. *Journal of Turkish Court of Accounts/Sayistay Dergisi*, (85).

Özdemirci, F. (2007). Üniversitelerde belge yönetimi ve arşivler. *Türk Kütüphaneciliği*, *21*(2), 218–229.

Paramonova, I. E. (2016). Electronic document-management systems: A classification and new opportunities for a scientific technical library. *Scientific and Technical Information Processing*, *43*(3), 136–143. doi:10.3103/S0147688216030047

Rui, C. (2006). Design and implementation of document management system. *Modern Electronics Technique*, *15*, 33.

Sánchez-Martinez, D., Marín-López, I., & Jiménez-García, T. (2008). *Electronic document management in the University of Murcia*. Academic Press.

Şen, C. G., Baraçlı, H., & Şen, S. (2009). A literature review and classification of enterprise software selection approaches. *International Journal of Information Technology & Decision Making*, *08*(02), 217–238. doi:10.1142/S0219622009003351

Sprague, R. H. Jr. (1995). Electronic document management: Challenges and opportunities for information systems managers. *Management Information Systems Quarterly*, *19*(1), 29–49. doi:10.2307/249710

van der Voet, E., van Oers, L., & Nikolic, I. (2004). Dematerialization: Not Just a Matter of Weight. *Journal of Industrial Ecology*, *8*(4), 121–137. doi:10.1162/1088198043630432

Van Laarhoven, P., & Pedrycz, W. (1983). A fuzzy extension of Saaty's priority theory. *Fuzzy Sets and Systems*, *11*(1), 199–227. doi:10.1016/S0165-0114(83)80082-7

Yager, R. R. (1978). Fuzzy decision making including unequal objectives. *Fuzzy Sets and Systems*, *1*(2), 87–95. doi:10.1016/0165-0114(78)90010-6

Yaldır, A., & Özgür Polat, L. (2016). Çok Kriterli Karar Verme Teknikleri İle Elektronik Belge Yönetim Sistemi Seçimi-Electronic Document Management System Selection With Multi-Criteria Decision Making Techniques. *Mehmet Akif Ersoy Üniversitesi Sosyal Bilimler Enstitüsü Dergisi*, *8*(14), 88–108. doi:10.20875b.56729

Yildiz, O. (2021). Changing Paradigms in the Digital Age and Entrepreneurial Universities. In G. Durmuş, A. Tuncer, & Y. Orkun (Eds.), *University-Industry Collaboration Strategies in the Digital Era* (pp. 1–21). IGI Global. doi:10.4018/978-1-7998-3901-9.ch001

Yildiz, O., Ersoy, A. S., & Yıldırım, İ. S. (2021). The Impact of Information and Communication Systems on Organizations. In Y. Orkun (Ed.), *Recent Developments in Individual and Organizational Adoption of ICTs* (pp. 1–25). IGI Global. doi:10.4018/978-1-7998-3045-0.ch001

Zantout, H., & Marir, F. (1999). Document management systems from current capabilities towards intelligent information retrieval: An overview. *International Journal of Information Management*, *19*(6), 471–484. doi:10.1016/S0268-4012(99)00043-2

# Chapter 5
# Farming-as-a-Service (FAAS) for a Sustainable Agricultural Ecosystem in India:
## Design of an Innovative Farm Management System 4.0

**Chandrani Singh**
*Sinhgad Institute of Management, India*

**Sunil Hanmant Khilari**
*Sinhgad Institute of Management, India*

**Archana Nandanan Nair**
https://orcid.org/0000-0001-7982-7235
*Sinhgad Institute of Business Administration and Research, India*

## ABSTRACT

*Agriculture being the prime means of livelihood, there is a basic need of re-inventing the farming best practices, combined with tech-driven innovations in this segment to ensure sustainability and eliminate poverty and hunger. In this chapter, the authors focus on introducing relevant technology-enabled services that will ensure economic sustainability, enhance food security through data-driven decision making by various stakeholders like farmers,agri-business and agri-tech start-ups, farmpreneurs, government, agronomists, and IT suppliers. The analyzed information will be used as a vantage by farmers to select precision farming practices to aid productivity to empower personnel to provide timely assistance and industries to implement real-time monitoring using sensors and devices. The chapter will help formulate concepts, methods, practices, benefits, and introducing several case scenarios to effectively propagate the service mode of farming that will imbibe pay-as-you go model ensuring cost optimization and operational ease.*

DOI: 10.4018/978-1-7998-8169-8.ch005

## OVERVIEW

India is primarily considered to be a nation where agriculture and its connected initiatives are considered as the chief source of livelihood for more than 80 percent population. The share of agriculture in the gross domestic product (GDP) has reached almost 20 percent in the year 2021 due to the resilience of farming communities within the current varieties. The agriculture sector has been the only entity that has clocked a positive growth in recent times and the consistent supply of tacks has enabled to provide food security for Indians as healthy as global citizens. Agriculture is the key means of livelihood, there is a basic need of re-inventing the farming best practices, combined with tech-driven innovations in this domain to ensure sustainability and reduce the poverty and hunger. Promoting new technologies to strengthen India's agricultural research and productivity is one of the most important needs for a sustainable agricultural ecosystem. To ensure efficiency, productivity, quality, capacity, and continuous supply of tacks, farmers in India are progressively adopting smart farming technologies operating drones and robots (Saraswathi & Kaushik, 2018). Successively with the introduction of Farming-as-a-Service (FaaS), various models are being created to build a sustainable eco-system to address the emerging issues in this domain. The awareness, accessibility, and availability of infrastructures, hard and soft resources to the majority of Indian farmers are to date scarce and very poor, and hence there is a dire need to familiarize and propagate the thoughts, ideas, studies, and researches concerning the implementation of Agriculture 4.0. The focus being information and technology-enabled farming practices. In this chapter the authors focus on introducing relevant technology-enabled services, that will ensure economic sustainability, enhance food security through data compelled decision making by various stakeholders like farmers, agri-business and agri-tech start-ups, 'farmpreneurs', government and non-government agencies, equipment suppliers, agronomists, IT suppliers, and vendors. The analyzed information will be used as a vantage by farmers to select precision farming practices to aid productivity, to invest personnel to provide appropriate assistance, and industries to implement real-time monitoring using sensors and devices. The chapter will help to formulate concepts, methods, practices, benefits and presenting several case scenarios to effectively proliferate the service mode of farming that will imbibe a pay-as-you-go model ensuring cost optimization and functioning ease.

## 1. FARMING-AS-A-SERVICE: AN INTRODUCTION

The forthcoming era necessitates, farming to be multi-functional and at the same time environmentally, profitably, and ethnically sustainable. The era is a proponent of ecosystem goods and services provisioning as well as ensure livelihoods to producers and the community at large. Farming needs to effectively and efficiently address local and global challenges. These challenges comprise of an absence of food security and also water and energy, change in climatic conditions, permeative rural economic condition, and degradation of earthy resources. Farming-as-a-Service (FaaS) offers modern, professional-grade methods for agriculture and related services via a subscription or pay-per-use model (Mitchell, Sehgal, Mathur & Priyanka,2020). These farm management offerings permit stakeholders to make data-driven decisions to aid productivity and skillfulness. Conversion of fixed upfront costs to changeable ongoing costs for farmers, make the methods more low-priced for most agriculturists. FaaS deals with tools that can broadly be categorized as in Table 1:

*Table 1. Farming as a service - Tools*

| Farm Management Solutions | Production Support | Access to Markets |
|---|---|---|
| Information sharing, analytic and precision farming tools | Advanced machinery rental and on-site support | Virtual platforms that connect farmers with suppliers of seeds, fertilizers, and other agrochemicals and their consumers |

Numerous organizations have started the initiation of RaaS & FaaS. Mahindra & Mahindra, John Deere, and ITC have actuated stellar initiatives in the production support and access-to-markets . with a concrete plan to offer farm management solutions. India being an agricultural country, the government has been taking initiatives to address diverse issues and boost innovation in this segment.

## 1.1 Farming-as-a-Service: Solutions, and Tools

Farming as a service can be visualized as a set of services that are customer-oriented and aim at making farming cost-effective, easy and efficient, in recurrence with the utilization of the latest tools and technologies. The solutions to effective farm management and assignment of due assistance to production along with advanced mechanisms make such a service extremely relevant for farmer's benefit.

**Farm Management Solutions -** The functioning model of a farm management solution can be subdivided as in Table 2 i.e. data collection, data pre-processing and information dissemination, and relevant usage by the stakeholders. While under the data collection phase relevant information is collected using the drones and the satellites, this information in the pre-processing stage undergoes cleaning, authentication, and validation and then is disseminated using alerts and through training. The information is then made available to relevant stakeholders like farmers, public and private enterprises,agri-tech and financial institutions, etc.

*Table 2. Operating model of a farm management solution*

| Farm Management Solution | | |
|---|---|---|
| Data-driven decision making for productivity and efficiency | | |
| **Data Collection** | **Data pre-processing and dissemination of information** | **Usage by stakeholders** |
| Information collected using drones and satellites<br>Data collected of seeds, fertilizers, associated costs, soil quality, and weather statistics | Information dissemination through mobile alerts and dashboards<br>Stakeholders training | Farmers to adopt precision farming<br>Government to provide the necessary support<br>Corporate to ensure real-time monitoring of crop output<br>Loan facilitation by the financial institution<br>Advisory bodies to be used for real-time advising to the farmers |

To have an efficient farm management solution in place there exists a dire need to have a deeper understanding, experience, insights, and reliable source of information. Technology experts who can collect, aggregate, and broadcast large-scale real-time accurate data (Christopher et.al. 2020), ensuring literacy and connectivity among the farmer's community, and the robust incursion of broadband or mobile communication can justify the usage of farm management solutions appropriately and optimally.

**Production Support -** Provide on-site entree to low-cost equipment, labor, and services, the service delivery model, and the consecutive impact on the farmer's requirements are presented in Table 3.

*Table 3. Operating model of production assistance*

<table>
<tr><th>Service types</th><th>Service Delivery</th><th>Impact on Farmers</th></tr>
<tr><td>Rental of equipment's for which two modes are commonly available- managed or self-service mode</td><td>Through Platform aggregation or service provisioning</td><td rowspan="5">Increase in farmer's capability and supplement of their workforce</td></tr>
<tr><td>On-demand skilled or unskilled workforce provisioning</td><td>Doorstep delivery</td></tr>
<tr><td>Veterinary services</td><td rowspan="3">Pay per use model with flexible EMI options as repayment</td></tr>
<tr><td>Workforce for equipment repair</td></tr>
<tr><td>Utility services such as water and electricity</td></tr>
</table>

The above conditions to be encountered, require such services to be available near the farms, be reliable and assure quality for an increase in acceptance and ensure higher usage of assets.

**Accessibility to Marketplace -** An efficient supply chain that connects farmers to vendors/suppliers at all ends and consumers on the other as direct connectivity to deliver quality services and products at reasonable prices that which is presented in Table 4

*Table 4. Marketplace accessibility*

| Supplier - Farmer | Farmer-Consumer |
|---|---|
| Establishing relevant network between farmers and suppliers (using virtual platforms like mobile apps or online stores) for timely procurement of seeds, fertilizer, pesticides | Establishing a relevant network between farmers and consumers (using virtual platforms like mobile apps or online stores) to get a reasonable price for their products grown |

Following is some use cases of Farming as a Service that portray the advancement made in the field of agriculture that range from soil DNA testing to cloud seeding and so on.

Soil DNA Testing
Weed control
Cloud seeding
Smart Sensors
Soil analysis
Self-Driving Tractors
Environmental monitoring
Online connect of farmers to the marketplace

### Services Offered Under FaaS

- Provides recommended services to help farmers schedule the agricultural cycle, create awareness to utilize the weather forecasting services appropriately, including periodic forecasts and weather predictions.
- Know how to use the Radio-frequency identification (RFID) tags for livestock, soil condition monitoring, and automation of agricultural cycle for an increase in farmer's productivity and profitability.
- Aerial surveying and mapping and usage of unmanned aerial systems (UAS), allow the farmers to improve land utilization, where identification of less-fertile land areas through the surveying mechanisms can yield maximum output. The surveys enable remote monitoring of crops to eliminate pests or weeds at an early stage.
- Using analytics to eliminate the intermediaries in order to assist farmers in getting fair prices for their goods and also continuity in the demands made by consumers. Similarly, at the consumer's end, fresh produce is received at competitive prices through doorstep delivery mode.

## 1.2 Farming-as-a-Service: A Case Study

FaaS offers tools and solutions such as Farm Management Solutions which consists of drones and robots to monitor activity and analyze real-time data to enable farmers to make data-driven decisions. In the case of irrigation, canal maintenance and water conservation, and allocation to the farmlands, the main problems encountered are as follows:

### The Problem

- Near to the water source, the utilization and consumption of water are more, resulting in shortages at the tail end.
- Illegal manipulation of canals and structures and subsequent water theft
- Low water levels due to canal erosion or over-topping of the canals

The wrong design or poor construction of an irrigation canal system may also be the chief cause or a canal may be too small to supply enough water for irrigation. The determination of water level in a canal may be inaccurate, or a significant reduction in water level might prohibit entry into the areas by gravity. Sometimes it can be the other way round wherein canals overflow due to more than adequate water release. Canal slopes that are too steep may be subjected to erosion on account of high speeds. In areas where construction materials are not well chosen, canals may not render benefits to farmers.

In addition, there can be unseen problems as well, such as complexities in water distribution for causing water wastage and farmer's crises against water distribution authority. This can have an adverse impact on plant growth and these problems can be solved by proper usage of technology.

### Technology-Based Solutions

Hence drones can be utilized, which can change the way the labor-intensive farming activities on a routine basis are carried out. Drones are remote aircraft systems having programmable controllers, features that encompass automated flight scheduling, and are able capable to carry devices such as cameras, spraying systems.

**Real-Time Information (Crop/Soil/Weather/Water as a resource):** Drones can provide real-time information about the crop status and livestock movement, and are equipped with sensors having digital imaging abilities, such as high-resolution camera systems and actuators, for surveying of fields and canals, crop monitoring, spraying of pesticides and surveillance of livestock, for real-time decision making. The drones can either be operated using remotes through wireless communication or can be programmed to maneuver using complex navigation algorithms running on controllers.

**Water Wastage Reduction:** Due to a high degree of leakages in a canal leading to subsequent water thefts, drones could be used to reduce the wastage and theft by utilizing sensors for surveillance, to detect the water consumption pattern by the crop and the land thereby optimizing on the consumption. Additionally, it could detect water leakage, wastage, and theft by making use of Artificial intelligence and Machine learning combined with imaging technology to produce high-resolution images of the locations from where wastage is envisaged based on the level of the terrain, the construction of the canal structure, the utilization of materials used to build the canal along with many other parameters

## 2. NATURAL AND SELF SUSTAINING ECOSYSTEM

*Figure 1. Natural Ecosystem*

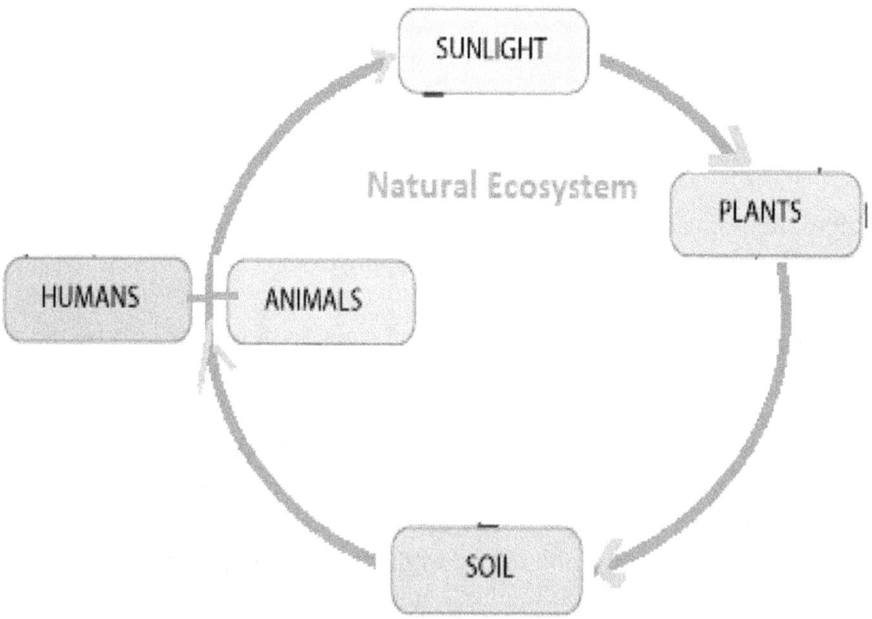


There's a huge transformation taking place in farming across the nation. An ecosystem of the same needs to be studied in its entirety as humans, animals, plants, microbes contribute to the keeping of the environmental balance in and around us. Natural ecosystems commonly are very complex and self-sustainable agricultural practices are anticipated to shelter the environment, increasing the soil's natural resource base, and improving soil fertility. A key theme connecting many of these farming as a service practices is the degree of diversification required to ensure the sustainability of this ecosystem. A self-sustainable agriculture ecosystem can be compared to a natural ecosystem as shown in figure 2 with the intervention of microbes and organic matter.

*Figure 2. Self-Sustaining ecosystem*

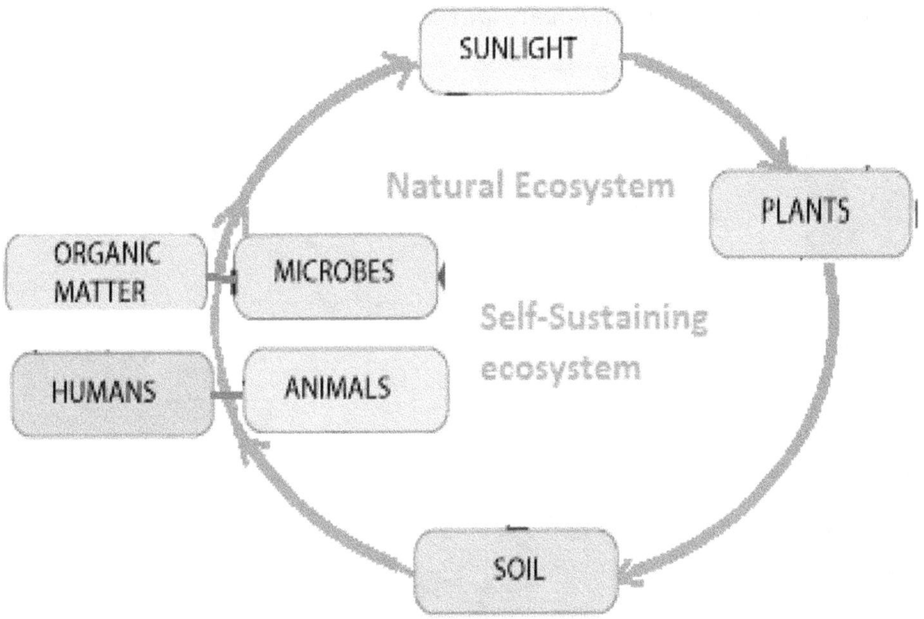


Data Source: Sunlight- Encyclopedia Britannica's editors, Plants: From Wikipedia- Forest cover by the state in India, Animal: National Dairy Development Board, Human: The World Bank –Data, Population, Total, India, Microbes: Statista, Global Survey, Soil: Fao, Fertilizer Association of India, 2003/04.

To be sustainable, there has to be recycling of waste and organic matter that are broken down by microbes like bacteria, fungi, and some larger organisms like worms and insects into soil humus and nutrients, for usage by plants. Within plants, animals, microbes, matters are large numbers of species, each performing their own set of tasks. In the food chain, the consumption pattern can be continuous and sequential. Interactions among the species, enable a balance to exist where species can co-exist together. Various eco-system components and their relevant statistics are shown in Fig 3. If a type of species is killed, they are substituted by others in their functioning. Thus a sustainable natural ecosystem can render many benefits to human beings, which are named eco-system services. Some of the major agricultural ecosystem services are Farming Services, Provisioning Services, Cultural services, regulating services, supporting services (R. Hinzl & T. B. Sulser, 2019).

The soil on formal farms is aerated with toxic chemicals and is organic matter deficient. Both organic matter and soil organisms make the soil permeable, and provide soil nutrients to the growing crops, prevent roots from soil-borne diseases and pests and also play an important part to avoid erosion of the soil. Plants that grow in healthy soil are likely to be robust. Healthy plants can showcase more immunity and can fight pests and diseases, similar to the human body's immune system. Also, healthy plants produce food rich in nutrients. Considering the several benefits, it only makes sense that the farmers do as much to work in natural conditions and ensure high fertility of the soil for good produce. High-quality crops can ensure higher market prices, thus making farming more profitable. Above in Fig. 2 is a self-sustaining agriculture ecosystem with each species doing its work and whereas Fig. 4 showcases practices aided by modern machines, high-quality raw materials, real-time data, and information and analytics'.

*Figure 3. Components of Eco-System and their statistics*

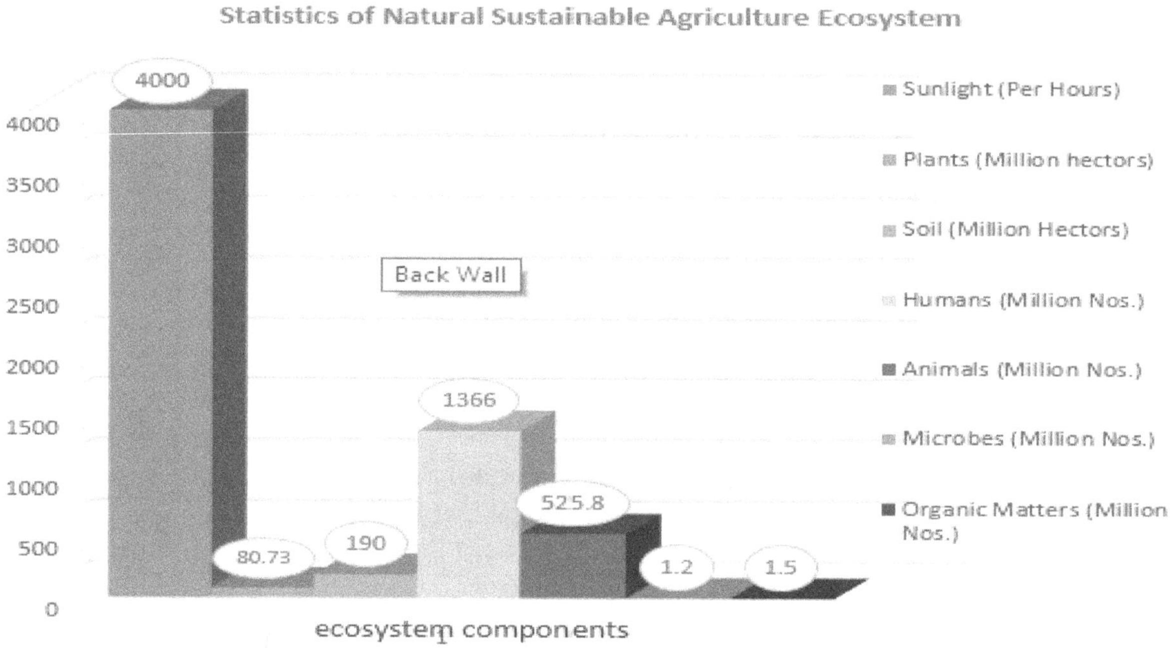


*Figure 4. Traditional practices vs emerging agriculture technology*

## 2.1 Agricultural Ecosystem in India

*Table 5. Integration of agriculture ecosystem*

| Types of ecosystem | Agro-Ecosystem | Agroforestry | Forest | Canal/ Tank ecosystem | Fresh Water | Climate regulation |
|---|---|---|---|---|---|---|
| **Types of Services** | | | | | | |
| **Provisioning Services** | Food, medical plants, fiber, bio-energy, | Food, timber, Medical plants, Fiber | Medicinal plants, Food, timber, freshwater, fiber, firewood | Silt collection, Food, fiber and | Paddy, freshwater fish, ducks, vegetables. | Timber, medicinal plants, fish, firewood, fodder |
| **Cultural Services** | Agro-tourism, aesthetic, landscapes | Cultural and amenity | Ecotourism | Festivals and other recreational | Aesthetic, recreational services, educational | Ecotourism |
| **Regulating Services** | Soil conservation, Air quality, and climate regulation | Carbon sequestration, bio-drainage, natural hazard regulation, air quality | Climate regulation, air quality, carbon sequestration, waste treatment, biological control | Groundwater recharge, Soil and water conservation, flood control, surface | Control of soil erosion, protection from storm and flood, detoxification, climate regulation | Carbon sequestration, waste assimilation, nutrient recycling, protection, shore-line protection |
| **Supporting services** | Biodiversity conservation, soil enrichment, wildlife habitat, soil fertility | Biodiversity conservation, nutrient cycling | Biodiversity conservation, genetic material, wildlife | Cropping diversity | Biodiversity conservation, nutrient cycling | Fish breeding nursery (ground) |

**Source:** Compiled from seminar proceedings of ICAR-National Institute of Agricultural Economics and Policy Research

India is the second-largest among the populous countries in the world, with huge diversity in climate and culture and the main source of livelihood being agriculture. The endeavor of Indian agriculture in ascertaining national food security and poverty reduction, thereby improvising the livelihood of the poor has been significantly evidenced in recent years. As a result, much of the focus has been shifted to agricultural production systems. Hence a balance between these production systems, natural resources, environment, and social systems needs to be established for enabling a robust agricultural man-made ecosystem that relies upon the services of the natural ecosystems. The chief eco-systems being mangroves, wetlands, and forests generating provisioning, regulating, and supporting services. A few important services under-provisioning are food, fiber, and fuel, whereas regulating and supporting services, range from soil conservation to climate regulation to eco-tourism. Few more contribute to the aesthetic and cultural services. Agriculture ecosystem exploration is a systematic analysis of an agricultural environment that considers aspects from sociology, ecology, economics, and governance. An agriculture ecosystem analysis is used to determine the sustainability of an agricultural system. This analysis provides increased levels of environmental services so that farmers can revise their crop production methods in diverse ways. Some of analytical and assessment areas are as follows:

- Changes in production systems
- Land diversion programs
- Conversion from forest to farming

Agricultural biodiversity provides humans with food, clothing, wood for shelter and fuel, plants and roots for medicines, and products for biofuels. Agriculture has the potency to make provisions for environmental balance through climate change mitigation, biodiversity conservation, watershed protection, etc, but agro-ecosystem has to be managed in altogether a very different manner. While biodiversity conservation and watershed protection services are generally location-specific, the former providing large benefits to the locales and the latter being of interest to the farmers. Table 1 lists the integration of four services vis-a-vis types of eco-system. Assuming that every ecosystem service provides multiple benefits, in the case of agricultural ecosystems, the benefits are of a larger order such as climate regulation and carbon sequestration, soil and water conservation, nutrient recycling, and protection against natural calamities as elaborated in Table 5.

Considering the maintenance of the agriculture ecosystem in India, with respect to prevention of soil erosion, detoxification, nutrient recycling both the government and technology companies are working together to improve on the environmental balance by ensuring efficient monitoring and service provisioning across the areas mentioned above. For nutrients re-cycling that implicates return of nutrient i.e. the crop residues to the soil by the plants, animal manure or the use of organic fertilizers derived from plant or animal or human excreta, several organizations public and private are using structured processes to do the needful. Some slow-release fertilizers enable the elimination of nutrient leaching and runoff prohibiting synthetic fertilizers not to damage the environment. Advanced nutrient recycling is helping communities to become resource-efficient and reduce spending, water usage, and landfill space. Similarly, for carbon capture and sequestration, there lies available 87 million hectares in India as in Rajasthan, Maharashtra, and Madhya Pradesh there lies the potential for carbon removal through agroforestry, which includes timber, fruits, fodder, and fuel with food crops. Tata Group and RIL companies are aggressively moving towards ensuring carbon neutrality and lowering carbon emission and using renewable energy forms for establishing environmental balance. As for shoreline protection that also plays a significant part in sustaining an eco-system, erosion avoidance is being incorporated using appropriate land management techniques as marsh planting, sand, and stone sills are installed as systems. Companies like Maccaferri India are working towards erosion protection using breakwaters or groynes systems to prevent the same to ensure a sustainable Eco-system. (web sr. no.37)

## 2.2 Sustainable Agriculture

Sustainable agricultural practices cater to protect the environment, increase the earth's natural resource base and improve soil fertility. Sustainable agriculture can contribute to the following:

- Increase in productivity and income
- Increase in production of food
- Promote environmental stewardship
- Enhance the quality of life for farmers and their families

Sustainable agriculture and integrated production practices are intended to produce continuous outcomes such as:

- Abundance of natural resources
- Creation of sufficient food, fiber, and fuel
- Protection of the environment
- Economic viability of agriculture structures

An increasing number of farmers and researchers are adopting farming methods that are environmentally, socially, and economically sustainable. The methods incorporate high-tech and advanced practices that increase not only productivity but also good yield while cutting down on undesired environmental impact.

In agriculture, sustainability is about better economic growth and social harmony of key stakeholders i.e. the farmers, and finally preservation of the environment. Environmental sustainability in agriculture aims at gaining support from the natural systems and resources and they are as follows:

- Maintain soil quality
- Optimize water utilization
- Minimize air, water pollution
- Encourage biodiversity

CropIn an agri-tech company, has been working in building Smart Farms, Smart Risk Solutions, Root Trace, and AcreSquare solutions that ensure improvised sustainability in agriculture domains. The systems are robust and flexible and cater to the following:

- traceability and output predictability
- alert log and management for pest infestation and diseases
- satellite and weather input based advisory
- crop reporting,geo-tagging, and insights
- crop risk assessment at a regional level
- risk-adjusted variable pricing
- end to end supply chain traceability
- replicable QR coding and tamper-proof labeling

Such organizations have been catering to farming and seed production companies, agri-input and financial lending providers, government advisories, and crop insurance providers.

### 2.2.1 Sustainable Agriculture -Best Practices

Sustainable agriculture desires to integrate social, environmental, and economic benefits. The goals of sustainable agriculture are to ensure accessibility and availability of food, reduce poverty and provide an improved quality of life for farming communities and incorporate farming methods that encourage soil health, reduction in pesticides and chemical fertilizers for environmental sustainability. Countless of the problems with the current agricultural sector accrue to environmental imbalance and have to be addressed in detail and with precision. Few of the methods pertaining to the best practices that can be implemented in a phased manner include crop rotation, Perma-Culture, soil enrichment through nutrient filling,bio-intensive pest management, Poly-culture Farming, Agroforestry, Bio-dynamic Farming, and improvised water management. While crop rotation implicates a multi-culture method of farming, crop alternation and even combining different crops in the same field can reduce the need for fertilizer and pesticides at subsequent stages. Perma-Culture one of the best practices refers to the intended design and upkeep of agriculturally cultivable systems that have the multifariousness, steadiness, and resilience of natural ecosystems and is the harmonious consolidation of the landscape with people and ensuring the provision of food, energy, shelter, and other material and non-material needs sustainably. Poly-culture Farming, another sustainable best practice refers to growing two or more plants at the same time and in the same place which enhances the soil properties, making it more suitable for crop production and controls soil erosion. This type of farming also increases local biodiversity. Below are some additional practices that ensure sustainability and conform to the best practices that range from inter-cropping to agroforestry practices. (web sr.no.38,39,40)

- Rotational crop plantation, inter cropping, and implementing diversity
- Planning and planting of crops in a way that will increase the soil nutrition levels
- Avoiding or considerable reduction of chemical-based fertilizers
- Combining cattle and crops production for maximum mutual benefit
- Adopting agroforestry practices

These best practices offer multiple benefits such as runoff and prevention of soil erosion, thereby reducing water loss, retention of organic matter and nutrients, ensure soil fertility and reduce toxicities, proper utilization of solar energy, reduction in diseases, augmentation of soil water availability, nitrogen fixation, root care and can provide a more diverse farm economy which in turn can impact the rural economy.

### 2.2.2 Implementation Challenges for Indian Farmers

To implement and incorporate the best practices, some challenges are still being faced by the Indian Farmers and they are as follows:

- dependency on the poor transportation availability in the rural areas
- the necessity of cognizance with respect to the crop management
- dependency on occasional monsoons
- and the imbalance in the division of urban-rural land segmentation
- reduced access to the latest farming techniques and methods
- inadequate storage facility
- high rates of interest and less access for cooperative/insurance credits and
- inability to repay loans along with poor governmental support

The water bodies in the Indian sub-continent are sufficient enough to irrigate the cultivation. Making the water available to the farms in the most efficient manner is the hurdle. Irrigation schemes have not been completely implemented in most parts and their reach is far less to the remotest of the areas.

Most farming activity relies only on the monsoon cycle and local irrigation setups. The average farm size is comparatively small, which leads to reluctance in using agricultural machinery. This increases dependency on labor availability and harms the profits made.

Superfluous growth of traditional crops is a problem that arises out of the lack of a nationwide agricultural plan. Storage of redundant production causes losses to farmers and amounts to wastage of the yield. Well facilitated storage go-downs, procedures, and packing material are insufficient in such a situation, forcing an immediate sale of the crops, as it is harvested, usually at a low market rate.

Upon harvest, the movement of material from the farm to the main market calls for reliable transportation means. Connectivity to highways, availability of useful modes of transportation that will carry the goods without damage is not available on-demand in rural areas. Thus a majority of farmers still rely on bullock-carts for transporting their crop to the marketplace. Moreover, many villages to market center's connectivity are poor, with temporary roads that become useless in certain seasons. Therefore, farmers cannot deliver their crop to the central market and sell it in the local market at a low price.

### 2.2.3 Current Advancement and Progression in India: By Examples

In India **BASF** India has launched crop protection and soil contamination techniques by offering seed treatments and for the latter has also developed a certified biodegradable mulch film from its eco via bioplastic. Adequate training for farmers and spray-men has happened with regards to the protection and quality retention through several outreach programs.

In Maharashtra, **A Climate-Smart Village Programme** was launched in 2016 to implement zero-till farming, integrated nutrient and water management, proper harvesting and storage.

Currently, Tata Chemicals(A Tata Group Company) has indulged in drone utilization for monitoring and improving farm and farmer's productivity, as the organization believes that along with the provision of making important analytic on soil and seeds available, a lot has to improve in the segment of storage, logistics, and transportation.

*Table 6. Agri-tech start-ups and their offerings*

| Name of the Company | Location/Start-up/Domain | Application |
|---|---|---|
| Fasal | Bengaluru based Agritech startup | Applications for farmers to plan and monitor pruning, sowing, spraying, fertilization, irrigation, harvesting and finally to reach the consumers |
| | | Fasal Sense is an IOT based application with data-driven decisions to be made by the farmers |
| DeHaat | Gurugram and Patna-based Agritech startup | Online marketplace for farmers providing farm advisory, access to financial services and institutions |
| Clover | Bengaluru based Greenhouse Agri startup | Provides superior quality, sale of naturally grown products through B2B and B2C channels |
| CropIn | Bengaluru-based CropIn AI and Data-Driven Agritech startup | SmartFarm Application helps improve output, adeptness, sustainability of the crop chains. Monitors high food safety standards |
| Intello Labs | Gurugram based startup | Implements artificial intelligence for quality testing and control. |

The agri-tech companies in India are building upon scalability, analytic, and inventiveness for precision farming, data-driven decision making, and modern farming gadgets, and implementation of farm to business (F2B) business models. Few notable examples of 2021 are shown in Table 6.

Population growth, changing food consumption habits, and climate change, calls Indians agriculture sector for a shift in the approach and initiate transformation to ensure global sustenance in areas such as

- Food Security
- Implementing an effective policy towards mitigation of climate change
- Use of water, energy, and land in the most maintainable ways.
- Infuse innovation & technology in agriculture
- Employment Generation
- Policy Interventions, Regulations, and Reforms
- Production and Producers

All these challenges underscore the need for a new vision for agriculture as we move forward in the 21st century (Chand, 2019). The paradigm shift has to begin with changing the mindset of policymakers from production-centric to sustainability-focused (Jyoti, Bikram, Chandel, Narendra & Agrawal, ,2020). Farmers should be exposed to some basic principles of agro-ecology and simple techniques, and then left free to experiment, innovate and implement what suits the local conditions (Shah, 2021).

FaaS based services can ensure the adoption of digital technology and make these services available through mobile, apps, and web and ERP-like software needed to be developed for the agriculture sector (Yildiz, 2021). Having discussed the technology integration for naturally sustainable agriculture ecosystem, various emerging agriculture services like FaaS, DaaS, RaaS, EaaS, the best practices, several agri-tech start-up's and their offerings, the current advancement envisioned is as follows:

- Increase in farmer's productivity and income
- Increase in production of food
- Promote environmental stewardship
- Enhance the quality of life for farmers and their families

## 3. AGRICULTURE 4.0

Agriculture 4.0, lays a greater focus on precision agriculture, the internet of things (IoT), and the use of big data to drive business efficiently and productively. The previous agricultural revolutions comprised of the following activities and initiatives:

- a transformation to cultivation and farming from hunting and gathering.
- The agricultural revolution brought about by the British in colonial India during the 18th century,
- The productivity surge as a result of the introduction of machinery and the Green Revolution (Proagrica & Relx Group,2018)

Agriculture 4.0 or Smart farming, include the use of Microsoft's Cortana Intelligence Suite, to determine optimal planting dates for crops around the world, such as in India and Colombia (López &

Corrales, 2018). Unmanned aerial vehicles, or drones, are being used to aid weed identification (Lottes, Khanna, Pfeifer, Siewart, & Stachniss, 2017), and robots are helping farmers to milk their cattle (Driessen & Heutinck, March 2014) and remove weeds (Fennimore, 2017), (Lottes, Khanna, Pfeifer, Siewart, & Stachniss, 2017).

In 2018, the World Government Summit published its report called Agriculture 4.0 – The Future of Farming. Agriculture 4.0, that mentions technology support for certain types of service provisioning and the below addresses the approach followed and the solutions to be implemented to technology.

*Table 7. Agriculture 4.0 and technology progression*

| Technology Type | Device/System | Use Case | Category of Service | Algorithm used |
|---|---|---|---|---|
| **Internet of Things (IoT)** | Drone, Robot,<br>Autonomous tractor<br>Sensors<br>pH probe<br>Capacitance hygrometer | Greenhouse monitoring<br>Drip irrigation, Leakage monitoring,<br>Canal water supply<br>Plant & Soil Management | FaaS<br>ADaaS<br>EaaS<br>RaaS<br>MaaS | Path-generating algorithms<br>Kernel-based clustering algorithms and heuristics,<br>Simulated annealing algorithm |
| **Blockchain** | Farm Management Software (FMS)<br>Immutable ledger system | Farm Inventory Management,<br>Agricultural Supply Chain,<br>Microloans and<br>Agricultural Subsidies,<br>Payments from Consumers to Farmers,<br>Security and Safety on Farms,<br>Controlling Weather Crisis<br>Managing Agricultural Finance | FaaS<br>ADaaS<br>EaaS<br>RaaS<br>MaaS | Proof of Work (PoW)<br>Proof of Stake (PoS)<br>Proof of Elapsed Time (PoET) |
| **Artificial Intelligence (AI)** | AI Sensors,<br>AI Chabot's | Detection of diseases in plants and poor plant nutrition in farms,<br>weather forecasting to<br>improve crop yields,<br>reduce food production costs | FaaS<br>ADaaS<br>EaaS<br>RaaS<br>MaaS | Computer vision algorithms<br>Deep learning algorithms and feature classification algorithms as<br>KNN, Logistic Regression, Probabilistic-Naïve Bayes,Adaboost, Ensemble-Random Forest,Markov etc |
| **Data Science** | MyCrop<br>real-time system<br>RFID chip | Optimize production cycles<br>Yield predictions<br>Digital Soil and Crop mapping<br>Fertilizer recommendation | FaaS<br>ADaaS<br>EaaS<br>RaaS<br>MaaS | Random forest algorithm<br>BigML<br>Partitioning Clustering algorithms |
| **Quantum Computing** | DNA mutation<br>Molecular modeling<br>Seed discovery system | Agrochemical discovery,<br>genomics data for plants<br>soil microbiome and<br>real-time analytics | FaaS<br>ADaaS<br>EaaS<br>RaaS<br>MaaS | Post-quantum algorithms<br>Grover's algorithm<br>Shor's algorithm |

To meet the above challenges and grab opportunities, from a concerted effort by the government, investors and farmers can be a success only by treading on the path of innovation and advancement of innovative agricultural technologies. Agriculture 4.0 will no longer depend on watering vast farmlands uniformly but will allow a greater degree of personalization based on soil, crop statistics, and availability of natural resources (Brozovic & Adma,2018). The farms and agricultural operations will have to be run very differently, primarily due to the inclusion of sensors, devices, machines, and applications at an operational and strategic level. It will make use of sophisticated technologies such as robots, temperature and moisture sensors, aerial images, and GPS technology. These advanced devices, precision agriculture, and robotic systems will allow farms to be more profitable, efficient, safe, and environment friendly. Smart data makes it possible for farmers to better understand changes that generate worth. A sector that utilizes disruptive technologies and benefits all entities of the agricultural and associated chain is what Agriculture 4.0 is all about.

The agricultural sector is provoked by the major challenges of increasing agriculture production for an increasingly prosperous population in a situation where there is the scarce availability of natural resources. Information and Communication Technologies (ICT's) in agriculture can increase efficiency, productivity, and sustainability by ensuring information and knowledge sharing. In this, the contribution of ICT to food security and a sustainable agriculture Eco-system is envisaged in developing countries (Yildiz, Ersoy, & Yıldırım, 2021). The researchers claim that developing solution architecture (e-agriculture framework) to expose farmers to the much-needed agricultural information can increase agricultural productivity. This framework must accommodate the dynamic trends in ICT tools, applications, adoption, and usage, and the development of such a framework to address the above will help improve agricultural productivity(Awuor, Kimeli, Rabah, & Rambim, 2013).

Farmer's requirement for experts knowledge to decide on soil preparation, seed selection, fertilizer management, pesticide management, water scheduling, weed management, etc. are a few of the important steps to optimize the resources and generate a high yield. For that, the systems that are heavily in use are the Expert Systems. These systems simulate human knowledge from an expert to assist an individual, to decide a level of or greater than a human expert. Expert systems help growers in making economically viable decisions related to effective crop management (Yelapure & Kulkarni 2012).

The application of Information and Communication Technology (ICT) in agriculture is progressively important. E-Agriculture involves the conceptualization, design, development, evaluation, and application of innovative traditions to use information and communication technologies (ICT) in the rural domain, with a primary focus on agriculture. Information and Communication Technology (ICT) can play a significant role in maintaining properties of information as it consists of three main technologies. These technologies are applied for processing, exchanging, and managing data, information and knowledge (Mahant, Shukla, Dixit & Patel, 2012).

Innovative methods to automatically grade the disease on plant leaves effectively inculcates Information and Communication Technology (ICT) in agriculture and hence promotes Precision Farming. The plant pathologists primarily rely on naked eye prediction and a disease recording scale to grade the disease. Hence a recommendation of an image processing based approach to automatically grade the disease spread on plant leaves by retaining Fuzzy Logic prove to be accurate and satisfactory in contrast to manual grading (Sannakki, Rajpurohit, Nargund, Kumar R & Yallur, 2011).

Green care, an innovative approach that combines simultaneously caring for people and caring for land through three elements that have not been previously connected through multifunctional agriculture and recognition of the variety of agricultural system values that includes social services and health care, and the opportunity of strengthening the farming sector and local communities. Hence the small enterprises operating as the agri-food vertical sustained by the social economy and following agro-ecological philosophies (community supported agriculture)incorporate the concept of social farming for societal betterment (García-Lorente, Rubio-Olivar & Gutierrez-Briceño, 2018).

Few more research conducted on automation and robotics in agriculture and related farming issues has led to the creation of the ICT-AGRI ERA-NET, which delivers a structured framework. Its main goal is to strengthen and coordinate research regarding ICT and robotics in agriculture and the creation of the Meta Knowledge Base (MKB), with a three-dimensional framework constituting of a task, technology, and scope (Mertens, Vangeyte, Van Weyenberg, Von Haselberg, Holpp, Doerfler & Thysen, 2012).

The usage of ICT can be realistic to help in transferring agricultural knowledge to farmers who live and work in rural and remote areas (Adamides & Stylianou, 2013).

The above literature review reveals that the future requires farming to be multi-functional and at the same time ecologically, economically, and socially sustainable. Enabling farming to deliver ecosystem goods and services as well as livelihoods to producers and society requires overcoming the challenges such as food, water, and energy insecurity, climate change, pervasive rural poverty, and degradation of natural resources.

### 3.1 The Analysis and Gap Finding

The literature review revealed Sustainable Agriculture Best Practices, Ecosystem and Design of an Innovative Farm Management System (IFMS)-4.0 as the major concern in Agriculture 4.0. The intervention of digital farming can be instrumental in revolutionizing the future of food with the help of technological components accompanied by sustainable good practices. Agriculture 4.0, including a focus on meticulous agriculture, the internet of things (IoT), and the use of big data to drive businesses efficiently and productively. Some of the analytical and assessment areas around which the chapter revolves are as follows:

- Changes in production systems
- Land diversion programs
- Conversion from forest to farming

Agriculture is considered the backbone of India. So it is essential to enhance traditional agriculture services and ecosystems with the latest technologies. There is a basic need for efficient re-inventions of existing agriculture farming practices, combined with tech-driven innovations. Promoting new technologies to strengthen India's agricultural research and productivity is one of the most important needs for agricultural growth. For disaster recovery from the economic crisis, natural calamities, farmers in India have to progressively adopt smart farming technologies and methods like Farming-as-a-Service (FaaS), Food-as-a-Service (FaaS), Agriculture Drone-as-a-Service (ADaaS), Equipment-as-a-Service (EaaS), Agriculture Robot-as-a-Service (ARaaS) and Software-as-a-Service (SaaS) models to address the emerging issues. To date, there is no unique software application having all FaaS available as a single entity. The importance of developing end-to-end innovative Agriculture Management Information System (AMIS) as a technology solution for all agriculture stakeholders like farmers, start-ups, 'farmpreneurs', governments, agri-entrepreneurs, equipment suppliers, agronomists, and IT vendors, it is the dire need to ensure the robustness of the entire agricultural supply chain, etc.

## 4. AGRICULTURE USE CASES

As tractor and harvester innovation brought mechanical innovation in the agriculture sector in the 20th century, today IoT is the key towards increased and sustainable production. IoT has made available to engineers and innovators, a wide opportunity to bring the smart farming solution to market.

Technology is playing a vital role in making farming smarter than ever before. The usage of smart farming techniques is enabling farmers to significantly increase crop and food production and raise the quality levels.

Focusing on some important functions, both the government and private players are working to improve the efficiency and productivity of Indian agriculture and exploring how Farming as a Service (FaaS) can act as a remedy for the continued sustenance of the agriculture eco-system in India. FaaS seeks to provide affordable technology solutions for efficient farming. It converts fixed costs into variable costs for farmers and enables improvised information sharing, surveillance, analytic's and precision tools for production assistance, on-site resources to aid production, like equipment rentals, access to markets, and also virtual platforms that connect farmers with suppliers of seeds, fertilizers, and other agro-chemicals.

*Figure 5. Real-time farm data capturing*

## 4.1 Food-as-a-Service (FaaS)

India is a country with over 1.30 billion people, out of which, over 70% of the population lives in rural areas (Hinz1 & Sulser,2019). Agriculture is a major industry and an influencer of the Indian economy. FaaS will push much-needed process and product innovations in Indian agriculture, including multipurpose agricultural equipment, tools for real-time data capturing and analysis, aggregation of farmland and farm produce, and financial technology for farmers. The growing population demands quality food on time and budget. Underlying these rapid changes are macro forces that influence the way India produces, distributes, buys, sells, and consumes food. The shift from rural to urban life will increase demands for future food stocks and shorter, more efficient supply chains. In addition, wealth inequality continues to widen, creating disparities in access to healthy food among varied socioeconomic and income groups. Consumers will continue to seek ways to improve their diets to manage health and wellness, to counteract escalating obesity and non-communicable diseases. Following are some of the commercial applications of FaaS that are predominant in the Indian landscape:

Delivery.com (iOS / Android)
DoorDash (iOS / Android)

GrubHub (iOS / Android)
Seamless (iOS / Android)
Uber Eats (iOS / Android)
Instacart (iOS / Android)
goPuff (iOS / Android)

## Services Offered Under Food as a Service

The $3 Trillion Meal Delivery Market offers cooked food delivered to customers who can enjoy it in the comfort of their homes. The mobile internet has given rise to meal ordering apps, that act as a platform for any restaurant. A structured and efficient supply chain is the underlying architecture that streamlines the movement of food from farms to homes. This has given rise to contract cultivation.

Contract cultivation is essentially a binding agreement that guarantees farmers' purchases from giant global companies, provided they agree and supply the preferred crops to the companies. For example, McDonald's currently has over 400 farmers cultivating potatoes for them in over 2000 acres of farmland in the state of Gujarat.

For meal delivery to replace a large percentage of home-cooked meals, it needs a nutritional profile that is closer to home cooking than fast food. A tech-led platform that plans meals for consumers in consultation with fitness experts, and nutritionists, acquires its raw material like vegetables and pulses from organic farms and then gets its in-house chefs to prepare them at its central kitchen, and finally, delivers the meal box to the consumer's doorstep are seen to evolve and grow in the recent years. These tech-led small and medium scale startups (Boyacioglu, & Yıldız, 2021) use artificial intelligence (AI) and machine learning (ML) algorithms to track consumers' progress towards their health goals and recommend meal plans. The next series of progressions made in the services segment range from weather forecasting to supply chain tracking, food security, and risk assessment.

## Big Data for Weather Forecasting

Essentially all agricultural production is reliant on natural conditions such as climate, soil, pests, and weather. With the help of data analysis for agri-businesses, farmers can witness the impact that weather conditions and others can have on their crops. But even more valuable is the capability to forecast and adjust to these things. Integrating big data in smart farming, one can understand changes in weather conditions in real-time. For example, data from sensors in soil and images taken by drones can help farmers form expected growth rates. When a smart system identifies what to expect, it can inevitably detect anomalies and advise farmers of them.

## Supply Chain Tracking

There are numerous stakeholders in an agricultural supply chain, and big data has established significant usage for all parties throughout all stages. At the production stage, automated systems handle data to display performance and tell issues in critical equipment. When dealing with seeds, plants, and food products, preventing spoilage is a matter of grave concern. Big data helps farmers and suppliers optimize fleet management to increase delivery reliability. Furthermore, big data tracking solutions, smart meters, and GPS-based analytic's enable routing and present innovative mapping of the locations of animals and vehicles.

### Risk Assessment

Big data analytic's in farming risk assessment is useful for benchmarking, sensor distribution, analytic's and predictive modeling. Applying these approaches to make predictions using big data can help farmers model and manage risks connected with livestock and growing crops. Farmers want to make their economic models more robust, while insurers demand to be more certain as to the insured events. Smart insurance contracts deal with various risks, including natural calamities. Insurers then calculate a premium based on the likelihood of a specific weather event and the impact it would have on livestock or crops at a precise point in time. Farmers get paid routinely when the number of occurrences exceeds a predefined edge.

### Food Security

In this case, big data help farmers and customers to establish confidence in food safety and security. This enables businesses to carefully collect and consider high-resolution data on humidity, temperature, fertilizers. Further, that data helps farmers and consumers to find where and how agricultural products were grown, transported, and processed

## 4.2 Agriculture Drone-as-a-Service (ADaaS)

Growing crops that are not common or regular in their land, farmers require information that can help them. Having a reference to similar information avoids farming errors. Typically, a farmer has access to local sources of information such as TV, radio, newspapers, agricultural agencies government and private, farm supply, and traders. An up-to-date and quicker response system is needed that allows farmers access to relevant information.

*Figure 6. Agricultural Drones*

Inclusions of farming drones help farmers deal with a wide range of challenges and secure a great number of benefits. Most of these benefits stem from eliminating any guesswork and reducing uncertainty. By gaining access to critical data, farmers can increase crop production, save time, reduce expenses and act with accuracy and precision. Machine learning is also among the trending technologies; hence, there exist several technologies and systems that run on a machine learning framework, and hence it is a very effective tool for efficient use of resources, prediction, and management, which are needed in agriculture (Adebiyi, 2020).

Indian government agencies, the Directorate of Plant Protection, Quarantine & Storage, Faridabad, and the Ministry of Civil Aviation, have initiated the inclusion of drones in the projects they undertake and to update local farmers on its usability. While the Directorate has come up with standard operating procedures (SOP's) on aerial spraying to curb the spread of desert locusts, the Aviation Ministry has issued a draft notification on a wider framework, namely "The Unmanned Aircraft System Rules, 2020." Following are some use cases of AD-a-a-S:

Aerial photography
Shipping and delivery
Geographic mapping
Crop surveillance
Disaster management
Precision agriculture
Search and rescue
Wildlife monitoring
Weather forecast

## Services Offered by Agriculture Drone-as-a-Service (ADaaS)

### Agriculture Drone

Empowers the farmers to adapt to specific environments and make mindful choices accordingly. The data gained through drone surveys helps regulate crop health, crop treatment, crop scouting, irrigation, and carry out field soil analysis and crop damage assessments.

The drone survey helps boost crop yields and minimize time and expenses. The drone-enabled technology could be very useful in soil analysis of the fields. This could also help in better irrigation management and maintaining correct nitrogen levels.

### Aerial Imagery Drones for Seed-Planting Drones

Aerial imagery benefits farmers by saving a lot of time by providing them with a bird's eye view of the crops. Farmers can rapidly assess the health of vegetation, insect issues, and weed growth. It permits them to determine the accurate amounts of fertilizers and seeds needed in the fields. The manufacturers of aerial imaging and seed planting drones are American Robotics, UAV Systems International, and Taranis. The agricultural robots and their significance in the farming industry are notable for all concerns.

## Crop Surveillance

It is very difficult to estimate the complete state of crops in large fields. Drones-based agriculture mapping can help farmers remain area-wise updated on the plant status and point out which field areas need consideration. Drones scrutinize the field with infrared cameras and regulate light absorption rates to estimate the state of crops. Based on real-time and correct information, farmers can take measures to progress the state of plants in any of the fields. This feature of crop surveillance and crop health assessment forms the basis of the use of drones for improving agricultural insurance tools for cross verifying farmers' insurance claims.

## Soil Analysis for Agri Field Planning

Drones can be used for soil and field analysis for irrigation, planting, planning the nitrogen and fertilizer level in the soil. A drone is helpful to provide accurate 3-D maps that can be used to conduct soil analysis on soil properties, moisture content, and soil erosion.

## Seed Plantation

Seed planting is critical for agriculture farming. Some companies have come up with additional supplements for the drone systems those that can shoot pod containing seed and plant nutrients into the soil. This serves to reduce planting costs.

## Crop Health Assessment

Plants replicate visible and near-infrared light and its intensity differ with health status and stress levels experienced by plants. Drones close-fitted with sensors are capable of scanning crops using observable and near-infrared light that can be used to track crop health over a period of time and to monitor reply to relieving measures.

## Controlling Pest, Insects, and Diseases

In addition to soil conditions, drones detect and notify farmers about field areas wrecked by weeds, disease, insects, and pests. Based on this evidence, farmers can optimize the use of chemicals needed to fight infestations, henceforth reducing the expenditures and contributing to better field health. Tree/crop biomass estimation from the ground surface can be measured using ultra-compact LiDAR sensors mounted on drones.

Following the services offered by drones are relevant services offered by modern farming technologies under the banner of equipment and machine as a service. Few types of equipment are listed in Figure 7.

## 4.3 Equipment-as-a-Service (EaaS)/ Machine-as-a-Service (MaaS)

*Figure 7. Equipment's for modern agriculture*

Soil Moisture Sensor

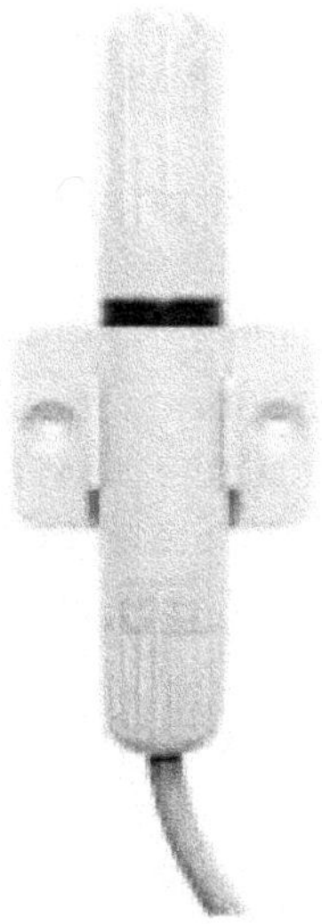

Temperature & Humidity Sensor

Pay-per-use for machines and equipment has become a successful business model in various agriculture industries, including farming, fishery, poultry, dairy equipment, and machinery (Driessen & Heutinck, 2014). EaaS front-runners in industrial manufacturing have already applied this model for emerging revenue streams to differentiate themselves in the marketplace and/or meet agriculture customer expectations. Equipment-as-a-service (E-a-a-S) is rapidly moving from a specialized notion established by the providers of agriculture to general adoption strategies. They provide the ease of connecting all sorts of equipment and devices in the internet of things (IoT). E-a-a-S is also becoming more feasible and affordable for farmers and agronomists due to industry-led equipment uptime and transparent pricing structure, wherein the vendors of the machines and equipment can also benefit from an E-a-a-S model. If done in the right way, it can be an attractive business model for a long-term sustainable revenue stream for agriculture equipment manufacturing companies. Following are the uses of E-a-a-S as mentioned:

Livestock Monitoring, AI-enabled system to detect pests, Soil management, Water Management, Disease Detection, Species management, Crop management.

### Services Offered under MaaS/EaaS

- Usage of Accelerometers to detect indication, activity level, disturbance in the agriculture farm.
- Humidity and temperature sensors are used for soil checking, air monitoring and livestock health monitoring. These devices convey critical input for IoT enablement in agriculture.
- A pressure sensor can distinguish atmospheric pressure that is ultimately used to measure altitude. Since a pressure sensor needs an initial diaphragm to detect the pressure, they are exposed majorly

to water and chemical pollution. Therefore, a pressure sensor is needed that can continue operating safely from chemicals like Chlorine and Bromine.

- Optical sensors have been manufactured to determine the organic matter and moisture content of the land and soil.
- Electrochemical radars deliver key information required in precision agriculture like soil nutrient levels. Few use cases under EaaS are as follows:

### a. Agriculture Equipment Manufacturers

These OEMs provide agriculture equipment to enterprises through a subscription-based model. In this model, the equipments are located at the facilities of the subscribing farmers. The manufacturer leases the machine for a definite period and the subscription fee covers maintenance, rent and repair tasks which leave the software update and spare parts replacements in the hands of the OEM vendor. As payback, the OEM will own the equipment data and use it for research and development, for predictive maintenance.

### b. Customer Manufacturer's

This model comprises manufacturers and OEMs outsourcing factory equipment to customers for definite periods. This means customers who do not have specific equipment that is needed for specialized farming applications due to equipment cost, can see service providers and use their equipment within the equipment provider's facilities. The payback for the service provider includes subscription payments. The value-added schemes of EaaS include:

- Improved Equipment Design
- Developing Predictive Maintenance Strategies
- Revenue Growth
- Reduced Capital Expenditure
- Increased Data Reliability etc.

Implementing an equipment-as-a-service (EaaS) model allows an individual to acquire the latest hardware and software while ensuring topmost performance through continued support services. Companies that provide these services can help develop a comprehensive approach that enables manufacturing companies to address farmer's requirements, fast-track technology migrations, and take advantage of new advancements. Companies like Kaeser -compressors and Atlas Copco-mining equipments are well-known examples of successfully applying this business model for agriculture machines and equipment.

## 4.4 Agriculture Robot-as-a-Service (AR-a-a-S)

In modern years, robots have found their place in agriculture. The occurrence of robots in agriculture has developed significantly in current years, overcoming a few of the challenges and difficulties of the agriculture sector. The primary task of a robotic system is to do basic agricultural operations like seeding, planting, weeding, spraying and monitoring, whereas the secondary task includes mobility, steering, navigation, manipulator and human-robot interaction as in Fig.8. R-a-a-S suppliers suggest robots as a service to an agriculture sector for handling repetitive and hazardous tasks (Mohiuddin, 2015). Since positioning robots could be pretty costly, companies face difficulties in receiving a return on investment. The RaaS model is becoming commonplace in agricultural robotics. Robots pick apples, gather strawberries, harvest lettuce, and strip away weeds. Drones gather aerial images that help farmers quickly assess crop health. And robotic greenhouses are located thousands of miles away from traditional farmland regions, growing vegetables in the backyards of high-consumption urban markets.

*Figure 8. Agricultural robot*

Agriculture can be a field as favorable as the industry for the application of automation (López, & Corrales, 2018). The challenges for robots in agriculture are diverse. Agricultural environments, in contrast to industrial facilities, are not structured and controlled. On the other hand, industrial processes can be designed by modules to apply specific robots to specific work, whereas the complex tasks of agriculture sometimes cannot be split into simple actions. For the above reasons, agricultural applications require more versatile and robust robots. Following are some use cases of R-a-a-S:

Seed planting (cloud seeding)
Precision Framing
Air humidity and Temperature
Weed and pest control
Greenhouse farming
Field mapping
Surface temperature
Human security guards for patrolling

## Services Offered under Robot as a Service:

- A robotic system is used for harvesting, weed management, spraying using semi-automatic teleoperation of an agricultural robotic system to enable improved performance and profit.
- A tech entrepreneur-turned farmer has made a robotic platform to harvest cotton, which was triggered by rice and cotton harvests he lost due to lack of farm labor.
- Robots are being used for weed control, which will help to reduce herbicide usage, and the produces will turn into organic fertilizers (Mohiuddin, 2015)

- Robots can be used for transplanting seedlings to avoid intensive labor(Mohiuddin, 2015).

Few more use cases which focus on Farming as a Service and also include the use of Robots are as follows:

## a. Monitoring of Climate Condition

Perhaps the most general smart agriculture tools are weather positions, bonding numerous smart farming sensors. Positioned across the area, they accumulate huge data from the environment and send it to the cloud. The delivered dimensions can be used to map the climate situations, select suitable crops, and take the essential actions to improvise on their capacity.

*Figure 9. Weather monitoring equipment*

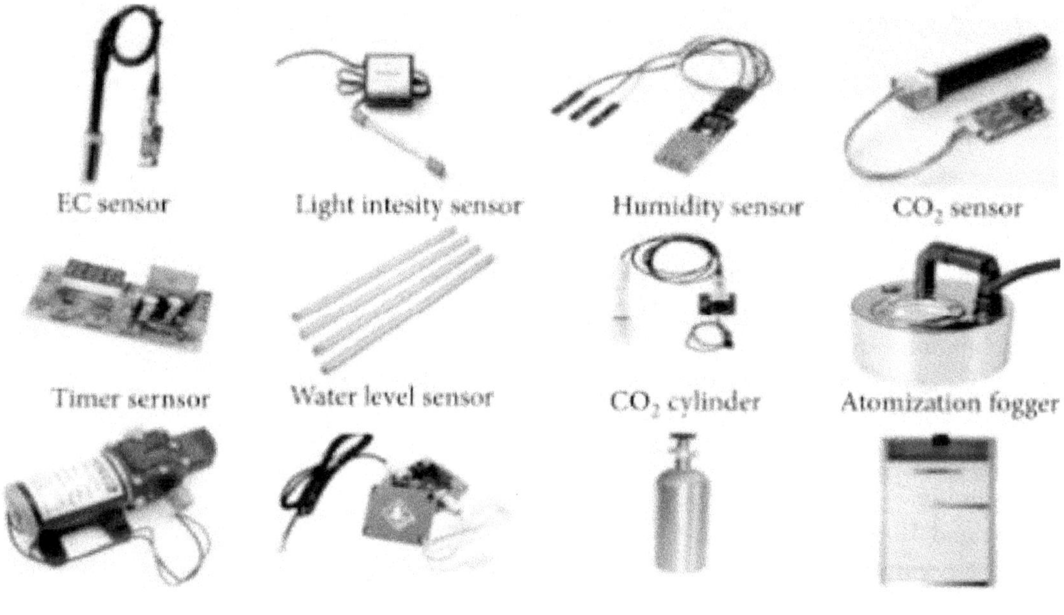


## b. Greenhouse Automation

Typically, farmers use labor-intensive involvement to control the greenhouse environment. The use of IoT sensors allows them to get exact real-time information on greenhouse conditions such as lighting, temperature, land, soil, and humidity condition. To outlining environmental data, weather stations can use robots, regulate the conditions to match the specified constraints. For example, Farmapp and Growlink are IoT-based that present the above capabilities. GreenIQ is another encouraging product that uses smart agriculture sensors. It is a smart sprinkler controller that permits to manage irrigation and lighting systems remotely.

### c. Crop Management

The weather stations should be situated in the park to collect data accurate to crop farming; from temperature and precipitation of water likely on the leaf and complete crop health. Thus, crop growth can be monitored as well as anomalies to effectively and efficiently prevent any diseases that can harm the crop. Arable and Semios are the few examples which can be functional in real life.

### d. Cattle Monitoring and Management

Cattle monitoring, the IoT sensors can be used to monitor animal health and capture performance. Livestock tracing and data gathering on livestock health can enable farmers to distinguish themselves from the herd and prevent infection. Using drones for real-time cattle tracking may also help farmers to minimize employment expenses. For example, Allflex and Cowlar use smart agriculture sensors to deliver temperature, health, activity, and nutrition aspects to each individual cow.

### e. Predictive Analytics for Smart Farming

In Precision Agriculture, the use of data analytic's benefits farmers to come up with significant predictions: crop harvesting time, the dangers of diseases and infestations, yield volume, etc. Data analytic's tools aid farming, which is extremely dependent on weather conditions and predictable. For example, the Crop Performance platform helps farmers access the volume and quality of yields, as well as their vulnerability to adverse weather conditions, such as floods and drought. It further enables farmers to improve the supply of water and nutrients for each crop and choose crop behaviors to increase quality. Solutions like Soil Scout delivers to farmers to save irrigation water, and decrease the cost of fertilizers.

### f. End-to-end Farm Management System

End-to-End Farm Management System comprises of several agriculture IoT devices and sensors, connected on the places as well as the dashboards with analytical competencies and in-built reporting parameters compromising of remote farm monitoring capabilities to streamline the business procedures as like FarmLogs and Cropio.

### g. Weed Control

Agbots differentiate weeds from useful crops and remove them by producing artificial soil disturbances using laser technologies. Agbots use smart sensors to decide plant density and cut farmlands with precision.

### h. Seeding

Seeder attachments to Agribots can accurately forecast the soil tendency and help in planting seeds at the right locations. Spraying – Agbots can help to identify weeds and crops that require pesticides and fertilizers, thus leading to a reduction in wastage of resources. It is also useful for sorting and packaging agricultural products.

## 5. DESIGN OF AN INNOVATIVE FARM MANAGEMENT SYSTEM-4.0

Innovative Farm Management System (IFMS) -4.0 should deliver the functioning of farming systems and support to the development of numerous alternative scenarios. Incremental development methodology has to be adopted for integrating technical and functional requirements of the latest technological components.

Applications embedded with Artificial Intelligence (AI), IoT, Data Science, Blockchain, Quantum Computing offer farmers a solution to replace manual agri-work.

As technology innovators look ahead at 2021 and beyond, it will be possible for few agri-tech companies to gain insights into the trends through mobile apps for agriculture transformation. Various parameters are required to be understood and are critical for the success of the design and delivery of Innovative Farm Management System 4.0. Some are, as given below:

- Security is becoming more and more important in every aspect of our digital life
- Enhanced analytical capabilities
- Mobile applications
- BI integration and remotely accessible, data, device, and internet infrastructure
- Provision of open source technologies
- Motivating and making more tech-savvy young farmers and agronomists
- Provision of agriculture services like - FaaS,ADaaS, EaaS,RaaS,MaaS
- Promotion of a subscription or pay-per-use basis
- Secure access and coordination between all the direct stakeholders (start-ups, investors, entrepreneur's governments, and corporations)

Addressing the key structural challenges, such as the lack of infrastructure, technology, and financing, is crucial and successful adoption of digital technology and web-enabled, mobile services can help in the creation of large-scale databases for the farmers. Also, the collection of data from farmers' fields over a period of time, enabling the stakeholders to make data-driven and precise decisions to boost productivity and efficiency is the key to successful farming.IT companies also play an important role in redefining the agri-domain through innovative results such as AI, Data Science, IoT, Quantum Computing. RFID and FaaS, ADaaS, EaaS, RaaS, and MaaS make it more efficient through improved access to technology, capital, and entrepreneurial skills. Some of the sub-solutions as proposed for an innovative farm management solution are as follows:

*Table 8. Farm management solution category*

| | |
|---|---|
| Digital Agriculture Solution | Collection of real-time data from a variety of sources drone, sensors, field equipment's, weather data, soil data |
| Precision Agriculture Solution | Reduce the risk of crop failure, minimize operating costs, Sell crops for the highest price, Test quality of fertilizing, soil, water, and seed |
| Connected Crop Solution | Connect to agricultural stakeholders, Supply Chain Management, Customer Relation Management, e-CRM |
| Integrated Farming Solution | Cloud-based analytics, smartphone applications |
| Decision support engine | Practical recommendations and actions for economic output |

In alliance with the conventional approach, System Requirement Specification (SRS) is prepared for both Function Requirements (FR) and System Requirements (SR). Both FR & SR are analyzed for scope, technical feasibility, operational feasibility, and financial feasibility of the proposed IFMS. Further requirement traceability matrix is prepared based on process and product standardization of Innovative Farm Management System 4.0. The architectural and detailed design of the proposed system has to be developed with the help of software design development tools. Further, both the designs, software quality factors, software quality matrix for the proposed system are evaluated based on the agriculture ecosystem. Following technical parameters are considered during the design of proposed systems as specified below in table 9.

*Table 9. Innovative farm management solution utility stack*

| **Software Modularity** | **Information Integration Platform** | **Component Availability** | **ITIL methodology (Service Strategy, Service Design, Service Transition, Service Support)** |
|---|---|---|---|
| Configuration Management and Support | COBIT framework | Standards and taxonomies applicable | |

In addition, to make it innovative several steps have to be carried out in contrast to simple problem-solving. Innovation initiatives solve agriculture issues by producing something completely new that does not yet exist (Falkowski & Drinkwater, 2020). Regardless of the initial point, the process of innovation needs extra background research and numerous sequences of experimentation.

The difference between problem solving and innovation as reformed from Boerma 2013 is listed below thus justifying our design of an innovative system:

*Table 10. Characteristics of problem solving and innovation*

<table>
<tr><th>Problem Solving</th><th>Innovation</th></tr>
<tr><td colspan="2">Transformations</td></tr>
<tr><td>Reactive to report a problem<br>Preserve the status quo<br>Motivated to solve a specific problem needs to be addressed near future</td><td>Proactive to take benefit of opportunities<br>Progress beyond the status quo<br>Motivated to uninterruptedly progress the farm system<br>Significant, but not essentially urgent</td></tr>
<tr><td colspan="2">Connections or Commonalities between the above</td></tr>
<tr><td colspan="2">Informal to do with clear goals and evaluate the accomplishment<br>Established on observing and understanding the farm system<br>Benefit from comprehensive background examination and networking<br>Consistency of experimentation reflects the risk that occurred<br>An improved complete methodical evaluation of outcomes<br>Classically repetitive, cyclical and depend on previous efforts<br>Permit to better understand the farming system and continue its feasibility</td></tr>
</table>

## 5.1 System Analysis

Things that needed to consider before and during the development of the Innovative Farming Management System are as under:

The research methodology used is "Design and Creation" for Design of an Innovative Farm Management System-4.0 that should lead to working of farming systems and provide support to develop several alternative setups. Incremental development methodology has to be adopted for integrating technical and functional requirements of the latest technological components. This farm management system is proposed to use technological components as Artificial Intelligence (AI), IoT, Data Science, Blockchain, and Quantum Computing

**The hardware:** To build a technology solution for agriculture, one needs to choose the sensors for a device. The choice depends on the types of information an individual wants to collect and the drive the solution in general. The quality of the sensors is critical to the success of agriculture products which depend on the accuracy of the collected data and its reliability.

**The Software:** Front-end and back-end software which are for developing systems based on the latest software technology platform and supporting agriculture multitasking and multi-user concurrently.

**Data collection:** There are varied data types and confirming the ideal data collection can be challenging. The data from field-based, floating and environmental sensors, apps, devices, and equipments, as well as processed analytical data, can be a subject of constraint and regulation. The safe and on-time delivery and distribution of data is the key to emerging smart farming challenges.

**The Knowledge:** Data analytics should be the key to every smart agriculture solution. For the collected data one needs to have actionable and influential data analytic's capabilities and apply predictive algorithms and machine learning to obtain actionable insights based on the collected data.

**The Mobility:** Smart farming applications should be custom-built for good practice in farming. A farmer should be able to access the information remotely via a smartphone or handheld device. Each connected device should be independent and have adequate bandwidth and range to communicate with the other devices and send data to the cloud or central server.

**The infrastructure:** To assure that smart farming application accomplishes zero defect or error-free, one needs a reliable internal infrastructure. Additionally, the internal systems have to be secure and safe. Failing to accurately secure the system only increases someone breaking into it, stealing important data, or taking control of farmer's autonomous tractors.

**The Connectivity:** To transmit data between several agricultural services still conveys a challenge for the acceptance of smart farming. The connection between these services should be reliable, effective, and efficient to survive bad weather circumstances and to guarantee for non-disruptive operations and agri-business should run during or after any disaster. The agriculture domain is the unique domain wherein below mentioned types of innovations are carried out as follows:

### Types of Agriculture Innovations

For designing and developing the innovative farm management system below are some of the inventive steps for designing IFMS 4.0

*Table 11. Agriculture innovations*

<table>
<tr><td>Agri-business model innovation</td><td>Farming workflow innovation</td><td>Agri System delivery innovation</td><td rowspan="2">Value innovation</td></tr>
<tr><td>Supply Chain Innovation</td><td>Agriculture Product Innovation</td><td>Farming Process Innovation</td></tr>
</table>

## Inventive steps for Farming Innovations

*Table 12. Farming innovations*

| **Identify opportunities** | **Prioritize innovation** | **Agriculture problem being solved** | **Initial small-scale trials** | **Differentiation from a traditional known solution** |
|---|---|---|---|---|
| The implementation method of the invented solution | Scale-up experimental approaches | Collect resources and delegate tasks | Estimating business and commercial value | Develop Insights for future farming |

*Table 13. Farm Management Solution as an Application*

| **The Phases (Layers)** | **Functional Area (Activities)** | **Work Breakdown Structure** |
|---|---|---|
| **Definition** | • Plot the farm<br>• Categorize resource inventory<br>• Cultivate complete farm plot<br>• Decide earnings of production<br>• Decide farm interactions | • Farm mapping and measurement<br>• Categorization of resources human/material and allocation of resources to tasks based on schedules and timelines<br>• Calculation of Investment, Return on Investment, Profit, Productivity, and utilization of resources. |
| **Information Gatherings** | • Farming site visit<br>• Capture observations & events<br>• Recognize patterns<br>• Perform regression testing<br>• Collect external observations<br>• Collect responses from farmers<br>• Collect feedback from all stakeholders<br>• Assess farming machinery and equipment | • Functional and System requirements inclusive of application, machines, land, water, climate and crop statistics<br>• Pattern recognition and observations collected from current and previous experiments to structure out the new ones based on requirement priority through the usage of requirement traceability matrix |
| **Appraise the farm system** | • Review farm schedules and benefit realization<br>• Analyze farm finances with innovation adopted<br>• Analyze past and current records<br>• Establish targets<br>• Review successes and failures<br>• Review earnings from production<br>• Identify important trends<br>• Prioritize problems and find solutions<br>• Rank opportunities | • Formal & Informal Review<br>• Farming innovation standards<br>• Farming good practices<br>• Change requests solicited and implemented<br>• Expected outcomes and benefits<br>• Tolerance for output based on the failures |
| **Design activities** | • Innovation Design<br>• Investigation of options<br>• Assess and analyses risks<br>• Select the best course of action<br>• Design prototype & conduct trial<br>• Classify success criteria | • Detailed Inspection checklist<br>• Risk Analysis, Prioritization, and Mitigation<br>• Implementation of Principle of Optimality<br>• Accuracy and relevance<br>• Realization and deliverable |
| **Go-Live (Deployment of Plan)** | • Accumulate resources<br>• Assign necessary timeline<br>• Assign roles & responsibilities<br>• Plan roll-out<br>• Collect data during the implementation<br>• Screening of results<br>• Review success criteria | • Infrastructure setup<br>• General and high-level objectives<br>• Evaluation criteria<br>• Training to farmers<br>• Operational manual<br>• Result sharing<br>• Future enhancement steps |

Following is an innovative farm management framework (Falkowski & Drinkwater, 2020) that the farmers and innovators have claimed to be supportive of building as presented in Table 12 that is also deployed via technology.

In alignment with the above, a case of Innovative Farming Management Information System (IFMS) 4.0 is presented herewith.

## Case Study: Developing and cultivating an innovative Agriculture farming System

**Agronomist Profile:** Mr.Laxman Karande has always cherished a desire to become a farmer in alignment with his ancestral culture. Beginning of his livelihood as a farmer, Mr.Laxman was familiar with the various types of crops. He and his family currently have a farm of around 10 acres. The majority of cultivated farm area is dedicated to crops like Sugarcane, Cotton, White Onion, Potato, Jawar, and Bajri, but he also grows several acres of tomatoes. He has been eager to implement innovative concepts in farming.

Disappointed by the vast corrosion he saw in his farmlands, Mr.Laxman transformed to direct drill farming in year-2000. From then onwards he has been constantly refining his farm system to elevate soil health and decrease chemicals usage to manipulate or regulate undesirable vegetation inputs.

### Paybacks of Association

Mr.Laxman collaborated with Dr. Tukaram who is self-practicing at Sangli for over 15 years to study soil health under varying conditions. This research association began in the year-2000 when they collaborated to appraise soil health under dissimilar situations. In association with a researcher and his team, Dr. Tukaram assisted Mr.Laxman to acquire innovative farming experience. Below is a snapshot of Mr.Laxman and his onion farm on which he wanted to experiment.

*Figure 10. Mr. Laxman (inset) and his harvest. Photo courtesy of Mr. Laxman*

He gathered and investigated the data for actionable insights, where he studied the constituents of soil organic matter, nutrient stages, crop yields, and weed populaces. This would have been very hard if he had struggled to do the project himself. Dr. Tukaram introduced Mr. Laxman to several innovative technologies and administration strategies that he might not have otherwise uncovered. For example, they tried and established the seeding edible root vegetable together, which Mr. Laxman advertised as a multifunctional cover crop.

## Ascertain Opportunities

Mr. Laxman was continuously looking for opportunities to advance his farm system. He regularly read newspapers, research papers, and agriculture farming reports. He got concepts from other peer farmers. He was always eager to converse on the issue as well as the results others were trying to achieve. For example, he was encouraged to use the onion transplanting machine as an output of extensive research made by agricultural start-ups in Krushi Exhibition. Also, Mr. Laxman used green manure for sustainable farming to improve soil quality where the cover crops or plants were grown, uprooted, or sown and left on the field to shrivel, proving mulch for soil cover and nutrients for enhancing soil fertility.

*Figure 11. Mr. Laxman and other farmers using white onion transplanting machine*

He considered the transportation challenges involved in the prototype with respect to the money, time, and effort needed for the pilot, and correlation to the expected results. Mr.Laxman was unsure whether the innovation would be fully accepted. Mr.Laxman tried a pilot for white onions in the year 2K's, but there was no market for this crop, but in due course growing white onion and selling them started becoming common in rural and the suburbs. All of these facets apprised his conclusion to kick-off the project.

## Preliminary Prototype Trials

If a specific crop seemed relevant and useful, Mr. Laxman appraised it using trials. This comprised of periodic assessment of diverse alternatives, permitting him to decide whether he desired to dedicate additional assets to the same. Mr. Laxman with an innovative mindset, to achieve the impossible with technology support saw his progression from a developmental and economic aspect.

## Upgrade Experimental Tactics

Mr. Laxman ensured scalability in his experiments and conducted them considering multiple environmental factors, the scope of innovation as well as the assets he had in existence. He conducted and attempted to replicate several experiments for few more years to guarantee that results were reliable and gave the expected outcome.

*Figure 12. Mr. Laxman's Farm - Traditional way of onion crop cultivation gathering assets and delegate responsibilities*

*Figure 13. Mr. Laxman's simulated cover crop trials for another crop variety- pomegranate*

To ensure a disciplined process of experimentation, Mr. Laxman delegated the tasks to the farmworkers and laborers of his unit. Mr. Laxman also used relevant applications for fertilizer claims, planting rates to aid him in taking the correct decisions.

## Conclusion

Mr. Laxman highlighted the need to couple the purpose with the concept for accomplishing the relevant milestone. Taking a technical expert aided in the provisioning of support.

### Planning is Crucial

Mr. Laxman had been making observations for subsequent innovation for some number of years. This provided him with time to arrange machinery, obtain the required assets, and experiment with his fieldwork. There are always unpredictable difficulties that need essential discussions and creativity and persistence to make it a success. Using pilot/prototype models, the innovative methodologies are tried and tested out effectively.

*Figure 14. An overall approach towards innovation in farming*

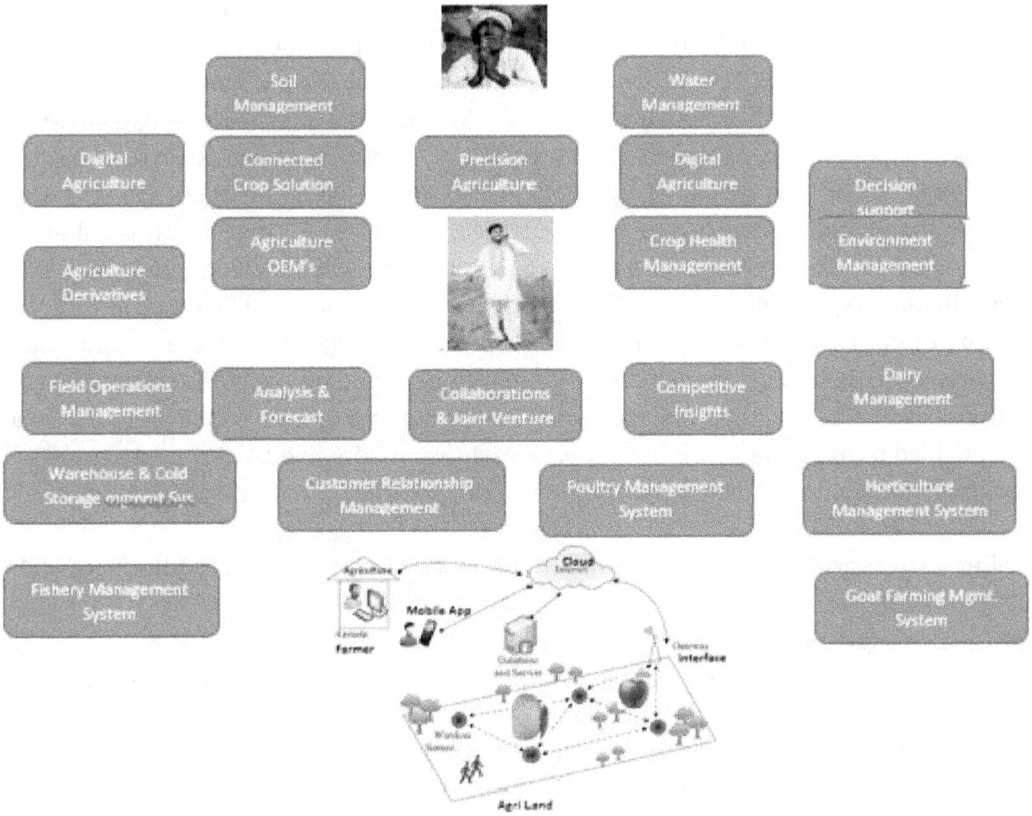

### Begin Lesser and Work Your Decent

While applying inventive farming approaches, binding the preliminary efforts to the number of acres was good to progressively measure the experimentation over few more years.

### Promise and Dedicate Assets to Experimentation

Although the basic philosophies of best farm management are appropriate around the nation, the particulars required to be operated at the local fields and the global level, with experimentation at each and every stage to infuse innovation in order to continuously improvise on the farming practices. Below are the indicators who self speak about the do's and the don'ts to improvise on the existing farming practices across large stretches of India's farmlands.

## DISCUSSION AND CONCLUSION

Innovative technologies are already disrupting the traditional methods of farming, with earlier unreasonable mechanisms and modern machinery and devices currently accessible and regularly installed on agriculture farms across the nation. IoT-based drones give a third eye in the investigation for pests which subsequently require more attention. The modern advances in sensor technology like robots, drones, chat-bots, and sensors are now able to use insights to assess crops, pests, insects, weeds and diseased crops, etc. Blockchain technology is on the rise, generating an innovative method of interaction in the electronic-Customer Relationship Management (e-CRM) and electronic-Supply Chain Management (e-SCM). Blockchain can decrease inefficiency and significantly enhance food safety and security. Traceability is upgraded, with regulators speedily checking the source of foods and investigating the scope of any contamination and also accessibility to the marketplace for raw and finished goods. These and other technological advancements in AI, Data Science, IIoT, Quantum Computing, RFID are acting as significant disruptors, driving change and inducing greater efficiency. The awareness, accessibility, and availability of infrastructures, hard and soft resources to the majority of Indian farmers are till date scarce and very poor and hence there is a dire need to introduce and propagate the thoughts, ideas, studies, and researches concerning the implementation of Agriculture 4.0 the focus being information and technology-enabled farming practices. In the opinion of the authors, the government should emphasize the below-mentioned points to make agriculture far more self-reliant and resilient.

- Forming more agri-entrepreneurs and support local farmers for the addition of values (Mr. Sandeepa, Dr. K. S. Sarala, 2019)
- Investments in agri-infrastructure containing storage, and supply chain (logistics and transport)
- Use Information Technology (IT) in farming to be made accessible to the remotest of the areas
- Process and analyze real-time information and data.
- Strengthen CRM & SCM chains to make them beneficial for farmers.
- Strengthening community-based enterprises for producers and farmers.
- Ensure visibility on an agri-insurance scheme
- Generate space for farming innovation in the agriculture domain.
- Motivate young farmers for more number of agricultural start-ups

- Motivate for infrastructure-related investments in the agriculture farming domain

The new wave of innovative technology goes to the agriculture sector and it looks a lot like the tech disruptions where cutting-edge tech like the self-driving tractor, digital farming are taking center stage (Cropin, 2021). This means they will also need to decide what the array of innovative technology means for increasing productivity, scaling a business, and driving sustainability and survival of human beings from starvation. To summarize, - FaaS, ADaaS, EaaS, RaaS, MaaS FaaS, hope to drive much-needed process and product innovations in Indian agriculture. Through this effort authors have tried to focus on and brought the attention of researchers to technology-enabled services that will ensure economic sustainability, enhance food security through data-driven decision making by various stakeholders like farmers, agri-business and agri-tech start-ups, 'farmpreneurs', government and non-government agencies, equipment suppliers, agronomists, IT suppliers, and vendors. The analyzed information will be used as a vantage by farmers to select precision farming practices to aid productivity, to empower personnel to provide timely assistance, and industries to implement real-time monitoring using sensors and devices. The chapter will help formulate concepts, methods, practices, benefits and introducing several case scenarios to effectively propagate the service mode of farming that will imbibe a pay-as-you-go model ensuring cost optimization and operational ease. The suggestion for organic farming, organic fertilizer production, modernization of farming techniques, education and skill up-gradation of farmers, awards, rewards and insurance schemes for young farmers, etc. are some initiatives that need to be kick-started to sustain the identity of India as an Agriculture Nation.

## REFERENCES

Adamides, G., & Stylianou, A. (2013). ICT and Mobile Phone Use for Agricultural Knowledge Sharing by Cypriot Farmers. *AGRIS On-Line Papers in Economics and Informatics*, *5*(2), 8.

Adebiyi. (2020). *Machine Learning-Based Predictive Farmland Optimization and Crop Monitoring System*. https://www.hindawi.com/journals/scientifica/2020/9428281/

Arun Kumar, R. (n.d.). Grading by Machine Vision and Fuzzy Logic. *Int. J. Comp. Tech. Appl., 2*(5), 1709-1716.

Awuor, F., Kimeli, K., Rabah, K., & Rambim, D. (2013). *ICT Solution Architecture for Agriculture*. IST.

Boyacioglu, C., & Yıldız, O. (2021). The Impact of Data Protection Regulations on Start-Up Enterprises. In *Recent Developments in Individual and Organizational Adoption of ICTs* (pp. 120–133). IGI Global. doi:10.4018/978-1-7998-3045-0.ch007

Chand, R. (2019). *102 Annual Conference Indian Economic Association (IEA) Transforming Agriculture for Challenges of 21st Century*. Academic Press.

Driessen, C., & Heutinck, L. F. M. (2014). Cows desiring to be milked? Milking robots and the co-evolution of ethics and technology on Dutch dairy farms. *Agriculture and Human Values*, *32*(1), 3–20. doi:10.100710460-014-9515-5

Fennimore, S. A. (2017). *Automated Weed Control: New Technology to Solve an Old Problem in Vegetable Crops*. Conference presentation at ASA Section: Agronomic Production Systems.

García-Llorente, M., Rubio-Olivar, R., & Gutierrez-Briceño, I. (2018). Farming for Life Quality and Sustainability: A Literature Review of Green Care Research Trends in Europe. *International Journal of Environmental Research and Public Health, 15*(6), 1282. Advance online publication. doi:10.3390/ijerph15061282 PMID:29914199

Hall. (2007). Challenges to Strengthening Agricultural Innovation Systems: Where Do We Go From Here? The Commonwealth Scientific and Industrial Research Organization.

Hinz & Sulser. (2019). *Agricultural Development and Land Use Change in India: A Scenario Analysis of Trade-Offs Between UN Sustainable Development Goals (SDGs).* https://agupubs.onlinelibrary.wiley.com/doi/pdf/10.1029/2019EF001287

Jyoti, B., Chandel, N., & Agrawal, K. (2020). *Application of Robotics in Agriculture: An Indian Perspective*. Academic Press.

Kate. (2020). *How Agriculture Affects Our Daily Life*. https://makebakegrow.com/2020/01/08/how-agriculture-affects-our-daily-lives/

López, I. D., & Corrales, J. C. (2018). A smart farming approach in automatic detection of favorable conditions for planting and crop production in the upper basin of Cauca River. *Adv. Intell. Syst. Comput., 687*, 223–233. doi:10.1007/978-3-319-70187-5_17

Lottes, P., Khanna, R., Pfeifer, J., Siewart, R., & Stachniss, C. (2017). UAV-based crop and weed classification for smart farming. *Proceedings – IEE International Conference on Robotics and Automation*, 3024–3031. 10.1109/ICRA.2017.7989347

Mahant, Shukla, Dixit, & Patel. (2012). Uses of ICT in Agriculture. *International Journal of Advanced Computer Research, 2*(3).

Mertens, Vangeyte, Van Weyenberg, Von Haselberg, Holpp, Doerfler, & Thysen. (2012). Web-Based Research Mapping and Analysis: ICT-AGRI's Meta Knowledge Base Centralizes ICT and Robotics Development in Agriculture and Related Environmental Issues. *Proceedings of the 9th International Conference on Education and Information Systems, Technologies and Applications: EISTA 2011.*

Mitchell, C., Sehgal, S., Mathur, H., & Chopra, P. (2020). *Indian Farming's Next Big Moment*. Bain & Company, Bain Capability Centre and CIIE.

Mohiuddin. (2015). Agricultural Robotics and Its Scope in India. *International Journal of Engineering Research & Technology, 4*(7).

Sandeepa & Sarala. (n.d.). Opportunities and Challenges of Agripreuership in India-Some Reviews. *Palarch's Journal of Archaeology of Egypt/Egyptology, 17*(7).

Saraswathi, & Kaushik. (2018). Use Cases and Challenges in Smart Farming System on the Verge of Cloud and Internet of Things (IoT). *American Journal of Computer Science and Information Technology, 6*(3), S1.

Shah, K. (2021). *The future of Indian agriculture lies with 'atmanirbhar' farmers*. https://www.downtoearth.org.in/ blog/ agriculture/ the- future- of- indian- agriculture- lies- with- atmanirbhar- farmers- 75228

Tomasz, B. (2020). Problem Solving and Innovation on the Farm- A How-To Manual. Academic Press.

Yelapure, S. J. (2012). Literature Review on Expert System in Agriculture. *International Journal of Computer Science and Information Technologies*, *3*(5), 5086–5089.

Yildiz, O. (2021). Changing Paradigms in the Digital Age and Entrepreneurial Universities. *University-Industry Collaboration Strategies in the Digital Era*, 1-21. https://www.researchgate.net/ publication/ 348767321_Changing_Paradigms_in_the_Digital_Age_and_Entrepreneurial_Universities/citations

Yildiz, O., Ersoy, A. S., & Yıldırım, İ. S. (2021). The Impact of Information and Communication Systems on Organizations. In *Recent Developments in Individual and Organizational Adoption of ICTs* (pp. 1–25). IGI Global. doi:10.4018/978-1-7998-3045-0.ch001

# Chapter 6
# Cloud Computing Service Provider Business Model Success Characteristics

**Ignitia Motjolopane**
*North West University, South Africa*

**Tshinakaho Relebogile Seaba**
*Tshwane University of Technology, South Africa*

## ABSTRACT

*In a digital arena, information technology services provision is shifting to a cloud computing ecosystem. Cloud computing is an enabler for digital transformation with cloud computing service providers central to the digital transformation of both companies and higher education. As cloud computing service providers play the role of an 'architect' for companies as supply chain is digitised and in supporting higher education institutions striving to deliver user-focused services in the face of increasing competition, an understanding of successful characteristics of cloud computing service provider business models is of main interest for providers and may also be of value for companies and higher education institutions when selecting cloud computing service providers. Despite the importance of cloud computing service providers' business models, information systems literature has provided limited analysis on the characteristics of successful business models. As such, the chapter aims to contribute to the emerging research on characteristics of successful business models.*

## INTRODUCTION

In the digital era, the provision of information technology (IT) services is shifting from traditional on premise to a cloud computing service with computing services delivered through an ecosystem. In this digital transformation, cloud computing plays a key role enabling companies to create competitive advantage and establishing useful links with other companies (Masenya, 2020). Digital transformation may be defined as the innovative use of IT to significantly change the model of how business operates in

DOI: 10.4018/978-1-7998-8169-8.ch006

generating and capturing value for customers and shareholders (Chan, 2020). Therefore, cloud computing will play a fundamental role in businesses in the future with IT as the backbone of digital transformation (Abolhassan, 2017), and cloud computing service providers playing 'architect of the digital future' for companies (Hottges, 2017). Furthermore, collaboration between higher education institutions and industry is increasingly viewed as a primary vehicle to enhance innovation through knowledge exchange (Gunay, 2021). As such, the value of cloud computing in the digital transformation journey for companies and higher education cannot be understated. More so, industries in areas such as manufacturing, transportation and logistics are experiencing a digital transformation across the value chain (Abolhassan, 2017). In higher education, the digital transformation has become a priority (Benavides et al., 2020) and is aimed at delivering user-focused services as changes occur in technology, competition and audience (Seres et al., 2018).

Companies and higher education institutions require a cloud computing provider that is able to provide flexibility and support progress towards successful digital transformation. More so, Higher Education business model paradigms have been shifting (Yildiz, 2021). Cloud computing providers are central in meeting the diverse companies and higher education institution needs and overseeing the value creation network.; hence the right IT partners are an important element for digital transformation (Abolhassan, 2017). Therefore, for the overall success in digital transformation, the cloud computing service providers' success is of importance to the digital transformation ecosystem's success. However, despite cloud computing's potential to fuel business model disruptions and digital transformation, value creation and capture comes with several challenges and concerns for cloud computing service providers (Sunyaev, 2020).

Some cloud computing service providers have reaped the rewards from the transition to cloud computing, and others have experienced substantial difficulties in formulating and operationalising effective business models (Clohessy et al., 2018) that contribute to economic success. As in moving to cloud computing for survival and retaining customers implies service providers' need to change existing business models revenue streams from upfront license fees, to periodic subscription fees (Xiao & Hedman, 2019). The cloud computing ecosystem further complicates business model creation as, while the actors bring almost unlimited creativity to the ecosystem, the actors also add complexity, interdependencies, and uncertainties that escalate the need for information (Wang, 2021). Consequently, to achieve business model agility, continuous business model development is needed (Bouwman et al., 2018), taking into account business model component interdependencies (Lanzolla & Markides, 2020) and testing business models under different scenarios (Bouwman et al., 2018).

Despite the importance of cloud computing service providers' economic success as an enabler of digital transformation, information systems literature on cloud computing has mainly been directed towards security, risk and adoption (Johansson & Muhic, 2017). Existing research provides limited analysis of how cloud computing service provider business models lead to economic success (Floerecke & Lehner, 2018). Moreover, the analysis of business models needs to address agility by including an element of stress testing (Bouwman et al., 2018) r. As such, this chapter examines cloud computing service providers' business model success characteristics and stress testing. Based on a systematic literature analysis, characteristics of successful business models in the various cloud computing services layers are identified and the potential contribution of business model component interdependencies outlined. Furthermore, cloud computing perspectives from South Africa are presented, highlighting how the COVID-19 pandemic has led to an increase in the use of public cloud services. In addition, the chapter conclusion and implications are discussed and potential areas for future research recommended.

## CLOUD COMPUTING AND BUSINESS MODELS

### Cloud Computing Service Delivery Models

In the provision of IT services, cloud computing service providers have four different models that may be adopted, and the decisions around the deployment models are influenced by the customer requirements. Therefore, deployment model decisions are important steps for successful cloud computing implementation, as the various types of deployment call for diversity in both skills and resources (Gaur et al., 2017). Furthermore, from a cloud computing service provider perspective, the varied deployment models address specific user requirements, user deployment choices have different characteristics and regulatory compliance restrictions and requirements, that can be complicated (Soni et al., 2017). A brief discussion of the deployment models is presented.

#### Public/External Cloud Model

A public cloud is hosted on the premises of the service provider offering open-use cloud infrastructure for the public and is managed by an academic or governmental organisation or another business (Mell & Grance, 2011). As such, public clouds facilitate a multi-tenant space that is managed by a third party (Indu et al., 2018). Public cloud services provided over the internet include application and storage (Magoules et al., 2012), with examples such as Microsoft Azure, and Apple's iCloud, which offers services such as Dropbox for file sharing, Instagram for photo and vide sharing and other social media sites (Karikari et al., 2018). Furthermore, El Alami et al. (2015) suggest public cloud deployment models focus on self-service and low-cost, pay-as-you-go and practically infinite scales, but cannot generally achieve a high performance level like the private cloud, mainly because of the strength of the internet link. However, Soni et al. (2017) caution that public clouds offer small and medium businesses lower overheads but face challenges such as poor performance, lost data, and security threats with protecting corporate data a driving factor for the use of private clouds.

#### Private/Internal Cloud Model

A private cloud is provided for exclusive single company use that may comprise of multiple business units and may be owned, managed and operated by this company or a third party, or some combination of either on- or off-premises (Mell & Grance, 2011). Therefore, private clouds services are dedicated to the needs of a specific company (Indu et al., 2018) with computing services enabling distribute access to a number of people usually via interior networks or extranets that remotely access the services and require authentication (Mazumdar & Alharahsheh, 2019). As such, according to El Alami et al. (2015) private clouds offer a more secure access, especially for critical business data and enable users to control fixed costs, but do not offer elasticity and upgradability that are offered by public clouds. Furthermore, Magoules et al. (2012) indicate that most companies prefer private cloud service so as to retain accurate control over own data whilst providing some of the scalability benefits presented by public cloud.

### Community Cloud Model

Mell and Grance (2011) indicate that a community cloud is operated, managed or owned by one or more organisations in a community, or provided by third party providers exclusively for a specific community of consumers from organisations that have shared concerns such as mission, policy, security requirements and compliance considerations. Therefore, in a community cloud, parties' conformance to the community requirements is of critical importance (Magoules et al., 2012). In a community cloud sharing infrastructure, software and hardware lead to a reduction in IT running costs (Gaur et al., 2017).

### Hybrid Cloud Model

A hybrid may combine any one of the other three types of the deployment models with the entities bound by standardised or proprietary technology that facilitates application and data portability enabling load balancing between the different cloud deployments (Mell & Grance, 2011). Therefore, a hybrid cloud enables the data and application sharing between the deployment models (Karikari et al., 2018), and hybrid cloud permits some nodes to run on real physical hardware and others on cloud server instances (Magoules et al., 2012).

Hybrid models may include a public being deployed for non-critical information while business-critical services and data run in private cloud for increased company control (Marston et al., 2011). However, El Alami et al. (2015) highlight that hybrid cloud model main challenge is the management of multiple clouds as a single entity. The four deployment models form the basis upon which the IT service provider delivers services to the customer. In addition to the deployment models, the services delivered to the customer are a key component in the delivery of services. The most common services are briefly examined.

## Cloud Computing Service Layers

The cloud service layers are key in the examination of cloud computing service providers' business models. There are a number of classification schemes for cloud computing services, such as Weinhardt et al.'s (2009) categorisation into software as a service (SaaS), platform as a service (PaaS), hardware as a service (HaaS), development/database/desktop as a service (DaaS), infrastructure as a service (IaaS), business as a service (BaaS), framework as a service (FaaS) and organisation as a service (OaaS). However, often, cloud computing service layers are commonly divided into three primary cloud service models, namely SaaS, PaaS and IaaS (Indu et al., 2018). According to Lindstrom et al. (2018), more specialised offerings that complement are emerging, such as security-as-a-service and identity-as-a-service, complementing the three main ones. Furthermore, El Alami et al. (2015) indicate that despite these common classifications into IaaS, PaaS and SaaS, there are new service models, some of which are starting to become prominent, including database as service (DbaaS), network as a service (NaaS), identity as a service (IDaaS), unified communications as a service (UCaaS), desktop as a service (DaaS), security as a service(SECaaS) and others with the format of XaaS, i.e. anything as a service. The multiple cloud computing services present a significant challenge for cloud computing service providers.

According to Marston et al. (2011), these service categories are depicted from end-users' viewpoint, and from cloud computing service providers' viewpoint, the services provided may incorporate various combinations customised to different customer needs. In addition to the three main categories of IaaS,

PaaS and SaaS, IDaaS will become more common. More so because identity management is considered a dominant challenge in the successful implementation of IaaS, PaaS and SaaS, with privacy and authentication (Ali et al., 2020) mechanisms that secure identities key for successful real platforms for multi-tenant applications (Goomaa et al., 2019). A brief overview of these four service categories of IaaS, PaaS, SaaS and IDaaS is provided.

## Software as a Service (SaaS)

SaaS offers the capability for customers to use the provider's applications running on a cloud infrastructure and the consumer does not manage or control the underlying cloud infrastructure, including networks, servers, operating systems, storage, or even individual application capabilities, with the exception of limited users' specific application configuration settings (Mell & Grance, 2011). Therefore, with SaaS, the cloud computing service provider licences an application to the customer for use as a service on demand offering consumers benefits such as operational efficiency and reduced costs (Subashini & Kavitha, 2010). The SaaS model's pay per use provides the customers much better control with services self-provisioned instantly (Subashini & Kavitha, 2010). In addition, from a customer's perspective, SaaS's features of on-demand self-service, rapid elasticity, measured service, broad network access and resource pooling are considered advantageous, strengthening business IT alignment with business strategy meeting service demands, accessibility needs, storage and resource needs, application customisability and cost-effectiveness (Ali et al., 2020).

SaaS's services empower developers and product managers to push features to production (Lakka et al., 2015). Furthermore, SaaS is widely used and depended on by a wide range of applications with the potential to offer services to a large number of customers having specific requirements, without encountering software quality problems (Ali et al., 2020). In addition, the ultimate goal of cloud computing service providers offering SaaS applications is to provide an easy to use, fully coordinated option software service (Ali et al., 2019). However, the main caveat with SaaS from the customer perspective is that most enterprises are still uncomfortable with the SaaS model due to a lack of visibility about the way customer data is stored and secured (Subashini & Kavitha, 2010).

## Infrastructure as a Service (IaaS)

IaaS entails the provision, processing, storage, networks, and other fundamental computing resources where the consumer does not manage or control underlying infrastructure, but has control over operating systems, storage, and deployed applications; and possibly limited control over select networking components such as host firewalls (Mell & Grance, 2011). The consumer installs the operating systems and the business applications required for deployment (El Alami et al., 2015). Therefore, a cloud computing service provider offering IaaS supplies the needed processing, networks storage, and additionally necessary resources of computing and the customers are allowed to implement and run the software that might be needed, such as operating applications and systems (Gaur et al., 2017). The global market for IaaS is dominated by global hyper-scalers, i.e. Alibaba, Amazon Web Services, Google and Microsoft, with a remaining 25% shared by a number of large international and national IT companies as well as a large number of small and medium-sized providers (Floerecke & Lehner, 2019). Therefore, the need arises for regional IaaS providers to successfully differentiate business models from the hyper-scalers to survive in the cloud computing ecosystem (Floerecke & Lehner, 2019).

### Platform as a Service (SaaS)

PaaS offers a computing platform and solution stack as services enabling the consumer to deploy applications without the cost and complexity of buying and managing the hardware and underlying software layers (Subashini & Kavitha, 2010). As such, the customer does not manage or control underlying cloud infrastructure, including networks, servers, operating systems, or storage, but has control over the deployed applications and possibly configuration settings for the application-hosting environment (Mell & Grance, 2011). Furthermore, PaaS may be based on the interfaces to the IaaS layer with flexible and programmable links to the infrastructure and development environment (Lakka et al., 2015).

### Identity as a Service (IDaaS)

In a cloud computing environment, there is growing need to ensure that users' identity and privacy are protected. As such, cloud computing forces a fundamental shift in how companies handle authentication, authorisation and provisioning (Ghazizadeh et al., 2020). According to Ates et al. (2011), the increasing amount of digital data leads to the emergence of a 'digital identity'; therefore, IDaaS is a third party-provided cloud-based management of authentication and authorisation service. Therefore, IDaaS is a cloud-based identity solution to manage cloud computing customers' identities, enabling cloud computing to manage their identity centrally (Ghazizadeh et al., 2020). Furthermore, Vo, Fuhrmann and Fischer-Hellmann (2018) add that IDaaS provides a federated identity for users to access multiple cloud services on demand, but may preserve user privacy with users registering to an IDaaS of choice to enable access to various cloud computing services and preserving user privacy according to user privacy policies.

The benefits of IDaaS include reduced on-site infrastructure, easier management and a broader range of integration options, availability, reliability and security (Firdhous, 2014). Moreover, IDaaS enhances the functionality of existing on premise implementations by working with them as part of the hybrid solution (2016). The third party approach to identity management, including creation and authentication, and privacy assurance is one of the corner stones of digital transformation, is that users may have different identities that may be used to access different services, especially in multi-tenant services like SaaS (Goomaa et al., 2019). Cloud computing services are articulated from the perspectives of the customers and are central to the key activities within the IT service provider business models. Furthermore, Magoules et al. (Magoules et al., 2012) suggest that, in terms of the cloud competing service provider business model, different levels of service may be offered at different prices in relation to uninterrupted service provision, storage requirements, access to applications, bandwidth, number of users and devices to be supported. In addition, from a cloud computing service provider's viewpoint, service delivery may incorporate various combinations of these services and different deployment models may be customised to different customers' needs (Marston et al., 2011). Therefore, the service layers should not be looked at in isolation due to the mutual interrelationships between the layers, and this has to be taken into account when designing business models (Duin et al., 2010). Consequently, the service layers will have a bearing on cloud computing service providers' business model decisions.

## Cloud Computing Service Providers' Business Model Decisions

The business model plays a fundamental role in cloud computing services providers' economic success. Osterwalder and Pigneur (2002) indicate that a business model identifies what value is offered by the company; to whom the value is offered and how the value is created, taking into account company architecture and partners and how much profit is made . Therefore, in delivering services to the customer's cloud computing service providers need to make decisions in answering these fundamental questions. The decisions that cloud computing service providers need to undertake are briefly discussed in the sections that follow.

## Business Model 'What' Decisions: Value Offering

The questions relating to the *what* are answered by the value offering (Krumeich et al., 2012), which includes value proposition specification that provides an answer as to what value is offered to the target customer (Alt & Zimmerman, 2001; Osterwalder, 2004; Taran et al., 2015) and value proposition for partners that are required to fulfil the value proposition to the customer (Stähler, 2002). In addition to the differentiation, the value offering will articulate the competitive model that illustrates the competing business models and the risk of the company's business model in relation to those of competitors. In a cloud-based environment (Krumeich et al., 2012), according to Lakka et al. (2015), the value propositions reflect problems that the customers are trying to solve and ultimately willing to pay for and revolves around the six key attributes of costs, namely flexibility, scalability, market adaptability, context-driven variability, market complicity and ecosystem connectivity. In addition, Chlohessy et al. (2016) indicate that from a service domain, cloud computing provides aggregate customer-oriented value propositions and new value propositions as a result of acquiring main cloud computing offerings and services and innovative delivery capability. In terms of SaaS services, cloud computing service providers use the cloud computing environment to rent resources while reducing customers' capital and operational expenditures, while enabling seamless, easy-to-use access to various applications (Alnumay, 2020). Having answered the questions relating to the *what* of the business model, the cloud computing service provider needs to determine how value will be created.

## Business Model 'How' Decisions: Value Creation

The business model *how* decisions specify the value configuration in terms the way in which key activities, resources and partners are organised to create value. According to Krumeich et al. (2012), the *how* decisions around value creation include aspects of resources, competencies, key activities and processes, organisational structure and key partnerships. Furthermore, the partnerships component needs to take into account the maturity of the partnership (Krumeich et al., 2012). Partnership maturity, drawing from Luftman (2015), in a cloud computing setting, may be defined as how each cloud computing service provider perceives the contribution of the other actors in the network and the trust that develops among the actors as well as the sharing of risks and rewards. In a cloud computing environment, the key activities are different cloud services provided (Lakka et al., 2015), and therefore key activities will depend on the service layers offered by the service provider and may include all four services of SaaS, IaaS, PaaS and IDaaS or different combination of these services based on user requirements. In a SaaS, key activities may provide services using four different maturity levels of service that may include, *ad hoc* and custom, configurable, configurable multitenant and scalable, configurable and multitenant (Alnumay, 2020). These answers on value creation will need to be supported by decisions in the financial model.

## Business Model 'How Much' Decisions: Financial Model

Decisions on *how much* stipulate the financial aspects in terms of how much value creation and delivery costs, as shown by the costs and revenue model, reflect the profit model for creating and delivering value to the target customer (Chesbrough & Rosenbloom, 2002; Morris et al., 2005; Pateli & Giaglis, 2004; Petrovic et al., 2001; Richardson, 2008). Revenue streams for cloud computing service models, by definition, are usage based or by subscriptions (Lakka et al., 2015). In addition, the economic model in cloud computing relies on multiple and flexible revenue models that may include freemium trial, pay-per-use, monthly, annual, licensing billing formats or consulting fees, purchasing order and financing packages (Clohessy et al., 2016). In a cloud computing environment, pricing for competition and fairness affects choices in the design of user applications and system infrastructures with the need for a more flexible pricing approach to ensure pricing fairness balancing user cost and cloud service provider profit (Mazrekaj et al., 2016). These financial model decisions will need to be optimised in relation to the value capture components in the business model.

## Business Model 'Who' Decisions: Value Capture

*Who*-based decisions examine the target customer, distribution channels and customer relationships, and therefore articulate who the target customer is to whom the company wants to offer value, specifying customer segments (Krumeich et al., 2012 ; Osterwalder et al., 2005; Pateli & Giaglis, 2004), delivery channels used (Krumeich et al., 2012 ; Osterwalder et al., 2005; Petrovic et al., 2001) and customer relationship strategies used per target market segment (Krumeich et al., 2012 ; Morris et al., 2005; Osterwalder, 2004; Osterwalder et al., 2005; Petrovic et al., 2001). A cloud computing environment enables the service providers to target private business-to-business and business-to-customer and public sector organisations, enabling the cloud computing service providers to target new and niche customer segments, which would not have been previously possible (Clohessy et al., 2016). In terms of the service layers, customer segments for IaaS are mainly developers, while customers for PaaS are mainly developers and SaaS providers with end-users as SaaS consumers (Lakka et al., 2015).

In managing customer relationships, cloud computing service providers need to adopt different strategies in different target market segments based on the desired objectives. In a SaaS environment, cloud computing service providers need a well-structured strategy to ensure that customisation will not result in alterations to the application source code and lack of such a strategy could be detrimental and hamper the development and maintenance of application code for individual customers (Ali et al., 2019). Furthermore, according to Lakka et al. (2015), in a cloud computing environment, value delivery IaaS adopts a self-service direct model often aggregated in broker portals, whose added value is in consolidated billing, self-service provisioning, IDaaS, and potentially some data integration, while SaaS and PaaS develop extensive partner programs with carefully planned and executed change management and master data alignment (Lakka et al., 2015).

In the analysis of cloud computing business models, prior studies such as that of Weinhard et al. (2009) have either used the types of services to categorise business models or combined deployment models and service categories. For example, Masiyev (2012) classifies business models into five types, namely infrastructure provider; platform provider; service provider; aggregate services provider and consulting business models. Furthermore, Chang (2010), using the Jericho Forum's cloud cube model, classifies cloud computing business models into eight different categories. Following on Weinhardt's

(2009) classification, the service layers are used to categorise the business models with the IDaaS layer added in the grouping. Using the Ostewalder and Pigneur (2010) elements of the business model canvass components, as depicted in the diagram, a systematic literature review is conducted to analyse the business models for each of these service categories. In addition to the business model components, the interdependencies between the components are examined. According to Lanzolla and Markides (2020), interdependencies among activities in a business model present a new 'lens' in developing strategies. This could be of value to cloud computing service providers connecting the business model components in a manner that builds superior interdependencies (Lanzolla & Markides, 2020). The next section will discuss the business model interdependencies and business model stress testing for robustness.

*Figure 1. Adapted from (Pigneur, 2006) Business Model Components and questions answered*

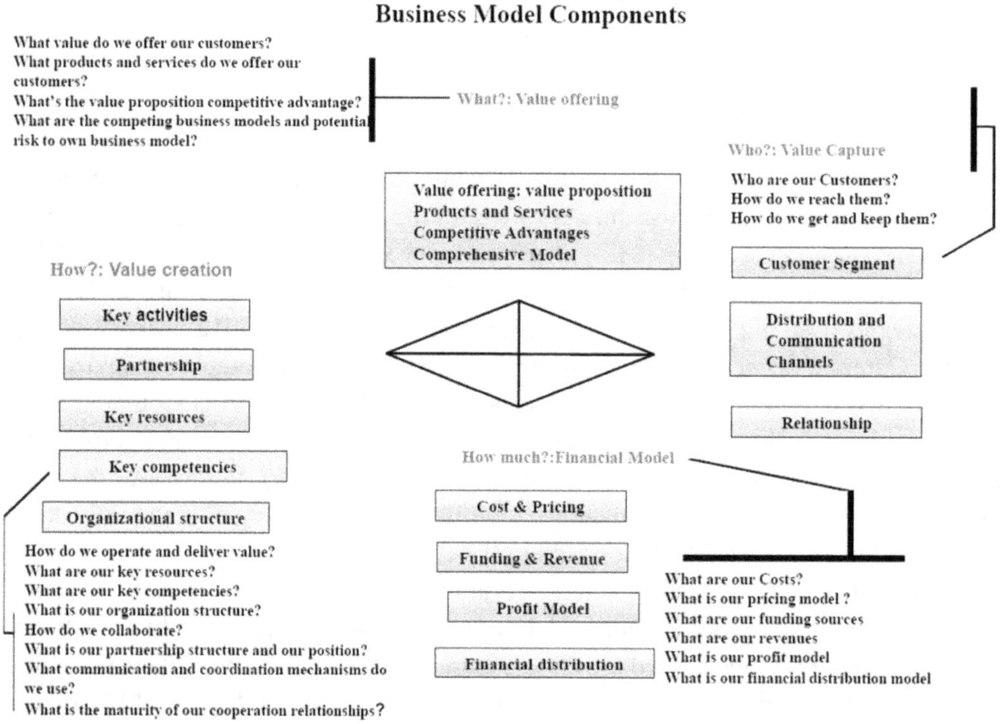


## Business Model Components Interdependencies and Stress Testing

Cloud computing service providers' understanding of the business model components interdependencies is key to formulating and operationalising business models that contribute to economic success. Schaffer et al. (2020) highlight that an understanding of the inherent business model components' dynamics offers insights into developing more sustainable business models that take into account the interrelations and facilitate transparency that enables the evaluation of profitability for the proposed business model. Moreover, the lack of knowledge of the structural relations and internal behaviour in a business model hampers the company's efforts to successfully innovate and transform business models (Krumeich et al., 2013). An understanding of the business model components supports companies to develop new insights into building superior strategies, especially where industry structure does not offer protection from imitation and resources, and capabilities are widely available and/or easily imitated (Lanzolla & Markides, 2020). According to Kruimech et al. (2013), the value offering in the business model is interrelated with the target, distribution channel, customer relations, price as well as with the competitive advantage, cost model and price. Another set of important interdependencies is between the value creation components of key resource partners, competencies, activities that are interdependent and further have an interrelationship with the value proposition, competitive advantage, target customer, distribution channel, customer relationship, revenue model, costs, coordination costs and financial distribution (Krumeich et al., 2013). In addition, an understanding of the interdependencies between the *how* in terms of the value creation and the *who* as value capture components is key in selecting the right competencies, resources, and activities, and ensuring appropriate target customers, customer relationships and communication (Schaffer et al., 2020).

The interrelationship extends to the value capture components of target customers and distribution channels and the revenue model, pricing, costs, partnerships and value propositions (Krumeich et al., 2013). The dynamic between the business model components will require cloud computing service providers to stress test business models. Business model stress testing decisions serve to support business model agility for cloud computing service providers' business models' robustness and agility. Stress testing is defined as validating the strong- and weak points of the business model by applying scenario analysis to determine the fit between the business model and future business environments (Bouwman et al., 2012). As such, stress testing is a practical approach to evaluate the robustness of business model components to enable testing individual components as well as the interrelation between components (Haaker et al., 2017). Stress testing evaluates business models against market scenarios, regulatory uncertainties, or technological uncertainties (Bouwman et al., 2018). The market uncertainties may be driven by changing customer needs and increasing competition. The changing customer needs are a result of the increased access to information and commoditisation (Chesbrough, 2007; Johnson et al., 2008; Teece, 2010). For example, while the global IaaS market continues to grow enormously, the market share of these regional IaaS providers has been decreasing for years, as IaaS services have become commoditised (Floerecke & Lehner, 2019). In addition to commoditisation, cloud computing services raise policy and regulatory challenges globally, more specifically on data security and privacy, among other issues (Mohlameane & Ruxwana, 2020).

Business model stress testing decisions focus on addressing these uncertainties, as misalignment between an organisation and its environment has been recognised as the main cause of company failure (Bouwman et al., 2012). Within the context of industry 4.0, Baloutsos et al. (2020) indicate six broad categories, and these may be of relevance to a cloud computing. These include management issues that entail lack of prioritisation or support by top management, corporate culture, and company rigidity, and economic issues in relation to unclear economic benefits, excessive investments, competing in-house programs as well as technological readiness that is affected by low maturity levels of required technologies, information and data security issues, non-seamless integration, and ineffective data management. Moreover, stress factors will include resource aspects such as lack of trained personnel either in the company or region, lacking industry standards, and contradicting regulations in different regions, data ownership issues, as well as powerful actors across the supply chain that may be resistant to change ecosystems (Baloutsos et al., 2020). The business model stress test process entails describing the business model, identifying stress factors, mapping the business model stress factors, creating a heat map, analysing the results and formulating improvement and actions to enable robustness (Haaker et al., 2017). Such enhancements to the business model need to take into account the interdependencies between the business model components. In the background of the importance of cloud service provider business model success for digital transformation, cloud computing layers, business model component success characteristics and stress testing a systematic literature review were conducted to identify the success characteristics and the approaches to business model stress testing. The analysis was focused on the business model success characteristics for the different cloud computing service layers.

## METHODOLOGY

An initial literature search, using Google Scholar to identify the most cited and most recent articles in the area of cloud computing business model, was conducted. Using the search terms 'business model', 'cloud computing', 'South Africa', and 'cloud computing business model', a quick scan indicated that the IDaaS business model was not included in the articles; the phrases 'business model' and 'identity management as a service' were used. The subsequent step was a search in the academic electronic databases, which included Emerald, Science Direct, IEEE, Springer and EBSCOHost, inclusive of conference proceedings from some of the top conference in information systems, such as ECSIS, AMSIS and ACM. Additional sources were identified from the citations in the papers that were reviewed. Based on the search, a total 121 articles were identified. These articles' abstracts were scanned, and those articles (46) that were not relevant were removed, as they do not focus on business models or used the term business model to refer to service categories, nor the underlying economic logic of how cloud computing service providers create and generate value when delivering services to the customer. An additional 25 articles were excluded as the business model was being discussed from the customer perspective.

A total of 52 relevant articles were generated from three of these articles that were using a Jericho Forum cloud cube model focus in the analysis, and as such provide limited avenues for understanding potential cloud computing service providers' business model elements in a cloud environment (Chang, Bacigalupo, et al., 2010; Chang, Wills, et al., 2010). In a similar manner, (Masiyev et al., 2012) provide a business model categorisation that is not business model component-centric. The remaining articles were analysed, of which some discussed the business model in general, not at a specific layer of cloud computing services, mostly comparing pricing mechanisms articulating advantages and disadvantage and in some cases elaborating on the fairness of these mechanisms to customers and to providers (Chun, 2020; Gupta & Vashisht, 2010; Ibrahimi, 2017 ; Mazrekaj et al., 2016). The other areas of focus for the articles that were not service layer specific included the transition of specific companies from a basic business model to a more dynamic business model (Clohessy et al., 2018), business models for machine-to-machine players and communication service providers (Juliandri, 2012). Additional areas were on special case business models such as B2B business models for medical imaging, building management and internet of things (Krueger, 2014), cloud computing service providers' business models within a manufacturing industry 4.0 context (Baloutsos et al., 2020) and the evaluation of a virtual enterprise cloud architecture for South African government as a PaaS provider (Mvelase et al., 2014), as well as examining the business model from a value net theory not using a business model component focus (Fang et al., 2010). A review of the remaining articles indicated that the SaaS business model was analysed in five papers, IaaS business model in three papers and PaaS in five papers, while the IDaaS business model was not discussed and extant literature was reviewed to identify some potential aspects of relevant business models. The research methodology is represented below.

*Figure 2. Authors own depiction research methodology*

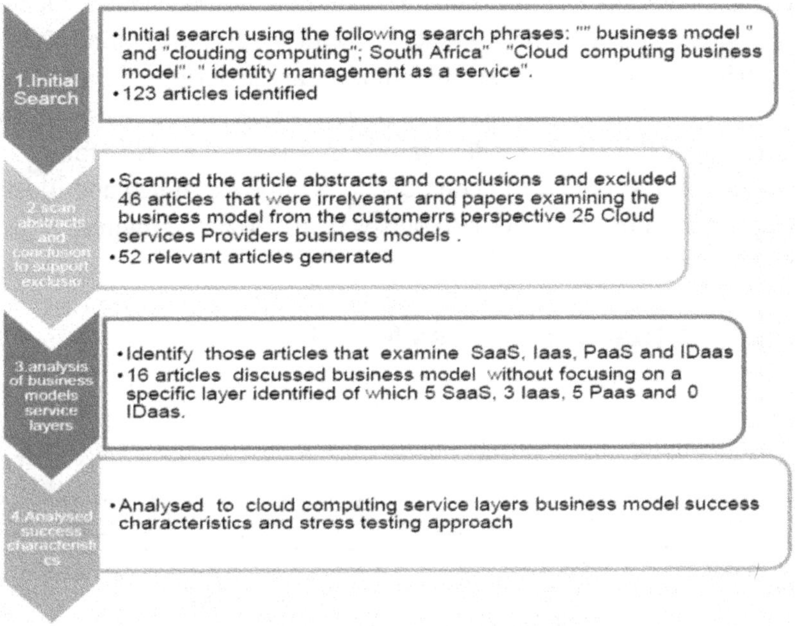


## FINDINGS

The articles that do not focus on the service layers have provided valuable input into the cloud computing service providers' decision-making regarding business models. The papers shed light on the aspects of some of the approaches that may be adopted by cloud computing service providers to transit from a generic to a more competitive business model. Labes et al. (2017) provide valuable insights for new comers, standardised mass-ware providers and specialised cloud computing service providers. In particular, newcomer providers in a crowded market are advised to define and understand own entry strategy, target market ranging from niche markets to wealthy customers and to take advantage of providers' small size and flexibility and develop lean and specialised services.

The standardised mass-ware providers who have high economies of scale and a good understanding of technology due to the standard service low trust level and less direct customer contact are advised to focus on building a sound customer relationship and finding an appropriate pricing model. Furthermore, these authors suggest that specialised cloud providers need to 'understand what, why and where they are doing what they are doing' with services that are highly innovative with a high degree of customer orientation, and a partner network that ensures the business models are not easy to imitate. Similarly, business model decision rules to transit from a basic foundational business model to proprietary business model to compete effectively have been proposed (Clohessy et al., 2018). In addition, Clohessy et al. (2016) shed light on how cloud computing has enabled both SME born-on-the-cloud and large business models' mature cloud computing service providers to commercialise their hardware and software along each of the four business model domains of service, technology, organisation and finance.

Pricing is a core element on the cloud computing service provider business model. Based on a comparison of subscription pricing and pay-per-use pricing, pay-per-use pricing is recommended in a social welfare environment (Chun, 2020). In addition, different pricing schemes have been compared regarding their advantages and disadvantages examined inclusive of these models' fairness features for both cloud computing service providers and customers (Gupta & Vashisht, 2010; Ibrahimi, 2017 ; Mazrekaj et al., 2016). These characteristics of successful business models in the various services layers would need to be interlinked with the business model components interdependencies and stress testing to validate the feasibility and viability of the business model options. In the sections that follow, the characteristics and potential options of the business model components will be examined and illustrated with a stress testing approach adapted from prior studies (Baloutsos et al., 2020; Bouwman et al., 2012; Bouwman et al., 2018; Haaker et al., 2017).

## Software as a Service (SaaS) Business Model

*Figure 3. Authors own depiction SaaS business model components success characteristics*

SaaS is the most visible layer of cloud computing for end-users, providing software that is owned, delivered and managed remotely by one or more providers (Masiyev et al., 2012). According to (Duin et al., 2010), in addition to the generic cloud advantage of low price, flexible contractual models' success factors for SaaS include best-of-breed support for the company processes that are mapped, the provider's economic reliability, integration and migration interfaces, references and flexible price models. The business model component variations for SaaS are illustrated below, with (Luoma et al., 2012) categorising SaaS business models into pure play and enterprise SaaS. SaaS service providers need to ensure timeliness, transparency and creativity to attract and retain customers and optimise profitability (Vaudour & Heinze, 2020). Moreover, to retain customers in the hyper-competitive SaaS, service providers may promote the cloud computing technology in general, rather than just focusing on the specific service, while ensuring customer satisfaction and investing in programs that may improve customer commitment to SaaS (Xiao et al., 2020). The component characteristics of successful business are illustrated, drawing from (Duin et al., 2010; Lakka et al., 2015; Luoma et al., 2012).

## Infrastructure as a Service (IaaS) Business Model

In an IaaS business model, the cloud computing service provider supplies infrastructural resources that include computing, storage and network (Floerecke & Lehner, 2018). Duin et al. (2010) identify key success factors in an IaaS environment as leveraging economies of scale, advantages in price/performance ratio, availability, security and network connection bandwidth. Based on the review, the variations of the IaaS business model are illustrated below drawing from (Duin et al., 2010; Floerecke & Lehner, 2018; Lakka et al., 2015).

*Figure 4. IaaS business model components success characteristics*

Key partners

**Weaving of partners in the core services (IaaS:** strictly avoiding having partners in one's core services)

**Building a partner ecosystem IaaS/PaaS:** thriving partner ecosystem serves as a sales and marketing channel

Key activities

**IaaS/PaaS: Conducting research:** high-level research and development is vital in the rapidly changing cloud ecosystem. The risk of lagging behind the technological development is high

Key resources

**Locating data centres in the target country (IaaS):** ensuring performance and latency and legal and cultural compliance
**Operating a worldwide network of interconnected data centres (IaaS):** To prevent loss of data, enable additional backup and recovery and addressing geographical risks
**Building and operating innovative, cost-efficient data centres (IaaS):** characterised by innovativeness and engineering performance. reduce energy costs ensuring scalability
**Possessing leading certificate IaaS/PaaS:**

**Having highly qualified employee's IaaS/PaaS:**
**Owning a large pre-cloud customer base IaaS/PaaS:**

Value propositions

**Multi-cloud management IaaS:** offer one's own IaaS service and additionally act as a broker for other providers.
**Managed services IaaS:** Extend basic virtual computing, storage and network resources with managed services such as back-up and monitoring services
**Hybrid IaaS:** offering the capability to combine legacy systems and new hybrid private and public cloud scenarios
**Extensive transition services from on-premise to cloud:** Offering strong support during transition from lots of accumulated on premise infrastructure additional strategic aspect of provider directly wining customers for own IaaS services
Storage, computing, systems administration services, self-service provision of virtual machines, application domains
**Guaranteed high availability IaaS/PaaS**

**High experience IaaS/PaaS**
**Broad integrated cloud portfolio PaaS/IaaS**
**Extensive Client Support IaaS/PaaS**

**Customer-specific service adaptation Success characteristics**
Best-of-breed support for the company processes that are mapped, The provider's economic reliability, integration and migration interfaces, references and flexible price models

Customer relationships

**Developers**: Establish and maintain a close contact with developer community
**Personalise IaaS/PaaS:** Offering personalised instead of self service. Initially explaining the cloud concept Conducting marketing activities and establishing cloud specific incentives for sales staff

Channels

Efficient mode of sales that can be efficiently used to target small and medium-sized
customers and buyers at all levels of an end-user organisation
**Enterprise SaaS:** Perform personal sales and employ channel partners
**Pure play SaaS:** Sales channel is push-oriented, and SaaS firms engage in inbound, high-pressure sales
**Self-services SaaS**: Outbound and viral marketing used to attract customers to the vendor's home page. Landing page critical in turning prospects into customers

Customer segments

**Ambitious**: Focusing on medium-sized and large companies: Offering possibility for all firms of all sizes to become a client Larger enterprises and their IT

Stress testing

**1. Stress factors identification:**
Management issue:
Economic issues:
Technology readiness:
Resource limitations:
Standards & regulations
Powerful actors supply chain
**2.Mapping business model to Stress factors** exploring causal relationship between identified stress factors and business model components
**3. Create heat map: business model:**
**Red:** Possible showstopper: needs attention from a strategy perspective
**Yellow**: Negative or positive effects cannot be excluded, but attention is required;
**Green:** No negative effects are expected;
**Grey:** No relevant influence
**4. Analyse results:** conduct sub-view analysis and pattern analysis
**5. Formulate improvement actions:** provide recommendations
on how to improve weak business model components or improve consistency across components. Provide reasoning behind the choice for a specific colouring

Cost structure

**Reducing electrical consumption:** Have varying marginal costs, owing to the long sales cycles and required support
**Achieving economies of scale:**

Revenue streams

**Keeping up with market price:** ensuring that market prices as the main sales argument
**Providing transparency IaaS/PaaS:** Simplicity in usage based pricing models
**Implementing a layer overarching pricing IaaS/PaaS:**
**Supporting bring your own licence IaaS/PaaS:**
**Price flexibility with pricing model**

## Platform as a Service (PaaS) Business Model

A PaaS business model allows cloud computing service providers to develop and deploy applications by offering a software development environment with programming languages, libraries and tools. A number of characteristics for success have been identified for PaaS and these include size of the community entrusted with developing the technology in question, simplicity of service deployment, and architecture frameworks that support automatic scaling (Duin et al., 2010). The potential business model components are depicted in the diagram below, drawing from business model success characteristics (Duin et al., 2010; Floerecke & Lehner, 2018).

*Figure 5. PaaS business model components success characteristics*

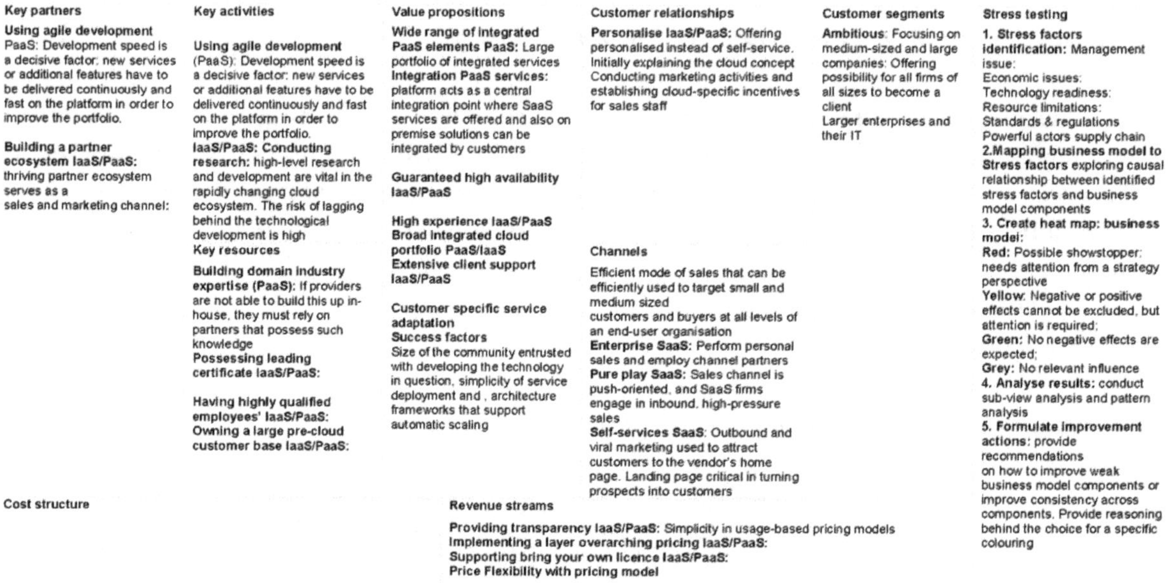


## Identity Access as a Service (IDaaS) Business Model

The analysis clearly reflects a dearth of research around IDaaS business models, and as such, adjacent literature in the area of identity management was used to identify the related business model components of the IDaaS business model. In an IDaaS business model, an independent trusted third party provides digital identity federation with authentication and authorisation mechanisms for access control in a cloud computing environment (Leandro et al., 2012). The core processes in IDaaS include management of users, authentication, authorisation, dissemination of access data, and audit and operational monitoring that would require the management of attributes, authorisation policies, external identities, compliance and authentication and authorisation centralisation (Manguic, 2012). IDaaS opens up a new business opportunity for cloud providers and vendors, broadening service offerings (Nunez & Agudo, 2014). Furthermore, Xiang et al. (Xiang et al., 2010) have indicated that IDaaS bridges the gap between end-customers and other cloud service providers that are delivering SaaS, IaaS and PaaS, as such a business model may be established for these providers to delegate to an IDaaS provider.

The value proposition for IDaaS would be enabling end-to-end confidentiality, authenticity, improved cloud-based identity management, and data sharing scenarios (Kostopoulos et al., 2017). For example, in a managed hosting, an IDaaS provider could maintain a complete set of employee data, and in another scenario, the IDaaS provider would maintain pseudonyms of employees, which the user companies would map to real employee identities (Leandro et al., 2012). In addition, with the growing number of users and thousands of identities, IDaaS offers increased flexibility, scalability and stability for high demand environments and improved compliance and business process audits, and due to the high specialisation and security standards that an IDaaS provider can achieve, they may lower costs through implementing common policies for customers (Nunez & Agudo, 2014). The target customers in an IDaaS business model would be cloud service providers for SaaS, IaaS and PaaS, both in both public and private deployments (Suresh et al., 2017). The success characteristics for ITO providers include the ability to balance load, and provide a single to multiple services, using cloud lifecycle management to deliver flexible services and providing privacy assurance through trust management, risk assessment and the use of standards to mitigate identity theft and improve strong authentication (Ghazizadeh et al., 2020).

## Perspectives on Cloud Computing Service Provision in South Africa

### Cloud computing and national information communication strategy in South Africa

Cloud computing presents potential for both IT service providers and customers; however, according to Addendorf and Smuts (2019), South Africa, like many other African countries, has unique conditions that require companies to apply special effort in order to realise the benefits of cloud computing with legacy issues from geographical and political isolation having hampered the evolution of cloud solutions. Historically, South African IT services have had challenges to influence customers to migrate to SaaS (Du Plessis & Mwalemba, 2016); moreover, although cloud computing awareness has increased in South Africa, cloud adoption in emerging economies is not prevalent (Adendorff & Smuts, 2019). This is due to a failure to invest in high performance internet connectivity needed for the successful adoption and usage of SaaS enterprise resource planning systems (Faasen et al., 2013; Schay, 2018). In addition, infrastructure limitations, poor bandwidth coupled with latency and high costs hamper the advancement of cloud adoption and lack of support by service providers in migrating legacy solutions into the cloud-raised concerns based on the number of service providers available in South Africa (Adendorff & Smuts, 2019).

However, despite these challenges, BMIT forecasts the cloud services market will grow at a CAGR of 28% over the next five years to R23.6 billion in 2023, with the local Microsoft Azure cloud officially going live, as well as the Huawei cloud being available in-country and the local AWS and Oracle clouds coming soon (BMIT, 2020). This growth may be boosted by the South African government's plans to make substantial use of ICTs in the delivery of governmental, informational and educational services in the long term between 2020 and 2030 (Gillwald et al., 2012). According to market research reports, the COVID-19 pandemic has prompted an increase in the use of public cloud services, and the next five years may be pivotal for public cloud service providers and customers with public cloud services such as IaaS and PaaS becoming convenient and cost-effective (Miemoukanda, 2020). South Africa accounts for 75 percent of Africa's cloud revenue, thereby making South Africa an important player in the evolution of cloud computing (Cruise, 2020). There is a need for South African companies to continuously develop a well-defined cloud migration strategy to avoid losses in the cloud migration process (Jaka & Van den Berg, 2020). Therefore, the value of IT service providers articulating creative business models cannot be understated. The use of data centres and security issues remain a concern as some of the existing international regulations require certain foreign governments to have direct access to the data existing within their country (Du Plessis & Mwalemba, 2016). It is on this basis that organisations are hesitant to send vital business data to third parties (Faasen et al., 2013).

### South African IT Service Providers' Cloud Computing Service Layers and Business Models

Information on the level of adoption of each service layers is still limited. Findings from a survey that was conducted indicated cloud e-mail, cloud storage and cloud productivity tools are the most adopted SaaS solutions in South African small, medium and micro-enterprises (SMMEs) (Maserumule, 2019). The least embraced were virtual team communication, IT support desk ticketing, cloud e-commerce and payroll software (Maserumule, 2019). In customer cloud migration, the service adopted will differ based on organisational need and the type of cloud service being adopted; as an example, for a franchisee in South Africa the path followed entailed a move to SaaS, PaaS, then IaaS (Jaka & van den Berg, 2020). Furthermore, (Schay, 2018) emphasised that IT decision-makers in South African SMMEs lack awareness of cloud computing and software-related concepts with disparate use of SaaS software companies for basic operations, but not generally an end-to-end cloud offering. In their research, Lechesa et al. (2012) reveal that South African organisations are aware of SaaS, but the value provided by SaaS to business is not always clear and the requisite network infrastructure hinders adoption where the value is clear. A study by Madisha and Van Belle (Madisha & Van Belle, 2012) showed that SaaS adoption is predominantly for productivity-suit applications within the context of South African SMEs, with just a few SMMEs using more advanced SaaS applications. Only a small percentage is preparing for the implementation of SaaS. Overall, the South African cloud adoption rate is very low in contrast to other countries (Mokwena & Hlebela, 2018). In addition, the emergence of cloud computing has exposed the existing South African policies and regulatory laws as being inadequate to address cloud computing developments, complexities and challenges, especially challenges related to public confidence regarding the use of cloud computing services and cloud competitiveness (Mohlameane & Ruxwana, 2020).

## DISCUSSION, CONCLUSION, LIMITATIONS AND FUTURE RESEARCH DIRECTIONS

This chapter. The chapter, while having limitations, is expected to make a valuable contribution to theory and practice. The chapter makes a theoretical contribution on cloud computing service providers' strategies and business models using an evidence-based analysis to consolidate what is known about designing and operationalising business models that may contribute to economic success and identify potential knowledge gaps in the area. One may conclude that research on the characteristics of successful business is beginning to emerge. However, there is still a need to link business model components' interdependencies in the assessment of business model success characteristics, inclusive of examining the mediating effect of stress testing to assure robustness of cloud computing service providers. Therefore, based on the review, future research may empirically explore the contribution of interconnectedness between the business model interdependencies, success characteristics and stress testing at the different cloud computing service layers when designing and operationalising business models for economic success. In addition, a comparative analysis of the interrelationships between business model components; interdependencies, success characteristics and stress testing between cloud computing service providers serving different industries may be examined. The chapter has practical implications for cloud computing service providers as the business model components, interdependencies and success characteristics based on previous empirical research may serve as a lens when designing and operationalising business models that contribute to economic success. The key limitation in the chapter is that the findings are based on a literature analysis, and as such, the findings still need to be validated using empirical research.

## ACKNOWLEDGMENT

The authors would like to acknowledge North-West University's Mrs Cecile van Zyl for language editing support with the manuscript.

This research received no specific grant from any funding agency in the public, commercial or not-for-profit sectors.

## REFERENCES

Abolhassan, F. (2017). Pursuing digital transformation driven by the Cloud. In F. Abolhassan (Ed.), *The drivers of digital transformation: Why there's no way around the cloud*. Springer Nature. doi:10.1007/978-3-319-31824-0_1

Adendorff, R., & Smuts, H. (2019). Critical success factors for cloud computing adoption in South Africa *Twenty-fifth Americas Conference on Information Systems*, Cancun, Mexico.

Ali, A. Q., Sultan, A. B., & Gani, A. A. A. (2019). A Systematic mapping study on the customization solutions of software as a service spplications. *IEEE Access: Practical Innovations, Open Solutions*, *7*, 88196–88217. doi:10.1109/ACCESS.2019.2925499

Ali, M. B., Wood-Harper, T., & Ramlogan, R. (2020, March 31-April 1). *Challnges of value creation through cloud SaaS: Business/It alignment in service oriented industries* 25th UK Academy for Information Systems International Conference, Oxford, UK.

Alnumay, W. S. (2020). A brief study on software as a service in cloud computing paradigm. *Journal of Engineering and Applied Sciences (Asian Research Publishing Network)*, *7*(1), 1–15. doi:10.5455/jeas.2020050101

Alt, R., & Zimmerman, H. (2001). Preface: Introduction to special section business models. *Electronic Markets*, *11*(1), 3–9.

Ates, M., Ravet, S., Ahmat, A. M., & Fayolle, I. (2011). An identity-centric internet: identity in the cloud, identity as a service and other delights. *Sixth International Conference on Availability, Reliability and Security*, Vienna, Austria. 10.1109/ARES.2011.85

Baloutsos, S., Karagiannaki, A., & Mourtos, I. (2020). Business model gneration for industry 4.0: A "lean startup" approach. *The International Technology Management Review*, *9*(1), 34–45. doi:10.2991/itmr.k.200630.001

Benavides, L. M. C., Arias, J. A. T., Serna, M. D. A., Bedoya, J. W. B., & Burgos, D. (2020). Digital transformation in Higher Education Institutions: A systematic literature review. *Sensors (Basel)*, *20*(11), 3291. doi:10.339020113291 PMID:32526998

BMIT. (2020). *BMIT 2020 Tech Trends* [Market research report]. Retrieved 14/11/2020, from https://www.bmit.africa/bmit-2020-tech-trends

Bouwman, H., de Reuver, M., Solaimani, S., Daas, D., Haaker, T., & Janssen, W. (2012). *Business models tooling and a research agenda* 25th Bled eConference, Bled, Slovenia.

Bouwman, H., Heikkilä, J., Heikkilä, M., Leopold, C., & Haaker, T. (2018). Achieving agility using business model stress testing. *Electronic Markets*, *28*(2), 149–162. doi:10.100712525-016-0243-0

Chan, J. O. (2020). Digital transformation in the era of big data and Cloud Computing. *International Journal of Intelligent Information Systems*, *9*(3), 16–23. doi:10.11648/j.ijiis.20200903.11

Chang, V., Bacigalupo, D., Wills, G., & De Roure, D. (2010). A Categorisation of Cloud Computing Business Models. *International Conference on Cluster, Cloud, and Grid Computing.*

Chang, V., Wills, G., & De Reuver, M. (2010). *A Review of Cloud business models and sustainability.* In the third International Conference on Cloud Computing, Miami, FL.

Chesbrough, H. (2007). Business model innovation:Its not just about technology anymore. *Strategy and Leadership*, *35*(6), 12–17. doi:10.1108/10878570710833714

Chesbrough, H., & Rosenbloom, R. S. (2002). The role of the business model in capturing value from innovation: Evidence from Xerox Corporation's technology spin-off companies. *Industrial and Corporate Change*, *11*(3), 529–555. doi:10.1093/icc/11.3.529

Chun, S. H. (2020). Cloud services and pricing Strategies for sustainable business models: Analytical and numerical approaches. *Sustainability*, *12*(1), 49. doi:10.3390u12010049

Clohessy, T., Acton, T., & Morgan, L. (2018). Contemporary digital business model decision making: A cloud computing supply-side perspective. *International Journal of Networking and Virtual Organisations*, *19*(1), 1–20. doi:10.1504/IJNVO.2018.093923

Clohessy, T., Acton, T., Morgan, L., & Conboy, K. (2016). The times they are a-chchanging for ICT service provision. *Twenty-fourth European Conference on Information Systems (ECIS)*, Istanbul, Turkey.

Cruise, A. (2020). South Africa to lead cloud adoption race on the continent. *Hi tech security solutions.* http://www.securitysa.com/10256r

Du Plessis, J. J., & Mwalemba, G. (2016). Adoption of emerging technologies into ERP Systems Landscape. A south African Study. *2016 IEEE International Conference on Emerging Technologies and Innovative Business Practices for the Transformation of Societies (EmergiTech).* 10.1109/EmergiTech.2016.7737373

Duin, H., Heindl, M., Marke, E., Suttner, H., Withalm, J., Wolfe, W., & Zand, D. (2010). *Green car environment - A vision of an electric ecosystem in automotive IEEE International Technology Management Conference (ICE)*, Lugano, Switzerland.

El Alami, A., Sadok, H., & Elhaoud, N. (2015). *Cloud computing & the organizational performance different approach of assessment International Conference on Cloud Technologies and Applications (CloudTech)*, Marrakesh, Morocco.

Faasen, J., Seymour, L. F., & Schuler, J. (2013). SaaS ERP adoption intent: Explaining the South African perspective. Academic Press.

Fang, Z., Chen, J., Yi, M., Wu, Z., & Qian, H. (2010). Cloud computing business model based on value net theory. *IEEE International Conference on E-Business Engineering*.

Firdhous, M. (2014). A Comprehensive taxonomy for the infrastructure as a Service in Cloud Computing. *Fourth International Conference on Advances in Computing and Communications*.

Floerecke, S., & Lehner, F. (2018). Success driving business model characteristics of IaaS and PaaS providers. *Computer Networks & Communications: An International Journal*, *2*(4), 1–22.

Floerecke, S., & Lehner, F. (2019). The Unequal Battle for Market Shares in the Infrastructure-as-a-Service Segment: Success-Driving Business Model Characteristics of Regional Providers in Competition with the Hyperscalers. *HMD*, *56*(6), 1334–1354. doi:10.136540702-019-00549-y

Gaur, A., Gaud, S., & Jain, A. (2017). Advance computing paradigm with the perspective of cloud computing-An analytical study. *International Journal of Advanced Networking and Applications*, *8*(6), 3257–3265.

Ghazizadeh, E., Cusack, B. H. D., & Shahzad, A. (2020). *Cloud surfing: A general comparison of cloud identity guidelines*. Americas Conference on Information Systems (AMCIS), Virtual Conference.

Gillwald, A., Moyo, M., & Stork, C. (2012). *Understanding what is happening in ICT in South Africa a supply and demand side analysis of the ICT sector*. Retrieved 20/02/2016, from https://www.researchictafrica.net/publications/Evidence_for_ICT_Policy_Action/Policy_Paper_7_-_Understanding_what_is_happening_in_ICT_in_South_Africa.pdf

Goomaa, I., Abd-Elrahma, E., & Ksentini, A. (2019). Virtual identity performance evaluations of anonymous authentication in IDaaS framework. *IEEE Access: Practical Innovations, Open Solutions*, *7*, 34541–34554. doi:10.1109/ACCESS.2019.2904854

Gunay, A. (2021). New features of higher education competitiveness in terms of university-industry collaborations. In *University-Industry Collaboration Strategies in the Digital Era* (pp. 22–39). IGI Global. doi:10.4018/978-1-7998-3901-9.ch002

Gupta & Vashisht, S. (2010). A nascent study in cloud pricing. *Amity Journal of Computational Sciences*, *3*(2), 28-32.

Haaker, T., Bouwman, H., Janssen, W., & de Reuver, M. (2017). Business model stress testing: A practical approach to test the robustness of a business model. *Futures*, *89*, 14–25. doi:10.1016/j.futures.2017.04.003

Hottges, T. (2017). Foreword. In F. Abolhassan (Ed.), *The drivers of digital transformation: Why there's no way around the cloud*. Springer Nature.

Ibrahimi, A. (2017). Cloud computing: Pricing model. *International Journal of Advanced Computer Science and Applications*, *8*(6), 434–441. doi:10.14569/IJACSA.2017.080658

Indu, I., Anand, P. M. R., & Bhaskar, V. (2018). Identity and access management in cloud environment: Mechanisms and challenges. *Engineering Science and Technology, an International Journal, 21*(4), 574-588.

Jaka, N., & van den Berg, G. (2020). *Learnings from a Cloud Migration Project at a South African Retailer. African Conference on Information Systems and Technology*, Addis Ababa, Ethiopia.

Johansson, B., & Muhic, M. (2017). Relativism in the cloud: Cloud sourcing in virtue of IS development outsourcing - A literature review. *International Journal of Information Systems and Project Management*, *5*(4), 55–65.

Johnson, M. W., Christensen, M. C., & Kagermann, H. (2008). Reinventing your business model. *Harvard Business Review*, 59–67.

Juliandri, A. M. (2012). Positioning cloud computing in machine to machine business models. *International Conference on Cloud Computing and Social Networking (ICCCSN).*

Karikari, A., Zhu, L., & Dara, R. (2018). Blockchain: The next step in the development of The Internet of Things. 9th Annual Information Technology, *Electronics and Mobile Communication Conference (IEMCON)*, Vancouver; Canada.

Kostopoulos, A., Sfakianakis, E., Chochliouros, I., Pettersson, J. S., Krenn, S., Tesfay, W. M. A., & Horandner, F. (2017). Towards the adoption of secure cloud identity services. *12th International Conference on Availability, Reliability and Security, Reggio Calabria*, Italy. 10.1145/3098954.3104061

Krueger, M. W. a. D. (2014). Analysis of Cloud Business Models for the Industrial B2B Market. *IT Convergence Practice (INPRA), 2*(2).

Krumeich, J., Burkhart, T., Werth, D., & Loos, P. (2012). Towards a component based description of business models: A state of the art analysis. *Americas Conference on Information Systems*, Seattle, WA.

Krumeich, J., Werth, D., & Loos, P. (2013). Interdependencies between business model components – A literature analysis. *Proceedings of the Nineteenth Americas Conference on Information Systems.*

Labes, S. N. H., & Zarnekow, R. (2017). Successful business model types of cloud providers. *Business & Information Systems Engineering*, *59*(4), 223–233. doi:10.100712599-016-0455-z

Lakka, S., Michalakelis, C., Stamati, T., & Anagnostopoulos, D. (2015). *A framework for the classification of Could Computing business models. PCI '15: 19th Panhellenic Conference on Informatics*, Athens, Greece. 10.1145/2801948.2802028

Lanzolla, G., & Markides, C. C. (2020). A Business Model View of Strategy. *Journal of Management Studies.*

Leandro, M. A. P., Nascimento, T. J., dos Santos, D. R., Westphall, C. M., & Westphal, C. B. l. (2012). Multi-tenancy authorization system with federated identity for cloud-based environments using shibboleth. *Proceedings of the Eleventh International Conference on Networks (ICN).*

Lindstrom, J., Hermanson, A., Blomstedt, F., & Kyosti, P. (2018). A multi-usable cloud service platform: A case study on improved development pace and efficiency. *Applied Sciences (Basel, Switzerland)*, *8*(2), 316. doi:10.3390/app8020316

Luftman, J. (2015). Strategic alignment maturity. In J. V. Brocke & M. Rosemann (Eds.), *Handbook on business process management 2: Strategic alignment, governance, people and culture* (pp. 5–43). Springer. doi:10.1007/978-3-642-45103-4_1

Luoma, E., Ronkko, M., & Tyrvainen, P. (2012). Current software-as-a-Service Business models: Evidence from Finland. *International Conference of Software Business*, Berlin, Germany. 10.1007/978-3-642-30746-1_15

Madisha, M., & Van Belle, J. P. (2012). Factors Influencing SaaS adoption by small South African organisations. *Conference on World Wide Web Applications*, Durban, South Africa.

Magoules, F., Pan, J., & Teng, F. (2012). *Cloud Computing data-Intensive computing and scheduling*. CRC Press.

Manguic, D. M. (2012). Cloud Identity and Access Management–A model proposal. Proceedings of the *7th International Conference Accounting and management information systems AMIS*.

Marston, S., Li, Z., Bandyopadhyay, S., Zhang, J., & Ghalsasi, A. (2011). Cloud computing— The business perspective. *Decision Support Systems*, *51*(1), 176–189.

Masenya, T. M. (2020). Cloud Computing as a Strategy for Preservation of Digital Resources in Academic Libraries in South Africa. In Research Anthology on Collaboration, and Resource Management for the Sustainability of Libraries. IGI Global. doi:10.4018/978-1-7998-2527-2.ch006

Maserumule, M. D. (2019). The adoption of cloud-based Software as a Service (SaaS): a descriptive and empirical study of South African SMEs [Research Report]. University of the Witwatersrand, Johannesburg, South Africa.

Masiyev, K. H., Qasymov, I., Bakhishova, V., & Bahri, M. (2012). Cloud computing for business. *6th International Conference on Application of Information and Communication Technologies (AICT)*, Tbilisi, Georgia.

Mazrekaj, A., Shabani, I., & Sejdiu, B. (2016). Pricing schemes in cloud computing: An vverview. *International Journal of Advanced Computer Science and Applications*, *7*(2), 80–86. doi:10.14569/IJACSA.2016.070211

Mazumdar, A., & Alharahsheh, H. (2019). Insights of Trends and Developments in Cloud Computing. *South Asian Research Journal of Engineering and Technology*, *3*(1), 98–107. doi:10.36346arjet.2019.v01i03.003

Mell, P., & Grance, T. (2011). *The NIST Definition of Cloud Computing*. Retrieved 10/08/2017, from https://csrc.nist.gov/publications/detail/sp/800-145/final

Miemoukanda, M. (2020). *South Africa Public Cloud Market 2019 Analysis and 2020–2024 Forecast*. Retrieved 18/11/2020, from https://www.idc.com/getdoc.jsp?containerId=META46871520

Mohlameane, M., & Ruxwana, N. (2020). Exploring the impact of cloud computing on existing South African regulatory frameworks. *South African Journal of Information Management, 22*(1), 1–9. doi:10.4102ajim.v22i1.1132

Mokwena, S., & Hlebela, C. (2018). Factors affecting the adoption of software as a service in South African small medium enterprises. *2018 Open Innovations Conference*, Johannesburg, South Africa. 10.1109/OI.2018.8535714

Morris, M., Schindehutte, M., & Allen, J. (2005). The entrepreneur's business model: Towards a unified perspective. *Journal of Business Research, 58*(6), 726–735. doi:10.1016/j.jbusres.2003.11.001

Mvelase, P., Dlamini, Z., Macleod, D., Dlodlo, N., & Sithole, H. (2014). A business model for a South African government public cloud platform. *IST-Africa 2014 Conference Proceedings.*

Nunez, D., & Agudo, I. (2014). BlindIdM: A privacy preserving approach for identity management as a service. *International Journal of Information Security, 13*(2), 199–215. doi:10.100710207-014-0230-4

Osterwalder, A. (2004). The business model ontology a proposition in a design science approach. Academic Press.

Osterwalder, A., & Pigneur, Y. (2002). *An e-Business model ontology for modelling e-Business.* 15th Bled Electronic Commerce Conference e-Reality: Constructing the e-Economy, Bled, Slovenia.

Osterwalder, A., & Pigneur, Y. (2010). *Business model generation.* John Wiley & Sons.

Osterwalder, A., Pigneur, Y., & Tucci, L. C. (2005). Clarifying business models: Origins, present, and future of the concept. *Communications of the Association for Information Systems, 16*, 1–25. doi:10.17705/1CAIS.01601

Pateli, A. G., & Giaglis, G. M. (2004). A research framework for analysing e-business models. *European Journal of Information Systems, 13*(4), 302–314. doi:10.1057/palgrave.ejis.3000513

Petrovic, O., Kittl, C., & Teksen, R. D. (2001). Developing business models for ebusiness *International Conference of Electronic Commerce*, Vienna. Austria.

Richardson, J. (2008). The business model: An integrative framework for strategy execution. *Strategic Change, 17*(5-6), 133–144. doi:10.1002/jsc.821

Schaffer, N., Drieschner, C., & Krcmar, H. (2020). *An Analysis of Business Model Component Interrelations.* Twenty-Fourth Pacific Asia Conference on Information Systems, Dubai, UAE.

Schay, W. M. (2018). *Adoption of ERP software as a service by franchisees in South Africa* [Research report]. Academic Press.

Seres, L., Pavlicevic, V., & Tumbas, P. (2018). *Digital transformation in Higher Education competing on analytics.* 12th International Technology, *Education and Development Conference*, Valencia, Spain.

Sharmaa, D. H., Dhoteb, C. A., & Poteyc, M. M. (2016). Identity and cacess management as security-as-a-service from Clouds. *Procedia Computer Science, 79*, 170–174. doi:10.1016/j.procs.2016.03.117

Soni, M., Naamjoshi, J., & Pillai, S. (2017). Robustness and oppurtuneness based approach for cloud deployment model selection. *International Conference on Advances in Computing, Communications and Informatics (ICACCI)*, Mysore, India.

Stähler, P. (2002). *Business models as a unit of analysis for strategizing*. Retrieved 10/05/2014, from http://www.hec.unil.ch/aosterwa/Documents/workshop/Draft_Staehler.pdf

Subashini, S., & Kavitha, V. (2010). A survey on security issues in service delivery models of cloud computing. *Journal of Network and Computer Applications, 31*, 1–11.

Sunyaev, A. (2020). Cloud Computing. In Internet Computing. Springer.

Suresh, V., Raju, P. S. G., Sri, A. J., Nikhil, S. A. S. R., & Naresh, B. (2017). Sensor cloud to monitor cold chain logistics using Internet of Things (IoT). *International Journal of Innovative Science and Research Technology, 2*(6).

Taran, Y., Rene, C. G., & Boer, H. (2015). *Managing business model innovation risks - lessons for theory and practice*. 16th International CINet conference on Pursuing Innovation Leadership, Stockholm, Sweden.

Teece, D. J. (2010). Business models, business strategy and innovation. *Long Range Planning, 43*(2-3), 172–194. doi:10.1016/j.lrp.2009.07.003

Vaudour, F., & Heinze, A. (2020). Software as a service: Lessons from the video game industry. *Global Business and Organizational Excellence, 39*(2), 31–40. doi:10.1002/joe.21982

Vo, T. H., Fuhrmann, W., & Fischer-Hellmann, K. P. (2018). Privacy-preserving user identity in Identity-as-a-Service. *21st Conference on Innovation in Clouds, Internet and Networks and Workshops (ICIN).*

Wang, P. (2021). Connecting the parts with the whole: Toward an information ecology theory of digital innovation ecosystems. *Management Information Systems Quarterly, 45*(1).

Weinhardt, C., Anandasivam, W. A., Blau, B., Borissov, N., Meinl, T., Michalk, W. B., & Stober, J. (2009). Cloud Computing – A classification, business models, and research directions. *Business & Information Systems Engineering, 1*(5), 391–399. doi:10.100712599-009-0071-2

Xiang, Y., Rieger, S., & Richter, H. (2010). *Introducing a dynamic federation model for RESTful cloud storage*. First International Conference on Cloud Computing, GRIDs, and Virtualization, Lisbon, Portugal.

Xiao, X., & Hedman, J. (2019). How a software vendor weathered the stormy journey to the cloud. *MIS Quarterly Executive, 18*(1), 37–50. doi:10.17705/2msqe.00007

Xiao, X., Sarker, S., Wright, R. T., Sarker, S., & Mariadoss, B. J. (2020). Commitment and replacement of existing SaaS delivered applications: A mixed method investigation. *MIS Quarterly, 44*(4), 1811-1857.

Yildiz, O. (2021). Changing Paradigms in the Digital Age and Entrepreneurial Universities. In *University-Industry Collaboration Strategies in the Digital Era* (pp. 1–21). IGI Global. doi:10.4018/978-1-7998-3901-9.ch001

## ADDITIONAL READING

Abolhassan, F. (2017). Pursuing digital transformation driven by the Cloud. In F. Abolhassan (Ed.), *The drivers of digital transformation: Why there's no way around the cloud*. Springer Nature. doi:10.1007/978-3-319-31824-0_1

Bouwman, H., Heikkilä, J., Heikkilä, M., Leopold, C., & Haaker, T. (2018). Achieving agility using business model stress testing. *Electronic Markets*, *28*(2), 149–162. doi:10.100712525-016-0243-0

Floerecke, S., & Lehner, F. (2019). The Unequal Battle for Market Shares in the Infrastructure-as-a-Service Segment: Success-Driving Business Model Characteristics of Regional Providers in Competition with the Hyperscalers. *HMD*, *56*(6), 1334–1354. doi:10.136540702-019-00549-y

## KEY TERMS AND DEFINITIONS

**Business Model:** A dynamic set of interrelated set of components that articulate how a business makes money, creates, and captures value in serving the target customer, taking into account key activities, resources and partnerships as well as the value exchanges between the company and its partners.

**Cloud Computing:** Delivery of both hardware and software services on-demand to customers over the internet independent of device and location.

**Digital Transformation:** Application of innovative digital technology to fundamentally how the business operates, and the way technology is delivered to support the overall business.

**Identity as a Service (IDaaS):** Cloud-based identity solution to manage cloud computing customers' identities enabling cloud computing to manage their identities centrally.

**Infrastructure as a Service (IaaS):** Provision, processing, storage, networks, and other fundamental computing resources where the service provider controls the underlying infrastructure.

**Platform as a Service (PaaS):** Offers a computing platform and solution stack as services enabling the consumer to deploy applications without the cost and complexity of buying and managing the hardware and underlying software layers.

**Software as a Service (SaaS):** Provider licences an application to the customer for use as a service on-demand offering consumers benefits such as operational efficiency and reduced cost.

# Section 3

# Digitalization and Internationalization Policies

# Chapter 7
# Inequalities in Access to and Outcomes of Higher Education in Africa

**Roy Alexander Carr-Hill**
*Institute of Education, University College London, UK*

## ABSTRACT

*There have been very few studies of the socio-economic background and outcomes for students in Africa because of the lack of data. This chapter draws on an institute which has information about their parental background and subsequent careers collected from surveys. In terms of access, the combination of parents not having more than primary education, renting and not owning land identified less than 1% of students whilst the percentage of entrants reporting that their parents had a post-secondary qualification is considerably higher (around 57%) than the norm at the time the parents would have been studying (around 7%). These students were upper middle class. In terms of outcomes, both current students and alumni say that the curriculum only partly fits their employment needs, but 85% of alumni would recommend AIMS to other students. In general, employers are satisfied with AIMS interns, but the percentage of AIMS graduates who are unemployed has risen from 2% in 2011 to 29% in 2016. Finally, rather than contributing to Africa, over one-third of graduates since 2012 are in the West.*

## 1 INTRODUCTION AND BACKGROUND

The new agenda for Africa, while giving priority to the challenges of sustainable development, should include promoting growth through improved rural development, increased sustainable manufacturing and having a far greater value-added input in the extractive industries.

Higher education can contribute towards these goals by producing skilled and employable graduates in the relevant fields. Tertiary education is an important element in national economic performance and a major determinant of a person´s life chances (Barr 2005). Higher education is booming in Sub-Saharan Africa. No longer only a consumption good enjoyed by a narrow elite, but it is recognised that there remain substantial inequalities. The brief review in $2, however, demonstrates that there is very little

DOI: 10.4018/978-1-7998-8169-8.ch007

hard data on those inequalities, which is the rationale for focusing on a pan-African institution which does collect such detailed data.

At the same time, there are several issues about the relationship between tertiary education and the labour market: what kind of skills and training should Higher Education Institutions be providing

In particular, although an emerging problem elsewhere in the world, the rate of growth of unemployed graduates is escalating at a rapid pace in Africa. In Nigeria, where the government recently declared itself to have Africa's biggest economy, nearly a quarter of graduates are unemployed. There are a number of causal factors that contribute to the accentuation of the problem; chief among these being the collapse of structured pathways from education and training into work in key areas of employment. These issues are reviewed in more detail in $3.

## 2 INEQUALITIES IN ACCESS TO HIGHER EDUCATION IN AFRICA

There are questions about whether widening participation in higher education is a force for differentiation or democratization (Ball 1998, David 2007). Initiatives that are promoted as a form of meritocratic equalisation can also be seen as reinforcement of existing social stratification processes. Between 2000 and 2010, moreover, enrolment in higher education in SSA more than doubled, increasing from 2.3 million to 5.2 million (UIS, 2011. However, whilst globally these figures meant an enrolment rate of 24 per cent; in Sub-Saharan Africa the figure was only 5 percent (UNESCO 2012, pp.126-9), and that figure was dominated (61%) by enrolments in Nigeria and South Africa. In 2014, global enrolment in higher education was 34.5% and 8.6% in sub-Saharan Africa. But educational expansion may simply magnify inequalities by expanding opportunities disproportionately for those who are already privileged, rather than reducing inequalities by providing more opportunities for persons from disadvantaged strata (Shavit et al. 2007:1). As Cloete (2005) said, 'Apart from the experience of a few countries such as Finland, Norway and the Netherlands, massification leads to differentiated systems. For example, as the US, UK and Australian systems massified, up to 50% of the age cohort entered higher education, but they entered into a large range of institutions in terms of mission and prestige.'

The relationship between higher education and wealth creation &/or poverty reduction can be seen in terms of micro levels of benefit streams (the premium for the individual for each additional year of schooling which tends to be higher with higher levels of schooling); or in terms of the increased potential opportunities for those with higher education. Because of the fees that need to be paid, contrary to Unterhalter and Oketch (2017), higher education is nearly always excludable in Africa; but there are some exceptions and the institution examined here is one such where all direct costs (travel, course fees, board and lodging and pocket money) are paid, although of course there may well be opportunity costs to the student and/or her/his parents.

McCowan (2014) comments that university is still for the privileged few in Sub-Saharan Africa, but does not give any data by parental wealth or similar. Nevertheless, whilst assuming that students from wealthier families attend better quality universities, the ratio of the numbers of entrants from wealthier to whose from poorer families may have reduced, simply because the numbers enrolled have increased very dramatically. Such a trend, would parallel the reduction in formal socio-economic disparities with widening participation in overall access to higher education in developed countries. Moreover, Higher Education has become heavily affected by neo-liberal globalisation pushing equity issues into the shadows (Ntshoe, 2003).

Overall, however, the major issue is the lack of any detailed data on student entrants and that is the rationale for focusing in S4 on a pan-African institution which does collect such detailed data

## 3 LABOUR MARKET ISSUES

### 3.1 Wrong Skills?

Too few graduates gain the skills they need to find work. Nowhere is this quality challenge more evident than the transition to the labour market. Graduate unemployment rates are high in many countries and employers across the region complain of a lack of basic, technical and transferable skills. Given the pressures for expansion outlined above, absorption of graduates into the labour market will be a significant undertaking. Preparing graduates for the workplace is the principal problem – and one that AIMS intends to tackle through:

- Broadening the learning experience for students to make them more employable -- through extra-curricular activities such as voluntary work.
- Providing better information for students about career opportunities, providing more chances for them to interact with employers, and introducing skills enhancement programmes in areas such as entrepreneurship and communication skills.

While there is increasing international evidence on the link between skills and productivity, firms in Africa generally do not rate skills as a top constraint. Self-reported shortages of skills tend to be higher in relatively capital-intensive industries. Skills also tend to become a constraint for high-performing firms: businesses that complain of a skills shortage consistently outperform those that do not (Barker and Mengistae, 2013). In addition to the limited availability of cognitive, soft, and technical skills among job seekers, a lack of "managerial capital" could also be constraining the competitiveness of African firms. There may be considerable scope for improving productivity (and hence raising employment) by investing in business and management skills training, and perhaps even in individualized management consulting. Several policy recommendations emerge from this evidence on the role of skills. They emphasize the need to focus on foundational skills and public goods such as quality assurance and information, the need for government to focus on building portable rather than job-specific skills, the need for special support to enable poor and disadvantaged groups to acquire skills, the need to develop international linkages, and the need for systems that link employers with trainers.

### 3.2 Need for Skilled Manpower

There is a close relationship between a country's economic growth and its proportion of skilled manpower, and human capital development is a major strategy used for national development. All the indicators show that there is an acute shortage of appropriately trained manpower in Africa and this could hamper its economic and social development at this crucial stage when the continent has emerged from a long period of turmoil and economic stagnation. The current tertiary enrolment in Africa (around 7%) is by far the lowest in any other world region (Ref: and more analysis in Annex). Africa has experienced laudable and consistent economic growth and development over the past decade which, for it to be sustained, would require more skilled manpower, especially in areas of science and technology. African countries therefore have a responsibility to continue to increase their tertiary enrolment to be at par with other developing countries.

However, this expansion must be cautiously planned, taking into account economic and social factors. In almost all African countries unemployment is high. Africa has the world's youngest population, which is expected to increase, and nearly 60% of its unemployed are aged between 15 and 24 (Ref), a significant number of whom are graduates. It is clear, then, that merely increasing tertiary enrolment – and thus the number of graduates – will not be sufficient to have a positive impact on growth. Graduate employment and employability must be considered.

## 3.3 Country Examples of Graduate (Un) Employment

At the same time, high-skilled non-routine cognitive jobs have been increasing steadily, making up more than 18 per cent of total employment. These trends are set to continue, although with significant regional variations (see figure 1.9, panel B). Medium-skill jobs are declining in advanced economies, partly replaced by low-skilled occupations, while they remain stable as a share of the global economy. The share of high-skilled occupations varies widely, ranging from less than 10 per cent in Sub-Saharan Africa to almost 40 per cent in developed economies (ILOo, World Employment and Social Outlook, p.23).

Africa's graduate unemployment is 16 per cent in low income countries and 46 per cent in middle income countries. [26]. The Economist magazine has reported that in South Africa there were more than 800,000 private sector vacancies in 2012. [13] Remarkably, in the same year, 600,000 university graduates were unemployed and had difficulties finding any job. Similar stories can be found all over Africa. The Economist explains this apparent paradox as reflecting the mismatch between skills acquired at university and those needed in jobs.

The key to successfully reforming graduate training is addressing both Africa's challenges as a whole and the local labour market's specific needs. This will involve making critical thinking and employability skills an integral part of learning and teaching, providing courses linked to industry needs and introducing quality assurance schemes. If they can do this, universities will be at the forefront of Africa's transformation. The 'USEM' model proposed by Knight and Yorke to describe the skills graduates need to increase their employability: [24]

- U: Deep Understanding: specialised expertise their chosen field.
- S: Skilful practice in: communication, management of time, self and resources, problem-solving and lifelong learning.
- E: Efficacious beliefs: about personal identity, self-worth and personal qualities. These help students feels they can 'make a difference'.
- M: Metacognition: 'knowing about knowing' — self-awareness about learning and the capacity to reflect on their actions.

World Bank: graduate unemployment in Africa

## 3.4 Tackling Factors Affecting Employment and Employability

For any higher education institution (HEI), the factors affecting graduate employment and employability can be grouped into three categories: exogenous factors related to the absorptive capacity of the country for its graduates; endogenous factors associated with the institution's efforts to ensure the employability of its graduates; and factors linking the exogenous and endogenous factors – in other words linking employment and employability. Some of the issues surrounding these factors are considered below.

### Engaging with Development Challenges

HEIs in Africa have a responsibility to ensure that students are sensitised to the continent's myriad development challenges, and that graduates not only find meaningful employment according to their skills, but are also equipped to create an informed and engaged citizenry – one that promotes sustainable development, multicultural understanding, tolerance and peace.

Over 60% of the population of sub-Saharan Africa, for example, live in rural areas where poverty is extreme. Agriculture is the main rural activity in these areas. Unfortunately, the agricultural departments in most HEIs focus on production agriculture – mainly crop and animal production; very few deal with the problems of rural development and food security. This emphasis on rural development should be mainstreamed in all areas of higher education. At present, most of the curricula in the professional areas, such as engineering and health, are geared towards work in an urban environment. It is not surprising, therefore, that few graduates are prepared to practice in rural areas. Engineering students, for example, should be made aware of rural technological traditions and innovations; medical students should be familiarised with traditional medicine and trained to practice in environments where advanced equipment is not available.

Africa's economic and technological development requires graduates not only from universities but also from other post-secondary institutions – technical colleges, professional schools, and so on. In fact, graduates of these institutions are often more employable than those from universities. Unfortunately, in order to meet the increasing demand for higher education, existing post-secondary institutions are converted into universities. The need for differentiation in higher education systems, accompanied by a valorisation of technical and vocational education, is crucial for Africa's growth. But sustained growth in Africa can only take place through an increase in the provision of skilled manpower, but it must be ensured that this manpower is productively employed.

### Role of the Private Sector

The private sector now offers greater opportunities for employment than the public sector and is the main beneficiary. The private sector should fund higher education as part of its social responsibility and governments should provide appropriate financial incentives. The private sector can also contribute by providing company-based training to new graduates to enhance their business skills and provide them with valuable work experience. Although a particular company may not employ all the trainees, the experience will greatly help the graduates in becoming more employable. To encourage such schemes, government should provide support and incentives.

## 3.5 What Should HEIs Provide?

Institutions must be responsive to labour market demands and provide the necessary competencies and skills to their students; and of course AIMS is trying to do that.

National manpower planning data is rarely up-to-date. Feedback from employers and from alumni tracer studies can be more useful. Indeed, it is often the number of applications received for a programme that signals its relevance –particularly true for private HEIs.

Besides the relevance of an institution's programmes, quality is also a key factor in employability. African higher education institutions are still in the process of assuring the quality of their programmes and, as a result, graduates from abroad tend to be favoured for employment.

Moreover, graduates need other attributes and competencies often referred to as 'soft' skills – indeed many employers place greater importance on soft skills than on qualifications. These skills include communication skills, analytical and problem-solving skills, and adaptability. It is important, then, for HEIs to embed these skills in their curricula. Extra-curricular activities – such as participation in sports, debating, student union activities, and community services also enhance graduates' soft skills; and, of course AIMS has done all of that.

Similarly, where opportunities for employment are limited, training students to become entrepreneurs can be very useful to the economy, especially as graduates then become job providers rather than job seekers. HEIs should integrate entrepreneurship training in their programmes or mount special entrepreneurship courses.

As well as the provision of skills, HEIs should assist students in their job-seeking activities through dedicated units. Such a unit could assist students in preparing applications for jobs, offer guidance about possible careers and in interview technique, and arrange job fairs to bring potential employers to the campus. The same unit could provide support to the institution's alumni association, through which the employment situation of graduates could be gauged.

Two further important issues need to be considered in relation to employability. First, graduates can no longer expect to be employed in just one sector throughout their professional life. They will need to be provided with skills that enable them to adapt to different situations as they move from one job to another. Second, students need to be made aware that they will operate in an increasingly globalised world. They will need to learn to take full advantage of the opportunities offered by globalisation, as well as be aware of its potentially negative consequences.

## 3.6 Higher Education and Business/Industry

Links between universities and business/industry can be enormously helpful in facilitating graduate employability, although the industrial sector in most African countries is not fully developed. Indeed, currently the main industries are mining and mineral extraction which, at present, offer few graduate employment opportunities as the resources are exported mostly unrefined. There is an urgent need in Africa to ensure more value-added to the resources and also to develop the manufacturing sector which will create employment.

In Section 5, we examine how successful AIMS has been in building these links and in placing their graduates into jobs

## 4. STUDENTS AT AIMS CENTRES

### 4.1 Background

AIMS, founded in 2003 in Cape Town, South Africa, is a pan-African network for one-year postgraduate education and research in mathematical sciences. Building on the success of its first centre in Cape Town, AIMS launched the Next Einstein Initiative (NEI) in 2008 to build a critical mass of scientific and technical talent in Africa, capable of driving economic, scientific and social advancement across the continent. Five new centres were established in Senegal (2011), Ghana (2012), Cameroon (2013), Tanzania (2014), and Rwanda (2016).

Applicants must be a national from an African country and have a four-year university degree in mathematics, physics, computer science, engineering, business or other scientific fields, but with a substantial mathematics component. Evaluating the applications relies on assessing their grade records from their undergraduate degrees. The number of applications has grown from 1,400 in 2013 to 2,500 in 2017 but, as the number of centres and places has increased, the percentage of applicants who are accepted has only dropped from 10% to 8%. It can be seen that the programme has become increasingly popular and, despite the expansion of the programme, increasingly competitive. This is especially important for female applicants as AIMS has set a target of a minimum of 1/3rd of successful entrants being female. Successful applicants receive a return flight ticket, free board and lodging, free tuition and a small amount of 'pocket money'.

### 4.2 Socio-Economic Status and Heterogeneity of Student Body

As mentioned above, admission of students is carried out primarily on the basis of merit, but there are other criteria. The entire student body at a centre during an academic year should have a minimum of 1/3rd women and 1/3rd of students coming from the home country, which is in line with the intended acceptance principles of AIMS. No particular attention is paid to socio-economic background or to minority groups (besides women who are positively discriminated as 16%-19% of the applicants are women).

*"Ensuring that an inability to pay is not a barrier to enrolling on the AIMS Masters program." (http://applications.nexteinstein.org/?application_type=Masters+Intake)*

On several occasions in our interviews with senior stakeholders in the organisation, we raised the issue of the rationale and viability of the *fully* funded model; the response almost invariably was that this was the only way in which "poor" African students could access Higher Education. We entirely agree that, even if access to the course were free, living costs would almost certainly inhibit and, in most cases, prevent poorer students from accessing Higher Education; but we thought that the presumption that the majority of students coming to AIMS are poor is misplaced.

In fact, this question could be addressed using the responses of successful applicants to questions in the Pre-Assessment form, which students complete on arrival at their centre, as to the most educated of their parents, whether or not the house they had lived in was owned or rented, whether or not the household owned any land, and their (previous) household income.

## Low Income

The obvious marker of poverty was the question about their monthly income (with the exception of the 2014-15 database, when the question referred to Household monthly income, which was probably what was intended in the other years). Unfortunately, the wording of the question varied across the years and, more importantly, the lowest response category is 'below US$501' and it can be seen (Table 1) that, with the exception of 2014-15, over 75% of responses are less than US$501 (although successful female applicant are more likely to report being in the 'more than US$500 bracket').

*Table 1. Housedhold monthly income*

| | | | | *Less than US$ 501* | | *More than US$500* | |
|---|---|---|---|---|---|---|---|
| | *Valid Replies* | *M* | *F* | *N* | *%* | *M* | *F* |
| *2013-14* | *63* | *49* | *14* | *52* | *83* | *16%* | *21%* |
| *2014-15* | *172* | *123* | *49* | *113* | *66* | *31%* | *43%* |
| *2015-16* | *161* | *103* | *58* | *121* | *75* | *20%* | *33%* |
| *2016-17* | *133* | *123* | *10* | *115* | *86* | *13%* | *20%* |

FOOTNOTE For the 2014-15 row in Table N1, it is more complicated because the question referred to household rather than individual income, so we have to assume a household size. An average of 3 has been taken for these students (either because they are living with partner, or because the parental household they are in, no longer has young children). Using these estimates, very few responses should have been below US$501

Breakdowns have also been computed by nationality and AIMS Centre but the numbers are so small, that there is nothing important to say other than that women were more likely to be from households in the higher income bracket than men in every year, Across all four years, given that the standard error of the difference is 5.1%, the difference between the 34.4% for women and the 21.4% for men is statistically significant.

The fact that more than two-thirds are in the lowest income bracket each year does not mean that they are 'poor'; because for all of the Centre countries except South Africa, the monthly per capita income in 2016 was between US$160 and US$360 per month so that it is not surprising that in response to the questions in 2013-14, 2015-16 and 2016-17, the majority of valid responses were below US$501. The majority would have been well above the absolute poverty line of $2 a day and many would have been above the average monthly per capita income in their country.

*Source:* https://data.worldbank.org/indicator/NY.GDP.PCAP.PP.CD *(accessed 08/07/2017)*

## Non-Income Poverty of Students in the Pre-Assessment Files

Given the ambiguity of the income variable, we have examined the non-income questions that were asked in the Pre-Assessment form, viz. the education attainment of parent or respected relative of the student, whether or not their family owned or rented the house they were living in (Roy and Chaudhuri, 2008); and whether or not the family owned any land (Maeshti, 2013). Since neither of the latter two questions were further specified (unless the respondent answered 'Other') it is not possible to know whether the house was large or small or whether the land owned was small or extensive. Except when constructing a sort of index of non-income poverty (see below), we have therefore finally relied on the Educational Attainment variable (Nachinaab et al., 2019).

### *''Poverty' or 'Wealth' of Parental/ Relatives Households*

Students had come from between 29 and 34 countries, depending on the year. Although we understood the importance of distinguishing between country of origin in terms of the prevalence and meaning of non-income poverty variables, we have restricted the breakdowns below to the 6 AIMS Centre countries; plus Kenya, Nigeria and Sudan, which were the most likely among other countries to be sending students, versus the other African countries sendng students to one of the Centres.

*Table 2. Percent parents or relative/ spouse with no formal schooling or only primary education; owning or renting a house; owning land or not*

| | 2013-14 | | 2015-16 | | 2016-17 | |
|---|---|---|---|---|---|---|
| *Parents/Relatives with No Formal Schooling or at most Primary* | | | | | | |
| Nine Countries | 12/75 | 16% | 29/134 | 22% | 59/195 | 30% |
| Other Countries | 9/49 | 18% | 12/55 | 22% | 15/81 | 19% |
| Total | 21/122 | 16% | 41/189 | 22% | 74/276 | 27% |
| *Parents/Relatives House Owners* | | | | | | |
| Nine Countries | 62/78 | 79% | 89/128 | 70% | 133/191 | 70% |
| Other Countries | 35/50 | 70% | 39/68 | 57% | 51/85 | 60% |
| Total | 97/128 | 76% | 128/196 | 65% | 184/276 | 67% |
| *Parents/ Relatives Land Owners* | 2013-14 | | 2015-16 | | 2016-17 | |
| Nine Countries | 56/80 | 70% | 86/136 | 63% | 125/196 | 64% |
| Other Countries | 34/51 | 67% | 32/59 | 54% | 55/74 | 74% |
| Total | 90/131 | 69% | 118/195 | 61% | 180/270 | 67% |

We constructeda very loose interpretation of a poor household:

(a) where the graduate's parents had only completed at most primary education. If we estimate an average 'generation gap' in most African countries of about 20 years and recall that, 20 years previously in 1997, the percentages with 'no schooling' or 'no schooling or incomplete primary' were considerably higher than now (compare GMR, 2005 and GMR 2017);
(b) are renting but don't own their house (but have somewhere to live) and
(c) don't own any land (why should they?).

With this 'definition' only 1 (one) out of 132 in 2013-14, 2 (two) out of 197 in 2015-16 and 3 (three) out of 296 in 2016-17 cohort are 'poor' (less than 1%). It didn't seem worthwhile to break these figures down between countries! Note that this is nowhere near the World Bank level of poverty where the person or the family will be living in precarious or vulnerable housing if any at all.

## Educational Attainment of Parents/ Relatives

We therefore looked at the opposite extreme: which of these student candidates had a relatively - non-income - but well-off – parental background, using the information on the educational attainment of their Parents or Guardians.

*Table 3. Parent or guardian with post-secondary education or more (from AIMS questionnaires)*

| | 2013-14 | | 2015-16 | | 2016-17 | | Across Three Years | |
|---|---|---|---|---|---|---|---|---|
| Nine Countries | 44/81 | 54% | 68/137 | 50% | 90/196 | 46% | 202/414 | 49% |
| Other Countries | 30/41 | 73% | 31/52 | 60% | 51/80 | 64% | 112/173 | 65% |
| Total | 74/122 | 61% | 99/189 | 52% | 141/276 | 51% | 315/587 | 54% |

We have to compare these with data on when these parents would have completed their secondary education and could potentially have been going to university or another course. As before, we estimate an average 'generation gap' in most African countries of about 20 years and have used data on tertiary education in 1998 - i.e. 20 years ago.

For comparison, the numbers in post-secondary non-tertiary, where reported in the GMR, were always considerably less than the numbers in tertiary at the time (20 years ago); but there would have been several people who added on a certificate/ diploma to their secondary education later on in life (to get a better job), so it is not clear what the correct estimate would be. In Table 4, we see that where there are estimates from both sources, those from DHS tend to be higher.

*Table 4. National estimates of post-secondary education in 1998*

| Estimates c. 1998 of Tertiary or 'More than Secondary'▼ | Country ▶ | Cameroon | Ghana | Kenya | Nigeria | Rwanda | Senegal | South Africa | Sudan | Tanzania |
|---|---|---|---|---|---|---|---|---|---|---|
| GER Tertiary around 1998 | | 5.1 | Est'd 5.0 | Est'd 7.0 | | 0.8 | 3.7 | 15.3 | 6.8 | 0.6 |
| DHS estimate for 'More than Secondary' (from Table N4) | | 7.6 | n.a | 0.2 | 15.9 | 2.5 | 5.0 | 11.1 | n.a. | n.a. |

Source for Row 1: UNESCO, Global Monitoring Report on Education for All for 2005 (includes figures for 1998).

Sources for Row2, all from DHS country reports: Cameroon 1998, Table 2.5.2; 2011, Table 2.11.12; Ghana 1998, Table 2.10; 2014, Table 2.12.2; Kenya: 1998, Table 2.5; Nigeria 1999, Table 2.5; Rwanda: 2000, Table 3.2.2; Senegal 2005, Table 2,4.1; 2016, Table 3.2.2; South Africa: Tanzania: 1999, table 2.5.2.

Comparing these figures with those in Table 3 it is clear that the percentage of entrants reporting that their parents had a post-Secondary qualification is considerably higher (around 54% on average) than the norm at the time the parents would have been studying (around 7% on average). These entrants are not poor; they are (upper) middle class.

### Breakdowns by Nationality and Centre

Breakdowns of the parents' educational qualifications according to own nationality and nationality of centre where they studied at have been carried out both across all four years of available data and for each year of available Pre-Assessment data. There are differences between Anglophones and Francophones in both breakdowns when all four years are considered together; and there are also some interesting trends across the four years.

## All Four Years Together

In both breakdowns, about 32% of both Anglophones and Francophones have a Bachelor or Post-Graduate qualification; about 24% of Anglophones have a post-secondary qualification (but not bachelor) compared to 12% of Francophones; for Anglophones about the same percentage (17%) have been to each of primary or secondary, whilst for Francophones 22% have been to secondary and 26% to Primary. There was clearly a difference for the parents in the availability of non-degree post-secondary qualification from Francophone centres or in the motivations of those of Francophone nationality to obtain them, as compared to Anglophones (whether by centre or nationality), which reflects the higher reported percentages of Francophone parents only having completed secondary (or primary) level.

*Table 5. Educational attainment of parents/ guardians (all four years of data)*

| | | Bachelor or PG | Post Sec Qualific | Secondary | Primary | Other | Missing | 100% |
|---|---|---|---|---|---|---|---|---|
| Nationality Phonic | Anglo | 32% (130) | 26% (105) | 18% (75) | 17% (68) | 2% (9) | 5% (19) | 406 |
| | Franco | 30% (93) | 11% (35) | 23% (71) | 26% (82) | 4% (12) | 6% (18) | 311 |
| Centre Country | Anglo | 34% (165) | 21% (102) | 17% (83) | 17% (82) | 2% (12) | 8% (39) | 483 |
| | Franco | 31% (120) | 13% (51) | 20% (79) | 25% (98) | 3% (12) | 8% (30) | 390 |

## Across the Four Years

The percentage reporting that their parents had a Bachelor or Post-Graduate degree was slightly higher for both Anglophones and those studying at an Anglophone Centre (around 39%) than for Francophones or those studying at a Francophone Centre (36%) in the first two years of data (2013-14 and 2014-15), compared to the second two years of data (2015-16 and 2016-17) when they were about the same. In contrast, the percentages reporting that their parents only had Secondary or at most Primary, has increased for Anglophones by nationality from an average of 15% to 20% and for Francophones by both nationality and Centre from 21% to 25%.

Given that the proportion of applicants who are accepted to AIMS centres has been more or less stable, together these trends suggest that the reviewers of those applications have become more egalitarian.

## 5 AIMS AND THE LABOUR MARKET

Most of this section is extracted from an evaluation carried out by the author of AIMS. Some of the material comes from a set of surveys

*Survey of Current Students*: An invitation to complete an online survey was sent to 255 students from the six centres. The response rate was 74% with 189 students replying. Figure 6 indicates the percentage of male and female responding by centre.

The purpose of the survey was to obtain information about the students' background, the application process, and students' experience with the program, their views of the courses and modules, the assessment process and their ambitions for the future.

*Alumni Survey* An invitation to complete an online survey was sent to 261 alumni from all centres except Rwanda, which was excluded because they have only been operating since 2016. The response rate was 63% with 164 (29% female, 71% male) completing the survey.

The survey focused on the same questions as were included in the student online survey, plus several questions regarding the search for employment and post-graduate situation.

*University and Employer Survey* This survey collected information on the employers' satisfaction with AIMS graduate(s) quality of work, comparison with other employees recruited elsewhere and their perception of AIMS. The following were invited to participate

- 31 employers
- 23 universities
- 8 companies who had given permission to be contacted

The response rate was 26% with 16 responses thereby being more anecdotal evidence rather than representative.

### 5.1 Increased Demand and Interest in Mathematical Sciences

AIMS intends not only to fill the existing demand for mathematical sciences training, but also to create new demand and enthusiasm among young Africans. The evidence suggests that this is indeed occurring, although it is difficult to attribute it to AIMS itself.

The number of applications submitted to AIMS has grown hugely along with the opening of new centres. There were 607 applications in 2013, climbing to 3,109 in 2016. This could indicate that demand and interest in mathematical sciences has increased, or it could simply mean that AIMS has become more visible or that the opening of centres in different parts of the continent makes AIMS accessible to a larger number of prospective students. Targets were met and surpassed in 2015 and 2016. With the development of new centres, the number of applications will likely continue to increase. Applications from women have shown a small but steady growth, starting at 16% in 2013 and rising to 19% in 2016. The number of female applicants surpassed the target, but because of the large number of male applicants, the proportion of females was below the target of 30%.

Another sign of increasing demand and interest is the rising number of attendees at AIMS-organized public lectures on the mathematical sciences. In 2015 there were 2,675 attendees, rising to 5,024 in 2016. These are impressive numbers, and well above the planned-for figures of 1,600 in 2015 and 1,800 in 2016. However, public lecture attendees are disproportionately distributed across the centres. In 2016,

Ghana had almost seven times as many attendees as planned for, South Africa had over three times as many as planned for, and Senegal had over twice as many as planned for. These are very impressive achievements. On the other hand, Ghana fell a bit short of its plan (127 attendees versus 200 planned for), and Tanzania had no attendees at all.

AIMS centres also organize teacher training courses on the mathematical sciences, and participation in these courses has been increasing, indicating rising interest in mathematical sciences: there were 237 participants in 2015, rising to 495 in 2016. Targets were met and surpassed in both years; in 2016, there were more than twice as many participants as planned for, an impressive achievement. Similar to the public lectures, however, participation in teacher training courses is unevenly distributed across the centres. All of the participants in 2016 were at just two of the centres (275 in South Africa and 220 in Ghana), both of which vastly surpassed their targets. However, Senegal, Cameroon, and Tanzania had no participants at all.

## 5.2 Employability of, and Employment Outcomes for, Graduates

This section assesses the extent to which AIMS students graduate with the necessary qualifications to succeed in business, government, academia, and civil society. This includes the actual skills/ knowledge that students have gained, as well as the perception of those skills/knowledge by potential employers and academic programs.

Between 2012 and 2017 (including those who graduated in July 2017) 1207 AIMS students graduated. Of these 67.7% are Male and 32.3% are Female. During the 2011-2016 period only 9 students dropped-out, mainly due to personal reasons and therefore a very large majority of AIMS students graduate. The total numbers of graduates per AIMS centre were 400 from South Africa, 252 from Senegal, 201 from Ghana, 170 from Cameroun, 140 from Tanzania and 44 from Rwanda.

*Acquisition of necessary skills*: most students and alumni indicate that they indeed gained each of the three kinds of skills that AIMS is intended to foster: mathematics, technology, and social/life skills. The centres are doing especially well on social skills. There is room for improvement on mathematics and technology: whilst Ghana and Rwanda are doing especially well on technology, there is significant room for improvement in Cameroon, Senegal, and South Africa, where around six in ten students feel they did not gain many technical skills, or none at all.

Another way to assess whether students gained the necessary skills is to conduct a blind expert review of the final research papers that students submitted. This was done for a small sample of papers (three papers randomly selected from each of the six centres) by a York University (Canada) mathematician. One paper was judged to be of excellent quality, three of good quality, ten of average quality, four of poor quality, and none of very poor quality. This suggests that most students graduate with the ability to produce a research paper of at least low-Master's-level quality. At the same time, it suggests that a significant minority of graduates are not able to produce a paper that would pass muster internationally. There should be an effort to raise the bar in this area.

Another area for improvement is the fit between the curriculum content and students' professional needs. The number of alumni who report that the curriculum did not fit their career aspirations is quite high. In Cameroon, South Africa, and Senegal, around half of alumni were of the opinion that the curriculum does not fit their future career aspirations. This mismatch is especially prevalent among female students: 52% of the female alumni say that the program was not much in line the work they envision themselves doing later, compared to only 35% of male alumni. On the other hand, in the online survey,

88% of students and alumni described the overall quality of AIMS as excellent (36%) or good (52%); 11% called it average. 65% said that the academic program had fully (20%) or largely (45%) met their expectations; 32% said somewhat and 8% said not at all. 84% were very satisfied (36%) or satisfied (48%) with the teaching and learning at AIMS; 11% were unsatisfied and 5% were very unsatisfied. 81% would fully or largely recommend AIMS to someone else. These are all fairly high levels of satisfaction.

*Alumni career trajectories*. According to the AIMS tracer study (averaged across years), the majority of graduates (63%) continue as students after they graduate from AIMS, while a smaller proportion (29%) enter employment. The percentage of unemployed graduates has, however, been increasing dramatically, from 2% in 2010 to 29% in 2016.

*Ability to be in successful in further graduate studies*: the target for the number of AIMS alumni who were in post-AIMS study programs six months after graduation was met and surpassed each year. A total number of 480 graduates have continued into a post-AIMS study program six months after graduation since 2003 (output 2.4). For the evaluation period 2010-2017 this is 386 or 31.9% of the total number of graduates for this period. In 2015, 21% of these alumni were women (falling short of the target of 30%), and in 2016 31% were women (meeting the target). The percentage hoping to be specifically in a PhD program has dropped from 74% in 2012-13 to 40% in 2016-17, partly, given the increasing competition for such places and partly the reduction in post-AIMS bursaries provided by the AIMS network itself from about 50% in 2012-13 to about 10% from 2014 onwards.

These graduates appear to be well qualified for success once they enter these further academic programs. Most university supervisors of AIMS graduates were very satisfied (39%) or satisfied (46%) with the overall performance of AIMS graduates. 54% mention that AIMS graduates perform on a similar level as graduates from other universities while 31% mention that they perform better than others. University lecturers overseeing Masters' students in Tanzania said the candidates were stronger technically (computer skills), better at articulating their viewpoints, and faster to adapt to the rigours of the program, despite starting at lower level of mathematical theory. This indicates that AIMS is equipping students with both the technical and the life skills necessary for success.

Graduates do, however, face challenges in seeking further graduate studies. The AIMS Master's degree is broader, less specialized, and harder to describe to outsiders than other Master's degrees, meaning that majority of students are only accepted into PhD programs if they begin again at the Master's level. The lack of summative examination makes it more difficult for admissions boards to assess graduates' skills. Degrees from the centres that are not yet fully accredited are less credible to admissions boards than degrees from the other centres; there are many hurdles to accreditation at the unaccredited centres, including the lack of a set curriculum and the lack of an exit examination. At the same time, nearly 30% of the 2016 graduates remained unemployed a year following graduation, a considerable increase from 5% in 2012. This percentage is higher than either the percentage in an academic position or in employment outside academia, even though both increased 11% to 21% and from 5% to 11% respectively.

*Ability to be successful in internships*: based on the AIMS monitoring reports (output 2.5), the target of 5% of AIMS alumni offered internships facilitated by AIMS was achieved, although the rate, excluding the Co-Op program in Senegal, where all students have an internship as part of the program, has stayed roughly constant at around 7% compared to the period (2010-2013) before the industry initiative. Although there is no systematically collected data on employer satisfaction with AIMS interns, anecdotal evidence suggests that AIMS alumni do tend to enter these internships with the skills required to succeed. Interviews with AIMS employers (in several countries and fields including finance, healthcare, and technology) were on the whole positive. In a few cases, the intern had to seek additional training before being able to effectively take up the internship; in one case, the company pre-trained a Co-Op student in Big Data; in another case, the company sent the student to a training course at the employer's expense.

Support towards attaining an internship is, in principle, facilitated by Student Development Officers (SDOs) at the centres. The coordination and recruitment of SDO's across the network has been and still is an ongoing effort and challenge. As the July –December 2016 report mentions: "it has proved very difficult to appoint suitably qualified SDO's". About a quarter of the 2016 alumni reported that they had received assistance from SDOs in preparing resumes and interview skills. 17% had received help from someone else in the centre, such as the Academic Director or international lecturers; in some cases, these individuals gave students jobs. There were varying levels of satisfaction with SDOs' services, ranging from 75% good/satisfactory in Ghana to 52% good/satisfactory in South Africa and Tanzania.

*Ability to be successful in permanent employment that uses AIMS training*. There have been challenges meeting targets for the number of graduates employed in positions using AIMS training six months after graduation. The numbers have lagged significantly behind targets for both men and women each year for which data was available (2014, 2015, and 2016). The situation is no worse for female graduates than male graduates, however, with about 30% of employed graduates being female (similar to their representation among AIMS alumni as a whole). Of those working in the public sector (first engagement of graduates from 2011-2016), 3 were in senior positions and 21 in junior positions. Of those in the private sector, 14 were in senior positions and 35 in junior positions. Of the graduates that are (self) employed, 31% work in the ICT sector followed by 10% each in education and research. Financial services (8.2%), energy (5.5%), government (5.5%), transport and construction (5.5%), health (4.1%) and non-profit (4.1%) are the biggest other sectors AIMS graduates work in. Computer science is the skills domain most often used (32%) followed by 13% using Engineering Science. As noted above, about twice as many AIMS graduates go on to further studies rather than employment; this indicates that AIMS graduates are not able to find work in their preferred fields, or that they wish to continue with further studies (often another MSc).

Other barriers to employment are similar to those for further graduate studies: the broad, difficult-to-describe nature of the coursework; the lack of an exit exam or grades beyond pass/fail; and the lack of accreditation of three of the centres by their host countries.

*Potential and Actual Employers Views* According to brief telephone interviews with potential employers in the AIMS targeted sectors (finance, insurance, health, and telecom) in all but one of the centre countries, there is a significant market demand for the skills of AIMS graduates. In most cases the Human Resource managers of the companies were prepared – some eager – to have initial discussions about internships and possible collaborations. Centres have yet to build strong partnerships with employers, with the result that internships tend to be supply- rather than demand-driven. Centres need the additional capacity of new staff with a private sector background and network, as well as capacity development of current staff, to be able to: assess the labour market, match course content to career needs, and build bridges with employers. This should be a priority given the large and increasing percentage of unemployed graduates.

Although no data was regularly collected to monitor employer satisfaction with the technical and entrepreneurial skills, a total of seven employers were interviewed as part of the evaluation process, three in Tanzania and four in Senegal. All employers were positive about the performance of AIMS graduates compared to other employees. In addition, University lecturers in Tanzania who are AIMS graduates were reported to be stronger in technical computer skills, to have adapted faster to tough demands and to be stronger at articulating their views. Based on this admittedly small sample, it seems that those who were employed were seen to have the necessary technical and entrepreneurial skill.

*Motivations and First Destinations.* Looking at motivation of students in 2014-15, 31/212 (15%) are seeing themselves as somewhere else than in a PhD programme or become a researcher. In 2016/17, 81 out of 276 (29%) wanted to do something else. The table below presents the distribution of first engagement of AIMS graduates by year of graduation. Students are the largest category, although their share has fallen from 73% in 2012 to 48% in 2015 and dropped again to 39% in 2016; the numbers employed have risen from 8% in 2012 to a high of 15% in 2015 but dropped back to 12% in 2016; academic (research/ teaching) increased from 14% in 2012 to 23% in 2015 and dropped back slightly to 21% in 2016.

Across all years, although men are more likely to be in an academic occupation (24% compared to 16% for women) and women were more likely to be employed (14% vs 9% for men) and unemployed (18% compared to 13% for men), none of these differences were statistically significant.

*Table 6. Percentage distribution of first engagements by year of graduation*

| | 2010 | 2011 | 2012 | 2013 | 2014 | 2015 | 2016 |
|---|---|---|---|---|---|---|---|
| Student (Masters or PhD) | 77 | 75 | 73 | 67 | 58 | 48 | 39 |
| Academic (Research/ Teaching) | 11 | 21 | 14 | 20 | 24 | 23 | 21 |
| Public/ Private/ Voluntary | 7 | 4 | 8 | 11 | 11 | 15 | 12 |
| Unemployed | 3 | 0 | 5 | 2 | 8 | 13 | 28 |
| | 98 | 100 | 100 | 100 | 101 | 99 | 100 |

A noteworthy change has been the rise in unemployed from 5% in 2012 to 13% in 2015 and doubled again to 28% in 2016 (higher than those employed or in an academic occupation). This happened whilst the number of graduates increased by 39% from 2014 (179) to 2016 (249). Very clear evidence on why this is the case is not available, from the data obtained, but the lower market demand in academia and employment, combined with limited availability of post AIMS bursaries, seems a logical explanation.

Although not as many AIMS graduates as expected have entered the work force, more graduates have gone on to other studies than anticipated. The total number in post-AIMS study programs exceeds the total planned amounts for all years. Relatively more women graduates proceed to employment than men as the student percentage is about 30% percent while employment percentage is between 40% and 50% for 2014-2016. It is difficult to obtain accurate, recent unemployment information for all of the countries where centres are located. Information from IMF and the World Bank indicates relatively high unemployment rates in South Africa (27%), Senegal (22.7%) and Rwanda 13.2%) while there is no recent data for Tanzania, Cameroon Ghana. High unemployment rates could account for difficulties in finding employment, and particularly lack of STEM-related employment opportunities.

Of those working in the public sector (first engagement of graduates from 2011-2016), 3 were in senior positions and 21 in junior positions. Of those in the private sector, 14 were in senior positions and 35 in junior positions. Of the graduates that are (self) employed, 31% work in the ICT sector followed by 10% each in education and research. Financial services (8.2%), energy (5.5%), government (5.5%), transport and construction (5.5%), health (4.1%) and non-profit (4.1%) are the biggest other sectors AIMS graduates work in. Computer science is the skills domain most often used (32%) followed by 13% using Engineering Science. This finding suggests that the requested competencies from the labour market are geared towards competencies in relation to computing, applied maths and statistics, programming and engineering.

Subsequent Occupations. Up to three subsequent occupations were recorded: compared to the 712 where details were provided on first occupation, there were 210 with a second occupation, 58 with a third and 12 with a fourth.

*Table 7. Numbers of graduates in broad categories of current occupation by year of graduation*

| | 2012 | 2013 | 2014 | 2015 | 2016 |
|---|---|---|---|---|---|
| Student | 26 | 36 | 48 | 10 | 6 |
| Academic | 22 | 24 | 27 | 4 | 6 |
| Private/ Public | 10 | 3 | 12 | 5 | 4 |
| Unemployed | 4 | 10 | 15 | 6 | 2 |

The breakdown of these current occupations was that 45% were still a student, 30% were in teaching or research, 13% are working and 13% are unemployed. Compared with the first occupation there are 9% fewer students, 8% more in teaching or research, 3% more are working, 1% fewer are unemployed. The pattern by gender has changed slightly with the same proportions of men and women being a student or in teaching or research and whilst women are still more likely to be unemployed, they are less likely to be employed; but none of these variations were significant.

For those with two or more jobs, comparisons have been made between their most recent job (2016) with their first job. Of those who started as students, 38% were still studying, 36% were engaged in academic research/teaching, 7% were working and 19% were unemployed. Of those who started out in teaching or research, only 18% had continued, with 60% now a student.

As is typical for developing countries, employment opportunities in more technical or managerial positions are likely limited because of limited foreign investment and jobs being given to foreign staff associated with the investing company. Despite the challenges facing graduates, and recognising the difficulties of interpreting self-report data, 53% of graduates indicated that their first job was directly STEM-related and an additional 18% indicated that their first job was indirectly STEM-related.

Preparation for STEM positions and the availability of STEM positions are often not synchronized, which can be discouraging for graduates. The emphasis placed by AIMS on entrepreneurship is appropriate for developing countries. Entrepreneurs can create their own jobs and occasionally start businesses that can grow into larger companies, hence creating jobs, although only a very limited number of graduates (3) have reported setting up their own business.

## 5.3 Wider Impacts

*Ability to contribute to government policies or wider socio-economic impact on Africa*:

There is limited information regarding the extent to which AIMS has contributed to Africa achieving its development goals.

While logically, AIMS graduates may appear to be in a better position to contribute to African development goals, it seems that at this point the opportunities to do so are not always available. Indeed, over a third of AIMS graduates since 2012 are now in Europe, America, or other parts of the 'Western world'. This is a loss of resources; although at the same time it is difficult to see what AIMS can do about it within the framework of the current funding model and continuous globalisation. Whilst the brain drain is much larger than the UIS (2008) estimate of 7.5% of tertiary students, the UIS estimate obviously includes undergraduates; and the figures of 34% is not out-of-line (indeed lower) than another – probably more relevant - estimate of 40% of African scientists living in OECD countries . Probably of more concern is the difficulty of translating attained knowledge and research into practical improvements.

*Research into Practice*: The development sector revolves around the principle that better use of research and evidence in policy and practice can help save lives, reduce poverty and improve quality of life. Yet, applying research to guide and inform the development sector's many actors (from donors and researchers to NGOs and policy makers) and shaping the policy agenda is a difficult task.

In practice, academic research typically has little influence on policy. When it does, the process is far more complex than the linear model of research-informing-policy-leading-to-change-on-the-ground. Why this is (partly) the case is described below:

Perverse incentives:

It may not always be evident, but traditional systems for incentivising and evaluating academics (i.e. measuring their success) are largely incompatible with practitioners needs and often discourage the integration of research into policy and practice. For example, the success of a university academic – say a professor – is primarily measured against the number of peer-reviewed journal articles he/she produces, and the number of times those papers are cited by their peers (typically other university academics). Yet academic articles rarely feature on a policy-makers radar. If they do, they are often found behind an expensive pay wall.

What's more, research often comes in a language that is incomprehensible to many policy-makers. Often technical research needs to be translated into practical and engaging recommendations that communicates uncertainties and relates strongly to a policy-maker's decision-making environment. Yet shorter non-technical outputs like policy briefs, blogs and other forms of grey literature are rarely recognised or rewarded from an academic's perspective.

In many European and North American countries, these problems are in part mitigated by systems of communication and communicability between researchers and practitioners.

Blame is not only attributable to the system of producing and communicating research. There are fora in Africa for mathematicians and scientists to discuss and promote research findings; but from a policy perspective, research is supposed to feed into decision-making and planning. However, only a few developing countries in Africa have been able to equip their technical officers with the resources and networks to be able to translate new research into policy relevant actions for key decision-makers (say the head of a district government).

## 6. DISCUSSION AND CONCLUSION

The potential for Africa to have a successful economic future depends, in large part, to educating and retaining students at tertiary level. This raises two important questions: to what extent is the tertiary sector accepting the brightest students on the continent; and how well are the graduated students able to translate their learning into productive employment opportunities,

*Inequalities in Access:* There has been considerable debate in developed countries about the relationships between widening participation in higher education, the formal inequalities in access to higher education by social class and the inequalities in terms of access to prestigious (presumed to reflect better quality) higher education institutions. Given the rapid expansion of higher education in sub-Saharan Africa over the last thirty years, this has now become an issue there.

This was investigated, based on data obtained during an evaluation of a pan-African institution (AIMS) finding that, contrary to the declarations of the organisers of that network of 6 institutions, it was clear that the majority of students were from upper middle class families. In particular, a very high proportion (relative to what one would expect from an African population at that time) had parents who had completed secondary education or been to university in or around 1997 which would have been very unusual. A very large proportion of the brightest students have been excluded from tertiary education.

*Employment Outcomes*: The same evaluation obtained information on what happened to the graduates from AIMS courses. A small percentage ranging from 7% in 2010 to 15% in 2015 had obtained employment in either the private or public sector, a larger percentage had become a teacher in a secondary school, and a much larger – although decreasing - percentage pursuing an academic career through a course leading to a PhD, ranging from 77% in 2010 to 39% in 2016. Moreover, there was disturbingly an increasing level of unemployment in the first year after graduation from 3% in 2010 to 28% in 2016.

*Labour Market*: There may well be a potential demand for highly skilled graduates in the African labour market but it is not, in general, articulated or responded to by either HEIs or employers; and there is absolutely no evidence about the demand for graduates in the mathematical sciences. The only point on which commentators agree is that, in general, graduates are not prepared for the labour market; and that university programmes should include appropriate courses on employability and internship experiences. Whilst the AIMS programme does include such modules, they do not appear to be having the desired affect (see Section 5).

*Research into Practice*: The problem of translating research into practice is worldwide; and, whilst there has been extensive research in Europe and North America, the answers are depressingly similar and difficult to implement: collaboration, mutual understanding between academia and industry. In Africa, the few studies confirm those findings but also show that the difficulties of implementation are even greater.

## REFERENCES

Ball, S. J. (1998). Big Policies/ Small World: An introduction to international perspectives in education policy. *Comparative Education, 34*(2), 119–130. doi:10.1080/03050069828225

Barker and Mengistae. (2005, June). *Raising Productivity in Africa's Modern Wage enterprises to Foster Job Growth for Youth.* Author.

Barr, N. (2005). Financing Higher Education. *Finance & Development, 42*(2).

Cloete, N. (2005). Transformation Tensions in Higher Education: Equity, Efficiency, and Development. *Social Research, 72*(3), 693–722.

McCowan, T. (2014). *Can higher education solve Africa's job crisis: Understanding Graduate employability in Sub-Saharan Africa*. Policy Brief for British Council.

Nachinaab J.O., Nelly, E., Kumah, M., & Alexander, Y. (2019). Parents' Socio-Economic Status As Determinants Of Young Adults' Educational Attainment In Ayeduase, Kumasi. *International Journal of Innovative Research and Advanced Studies, 6*(2).

Ntshoe, I. M. (2003). The Political Economy of Access and Equitable Allocation of Resources to Higher Education. *International Journal of Educational Development, 23*(4), 381–398. doi:10.1016/S0738-0593(02)00070-6

Shavit, Y., Arum, R., & Gamoran, A. (Eds.). (2007). *Stratification in Higher Education: A Comparative Study*. Stanford University Press. http://report.post2015hlp.org/digital-report-executive-summary.html

UNESCO Institute for Statistics (UIS). (2009). *Comparing Education Statistics Across the World.* Montreal: UIS.

UNESCO Institute of Statistics. (2010). *Trends in Tertiary Education in Sub-Saharan Africa*. Fact Sheet No. 10. UNESCO.

United Nations Educational, Scientific and Cultural Organization (UNESCO) Secretariat. (1998). Women in Higher Education and Research in Africa. In *UNESCO World Conference on Higher Education*. Paris: UNESCO.

Unterhalter, E., & Oketch, M. (2017). *Higher education has considerable potential for benefitting all segments of society. Seminar*. UCL Institute of Education.

World Bank. (2014). *Africa's Pulse: An analysis of issues shaping Africa's economic future*. https://data.worldbank.org/indicator/NY.GDP.MKTP.KD.ZG?order=wbapi_data_value_2012+wbapi_data_value+wbapi_data_value-last&sort=desc

World Bank. (2014). *Youth employment in Sub-Saharan Africa: Africa Development Forum*. World Bank.

# Chapter 8
# Internationalization Policies and Strategies From the Comparative Standpoint of Student Mobility in Slovenian and Turkish Higher Education

**Maruša Hauptman Komotar**
https://orcid.org/0000-0002-5061-8357
*Alma Mater Europaea - Faculty of Humanities, Institutum Studiorum Humanitatis, Ljubljana, Slovenia*

**Tugba Elif Toprak-Yildiz**
https://orcid.org/0000-0003-0341-229X
*Izmir Democracy University, Turkey & University of Hamburg, Germany*

## ABSTRACT

*This chapter explores the development and implementation of internationalization policies, strategies, and practices from the standpoint of student mobility. It considers Slovenia and Turkey as the two countries forming the European Higher Education Area which have not received much attention from comparative researchers dealing with higher education. To this end, it initially investigates each country case individually by analyzing student mobility in national and institutional internationalization policies and strategies and its implementation in practice. On this basis, it provides the necessary background for the continuing debate, in which it evaluates the main similarities and differences in the field from the comparative perspective of both countries examined. Methodologically, the chapter is based on a thorough analysis of multiple documentary sources and most recent secondary data obtained from national and international statistical databases.*

DOI: 10.4018/978-1-7998-8169-8.ch008

## INTRODUCTION

This chapter explores the internationalization of Slovenian and Turkish higher education from the comparative standpoint of policies, strategies and practices in student mobility as the activity most frequently associated with the internationalization of higher education (abroad) (see Knight, 2008; Bista & Foster, 2016; Pawar, 2017). In European higher education, the start of the Bologna Process in 1999 was strongly influenced by positive experiences with the Erasmus mobility program which was launched in 1987 and paved the way for further harmonization of internationalization and mobility policies in the last decade of the past century (de Wit, 2002). But from the mid-1990s onwards, internationalization already started to develop as a strategic process in some Western European countries where economic rationales in the sense of attracting non-European students who pay tuition fees were strengthened under complex effects of globalization on higher education (de Wit, 2002; Teichler, 2010; de Wit et al., 2015). In 1998, the Sorbonne Declaration (1998) pointed to the need for a harmonized architecture of the European higher education system to establish "a framework for teaching and learning, which would enhance mobility and an ever-closer cooperation" (p. 1). A year later, 29 ministers responsible for higher education signed the Bologna Declaration (1999) in which they agreed to strengthen the mobility of students, academic staff, researchers, and administrative staff as one of the six principal objectives of building the European Higher Education Area (EHEA) by 2010. In 2009, they highlighted that by 2020, at least one-fifth of graduates from EHEA countries would complete a part of their study or training abroad (Leuven Communiqué, 2009). In 2012, they called for a more balanced mobility, and urged all EHEA countries to develop and implement internationalization and mobility strategies and policies in accordance with their profile, provide fair recognition of competencies acquired abroad and ensure other opportunities for mobile and non-mobile students (Working Group on Mobility, 2012, pp. 2–5). More recently, the ministers responsible for higher education maintained that they paved the way for large-scale student mobility along with increasing the quality and attractiveness of mobility practices (Paris Communiqué, 2018). The ministers stressed that achieving the Leuven target, which envisages 20% of EHEA graduates experiencing a study or training period abroad, is essential. They emphasized that "all learners [...] experience some form of mobility, whether in physical, digitally enhanced (virtual) or blended formats" (Rome Ministerial Communiqué, 2020, p. 6).

In 2013, also the European Commission published the communication *European Higher Education in the World* which exposed the need to develop comprehensive internationalization strategies focusing on international mobility, internationalization at home, and strategic partnerships (European Commission, 2013). As reported in the study of the European University Association (EUA), which involved 175 higher education institutions from 38 European countries, 56% of participating institutions stated that they have adopted the internationalization strategy, 30% noted that it makes part of other strategies and 13% underlined that it is in the process of its design (EUA, 2013). But as revealed by de Wit et al. (2015), a substantial majority of EHEA countries continue to support student mobility in their national and institutional internationalization policies and strategies, and to this end, this study explores it comparatively in more detail in the context of Slovenia and Turkey. Although both countries are Bologna Process signatory countries (from 1999 and 2001 onwards), they usually do not make part of comparative studies in higher education, despite the ever-growing need for their conduct in less-known (European/EHEA) higher education contexts. To overcome this notable research limitation, the chapter explores internationalization from the perspective of student mobility in the framework of the following research questions:

(1) How is student mobility addressed in national and institutional internationalization policies and strategies in Slovenian and Turkish higher education?
(2) How is student mobility implemented in practice in Slovenian and Turkish higher education systems?
(3) What similarities and differences between Slovenia and Turkey exist in terms of the implementation of national and institutional internationalization policies and strategies with respect to student mobility?

To provide answers to the above questions, each country's case is first analyzed individually (research questions 1 and 2) and then, the obtained results are discussed from the comparative standpoint (research question 3). Answers to the three research questions are provided through the documentary analysis of academic literature, recent studies and reports, national and institutional internationalization strategies, mobility strategies, development programs, and complemented with the review of most recent secondary data obtained from national and international statistical databases (e.g., the Statistical Office of the Republic of Slovenia (SORS), I-STAT Turkey, UNESCO Institute for Statistics (UIS), etc.).

## SLOVENIA

In this section, firstly some general characteristics of the higher education system are presented. Afterward, national and institutional internationalization policies and strategies from the perspective of student mobility are investigated. In the continuation, student mobility is also analyzed in practice, in order to adequately establish the starting point for the continuing comparative debate (after the presentation of each country's case).

## THE HIGHER EDUCATION SYSTEM

In Slovenia, higher education is provided by the Higher Education Act (HEA) which was first adopted in 1993, after the country's independence from the Socialist Federative Republic of Yugoslavia (SFRY) in 1991. As part of the country's involvement in the Bologna Process (since 1999), the amended HEA was published in 2004 and introduced undergraduate (bachelor's) and graduate (master's and doctoral) study programs, as shown by the below figure (see Figure 1).

Figure 1 showcases that three- and four-year university and higher professional study programs (180 to 240 ECTS) are implemented by Slovenian higher education institutions at the bachelor's level, whilst one-to two-year master's study programs (60 to 120 ECTS), uniform master's study programs, and three-year doctoral study programs (180 ECTS) are delivered at the postgraduate level (Republic of Slovenia, 2012, 2016, Articles 33 and 36).

*Figure 1. The structure of the Slovenian HE system*
*Source: Adapted from Republic of Slovenia (2012, Articles 33 and 36); Republic of Slovenia (2016, Article 11).*

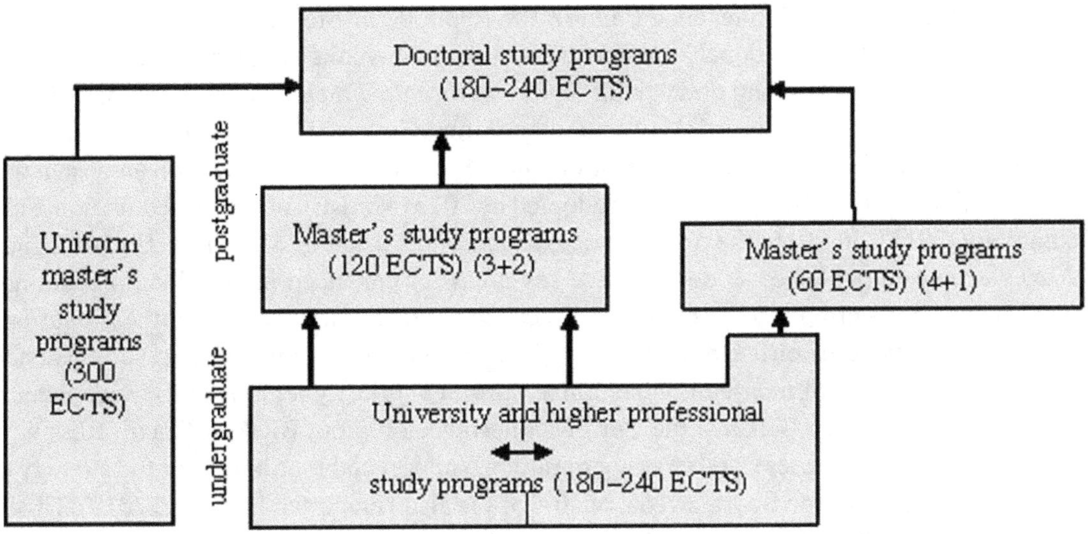


Higher education studies are offered by public and private universities and self-standing mostly private (and private with concession) higher education institutions (e.g., faculties, art academies, and professional colleges). Whilst universities, faculties and art academies are allowed to provide study programs at all three study cycles, higher professional colleges implement bachelor's and master's study programs (Republic of Slovenia, 2012, Article 4). In 2021, the number of accredited higher education institutions increased to six universities (3 public and 3 private) and 39 independent higher education institutions (Slovenian Quality Assurance Agency (SQAA), 2021); on the other hand, the number of students enrolled was decreasing for more than a decade, but in 2020/21, it increased to 82,694 students or almost 8% (or 6,000) more than a year before (SORS, 2021c). Hence, the internationalization of Slovenian higher education is "crucial for its development [...] [through] cooperation with other countries and regions in those areas where we will not reach critical mass on our own" (Ministry of Higher Education, Science, and Technology, 2011; see also Hauptman Komotar, 2019).

## NATIONAL LEVEL: INTERNATIONALIZATION POLICIES AND STRATEGIES FROM THE STANDPOINT OF STUDENT MOBILITY

From the above discussion, it is evident that internationalization presents a key element of the quality of the higher education system (e.g., Ministry of Education, Science, and Sport, 2016a). Already in 1994, Slovenia was one of the founding members of the Central European Exchange Program for University Studies (CEEPUS), which promotes partnerships, inter-university networks and student and staff mobility exchanges among member countries. In the year of joining the Bologna Process (1999), the country started to participate in Erasmus; in 2003, also the Centre of the Republic of Slovenia for Mobility and European Educational and Training Programmes (CMEPIUS) was established as a responsible body for the implementation of Erasmus and CEEPUS, bilateral agreements and other programs (CMEPIUS, n.d.a). The management of scholarships for domestic and foreign students, the provision of additional funding for Erasmus+ and Fulbright programs falls under the responsibility of the Public Scholarship, Development, Disability and Maintenance Fund of the Republic of Slovenia (hereafter: Public Fund) (Eurydice, 2021), whilst international(-ization) activities of Slovenian higher education institutions abroad are promoted through a joint entry point *Study in Slovenia* which is managed by CMEPIUS.

Nevertheless, in 2011, it was argued that "a number of immediate national and institutional measures must be adopted to increase the internationalization of the Slovenian higher education area" and that the national internationalization strategy should be adopted by 2013 (Ministry of Higher Education, Science, and Technology, 2011). In 2016, the *Strategy of Internationalization of Slovenian Higher Education 2016–2020* was indeed published; it defined five key areas for enhanced internationalization, namely (1) long-term and short-term mobility of students, academic and administrative staff, (2) international cooperation in scientific research and development, (3) the development of intercultural competencies of graduates in the framework of internationalization at home, (4) priority regions or individual countries (e.g., those from the Western Balkans, the Euro-Mediterranean region, BRICS (Brazil, Russia, India, China and South Africa countries), and (5) the promotion, support and monitoring of the strategy (Ministry of Education, Science, and Sport, 2016a, pp. 6–13; see also Hauptman Komotar, 2019). Given that the strategy points out that (student) mobility is "a key component of a high-quality and open higher education area" (Ministry of Education, Science, and Sport, 2016a, p. 11), it is adequate to also present the governmental (overall and specific) objectives for increasing long-term and short-term mobility in Slovenian higher education.

*Table 1. Student mobility objectives in the national internationalization strategy*

<table>
<tr><th>Overall objective</th><th>Specific objectives</th></tr>
<tr><td rowspan="3">Encouraging the mobility of international students to Slovenia</td><td>Increasing the number of international students participating in student exchanges, internships or full-time study in Slovenia (Objective 5).</td></tr>
<tr><td>Enabling the placement of international students in public student housing (Objective 6).</td></tr>
<tr><td>Informing international students on Slovenian culture, society, and language (Objective 7).</td></tr>
<tr><td rowspan="4">Encouraging the mobility of Slovenian students abroad</td><td>Increasing the number of Slovenian students on student exchanges and student internships abroad (Objective 1).</td></tr>
<tr><td>Increasing the number of Slovenian students studying abroad full-time (Objective 2).</td></tr>
<tr><td>Strengthening support environments for the improved quality of international mobility (Objective 3).</td></tr>
<tr><td>Implementing a pilot project to promote student competencies gained from mobility abroad (Objective 4).</td></tr>
</table>

Source: Ministry of Education, Science and Sport (2016a, 2017).

Already in 2011, it was outlined that 20% of domestic students will participate in exchanges abroad by 2020 (Ministry of Higher Education, Science, and Technology, 2011) but in 2017, this quantitative target was lowered to 5% in the two-year action plan (2016-2018) which was adopted as part of the internationalization strategy (see Ministry of Education, Science, and Sport, 2017). The document also noted that legislative basis regarding the language of instruction should be regulated, Slovene language and culture courses and support activities for the internationalization at home implemented and scholarships for domestic and foreign degree-seeking students provided (Ministry of Education, Science, and Sport, 2017). In terms of funding student mobility, Public Fund and CMEPIUS offer different types of scholarships, such as bilateral scholarships based on governmental agreements (e.g., with Poland, Switzerland, Slovakia, Hungary), *Ad futura* scholarships (for education, study visits, participation in knowledge or research competitions abroad and education of foreigners in Slovenia), scholarships for Slovene students abroad (from neighboring countries, descendants of Slovene emigrants), etc. (Public Fund, 2021). Based on the governmental agreement, the so-called Turkish scholarships are also available for domestic students wishing to study at prestigious Turkish universities (Public Fund, 2021).

## INSTITUTIONAL LEVEL: INTERNATIONALIZATION POLICIES AND STRATEGIES FROM THE STANDPOINT OF STUDENT MOBILITY

At the institutional level, one measure of the national higher education program from 2011 was to prepare and implement institutional internationalization strategies by 2014 (Ministry of Higher Education, Science and Technology, 2011, Measure 29). Gradually, the number of Slovenian higher education institutions with this document published is increasing, although it is frequently published in a separate document or as part of broader developmental strategies (see Hauptman Komotar, 2019). In the following table (Table 2), internationalization strategies from two public universities are presented in terms of key objectives in the field of student mobility.

*Table 2. Internationalization strategies and their reference to student mobility – the example of University of Ljubljana and University of Maribor*

| University | Internationalization Objectives | Student Mobility Objectives |
|---|---|---|
| University of Ljubljana<br>*Strategy for the Internationalization of the University of Ljubljana 2014 – 2020* | *General objectives*<br>10-20 strategic partnerships with excellent universities across the world and in the region<br>To achieve 500 international ambassadors of the university by 2017<br>*Objectives in the field of education*<br>To increase the number of programs and summer schools in foreign languages by 50 percent by 2017<br>To increase the number of programs that lead to double or joint degrees by 50 percent<br>To increase the implementation of educational programs abroad (e.g., in the Western Balkans, South-Eastern Europe, the Mediterranean)<br>To provide 2-3 programs annually for students in these regions, to increase the number of units and program offer by a third<br>To increase the scope of participation in existing networks and partner institutions | To increase the exchange of students by a third<br>To increase the number of international students by a quarter |
| University of Maribor<br>*Internationalization as Quality Development of the University of Maribor 2013-2020* | To increase the number of joint (postgraduate) degree programs conducted in cooperation with foreign institutions<br>To establish an international medical school par excellence attracting the best international scholars and students<br>To establish an International Summer University consisting of the existing and new individual international summer schools<br>To cooperate with neighboring regions (the Western Balkans, Central and Eastern Europe) and expand the activity in cooperation with regional partners (in Africa, Middle East, and Asia) | To encourage mobility of students, regular enrolment of international students (primarily in postgraduate programs)<br>To provide best possible conditions for housing, administrative support, and academic transfer of competencies<br>To continue to systematically regulate scholarships for students from disadvantaged regions, with governmental support |

Source: University of Ljubljana (2014), University of Maribor (2013, p. 4)

The increase in the number of internationalization and/or student mobility strategies published may also be associated with the start of a new Erasmus+ funding period in 2021 and the adoption of the

Erasmus Policy Statement to apply for funding sources. This also means that (student) mobility is an indispensable "part of the internationalized higher education community" (Ministry of Education, Science and Sport, 2019, p. 2) and, as such, needs to be examined in more detail in practice.

## STUDENT MOBILITY IN PRACTICE

To address student mobility flows in Slovenian higher education comprehensively, the following analysis investigates separately long-term (degree) and short-term (credit) mobility flows and considers incoming and outgoing internationally mobile students. In the context of degree mobility, students go abroad for the whole study period to obtain (undergraduate or postgraduate) degree, whereas in the framework of credit mobility students spend a study period, up to one year, at a higher education institution abroad and obtain credit points for modules of study or training completed which are also recognized by the home institution (Teichler, 2010).

### Degree Mobility Flows

#### Incoming Degree Mobility

In recent years, the number of foreign students enrolled at Slovenian higher education institutions is increasing year by year and the population of students from abroad is becoming more and more diverse. As shown in Figure 2, the number of students with the country of permanent residence abroad increased from 3,090 in 2016/17 to 7,607 in 2020/21[1] (SORS, 2017, 2021a).[2]

*Figure 2. Number of mobile students with the country of permanent residence abroad in Slovenian tertiary education (2016–2021)*
*Source: SORS (2017, 2018, 2019, 2020, 2021a).*

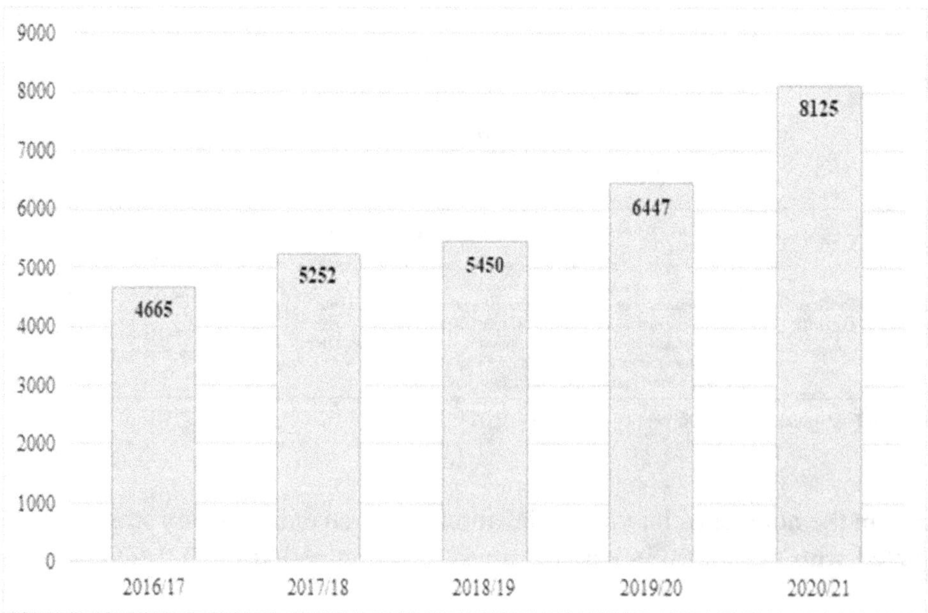

In the 2020/21 academic year, 4,565 or 61.2% of students with permanent residence abroad came to study in Slovenia from ex-Yugoslav countries (i.e., Bosnia and Herzegovina, North Macedonia, Croatia, Serbia, Kosovo, and Montenegro), 2,144 or 28.2% from EU member states and 1,651 or 21.7% from other countries (SORS, 2021a). This means that Slovenia is (still) not a preferred study destination for Western (European) students, as revealed in the following table.

*Table 3. Distribution and percentages of students with country of permanent residence abroad in Slovenian tertiary education, 2020/21*

| Country | Number of Students | Share in the Total |
|---|---|---|
| Bosnia and Herzegovina | 1476 | 19.4% |
| Croatia | 1430 | 18.8% |
| Serbia | 1354 | 17.8% |
| North Macedonia | 1331 | 17.5% |
| Italy | 365 | 4.8% |
| Other countries | 1651 | 21.7% |
| Total | 6447 | 100.0% |

Source: SORS (2021a).

The high proportion of incoming students from ex-Yugoslav countries is to be attributed to (common) historical patterns, the knowledge (and similarity) of the Slovene language, and especially to the priority governmental aim of establishing "cooperation with the Western Balkans region as an example of good practice in the field of regional mobility by 2020" (Ministry of Higher Education, Science, and Technology, 2011, Measure 30). This means that the governmental objective of at least 10% of foreign students at Slovenian higher education institutions by 2020 (Ministry of Higher Education, Science, and Technology, 2011) was almost achieved in the 2020/21 academic year and even considerably increased from 2019/20 (from 7.8% in 2019/20 to 9.2%), despite the ongoing pandemic of Covid-19 (SORS, 2021a).

## Outgoing Degree Mobility

In the framework of outgoing degree mobility, the latest data from UIS[3] conversely show that Austria (675 or 21.1%) Germany (429 or 13.4%) and the United Kingdom (393 or 12.3%) are the three main destination countries of Slovenian students, demonstrating that apart from Croatia and Serbia, domestic students do not choose to study in former Yugoslav countries, and that Western (European/EU) countries and the US are their most popular countries to obtain a degree abroad (UIS, 2021).

*Table 4. Distribution and percentages of Slovenian students in tertiary education abroad, 2021*

| Country | Number of Students | Share in the Total |
|---|---|---|
| Austria | 675 | 21.1% |
| Germany | 429 | 13.4% |
| United Kingdom | 393 | 12.3% |
| The Netherlands | 258 | 8.1% |
| Croatia | 246 | 7.7% |
| United States | 214 | 6.7% |
| Italy | 197 | 6.2% |
| Serbia | 104 | 3.3% |
| Switzerland | 91 | 2.8% |
| Denmark | 75 | 2.3% |
| Other countries | 513 | 16.1% |
| Total | 3195 | 100.0% |

Source: UIS (2021).

The above table also showcases that Austria, Germany, and the UK jointly hosted almost half (46.9%) of all domestic tertiary students abroad, whilst Croatia and Serbia became the fifth and the eighth most popular study destinations of Slovenian tertiary students (UIS, 2021) but this is quite a recent event. The latest data also show that 44 Turkish students came to study in Slovenia and 12 Slovenian students went to study in Turkey (UIS, 2021).

In summary, the proportion of students with the country of permanent residence abroad in Slovenian tertiary education (9.2%) (SORS, 2021a) (or 9.8% of students with foreign citizenship) (SORS, 2021b) is more than twice as high as the percentage of domestic students in tertiary education abroad, given that the outbound mobility ratio is currently 4.2%, according to UIS (2021).

## Credit Mobility Flows

In the framework of short-term mobility, the number of incoming and outgoing exchange students markedly decreased in 2020 when only 411 incoming exchange students participated in EU mobility programs (predominantly in Erasmus+) and most frequently originated from Germany (87), France (52) and Czech Republic (37) (CMEPIUS, n.d.b). In 2020, the number of outgoing exchange students was approximately the same as the number of incoming ones, given that 391 domestic students participated in (Erasmus+) exchanges abroad (for study and internship purposes), most frequently in Austria (63), Germany (53), and the Czech Republic (51) (CMEPIUS, n.d.b). Figure 3 additionally displays the increase in the absolute number of incoming and outgoing exchange students from 2016 to 2019, and the notable decrease in their number in 2020 when the Covid-19 pandemic started.

*Figure 3. The number of incoming and outgoing exchange students between 2016 and 2020 within the Slovenian HE system*
*Source: CMEPIUS (n.d.b).*

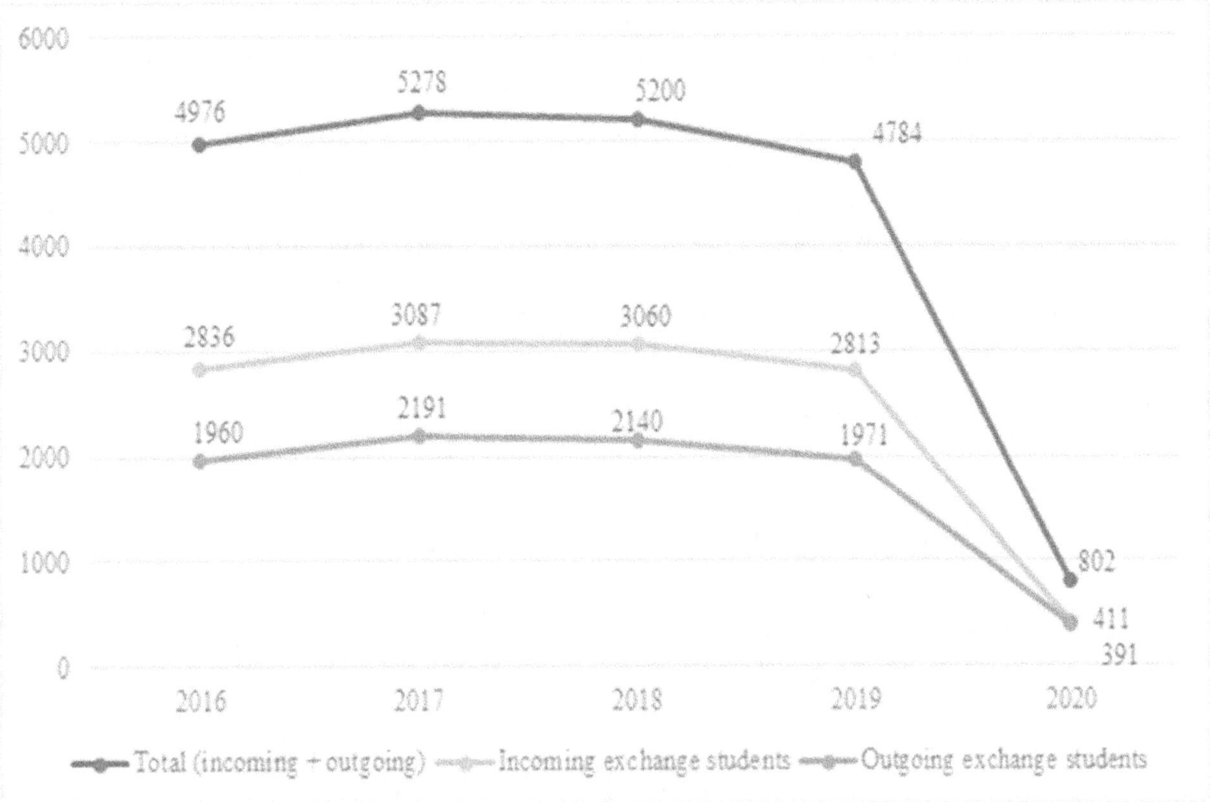


As shown in Figure 3, the number of incoming exchange students was slightly higher than the number of outgoing ones over the five-year period. However, the governmental aim of 20% of graduates participating in exchanges abroad by 2020 (Ministry of Higher Education, Science, and Technology, 2011) was not accomplished to date and to this end, the government defined a more realistic objective of 5% of domestic students participating in exchanges abroad in the action plan of the internationalization strategy in 2017 (Ministry of Education, Science, and Sport, 2017; see also Hauptman Komotar, 2019). On the other hand, the number and percentage of incoming degree mobile students in Slovenian higher education is (still) growing (9.8% and 4.2%, respectively in the 2020/21 academic year) and despite being much higher than the share of exchange students (about 0.5% in 2020), long-term mobility flows in Slovenian higher education are much more unbalanced than short-term ones.

## TURKEY

### The Higher Education System

The Turkish higher education system was reconstructed to a considerable extent in accordance with the new Higher Education Law (numbered 2547) in 1981 (Council of Higher Education, 2019). Since the system is considerably centralized, all higher education bodies in Turkey function under the Council of Higher Education. Moreover, admissions to universities are managed through a central university entrance exam. These universities can be divided into two groups as public and non-profit foundation universities. After successfully earning their high school certification and taking the central university exam, students can enroll in universities based on their score in the university entrance exam. Turkish universities are compatible with the Bologna three-cycle system (see Figure 4).

*Figure 4. The general structure of the Turkish education system*
*Source: Council of Higher Education (2019).*

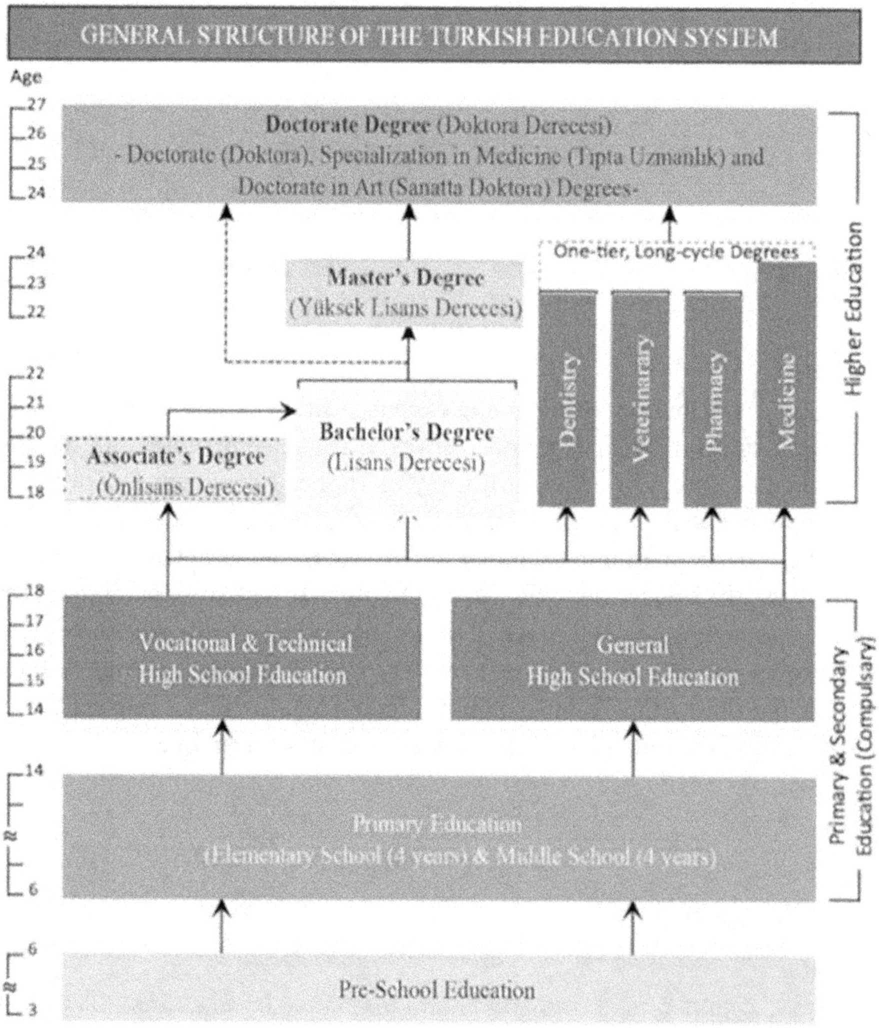

Within the higher education system, there are different types of higher education institutions and academic units, including faculties (colleges), which typically last four years, and result in a bachelor's degree, graduate schools that award students' masters and doctorate degrees, and conservatories that train artists during an eight-semester period. Apart from these institutions, post-secondary vocational schools train individuals in specific professions during four semesters.

Higher education institutions within the Turkish education system award various degrees such as associate's (short cycle), bachelor's (1st cycle), master's (2nd cycle), and Doctoral degrees (3rd cycle). Besides these degrees, Turkish higher education institutions award specialization in medicine programs, which are equivalent to doctoral degree programs and based on a competitive selection among graduates of medicine, and proficiency in art, which is equivalent to a doctorate and requires the rendition of original artwork. Currently, there are 209 higher education institutions, including 129 state and 75 foundation universities, and four foundation vocational schools in the Turkish higher education system (Council of Higher Education, 2019). All 81 cities in Turkey host a university or several universities.

## NATIONAL LEVEL: INTERNATIONALIZATION POLICIES AND STRATEGIES FROM THE STANDPOINT OF STUDENT MOBILITY

Establishing international collaborations and supporting internationalization and mobility practices in close cooperation with other countries and international institutions have been among the primary objectives of the Turkish higher education system. Consequently, Turkey has taken an active role in the decision-making processes of international organizations, such as The United Nations Educational, Scientific and Cultural Organization (UNESCO) and the Organization for Economic Cooperation and Development (OECD) regarding internationalization and global education. Moreover, the Turkish Ministry of National Education has formed strong bonds with international bodies and organizations, including the United Nations (UN), OECD, World Bank, and the Black Sea Economic Cooperation Organization (BSEC) (European Commission, 2020a).

Turkey has occupied a crucial role in several EU-based initiatives that are launched to foster internationalization, mobility, and intercultural relations (Council of Higher Education, 2017). Furthermore, Turkey has been one of the members of the Bologna Process, which commenced in 1999 as an initiative to boost transparency, familiarity, and mobility within the European higher education system. Turkey ranks second in the European Higher Education Area in terms of the number of students. Correspondingly, Turkey has paid a considerable effort to ensure the implementation of various schemes, such as Education and Training 2020, the Bologna Process, Lifelong Learning Program (LLP), and Youth in Action program (European Commission, 2020c). Moreover, during the 2014-2020 period, the Erasmus+ program replaced Lifelong Learning and Youth programs. According to the Turkish National Agency, the Erasmus+ program has funded a great number of projects that concentrated on the training of individuals and institutions. Besides these, the Erasmus+ program has supported and facilitated mobility practices both within the EU zone and in partner countries and regions, including Western Balkans, East Partnership Countries, Southern Mediterranean countries, Russian Federation, the Asian region, Latin America, Australia, Canada, Hong Kong, Japan, South Korea, New Zealand, Singapore, and the USA. In particular, Jean Monnet activities under the Erasmus+ scheme have provided support in research and teaching activities. By attending this particular program, participants have been able to extend their knowledge-base and skills in various EU-related topics such as comparative regional studies, EU communication, information studies, EU international relations diplomacy, EU law studies, and EU political and administrative studies. Additionally, Turkey is involved in the Fulbright program, which is one of the United States Cultural Exchange Programs that aims to improve intercultural relations.

Apart from these schemes, Turkey has been promoting internationalization policies by sending Turkish graduate students to international graduate programs located mainly in the UK, USA, Germany, and France to receive education based on a compulsory service system. Another ambitious internationalization scheme has been the Mevlana program, which was initiated to facilitate student and academic staff exchange within domestic and international higher education institutions. Contrary to other exchange programs, the Mevlana Program has been supporting the exchange activities without any geographical restrictions. Finally, the Turkish Council of Higher Education has recently introduced a major scheme to boost Turkish universities' internationalization activities elaborated in the Turkish Council of Higher Education Internationalization Strategy Document released on June 30, 2017 (Council of Higher Education, 2017). The plan covers the period between 2018-2022 and divides internationalization strategies into three broad areas: Access to higher education, quality, and institutional capacity. One of the most significant aims of the plan is to support the internationalization efforts of universities that are featured in international ranking systems such as The Times Higher Education World University Rankings, QS World University Rankings, Academic Ranking of World Universities, and CWTS Leiden Ranking Academic Ranking.

With this goal in mind, 20 pilot universities have been appointed to implement various internationalization strategies and set an example for other universities. These pilot universities have been listed as Anadolu University, Ankara University, Ataturk University, Bogaziçi University, Cukurova University, Dokuz Eylul University, Ege University, Erciyes University, Gazi University, Gebze Technical University, Hacettepe University, Istanbul Technical University, Istanbul University, Izmir Institute of Technology, Karadeniz Technical University, Marmara University, Middle East Technical University, Selcuk University, Uludag University, and Yildiz Technical University. The majority of these universities are located in the most populated and metropolitan cities in Turkey, such as Istanbul, Ankara, and Izmir, along with cities that have remained culturally, economically, and industrially developed within their surrounding regions (e.g., Adana, Bursa, Konya, and Trabzon).

Council of Higher Education (2017) has laid out several key objectives in the internationalization strategy document that could also function as guiding principles for both pilot universities and universities that are not included in the current internationalization scheme. According to the Council of Higher Education (2017), these objectives are ensuring that Turkish universities become a center of attraction and increasing the institutional capacity in internationalization. Council of Higher Education (2017) aims to realize the first main objective by increasing the number of international students and scholars, attracting qualified academic staff with a reverse brain drain, increasing the participation in international exchange programs, creating accommodation opportunities for international students, developing the international cooperation potential of universities, raising universities' international visibility, increasing the number of foreign language medium instruction programs, improving scholars' teaching skills in a foreign language, and signing cooperation agreements with foreign governments and multinational institutions. Council of Higher Education (2017) aims to realize the second main objective by establishing a department of international relations, employing qualified human resources in the field of international relations, establishing communication mechanisms regarding legislation, current developments, and trends in internationalization, and employing higher education academic advisors in target/focus countries.

## INSTITUTIONAL LEVEL: INTERNATIONALIZATION POLICIES AND STRATEGIES FROM THE STANDPOINT OF STUDENTS MOBILITY

For decades, a significant number of Turkish higher education institutions have actively engaged with international mobility, which constitutes a significant part of internationalization activities, along with launching and maintaining partner study programs and attracting an increasing number of international students (Council of Higher Education, 2017). The strategic internationalization scheme introduced by the Council of Higher Education (2017) seems to have inspired many Turkish universities, including pilot internationalization universities, to reconsider, reformulate and systemize their internationalization policies. Table 5 provides details about two pilot universities' internationalization strategies (e.g., Cukurova University and Dokuz Eylul University). These universities are both characterized as research universities and located in different geographical regions in Turkey.

*Table 5. Internationalization strategies and some institutional examples*

| University | Internationalization Objectives |
|---|---|
| Cukurova University<br>*Cukurova University, Internationalization Strategic Plan (2019-2023)*[4] | To increase the number of international students.<br>To boost international cooperation by increasing the participation in student/staff exchange programs.<br>To increase the visibility of Cukurova University in international rankings.<br>To increase the University's collaboration potential in international research.<br>To boost university-industry collaboration.<br>To improve research infrastructure and increase resources for research.<br>To increase the number of visiting/foreign scholars and the share of programs offered in foreign languages.<br>To enhance academics' teaching skills in a foreign language.<br>To develop an internationalized curriculum. |
| Dokuz Eylul University<br>*Dokuz Eylul University Internationalization Strategy*[5] | To increase the number of international students, academics/researchers.<br>To increase the rate of participation in exchange programs.<br>To expand the University's international research collaboration capacity.<br>To raise the University's international visibility and reputation.<br>To improve international funding opportunities.<br>To offer greater accommodation opportunities for international students.<br>To prevent brain drain.<br>To increase the number of English medium instruction programs.<br>To form an international relations administrative unit and recruit qualified personnel.<br>To follow the current trends, legislation, and regulations concerning internationalization. |

Apart from Cukurova University and Dokuz Eylul University, all pilot universities included in the Council's internationalization scheme have been investing considerable effort in reshaping and improving their internationalization policies.

## STUDENT MOBILITY IN PRACTICE

To address student mobility flows in the Turkish higher education system, secondary data on degree and credit mobility flows have been examined.

## Degree Mobility Flows

### Incoming Degree Mobility

Recently, the number of foreign students enrolled at Turkish universities has been increasing steadily. Moreover, the Turkish higher education system's foreign student population has become more diverse over the years. This increase is evident in both student numbers and diversity (see Figure 5).

*Figure 5. The number of international students in the Turkish tertiary system (2013-2020)*
*Source: Council of Higher Education (2019).*

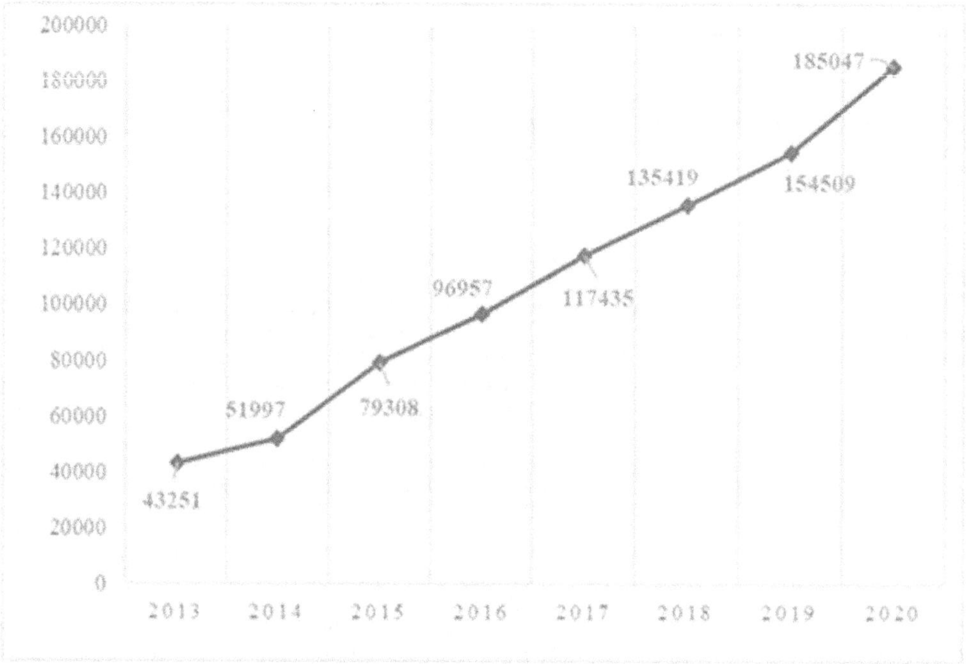


The numbers of international students in the Turkish HE between 2013-2020 as shown in Figure 5 may suggest that the Turkish higher education system has grown more international and diverse over the years, and there is a steady increase in the number of students with foreign citizenship. Table 6 below shows the recent distribution of students with foreign citizenship (2018-2019) that attend Turkish universities, along with students' home countries. The percentages presented below have been calculated for the top 30 sending countries.

*Table 6. Distribution and percentages of students in Turkish HE with foreign citizenship (2018-2019)*

| Country | N of Students | Share in the Total | Country | N of Students | Share in the Total |
|---|---|---|---|---|---|
| Syria | 27034 | 17.5 | Kazakhstan | 2191 | 1.4 |
| Azerbaijan | 19383 | 12.6 | Pakistan | 2115 | 1.4 |
| Turkmenistan | 17571 | 11.4 | Kyrgyzstan | 1937 | 1.3 |
| Iraq | 7608 | 4.9 | Libya | 1756 | 1.1 |
| Iran | 7154 | 4.6 | Nigeria | 1562 | 1.0 |
| Afghanistan | 6804 | 4.4 | Russian F. | 1407 | 0.9 |
| Germany | 4378 | 2.8 | Kosovo | 1322 | 0.9 |
| Somalia | 3764 | 2.4 | Indonesia | 1218 | 0.8 |
| Yemen | 3076 | 1.9 | Albania | 1148 | 0.7 |
| Bulgaria | 3010 | 1.9 | Uzbekistan | 1075 | 0.7 |
| Egypt | 2910 | 1.8 | Morocco | 1071 | 0.7 |
| Greece | 2713 | 1.7 | Chad | 989 | 0.6 |
| Jordan | 2643 | 1.7 | N. Cyprus | 888 | 0.6 |
| Palestine | 2483 | 1.6 | Macedonia | 883 | 0.6 |
| China | 2257 | 1.5 | Serbia | 795 | 0.5 |

Note: Frequencies and percentages have been calculated based on the data available on the Turkish Higher Education Information Management System https://istatistik.yok.gov.tr/

The total number of students with foreign citizenship enrolled in Turkish universities is 154.446 based on 2018-2019 statistics available on the Turkish Higher Education Information Management System. The figures reveal that Turkish universities attract a significant body of foreign students from 126 countries/regions, yet due to space limitations, top 30 sending countries have been listed in Table 6. Syrian students make up the largest group of students with foreign citizenship due to ongoing conflicts and civil war in Syria. Moreover, the figures indicate that a substantial number of students that have chosen Turkey as a study destination are from neighboring countries (e.g., Iraq, Iran), Turkic countries (e.g., Turkmenistan, Azerbaijan, and Kazakhstan), or countries where a great many Turkish origin individuals live (e.g., Germany, Bulgaria). Furthermore, Turkish universities seem to attract a considerable number of students from the Middle East (Egypt, Jordan, Palestine, and Yemen) and African countries (e.g., Somalia). A wide diversity is evident considering even students from Indonesia, Thailand, Mexico, and Spain attend Turkish universities. Based on the information presented in Table 6, it would be safe to posit that the Turkish higher education system has grown more internationalized within the last decade, and it attracts a more significant number of students, mainly from neighboring countries and countries with close cultural and historical bonds with Turkey.

## Outgoing Degree Mobility

In the framework of outgoing degree mobility, the UNESCO Institute of Statistics (UIS, 2021) reveals 45,588 Turkish students have chosen 69 counties for study purposes. The most popular study destinations of Turkish students are the United States (21%), Germany (17%), United Kingdom (8%) and Italy (5%), and Austria (5%) (see Figure 6 below).

*Figure 6. Countries with the highest proportion of Turkish students enrolled in tertiary education abroad*
*Source: UIS (2021).*

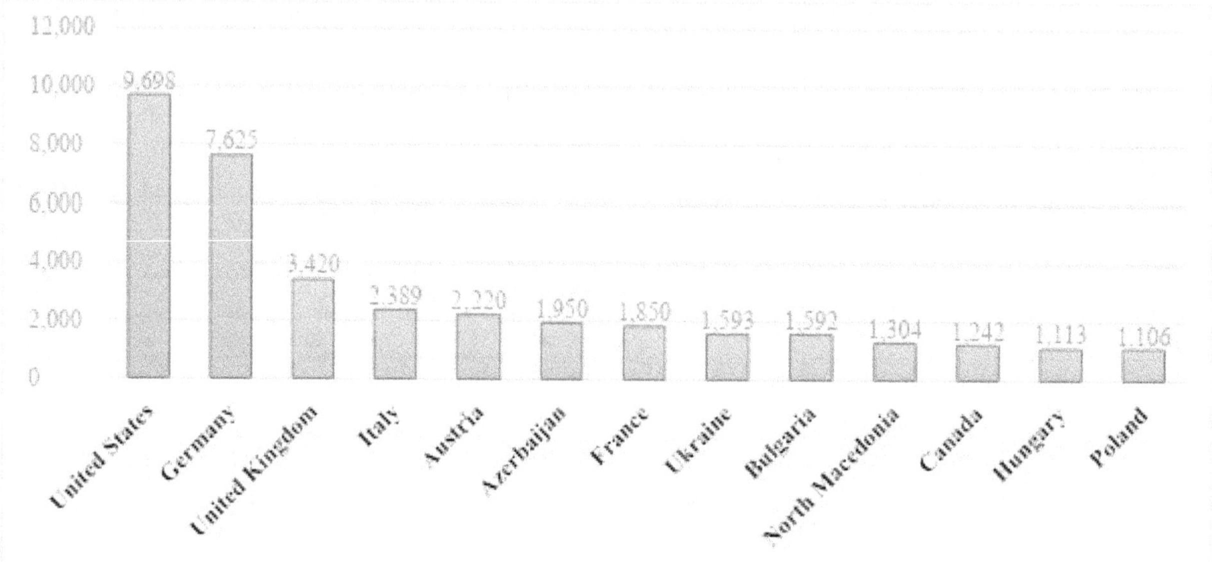


Since the number of study destinations is quite large, Figure 6 exhibits only the countries with student numbers exceeding 1,000. The figures suggest that many Turkish students opt for countries that attract foreign students on an international scale (e.g., the USA, the UK, and Germany). European countries, such as Italy, Austria, and France are also popular study destinations for Turkish students. Turkish students also prefer neighboring countries such as Azerbaijan, Bulgaria, and Ukraine for study purposes. Apart from the countries shown in Figure 6, a considerable number of Turkish students preferred Bosnia/Herzegovina (893), Netherlands (825), Australia (716), and Switzerland (687) as well.

## Credit Mobility Flows

The Erasmus program was put into effect in the 2003-2004 academic year with the establishment of the Turkish National Agency. The Agency was established in 2003, in accordance with the 25191 numbered Official Gazette as an institution with administrative and financial autonomy to ensure that all individuals, institutions, and organizations in the fields of education, youth, and sports would benefit from the European Union Programs in the most effective way (Turkish National Agency, 2021). Turkish National Agency started implementing the Erasmus program as a pilot study in 2004 and has since become an active participant in the program (Boyaci, 2011). Since 2004, the number of institutions participating in the Erasmus program seems to be increasing. To illustrate, at the end of 2009, 114 out of 152 Turkish higher education institutions had their Erasmus Declaration document and started actively participating in short-term mobility exchanges (Center for EU Education and Youth Programs, 2009). In the 2008-

2009 academic year, the number of students who benefited from the Erasmus program was 7,795, while the number of incoming students from 28 European countries was 2,453 (Center for EU Education and Youth Programs, 2009). Between the years 2004-2015, the number of outgoing students exceeded 100,000 whereas the number of incoming students was around 40,000 (European Commission, 2020b). Since Erasmus was launched in 2004, the number of outgoing students benefiting from the scheme is estimated to exceed 130,000 while the number of incoming students exceeds 50,000 (European Commission, 2020b). Figure 7 below shows the increase in incoming and outgoing students benefiting from the Erasmus program between 2014-2019.

*Figure 7. The number of incoming and outgoing students benefiting from the Erasmus program between 2014-2019 within the Turkish HE system*

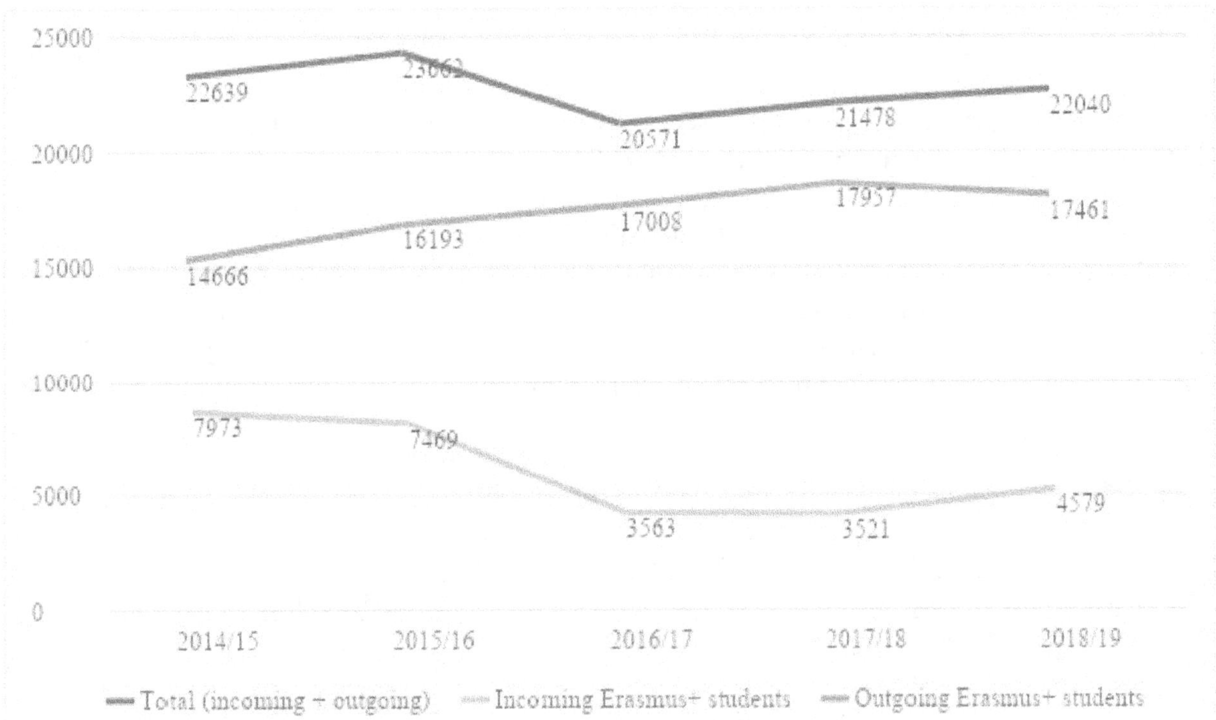


The statistics regarding the number of incoming and outgoing students benefiting from the Erasmus program between 2014-2019 indicate that Turkish higher education institutions have actively participated in short-term mobility practices since the Erasmus program started to be implemented in 2014. Although there seems to be a decline in the number of incoming students in the 2016-2017 and 2017-2018 periods, the number of outgoing students seems to be in a steady increase over the years. Overall, the total number of both incoming and outgoing students seems to be steady, except for the 2016-2017 period, in which mainly the number of incoming students is the lowest over the years. Note that the figure does not feature the statistics concerning the 2020-2021 academic year since European Commission's report on the Erasmus mobility within this particular period is not available at the moment.

According to the Erasmus+ Annual Report 2019 (European Commission, 2020d), the top three sending higher education institutions in Turkey are Marmara University (Istanbul), Anadolu University (Eskisehir), and Yildiz Technical University (Istanbul). Moreover, three receiving countries which are the most popular study destinations among Turkish university students, are Poland, Germany, and Spain. In 2018, Ankara University (Ankara), Anadolu University (Eskisehir), and Hacettepe University (Ankara) were the top sending Turkish universities, while Poland, Germany, and Italy were the most popular receiving countries (European Commission, 2019b). In 2017, Anadolu University (Eskisehir), Ankara University (Ankara), and Hacettepe University (Ankara) were again the top sending institutions, whereas Poland, Germany, and Italy were also the most popular receiving countries (European Commission, 2018). Based on these figures concerning 2017, 2018, and 2019, it could be deduced that, in particular, Poland, Germany, and Italy have been the most attractive study destinations for Turkish university students.

## COMPARATIVE DISCUSSION

### Internationalization Policies and Strategies in Slovenian and Turkish Higher Education from the Viewpoint of Student Mobility

In the following section, the comparison of internationalization policies and strategies in Slovenian and Turkish higher education are firstly presented. In the continuation, student mobility flows in both country cases are comparatively investigated. On this basis, similarities and differences in the development and implementation of internationalization policies and strategies in the field of student mobility are discussed and answers to the third research question are given.

*Table 7. Key information on the Slovenian and Turkish HE system*

| | Slovenia | Turkey |
|---|---|---|
| **Population** | 2,108,977 (2021) | 84,979,457 (2020) |
| **Number of students in higher education** | 72,130 (2020/21) | 7,940,615 (2019/20) |
| **Higher education institutions** | 6 universities (3 public, 3 private)<br>39 self-standing higher education institutions | State universities: 129 (62%)<br>Foundation universities: 74 (36%)<br>Vocational universities: 4 (2%) |
| **Number of study programs (total BA, MA, PhD)** | Around 970 | 26,476 |
| **Types of study programs with credit valuation** | University and higher professional study programs (bachelor's): 180–240 ECTS | Associate degree (short cycle): 120 ECTS<br>Bachelor's: 240 ECTS |
| | Master's study programs (3+2): 120 ECTS; (4+1): 60 ECTS<br>Uniform master's study programs: 300 ECTS | Master's: 120 ECTS |
| | Doctoral study programs: 180–240 ECTS | Doctorate: 240 ECTS |

Source: Republic of Slovenia (2012, 2016); Council of Higher Education (2019); Eurydice (2021); SORS (2021c).

As shown in Table 7, Slovenia has 6 universities and 39 self-standing (mostly private and private with concession) higher education institutions, whilst Turkey has 207 universities (of state, foundation, and vocational type). In terms of study programs, their number is in both cases above the European average of 250 study programs per million inhabitants (462 in Slovenia and 331 in Turkey) (SQAA, 2021; Council of Higher Education, 2019). Both countries have also the Bologna three-cycle system (bachelor's, master's, doctoral study programs); whilst Turkey offers the associate degree or short-cycle (two-year) education as part of higher education offered by universities and foundation postsecondary vocational schools, the Slovenian tertiary education system also includes practically-oriented short-cycle (two-year) higher vocational education offered by higher vocational colleges.

Both in Slovenia and Turkey, the inclusion in the Bologna Process (in 1999 and 2001, respectively) meant the further promotion of student and staff mobility. In the words of Özer (2016), the Bologna Process and its key objective of increasing student and staff mobility "made significant contributions to the internationalization experiences of [...] [Turkish] higher education institutions, and public universities, in particular, have engaged in competition with each other" (p. 56). However, the adoption of internationalization strategies, in which student mobility objectives are additionally and more precisely outlined, is of a more recent origin. Whereas in Slovenia, the government adopted the national internationalization strategy in 2016, the Turkish Council of Higher Education adopted this strategic document a year later (in 2017) (Council of Higher Education, 2017). In Slovenia, the national internationalization strategy considers internationalization as an element of quality and international mobility as one of the five key areas that should stimulate its development (Ministry of Education, Science, and Sport, 2016a). In Turkey, the Council's plan for the 2018-2022 period emphasizes access to higher education, quality, and institutional capacity as key areas of the internationalization strategy, and supports the internationalization efforts through the inclusion of Turkish universities on the most influential international rankings. In Slovenia, national ranking policies are not observable, but at the university level, the improvement of ranking position is an important strategic objective (e.g., University of Ljubljana, 2014; Hauptman Komotar, 2021).

Hence, in recent years, both countries made strategic efforts to enhance the internationalization of their higher education systems. In the following table (Table 8), the main similarities and differences between Slovenian and Turkish internationalization strategies are summarized.

In terms of institutional internationalization strategies, the Turkish government selected 20 pilot universities for their implementation in 2017, whilst in Slovenia, it was declared that these strategies should be adopted by 2014; to date, the number of institutions with the strategy published, either in a separate document or as part of broader strategies, is slowly growing (see also Hauptman Komotar, 2019). Next to student mobility, other types of internationalization are considered by institutional internationalization strategies from both countries examined, such as the implementation of study programs in foreign (English) language, joint or degree programs, the internationalized curriculum, the internationalization at home, the improvement of accommodation opportunities for international students, etc. (e.g., University of Maribor, 2013; Dokuz Eylul University; see also Knight, 2008; Toprak, 2019). However, student mobility is in both cases an essential part of national and institutional internationalization policies and strategies and in the following, we evaluate its implementation in practice from the comparative standpoint.

*Table 8. Internationalization strategy in Slovenian and Turkish HE from the comparative perspective*

| | Slovenia | Turkey |
|---|---|---|
| **National internationalization strategy (title)** | Strategy for the internationalization of Slovenian higher education 2016-2020 | The Turkish Council of Higher Education Internationalization Strategy Document 2018-2022 (Yükseköğretimde Uluslararasılaşma Strateji Belgesi 2018-2022) |
| **Year of adoption** | 2016 | 2017 |
| **Responsible body** | Ministry of Education, Science, and Sport; CMEPIUS; Public Fund | The Council of Higher Education |
| **Key objectives of the internationalization strategy** | Encouraging the mobility of domestic students abroad<br>Encouraging the mobility of international students to Slovenia<br>Encouraging the mobility of domestic higher education teachers and professional associates abroad<br>Encouraging the mobility of higher education teachers and professional associates to Slovenia<br>Encouraging quality international scientific research and development cooperation<br>Encouraging the development of intercultural, social and civic competencies of students and academic staff<br>Targeting priority regions and countries<br>Promotion, support, and monitoring of the strategy | Two main objectives<br>1. Ensuring that Turkish HE becomes a center of attraction<br>Increasing the number of international students<br>Increasing the number of international scholars<br>Attracting qualified academic staff with a reverse brain drain<br>Increasing the number of participants in international exchange programs<br>Creating increased accommodation opportunities for international students<br>Developing the cooperation potential of universities<br>Increasing Turkish universities' international visibility<br>Increasing the number of foreign language medium instruction programs<br>Boosting academicians' teaching skills in a foreign language<br>Signing cooperation agreements with foreign governments and multinational institutions<br>2. Increasing the institutional capacity of Turkish universities in internationalization<br>Establishing a department of international relations within higher education<br>Employing qualified human resources in the field of international relations<br>Establishing communication mechanisms regarding legislation, current developments, and trends in internationalization<br>Employing higher education academic advisors in representative offices in target/focus countries |

Source: Ministry of Education, Science, and Sport (2016a); Council of Higher Education (2017).

## STUDENT MOBILITY FROM THE COMPARATIVE VIEWPOINT OF SLOVENIA AND TURKEY

In the field of incoming degree mobility, the number of foreign students is continuously increasing both in Slovenia and Turkey. In Slovenia, for example, 9.2% (7,607) students with country of permanent residence abroad were enrolled in tertiary education in 2020/21 (SORS, 2021a), whilst in Turkey, this percentage is much lower and accounted for 2.3% in 2020, despite the yearly increase in the absolute number of students from abroad (https://istatistik.yok.gov.tr/). In terms of the 'top 3' countries of origin of incoming students, these are ex-Yugoslav ones in Slovenia (Bosnia and Herzegovina, Croatia, and Serbia, representing together over half of all foreign students in Slovenian tertiary education in 2020/21).

In Turkey, Syria, Azerbaijan, and Turkmenistan were 'top 3' countries of origin of international students in 2018/19 (https://istatistik.yok.gov.tr/). Therefore, "Turkey receives very few foreign students from the countries sending the highest numbers of students abroad, and the ratio of the students Turkey receives from these countries is very low compared to the total number of students it sends abroad" (Özer, 2016, p. 58). In both countries, the proportion of domestic students enrolled in tertiary education abroad is lower, especially in Turkey with only 0.6% of the total student population in 2021, according to UIS (2021). Hence, the ratio between incoming and outgoing students is much more unbalanced than in Slovenia, where it currently accounts for 4.2% (UIS, 2021). In terms of the 'top 3' main destination countries, these are Austria, Germany, and the United Kingdom for Slovenian students, and the United States, Germany, and the United Kingdom for Turkish ones (UIS, 2021).

In the framework of short-term mobility, Germany is in both cases among the 'top 3' sending and receiving countries of Erasmus+ students. But in Turkey, the ratio between incoming and outgoing exchange students is comparably more unbalanced than in Slovenia, as the number of incoming exchange Erasmus+ students is lower than the number of Turkish ones going abroad (Özer, 2016).

In terms of implementing English-taught study programs, "opening graduate level courses with languages of instruction completely in English, French, and Arabic is a must" in Turkey (Özer, 2016, p. 62). In Slovenia, the implementation of study programs in foreign languages is also supported at the master's and doctoral level, but as reported by Wächter and Maiworm (2014), the percentage of institutions offering study programs in the English language was in both countries below 20 in 2014, resulting from "a 'north-south' rift" (p. 41). Moreover, in Slovenia, English-taught study programs are allowed to be implemented if they are also conducted in Slovene; conversely, in the Turkish case, it is "recommended that the university departments should be permitted to choose between English or Turkish as the medium of instruction" (Kırkgöz, 2009, p. 9). Considering that the availability of English-medium instruction (EMI) programs may create increased opportunities for degree and credit mobility, international research and development collaborations, and intercultural learning (Toprak, 2019), it is no surprise that the number of EMI programs in the Turkish higher education system has increased considerably within the last decade.

In summary, activities related to student mobility are still a priority in internationalization policies and strategies in both cases examined. But despite being argued that the promotion of student mobility strengthens the trend of homogenization of national internationalization policies in the EHEA region (de Wit et al., 2015), the two cases showcase that the EHEA is not a homogenous region (de Wit, 2002), as the percentage of international students varies considerably not only between different higher education systems and institutions, but also among study programs or disciplines (e.g., EUA, 2013). Moreover, "[e]nrolling qualified international students in graduate programs [...] positively contributes to [...] [Turkey's] power of economic competition" (Özer, 2016, p. 61), while in Slovenia, the internationalization of higher education "shall proceed as a part of a long-term and sustainable process based on high-quality, holistic and balanced international partnerships" (Ministry of Education, Science, and Sport, 2016a, p. 6). What is then needed is "the establishment of a recognizable, integrated, national identity for Slovenian higher education, which will improve the global visibility of Slovenia and the Slovenian higher education and research area" (Ministry of Education, Science, and Sport, 2016a, p. 6). Hence, the development of internationalization and its key activity – student mobility is influenced by diverse rationales of various actors and stakeholders inside and outside higher education which answer differently why to internationalize Slovenian and Turkish higher education space (see also de Wit, 2002; Knight, 2008; de Wit et al., 2015; Bista & Foster, 2016).

## CONCLUSION

This study reveals that internationalization policies and strategies have received increasing attention, especially in the last decade within both Slovenian and Turkish higher education systems. This increasing attention is evident in the implementation of major and ambitious internationalization schemes that aim to maintain long-term and short-term mobility of students and staff, foster international cooperation in scientific research, increase the competitiveness of universities in the global educational market, and boost intercultural and linguistic competences of university students across both countries (see also Kenebayeva, 2019). Even though the implementation of such international strategies and policies seems to have been effective so far, we must not overlook the complex effects of the pandemic of Covid-19 on the future of internationalization, and student mobility in particular.

Future research endeavors should therefore focus their attention on the implementation of national and institutional internationalization strategies in times of the pandemic and hence, on the achievement of their stated objectives. In this respect, the pandemic influences on long-term and/or short-term student mobility flows in other EHEA and non-EHEA countries or emerging economies outside the Western context could be examined, since the selection of Slovenia and Turkey narrowed the comparative analysis to the European context. Moreover, the increasingly relevant role of technology (see Yildiz, 2021a, 2021b) calls for a more detailed exploration of links between physical and virtual forms of student mobility; as reported in the recent study on the impact of Covid-19 on student mobility in Mainland China and Hong, 84% of responding mobile students "showed no interest to study abroad after the pandemic" (Mok et al., 2021, p. 1).

Therefore, designers and implementers of internationalization policies and strategies should also put greater attention to the implementation of the 'at home' dimension of internationalization (Knight, 2008) and hence, to "the importance of internationalizing learning outcomes for all students, not simply those who study abroad" (Jones and Reiffenrath, 2018). After all, the internationalization of higher education is "the intentional process of integrating an international, intercultural or global dimension into the purpose, functions, and delivery of post-secondary education, in order to enhance the quality of education and research for all students and staff, and to make a meaningful contribution to society" (de Wit et al., 2015, p. 281).

## REFERENCES

Bista, K., & Foster, C. (Eds.). (2016). *Global perspectives and local challenges surrounding international student mobility*. IGI Global. doi:10.4018/978-1-4666-9746-1

Bologna Declaration. (1999). https://www.ehea.info/media.ehea.info/file/Ministerial_conferences/02/8/1999_Bologna_Declaration_English_553028.pdf

Boyaci, A. (2011). Erasmus exchange students' comparative views on classroom management in Turkey and in their country (Anadolu University case). *Education in Science*, *36*(159), 270–282.

Center for EU Education and Youth Programmes. (2009). *2009 yılı hayatboyu öğrenme programı (LLP) ve gençlik programı uygulama raporu* [Lifelong learning program (LLP) and youth program implementation report in 2009]. https://www.ua.gov.tr/media/eylif3cm/35_reduced-uygulama-raporu_bask%C4%B1-min.pdf

CMEPIUS. (n.d.a). *Basic info*. https://eng.cmepius.si/about-us/basic-info/

CMEPIUS. (n.d.b). *Mednarodno sodelovanje v številkah 2007–2020* [International cooperation in numbers 2007 –2020]. http://statistike.cmepius.si/

Council of Higher Education. (2017). *Yükseköğretimde uluslararasılaşma strateji belgesi 2018-2022* [Internationalization in higher education strategy document]. https://www.yok.gov.tr/Documents/AnaSayfa/Yuksekogretimde_Uluslararasilasma_Strateji_Belgesi_2018_2022.pdf

Council of Higher Education. (2019). *Study in Turkey*. https://www.studyinturkey.gov.tr/

de Wit, H. (2002). *Internationalisation of higher education in the United States of America and Europe*. Greenwood Press.

de Wit, H., Hunter, F., Howard, L., & Egron-Polak, E. (2015). *Internationalisation of higher education*. European Parliament, Directorate-General for Internal Policies.

EUA. (2013). *Internationalisation in European higher education: European policies, institutional strategies and EUA support*. European University Association.

European Commission. (2013). *European higher education in the world: Communication from the Commission to the European Parliament, the Council, the European economic and social committee and the Committee of the regions*. https://eur-lex.europa.eu/legal-content/EN/TXT/PDF/?uri=CELEX:52013DC0499&from=NL

European Commission. (2018). *Erasmus+ 2017 in numbers*. https://ec.europa.eu/programmes/erasmus-plus/resources/documents/erasmus-annual-report-factsheets-turkey_en

European Commission. (2019). *Erasmus+ country factsheets 2017*. https://ec.europa.eu/programmes/erasmus-plus/about/factsheets#fsTitle

European Commission. (2019b). *Erasmus+ 2018 in numbers*. https://ec.europa.eu/programmes/erasmus-plus/resources/documents/turkey-erasmus-2018-numbers_en

European Commission. (2020a). *Turkey/Mobility and internationalisation*. https://eacea.ec.europa.eu/national-policies/eurydice/content/mobility-and-internationalisation-85_en

European Commission. (2020b). *Erasmus+ 2019 in numbers*. https://ec.europa.eu/assets/eac/factsheets/factsheet-tr-2019_en.html

Eurydice. (2021). *Mobility in higher education (Slovenia)*. https://eacea.ec.europa.eu/national-policies/eurydice/content/mobility-higher-education-68_en

Hauptman Komotar, M. (2019). Comprehensive internationalisation of Slovenian higher education? The rhetoric and realities. *Higher Education*, *77*(5), 871–887. doi:10.100710734-018-0306-6

Hauptman Komotar, M. (2021). Global university rankings in European higher education policy and practice: Institutional and national responses from Slovenia and the Netherlands. In D. Günay, T. Asunakutlu, & O. Yildiz (Eds.), *University-industry collaboration strategies in the digital era* (pp. 62–83). IGI Global. doi:10.4018/978-1-7998-3901-9.ch004

Jones, E., & Reffenrath, T. (2018, August 21). Internationalisation at home in practice. *EAIE Blog*. https://www.eaie.org/blog/internationalisation-at-home-practice.html

Kenebayeva, A. S. (2019). Internationalization of higher education in Kazakhstan: National capacity-building initiatives. In F. Silman, F. Altinay Aksal, & Z. Altinay Gazi (Eds.), *Policies and initiatives for the internationalization of higher education* (pp. 153–174). IGI Global. doi:10.4018/978-1-5225-5231-4.ch009

Kırkgöz, Y. (2009). Globalization and English language policy in Turkey. *Educational Policy*, *23*(5), 663–684. doi:10.1177/0895904808316319

Knight, J. (2008). *Higher education in turmoil: The changing world of internationalisation*. Sense Publishers. doi:10.1163/9789087905224

Leuven Communiqué. (2009). http://www.ehea.info/Upload/document/ministerial_declarations/Leuven_Louvain_la_Neuve_Communique_April_2009_595061.pdf

Ministry of Education, Science, and Sport. (2016a). *Strategy for the internationalisation of Slovenian higher education 2016-2020*. https://eng.cmepius.si/wp-content/uploads/2015/08/Strategija-internacionalizacije-slovenskega-visokega-solstva_ENG_2016%E2%80%932020_WEB.pdf

Ministry of Education, Science, and Sport. (2016b). *Pregled stanja v slovenskem visokem šolstvu na področju internacionalizacije* [An overview of the situation in Slovenian higher education in the field of internationalization]. http://mizs.arhiv-spletisc.gov.si/si/delovna_podrocja/direktorat_za_visoko_solstvo/sektor_za_visoko_solstvo/internacionalizacija_vs/

Ministry of Education, Science, and Sport. (2017). *Action plan strategy for the internationalisation of Slovenian higher education 2016–2018: Collected objectives, measures, indicators, responsibilities with a time plan*. https://eng.cmepius.si/wp-content/uploads/2015/08/Akcijski-nacrt-2016-2018_ANG_WEB.pdf

Ministry of Education, Science, and Sport. (2019). *Akcijski načrt za obdobje do leta 2020 - Uresničevanje akcijskega načrta* [Action plan for the period until 2020 - Implementation of the action plan]. https://www.gov.si/teme/internacionalizacija-visokega-solstva/

Ministry of Higher Education, Science, and Technology. (2011). *Nacionalni program visokega šolstva 2011–2020 ter Raziskovalna in inovacijska strategija Slovenije 2011–2020* [The national higher education program 2011–2020 and the research and innovation strategy of Slovenia 2011–2020]. http://www.drznaslovenija.mvzt.gov.si/

Mok, K. H., Xiong, W., Ke, G., & Cheung, J. O. W. (2021). Impact of COVID-19 pandemic on international higher education and student mobility: Student perspectives from mainland China and Hong Kong. *International Journal of Educational Research*, *105*, 101718. doi:10.1016/j.ijer.2020.101718

Özer, M. (2016). The internationalization of higher education in Turkey: Realities, motivations and opportunities. *Insight Turkey*, *18*(4), 53–63.

Paris Communiqué. (2018). http://www.ehea.info/media.ehea.info/file/BFUG_Meeting/48/8/BFUG_BG_SR_61_4_FinalDraftCommunique_947488.pdf

Pawar, S. K. (2017). International student mobility in Indian higher education. In H. Alphin Jr, R. Chan, & J. Lavine (Eds.), *The future of accessibility in international higher education* (pp. 51–68). IGI Global. doi:10.4018/978-1-5225-2560-8.ch004

Public Fund. (2021). *Letno poročilo 2019* [Annual Report 2019]. https://www.srips-rs.si/storage/app/media/dokumenti/LP_in_PFN/Letno%20poro%C4%8Dilo%202019.pdf

Republic of Slovenia. (2012). *Zakon o visokem šolstvu* [Higher education act]. Uradni list RS [Official gazette RS], no. 32/12.

Republic of Slovenia. (2016). *Zakon o spremembah in dopolnitvah Zakona o visokem šolstvu (ZViS-K)* [Act amending the higher education act (HEA-K)]. *Uradni list RS, 75*(16).

Rome Ministerial Communiqué. (2020). https://www.eqar.eu/assets/uploads/2020/11/Rome_Ministerial_Communique.pdf

Sorbonne Declaration. (1998). http://ehea.info/media.ehea.info/file/1998_Sorbonne/61/2/1998_Sorbonne_Declaration_English_552612.pdf

SORS. (2017). *Student enrolment in tertiary education, Slovenia, academic year 2016/2017.* https://www.stat.si/StatWeb/en/News/Index/6665

SORS. (2018). *Student enrolment in tertiary education, Slovenia, academic year 2017/2018.* https://www.stat.si/StatWeb/news/Index/7433

SORS. (2019). *Student enrolment in tertiary education, Slovenia, academic year 2018/2019.* https://www.stat.si/StatWeb/en/News/Index/8148

SORS. (2020). *Student enrolment in tertiary education, Slovenia, academic year 2019/2020.* https://www.stat.si/StatWeb/en/News/Index/8802

SORS. (2021a). *Student enrolment in tertiary education, Slovenia, academic year 2020/2021.* https://www.stat.si/StatWeb/en/News/Index/9537

SORS. (2021b). *Foreign and mobile students in tertiary education by type of education, group of countries, sex and type of mobility, Slovenia, annually.* https://pxweb.stat.si/SiStatData/pxweb/en/Data/Data/0955066S.px/

SORS. (2021c). *Population.* https://www.stat.si/StatWeb/en/Field/Index/17

SQAA. (2021). *Public Records.* https://www.nakvis.si/accreditations-and-evaluations/public-records/?lang=en

Teichler, U. (2010). Internationalising higher education: Debates and changes in Europe. In D. Mattheou (Ed.), *Changing educational landscapes* (pp. 263–283). Springer. doi:10.1007/978-90-481-8534-4_15

Toprak, T. E. (2019). Internationalization, mobility and englishization in higher education across OECD countries. *Journal of University Research*, *2*(1), 12–17.

Turkish National Agency. (2021). *Turkish National Agency official homepage*. https://www.ua.gov.tr/en

UIS. (2021). *Global flow of tertiary-level students*. http://uis.unesco.org/en/uis-student-flow

University of Ljubljana. (2014). *Strategy for the internationalisation of the University of Ljubljana 2014– 2020*. https://www.uni-lj.si/study/news/strategy-internationalisation

University of Maribor. (2013). *Internationalisation strategy "Internationalisation as Quality Development of the University of Maribor 2013-2020"*. https://www.um.si/en/quality/re-accreditation/Documents/INTERNATIONALISATION%20STRATEGY.pdf

Working Group on Mobility. (2012). *Mobility for better learning: Mobility strategy 2020 for the European Higher Education Area (EHEA)*. https://www.ehea.info/cid101043/ministerial-conference-bucharest-2012.html

Yildiz, O. (2021a). Changing paradigms in the digital age and entrepreneurial universities. In D. Günay, T. Asunakutlu, & O. Yildiz (Eds.), *University-Industry Collaboration Strategies in the Digital Era* (pp. 1–21). IGI Global. doi:10.4018/978-1-7998-3901-9.ch001

Yildiz, O. (Ed.). (2021b). *Recent developments in individual and organizational adoption of ICTs*. IGI Global. doi:10.4018/978-1-7998-3045-0

## ADDITIONAL READING

Aba, D. (2014). Internationalization of higher education and student mobility in Europe and the case of Turkey. *Cukurova University Faculty of Education Journal*, *42*(2), 99–110.

Colucci, E., Ferencz, I., Gaebel, M., & Wächter, B. (2014). *Connecting mobility policies and practice: Observations and recommendations on national and institutional developments in Europe: MPPC, Mobility Policy-Practice Connect*. European University Association.

Grabher, A., Wejwar, P., Unger, M., & Terzieva, B. (2014). *Student mobility in the EHEA: Underrepresentation in student credit mobility and imbalances in degree mobility*. Institute for Advanced Studies.

Gürüz, K. (2011). *Higher education and international student mobility in the global knowledge economy: Revised and updated* (2nd ed.). SUNY Press.

Klemenčič, M., & Flander, A. (2013). *Evaluation of the impact of the Erasmus programme on higher education in Slovenia*. CMEPIUS.

Knight, J. (2012). Student mobility and internationalization: Trends and tribulations. *Research in Comparative and International Education*, *7*(1), 20–33. doi:10.2304/rcie.2012.7.1.20

Kotsi, F., & Agiomirgianakis, G. M. (2013). Mobility of higher education students in Europe: The South–North differences. *International Journal of Educational Development*, *4*(3), 233–254.

## KEY TERMS AND DEFINITIONS

**Comparative Research:** A research methodology that aims to identify and contrast commonalities and differences between two or more units of analysis (e.g., countries, universities).

**Credit Mobility:** Credit mobility refers to a limited period of study or traineeship at an institution abroad to earn credits.

**Degree Mobility:** Degree mobility refers to an entire degree program that is completed abroad.

**Higher Education:** Higher education, also referred to as post-secondary education, is a part of tertiary education which results in an academic degree.

**Internationalization:** In the context of higher education, internationalization refers to the deliberate and active process of developing and incorporating an international, intercultural, and global dimension into the aim, functions, and delivery of higher education.

**Internationalization Policy:** A set of official agreements or a plan concerning the internationalization adopted by an organization, such as the EU at the supranational level, the government at the national level or the university at the institutional level.

**Internationalization Strategy:** A plan of decisions of an organization to achieve the desired (strategic) objectives in the field of internationalization over a certain time period.

## ENDNOTES

1 Data for the 2020/21 academic year are available for tertiary education.

2 Next to data on mobile students permanently residing abroad, SORS also collects data on students with foreign citizenship and mobile students with high school completed abroad. Data for the 2020/21 academic year reveal that 8,125 students with foreign citizenship represented 9.8% of the total student population in Slovenian tertiary education (SORS, 2021b).

3 Data is available for tertiary education (ISCED 5-8).

4 Available on https://www.cu.edu.tr/cu/international/internationalization-strategy-document

5 Available on https://international.deu.edu.tr/en/uluslararasilasma-stratejisi

# Chapter 9
# Internationalisation and Language Policy in European Higher Education:
## The Case of Austria and the Czech Republic

**Tugba Elif Toprak-Yildiz**
https://orcid.org/0000-0003-0341-229X
*Izmir Democracy University, Turkey & University of Hamburg, Germany*

## ABSTRACT

*The internationalisation of higher education has received considerable attention over the last three decades, and the phenomenon has transformed into a strategic goal in its own right. Consequently, internationalisation has caused higher education institutions to tailor their language policies to better compete in the global market and promote progressive values such as collaboration and harmony. While macro-level European initiatives have encouraged institutions to foster societal and individual multilingualism, an increasing number of institutions seem to favour English-medium instruction (EMI) over other alternatives. Taking the links between internationalisation and language into account, the present chapter examines the meso-level language policy of two European countries, Austria, and the Czech Republic, which have developed formal and comprehensive frameworks of internationalisation strategy in higher education. The chapter particularly examines the language management component of language policy in these countries by considering internationalisation, EMI, and multilingualism.*

## INTRODUCTION

Since the 1990s, the term internationalisation has become widely used in higher education, and the literature on internationalisation has proliferated (Soliman, Anchor, & Taylor, 2019). There have been various perspectives on internationalisation in the higher education context in terms of its objectives,

DOI: 10.4018/978-1-7998-8169-8.ch009

practices, and implications in the relevant literature. For instance, according to Knight (1994), internationalisation can be defined as the process of incorporating an international dimension into the teaching/learning activities, research and service functions of a higher education institution. What is meant by this international dimension is a perspective or activity that facilitates an international, intercultural and global point of view. On the other hand, Soderqvist (2002, p. 29) described internationalisation as "a change process from a national higher education institution to an international higher education institution leading to the inclusion of an international dimension in all aspects of its holistic management to enhance the quality of teaching and learning and to achieve the desired competencies."

Over time, the definition of internationalisation has changed considerably to include several other aspects. For instance, Yemini (2015) defined internationalisation as the process of supporting the incorporation of multicultural, multilingual, and global aspects into the education system in the hope of helping learners develop a sense of global citizenship. On the contrary to previous definitions, this specific definition recognises the significance of cultural and linguistic barriers to help international students become global citizens in an increasingly globalised world (Soliman et al., 2019). The concept of internationalisation, which has initially been associated with mobility and exchange practices, has broadened significantly to encompass international collaborations, international research and learning and define a higher education institution's culture and structure (Middlehurst, 2008). It has also been shown that there are many aspects to this complex phenomenon, such as language policy. Even though relatively underestimated in the literature, the interactions between language and internationalisation also deserve further attention (Llurda, Cots, & Armengol, 2014; Meyer, Gekeler, Manger, & Urank, 2013).

Internationalisation seems to exert a profound impact on the language policy of higher education institutions. Particularly, the English language has taken the lead due to its status as the lingua franca of academia (Lasagabaster, 2015; Meyer et al., 2013). According to Jenkins (2013), English as a lingua franca refers to the use of English as a contact language among individuals with different native languages. To illustrate, apart from serving as the medium of instruction in various parts of the world, English is also used as the medium of written communication among non-Anglophone academics who would like to publish in prestigious international journals in their respective fields.

The conception that the English language facilitates and exerts a profound impact on internationalisation in the higher education context has previously been echoed in the relevant literature (Lasagabaster, 2015; van der Walt, 2013). Apparently higher education institutions have begun to adjust their language policies in line with this conception, particularly favouring English medium instruction (EMI) over other alternatives. Though reasons behind the steady and rapid spread of EMI might vary across countries and institutions, the following could be major determining factors: increasing the share of international students and researchers in the highly competitive global education market, fostering dissemination and access to knowledge, broadening mobility and abroad opportunities, expanding students' job prospects in the market, increasing students' motivation and linguistic competence, and improving university rankings (Doiz, Lasagabaster, & Sierra, 2013; Kirkpatrick, 2011; Lasagabaster, 2015).

While an increasing number of higher education institutions all around the world, especially in the European context, continue to reformulate their language policy and offer study programmes and courses in EMI (Wächter & Maiworm, 2014), macro-level European initiatives (e.g., European Commission, 2004, 2013) have considered higher education institutions as vital agents in fostering societal and individual multilingualism and linguistic diversity. Likewise, over two decades ago, the Bologna Process (1999) was launched as a major initiative to foster internationalisation, transparency, harmony, and diversity in Europe. On the other hand, it seems that, at least in practice, the Englishisation process in the higher education context has undermined the European goal of multilingualism policy (Lasagabaster, 2015).

Even though language policy could be affected by a set of non-linguistic factors including but not limited to economic, social, and demographic features, religion, politics, and bureaucracy (Lasagabaster, 2015), Spolsky (2004) argues that language policy comprises three main components, namely language practices, language management and language beliefs or ideologies. In higher education, language practices might mean the actual use of a language or different languages in various academic settings. On the other hand, language management would refer to the development and declaration of an explicit policy about language use, such as which language to use for teaching, research and publishing activities. Language beliefs or ideology refers to individuals' beliefs about language and language use. In the European higher education context, language policy could also be distinguished and examined at different levels, namely the macro-level (i.e., European institutions' schemes), the meso level (i.e., European states' initiatives), the micro-level (higher education institutions' initiatives), and the nano-level (characterised by the higher education institutions' stakeholders) (Lasagabaster, 2015). Although European Commission (2013) has called for more centralised and broad strategies at European higher education institutions and fostered EU-level internationalisation strategies, language policies at European higher education institutions might differ considerably in how they are constructed and communicated. To illustrate, European University Association's (EUA, 2013, 2020) reports on internationalisation have revealed that institutions across the continent pose different approaches to internationalisation, are at different stages of internationalisation, and vary in the degree of explicitness they communicate their internationalisation policy.

Considering internationalisation has caused higher education institutions to reformulate and reshape their language policy to varying degrees amid the discussions on EMI and multilingualism, the present chapter aims to examine the language policy of European higher education institutions at the meso, in other words, at the country level. Since previously it has been documented that the number of countries that have comprehensive internationalisation strategies for higher education is currently not high (Matei & Iwinska, 2015), this chapter focuses particularly on two countries, Austria and the Czech Republic, which have formal, well-articulated and comprehensive internationalisation strategies for higher education. To be more specific, the present chapter seeks answers to these questions: 1) Within the context of internationalisation, how is language policy, particularly language management, considered in the Austrian and Czech higher education systems? and 2) Are there any discrepancies and similarities between the Austrian and Czech higher education language policy within the context of internationalisation?

## BACKGROUND

### The Concept of Internationalisation and Approaches to Internationalisation

Even though the term internationalisation needs to be international by definition, the conceptualisation of internationalisation may vary across countries and higher education institutions. To illustrate, while in some cases the term is used to refer to border-crossing phenomena such as knowledge transfer, mobility and collaboration, in other cases, internationalisation could be associated with diversification, change, internationality, and growth (Teichler, 2017). Besides, internationalisation has been associated with progressive and liberal values such as multiculturalism, diversity and cosmopolitanism, but has also been linked with competition, markets and stratification (Jones, Leask, Brandenburg, & de Wit, 2021).

To date, one of the most commonly accepted definitions has been provided by Knight (2008, p. 21), who defined internationalisation as "the process of integrating an international, intercultural, or global dimension into the purpose, functions or delivery of higher education at the institutional and national levels". Moreover, more updated definitions of internationalisation have emphasised the contribution of internationalisation to society and communities at home and abroad (de Wit, Hunter, Howard, & Egron-Polak, 2015). According to Teichler (2017, p. 180-181), there are six primary meanings of internationalisation which can be listed as worldwide knowledge transfer, student/faculty/staff physical mobility, international cooperation and communication across countries and institutions, international education, and research in terms of intercultural learning, socialisation, international similarity including Europeanisation and globalisation, and international reputation. Likewise, in Curaj, Matei, Pricopie, Salmi, & Scott (2015), these were some of the aspects of internationalisation that were dealt with: student mobility, internationalisation as a catalyst of change, intercultural competence, and the quality of internationalisation.

The significance of internationalisation has increased steadily over time, and these days internationalisation has become a key indicator for the competitiveness and visibility of higher education institutions. For this reason, higher education institutions worldwide have taken the concept of internationalisation seriously and implemented a series of actions to unlock their potential for internationalisation. Although these actions and the degree of importance attached to this concept may vary from institution to institution, developing detailed internationalisation strategic plans, increasing the number of international students and teaching staff (Mosneaga & Agergaard, 2012), updating and internationalising the curriculum (Luxon & Peelo, 2009), supporting student and teaching staff research mobility (Jacob & Meek, 2013), opening satellite campuses in different countries (Wilkins & Huisman, 2012) and improving linguistic and intercultural skills of the students (Stier, 2006) could be considered the most common internationalisation efforts. To date, internationalisation has transformed into one of the most crucial performance measures in its own right, as manifested in several international ranking systems such as the Times Higher Education and the QS World University Rankings (Soliman et al., 2019).

In a similar vein, European Commission (2013) suggested that a broad internationalisation strategy should encompass significant areas divided into three categories, namely, international student and staff mobility, the internationalisation and improvement of curriculum and digital learning, and strategic cooperation, partnerships and capacity building. Partially in line with this view, many higher education institutions have focused most of their efforts on mobility practices and attracting international students. On the other hand, it is safe to posit that mobility practices, although showing a steady increase over the years, still constitute only a portion of internationalisation since a significant number of students and staff are not internationally mobile. Hence, bringing an international dimension to study programmes at all levels is needed to ensure that all students and staff can enhance their international skills without changing their location, a process named internationalisation at home (European Commission, 2013). At this point, bringing an international dimension to teaching, learning, and research practices grows highly significant.

## The Benefits of Internationalisation

Internationalisation may offer many benefits to students, higher education institutions and countries. Internationalisation can offer students quality education and experiential learning opportunities that are difficult to seize in their home contexts. Moreover, it may help students increase their awareness of global issues, cultures, and languages. When it comes to organisations, internationalisation can help higher education institutions attract better-skilled students and boost their visibility and reputation among other institutions. Furthermore, internationalisation can help higher education institutions in forming strategic partnerships with other institutions, supporting their academic staff's academic development and efforts by enlarging the academic community, mobilising intellectual resources, and establishing research groups (Hénard, Diamond, & Roseveare, 2012; Yildiz, 2021). Finally, countries may also benefit from internationalisation practices since internationalisation can help countries build a skilled workforce, create revenue, boost exchange and cooperation practices in research and development initiatives, and present more affordable alternatives to education opportunities at home (OECD, 2018).

## Language Policy, Multilingualism, and EMI in the Process of Internationalisation

As pointed out earlier, bringing an international dimension to the internationalisation processes in higher education accentuates the significance of language and language policies implemented at higher education institutions. Even though a vast majority of literature on internationalisation has focused on more visible components of internationalisation such as student mobility, the concept of internationalisation is broad enough to encompass linguistic and intercultural aspects of teaching, research and extracurricular activities that help hone students' intercultural and linguistic skills (Wächter, 2003). Besides, language could be considered one of the most powerful tools for internationalisation (Doiz et al., 2013). Hence, exploring the links between language and internationalisation would be a fruitful endeavour.

In our age, multicultural awareness is regarded as one of the most sought-after assets. In the job market, individuals are expected to possess international networking, multicultural and multilingual skills to effectively interact in various international settings (Hénard et al., 2012). In the higher education sector, the current OECD figures indicate that the number of students attending higher education institutions outside their country of citizenship has been steadily rising (Toprak, 2019). Additionally, special programmes and campuses are launched to host an increasing number of international students (Hénard et al., 2012). It is expected that this trend will continue in the future, and internationalisation will connect more students and faculty from various cultural, linguistic, and educational backgrounds. Consequently, a great number of universities all around the world are occupied with updating their study programmes to meet the needs of these international and heterogeneous student populations and the labour market (Holmen, 2015). To illustrate, a model on how to consider faculty, culture, and context has been developed at the University of Nottingham to ensure that the content, instruction and learning styles can be culturally adopted (Hughes, 2011). On the other hand, there have also been many higher education institutions anticipating that international students would automatically adapt to their new academic context abroad (Kelly & Moogan, 2012), an expectation that could prove unrealistic in many higher education settings.

It has been acknowledged that internationalisation can contribute to the development of higher education institutions by supporting multiculturalism and cross-cultural awareness (Hénard et al., 2012). On the one hand, according to the action plan provided by the European Commission (2004), higher education institutions are regarded as pivotal actors in promoting societal and individual multilingualism. Especially in the European context, multilingualism is deemed a highly valuable asset that should be recognised and fostered (European Commission, 2013). Closely parallel to this view, adding multiple languages in one's linguistic gearbox is considered to expand career prospects, ease integration processes at the host country/institution, and boost intercultural competence. On the other hand, the English language has become highly associated and almost synonymous with internationalisation (Coleman, 2006). Several reports have suggested that the Commission's emphasis on multilingualism remains an ideal rather than reality in many higher education settings (OECD, 2018, 2019; Wächter & Maiworm, 2014).

It seems that whilst the landscape of internationalised higher education changes rapidly, the English language continues to dominate other languages as the language of academia. To be more precise, the direction of international students' flow to English-speaking countries for study purposes and the steady increase in the number of EMI programmes in non-Anglophone countries might suggest that higher education institutions embrace Englishisation or EMI rather than multilingualism in their race for internationalisation. This tendency might have to do with the observation that offering EMI programmes and courses has increased the attractiveness of many higher education institutions and the fact that the English language is assuming the role of academic lingua franca (Doiz, Lasagabaster, & Sierra, 2011). This situation is hardly surprising considering that EMI has also been reported to bring about many personal, linguistic, and occupational benefits, including but not limited to broadening individuals' minds, increasing students' motivation, promoting students' linguistic competence and performance, and providing increased mobility and abroad opportunities (Doiz et al., 2013). As a result, a vast number of higher education intuitions have embraced EMI to increase their capacity to compete in the global education market (Wächter & Maiworm, 2014). EMI programmes are reported to increase exponentially not only in Europe but also in various parts of Asia (Arik & Arik, 2014; Fenton-Smith, Humphreys, & Walkinshaw, 2017; Kirkgöz, 2009; McMullen, 2014; Wächter & Maiworm 2008, 2014). Thus, contrary to the European Commission's efforts and calls to boost multilingualism and multiculturalism in higher education, it seems that many institutions would continue to pay more attention to EMI to attract better-skilled students and researchers and boost their students' competitiveness in the job market.

Even though the perceived benefits of the increasing use of English have been reported in the relevant literature, some scholars also argue that the links between internationalisation and Englishisation or any other powerful language cannot be considered neutral (Doiz et al., 2013; Phillipson 2009; Shohamy 2007). As a consequence, it has been claimed that internationalisation is likely to trigger tensions or conflicts between the languages (i.e., local languages, English as a lingua franca and international students' home languages) used in a particular HE context (Doiz et al., 2013). Likewise, although a substantial portion of students attending higher education institutions located in English-speaking countries comes from a highly heterogonous multilingual and multicultural background (OECD, 2018, 2019, 2020), these institutions seem to remain highly monolingual and multilingual students are anticipated to maintain a certain kind of language practices (Doiz et al., 2011). Taking all these issues into account, the present chapter focuses on the language policy proclaimed in two countries of interest (i.e., Austria and the Czech Republic) in the context of internationalisation of the higher education.

## METHODS

### Materials and Data Analysis

The present study is based on an examination of national policy documents in the countries of interest (i.e., Austria and the Czech Republic), particularly concentration on their internationalisation strategy at the higher education level. The study uses document analysis, which can be defined as a form of qualitative analysis, a systematic procedure for reviewing and examining both printed and electronic material such as newspapers, organisation reports, radio and television program scripts, diaries, and journals. (Bowen, 2009; Frey, 2018). Document analysis involves repeated review, examination, and interpretation of the data to understand the phenomenon at hand.

The primary strategy documents that were closely and iteratively examined within the scope of the present study were "National Mobility and Internationalisation Strategy for Higher Education "2020 – 2030 "There are many routes to internationalisation" released by the Austrian Federal Ministry of Education, Science and Research in 2020, and "Strategy for the internationalisation of higher education for the period from 2021" published by the Czech Ministry of Education, Youth and Sports (MEYS) in 2020. Apart from these documents, European University Association's (EUA) reports on internationalisation in the European higher education area (2013, 2020) and European Commission's (2013) report on European higher education in the world were examined to better understand the ecology of internationalisation. Finally, Wächter and Maiworm's (2014) report entitled "English-taught programmes in European higher education" was examined to gain more insights into language policies that have been implemented in these two countries.

These documents were processed by using skimming (superficial examination), reading (thorough examination), and interpretation in an iterative fashion (Bowen, 2009). Since document analysis combines the elements of content analysis and thematic analysis, relevant information was coded and organised into categories based on the research questions of the study.

## RESULTS

### An Overview of the Austrian Internationalisation Strategy

Austria's strategy named "National Mobility and Internationalisation Strategy for Higher Education" (Austrian Federal Ministry of Education, Science and Research, 2020) considers four sectors: public universities, universities of applied sciences, private universities, and teacher education colleges. Since each sector has very different objectives, priorities, and conditions, the strategy does not suggest a one-size-fits-all approach to internationalisation. Higher education institutions are expected to choose suitable objectives from five overarching objectives based on their profiles and objectives. These overarching objectives can be summarised as follows: promoting an all-encompassing culture of internationalisation at higher education institutions, promoting mobility for all members of higher education institutions, developing and implementing the innovative digital forms of mobility, supporting the effective skills improvement and institutional learning, and developing a global mindset. Internationalisation is regarded as a key to raising the country's profile as a global higher education centre. Austria's internationalisation strategy is reported to be based on the notion of "internationalisation of curriculum", which refers to integrating global, international and intercultural aspects into the goals and content of higher education by using a holistic approach. Accordingly, internationalisation is taken into account while arranging course content, teaching methods, and assessment criteria.

## Language Policy in the Austrian Strategy

In the vision for 2030 statement, the strategy clarifies that the Austrian higher education students are envisioned as individuals with great international and intercultural skills, speaking several languages. Even though none of the overarching objectives is directly related to language policy, all objectives specified in the strategy document have direct references to foreign language and intercultural skills, except for the last objective. To accomplish the first objective, "promoting an all-encompassing culture of internationalisation at higher education institutions", higher education institutions are recommended to increase the number of courses taught in a foreign language and the number of foreign language degree programmes, especially at the universities of applied sciences. The strategy suggests that the number of foreign language courses for lecturers and staff is increased as well. Under the "Internationalisation@ Home" umbrella, the strategy lists all measures that are intended to develop an international environment at a higher education institution. This scheme offers a wide range of courses taught in foreign language and language learning courses, supports students' interaction with foreign higher education students and calls for a welcoming culture for incoming students and lecturers.

In line with the second objective, "promoting mobility for all members of higher education institutions", the strategy asserts that improving the foreign language skills of lecturers is highly crucial to mobility experiences. Furthermore, launching language courses, summer/winter schools and excursions is recommended to support student mobility. The third objective, "developing and implementing innovative digital forms of mobility", is closely related to the "Internationalisation@Home" scheme, and it seeks to promote intercultural, international and foreign language skills in a virtual mobility setting. Based on the third objective, the strategy refers to a specific type of digital mobility called blended mobility. Blended mobility, as its name already suggests, blends the elements of physical mobility with virtual mobility. One specific example for this kind of mobility, according to strategy, could be a mixed face-to-face and online language course at a higher education institution with a different language abroad. Finally, the fourth objective, "ensuring effective skills improvement and institutional learning", puts forward that incorporating intercultural skills into all curricula, especially at the graduate level, is highly essential.

## An Overview of the Czech Internationalisation Strategy

The internationalisation strategy is intended to contribute to the attainment of the goals in international cooperation, as laid out in the Czech Republic Innovation Strategy to 2030. The strategy appreciates the significance of the internationalisation of the curriculum at higher education institutions to improving the quality of study programmes and helping students develop their international and intercultural skills. The vision of the Czech higher education system can be summarised as preparing students for a leading role in the global world and contributing to the sustainable development of communities and groups both in the Czech Republic and abroad (Ministry of Education, Youth and Sports, 2020). Besides these, incorporating the elements of internationalisation as a part of the courses in a foreign language and improving intercultural skills are also mentioned in the vision statement. The overarching objectives of the Czech internationalisation strategy can be summarised as follows: developing global competences of students and staff, ensuring the internationalisation of study programmes, simplifying the recognition process of foreign education credentials, building an international environment at higher education institutions and promotion, reinforcing the strategic management of internationalisation, and maintaining internationalisation activities of the National Accreditation Bureau. The document regards internationalisation as a cross-cutting area encompassing a comprehensive set of activities and policies at national, institutional, continental, and global levels.

## Language Policy in the Czech Strategy

Throughout the strategy, there are many explicit references to language and intercultural competences. To illustrate, the first overarching objective, "developing global competences of students and staff", includes a secondary objective named "support for language and intercultural training of university students and staff". In line with this secondary objective, it is suggested that students and staff be equipped with language and intercultural competences, which are fundamental prerequisites for internationalisation. The crucial role of the language and intercultural competences in maintaining international mobility, international projects and partnerships, and the need for delivering study programmes in English or other world languages are recognised. Moreover, the strategy suggests higher education institutions take measures to use foreign languages as a central part of studies at institutions, make sure that students, faculty and staff are provided with a wide range of foreign language courses, expand the share of occupational subjects taught in foreign languages, ease access to foreign language study materials, and allow students' final theses to be written in foreign languages. Apart from language-related issues, this particular objective asks higher education institutions to launch courses that target fostering students' intercultural competences to help them understand the culture of partner institutions, heterogonous groups of international students and staff. Financial support needed to accomplish these objectives would be provided by the Ministry of Education, Youth and Sports. Under the umbrella of the first overarching objective, the strategy also recognises the importance of linguistic and intercultural preparation before joining mobility practices.

The second overarching objective, "ensuring the internationalisation of study programmes", is directly and explicitly linked to language policy since it primarily focuses on expanding the number and quality of study programmes taught in foreign languages. It is pointed out that study programmes taught in foreign languages would be the only way to attract a more diverse and sufficient number of international students to the Czech higher education institutions for more extended periods, as in degree mobility. The unique perspectives and experiences international students would bring with them, the financial benefits of recruiting international students (e.g., tuition fees) and increasing global prestige are considered to be the most obvious advantages of the foreign language medium instruction policy. Apart from these substantial benefits, foreign language medium instruction is expected to facilitate the integration of international students into the local student and academic community and to support internationalisation at-home activities, thereby providing domestic students with international experiences at home. In order to ensure the accomplishment of this specific objective, the strategy recommends higher education institutions take the following actions: launching foreign language medium instruction programmes that are attractive in terms of quality and price by considering the demands of international students, ensuring faculty teaching these programmes are equipped with sufficient linguistic and intercultural competence, and ensuring that the quality of foreign language medium instruction study programmes matches the quality of the programmes provided in the Czech language.

The strategy states that the Ministry, in close collaboration with the Czech National Agency for International Education (DZS), will contribute to the development of faculty's competences to teach in foreign languages through trainings provided by domestic and international experts. Furthermore, the quality of the theses written by students from foreign language study programmes will be monitored by The National Accreditation Bureau for Higher Education (NAB). The fourth overarching objective, "building an international environment and promotion", describes the country as a medium-sized, open economy that needs collaboration in education to reinvigorate individuals' professional and language skills. In particular, the Ministry supports a scholarship programme that welcomes international students and faculty and facilitates the spread of the Czech language and national aspects among international experts. Closely related to these efforts, the Ministry also backs up a scholarship programme for Czech language courses, which aims to spread the Czech language and maintain the positive image of the Czech Republic in the international arena.

## A COMPARATIVE LOOK AT THE AUSTRIAN AND CZECH STRATEGIES

Both the Austrian and Czech higher education internationalisation strategies seem to attach great importance to the concepts of "internationalisation of curriculum" and "internationalisation at home" in order to maximise the benefits that internationalisation could offer and raise the countries' profiles as a global higher education hub (Austrian Federal Ministry of Education, Science and Research, 2020; Ministry of Education, Youth, and Sports, 2020). Specifically, the two strategies of these countries recognise the utmost significance of language and intercultural skills to the development and maintenance of internationalisation processes. They suggest equipping domestic students with these essential skills to compete in the domestic and global markets. For instance, the Austrian strategy explicitly mentions the vision of higher education students who speak multiple foreign languages and possess intercultural skills. Although none of the main objectives is straight-forwardly about language policy, four out of five objectives strongly emphasise the significance of language and intercultural competence to internationalisation processes. The strategy proposes expanding courses taught in a foreign language and increasing the number of foreign language degree programmes. The strategy also indicates that fostering the foreign language skills of lecturers is essential for mobility practices. It also aims to promote linguistic and intercultural skills by using innovative digital initiatives and information/communication technologies under the initiative of "internationalisation@home" and "blended mobility". This way, it becomes possible to develop and maintain internationalisation practices even during extraordinary conditions that do not allow physical mobility, such as a pandemic. Nevertheless, it should be noted that what is meant by "a foreign language" remains rather vague since the strategy does not name a specific language. Moreover, although the term foreign languages is used several times, there is no exact reference to multilingualism or linguistic diversity.

The Austrian strategy seems to pose a more flexible and autonomous approach when laying out the objectives and possible implementations. This might have to do with the range of institutions (e.g., public universities, applied sciences universities, and teacher colleges) covered in the strategy. Since each type of institution might have different remits, the strategy adopts a comprehensive approach rather than favouring a one-size-fits-all approach. The strategy focuses on laying the cornerstones of the internationalisation process and allows greater flexibility to the institutions with diverse characteristics and needs.

To illustrate, even though the strategy underscores the importance of foreign language skills, details on existing or envisioned language policy and implementations are relatively scarce.

When it comes to the Czech internationalisation strategy, as in its Austrian counterpart, the significance of foreign language and intercultural skills is emphasised throughout the strategy. On the other hand, the Czech strategy is highly detailed concerning language policy to be implemented in the future. The secondary objective of the first overarching objective, labelled "support for language and intercultural training of university students and staff", sets forth the prominence of delivering study programmes in the English language or other world languages. As in the Austrian strategy, the Czech strategy does not refer to specific languages, apart from this exception. The strategy provides quite detailed guidelines about how to promote foreign language and intercultural skills and lists the measures to be taken by the institutions and the Ministry, including easing access to foreign language study materials, allowing students' final theses to be written in foreign languages and fostering lecturers' intercultural skills. The second overarching objective labelled "ensuring the internationalisation of study programmes" does not feature a specific reference to language policy, but it is completely intended to address the number and quality of the study programmes taught in foreign languages. The strategy names these programmes as study programmes taught in foreign languages without explicitly mentioning a language. However, since these programmes are intended to attract a more diverse and sufficient number of international students, increase revenues obtained from fees, foster global prestige and support internationalisation at-home activities, we may safely assume that these functions are provided mainly by EMI programmes. In addition to presenting general guidelines, the strategy lays out several actions to be taken by institutions, such as considering the demands of international students, checking the quality and price of these study programmes, monitoring the linguistic and intercultural skills of lecturers teaching these programmes by using a quality control system, and checking the quality of foreign language programmes against the Czech language programmes. The strategy briefly deals with the quality assurance and accreditation procedures and the promotion of the Czech language and culture. The Czech strategy does not feature any policy regarding the use of technology during internationalisation or language learning processes, except for the Single Digital Gateway. This platform provides online information about study opportunities, scholarship and study applications, and diploma recognition.

## DISCUSSIONS AND CONCLUSIONS

Even though both strategies acknowledge and emphasise the critical role of linguistic and intercultural skills in the internationalisation processes, explicit and direct references to multilingualism and EMI have been relatively scarce. Both strategies underscore the significance of speaking foreign languages rather than a single foreign language or a specific language, except one instance, where the Czech strategy mentions the preparation and teaching of study programmes in English. Since the Austrian strategy is intended to provide a road map for the institutions to design and implement their internationalisation strategies based on their conditions and priorities, overall, it remains relatively general and less detailed than the Czech strategy. On the other hand, the Czech strategy provides many details about the motivations behind foreign language medium instruction programmes, even though it does not refer to a specific language. However, considering that English has turned into the lingua franca of academia and there has been a shift from monolingual institutions to a new bilingualism where English is now an assumed basic skill (Meyer et al., 2013), it possible that foreign language medium instruction could refer to EMI in these two particular contexts. Llurda et al. (2014) also argue that among all associated factors, language has exerted relatively little impact on internationalisation policies in non-Anglophone countries since the majority of leading higher education institutions are located in Anglophone countries. Hence, the lack of explicitly defined and declared language policy guidelines may have resulted in an approach that automatically considers preferential language as English in these settings.

As a response to the pressures caused by internationalisation, higher education institutions have mostly resorted to these three language policies: a monolingual policy using only English, a bilingual policy using English along with the national language, and a trilingual policy where English is used along with the national and regional languages (Risager, 2012). In the long run, the two countries' strategies seem to attach greater significance to a bilingual policy considering that they support foreign language medium instruction programmes due to the benefits that these programmes could offer in terms of internationalisation. This tendency is more accentuated in the Czech strategy, which devotes an overarching objective to the effective launch and maintenance of foreign language instruction programmes and explicitly lays out each action to be taken by higher education institutions. At the same time, the Czech strategy also focuses on supporting the introduction and spread of the Czech language and culture by allocating scholarships and funding. This might be a reflection of the tension in non-Anglophone countries that favour internationalisation through English but also aim to protect and promote their national languages and culture (Cots, Lasagabaster, & Garrett, 2012; Lindström, 2012).

As pointed out earlier, both the Austrian and Czech internationalisation strategies consider the ability to speak multiple foreign languages and possessing foreign language and intercultural skills as valuable assets in an increasingly internationalised higher education system and labour market. On the other hand, they do not reveal any specific languages to be promoted within their internationalisation initiatives, except one case where the Czech strategy particularly cites the English language. Wächter and Maiworm's (2014) comprehensive survey on English-taught programmes in European higher education, one of the most important studies to date to investigate the spread of EMI, revealed that the share of EMI providing institutions of all institutions was 46.6% in Austria and 27.8% in the Czech Republic. Furthermore, the proportion of EMIs of all programmes was 9.4% in Austria and 6.3% in the Czech Republic. Note that these figures are pertaining to the year 2014, and the share of these programmes is most likely to have substantially increased considering the steady increase in the number of EMIs worldwide (Macaro, Curle, Pun, An, & Dearden, 2018). In a similar vein, the report demonstrated that Austria (88%) and Czech Republic (84%) had the highest proportions concerning the English proficiency of administrative staff members involved in the EMIs. Furthermore, all programme directors from Austria (100%) rated the English proficiency of their instructors as very good or good.

Notably, the internationalisation at home initiative embraced by the two strategies is worth mentioning especially considering the unprecedented changes and struggles that higher education institutions have needed to face since the beginning of the COVID-19 pandemic. Even though internationalisation at home is not foreseen to be a viable alternative to actual internationalisation practices, it can, to some extent, help overcome the difficulties that the pandemic has caused by dismantling the national borders and overcoming particularly legal and practical barriers (e.g., travel restrictions and visa requirements) to actual international activities requiring physical mobility amid the pandemic. Furthermore, it can support the foreign language, intercultural, networking and professional skills of students, faculty and staff in a virtual space, by bringing people from different institutions, countries and continents together.

Finally, it should be noted that the scope of this chapter has been limited to the language management component of the language policy at the meso, in other words, country level. In line with the focus of the present chapter, the analysis reported here was limited to the official higher education internationalisation strategy frameworks of the two countries. Language management concerns itself with developing and introducing an explicit policy about language use rather than focusing on the actual use of a language in various settings. Consequently, we should bear in mind that at the institutional, department, programme and even individual level, there could be cases where the actual language related implementations might be different from or even contradict the policy introduced. Hence, to what degree these policies have been or are being implemented at the Austrian and Czech higher education institutions could be a subject matter for another scholarly effort.

This research received no specific grant from any funding agency in the public, commercial, or not-for-profit sectors.

## REFERENCES

Arik, B. T., & Arik, E. (2014). The role and status of English in Turkish higher education. *English Today, 30*(4), 5–10. doi:10.1017/S0266078414000339

Austrian Federal Ministry of Education, Science and Research. (2020). *National mobility and internationalisation strategy for higher education 2020 – 2030*. Austrian Federal Ministry of Education, Science and Research.

Bologna Declaration. (1999). *The European higher education area*. Joint declaration of the European Ministers of Education convened in Bologna on the 19th of June 1999.

Bowen, G. A. (2009). Document analysis as a qualitative research method. *Qualitative Research Journal, 9*(2), 27–40. doi:10.3316/QRJ0902027

Coleman, J. A. (2006). English-medium teaching in European higher education. *Language Teaching, 39*(1), 1–14. doi:10.1017/S026144480600320X

Cots, J. M., Lasagabaster, D., & Garrett, P. (2012). Multilingual policies and practices of universities in three bilingual regions in Europe. *International Journal of the Sociology of Language, 216*(216), 7–32. doi:10.1515/ijsl-2012-0037

Curaj, A., Matei, L., Pricopie, R., Salmi, J., & Scott, P. (Eds.). (2015). *The European higher education area Between critical reflections and future policies*. Springer. doi:10.1007/978-3-319-20877-0

De Wit, H., Hunter, F., Howard, L., & Egron-Polak, E. (2015). Internationalisation of higher education: A study for the European Parliament. *European Union*.

Doiz, A., Lasagabaster, D., & Sierra, J. (2013). Globalisation, internationalisation, multilingualism and linguistic strains in higher education. *Studies in Higher Education, 38*(9), 1407–1421. doi:10.1080/03075079.2011.642349

Doiz, A., Lasagabaster, D., & Sierra, J. M. (2011). Internationalisation, multilingualism and English-medium instruction: The teachers' perspective. *World Englishes, 30*(3), 345–359. doi:10.1111/j.1467-971X.2011.01718.x

European Commission. (2004). *Promoting language learning and linguistic diversity: An action plan 2004–2006*. European Commission.

European Commission. (2013). *Communication from the Commission to the European Parliament, the council, the European economic and social committee and the committee of the regions: European higher education in the world*. European Commission.

European University Association (EUA). (2013). *Internationalisation in European higher education: European policies, institutional strategies and EUA support*. European University Association.

European University Association (EUA). (2020). *Learning & teaching paper: Internationalisation in learning and teaching*. European University Association.

Fenton-Smith, B., Humphreys, P., & Walkinshaw, I. (2017). *English medium instruction in higher education in Asia-Pacific*. Springer. doi:10.1007/978-3-319-51976-0

Frey, B. (2018). *The SAGE encyclopedia of educational research, measurement, and evaluation* (Vol. 1–4). Sage. doi:10.4135/9781506326139

Hénard, F., Diamond, L., & Roseveare, D. (2012). *Approaches to internationalisation and their implications for strategic management and institutional practice*. OECD.

Holmen, A. (2015). Linguistic diversity among students in higher education: A resource in a multilingual language strategy? In A. H. Fabricius & B. Preisler (Eds.), *Transcultural interaction and linguistic diversity in higher education: The student experience* (pp. 116–141). Palgrave. doi:10.1057/9781137397478_6

Hughes, R. (2011). Strategies for managing and leading an academic staff in multiple countries. *New Directions for Higher Education, 155*(155), 19–28. doi:10.1002/he.441

Jacob, M., & Meek, V. L. (2013). Scientific mobility and international research networks: Trends and policy tools for promoting research excellence and capacity building. *Studies in Higher Education, 38*(3), 331–344. doi:10.1080/03075079.2013.773789

Jenkins, J. (2013). *English as a lingua franca in the international university: The politics of academic English language policy*. Routledge. doi:10.4324/9780203798157

Jones, E., Leask, B., Brandenburg, U., & de Wit, H. (2021). Global social responsibility and the internationalisation of higher education for society. *Journal of Studies in International Education, 25*(4), 330–347. doi:10.1177/10283153211031679

Kelly, P., & Moogan, Y. (2012). Culture shock and higher education performance: Implications for teaching. *Higher Education Quarterly, 66*(1), 24–46. doi:10.1111/j.1468-2273.2011.00505.x

Kirkgöz, Y. (2009). Globalization and English language policy in Turkey. *Educational Policy, 23*(5), 663–684. doi:10.1177/0895904808316319

Kirkpatrick, A. (2011). English as a medium of instruction in Asian education (from primary to tertiary): Implications for local languages and local scholarship. *Applied Linguistics Review, 2*(2011), 99–120. doi:10.1515/9783110239331.99

Knight, J. (1994). Internationalization: Elements and Checkpoints. Research Monograph No. 7. Ottawa: Canadian Bureau for International Education.

Knight, J. (2008). *Higher education in turmoil: The changing world of internationalization*. Sense. doi:10.1163/9789087905224

Lasagabaster, D. (2015). Language policy and language choice at European Universities: Is there really a 'choice'? *European Journal of Applied Linguistics*, *3*(2), 255–276. doi:10.1515/eujal-2014-0024

Lindström, J. (2012). Different languages, one mission? Outcomes of language policies in a multilingual university context. *International Journal of the Sociology of Language*, *216*(216), 33–54. doi:10.1515/ijsl-2012-0038

Llurda, E., Cots, J. M., & Armengol, L. (2014). Views on multilingualism and internationalisation in higher education: Administrative staff in the spotlight. *Journal of Multilingual and Multicultural Development*, *35*(4), 376–391. doi:10.1080/01434632.2013.874435

Luxon, T., & Peelo, M. (2009). Internationalisation: Its implications for curriculum design and course development in UK higher education. *Innovations in Education and Teaching International*, *46*(1), 51–60. doi:10.1080/14703290802646172

Macaro, E., Curle, S., Pun, J., An, J., & Dearden, J. (2018). A systematic review of English medium instruction in higher education. *Language Teaching*, *51*(1), 36–76. doi:10.1017/S0261444817000350

Matei, L., & Iwinska, J. (2015). National strategies and practices in internationalization of higher education: Lessons from a cross-country comparison. In *Higher education reforms in Romania: Between the Bologna Process and national challenges* (pp. 205–226). Springer. doi:10.1007/978-3-319-08054-3_11

McMullen, G. (2014). The value and attributes of an effective preparatory English program: Perceptions of Saudi university students. *English Language Teaching*, *7*(7), 131–140. doi:10.5539/elt.v7n7p131

Meyer, S., Gekeler, P., Manger, S., & Urank, D. (2013). Plurilingualism, multilingualism and internationalisation in the European Higher Education Area: Challenges and perspectives at a Swiss university. *Language Learning in Higher Education*, *2*(2), 405–425. doi:10.1515/cercles-2012-0022

Middlehurst, R. (2008). Changing Patterns of Internationalisation: Implications for Higher Education. In K. Clarke (Ed.), *Quality in Partnership: 25 Years of the Council of Validating Universities* (pp. 83–105). Open University Press.

Ministry of Education, Youth, and Sports. (2020). *Strategy for the internationalisation of higher education for the period from 2021*. https://www.msmt.cz/areas-of-work/tertiary-education/strategic-plan-of-the-ministry-for-higher-education-for-the

Mosneaga, A., & Agergaard, J. (2012). Agents of internationalisation? Danish universities' practices for attracting international students. *Globalisation, Societies and Education*, *10*(4), 519–538. doi:10.1080/14767724.2012.690309

OECD. (2018). *Education at a glance 2018: OECD indicators*. OECD Publishing.

OECD. (2019). *Education at a Glance 2019: OECD Indicators*. OECD Publishing.

OECD. (2020). *Education at a Glance 2020: OECD Indicators*. OECD Publishing.

Phillipson, R. (2009). English in higher education: Panacea or pandemic? *ANGLES on the English-Speaking World, 9*, 29–57.

Risager, K. (2012). Language hierarchies at the international university. *International Journal of the Sociology of Language, 216*, 11–130.

Shohamy, E. (2007). Reinterpreting globalisation in multilingual contexts. *International Multilingual Research Journal, 1*(2), 127–133. doi:10.1080/19313150701495421

Soderqvist, M. (2002). *Internationalisation and Its Management at Higher Education Institutions: Applying Conceptual, Content, and Discourse Analysis*. Helsinki School of Economics.

Soliman, S., Anchor, J., & Taylor, D. (2019). The international strategies of universities: Deliberate or emergent? *Studies in Higher Education, 44*(8), 1413–1424. doi:10.1080/03075079.2018.1445985

Spolsky, B. (2004). *Language policy*. Cambridge University Press.

Stier, J. (2006). Internationalisation, intercultural communication and intercultural competence. *Journal of Intercultural Communication, 11*(1), 1–12.

Teichler, U. (2017). Internationalisation trends in higher education and the changing role of international student mobility. *Journal of International Mobility, 1*(1), 177–216. doi:10.3917/jim.005.0179

Toprak, T. E. (2019). Internationalization, mobility and Englishization in higher education across OECD countries. *Journal of University Research, 2*(1), 12–17.

Van der Walt, C. (2013). *Multilingual higher education: Beyond English medium orientations*. Multilingual Matters. doi:10.21832/9781847699206

Wächter, B. (2003). An introduction: Internationalisation at home in context. *Journal of Studies in International Education, 7*(1), 5–11. doi:10.1177/1028315302250176

Wächter, B., & Maiworm, F. (2008). *English-taught programmes in European higher education: The picture in 2007*. Lemmens.

Wächter, B., & Maiworm, F. (2014). *English-taught programmes in European higher education: The state of play in 2014*. Lemmens.

Wilkins, S., & Huisman, J. (2015). Factors affecting university image formation among prospective higher education students: The case of international branch campuses. *Studies in Higher Education, 40*(7), 1256–1272. doi:10.1080/03075079.2014.881347

Yemini, M. (2015). Internationalisation discourse hits the tipping point: A new definition is needed. *Perspectives: Policy and Practice in Higher Education, 19*(1), 19–22.

Yildiz, O. (2021). Changing paradigms in the digital age and entrepreneurial universities. In D. Gunay, T. Asunakutlu, & O. Yildiz (Eds.), *University-Industry collaboration strategies in the digital era* (pp. 1–21). IGI. doi:10.4018/978-1-7998-3901-9.ch001

## ADDITIONAL READING

Altbach, P. G., & Knight, J. (2007). The internationalization of higher education: Motivations and realities. *Journal of Studies in International Education, 11*(3–4), 290–305. doi:10.1177/1028315307303542

Cenoz, J. (2013). Defining multilingualism. *Annual Review of Applied Linguistics, 33*, 3–18. doi:10.1017/S026719051300007X

Dafouz, E., & Smit, U. (2016). Towards a dynamic conceptual framework for English-medium education in multilingual university settings. *Applied Linguistics, 37*(3), 397–415. doi:10.1093/applin/amu034

De Wit, H. (2002). *Internationalization of higher education in the United States of America and Europe: A historical, comparative, and conceptual analysis*. Greenwood Publishing Group.

Doiz, A., Lasagabaster, D., & Sierra, J. M. (Eds.). (2012). *English-medium instruction at universities: Global challenges*. Multilingual Matters. doi:10.21832/9781847698162

Jenkins, J. (2013). *English as a lingua franca in the international university: The politics of academic English language policy*. Routledge. doi:10.4324/9780203798157

Knight, J. (2004). Internationalization remodeled: Definition, approaches, and rationales. *Journal of Studies in International Education, 8*(1), 5–31. doi:10.1177/1028315303260832

Knight, J., & de Wit, H. (1995). Strategies for internationalization of higher education: Historical and conceptual perspectives. In H. de Wit (Ed.), *Strategies for Internationalization of Higher Education: A Comparative Study of Australia, Canada, Europe and the United States of America*. EAIE.

Liyanage, I. (2018). Internationalization of higher education, mobility, and multilingualism. In *Multilingual Education Yearbook 2018* (pp. 1–20). Springer. doi:10.1007/978-3-319-77655-2_1

## KEY TERMS AND DEFINITIONS

**English-Medium Instruction:** English-medium instruction refers to the use of the English language to teach academic subjects, other than the English language itself, in settings where the first language is not English.

**Foreign Language:** A foreign language is a language that is neither one's native language nor used for communicative purposes among the members of the community.

**Higher Education:** Higher education, also named post-secondary education, can be defined as tertiary education resulting in an academic degree.

**Internationalisation:** Internationalisation can be defined as the process of bringing an international, intercultural, or global dimension into the objectives, functions, and delivery of higher education at the national and institutional levels.

**Language Management:** Language management is a component of language policy and refers to the development and specification of an explicit policy about language use, including decisions about which language to use for teaching, research, and publishing activities.

**Language Policy:** A language policy can be defined as a set of regulations and practices that help bring about the planned language change within a society or system.

**Multilingualism:** Multilingualism can be defined as the use of more than one language, either by an individual speaker or a community of speakers.

# Chapter 10
# Integration of International Students With Education Processes Through Information Systems

**Ömer Güleç**
*Pamukkale University, Turkey*

**Leyla Özgür Polat**
https://orcid.org/0000-0002-5143-359X
*Pamukkale University, Turkey*

## ABSTRACT

*In the globalizing world, students can cross the boundaries and benefit from the education systems from other cultures. Management of the international students' acceptance processes are given under the responsibility of higher education institutions within the bounds of criteria determined by the Higher Education Council in Turkey. Therefore, selection process shows differences in each institution and the management of the process becomes difficult because of the increase in applications. Consequently, it has been an inevitable need to use digitalization and information systems to conduct this process correctly. In this chapter, digital transformation and integration in educational activities through the international student application process is discussed. This chapter involves different application methods used in universities and some enhanced processes. This chapter is to be a guide for effectively conducting the process of international student applications in universities using information technologies and how to perform integration with educational practices.*

## INTRODUCTION

Education is one of the most fundamental necessities of a society for its development. Each society has its own education system, depending on its culture, history and regime (Erginer, 2006). These differ-

DOI: 10.4018/978-1-7998-8169-8.ch010

ences of education systems among countries have an important role in supporting scientific and artistic improvements, raising successful individuals in the society, increasing the level of welfare of the community, and indirectly helping the countries develop (Erarslan, 2009). For this reason, students do not want to be limited to their own countries' education but want to benefit from the education facilities of high-ranking universities abroad. In Mazzarol et al. (1997)'s study, the six pull factors have been found to influence international student selection of a host country. These factors are knowledge and awareness levels of the host country, referrals and recommendations, costing issues, climate, geographic proximity and social links, respectively. At the same time according to González et al. (2011), the factors such as the university ranking, scholarship availability from European Union (EU), language, the population of the country could positively affect international students' choice. This demand leads the developing countries to make reforms in their own education systems. Changes made in education systems for international students coming from different countries and cultures and renovating the education with universal languages leave a positive impression on the education systems of developing countries. Besides, universities have been culturally and educationally enriched and economically benefited with the enrolment of these students (Martirosyan et al., 2019). In literature, these students are named as international student, student from abroad or overseas student. In this chapter, the term "international student" has been adopted.

The global mobility of international students in the 1998 was about 2 million, it reached to 5.6 million in 2018 with an average increase of 4.8% per year and it is expected to double in the following years (OECD, 2020). Developed countries give importance to this issue by hosting numerous international students (Şimşek & Bakır, 2016). According to the report prepared by OECD in 2020, while OECD countries are accepting approximately 70% of the globally existing international students where USA, Australia, UK and Germany are the top destinations in OECD countries, respectively (OECD, 2020). Every year, more acceptance of international students is aimed in the developing countries. This aim does not only increase the scientific and academic productivity, but also it supports the sociocultural and economic developments of the countries in a positive way. International students contributed approximately 300 billion dollars to the world economy in 2016 (ICEF Monitor, 2019). This contribution for only the United States of America's budget was more than 44 million dollars in 2019-2020 academic year (Institute of International Education, 2020). Turkey, in order to get more share from student mobility, sped up the movements on international student procurement through The Department of International Students which was founded within The Presidency for Turks Abroad and Related Communities.

Over the years, there has been an observable increase in the demands of international students for getting an education in Turkey (Gündüz et al., 2020). This increase is an important development for higher education institutions as well. In the recent years, there has been a notable increase in the number of international students who come to Turkey. This number is 153 thousand and 662 in 2018-2019 academic year, while it was 126 thousand and 681 in the 2017-2018 academic year (Higher Education Institution University Monitoring and Evaluation General Report, 2020). This increase brought the need for organizing students' preference and placement processes in a proper way. The international students chose to study in Turkey due to cultural, historical, ethnic and religious affinities as main factors. The other pull factors are identified as funding opportunities, lower cost of living and education, family's or friend's recommendations and receiving scholarships at least in one quarter (Özoğlu et al., 2015).

Many fields have been growing fast thanks to technology under the circumstances of the globalizing world. Improvements in Internet technologies and increases in communication speeds have directly influenced education processes (Yildiz et al., 2021; Günay et al., 2021). In the process, education should not be limited to the specified sources, but should be supported by technology (Güllüpınar et al., 2013). Education practices supported by technology make it easier for higher education institutions to globalize. According to this view, online education applications that provide benefit for learning motivation have been developed (Barak et al., 2016). In addition to Internet applications that involve hundreds of sources in its database and make learning foreign languages easier and enjoyable; there has been an increase since 2012 in the number of open-source education applications through which lecturers from many reputable universities publish their lectures online in their own branches (Chapman, et al., 2016). Thanks to Internet technologies, users can access lecture contents and materials whenever and wherever they want.

Due to the COVID-19 pandemic that started around the world in January 2020, the education of 1.6 billion students was interrupted (UNESCO, 2020), and accordingly e-learning activities and educational technology initiatives have increased (Shivangi Dhawan, 2020; Teräs et al., 2020). The course materials used during the pandemic process were transferred to digital environment and the training activities carried out were recorded. In this way, in addition to online learning, students have the flexibility to access course repetitions and all kinds of course materials whenever they want (Bozkurt, 2020). Today, it is seen that the use and development of educational technologies is very important in order to prevent disruption of education and ensure equality opportunities in unpredictable situations such as pandemics where urgent measures need to be taken.

According to Taylor (2001), distance education involves five learning zones and today's education system uses smart and flexible learning model that contains Internet based sources (Yorgancı, 2015). By using online education applications, students have more interesting, attractive, enjoyable and interactive education environment which can make presentations with ease with its instructive and rich contents (Uluuysal et al., 2014). For this purpose, Movement to Enhance Opportunities and Improve Technology or FATIH project, which was founded in 2010 with the aim of providing an integration between the opportunities and conveniences of information technologies and education activities in Turkey, was launched in 2011-2012 academic year. Within this project, it was aimed to create equal opportunities in education and improve education with the help of technology by equipping every school in Turkey with interactive boards, laptops, tablets, projectors and such.

Meeting the need for integration of today's education with simple, fast, reliable and advanced Internet technologies will take the targeted education quality to a fairly modern level. For proper and suitable use of Internet technologies in education, education goals should be set according to the necessities of the time. Within the frame of these goals, IT specialists should develop applications special to education systems, visual media materials that improve creativity should be generated, support should be given to reduce the costs of research and development and libraries and storages like cloud storages that can be accessed and shared anywhere, anytime should be created. For this reason, the development of Internet technology applications and their integration with education is very important at every level of the education system, especially in higher education.

In the recent years, distance education programs and applications have gained popularity also in many universities in Turkey. According to the information published by Higher Education Council of Turkey (Higher Education Council of Turkey, 2020a), courses are supported by distance education in many universities and distance education research and application centers have been also established within 120 universities. With the COVID-19 pandemic, distance education applications have been developed rapidly in higher education institutions or existing applications have been integrated with the education systems of the universities (Dikmen & Bahçeci, 2020). As a result, higher education institutions can easily conduct processes of education, assessment and evaluation, and feedback with the help of Internet technologies independent of time and place, even in unforeseen situations such as pandemics (Karadağ & Yücel 2020; Balta & Türel, 2013). In addition, Higher Education Council of Turkey has also created a distance education platform called "Higher Education Council of Turkey Courses Platform" for universities that cannot provide distance education support yet (Higher Education Council of Turkey, 2020b). The developments in the digital era requires comprehensive revaluations in managerial processes at universities (Yildiz, 2021).

In this chapter, an international student information system model for a university in Turkey is proposed. This system is designed to be a guide both for the applicants and the international students which is directly integrated with student information system and education support system. The purpose of this system is to support the application, selection, placement and admission processes of international students with the help of digital transformation techniques. To the best of our knowledge, there exists no information system model for international students in the literature.

Within the cover of this chapter, application and selection process is explained in general. In the following parts, stages of development since 2011 in the university that application has been developed is explained along with recently applied application and selection process. Statistical charts about the number of students who make application and certain registration and country-based numbers and rates of students who register to the university for annually are also given in this context. At the same time, integration of the international student information system with the university's other information systems is explained. In discussion, conclusion and suggestion part, achievements obtained by this work are scrutinized.

## LITERATURE

In the literature, many studies exist about international students in different topics. Even the countries can benefit from the enrolment of international students, some research rely on the income from international students in the literature. Thus, Bound et al. (2021) explored the role of international students in the US Higher Education System and the marketing of the US on an economic perspective.

Some of the studies about international students are about the effects of social issues on their education periods. Therefore, Ebinger (2011) and Jackson et al. (2013) examined some social adjustment factors of international students. Hung (2021) proposed a mixed model in Higher Education for international students' choice to study in Taiwan. Nguyen & Phuong (2021) investigated the physiological effects of returning home for studying due to COVID-19 pandemic of international students. According to the study, the pandemic has affected the international students' future plans and changed their behaviours. Khoshlessan & Das (2017) explored international students' study anxiety in a university under the parameters such as nationality, gender, age, degree and stage of education. Ammigan (2019) investigates the role of satisfaction variables of higher education institutes for international students and recommends the university administrations how to enhance this satisfaction. According to Gündüz et al. (2020), the common cultural and artistic activities of the host students in the classroom, school, and campus and the communication with the public in the settlement will enable the cultures to get to know each other better. Angove (2019) compares work-based learning performances of international commerce degree students in Germany. International students are evaluated according to key skills including problem solving and decision making, numeracy and quantitative skills, communication and information technology, self-management, learning to learn, self-awareness and application of research skills to business and management issues with the help of their developed methodology.

Zhang et al. (2020) investigated international students' perception in Medicine Faculty for online learning. According to the study, online learning is an effective alternative when classroom learning is suspended due to the factors such as COVID-19 pandemic although it could not give all the needs despite the face-to-face education for international students. Susanto et al. (2020), proposed an emotional geography of international students learning Bahasa Indonesia online during COVID-19 pandemic. According to the study, the students experienced positive feelings such as intimacy, safety, happiness, seriousness and successfulness and negative feelings such as confusion and anxiety. Zhang & Kenny (2010) explored distance learning experiences of international students who were studying in Canada. Wiranota & Wijaya (2021) investigated international students' perception towards online learning during COVID-19 outbreak in China.

When the literature about international students is examined, it can be observed that works done in this field dwells on socioeconomic and sociocultural problems of the students studying in Turkey. According to Kıroğlu et al. (2010), it was revealed that to get a good education, students coming to Turkey that is kilometres away from their countries, face adaptation, accommodation and social relationship problems and miss their home countries. In addition to this, Ülper (2020), Gürbüz & Güleç (2016) and Özyürek (2009) talked about the difficulties faced when learning Turkish.

Yabanova & Özerbas (2020) conducted a study on the characteristics, the problems and possible solutions of the selection process of international students in higher education institutions in Turkey. According to the study, management problems encountered during the applications, transparency problems in the organization and the exams, coordination problems between institutions, document verification problems, application tracking problems, quota problems, special talent exam problems, shortcomings of legislation, lack of a common database, lack of a central control mechanism and lack of personnel are determined during the selection process of international students. However, no work exists in literature which deals with the digitalization of the processes of examination, application, placement, registration and pupillage, and the use of technology to conduct these processes. Therefore, it is aimed to fill this space in literature with this work.

After all, the studies in the literature are mainly focuses on the language learning, distance learning, culture and social life problems of the international students. On the other hand, this chapter focuses on the digitalization of international students' examination, approval and placement processes first time in the literature. In this chapter, a sample application supported by internet technologies has been developed for international students for the processes of application, examination and placement in a higher education institution in Turkey. At the same time, information about different application and placement processes in the university that this application was developed was given along with statistical data and step by step development of the system. For this reason, this work is aimed to be a guide to increase the activity of process in universities on selection and placement of international students.

## METHODOLOGY

Case study examples of qualitative research methods were used in the chapter. Case study is an empirical research, which use multiple sources and investigate the events that occur in real life when the boundaries between the event and the place where the event took place is not clear (Anderson, 1990). Observation, interviews and document analysis techniques were used altogether in order to cover triangulation as a data collection technique. Statistical data given in the chapter cover the students applied between 2012-2013 and 2020-2021 academic years. The selected sample was analysed and interpreted through the actual data.

## System Design and Findings

### Application and Selection Process of International Students

The selection process of international students has been started to be taken under review by universities' own constitutions with the following notice from the Higher Education Council in Turkey: *"In the meeting of the Higher Education Council dated on 21.01.2010, International Students Examination (ISE) was decided to be repealed beginning from 2010-2011 academic year.* International *students who want to get associate and bachelor's degrees with their own means in our country need to be graduated from a secondary education institution and having examinations and scores which are deemed as appropriate by our chairmanship and determined by each university.* International *students need to apply directly to universities with beforementioned documents along with other documents that universities demand, and taken under review by universities* (Higher Education Council of Turkey, 2021)*."*

For this reason, universities should primarily prepare their application and selection criteria and instructions in this field. When overall tendency is observed in universities, it can be seen that some universities conduct the process with coordinatorship units while others prefer Registrar's Office. However, it is seen that every university that has acceptance for international students has an instruction. Lists of examinations which will have influence in the selection process also differ from university to university. In addition to the high-school exit exam, also called as "maturity diploma" in some countries, exams that are prepared by consulates and ISE exams made by universities themselves are used in the review processes of the students. Since these exams are reviewed in different scales, it is important for universities to prepare their conversion tables. ABITUR exams, for instance, are in the scale of 1-6, 1 being the score of the most successful student. For this reason, a conversion table which would levelized 100 score in 0-100 scale system to 1 in 1-6 scale system should be prepared. After all the processual processes, program vacancies should be reported to the relevant department and if an ISE exam will be made, examination committees should be determined. As seen in the general flow of the applications of international students in Figure 1, in the following stage, universities should accept applications within the compass of their academic calendars. Application and membership procedures are again within the structures of universities, where they are carried out in different methods such as conducting the application procedures online and receiving the documents by postal service or by hand; downloading the application forms through websites and again receiving the documents required by hand or by postal service, or applicants' applying to university in person along with the documents required. After receiving the applications, genuineness of the documents required and the suitability of the applicants under the criteria determined by the Higher Education Council should be checked over before the placements of the applicants to the programs. Checking process is done by university-authorized unit personnel during the application or after the application procedures depending on universities' application receiving methods. Placements should be done considering the order of preferences and scores within the compass of the converted scores among the suitable applicants decided after the checking process. Placements can be done manually or automatically by the systems depending on universities. Lining the applications up from the highest to lowest scores and making their placements considering their positions and

*Figure 1. Overall flow of the acceptance process of international students*

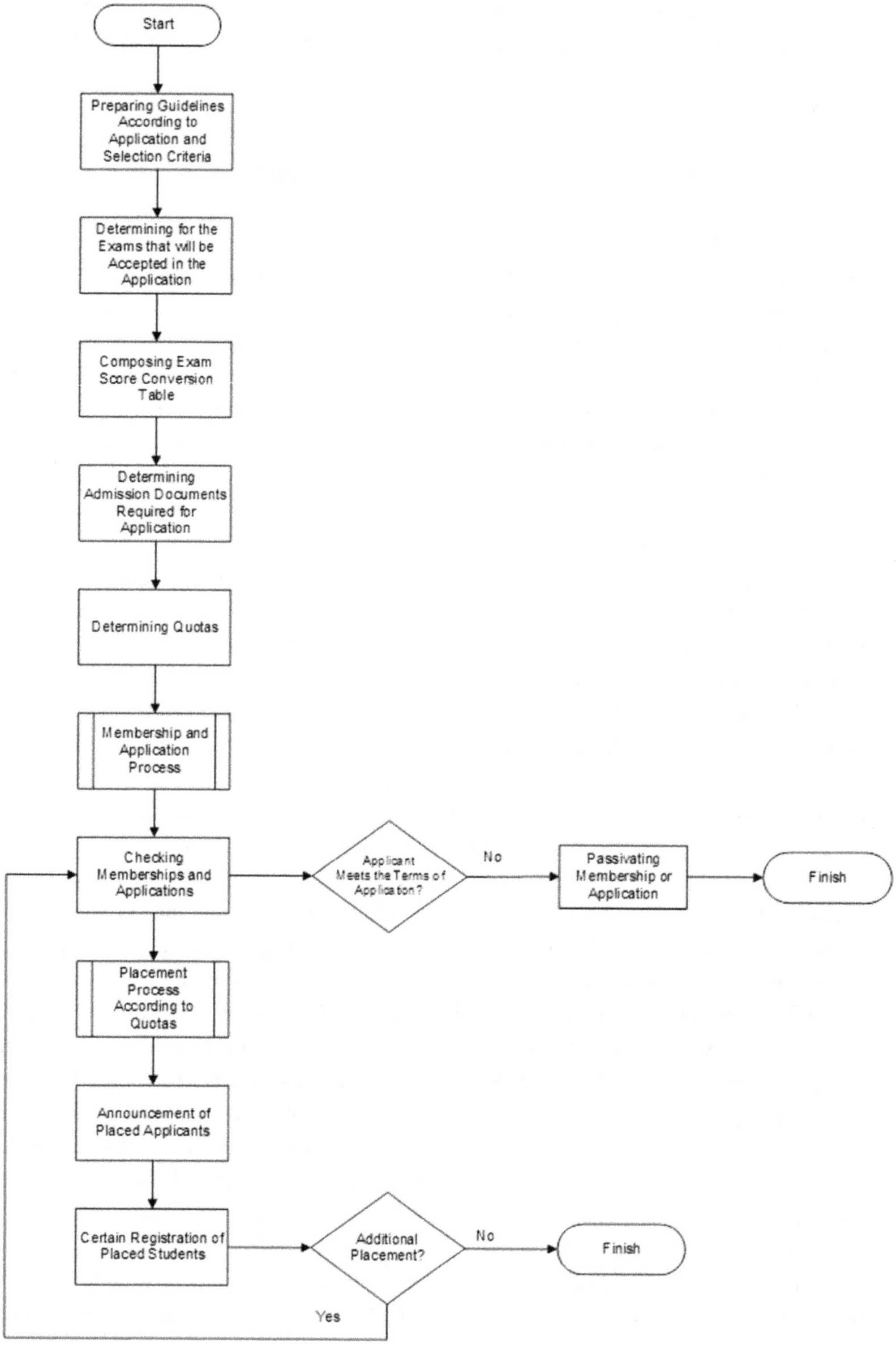

preferences will make the procedures easier. Another issue that should be paid attention is determining the precedence between two applicants with the same scores. After the announcements of the applicants that are placed in their program preferences, certain registration procedures of the main students begin. In the final stage of the process, in the case of an unfilled quota, the decision whether there will be additional placements will be made or not is stated by the relevant units of universities. Depending on the decision, the process can be restarted by accepting new applications or it can be ended when no additional placement is decided to be made. Since this process stands for the overall flow, not many details have been given at this stage. This issue will be mentioned in detail in the following part.

## Case Study

An application which was developed as a part of this work, was put into practice in a state university in Turkey after a period of trial and it is being actively used in present. Stages that are before the application procedure in the overall flow on Figure 1, are completed according to the principles determined by the Higher Education Council. Exam conversion table is prepared by lecturers who are experts in the field of assessment and evaluation. This university accepts international students since 2011-2012 academic year. Their first student acceptance took place with a method in which the documents were received by hand or by postal service and data were entered by the coordinatorship and only the placements were made from a system with a simple function. In the next stages a new method was developed which uses online system for applications, checking process and placements. Each year new methods were tried with the aim of using online system more efficiently, and in the last stage it was decided on the system which was used for applications and placements of students in 2020-2021 academic year. Existing system which provides a top-notch user satisfaction is being used actively.

Below follows the chronological stages and steps of the whole process:

***2011-2012 Academic Year Applications:*** In this academic year, there was not an online application system existed and application documents and preferences were accepted by hand or by postal service. Because of the difficulty of the placement system, a simple placement and data entry page was created. Information and preferences of the applicants were manually entered by the coordinatorship, only placements were made by the system.

***2012-2013 Academic Year Applications:*** In this academic year, applications were received online because of the difficulties that the coordinatorship experienced. However, documents required for the application were received by hand or by postal service. Applicants completed the application procedures and gathered their application documents from the system and gave their signed documents to the coordinatorships along with other documents required. Those who applied for ISE exams which are organised in universities and those who applied with other exams made their applications and program preferences on the same screen. At this stage, those who applied for ISE made their program preferences before their exam scores revealed.

***2013-2014 Academic Year Applications:*** In this academic year, applications were conducted the same way as the previous year. However, those who applied for ISE were provided to enter exams after receiving their applications until a particular date. Later, while other exams and applications were in progress, these applicants made their preferences.

***2014-2015 Academic Year Applications:*** In this academic year, applications and placement procedures were received online and documents required were also started to be received online, and no documents were received by hand or by postal service. After this stage, applications with ISE and applications with other exams were divided. Firstly, applications with ISE were received and after their exam results were revealed, applications with other exams were received at the same time.

***2015-2016 Academic Year Applications:*** Same system was used with 2014-2015 academic year. However, this year, exam fees for ISE were started to be taken. By communication with the contracted bank, list of payments was checked, and the payment information of the applicants was entered into the system by coordinatorship. Applicants without payments were not accepted for exams.

***2016-2017 Academic Year Applications:*** Applications are conducted the same way as 2015-2016 academic year. In the current active academic year, because of the difficulty of ISE which is prepared only by the university, program quotas are applied by determining quotas separately for applicants who will apply with ISE and other exams, and placements are made according to these determined quotas.

***2017-2018 Academic Year Applications:*** Applications are conducted the same way as 2016-2017 academic year. In this term, it was ensured that only ISE exams could be held simultaneously in different countries. For this reason, the applicant has been given the opportunity to choose the country and the exam center to take the exam.

***2018-2019 Academic Year Applications:*** Applications are conducted the same way as 2018-2019 academic year. In this term, quotas were determined according to the countries during the placement. The placement order is determined as one applicant from each nationality for each program to be placed.

***2019-2020 Academic Year Applications:*** For applications made until this period, a separate record is kept for each application of the applicant. In every application, even if the applicant will not change any information, all information is recorded in the system repeatedly. While this situation causes a waste of time for the applicant, it becomes difficult to control the applications by the coordinatorship. Systematically, all kinds of repetitive data causes wasted use of the resources. For this reason, the membership system has been put into use for applications in this period. Firstly, an applicant records the information needed only for one time, such as identity information, education information, residence information, contact information, exam information. After completing the membership process, the applicant can easily make all the applications on the calendar, regardless of the period of their membership. In this way, applicant does not have to save the information again and again in each application period but can update if it is needed. Every application is associated with a unique membership ID of the applicant.

***2020-2021 Academic Year Applications:*** Applications are conducted the same way as 2020-2021 academic year through the membership system.

After having face to face meetings with coordinatorship personnel and examining their problems that they faced in every stage, it was revealed that delays in postal services and manual data entering had been a loss of time and labour force in 2011-2012 academic year. In 2012-2013 and 2013-2014 academic years, it was observed that the delays in postal services and checking posts one by one and finding student registrations caused time losses and difficulties in the process of application approval. In addition, in 2012-2013 academic year, it was seen that applicants who made applications before learning their ISE exam results and having no other exam results, made unrealistic preferences. Since applications have been received online since 2014-2015 academic year, it has been observed that no problems experienced with the postal service and online system has proved to be more practical.

The overall flow of the system which is actively used is given in Figure 2 and Figure 3. When Figure 2 and its follower Figure 3 are examined, preparations of application systems and carrying out system checks should primarily be done in accordance with the academic calendar. It is very important for application and updating screens to be simple, easy to understand and involving indicators to guide applicants. Later, program quotas should be determined by departments and forwarded to the coordinatorship for entering quota entries.

The system that is actively used is a membership-based system in which applicants become a member of the system at first. The membership system is always open regardless of applications and applicants can become a member whenever they want. In the membership application, applicants save their personal information, contact information, education information and upload necessary documents to the system. Before creating a membership, it first goes through the membership control. According to this control, if the applicant has a previous membership, a new membership will not be created. If the applicant has been registered to the information system before and does not have a membership yet, the information required for membership is automatically displayed and a new membership is later created. If the applicant is not registered in the information system before but is already registered in the MERNIS System (Demir et al., 2010), a new membership is created by bringing all personal information from the MERNIS System. In this way, duplicate records in the information system are prevented and data integrity is ensured by working integrated with the MERNIS System. Once an applicant becomes a member, applicant can easily apply for any application opened at any time using this unique membership ID. This way, applicant does not have to save any information over and over again for each application. In addition, the applicant can update any information if it is necessary. This situation provides time saving for the applicant and ease of control for the coordinatorship.

In the next step, ISE applications are opened in accordance with the academic calendar. During this application, applicants should upload documents required along with some other information. Suitability of the applicants for the application conditions and the genuineness of the documents uploaded are carried out by the coordinatorship and the application status of the applicants are updated. If applicants are not suitable for the application conditions, their applications are passivized, and they are not accepted for examination. In case they upload wrong documents, they enter the system with their username and password and upload required documents if the deadline for applications and updating is not over. In case of deadline expiration, these applicants are again passivized. Applicants who are found suitable in the application checks are taken to approved status and accepted to take exams in determined dates, locations and times with their entrance documents. Data are entered into the system and applicants can access to their exam result documents with the announcement of the result of the exams. In the next step, applications for program preferences should be made in accordance with academic calendar. Those who make applications through ISE and those who make application through other exams make their applications through two different pages. Applicants with ISE applications enter the website with their usernames and passwords and just enter their preferences. Applicants with other exams applications, enter their preferences to the system along with their personal information and documents. Accordingly, controls of the applicants with other exams applications are checked and approved or passivized in the same way as the applicants with ISE applications. In this way, the list of applicants who gained the right for placements appears. First of all, exam scores of the applicants are updated in accordance with the conversion table. Now the coordinatorship makes the placements of the suitable applications in accordance with their preferences by clicking make placement button. In the procedure of placement, applicants are listed regarding their exam scores. In case of a same score situation, younger applicant is placed above the older one and if their date of birth is also the same, then female student is placed above the male student. After the procedure of placement, applicants are placed to programs in accordance with their preference lists. By registering applicants to student information system through the procedure of certain registration, applicants gain student status. After this step, it is decided whether the coordinatorship will make additional placements with a fast access to the reports of certain registrations thanks to information systems. In case of an additional placement, it should be decided whether new applications will be received or preference updates among existing applications will be allowed; or in case of a lack of certain registration, it should be decided whether placements will be made by existing applications and preferences using available quotas and disallowing any applications and application updates. In this current situation, since new applications continue to be received, decision on additional quotas has not been made yet. However, each decision was tried in previous years and the system was parametrically designed to be ready for these changes.

After the completion of all processes, statistical data can easily be accessed thanks to the information stored in central database. In this way, determination of international student strategies which will be practised in the future, such as the analysis of the current status and how the distribution of quotas can be made. Figure 4, Figure 5, Figure 6, Figure 7 and Figure 8 involve sample data on the university in which the application is executed. In order to show data in a proper way, data in 2011-2012 academic year in which the online system was not used, is not taken into account. At the same time, current data on May 15, 2021, are used as a base since placements for 2021-2022 academic year is still in progress. Figure 4 shows the proportional distribution of the applications in accordance with ISE and other exams. As seen in the figure, applications with other exams are denser and this density reaches up to the highest level of 94% in 2020-2021 academic year.

Figure 5 shows the number of applications, placements and certain registrations of international students according to academic years. As seen in the figure, academic year with the most applications, which is 7678, is 2020-2021 academic year, which is also the year with the most placements. However, as it will be seen in Figure 6, this academic year holds the lowest certain registration rate with 24% of the placements. The reason for having the lowest registration rates despite having the most applications and placements for this year can be explained by saying that students also applied to other universities and preferred the programs in those universities, or they gave up on the programs they were placed.

Figure 7 shows the most popular 10 programs according to the applications made so far. So, it is seen that the program of computer engineering has been the most preferred program with 7932 applications. In addition to the preference rates, quota occupancy rates can also be examined in order to support for determining program quotas in the following years.

Figure 8 involves the rates of students that started their educations according to the first 10 countries with the most applications. These 10 countries contain a scale of 51.20% within the total ratio. Students coming from Afghanistan hold the registration record with a rate of 25.14%. This country is followed by Syrian Arab Republic and Azerbaijan with the rates of 21.90% and 13.30% respectively. The rate of students who are holding a Turkish Republic citizenship who have dual citizenship is 21.62% of all applications.

These data in the university that this application is applied are presented in order to serve as a model for other universities that are accepting international students. Along with these data, it is possible to carry out different evaluations in accordance with the demographic features of the students and analyse different data depending on the needs of universities. In this way, universities can instantly scan their current international students' status and take support from existing data in order to determine their future international student strategies.

*Figure 2. Overall flow of the currently used application process of international students*

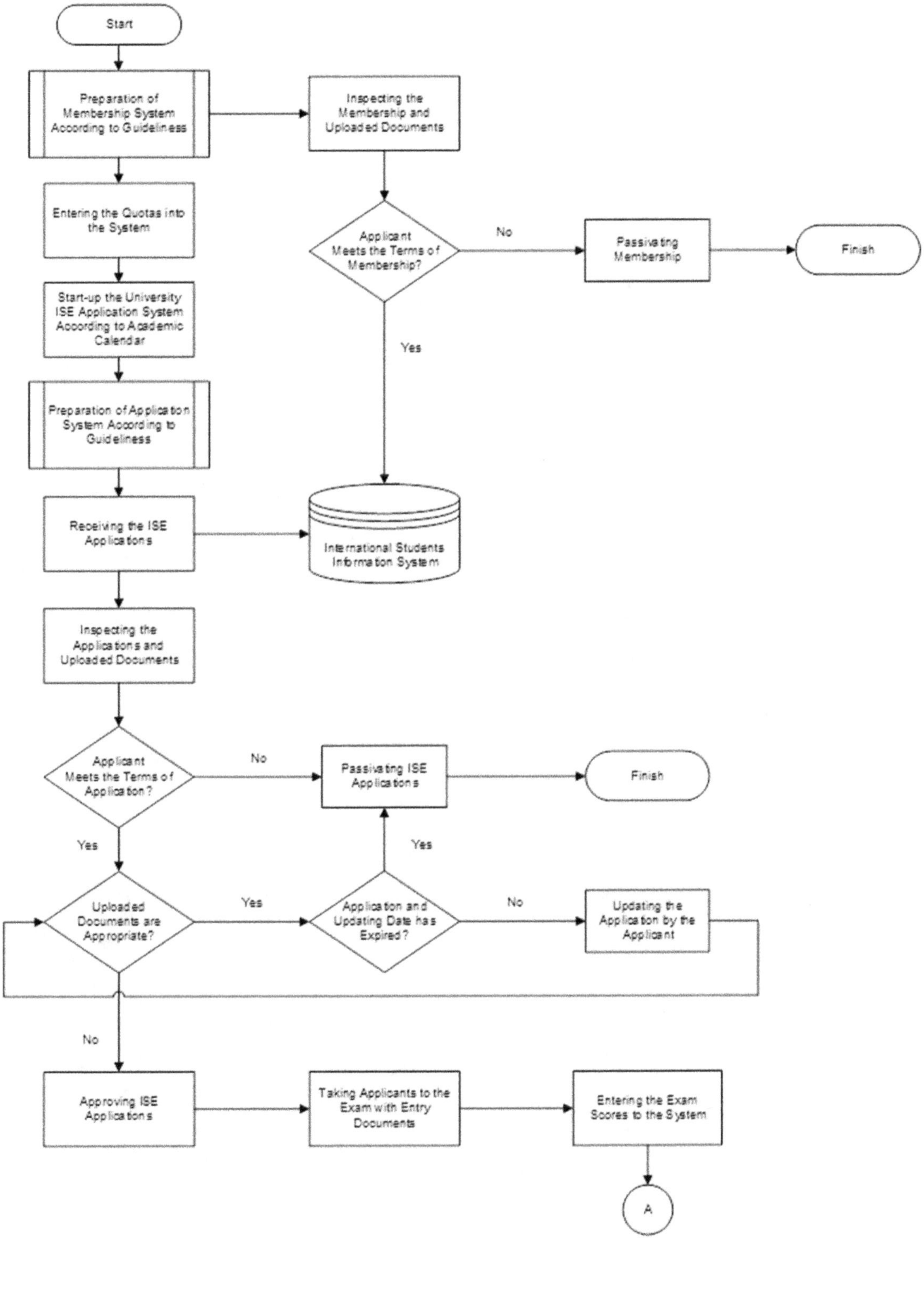

*Figure 3. Overall flow of the currently used application process of international students (cont.)*

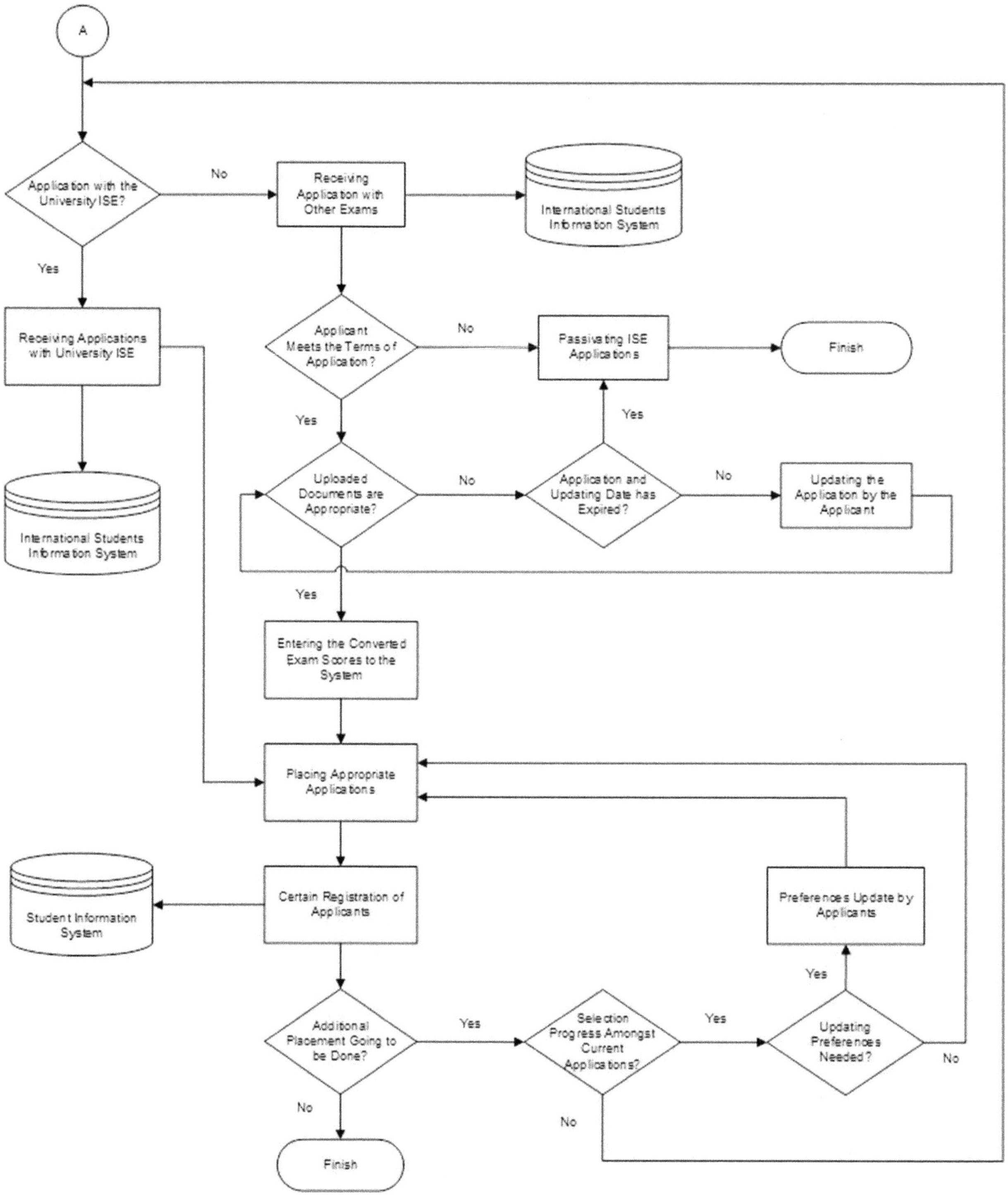

*Figure 4. Distribution of applications according to academic years*

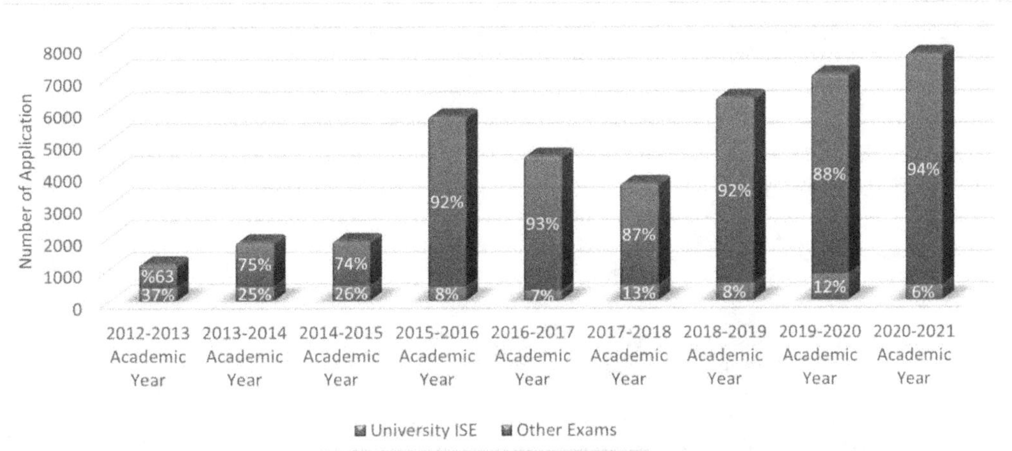


*Figure 5. Distribution of students with applications, placements and certain registration according to academic years*

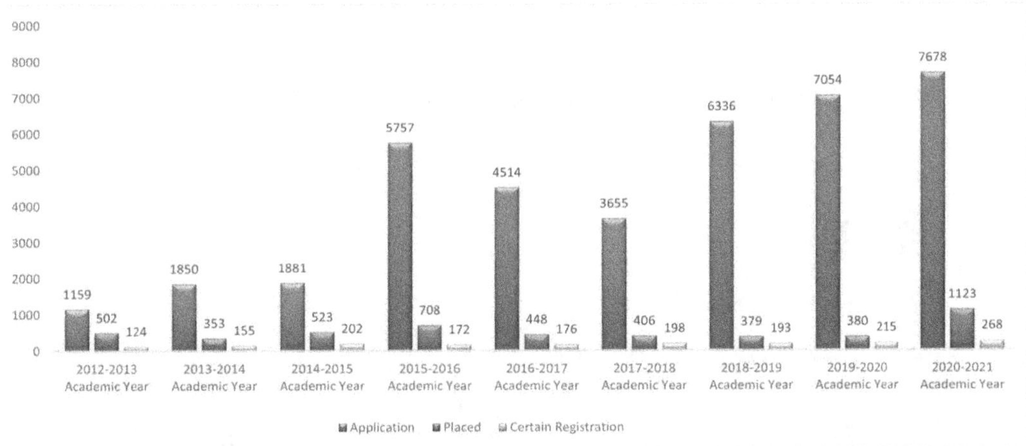

*Figure 6. Comparison of students with certain registrations and students with placements according to academic years*

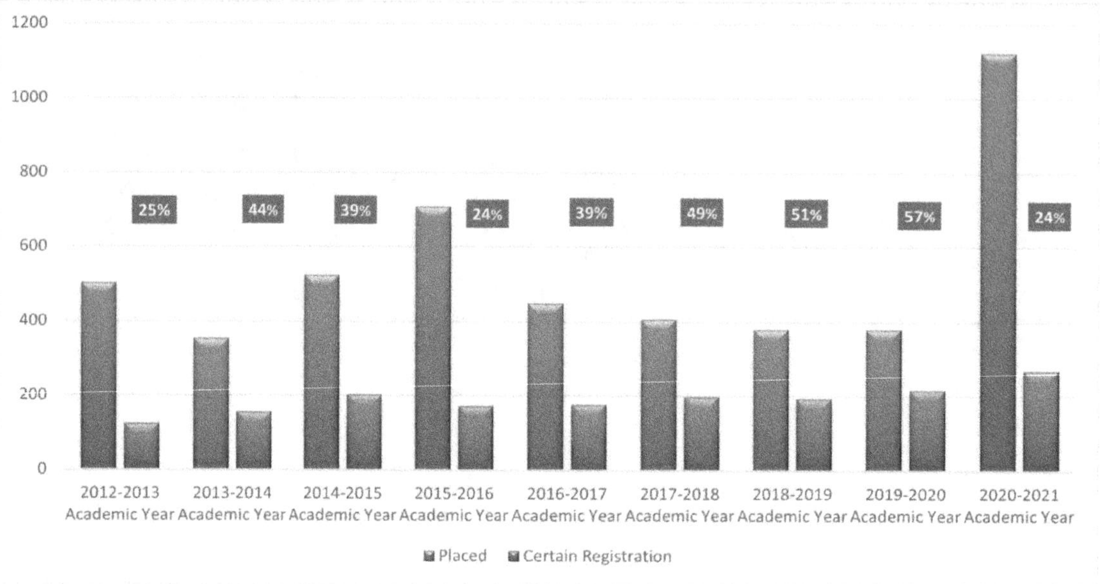


*Figure 7. The most popular 10 programs according to overall applications*

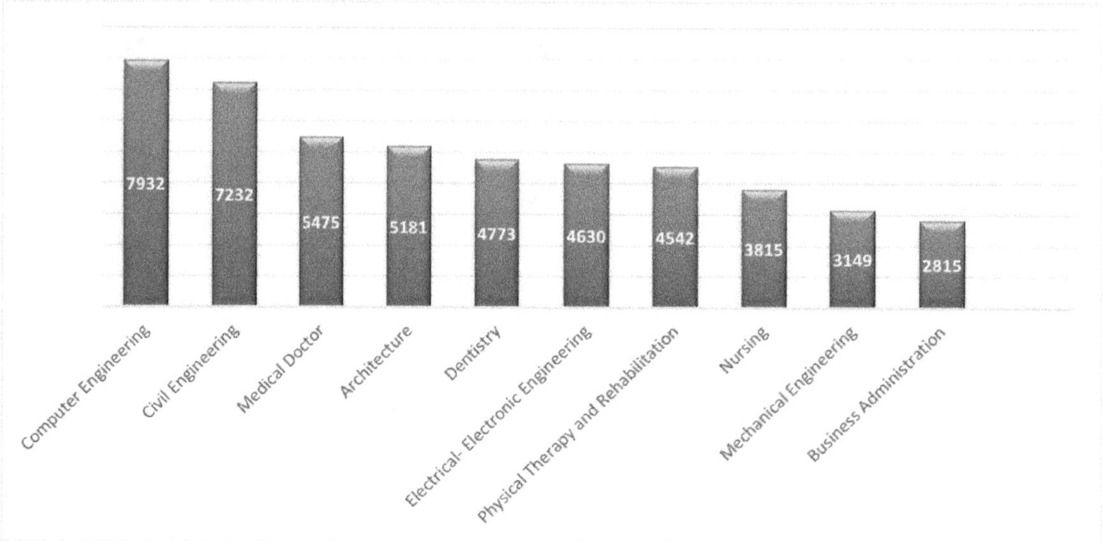

*Figure 8. The rate of international students according to the first 10 countries with the most applications*

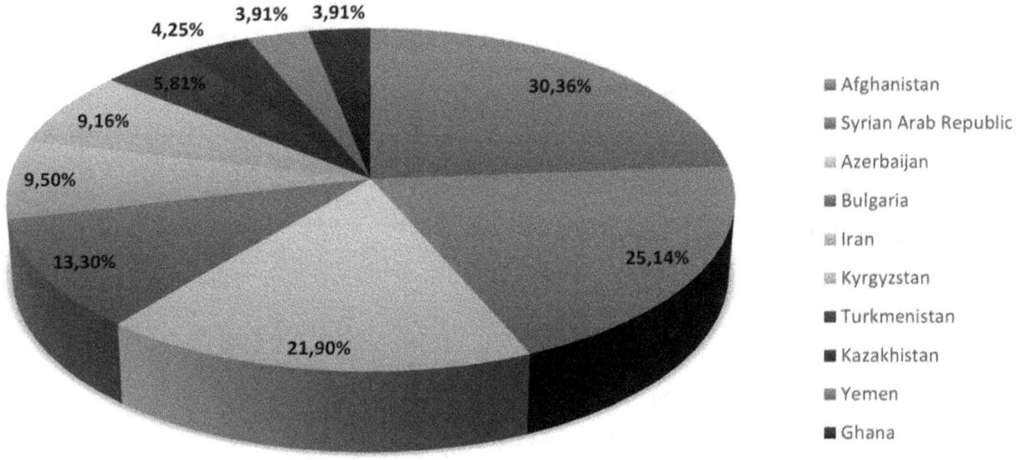


## Integration Among Education Applications

After the placements of the international students, certain registrations of the students are made in the related university. Unlike other students, these students need to go to universities in person and complete their registration procedures by handing their documents since they are holding a foreign nationality and not connected to the databases of the Higher Education Council and Civil Registry in Turkey. The certain registrations of the applicants are conducted by the coordinatorship along with the control of the documents required for the registration. With the completion of the registrations, students are registered in the Student Information System with their personal information, the program they are placed and their Turkish and foreign language qualification information. In this way, students who do not meet the requirements for the conditions of Turkish and/or foreign languages, need to spend a preparatory year or attend a course.

After the approval for studentship, if there is an obligation for foreign language in the program that the student is placed or if the student is not exempted from foreign language, student who had been automatically registered into Student Information System is automatically registered into Preparation Information System. In this case, information and scores of foreign language classes that the international student needs to accomplish along with attendance status are stored in Preparation Information System. If the program that the student is placed to does not obligate foreign language or if the student is exempted from foreign language, this student can now manage their educational procedures through the system such as selection of classes, checking of lectures and homework. Thanks to the integrated systems, this student, like other students do, can also check their scores, classes they need to take, course syllabi, weekly class schedules and locations, times and seating charts of the exams. Assignments of the classes that students select and assigning instructors to these assignments are again managed through the Student Information System. On the other hand, all, personnel information of every instructor is stored in Personnel Information System. For this reason, this application's compatibility with Student Information System, Education Support System, Preparation Information System and Personnel Information System as seen in Figure 9 makes it easier to follow up the successes of the international students. At the same time, in Figure 9, it is explained how International Students Information System is integrated with other information systems and on which fields data exchange is made for education practices.

*Figure 9. Integration among education applications*

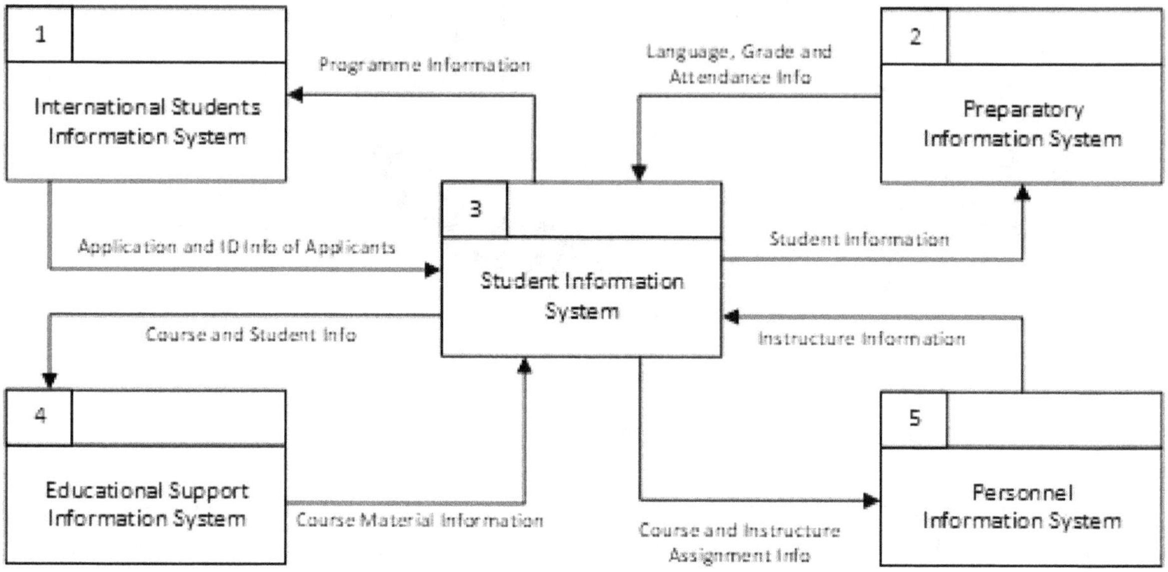


Personal information about the students is sent from International Students Information System where the placements of international students are made as seen in Figure 9 to Student Information System. In Student Information System, certain registrations of the students are made, and students are given student numbers. On the other hand, information on programs in which quotas will be opened, are sent from the Student Information System to International Students Information System. Student Information System contains information such as classes that international students who gained the studentship by certain registration have to select, credits of the classes, scores, attendances, weekly class schedules and the syllabi of the courses. If the program that the student is placed has an obligation for foreign language, student is registered into Preparation Information System as preparation student. With this registration, studentship information of the student is transferred from the Student Information System to Preparation Information System. Foreign language information, scores and attendance are stored in Preparation Information System. Success status and scores of international students who successfully complete preparation class are transferred to Student Information System. In this way, information about the compulsory foreign language that the student must accomplish appears on the student transcript. Information of the instructors who are assigned to the classes that students will take are stored in Personnel Information System. Education Support System is a system through which students attend classes and access class materials. Access to homework, practice exams, visual, aural and written class materials are managed through this system. All the desks belonging to every class opened in the university in the relevant period are added into the module of Education Support System. Within the compass of these classes, relevant instructors can follow an interactive lecture process with their students. Instructors are able to assign homework for students or check homework uploaded to the system by students again using Education Support System. In the same way, every exam related to classes is managed through this system. Evaluation of each homework, examination, and application uploaded by students can also easily be managed. Through Education Support System, instructors can start a debate related to lessons and can quickly reply to the questions of students. By the way, an active communication between students and instructor is provided. On the other hand, instructors can get feedback by preparing online surveys. Since Education Support System provides an interactive class environment, it is observed that the interests of students on the lecture increase. Additionally, in the examinations which are needed to be made in a computer environment such as programming and modelling, it is provided for the instructor who actively uses the system to conduct a fairer examination and reach data whenever and wherever he is. Thus, effectiveness and time losses of the examinations are prevented.

Consequently, applicants in Student Information System are transferred to Student Information System after certain registrations and benefit from interactive education activities through Education Support system like other students do.

## CONCLUSION AND SUGGESTIONS

It is important for students to get out of the passive status and take active actions and it is also important to make learning permanent in education practices by using interactive visual tools. In this stage, keeping pace with today's conditions in the globalizing world and reaching correct information not to be behind the times is possible by increasing both the technology and student awareness. Aggregation and cooperation of different cultures are inevitable, particularly in our day in which interactions grew up along with the globalization of education within international scale. Therefore, every process should be supported by information technologies in institutions such as universities where socializing and education practices are intensely experienced. In this work, it is explained on an actual application about how international students can be adapted into the university information system and how the application and placement processes of these students can effectively be managed. In this way, it is aimed to increase the awareness of universities and guide them in this process. At the same time, information is given on different systems which have been used since 2011-2012 academic year. By this means, development stages of the current system in use are revealed. Thanks to all these stages, there have been many advantages gained such as a better management of the process and a faster obtaining of reports by decreasing the losses of budget, labour force and time both for the coordinatorship and applicants by activating the online system and enabling document upload. In this way, satisfactions of the coordinatorship personnel have increased. Within the scope of this work, information on sample statistical data and fields they can be used is presented along with integration and information exchanges of the system which involves data and the applications of international students with other information systems used in universities.

Consequently, for institutions such as universities, education practices supported by information technologies play a significant role in memorability of knowledge and acceleration in learning speed. Benefiting from information technologies is also important for these institutions to bring different cultures together and increase their preferability in the process of internationalization. Digital transformation of student exchange programs and supporting them with Internet applications play an important role for international students to gather correct information about these institutions, communicate with them and prefer them. Additionally, getting assist from information technologies will also prevent unnecessary labour force and time losses with a fast access to the information that they would need to send to the

Higher Education Council, or they would need for determining their future strategies for international students. In the following works, surveys can be applied to international students in order to measure the benefits and effectiveness of the system that is provided by application and placement system. At the same time, works on every student's benefiting from information systems, especially from Education Support System and their effects on education practices can be done.

## REFERENCES

Ammigan, R. (2019). Institutional satisfaction and recommendation: What really matters to international students. *Journal of International Students*, *9*(1), 262–281. doi:10.32674/jis.v9i1.260

Anderson, G. (1990). *Fundamentals of Educational Research*. The Felmer Press. doi:10.4324/9780203978221

Angove, M. (2019). Work-Based Learning and Innovation: A Study of International Commerce Degree Students. In *Innovation and Social Capital in Organizational Ecosystems* (pp. 173–193). IGI Global. doi:10.4018/978-1-5225-7721-8.ch009

Balta, Y., & Türel, K. Y. (2013). Çevrimiçi uzaktan eğitimde kullanılan farklı ölçme değerlendirme yaklaşımlarına ilişkin bir inceleme. *Turkish Studies-International Periodical For The Languages. Literature and History of Turkish or Turkic*, *8*(3), 37–45.

Barak, M., Watted, A., & Haick, H. (2016). Motivation to learn in massive open online courses: Examining aspects of language and social engagement. *Computers & Education*, *94*, 49–60. doi:10.1016/j.compedu.2015.11.010

Bound, J., Braga, B., Khanna, G., & Turner, S. (2021). The globalization of postsecondary education: The role of international students in the US higher education system. *The Journal of Economic Perspectives*, *35*(1), 163–184. doi:10.1257/jep.35.1.163

Bozkurt, A. (2020). Koronavirüs (Covid-19) pandemi süreci ve pandemi sonrası dünyada eğitime yönelik değerlendirmeler: Yeni normal ve yeni eğitim paradigması. *Açıköğretim Uygulamaları ve Araştırmaları Dergisi*, *6*(3), 112–142.

Chapman, S. A., Goodman, S., Jawitz, J., & Deacon, A. (2016). A strategy for monitoring and evaluating massive open online courses. *Evaluation and Program Planning*, *57*, 55–63. doi:10.1016/j.evalprogplan.2016.04.006 PMID:27213994

Demir, A. H. E., Bayram, A. E., & Kocaoğlu, S. A. B. (2010). Mernis Projesi ve Adrese Dayalı Nüfus Kayıt Sistemi Çevresinde 7201 Sayılı Tebligat Kanunu ve Bu Kanuna Dayalı Çıkarılan Tebligat Tüzüğünde Yapılması Gerekli Değişiklik Önerisi. *Ankara Barosu Dergisi*, (3).

Dhawan, S. (2020). Online learning: A panacea in the time of COVID-19 crisis. *Journal of Educational Technology Systems*, *49*(1), 5–22. doi:10.1177/0047239520934018

Dikmen, S., & Bahçeci, F. (2020). Covid-19 pandemisi sürecinde yükseköğretim kurumlarının uzaktan eğitime yönelik stratejileri: Fırat Üniversitesi örneği. *Turkish Journal of Educational Studies*, *7*(2), 78–98. doi:10.33907/turkjes.721685

Ebinger, S. E. (2011). *International students' perceptions of university assistance with their social adjustment* (Doctoral dissertation).

Eraslan, A. (2009). Finlandiya'nın PISA'daki Başarısının Nedenleri: Türkiye için Alınacak Dersler. *Necatibey Eğitim Fakültesi Elektronik Fen ve Matematik Eğitimi Dergisi, 3*(2), 238–248.

Erginer, A. (2006). *Avrupa Birliği Eğitim Sistemleri ve Türkiye Eğitim Sistemiyle Karşılaştırmalar.* PEGEM Akademi Yayıncılık.

González, C. R., Mesanza, R. B., & Mariel, P. (2011). The determinants of international student mobility flows: An empirical study on the Erasmus programme. *Higher Education, 62*(4), 413–430. doi:10.100710734-010-9396-5

Güllüpınar, F., Kuzu, A., Dursun, Ö. Ö., Kurt, A. A., & Gültekin, M. (2013). Milli Eğitimde Teknoloji Kullanımı ve Sonuçları: Velilerin Bakış Açısından Fatih Projesi'nin Pilot Uygulamasının Değerlendirilmesi. *SDÜ Fen Edebiyat Fakültesi Sosyal Bilimler Dergisi,* (30), 195–216.

Günay, D., Asunakutlu, T., & Yildiz, O. (Eds.). (2021). *University-industry Collaboration Strategies in the Digital Era.* IGI Global., doi:10.4018/978-1-7998-3901-9

Gündüz, M., Alakbarov, N., & Demirci, A. (2020). Improving the Communication Skills of International Students: Case Study of Usak University. In *Academic Language and Learning Support Services in Higher Education* (pp. 140–162). IGI Global. doi:10.4018/978-1-7998-2878-5.ch006

Gürbüz, R., & Güleç, İ. (2016). Türkiye'de eğitim gören yabancı öğrencilerin Türkçeye ilişkin görüşleri: Sakarya Üniversitesi örneği. *Sakarya University Journal of Education, 6*(2), 141–153. doi:10.19126uje.18712

Higher Education Council of Turkey. (2020a). https://www.yok.gov.tr/Sayfalar/Haberler/2020/coronavirus_bilgilendirme_1.aspx

Higher Education Council of Turkey. (2020b). https://yokdersleri.yok.gov.tr/

Higher Education Council of Turkey. (2021). https://www.yok.gov.tr/ogrenci/yurt-disinda-kabul-edilecek-ogrenci-kontenjanlari

Hung, N. T. (2021). Higher education in business: A model for international students' choice. *Business Process Management Journal.* Advance online publication. doi:10.1108/BPMJ-11-2020-0516

ICEF Monitor. (2019). *International students generate global economic impact of US$300 billion.* https://monitor.icef.com/2019/08/international-students-generate-global-economic-impact-of-us300-billion/

Institute of International Education. (2015). *Open Doors Data.* https://www.iie.org/Who-We-Are/News-and-Events/Press-Center/Press-Releases/2015/2015-11-16-Open-Doors-Data

Jackson, M., Ray, S., & Bybell, D. (2013). International students in the U. S.: Social and psychological adjustment. *Journal of International Students, 3*(1), 17–28. doi:10.32674/jis.v3i1.515

Karadağ, E., & Yücel, C. (2020). Yeni tip Koronavirüs pandemisi döneminde üniversitelerde uzaktan eğitim: Lisans öğrencileri kapsamında bir değerlendirme çalışması. *Yükseköğretim Dergisi, 10*(2), 181–192. doi:10.2399/yod.20.730688

Khoshlessan, R., & Das, K. P. (2019). Analyzing international students' study anxiety in higher education. *Journal of International Students*, *7*(2), 311-328.

Kıroğlu, K., Kesten, A., & Elma, C. (2010). Türkiye'de Öğrenim Gören Yabancı Uyruklu Lisans Öğrencilerinin Sosyo-Kültürel ve Ekonomik Sorunları. *Mersin Üniversitesi Eğitim Fakültesi Dergisi*, *6*(2), 26–39.

Martirosyan, N. M., Bustamante, R. M., & Saxon, D. P. (2019). Academic and social support services for international students: Current practices. *Journal of International Students*, *9*(1), 172–191. doi:10.32674/jis.v9i1.275

Mazzarol, T., Savery, L. K., & Kemp, S. (Eds.). (1996). *International students who choose not to study in Australia: An examination of Taiwan and Indonesia*. AEIF Policy, Research and Analysis Section.

Nguyen, B. H., & Phuong, P. N. (2021). The Effect of the Covid-19 Pandemic Risk Perception On Students' behavioural Intention Towards Returning Home For Studying. *UED Journal of Social Sciences. Humanities and Education*, *11*(1), 122–136. doi:10.47393/jshe.v11i1.964

OECD. (2020). *Education at a Glance 2020*. https://www.oecd-ilibrary.org/education/education-at-a-glance-2020_69096873-en

Özoğlu, M., Gür, B. S., & Coşkun, İ. (2015). Factors influencing international students' choice to study in Turkey and challenges they experience in Turkey. *Research in Comparative and International Education*, *10*(2), 223–237. doi:10.1177/1745499915571718

Özyürek, R. (2009). Türk Devlet ve Topluluklarından Türkiye Üniversitelerine Gelen Türk Soylu Yabancı Uyruklu Öğrencilerin Türkçe Öğrenimlerinde Karşılaştıkları Sorunlar. *Turkish Studies*, *4*(3), 1819–1862.

Şimşek, B., & Bakır, S. (2016). Uluslararası Öğrenci Hareketliliği ve Atatürk Üniversitesi'nin Uluslararasılaşma Süreci. *Atatürk Üniversitesi Türkiyat Araştırmaları Enstitüsü Dergisi*, (55), 509–542.

Susanto, G., & Rahayu, E. Y. (2020). The Emotional Geography of International Students in Online Bahasa Indonesia Learning during the COVID-19 Pandemic. *Journal of International Students*, *10*(S3), 161–179. doi:10.32674/jis.v10iS3.3205

Taylor, J. C. (2001). Fifth generation distance education. *Instrumentation Science & Technology*, *4*(1), 1–14.

Teräs, M., Suoranta, J., Teräs, H., & Curcher, M. (2020). Post-Covid-19 education and education technology 'solutionism': A seller's market. *Postdigital Science and Education*, *2*(3), 863–878. doi:10.100742438-020-00164-x

Ülper, H. (2020). Yabancı Öğrencilerin Türkçe Söyleyiş Akıcılıklarına İlişkin Algılarını Etkileyen Etmenler. *Başkent University Journal of Education*, *7*(2), 328–338.

Uluuysal, B., Demiral, S., Kurt, A. A., & Şahin, Y. L. (2014). Bir Öğretmenin Teknoloji Entegrasyonu Yolculuğu. *Turkish Online Journal of Qualitative Inquiry*, *5*(4).

UNESCO. (2020). *Startling digital divides in distance learning emerge*. https://en.unesco.org/news/startling-digital-divides-distance-learning-emerge

Wiranota, H., & Wijaya, T. T. (2021, March). The international students' perception towards online learning using the tencent meeting during covid-19 outbreak. Journal of Physics: Conference Series. doi:10.1088/1742-6596/1823/1/012011

Yabanova, U., & Özerbas, D. H. (2020). International Student Selection Process in Turkey: Characteristics, Challenges and Opportunities. *International Journal of Progressive Education*, *16*(2), 137–156. doi:10.29329/ijpe.2020.241.10

Yildiz, O. (2021). Changing Paradigms in the Digital Age and Entrepreneurial Universities. *University-Industry Collaboration Strategies in the Digital Era*, 1-21. doi:10.4018/978-1-7998-3901-9.ch001

Yildiz, O., Ersoy, A. S., & Yıldırım, İ. S. (2021). The Impact of Information and Communication Systems on Organizations. In *Recent Developments in Individual and Organizational Adoption of ICTs* (pp. 1–25). IGI Global. doi:10.4018/978-1-7998-3045-0.ch001

Yorgancı, S. (2015). Web Tabanlı Uzaktan Eğitim Yönteminin Öğrencilerin Matematik Başarılarına Etkileri. *Kastamonu Eğitim Dergisi*, *23*(3), 1401–1420.

Zhang, Q., He, Y. J., Zhu, Y. H., Pan, M. M., Wu, J. Q., Zhang, X., ... Qu, F. (2020). The evaluation of online course of Traditional Chinese Medicine for Medical Bachelor, Bachelor of Surgery international students during the COVID-19 epidemic period. *Integrative Medicine Research*, *9*(3), 14–14. doi:10.1016/j.imr.2020.100449 PMID:32632357

Zhang, Z., & Kenny, R. (2010). Learning in an online distance education course: Experiences of three international students. *The International Review of Research in Open and Distributed Learning*, *11*(1), 17–36. doi:10.19173/irrodl.v11i1.775

# Chapter 11
# Internationalizing Quality Assurance Systems With International Accreditations in Slovenian Higher Education:
## Globalization and Regionalization Influences

**Maruša Hauptman Komotar**
https://orcid.org/0000-0002-5061-8357
*Alma Mater Europaea - Faculty of Humanities, Institutum Studiorum Humanitatis, Ljubljana, Slovenia*

## ABSTRACT

*This chapter addresses the internationalization process from the standpoint of international accreditations. More precisely, it explores whether in Slovenia their implementation is affected primarily by globalization or regionalization of (quality assurance in) higher education. Initially, it discusses globalization and regionalization from the standpoint of internationalization and Europeanization of higher education. Then, it overviews the main international (professional) accreditors, which are relevant for Slovenian higher education (institutions). In the continuation, it outlines the internationalization of Slovenian quality assurance system at the national level, whilst afterwards, it concentrates in more detail on the analysis of institutional (internationalization) strategies and official websites of Slovenian higher education institutions with respect to international accreditations. In conclusion, it highlights that having more international accreditations does not necessarily mean more internationalization of (Slovenian) higher education.*

DOI: 10.4018/978-1-7998-8169-8.ch011

## INTRODUCTION

This chapter seeks to explain the internationalization process from the perspective of international accreditations, which are perceived by many as one of the key drivers for the internationalization of quality assurance systems at the institutional level of higher education. Today, many higher education institutions worldwide internationalize their quality assurance activities with international accreditations (evaluations, audits, etc.), which are performed by various international accreditors, especially those specialized in the particular disciplinary field (Alphin, 2014). In the United States, regional accreditation agencies already started to perform accreditation activities at secondary schools, colleges, and universities in the late 19th and early 20th century (Harcleroad & Eaton, 2005), whilst in some (Western) European countries, their emergence and development strengthened in the early 1990s. At that time, it was argued that by choosing a specific accreditation agency, higher education institutions would be "able to show to whom they want to be held accountable for their activities and products" (Vroeijenstijn, 1999, p. 245; van der Wende, 1999). With the start of the Bologna Process (in 1999) and its goal of creating the European Higher Education Area (EHEA), accreditation indeed became the key topic of the political agenda and the dominant quality assurance approach in both Western and non-Western European countries (Schwarz & Westerheijden, 2004).

Under the influence of globalization and regionalization on higher education, the accreditation 'marketplace' strengthened at program, institutional, national, and international levels of higher education (Alphin, 2014; Brahimi et al., 2018). On this basis, international accreditations developed into "a booming business" (Vroeijenstijn, 1999, p. 238) not only in Europe but worldwide. At present, numerous specialized international accreditors are offering their services in the form of institutional and program accreditations either additionally or together with the obligatory accreditation, evaluation, or other assessment procedure conducted by the national or foreign quality assurance and/or accreditation agency.

Higher education institutions can benefit from international accreditations in a variety of ways. They give them the opportunity to choose the accrediting body in compliance with their own profile and mission, assess their institutional performance according to the internationally-accepted standards, identify strengths and weaknesses of study programs (for example, in terms of designing the curriculum or developing academic and administrative staff), etc. (Hou et al., 2015). According to Urgel (2007), "some of the value added is specific and unique to having international accreditation, and is therefore unobtainable by any other means" (p. 68). Also, for 62% of about 1,300 participating students in the Carrington Crisp's (2013) survey *A change of direction? Tomorrow's Masters*, international accreditations represent an important or very important factor for considering where to study, and over a third of students think that the most important international accreditations are those awarded by professional accreditation bodies.

However, due to the growing diversity and commercialization of international (professional) accreditors, individual higher education systems may react differently to the expansion of this internationally-oriented quality assurance instrument. In some countries, the growth in the number of higher education institutions with international accreditations is strongly affected by the globalization of quality assurance in higher education, where predominantly overseas accreditors (for example, from the United States) are assuming the leading role (Altbach, 2015). In other countries, for example, those from Europe, their expansion results primarily from the increased regionalization of quality assurance systems in the framework of the Bologna Process, where regional (or European/EHEA) accreditation organizations are undertaking the relevant role.

Along these lines, the chapter addresses the internationalization of quality assurance systems in higher education from the perspective of globalization and regionalization of higher education. On this basis, it determines whether in Slovenia, the emergence and implementation of international (professional) accreditations should be perceived primarily as the result of globalization of (quality assurance in) higher education or the principal outcome of regionalization of (quality assurance in) higher education. In Slovenia, this topic is still under-studied, although the country is not an outsider to this international trend.

To provide a proper background for the continuing debate on the Slovenian case, this study initially discusses complex relationships between globalization and regionalization from the perspective of internationalization and Europeanization of higher education. Then, it overviews main international (i.e., global and regional) accreditation organizations, which are relevant for Slovenian higher education institutions. In the next part on the Slovenian case, it firstly outlines the national context in terms of the internationalization of the Slovenian Quality Assurance Agency for Higher Education (SQAA) and from the perspective of the ministerial support for the achievement of international (professional) accreditations. In the continuation, it positions the trend of obtaining international accreditations in the framework of internationalization and development strategies of Slovenian higher education institutions. To better understand the extent of internationalization of institutional quality assurance systems in the setting of international accreditations, the study considers all Slovenian higher education institutions (i.e., faculties, art academies, and professional colleges) with valid international (professional) accreditations. In conclusion, it highlights some trends and challenges, which may affect the performance of higher education institutions awarded with international accreditations. On this basis, it showcases that having more international accreditations does not necessarily mean the increased internationalization of quality assurance systems in (Slovenian) higher education (Knight, 2013).

The study focuses on the analysis of different documentary sources, such as academic literature, institutional and national policy documents (such as institutional internationalization strategies, development strategies, legislation, regulations, programs, etc.), national and international studies, research and review reports in this field, etc. Also, it gives considerable attention to the examination of most recent data on international accreditations from different web sources, such as official websites of Slovenian higher education institutions and international (professional) accreditation organizations; in the words of Elsayed (2017), they represent "a major source of information and the largest communication tool between the university and internal or external audiences" (p. 479).

To gain a thorough insight into the complex topic of research, this study additionally considers findings from semi-structured interviews, which were conducted between May and December 2016 as part of the broader research project on the internationalization and quality assurance in Slovenian and Dutch higher education (Hauptman Komotar, 2018a). Interviews involved a total of 18 actors and stakeholders operating in the field of internationalization and/or quality assurance in higher education, such as representatives of quality assurance and internationalization agencies, the ministry responsible for higher education, staff from institutional internationalization and quality assurance departments, institutional leadership, independent experts, etc. (see Hauptman Komotar, 2018a). Eight interview respondents originated from Slovenia, seven from the Netherlands, and three from the broader EHEA region; their selection was based on the nature of their involvement in the internationalization and/or quality assurance processes or their expertise in this field. Interviews included open-ended questions, which addressed (1) the concept of internationalization and/or quality assurance in higher education, (2) the development of internationalization and/or quality assurance (policies) at the institutional, national, and international levels of higher education, (3) the relationship between the two key concepts (i.e., the internationalization of quality assurance in higher education, quality assurance of the internationalization in higher education), and (4) future trends. In this study, interviewees' responses to the third group of questions on the internationalization of (institutional) quality assurance systems in (Slovenian) higher education are primarily considered. The analysis of textual data was based on content analysis; according to Cohen et al. (2007), content analysis is a useful research method for the analysis of different types of written material, both documents and transcripts of interviews.

Key findings of this study are therefore principally valuable to the institutional leadership and staff interested in applying for international accreditations, national and supranational policy-makers, (prospective) students, graduates, and the research community itself.

## GLOBALIZATION AND REGIONALIZATION OF HIGHER EDUCATION FROM THE STANDPOINT OF INTERNATIONALIZATION AND EUROPEANIZATION OF HIGHER EDUCATION

For the continuing discussion, it is essential to firstly examine the concept of globalization and regionalization of higher education through the lens of their relationship with the concept of internationalization and Europeanization of higher education. On this basis, the chapter provides the necessary background for the subsequent investigation of the main international accreditors operating at the global and regional levels, which are relevant for Slovenian higher education (institutions and their study programs).

As argued by many, the complex nature of globalization creates demanding challenges for higher education worldwide (Knight, 2008; Marginson & van der Wende, 2009; Teichler, 2010). In the opinion of Beerkens (2004), globalization is "a process in which basic social arrangements within and around the university become disembedded from their national context due to the intensification of transnational flows of people, information and resources" (p. 24). However, globalization of higher education needs to be distinguished from globalization of other social or economic processes (Beerkens, 2004). As stated by Knight (2008), globalization in higher education means "the flow of people, culture, ideas, values, knowledge, technology, and economy across borders resulting in a more interconnected and interdependent world" (p. 4). The effects of globalization on higher education are supported by a number of examples, such as the emergence of new, non-traditional higher education providers, the establishment of university branches and campuses outside the home country, physical and virtual mobility, the use of English language as a lingua franca, the emergence and development of world university rankings, the use of ICT in higher education, the increase in investments in infrastructure, publishing, etc. (Altbach & Knight, 2007; Knight, 2008; Marginson & van der Wende, 2009; Teichler, 2010).

In European debates on higher education, globalization began to gradually replace the term internationalization from the mid-1990s onwards (Teichler, 2010); however, the relationship between the two trends is still quite ambiguous, since both terms are frequently confused with one another, and, as such, need to be further clarified. In the broader sense, "[i]nternationalization means setting up flows (connections) between two or more *countries*, while globalization refers to a process where social arrangements that shape these connections become integrated on a world-wide scale" (Beerkens, 2004, p. 17). In the setting of higher education, internationalization refers to "the process of integrating an international, intercultural, and global dimension into the purpose, functions (teaching, research, and service), and delivery of higher education at the institutional and national levels" (Knight, 2008, p. xi). This means that globalization is "a phenomenon that impacts internationalization" (Knight, 2008, p. 4), whilst the latter is "both a reaction to and a driver for globalisation" (Beerkens, 2004, p. 24). Hence, the link between the two concepts cannot be denied; de Wit et al. (2017) even argue that in the changing environment of the 21st century, it is possible to speak about the globalization of internationalization, which strengthened under the influence of increasingly relevant economic rationales and more commercial forms of internationalization in the global higher education space.

An unexpected outcome of globalization is also the rise of regionalization, which can be broadly understood as "the integration of nations or the formation of groups of countries, usually around specific themes or interests such as trade or security issues" (Beerkens, 2004, p. 29). When promoting shared beliefs and values, regionalization can reinforce the sense of regional identity; however, it can also acquire different meanings in different contexts or regions, for example, in Europe or Africa (Knight, 2008; Huang, 2014). In European higher education, regionalization can be understood as Europeanization or "the regionally oriented version of mostly internationalisation or occasionally globalisation" (Teichler, 2010, p. 266). This means that regionalization (or Europeanization) should not be viewed as an opponent to globalization (or internationalization), but as a response to and a driver for globalization and hence, its specific feature (Beerkens, 2004; Huang, 2014).

To provide the necessary background for the continuing debate, the chapter now expands this conceptual discussion to the context of the main international (i.e., global and regional) accreditation agencies, which are considered relevant for the further investigation of the Slovenian case.

## International (Professional) Accreditation Agencies: An Overview

In the United States, the Association to Advance Collegiate Schools of Business (AACSB) was founded in 1916, and in 1919, it established the first standards for degree programs in business administration. In the 1980s, AACSB adopted additional standards for undergraduate and graduate degree programs in accountancy, whilst in 1991, it started to operate as AACSB International, whose vision is "to transform business education for global prosperity" (AACSB, 2018, p. 1). Until the mid-1990s, only large and research-oriented institutions could obtain accreditation; after that, AACSB adopted a mission-based approach with more flexible standards also for teaching-oriented institutions (Hunt, 2015). To become a member of AACSB, institutions must meet a set of 15 standards, which were updated in 2018; these standards are organized into four categories, namely, Management and innovation, Participants – students, Faculty and professional staff, Learning and teaching, and Academic and professional engagement (AACSB, 2018). To be eligible for accreditation (and obtain the membership), institutions must successfully pass the process of self-evaluation and peer-review, whilst after obtaining AACSB accreditation, they must undergo periodic peer-reviews each five years to provide the evidence of "continuous quality improvement in three vital areas: engagement, innovation, and impact" (AACSB, 2018, p. 2). In the period from 1919 to 1988, 260 business schools were AABSB-accredited (Hunt, 2015), whilst currently, more than 1,700 member organizations and over 800 business schools make part of AACSB (AACSB, n.d.). Skikne (2019) highlights advantages of having AACSB accreditation by claiming that only 5% of business schools worldwide hold AACSB accreditation, and 94% of higher education institutions listed in the Financial Times' Global MBA Rankings 2019 are AACSB-accredited.

In 1988, the Accreditation Council for Business Schools and Programs (ACBSP) was also established in the United States whose vision is that "[e]very business program of quality [should be] accredited and pursuing continuous improvement" (ACBSP, n.d.a). ACBSP awards accreditation at the associate, baccalaureate, and graduate degree levels; unlike AACBS, it focuses on individual programs and not on the whole institution (ACBSP, n.d.a). The accreditation process is based on the Baldrige Education Criteria for Performance Excellence and consists of seven standards, namely Leadership, Strategic planning, Student and stakeholder focus, Student learning assessment, Faculty focus, Curriculum, and Business unit performance (ACBSP 2021b). As of June 2021, the ACBSP global network had 1,200 member campuses located in 60 countries and geographically divided into 11 regions (ACBSP, n.d.a). Also, ACBSP is recognized by the Council for Higher Education Accreditation (CHEA), the U.S. organisation of degree-granting colleges and universities, which currently recognizes approximately 60 institutional and program accreditation organizations. In the words of one professor from the ACBSP-accredited higher education institution, "ACBSP accreditation legitimizes our program and department. We get recognition from our administrators and others around the college. In fact, we have faculty members outside of the department asking about our assessment methods for their own programs" (ACBSP, n.d.c).

In 1967, the Association of MBAs (AMBA) was also founded in the United Kingdom in response to the lack of awareness of the value of master's degree in Business Administration (MBA) in Europe, which was predominantly an American qualification. AMBA focuses principally on the membership of business schools in the association; it accredits postgraduate MBA, DBA, and master's degree programs and, as such, differs from ACBSP, which also covers undergraduate programs. To date, over 290 business schools from more than 70 countries obtained AMBA accreditation (AMBA, 2019) whose criteria are based on ten principles (such as The MBA portfolio, Institutional integrity, Sustainability and distinctiveness, Faculty quality and sufficiency, Programme design and leadership, The student cohort experience, Competences, Graduate attributes and learning outcomes, Curriculum breadth and depth, Assessment rigor and relevance, Delivery and interaction, and Impact and lifelong learning) (AMBA, 2016, p. 1). According to Mark (2018), one of the lesser-known benefits of AMBA accreditation is inter-institutional mobility, which can facilitate the transfer of credits if students seek to move from one (business) school to another.

Moreover, in 1998, the European Foundation for Management Development (EFMD) launched the European Quality Improvement System also known as EQUIS, which focuses on the whole institution, that is business and management schools (and hence, not their units or specific portfolios of programs) (EQUIS, 2020a). The accreditation process is based on benchmarking in ten areas, namely Governance, Programs, Students, Faculty, Research, Internationalization, Ethics, Responsibility, Sustainability, and Engagement with the world of practice (EQUIS, 2020a). Unlike the accreditation process of AACSB, ACBSP, or AMBA, internationalization is a strict requirement of EQUIS accreditation, since accredited business schools must demonstrate that they operate outside the national setting (Urgel, 2007). Currently, EQUIS has over 900 institutional members from 91 countries worldwide, including Slovenia (EQUIS, 2020b). Wanot (2018) sees the benefits of EQUIS accreditation in "a rigorous quality control, benchmarking the school against international standards [...] as well as corporate engagement. [...] Simply put, it allows students to evaluate their prospective learning experiences before embarking on a course of study".

With respect to the three above-presented accreditors (AACSB, AMBA, and EQUIS), it should be noted here that institutions awarded with these three accreditations are often called 'Triple Crown' institutions. In August 2020, 102 business schools worldwide had triple accreditation of this kind, of which 65% were located in Europe (MBA Today, n.d.). The available data also expose that the United Kingdom has the highest number of triple-accredited business schools (22), following France (18), and China (9); three other countries have three higher education institutions with a triple accreditation, and another 18 countries, including Slovenia, have one triple-accredited business school (MBA Today, n.d.).

The next accrediting body, which operates globally but is European-based, is the European Council for Business Education (ECBE); it was founded in 1995 and accredits study programs of private business schools in the field of Economics, Business, Management, and related fields for five years or a shorter period (of two to four years) (ECBE, 2019a). ECBE's accreditation standards are based on the Standards and Guidelines for Quality Assurance in European Higher Education Area (ESG) (ENQA et al., 2015), since ECBE is an affiliated member of the European Association for Quality Assurance in Higher Education (ENQA) and a member of the European Quality Assurance Register for Higher Education (EQAR) (ECBE, 2019b). Currently, 29 member institutions from 12 countries have ECBE accreditation for some of their programs, of which seven are from Russia, five from Switzerland, four from Slovenia, two from the Czech Republic, and other countries have one ECBE accreditation (ECBE, 2019c). ECBE (2019d) sees the following benefits of program accreditation for higher education institutions: "[n]etworking, support, motivation and advice to provide a dynamic quality program of education meeting both the demands of students and the market" (ECBE, 2019d).

Moreover, the International Association for Management Development in Dynamic Societies (CEEMAN) was founded in 1993 to increase the quality of management development in Central and Eastern Europe (CEEMAN, n.d.a). In 1998, CEEMAN established the international quality accreditation CEEMAN IQA, which considers seven areas of assessment, such as Strategy, Governance, Research, Education, Resources, Continuous improvement/innovation, and Responsible practices (CEEMAN, n.d.a). Currently, CEEMAN has 200 members from 500 countries worldwide; it is an affiliate member of ENQA and a full member of INQAAHE (CEEMAN, n.d.a). As such, CEEMAN IQA "provides international acknowledgment that the accredited institution delivers management education and engages in research, which is not only excellent by internationally recognized quality standards but well adapted and relevant to the customers and markets in which it operates" (CEEMAN, n.d.b).

The Accreditation Agency for Degree Programs in Engineering, Computer Science, Natural Sciences, and Mathematics eV (ASIIN) is another international accreditor located in Germany. ASIIN started to operate in 1999 and is a member of ENQA (since 2007) and EQAR (since 2008). It represents itself as the "global leader in quality assurance in higher education" (ASIIN, 2021a), which accredits bachelor and master's programs in Engineering, Computer science, Natural sciences, Mathematics, Medicine, and all interdisciplinary fields that involve these subject areas (ASIIN, 2021b). After successful completion of the process, study programs can obtain different quality seals or labels, which ASIIN awards internationally (ASIIN, 2021b). In addition to accreditation, ASIIN conducts other activities within the scope of ESG, such as evaluation, certification, and reviews (called EUR-ACE, EUR-INF, Eurobachelor, Euromaster, etc.) (EQAR, n.d.a). To date, ASIIN carried out (international) accreditations of 5,382 study programs and 287 institutions in 43 countries (including Germany) (ASIIN, 2021a). In the survey on ASIIN accreditation seals, Niemelä et al. (2014) that "accreditations have had an important effect on the curriculum work and thereby on the development of teaching and education. However, the effects on single courses were considered less significant" (p. 226). On the other hand, Habermann (2020) noted that ASIIN advances the development of quality of study programs, given that more than 80% of assessed study programs with the ASIIN seal or label were accredited with requirements.

Another interdisciplinary accreditation agency of German origin is the Accreditation Agency in Health and Social Sciences (AHPGS), which was established in 2001 and operates both nationally and internationally (in 13 European and non-European countries) (AHPGS, n.d.). AHPGS conducts accreditation of bachelor and master's study programs in the field of Health and Social Sciences (and other related areas) based on the Criteria for the assessment and accreditation of study programs and the

ESG. In the accreditation procedure of foreign higher education institutions, AHPGS considers seven criteria, such as Aims and implementation, Structure of the study program, Admission and feasibility, Examination system and transparency, Teaching staff and material equipment, Quality assurance, and Gender equality and equal opportunities (AHPGS, 2019a). The agency also conducts national and international institutional audits based on the criteria, which are grouped into five areas (Profile, objectives, and strategy of the institution, Quality assurance and quality management system, Institutional management and administration, Educational activities, including study programs, Infrastructure and functional resources) (AHPGS, 2019b). AHPGS is a member of various international organizations, including ENQA, EQAR, the International Network of Quality Assurance Agencies in Higher Education (INQAAHE), etc. (AHPGS, n.d.). In the study on international accreditations or certifications in pharmacy education, which also included the ACBSP accreditation, Alkhateeb et al. (2018) concluded that such procedures represent a tool for enhancing the quality of education, although their choice may be influenced by previous experiences of higher education institutions.

*Table 1. Comparison of the main international (professional) accreditation agencies relevant for the study*

| | AACSB | ACBSP | AMBA | EQUIS | ECBE | CEEMAN | ASIIN | AHPGS |
|---|---|---|---|---|---|---|---|---|
| **Year of establishment** | 1916<br>1991<br>(AACSB International) | 1989 | 1967 | 1998 | 1995 | 1993 | 1999 | 2001 |
| **Scope** | global | global (10 regions) | global | global (network) | operates globally but European-based | Central and Eastern European, global | National and international | National and international |
| **Location** | The United States (Tampa, Florida) | The United States (Kansas City, Kansas) | The United Kingdom (London) | Belgium (Brussels) | Belgium (Brussels) | Slovenia (Bled) | Germany (Düsseldorf) | Germany (Freiburg am Breisgau) |
| **Members** | Over 1,700 member associations, over 800 accredited schools | 1,200 member campuses from 60 countries | More than 240 accredited schools in over 70 countries | 945 institutional members from over 90 countries | 56 institutions from 27 countries | 200 institutions from 50 countries | 152 institutions from 33 countries | n.a. |
| **Focus** | institution | program | program (MBA) | institution | program | institution | program, institution | program, institution |
| **Review cycle** | 5 years | 5 years | 5 years | 3–5 years | 5 years or shorter period (2–4 years) | 6 years | 5 years | 5 years |
| **Standards / Criteria** | 15 standards, 4 categories | The Baldrige Education Criteria for Performance Excellence, 7 standards | Criteria as benchmarks, 10 principles | Benchmarking in 10 areas | ESG | 7 areas of assessment | ESG | 7 standards based on the ESG and the Criteria for the Accreditation of Study Programs |
| **Review outcomes** | Accreditation or membership | Accreditation or membership | Accreditation, certificate accreditation (for member campuses) | Accreditation | Accreditation, certification | Accreditation or membership | Accreditation, evaluation, certification, review | Accreditation, recommendation for accreditation, review |

Data Source: AACSB (n.d.; 2018), ACBSP (n.d.a; n.d.b), AMBA (2016; 2019), ASIIN (2021a; 2021b), AHPGS (n.d.), CEEMAN (n.d.a), ECBE (2019a; 2019b), EQUIS (2020a; 2020b)

Table 1 summarizes key information on the above-presented international (professional) accreditation agencies.

In summary, this overview of the main international (professional) accreditors offers a suitable starting point for the continuing investigation of the Slovenian case. In the following, the study focuses its attention to the analysis of institutional internationalization and development strategies with respect to international accreditations (and evaluations); additionally, it also examines official websites of Slovenian higher education institutions with valid international (institutional and/or program) accreditations. But firstly, it provides some general information about the internationalization of the national quality assurance system from the standpoint of the Slovenian Quality Assurance Agency for Higher Education (SQAA) and the ministry responsible for higher education.

## THE CASE OF SLOVENIA

In Slovenia, six universities (three public and three private) and 39 self-standing (independent) higher education institutions presently make part of the higher education system. According to the law, they must obtain institutional accreditation by the SQAA every five years, whilst their study programs are accredited for an indefinite period after successful first accreditation (Republic of Slovenia, 2016). SQAA is the only national agency responsible for accreditation and evaluation procedures, which started to operate in 2010. The agency has its own Criteria for the accreditation and external evaluation of higher education institutions and study programs (SQAA, 2019), which are ESG-compliant (ENQA et al., 2015). These criteria distinguish between different types of accreditations and external evaluations, such as initial institutional accreditation, program accreditation, institutional re-accreditation, accreditation of institutional transformations, regular institutional evaluation, extraordinary institutional or program evaluation, and evaluation of a sample of study programs (SQAA, 2019, Articles 4 and 5).

The internationalization of SQAA represents one of its key strategic objectives, and also refers to the extension of ENQA and EQAR membership and the strengthening of agency's international cooperation (SQAA, 2017). However, one notable obstacle for the agency's internationalization is the legislative constraint on its competence to operate outside the national setting. Another challenging barrier is that international accreditations (evaluations, audits, etc.) can only be obtained in addition to the mandatory national accreditation, which is performed by the national agency (i.e., SQAA). As stressed by the ministry responsible for higher education, "[t]he system of obtaining prestigious accreditations from international professional associations is, in contrast to mandatory national accreditations, voluntary [..]. [I]t means the added value that increases the institutional reputation or prestige at home and especially abroad" (Court of Audit of the Republic of Slovenia, 2016, p. 104).

To this end, the ministry issued in 2012 the public tender whose objective was also to co-fund various institutional quality assurance activities, and provided funding for "the implementation of international evaluations/accreditations as the support for the development of the system of external evaluations/accreditations performed by the competent national agency" (Ministry of Education, Science, Culture, and Sport, 2012, p. 2). With the public tender, both public and private higher education institutions obtained the possibility to undertake international professional accreditations from the field of study for which they are accredited (Ministry of Education, Science, Culture, and Sport 2012, p. 3). For each international accreditation, they were eligible to receive up to 30,000 EUR but under the condition that the accreditor is listed in EQAR (Ministry of Education, Science, Culture, and Sport, 2012). This means that the ministerial support for the implementation of international accreditations was quite influential, especially in terms of funding. In the words of one interviewee, this type of initiative is worth mentioning:

*I think it [i.e., the public tender] was very beneficial because institutions had the opportunity to get extra funding for that. So, I think that this was quite a noteworthy example in Europe because we are facilitating international quality assurance by some policy support from the Ministry. (EQAR Representative, Interview 17)*

But in 2016, the Court of Audit of the Republic of Slovenia examined whether the responsible ministry and SQAA were effective in arranging and implementing (international) accreditations and evaluations. It concluded that:

*the funding obtained for the accreditation abroad to which we do not recognize formal validity [...] does not contribute to simplifying the accreditation process for the agency, [and] is not economical. To avoid the duplication of costs, we estimate that it would make sense [...] to consider whether accreditation obtained from a foreign EQAR-listed agency should be recognized in the Slovenian system as the equivalent of accreditation granted by the agency's Council. (Court of Audit of the Republic of Slovenia, 2016, p. 105)*

The same conclusions were made by the EQAR project RIQAA (*Recognizing International Quality Assurance Activity in the European Higher Education Area*), which emphasized that international accreditations (or evaluations) "often happen in addition and parallel to the national, mandatory external quality assurance, rather than being recognised as part of it" (EQAR, 2014, p. 6). Therefore,

*it is a small group of agencies that really do a lot of activities across borders [...]. [I]n most cases, going for accreditation or evaluation from a foreign agency, basically you do an addition to the national requirement, so, it is a duplication. But still, a lot of institutions do it when they see benefits for their international profile. (EQAR Representative – Interview 17)*

## International (Professional) Accreditations in the Context of Institutional Internationalization Strategies

In the continuation, the chapter focuses its attention to Slovenian higher education institutions with valid international accreditations at the institutional and study program levels. To tackle this issue thoroughly, it investigates institutional internationalization (and development) strategies with respect to international accreditations, and supports these findings with the analysis of official_websites of Slovenian higher education institutions and quotes from interviews.

In the long-term strategy, the University of Ljubljana (UL), which is the oldest and largest public Slovenian university (founded in 1919), acknowledges that it "lags behind in using other, more sophisticated forms of internationalization [...] [and] has a limited impact on this phenomenon and a mostly adaptive role" (University of Ljubljana, 2013). In the internationalization strategy, the university further stresses that this weakness mostly results from "[l]arge differences between the internationalization of members and the promotion of internationalization across members and UL" (University of Ljubljana, 2014, p. 25). On the other hand, it also highlights that the "[e]ncouragement of international quality evaluations, program, and institutional accreditations in the relevant areas" is one of the key measures to increase the university's international recognition (University of Ljubljana, 2013). In this respect, the university reports that since 2010, its members obtained a total of 51 international accreditations of study programs (27 at bachelor and 24 at master's level) and six institutional international accreditations (University of Ljubljana, n.d.). According to the university, international accreditations "increase the visibility of UL, individual members, and programs in the international space and within individual professions" (University of Ljubljana, n.d.).

Among its members, the School of Economics and Business UL is (most) actively involved in acquiring international accreditations in the field of business education, although these were not funded by the ministerial call for tender. At present, it is the only Slovenian triple-accredited higher education institution (with AACSB, EQUIS, and AMBA accreditation); it obtained EQUIS accreditation for the five-year period, and officially obtained AMBA accreditation for its FELU MBA program in 2016 (School of Economics and Business UL, n.d.). Also, three other faculties from the University of Ljubljana (namely, the Faculty of Civil Engineering and Geodesy UL, the Faculty of Mechanical Engineering UL, and the Faculty of Computer and Information Science UL) have altogether 18 study programs accredited by ASIIN for the period of maximum six years; also, they all obtained different (18) quality seals (such as EUR-ACE or Euro-Inf), which ASIIN awards internationally in addition to program accreditation (EQAR, n.d.b).

The University of Maribor (UM), which is the second oldest public university (founded in 1975), also stresses in its internationalization strategy that "the strengthening of the university's international visibility [...] [and] its active involvement in international bilateral and regional networks and associations" is in the forefront of institutional (internationalization) policy (University of Maribor, 2013, p. 16). This also means that "the implementation of permanent national and international institutional and program evaluations and accreditations, which will enable the external international recognition of the university", is one of key strategic goals for the quality development (University of Maribor, 2013, p. 17). Among its members, the Faculty of Economics and Business UM is ACCSB-, ACBSP-, and ECBE-accredited (Faculty of Economics and Business UM, n.d.), the Faculty of Logistics UM obtained ECBE and ACBSP accreditation (Faculty of Logistics UM, 2019), and the Faculty of Organizational Sciences UM received ECBE accreditation for its master's study program (Faculty of Organizational Sciences UM, 2020).

The analysis revealed that in the mid-term strategy of the University of Primorska (UP), which is the third public university (founded in 2003), no reference is made to the issue of international accreditations, as the university stresses the achievement or prolongation of accreditation by the national quality assurance agency (i.e., SQAA) (University of Primorska, 2020). Among its members, the Faculty of Management UP obtained international professional accreditation for its master's study program Management from the Foundation for International Business Administration Accreditation (FIBAA), which was granted as part of the aforementioned public tender but expired in September 2020 (Faculty of Management UP, 2015).

Some private Slovenian higher education institutions are also actively involved in the international accreditation race. Alma Mater Europaea – European Centre, Maribor, for example, received ECBE accreditation for its bachelor and master's study program, and was also awarded with the ACBSP membership (Alma Mater Europaea – European Centre, Maribor, 2021). The private DOBA Faculty of Applied Business and Social Studies Maribor is, on the other hand, the only higher education institution in South-Eastern Europe with UNIQUe accreditation for online studies, which was awarded by the

European Foundation for Quality in e-Learning (EFQUEL) (DOBA Faculty, 2021). In the interview, its representative discussed some benefits of this type of accreditation:_

*In fact, on all materials we have on our website, we can write that we have a top European accreditation. [...] This is the only accreditation for online studies and we want to separate ourselves from others, and it is also very important to have the [quality] seal for the market. This also means that we do not use other accreditations so much. Why? Because we find ourselves in the company with those who have or are far from having this mode [of teaching and learning] that we have. And here, we want to be different, so, we have only one accreditation, and we will stay with it. (Representative of DOBA Faculty, Interview 13)*

Another private higher education institution with valid international accreditations is the International Executive Development Center (IECD) – Bled School of Management, which obtained CEEMAN International Quality Accreditation (IQA) in 1999, and AMBA accreditation for all three MBA programs in 2005. In 2012, AMBA recognized the Executive MBA Program "as one of the four most innovative MBA programs in the world, among 700 business schools" (IECD, n.d.). Moreover, the Faculty of Health Care Angela Boškin Jesenice achieved the international accreditation for two Nursing Care study programs from the German Accreditation Agency in Health and Social Sciences (AHPGS), whilst the Faculty of Medicine UL, for example, participated in institutional audit, which was conducted by AHPGS (EQAR, n.d.b).

Additionally, the Agency for Quality Assurance and Accreditation Austria (AQ Austria) and the Agency for Quality Assurance through Accreditation of Study Programmes (AQAS) carried out the procedure of the European Approach of Joint Programs at two Slovenian higher education institutions, which offer joint programs with foreign universities and other higher education institutions from abroad (EQAR, n.d.b). As explained in the interview:

*The basic idea of the [launch of] European approach was to really have one consistent approach for quality assurance of joint programs, independent of all kind of different national particularities. [...] Because there was a lot of approaches for single procedures but it is usually that different agencies had to cope with different frameworks together at one basis, and there were all kinds of different national requirements, sometimes very contradictory. (EQAR Representative, Interview 17)*

The following chart (Figure 1) displays all Slovenian higher education institutions with valid international (professional) accreditations at the institutional or study program level. The chart also considers those Slovenian higher education institutions with joint accreditation based on the European Approach of Quality Assurance of Joint Programs.

As Figure 1 reveals, a total of 11 international accreditors awarded institutional and program accreditations to 12 higher education institutions (of which eight are public, four are private, and three of them received more than one international accreditation), including those with joint accreditations of (master's) study programs as part of the European Approach for Quality Assurance of Joint Programs. Five international accreditations were granted at the institutional level (AACSB, AMBA, EQUIS, UNIQUe, and CEEMAN), and other six were obtained at the program level (AHPGS, ASIIN, ACBSP, ECBE, AQ Austria, and AQAS). Therefore, out of 103 higher education institutions currently operating in Slovenia, 12% have a valid international accreditation.

*Figure 1. Number of Slovenian higher education institutions and study programs with valid international accreditation at the level of institution and study program*

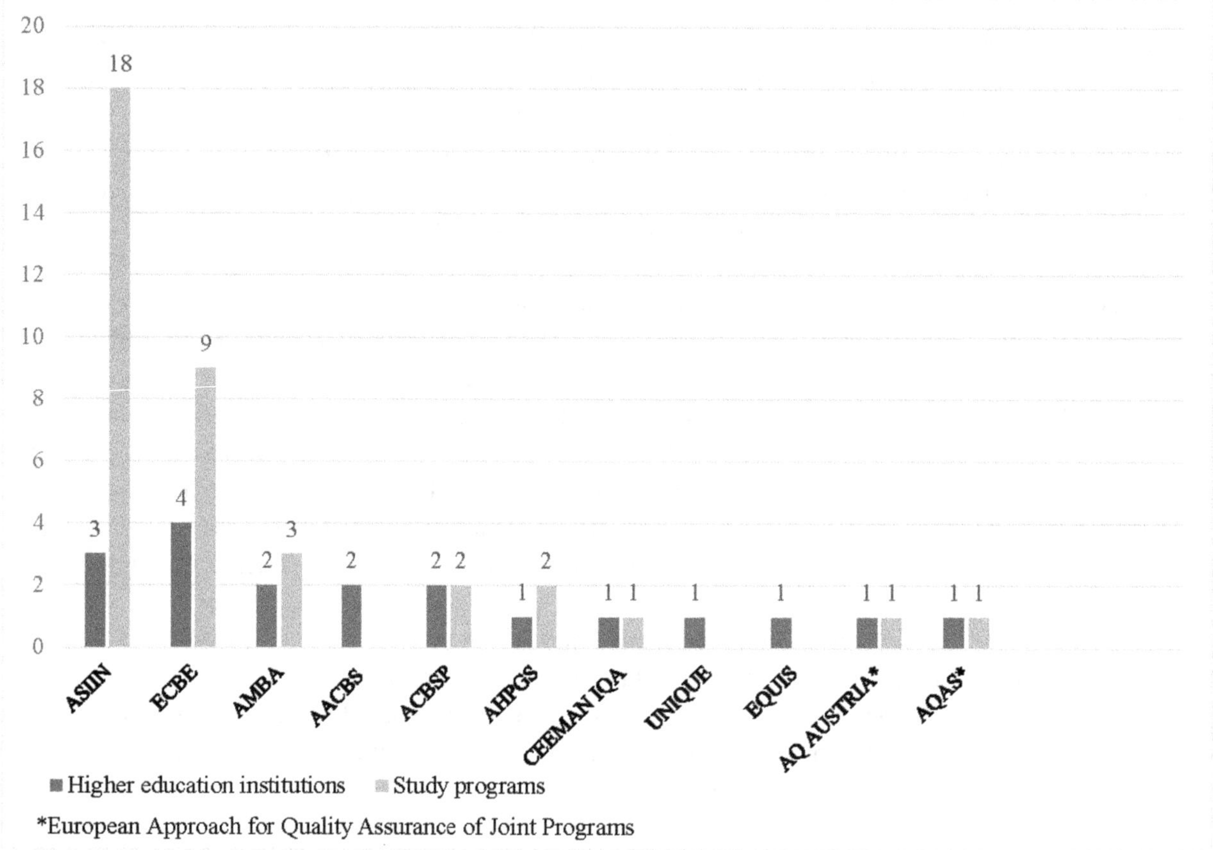


Figure 1 also showcases that (only) four Slovenian higher education institutions are currently accredited by the two accreditation organisations from the United States, namely AACSB and ACBSP. In the words of Brink and Smith (2012), public higher education institutions have the tendency to be AACSB-accredited, whilst private ones are more prone to have ACBSP (or IACBE) accreditation of their (business) programs. But as Altbach (2015) emphasizes, "American accreditation is designed for the realities of American higher education. It reflects the history, norms, and values of the U.S. academic system" (p. 6). Similarly, one interviewee highlighted that

*there is also a tradition of accreditation in the U.S. and, of course, European countries often look how it is in the U.S. [...], although sometimes the accreditation in the U.S. is quite different from the accreditation in Europe, or in the standards or in the concept. [...] I think actually that the accreditation in Europe and the accreditation in the U.S. have started with very different ends and they have not both moved in the same directions and become more similar. (EQAR Representative, Interview 17)*

Additionally, some Slovenian higher education institutions participate in the Institutional Evaluation Program (IEP) of the European University Association (EUA), which complies with the ESG (ENQA et al., 2015) and focuses on the institution as a whole. Already in the 1990s, the two then-existing universities (UL and UM) successfully passed this international evaluation procedure; more recently, in 2015, it was carried out at other five Slovenian higher education institutions (EUA, n.d.) as part of the aforementioned ministerial call. One of them was the (private) University of Nova Gorica, which acknowledges the importance of international evaluations and its high position on international university rankings for the university's internationalization (University of Nova Gorica, n.d.). Furthermore, the University of Ljubljana, which obtained two international evaluations by the EUA's IEP (in 1995 and 2007), plans "to carry out the third international accreditation through the Finnish National Quality Agency Finish Education Evaluation Center (FINEEC)" (University of Ljubljana, n.d.). However, the university wrongly states that it aims to apply for the international accreditation, since the (correct) approach is international evaluation. Based on this example, it can be argued that sometimes, the distinction between accreditation and evaluation is (still) blurred, despite the existence of some notable differences between both quality assurance approaches. Whilst accreditation includes a final yes/no decision on granting accreditation, (external) evaluation is primarily oriented towards the improvement, and can be or not the outcome of accreditation.

In summary, altogether 12 Slovenian higher education institutions have currently a valid international accreditation, whilst seven higher education institutions have successfully passed the EUA's international institutional evaluation. Also, one Slovenian higher education institution was involved in the procedure of international audit, and two of them were involved in the European Approach of Quality Assurance of Joint Programs. In the RIQAA project (EQAR, 2014), three quarters of participating higher education institutions also reported that they use such international assessments (i.e., accreditation, evaluation, audit, etc.) as a tool for enhancing their internationalization. They give them the possibility to adapt assessment procedures to their mission and profile, obtain appropriate feedback and develop their internationalization strategies (EQAR, 2014). At the same time, participating institutions also mentioned some challenges they confront, such as the search for a suitable foreign agency, additional costs, and the explanation of context to foreign experts (EQAR, 2014).

## DISCUSSION

So far, the chapter revealed that the significant majority of international (professional) accreditors in Slovenian higher education (i.e., a total of nine) are regionally- or European-based, thereby manifesting the more evident trend of regionalization of accreditation procedures at the international level. Out of these nine agencies located in Europe, three are listed in EQAR (ACQUIN, AHPGS, ASIIN), and except for CEEMAN, other ones (AMBA, ECBE, UNIQUE, EQUIS) are of Western European origin. This means that the trend of regionalization of international accreditation procedures in Slovenian higher education results from the increased governmental support for achieving international accreditations from EQAR-listed quality assurance and/or accreditation agencies. However, the majority of business-oriented Slovenian higher education institutions did not apply for the governmental funding but have invested their own resources to obtain accreditations from international accreditors.

Also, such regionalization of international accreditations results from broader processes of Europeanization of higher education in the framework of the Bologna Process, which Slovenia joined in 1999. But as in many other countries from Central and Eastern Europe, the accreditation practice was developed under different circumstances than in Western European countries. It emerged in the 1990s in response to the ever-growing need to assure the quality of academic offer in times of massification, diversification, and differentiation of higher education institutions and their study programs (Rozsnyai, 2003; Hauptman Komotar, 2018b). In Western Europe, accreditation replaced the previously dominant approach of evaluation under the influence of globalization of higher education and the Bologna Process (Schwarz & Westerheijden, 2004; Teichler, 2010). However, globalization of higher education is often associated with the standardized accreditation practice at the global level where "the poor and weak and peripheral copy the rich and strong and central" (Meyer et al., 1997, p. 164; see also Alphin, 2014). But as the Slovenian example showcases, globalization does not necessarily contribute to such international convergence. As Knight (2008) underlines, globalization is "a multifaceted process that can impact countries in vastly different ways – economically, culturally, politically, and technologically" (p. 4; see also Günay et al., 2021; Yildiz, 2021).

Moreover, obtaining and maintaining international accreditations is usually a costly process, especially if the accreditor operates overseas, for example, in the United States. But given that institutional financial resources are often limited, the amount of funding may be a decisive factor in the choice of the appropriate international accreditor. On the other hand, "the opposite relationship is also plausible: Accreditors, because of their different requirements, might cause institutions to secure different levels of resources" (Brink & Smith, 2012, p. 10). In addition, the achievement of international accreditation is a time-consuming process with the increased administrative workload, and this may also lead to certain resistance from those involved in the process (Hou et al., 2015). But as Lowrie and Wilmott (2009) underline for the AACBS model, "accreditation is nonetheless comparatively straightforward even if it is lengthy, costly, and administratively demanding" (p. 414). Furthermore, an important role in this process is also played by the knowledge of English language; its global dominance increases the linguistic hegemony and academic imperialism, and, as such, creates difficulties for non-English speaking countries – peripheries (Altbach, 2013), such as Slovenia.

In the context of the 'glonacal' quality assurance system (see Hou et al., 2015 for the Taiwanese case), it can be argued that the Slovenian quality assurance system is (much) less 'glonacal' than in some (Western) European countries where international accreditors from other continents, especially from the United States, prevail. As Hou et al. (2015) explain, the 'glonacal' system is a feature of quality assurance systems with longer tradition; here the globalization of internationalization intensified under increasingly influential economic rationales (de Wit et al., 2017). Hence, the institutional race for international accreditations should also be viewed as the product of commercialization, commodification, and marketization of higher education (Knight, 2013). However, the "[i]nternational higher education [marketplace] will provide substantial access in some countries and will be a 'niche market' in others" (Altbach & Knight, 2007, p. 304).

## CONCLUSION

In conclusion, it can be argued that in Slovenia, the achievement of accreditations from international accreditation agencies is still in the early stage of its development, since only slightly more than one tenth of higher education institutions (12% or 12 higher education institutions) currently make use of this internationally-oriented quality assurance instrument. Furthermore, the analysis also exposed that Slovenian higher education institutions from certain scientific fields, such as Economics and Business, Management, Administration, Engineering, Nurse Care, etc. typically decide to embark in the process of obtaining international accreditations. At other Slovenian higher education institutions, for example, those operating in the field of Humanities or Educational Sciences, international accreditations are not a widespread phenomenon.

For this reason, one may claim that even though all Slovenian higher education institutions are in one way or another affected by the processes of globalization and/or internationalization of higher education, some of them experience a (much) higher level of the internationalization of their quality assurance systems than others. Therefore, when conducting institutional or program accreditations, international accreditors and others interested in this issue must also consider the diversity of national, institutional, and disciplinary contexts in which their development is embedded "to understand different academic systems and [their diverse] traditions" (Altbach, 2015, p. 6). Therefore, having more international accreditations does not necessarily mean more internationalisation; according to Knight (2013), this is a myth.

In these complex times of the worldwide pandemic of Covid-19, it became even more important to acknowledge that the achievement of international accreditations should be, on the one hand, viewed as an opportunity to improve the quality of higher education provision. On the other hand, however, it should be perceived as a risk, especially if their achievement is supported by profit-oriented rationales of commercialization and competition by providers of dubious origin, which "may not offer objective assessments and may be more interested in racing for accreditation 'stars' than in improving quality" (Altbach & Knight, 2007, p. 301; Knight, 2013; Altbach, 2015).

## REFERENCES

AACSB. (2018). *2013 Eligibility procedures and accreditation standards for business accreditation.* https://www.aacsb.edu/accreditation/standards/business

AACSB. (n.d.). *Who we are.* https://www.aacsb.edu/about

ACBSP. (n.d.a). *Who we are.* https://www.acbsp.org/page/about-who-we-are

ACBSP. (n.d.b). *Accreditation standards.* https://www.acbsp.org/page/accreditation-standards

ACBSP. (n.d.c). *ACBSP accreditation overview.* https://acbsp.org/page/accreditation-overview

AHPGS. (2019a). *Handbook for program accreditation.* https://ahpgs.de/wp-content/uploads/2020/01/Handbook_for_Programme_Accreditation_AHPGS_January_2020-2.pdf

AHPGS. (2019b). *Handbook for institutional audit.* https://ahpgs.de/wp-content/uploads/2020/01/Handbook_for_Institutional_Audit_January-2020.pdf

AHPGS. (n.d.). *The accreditation agency.* https://ahpgs.de/en/about-us/

Alkhateeb, F. M., Arkle, S., McDonough, S. L. K., & Latif, D. A. (2018). Review of national and international accreditation of pharmacy programs in the Gulf Cooperation Council Countries. *American Journal of Pharmaceutical Education, 82*(10), 1162–1175. doi:10.5688/ajpe5980 PMID:30643306

Alma Mater Europaea – European Centre Maribor. (2021). *Accreditation.* https://en.almamater.si/accreditation-s88

Alphin, H. C. (2014). Global accreditation for a knowledge-oriented community: Foundational change breeds global access to educational and economic opportunity. In S. Mukerji & P. Tripathi (Eds.), *Handbook of Research on Transnational Higher Education* (pp. 303–328). IGI Global. doi:10.4018/978-1-4666-4458-8.ch016

Altbach, Ph. G. (2013). The imperial tongue: English as the dominating academic language. In Ph. G. Altbach (Ed.), *The international imperative in higher education* (pp. 1–6). Sense Publishers.

Altbach, Ph. G. (2015). Academic colonialism in action: American accreditation of foreign universities. *Industry and Higher Education, 32*, 5–7.

Altbach, Ph. G., & Knight, J. (2007). The internationalization of higher education: Motivations and realities. *Journal of Studies in International Education, 11*(3/4), 290–305. doi:10.1177/1028315307303542

AMBA. (2016). *MBA accreditation criteria.* https://www.mbaworld.com/accreditation/become-an-accredited-business-school

AMBA. (2019). *AMBA-accredited business schools.* https://www.associationofmbas.com/business-schools/accreditation/accredited-schools/

ASIIN. (2021a). *ASIIN - Global leader in quality assurance in higher education.* https://www.asiin.de/en/home.html

ASIIN. (2021b). *Accreditation degree programmes.* https://www.asiin.de/en/quality-management/accreditation-degree-programmes.html

Beerkens, H. J. J. G. (2004). *Global opportunities and institutional embeddedness: Higher education consortia in Europe and South East Asia.* [Doctoral dissertation]. University of Twente/CHEPS.

Brahimi, T., Sarirete, A., & Khalifa, S. (2018). Impact of accreditation on engineering education. In M. Lytras, L. Daniela, & A. Visvizi (Eds.), *Enhancing knowledge discovery and innovation in the digital era* (pp. 91–106). IGI Global. doi:10.4018/978-1-5225-4191-2.ch005

Brink, K. E., & Smith, C. A. (2012). A comparison of AACSB, ACBSP, and IACBE accredited U.S. business programs: An institutional resource perspective. *Business Education & Accreditation, 4*(2), 1–15.

Carrington Crisp. (2013). *A change of direction? Tomorrow's Masters.* Executive summary 2013. https://www.carringtoncrisp.com/images/PDFs/Tomorrows_Masters_(Exec_Summary).pdf

CEEMAN. (n.d.a). *About us.* http://www.ceeman.org/about-us

CEEMAN. (n.d.b). *Benefits of CEEMAN IQA accreditation.* http://www.ceeman.org/accreditation/benefits-of-ceeman-iqa-accreditation

Cohen, L., Manion, L., & Morrison, K. (2007). *Research methods in Education.* Routledge. doi:10.4324/9780203029053

Court of Audit of the Republic of Slovenia (2016). *Revizijsko poročilo: Postopki evalviranja, akreditiranja ter podeljevanja koncesij v višjem in visokem šolstvu* [Audit report: Procedures for evaluation, accreditation and granting concessions in higher vocational and higher education]. Court of Audit of the Republic of Slovenia.

de Wit, H., Gacel-Ávila, J., Jones, E., & Jooste, N. (Eds.). (2017). *The globalization of internationalization: Emerging voices and perspectives*. Routledge. doi:10.4324/9781315657547

DOBA Faculty. (2021). *Quality assurance*. https://www.dobabusiness-school.eu/why-doba/quality-assurance

ECBE. (2019a). *The accreditation process*. https://www.ecbe.eu/index.php/accreditation/accreditation-process

ECBE. (2019b). *Welcome to European Council for Business Education*. https://www.ecbe.eu/

ECBE. (2019c). *Members of ECBE*. https://www.ecbe.eu/index.php/members/members-of-ecbe

ECBE. (2019d). *Benefits of accreditation*. https://www.ecbe.eu/index.php/accreditation

Elsayed, A. M. (2017). Web content strategy in higher education institutions: The case of King Abdulaziz University. *Information Development, 33*(5), 479–494. doi:10.1177/0266666916671387

ENQA, EUA, ESU, & EURASHE. (2015). *Standards and guidelines for quality assurance in the European Higher Education Area (ESG)*. https://www.enqa.eu/wp-content/uploads/2015/11/ESG_2015.pdf

EQAR. (2014). *Recognising International Quality Assurance Activity in the European Higher Education Area (RIQAA): Final project report*. European Quality Assurance Register for Higher Education.

EQAR. (n.d.a). *ASIIN - ASIIN e. V.* https://www.eqar.eu/register/agencies/agency/?id=19&cn-reloaded=1

EQAR. (n.d.b). *Slovenia*. https://www.eqar.eu/kb/country-information/country/?id=157

EQUIS. (2020a). *2019 EQUIS standards and criteria*. https://efmdglobal.org/accreditations/business-schools/equis/equis-guides-documents/

EQUIS. (2020b). *About us*. https://efmdglobal.org/about-efmd-global/

EUA. (n.d.). *IEP – Institutional Evaluation Programme*. https://www.iep-qaa.org/

Faculty of Economics and Business UM. (n.d.). *International accreditations of study programmes FEB AACSB, ECBE and ACBSP*. https://www.epf.um.si/en/about-faculty/introduction/international-accreditations-of-study-programmes/

Faculty of Logistics UM. (2019). *Accreditations*. https://fl.um.si/en/akreditacije/

Faculty of Management UP. (2015, June 24). *Mednarodna akreditacija FIBAA za magistrski program management* [International FIBAA accreditation for the master's program management]. https://www.fm-kp.si/novice/mednarodna_akreditacija_fibaa_za_magistrski_program_management

Faculty of Organizational Sciences UM. (2020, February 11). *ECBE akreditacija študijskih programov FOV* [ECBE accreditation of study programs FOS]. https://fov.um.si/sl/studij/ecbe-akreditacija-studijskih-programov-fov

Günay, D., Asunakutlu, T., & Yildiz, O. (Eds.). (2021). *University-industry Collaboration Strategies in the Digital Era*. IGI Global. doi:10.4018/978-1-7998-3901-9

Habermann, C. (2020). *Study on the impact of ASIIN's programme accreditation in the field of engineering and management.* ASIIN. https://www.asiin.de/files/content/dokumente/Study_on_the_Impact_of_ASIIN_-_FA_06_Engineering_and_Management.pdf

Harcleroad, F. F., & Eaton, J. S. (2005). The hidden hand: External constituencies and their impact. In Ph. G. Altbach, R. O. Berdahl, & P. J. Gumport (Eds.), *American higher education in the twenty-first century: Social, political, and economic challenges* (2nd ed., pp. 253–283). The John Hopkins University Press.

Hauptman Komotar, M. (2018a). *Internacionalizacija in zagotavljanje kakovosti v visokem šolstvu v Sloveniji in na Nizozemskem* [Internationalization and quality assurance in higher education in Slovenia and the Netherlands] [Doctoral dissertation, University of Ljubljana]. Repository of University of Ljubljana.

Hauptman Komotar, M. (2018b). The evolutionary dynamics of quality assurance systems in European higher education: The view from Slovenia. *Quality in Higher Education, 24*(3), 203–220. doi:10.1080/13538322.2018.1553274

Hou, A., Morse, R., Ince, M., Chen, H.-J., Chiang, C.-L., & Chan, Y. (2015). Is the Asian quality assurance system for higher education going glonacal? Assessing the impact of three types of program accreditation on Taiwanese universities. *Studies in Higher Education, 40*(1), 83–105. doi:10.1080/03075079.2013.818638

Huang, F. (2014). The internationalisation of the academic profession. In F. Huang, M. J. Finkelstein, & M. Rostan (Eds.), *The internationalization of the academy: Changes, realities and prospects* (pp. 1–21). Springer. doi:10.1007/978-94-007-7278-6_1

Hunt, S. C. (2015). Research on the value of AACSB business accreditation in selected areas: A review and synthesis. *American Journal of Business Education, 8*(1), 23–30. doi:10.19030/ajbe.v8i1.9014

IECD. (n.d.). *About the school.* https://www.iedc.si/about-iedc/about-the-school

Knight, J. (2008). *Higher education in turmoil: The changing world of internationalisation.* Sense Publishers. doi:10.1163/9789087905224

Knight, J. (2013). The changing landscape of higher education internationalisation – for better or worse? *Perspectives: Policy and Practice in Higher Education, 17*(3), 84–90. doi:10.1080/13603108.2012.753957

Lowrie, A., & Wilmott, H. (2009). Accreditation sickness in the consumption of business education: The vacuum in AACSB standard setting. *Management Learning, 40*(4), 411–420. doi:10.1177/1350507609335851

Marginson, S., & van der Wende, M. (2009). The new global landscape of nations and institutions. In Higher Education to 2030, Volume 2: Globalisation (pp. 17–62). OECD. doi:10.1787/9789264075375-3-en

Mark, C. (2018, April 30). *Why is MBA accreditation important?* https://www.businessbecause.com/news/admissions-stories/5174/why-mba-accreditation-important

Meyer, J. W., Boli, J., Thomas, G. M., & Ramirez, F. O. (1997). World society and the nation state. *American Journal of Sociology, 103*(1), 144–181. doi:10.1086/231174

Ministry of Education, Science, Culture, and Sport. (2012). Javni razpis za vzpostavitev sistema zagotavljanja kakovosti na visokošolskih zavodih v Republiki Sloveniji v letih 2012–2015 [Call for tender for establishing a quality assurance system in higher education in the Republic of Slovenia in 2012–2015]. *Uradni list RS, 77.*

Niemelä, H., Okkola, T., Nurkka, A., Kuisma, M., & Tuunila, R. (2014). Is an accreditation seal worth the effort? Observations of programme accreditations in Lappeenranta University of Technology, Finland. *Quality Assurance in Education, 22*(3), 226–239. doi:10.1108/QAE-01-2013-0007

Republic of Slovenia (2016). Zakon o spremembah in dopolnitvah zakona o visokem šolstvu (ZViS-K) [Act amending the higher education act (HEA-K)]. *Uradni list RS, 77.*

Rozsnyai, C. (2003). Quality assurance before and after 'Bologna' in the Central and Eastern region of the European higher education area with the focus on Hungary, the Czech Republic and Poland. *European Journal of Education, 38*(3), 271–284. doi:10.1111/1467-3435.00146

School of Economics and Business UL. (n.d.). *Awards of excellence.* http://www.ef.uni-lj.si/awards_of_excellence

Schwarz, S., & Westerheijden, D. F. (Eds.). (2004). *Accreditation and evaluation in the European higher education area.* Kluwer Academic Publishers. doi:10.1007/978-1-4020-2797-0

Skikne, C. (2019). *AACSB accredited business schools—Key advantages.* https://www.businessbecause.com/news/mba-degree/6342/aacsb-accredited-business-schools

SQAA. (2017). *Strateški razvoj Nacionalne agencije Republike Slovenije za kakovost v visokem šolstvu, NAKVIS, za obdobje 2017–2020* [Strategic development of the Slovenian Quality Assurance Agency for Higher Education of the Republic of Slovenia, SQAA, for the period 2017-2020]. https://www.nakvis.si/wp-content/uploads/2018/11/Strategija-agencije-2017-2020.pdf

SQAA. (2019). *Regulations.* https://www.nakvis.si/accreditations-and-evaluations/regulation-and-legislation/?lang=en

Teichler, U. (2010). Internationalising higher education: Debates and changes in Europe. In D. Mattheou (Ed.), *Changing educational landscapes* (pp. 263–283). Springer. doi:10.1007/978-90-481-8534-4_15

Today, M. B. A. (n.d.). *The triple accredited business schools (AACSB, AMBA, EQUIS).* https://www.mba.today/guide/triple-accreditation-business-schools

University of Ljubljana. (2013). *Strategy.* https://www.uni-lj.si/university/strategy/

University of Ljubljana. (2014). *Strategy for the internationalisation of the University of Ljubljana 2014 – 2020.* https://www.uni-lj.si/study/news/strategy-internationalisation

University of Ljubljana. (n.d.). *International evaluations and accreditations.* https://kakovost.uni-lj.si/mednarodne-evalvacije-in-akreditacije/?lang=en

University of Maribor. (2013). *Development strategy of the University of Maribor 2013–2020: Create your future!* https://www.um.si/en/research/human_resources/Documents/Development%20Strategy%20of%20the%20University%20of%20Maribor%202013%202020.pdf

University of Nova Gorica. (n.d.). *International assessments and rankings of University of Nova Gorica*. http://www.ung.si/en/about/quality-assurance/international-assessments/

University of Primorska. (2020). *Internal acts of the UP*. https://www.upr.si/en/university/regulations/internal-acts-of-the-up/

Urgel, J. (2007). EQUIS accreditation: Value and benefits for international business schools. *Journal of Management Development*, *26*(1), 73–83. doi:10.1108/02621710710721698

Van der Wende, M. C. (1999). Quality assurance of internationalisation and internationalisation of quality assurance. In J. Knight & H. de Wit (Eds.), *Quality and internationalisation in higher education* (pp. 225–240). IMHE/OECD.

Vroeijenstijn, A. I. (1999). The international dimension in quality assessment and quality assurance. *Assessment & Evaluation in Higher Education*, *24*(2), 237–247. doi:10.1080/0260293990240211

Wanot, M. (2018, June 20). Advantages of attending an EQUIS accredited business school. *EFMD Global*. https://blog.efmdglobal.org/2018/06/20/advantages-of-attending-an-equis-accredited-business-school/

Yildiz, O. (2021). Changing paradigms in the digital age and entrepreneurial universities. In D. Günay, T. Asunakutlu, & O. Yildiz (Eds.), *University-industry collaboration strategies in the digital era* (pp. 1–21). IGI Global. doi:10.4018/978-1-7998-3901-9.ch001

## ADDITIONAL READING

Hawawini, G. (2016). *The internationalization of higher education and business schools: A critical review*. Springer. doi:10.1007/978-981-10-1757-5

Hou, A. Y. (2011). Quality assurance at a distance: International accreditation in Taiwan higher education. *Higher Education*, *61*(2), 179–219. doi:10.100710734-010-9331-9

Hudzik, J. K. (6 June 2020). How to strengthen internationalisation post-COVID-19. *University World News*. https://www.universityworldnews.com/post.php?story=20200605072319401

Job, J., & Sriraman, B. (2013). A framework for quality assurance in globalization of higher education: A view toward the future. *Interchange*, *43*(2), 75–93. doi:10.100710780-013-9186-y

Knight, J. (2011). Five myths about internationalization. *Industry and Higher Education*, *62*(62), 14–15. doi:10.6017/ihe.2011.62.8532

Mhlanga, E. (2012). Regionalisation and its impact on quality assurance in higher education. *Creative Education*, *3*(06), 1079–1086. doi:10.4236/ce.2012.326162

Nguyen, H. C. (2007). Impact of international accreditation on the emerging quality assurance system: The Vietnamese experience. *Change Management: An International Journal*, *17*(3), 1–9. doi:10.18848/2327-798X/CGP/v17i03/1-9

## KEY TERMS AND DEFINITIONS

**Accreditation:** The quality assurance procedure next to evaluation, audit, licensing, etc., which establishes the status of a certain institution or a program on the basis of minimum standards.

**Accreditation Body:** National or international organization, for example, an agency or council, which issues a license or certification after determining whether an institution or program meet the minimum threshold standards.

**Globalization:** The multidimensional process of movement of people, knowledge, economy, technology, ideas, etc. outside the national context, which results in a more interconnected world.

**Higher Education Institution:** The institution in the field of higher education that offers study programs, which lead to the undergraduate (bachelor or equivalent) or graduate (master's, doctoral) degree.

**Quality Assurance:** The systematic monitoring of pre-determined minimum standards to fulfil the stakeholders' needs and expectations.

**Regionalization:** The process of intensification of social, economic or other collaboration within specific geographic regions, such as the European Union, or the European Higher Education Area in the field of higher education.

**Slovenian Higher Education System:** The group of public and private higher education institutions in Slovenia, namely faculties, art academies, and higher professional colleges, which offer bachelor, master's, and doctoral study programs.

# Chapter 12
# A Strategic Model to Promote University of Choice Decisions Among the International Students

**Andre P. Calitz**
https://orcid.org/0000-0002-2555-9041
*Nelson Mandela University, South Africa*

**Margaret D. Cullen**
*Nelson Mandela University, South Africa*

**Carlien Jooste**
*Nelson Mandela University, South Africa*

## ABSTRACT

*The internationalisation of higher education has become increasingly important for many higher education institutions (HEIs) globally. To recruit national and international students, HEIs must invest in effective digital marketing and recruitment strategies. This study investigated the development of a strategic university of choice model that can assist universities in the recruitment of international students. A survey was completed by 306 international students studying at a South African university. The factors identified in this study included academic programme and quality, visa requirements, country/city attractiveness, lectures in English, costs, student life, safety and security, university location, university reputation, and assistance from the international office. The strategic university of choice model could assist university marketing personnel to develop a focused, targeted, and cost-effective digital marketing and recruitment strategy to recruit international students.*

DOI: 10.4018/978-1-7998-8169-8.ch012

## INTRODUCTION

Globally, the Internationalisation of Higher Education has become a key focus area included in universities' strategic institutional plans. Universities across the globe have essentially been tasked, of their own accord or by their respective governments, with the responsibility of being agents of internationalisation as the globalisation of higher education increases the contest for international and national students (Mosneaga & Agergaard, 2012). Internationalisation within the higher education sector is defined as "the intentional process of integrating an international, intercultural or global dimension into the purpose, functions and delivery of higher education, in order to enhance the quality of education and research for all students and staff and to make a meaningful contribution to society" (De Wit & Hunter, 2015, p. 29).

Internationalisation is an intentional activity ingrained in every aspect of higher education to produce global citizens who can actively contribute to the broader society. Internationalisation in higher education is beneficial to both students and Higher Education Institutions (HEIs). Internationalisation results in stronger brand recognition globally, increased revenue for the university and cross-fertilisation of academic and research intellectual knowledge (Yeravdekar & Tiwari, 2014). Students who are exposed to internationalisation have the skills set to enter the international market with a globally acceptable qualification, which allows them to work within a culturally diverse environment (EDUCBA, 2019).

Internationalisation facilitates activities, which foster the understanding and cooperation between individuals and entities, whereas globalisation relates more to nations and their economies (Yeravdekar & Tiwari, 2014; EDUCBA, 2019). Globalisation is defined as the altering or disregarding of national borders and economic systems to form one global economy. This global economic integration of many national economies includes free trade and free capital mobility as well as easy or uncontrolled migration (Teichler, 2009).

Higher education has entered into a market-driven environment, where education programmes (degrees, diplomas, etc.) are seen as products sold to customers (students). Globalisation, as well as the reduction in government subsidies and the need for the university to make a profit have influenced the market-driven approach (Bezuidenhout & De Jager, 2014). Similar to the competition for customers in other sectors, the recruitment of students has become a perplexing and competitive practice (Wiese, Jordaan & Van Heerden, 2010; Adams & De Wit, 2011; Sheppard & Smith, 2016).

The higher education sector has become more competitive and universities are forced to become more self-funded (Mosneaga & Agergaard, 2012; Rumbley & Altbach, 2016). With the increased demands for online programmes and virtual internationalisation brought on by digitalisation, the sector has become even more competitive. The need to recruit international students to provide additional income to an institution has evolved and changed into a consumer driven recruitment strategy (Mosneaga & Agergaard, 2012). However, universities and the higher education sector are globally being forced to re-evaluate their place in society and their relationships with industry, employers of students and other stakeholders (Gaulee, Sharma & Bista, 2020).

The massification and commercialisation of higher education has led to the increase in the number of higher education students globally (Boshoff & Quinlan, 2016). Student mobility has increased and students can now study at their university of choice, whether that means studying online or travelling to distant countries and continents (ICEF Monitor, 2015; Hearps, 2016). The COVID-19 pandemic has forced HEIs to move academic offerings on-line and use new digital technologies. The need for digitalisation and virtual internationalisation has drastically hastened the need for a re-evaluation of higher education in terms of market and student needs (Bruhn, 2017; Rumbley, 2019). The growing trend to offer qualifications partially or fully online, combined with an international study collaboration, has not only blurred the lines between conventional and distance learning, but has also made internal learning accessible from anywhere in the world (Bruhn, 2017; Lääts et al., 2019). This trend, further accelerated by the COVID-19 pandemic, has increased the competition for students on a global scale.

The recruitment of international students globally is addressed in this study. By understanding what factors influence an international student's university of choice and what information avenues the students use to make their decisions, could assist marketing departments responsible for the recruitment of international students to develop cost-effective, targeted digital recruitment plans. The chapter develops a strategic university of choice model for the recruitment of international students by universities, by ascertaining which factors influence international students' decisions when choosing a university.

## Background

Stakeholders in the higher education sector have observed the rapid marketisation of the sector, due to the increasing use of business and marketing principles and methods, digitilisation, as well as the commercialisation of education (Hemsley-Brown & Oplatka, 2006; Guilbault, 2016, Chapleo & O'Sullivan, 2017). Guilbault (2016) identifies the key drivers of the marketisation and the increase in the number of HEIs. The drivers are the subsequent competition that developed due to an increase in these institutions, a decline in subsidy from governments (Chapleo & O'Sullivan, 2017), the cost to students of studying at HEIs and the effects of globalisation (Hemsley-Brown & Oplatka, 2006). The marketisation of the higher education sector and the subsequent competitive nature it created, compelled HEIs to make use of business marketing principles to promote the institution and its offerings, in an endeavour to recruit students and secure additional third-stream income (Hemsley-Brown & Oplatka, 2010). Yildiz (2021) identified the properties that universities need to have in order to be labelled an entrepreneurial university.

Early research on competitiveness in the higher education sector indicated that due to the evolving economic climate and government and industry needs, universities had to start competitively vying for students (Chapman, 1981). Universities primarily used a paper-based recruitment strategy to recruit students and ultimately persuade them to enrol at their institution. The recruitment strategies included advertisements, flyers and as technology evolved, university websites later assisted with the recruitment of students. The recruitment of students was regarded as an important growth area, not only to ensure that a HEI stays relevant and operational, but also for revenue purposes.

However, this standard and dated approach to recruiting students has become increasingly irrelevant (Maringe, 2006; Hanover Research, 2014; Fleming, 2017). Recruitment approaches that ignore the factors, which influence a student's university of choice decisions, will no longer be able to satisfy the information needs and curiosity of an ever-evolving, globally aware individual. HEIs must invest in effective digital marketing approaches to persuade students to apply. The impact of modern Information Technology applications on organisational structures and processes are reported by Günay, Asunakutlu and Yildiz, (2021).

Students are culturally diverse, they have different information needs and access information digitally, thus a generalist approach may not apply to international students. Various factors influence a student's ultimate university of choice. Some factors are universal, but others develop due to current political or social activities affecting countries (Hearps, 2016; Altbach & De Wit, 2017). In order to understand how students decide on a university, research suggests investigating social and academic stimuli that influence prospective students' decisions (Maringe, 2006; Sánchez, 2012; Sheppard & Smith, 2016).

These factors differ from country to country, as students are influenced by costs; culture; tradition; social activities on- and off-campus; accommodation; facilities and socio-economic issues such as protests, terrorist activities, country instability and economic downturn. (Jooste, Cullen & Calitz, 2020).

The global factors, identified prior to 2012, which influence university of choice decisions by students were programmes and quality of programmes, ranking, location, accommodation, fees, bursaries, university brand and student life (Sorrells & Cole, 2011; Sánchez, 2012). The International Consultants for Education and Fairs (ICEF) found that since 2012, the factor of safety has increased in importance when selecting a study destination (ICEF Monitor, 2012). A difference is observed in current factors influencing university of choice compared to the factors identified by researchers, pre-2012 (Maringe, 2006; Sorrells & Cole, 2011; Sánchez, 2012). A study by Bezuidenhout and De Jager (2014) focused on students enrolled at private HEIs in South Africa. The study found that students considered security and safety conditions on-campus as the most important factor when deciding where to study. Other factors included employment prospects, computer facilities, well-equipped classrooms and international links (linked to study and job opportunities).

Prospective students and university stakeholders use university rankings as criteria for university of choice decisions (Vidal & Ferreira, 2020). Internationally, university rankings are used as an information source, for example by domestic German students and by international students studying at a German university (Koenings, Di Meo & Uebelmesser, 2020). South African students consider university ranking as an important factor when deciding where to study (Jooste et al., 2020). A longitudinal study on university rankings indicated that the criteria used to construct the major university rankings by the three major ranking institutions, Academic Ranking of World Universities (ARWU), Times Higher Education (THE) World University Ranking and Quacquarelli Symonds (QS) World University Ranking, primarily measure two underlying factors, namely a university's reputation and the institution's research performance by academics (Selten, Neylon, Huang & Groth, 2020).

An underpinning theory applied to studies of students' university of choice decisions is the Means-End Theory (MET). The MET is conventionally discussed in terms of understanding the decision-making process of customers, specifically in the retail sector. As this study posits that university students are in actual fact 'customers', this theory applies to the HE sector as well. The MET perceives consumers as goal-oriented decision-makers, who will engage in activities and make decisions that will likely lead them to their desired outcomes (Costa, Dekker & Jongen, 2004). Research on university of choice and why students enrol at their chosen university indicates that there are various factors that influence a student's decision (Sorrells & Cole, 2011; Sánchez, 2012). However, it can be posited that all students opt to study at a specific university of their choice with a certain end-goal in mind. This research will add to the body of knowledge regarding Means-End Theory as it relates to the HE context and student decision making. In addition, prospective students are external stakeholders and registered students internal stakeholders of an institution.

Stakeholder theory proposes that stakeholders exert different levels of influence or power on an institution. Stakeholders can be defined as the individuals or groups who are either affected by the activities and consequences of an organisation or those who have an influence on the organisation (Caballero, Vázquez, & Quintás, 2015). A core concept of the stakeholder theory is that all stakeholders must have decision-making power. A mutual agreement and relationship between the stakeholder and the organisation must exist, through participation, consultation and information exchange. HEIs need to rank those stakeholders and decide which ones have the most influence on their future. International students are important stakeholders for universities for a number of reasons. These include additional revenues, the internationalisation of the institution and improved reputation.

## MAIN FOCUS OF THE CHAPTER

In the higher education context, Chapman (1981) suggests studying the forces and stimuli, which influence prospective students in their university of choice. These factors are further swayed by culture, tradition and socio-economic influences. The following factors have all been identified through global research and are believed to influence university of choice decisions; programmes and quality of programmes; ranking; location; accommodation; fees; bursaries; university brand and student life (Maringe, 2006; Sorrells & Cole, 2011; Sánchez, 2012). The criteria identified by previous research on criteria used by students to make university choice decisions included cost of living, university fees, admission requirements, presentation language, accommodation, career and employment opportunities, institution facilities, security and location (Jooste et al., 2020; Koenings et al., 2020).

Prospective students further use university rankings, published by international ranking organisations as criteria for university of choice decisions (Dearden, Greal & Lilien, 2019; Vidal & Ferreira, 2020). The university ranking criteria have been included in a ranking model that could assist students to make a decision regarding a university of choice (Dearden et al., 2019). The criteria international students consider important in university choice decisions in South Africa has not been thoroughly investigated. This research endeavours to ascertain which factors influence international students' South African university of choice. This study surveyed international students enrolled at Nelson Mandela University (NMU) in South Africa. This chapter proposes a strategic university of choice model that could be used for the recruitment of international students by management and recruiters at HEIs.

## RESEARCH METHODOLOGY

The study followed a positivistic research philosophy and the approach was deductive, exploratory and quantitative. Data were collected from international students studying at the NMU, in South Africa. The NMU is one of 26 public universities in South Africa and the institution has five campuses and approximately 26 000 students. Through convenience sampling, non-probability sampling was used to identify the participants of this study, specifically registered international students at the NMU. In addition, snowball sampling was used, whereby the questionnaire was distributed via an online link to students, who were requested to complete the survey and to share the link with peers in their networks.

The *International Student University of Choice* questionnaire was divided into three sections, namely *Demographics, Sources of Information* and *Influence and Factors of Significance*. In section three, *Factors of significance*, the respondents were asked to rate 46 statements on a Likert scale on the level of importance (1=Not important, 2=Neutral, 3=Important). A pilot study was conducted amongst 2909 students in 2015 to test the validity and reliability of the questionnaire (Jooste, 2020). The results from the pilot study were used to update the conceptual model and the questionnaire used in this study. The NMU international students were surveyed during the period 2017 to 2018 for this study. The international student population at NMU during the period was approximately 1950 and a total of 320 responses were received.

The data from the NMU surveys completed by the international students were captured on QuestionPro and the raw data were exported as a Microsoft Excel file. All unusable or incomplete responses were removed and 306 complete responses were analysed in this research study, equating to a 16% response rate. The NMU statistician conducted the statistical analysis using the statistical software package, Statistica. Both descriptive and inferential statistics were used to analyse the data. The descriptive statistics were used to describe the profile of the respondents, while inferential statistics were used to make inferences about the factors identified in the study.

## RESULTS

The results of the statistical analysis indicated that of the 306 respondents, 82% (n=252) were international undergraduate students and 18% (n=54) were international postgraduate students. Table 1 indicates that 49% (n=150) of the respondents were full-time international students studying at NMU for a minimum period of three years. A significant number of the respondents (34%, n=105) were study abroad students, students from international universities studying at NMU for a 3 to 6 month period. Forteen percent (n=44) were part-time exchange students, that formed part of the exchange agreement between universities, where students from international universities come to NMU for a 3 to 12 month period and NMU sends students to the international partner university.

Table 1 indicates that 50% (n=153) of the respondents were from Africa, while 37% (n=112) were from Europe and 12% (n=36) were from North America. The number of African students studying at the university supports Lee and Sehoole's (2015) findings regarding the migration of African students across borders. According to Lee and Sehoole (2015), African countries deemed to offer a better life to students (human capital perspective) or countries whose education systems are deemed better (consumption perspective) are popular study destinations.

*Table 1. Demographic variables: Study Level, Type and Continent (n=306)*

| Study Level | % | Student Type | % | Continent of Origin | % |
|---|---|---|---|---|---|
| Undergraduate | 82% (n=252) | Exchange/ Part-time | 14% (n=44) | Asia | 0.5% (n=3) |
| Postgraduate (Graduate) | 18% (n=54) | Study Abroad | 34% (n=105) | Africa | 50% (n=153) |
| | | Full-Time | 49% (n=150) | Europe | 37% (n=112) |
| | | Research only | 2% (n=7) | South America | 0.5% (n=2) |
| | | | | North America | 12% (n=36) |

The gender breakdown of the respondents (n=306) indicates that 54% (n=166) were female and 46% (n=140) were male. Table 2 further indicates that 55% (n=168) of the respondents were between the ages of 18 to 21 years; while 29% (n=90) were between the ages of 22 to 25 years. However, this bias is not be deemed negative, as the 18 to 21 year age group, as well as the 22 to 25 year age group are deemed to be the traditional age of a university student (Guidry, 2018).

A list of the home language of families was compiled because of the vast number of home languages identified by the respondents. The majority of the respondents' home language (62%, n=190) identify with the Germanic home language family. This home language family is inclusive of English, German, Dutch, Danish, Swedish, Icelandic, Norwegian and Faroese (Moulton & Buccini, 2019). Only the languages which illustrated a large contribution to the Germanic language family were included in Table 2. The majority of the respondents' home language is English (30%, n=92) and German (26%, n=79). Other dominant home language families identified were Atlantic-Congo (27%, n=84) and Romance (7%, n=22). Atlantic-Congo language families are mostly found in Africa and are spoken in Cameroon, Liberia, Nigeria, Sudan and Senegal (Bendor-Samuel, 2019). The majority of these respondents' home language is Shona (13%, n=41).

*Table 2. Demographic variables: Gender, Age, Home Language Family, University and Country of Choice and Qualification (n=306)*

| **Gender** | | **Age** | | **University of Choice** | | **Qualification** | |
|---|---|---|---|---|---|---|---|
| Female | 54% (n=166) | 18 - 21 | 55% (n=168) | Yes | 74% (n=225) | Arts | 8% (n=26) |
| Male | 46% (n=140) | 22 - 25 | 29% (n=90) | No | 26% (n=81) | Business | 34% (n=105) |
| **Home Language of Family** | | 26 - 30 | 6% (n=18) | **Country of Choice** | | Education | 2% (n=5) |
| Atlantic-Congo | 27% (n=84) | 31 - 40 | 7% (n=22) | Yes | 78% (n=240) | Engineering & Built Environment | 18% (n=54) |
| Germanic | 62% (n=190) | 41 - older | 3% (n=8) | No | 22% (n=66) | Health Sciences | 13% (n=40) |
| Romance | 7% (n=22) | **Language** (majority only) | English | 30% (n=92) | | Law | 8% (n=23) |
| | | | German | 26% (n=79) | | Sciences | 12% (n=37) |
| | | | Shona | 13% (n=41) | | Various modules | 5% (n=16) |
| | | | French | 6% (n=17) | | | |

Seventy-eight percent (n=240) of the respondents indicated that South Africa was their initial country of choice, while 74% (n=225) indicated that NMU was their initial university of choice. Table 2 further illustrates that the respondents were registered in a variety of faculties, ensuring that the university of choice factors can be deemed applicable to the university as a whole and not just one faculty. However, the study can demonstrate bias as the majority of the respondents (34%, n=105) were registered for Business-related qualifications. Eighteen percent (18%, n=54) were registered for Engineering and Built Environment qualifications, 13% (n=40) were registered for Health Sciences-related qualifications and 12% (n=37) were registered for Sciences-related qualifications.

Section B of the questionnaire established the frequency distribution for the sources of information and influence factors. Table 3 summarises the responses to the question: *Why did you choose to study in South Africa?* The results in Table 3 show that 68% (n=208) of NMU respondents identified the *location of the university* as very to extremely important and thus had the greatest influence overall in these respondents' country-to-study in decision-making process. The results in Table 3 are rated from greatest to least influence. Other factors of influence were *cost of study* (67%, n=207), *wanted to experience the culture* (65%, n=19), *cost of living* (62%, n=190) and *university's concern for international students* (57%, n=176). The factor, *university's concern for international students* corresponds with the CBIE (2014) study conducted on Brazilian students in Canada. The Brazilian students surveyed indicated that they chose Canada due to the perceived tolerant, non-discriminatory nature of the country, as well as the country's positive attitude towards international students.

*Table 3. Why did you choose to study in South Africa? (n=306)*

| Why did you choose to study in South Africa? (n=306) | Ranked | Not Important | Neutral | Important |
|---|---|---|---|---|
| Location of the university | 1 | 55 (18%) | 43 (14%) | 208 (68%) |
| Cost of study | 2 | 52 (17%) | 47 (15%) | 207 (68%) |
| Wanted to experience the culture | 3 | 73 (24%) | 35 (11%) | 198 (65%) |
| Cost of living | 4 | 53 (17%) | 63 (21%) | 190 (62%) |
| University's concern for international students | 5 | 60 (20%) | 70 (23%) | 176 (58%) |
| Opportunity to stay in the country | 6 | 72 (23%) | 64 (21%) | 170 (56%) |
| Reputation of the country's education system | 7 | 52 (17%) | 95 (31%) | 159 (52%) |
| Opportunity to improve my English language skills | 8 | 128 (42%) | 29 (9%) | 149 (49%) |
| To get away from my home country | 9 | 116 (38%) | 51 (17%) | 139 (45%) |
| Reputation of the lecturers at the university | 10 | 68 (22%) | 100 (33%) | 138 (45%) |
| Ranking of the university | 11 | 76 (25%) | 96 (31%) | 134 (44%) |
| Stable political environment in the country | 12 | 78 (25%) | 104 (34%) | 124 (41%) |
| Reputation of the research conducted at the university | 13 | 84 (27%) | 101 (33%) | 121 (40%) |
| Ease of obtaining a study visa | 14 | 124 (41%) | 84 (27%) | 98 (32%) |
| Job prospects in the country | 15 | 159 (52%) | 50 (16%) | 97 (32%) |
| Courses not available in any other country | 16 | 172 (56%) | 51 (17%) | 83 (27%) |
| Desire to immigrate to the country | 17 | 187 (61%) | 54 (18%) | 65 (21%) |
| Family in the country | 18 | 218 (71%) | 42 (14%) | 46 (15%) |
| Friends in the country | 19 | 209 (68%) | 54 (18%) | 43 (14%) |
| Government funding received dictated that I study in this country | 20 | 218 (71%) | 53 (17%) | 35 (12%) |

Respondents were also asked to identify the influence of generic, social reasons in their decision to attend NMU. The results in Table 4 indicate that 83% (n=254) of respondents identified *to develop a broad-based set of skills* as very to extremely important in their decision-making process. Other reasons deemed of greatest influence were: *to increase my knowledge in an academic field* (81%, n=135), *to get a good general education* (75%, n=228), *to become a more culturally adapted person* (73%, n=224) and *to prepare for a specific career* (65%, n=197). The results in Table 4 contradict Lee and Sehoole's

(2015) finding that among African international students opting to study in South Africa, the main reasons for choosing the country as their preferred destination were career mobility and academic research. According to the study (Lee & Sehoole, 2015) both reasons were linked to the "country's role in developing human capital".

*Table 4. Social reasons for wanting to attend NMU (n=306)*

| Reasons for University Choice – NMU (n = 306) | Ranked | Not Important | Neutral | Important |
|---|---|---|---|---|
| To develop a broad-based set of skills | 1 | 19 (6%) | 33 (11%) | 254 (83%) |
| To increase my knowledge in an academic field | 2 | 27 (9%) | 34 (11%) | 245 (80%) |
| To get a good general education | 3 | 31 (10%) | 47 (15%) | 228 (75%) |
| To become a more culturally adapted person | 4 | 43 (14%) | 39 (13%) | 224 (73%) |
| To prepare for a specific career | 5 | 56 (19%) | 53 (17%) | 197 (64%) |
| To get a good job | 6 | 56 (19%) | 56 (18%) | 194 (63%) |
| To have fun | 7 | 77 (25%) | 42 (14%) | 187 (61%) |
| To meet new friends | 8 | 68 (22%) | 60 (20%) | 178 (58%) |
| To meet my host university's programme requirements | 9 | 89 (29%) | 60 (20%) | 157 (51%) |
| To meet my parents' expectations | 10 | 181 (59%) | 49 (16%) | 76 (25%) |

Respondents were asked to rate the importance of a variety of marketing and recruitment tools in their decision-making processes. Respondents were given a list of 23 marketing and recruitment tools varying from traditional tools (print adverts, radio adverts, brochures, etc.), electronic tools (social media, website, etc.), Word-of-Mouth (WOM - friends recommendations, alumni recommendations) to recruitment activities conducted by the university (open days, agents, etc.). Table 5 provides a summary of the frequency distribution. Respondents identified WOM factors: *recommendation from a former student* (60%, n=183) and *friends' recommendation* (50%, n=154) as influential. Other factors which ranked highly can be placed in two categories: *University website* and *International Office*. Fifty-two percent of NMU respondents (52%, n=159) identified the *university website* as influential and 51% of NMU respondents (51%, n=155) identified *information from your International Office* as influential. The top three marketing and recruitment tools, which were deemed of no importance and thus having no influence on the respondents' university of choice decision were Advert on radio/TV (79%, n=242), Advert in a newspaper (78%, n=238) and WOM option by Sponsor (72%, n=219) and Employer (72%, n=221).

Respondents were also asked to rate the importance of a variety of factors, which they may have considered in their university of choice decision-making process. Respondents were given a list of 46 factors. Table 6 illustrates that NMU respondents (n=306) relied on a variety of factors in their decision-making process. However, the five most influential factors were: (1) *classes offered in English* (84%, n=257), (2) *personal safety and security on campus* (78%, n=240), (3) *cost of living* (76%, n=234), (4) *quality of academic programmes* (75%, n=230) and (5) *tuition fees* (74%, n=225). Academic quality, factors related to academic programmes, financial factors and safety and security factors are thus main factors, which best describe the most influential factors identified by the respondents.

*Table 5. Marketing and recruitment tools and university of choice*

| Marketing and Recruitment Tools (n= 306) | | | | |
|---|---|---|---|---|
| **Factor** | **Ranked** | **Not Important** | **Neutral** | **Important** |
| Recommendation from a former student | 1 | 91 (30%) | 32 (10%) | 183 (60%) |
| University website | 2 | 90 (29%) | 57 (19%) | 159 (52%) |
| Information from your International Office | 3 | 121 (39%) | 30 (10%) | 155 (51%) |
| Friends recommendation | 4 | 116 (38%) | 36 (12%) | 154 (50%) |
| University brochure | 5 | 162 (53%) | 34 (11%) | 110 (36%) |
| University information email | 6 | 171 (56%) | 47 (15%) | 88 (29%) |
| Relatives/siblings recommendation | 7 | 175 (58%) | 44 (14%) | 87 (28%) |
| Lecturer/Professor/Mentor recommendation | 8 | 174 (57%) | 49 (16%) | 83 (27%) |
| Prior visit to the country | 9 | 184 (60%) | 47 (15%) | 75 (25%) |
| University Social Media | 10 | 170 (55%) | 61 (20%) | 75 (25%) |
| Career advisor | 11 | 189 (61%) | 45 (15%) | 72 (24%) |
| Advert online | 12 | 189 (62%) | 53 (17%) | 64 (21%) |
| Invitation to attend an information session on this university | 13 | 196 (64%) | 46 (15%) | 64 (21%) |
| Agent of the university | 14 | 195 (63%) | 51 (17%) | 60 (20%) |
| Cultural day on your campus | 15 | 205 (67%) | 49 (16%) | 52 (17%) |
| Visit by University representatives | 16 | 210 (69%) | 49 (16%) | 47 (15%) |
| Home country government advisory service | 17 | 209 (68%) | 51 (17%) | 46 (15%) |
| Exhibition or fair | 18 | 205 (67%) | 56 (18%) | 45 (15%) |
| Independent website | 19 | 204 (67%) | 58 (19%) | 44 (14%) |
| An employer | 20 | 221 (72%) | 45 (15%) | 40 (13%) |
| Sponsor | 21 | 219 (72%) | 47 (15%) | 40 (13%) |
| Advert in a newspaper | 22 | 238 (78%) | 49 (16%) | 19 (6%) |
| Advert on radio/TV | 23 | 242 (79%) | 49 (16%) | 15 (5%) |

As this research study wanted to reduce the number of factors to only those factors deemed influential by international students, the main factors, supported by sub-factors were identified. The sub-factors are thus the list of factors of significance in Table 6, the sources of information and influence in Table 3, the reasons for wanting to attend a university in Table 4, as well as the marketing and recruitment tools in Table 5. Table 7 illustrates the main factor and its subsequent sub-factors, which informed the strategic model.

The main factors in terms of factors of significance, sources of information and influences and reasons for wanting to attend a university were *academic programme*, *academic quality*, *visa requirements*, *country/city attractiveness*, *English language*, *financial*, *International Office*, *safety and security*, *student life*, *university location* and *university reputation*. The main factors in terms of marketing and recruitment tools were *adverts in media*, *government advisory service*, *university information* and *WOM*. It must be noted that items related to factors of significance and marketing and recruitment tools are not analysed together as marketing and recruitment tools are deemed not an attribute of the university of choice, but instead an information gathering tool (consultative in nature).

*Table 6. Factors of significance and university of choice*

| Factors of Significance (n=306) | Ranked | Not Important | Neutral | Important |
|---|---|---|---|---|
| Classes offered in English | 1 | 32 (10%) | 17 (6%) | 257 (84%) |
| Personal safety and security on campus | 2 | 36 (12%) | 30 (10%) | 240 (78%) |
| Cost of living | 3 | 40 (13%) | 32 (11%) | 234 (76%) |
| Quality of academic programmes | 4 | 30 (10%) | 46 (15%) | 230 (75%) |
| Tuition fees | 5 | 41 (13%) | 40 (13%) | 225 (74%) |
| Location of university (country and city) | 6 | 44 (14%) | 38 (13%) | 224 (73%) |
| Variety of academic programmes | 7 | 32 (10%) | 52 (17%) | 222 (73%) |
| Personal safety and security in the city | 8 | 35 (11%) | 52 (17%) | 219 (72%) |
| Quality of teaching/lecturers | 9 | 35 (11%) | 58 (19%) | 213 (70%) |
| Opportunities to travel and visit tourist attractions | 10 | 55 (18%) | 40 (13%) | 211 (69%) |
| How people would behave towards you as an international student | 11 | 52 (17%) | 44 (14%) | 210 (69%) |
| Opportunities to experience the culture of the country | 12 | 56 (18%) | 42 (14%) | 208 (68%) |
| Accommodation options available | 13 | 59 (19%) | 41 (14%) | 206 (67%) |
| Personal safety and security in the country | 14 | 42 (14%) | 60 (19%) | 204 (67%) |
| Assistance provided to international students | 15 | 64 (21%) | 48 (16%) | 194 (63%) |
| Accessible facilities on campus | 16 | 63 (21%) | 51 (16%) | 192 (63%) |
| University culture | 17 | 61 (20%) | 55 (18%) | 190 (62%) |
| University's level of technology | 18 | 54 (18%) | 62 (20%) | 190 (62%) |
| Social activities in the city | 19 | 62 (21%) | 65 (21%) | 179 (58%) |
| Campus social life | 20 | 79 (26%) | 53 (17%) | 174 (57%) |
| Cultural activities in the city | 21 | 64 (21%) | 68 (22%) | 174 (57%) |
| Ease of travelling to university | 22 | 71 (23%) | 63 (21%) | 172 (56%) |
| City facilities | 23 | 59 (19%) | 76 (25%) | 171 (56%) |
| Length of programme | 24 | 62 (20%) | 74 (24%) | 170 (56%) |
| University accreditation | 25 | 63 (21%) | 74 (24%) | 169 (55%) |
| Specific career-related programmes | 26 | 72 (23%) | 66 (22%) | 168 (55%) |
| Quality of research/researchers | 27 | 68 (22%) | 71 (23%) | 167 (55%) |
| University ranking | 28 | 77 (25%) | 74 (24%) | 155 (51%) |
| Reputation of International Office | 29 | 89 (29%) | 71 (23%) | 146 (48%) |
| Ease of obtaining a visa | 30 | 94 (31%) | 73 (24%) | 139 (45%) |
| Recommendation from current students | 31 | 118 (39%) | 50 (16%) | 138 (45%) |
| Availability of public transport | 32 | 89 (29%) | 80 (26%) | 137 (45%) |
| Frequent contact with faculty | 33 | 97 (32%) | 77 (25%) | 132 (43%) |
| Size of city | 34 | 87 (28%) | 87 (29%) | 132 (43%) |

*Table 7. Main and sub-factors pertaining to university of choice and marketing and recruitment tools*

| Main Factors | Sub-Factors |
|---|---|
| **Academic programme** | (1) Courses not available in any other country |
| | (2) To prepare for a specific career |
| | (3) To get a good general education |
| | (4) To develop a broad-based set of skills |
| | (5) To increase my knowledge in an academic field |
| | (6) To get a good job |
| | (7) To meet my host university's programme requirements |
| | (8) Quality of academic programmes |
| | (9) Variety of academic programmes |
| | (10) Length of programme |
| | (11) Specific career-related programmes |
| | (12) Opportunities for you to work while you study |
| **Academic quality** | (1) Size of university (and student population) |
| | (2) Quality of teaching/lecturers |
| | (3) Quality of research/researchers |
| | (4) Number of international staff at the university |
| | (5) Student to lecturer ratio |
| | (6) Frequent contact with faculty |
| | (7) Centres of Excellence |
| | (8) Job placement rate |
| **Visa requirements** | (1) Ease of obtaining a study visa |
| | (2) Ease of obtaining a visa |
| **Country/City attractiveness** | (1) Opportunity to stay in the country |
| | (2) Family in the country |
| | (3) Friends in the country |
| | (4) Desire to immigrate to the country |
| | (5) Job prospects in the country |
| | (6) To get away from my home country |
| | (7) Wanted to experience the culture |
| | (8) Prior visit to the country |
| | (9) Cultural activities in the city |
| | (10) Social activities in the city |
| | (11) City size and facilities |
| | (12) Opportunities to experience the culture of the country |
| | (13) Opportunities to travel and visit tourist attractions |
| **English language** | (1) Opportunity to improve my English language skills |
| | (2) Classes offered in English |
| **Financial** | (1) Cost of living (country) |

*continues on following page*

*Table 7. Continued*

| Main Factors | Sub-Factors |
|---|---|
| | (2) Cost of study |
| | (3) Government funding received dictated that I study in this country |
| | (4) Availability of public transport |
| | (5) Cost of living (university/city) |
| | (6) Tuition fees |
| | (7) Scholarships/bursaries available |
| **International Office** | (1) University's concern for international students |
| | (2) Reputation of International Office |
| | (3) Assistance provided to international students |
| **Safety and security** | (1) Stable political environment in the country |
| | (2) Personal safety and security in the country |
| | (3) Personal safety and security in the city |
| | (4) Personal safety and security on campus |
| **Student life** | (1) To become a more culturally adapted person |
| | (2) To meet new friends |
| | (3) To have fun |
| | (4) Ease of travelling to university |
| | (5) Campus social life |
| | (6) University culture |
| | (7) Athletic opportunities |
| | (8) Accommodation options available |
| | (9) Accessible facilities on campus |
| | (10) University's level of technology |
| | (11) How people would behave towards you as an international student |
| **University location** | (1) Location of the university |
| | (2) Proximity to home (closeness) |
| | (3) Proximity to home (far away from home) |
| | (4) Location of university (country and city) |
| **University reputation** | (1) Reputation of the country's education system |
| | (2) Reputation of the lecturers at the university |
| | (3) Reputation of the research conducted at the university |
| | (4) Ranking of the university |
| | (5) Friends attending |
| | (6) Recommendation from current students |
| | (7) Alumni network |
| | (8) University ranking |
| | (9) University accreditation |
| | (10) To meet my parents' expectations |

*continues on following page*

*Table 7. Continued*

| Main Factors | Sub-Factors |
|---|---|
| **Marketing and Recruitment Tools** | |
| **Advert in media** | (1) Advert in a newspaper |
| | (2) Advert online |
| | (3) Advert on radio/TV |
| | (4) Independent website |
| **Government advisory service** | (1) Home country government advisory service |
| **University information** | (1) University Social Media |
| | (2) University website |
| | (3) Agent of the university |
| | (4) Invitation to attend an information session on this university |
| | (5) Information from your International Office |
| | (6) Visit by University representatives |
| | (7) Cultural day on your campus |
| | (8) University brochure |
| | (9) University information email |
| | (10) Exhibition or fair |
| **WOM** | (1) Recommendation from a former student |
| | (2) Lecturer/Professor/Mentor recommendation |
| | (3) Friends recommendation |
| | (4) Relatives/siblings recommendation |
| | (5) Career advisor |
| | (6) An employer |
| | (7) Sponsor |

The sub-factor *to meet my parents' expectations* was excluded, as it could not be combined with any of the above factors. The sub-factor *prior visit to the country* was initially part of the marketing and recruitment tool list. It was excluded from the marketing and recruitment tool list and included in the factors of significance list as part of the *country/city attractiveness* main factor.

The majority of the Cronbach's alpha coefficients for the factors as indicated in Table 8, meet the minimum requirements of 0.80, indicating excellent reliability, while others meet the minimum requirement of 0.70 – 0.79, indicating good reliability and some meet the minimum requirement of 0.50 – 0.69 for acceptable reliability. The factors highlighted in italics with a reliability coefficient of < 0.50 are considered unacceptable.

## SOLUTIONS AND RECOMMENDATIONS

A HEI can develop a digital marketing and recruitment plan, which addresses relevant issues of a target market by understanding the factors, which influence a prospective student. By creating depth in the relationship between the HEI and the prospective student, the HEI facilitates the development and growth of a long-term relationship. This concept applies to the higher education sector and specifically HEIs as relationship marketing suggests that there is no beginning or end to the relationship, but instead a continuation of the relationship (current student to Alumni for example).

Based on the focus of this study, students are an important stakeholder. HEIs can use the information to assist students to make informed decisions (creating further value) by understanding the factors, which influence a student's decision-making. Furthermore, the information can be used to improve the student's experience during the information-seeking phase, application phase, registration phase and studying phase and as alumni. WOM is an important influencer of university of choice and a good experience leads to positive WOM. Positive WOM benefits the university and the student. The graduates of a university then join society as citizens who can contribute to the community, not only professionally but also socially.

The information gained from the research allows universities to understand the way the student relates to the university and the factors, which influence the student's university of choice. Attributes, which include both the consultative factors and influential factors, influence the international student's decision-making process. These attributes are concrete, for instance location of the university or abstract, for instance perceived safety and security on campus. The questionnaire, developed as part of the study, can guide a university in determining the consultative factors and influential factors relevant to that university. The result of the university of choice decision has on an international student can be functional (obtaining a qualification, experience) or psychosocial (a student who would like to study in close proximity to his/her home). The student determines the value of the university of choice decision. Understanding the values that drive the international student's decision is important. These values are formed by the international student's immediate surroundings, as well as opinions of people who the student deems important.

The recruitment of students, whether local or international, forms part of the strategic intent of a university. Universities determine the number of students they would like to recruit locally and internationally on an annual basis. Some universities further determine that they would like to increase their numbers of a specific type of student. For example, Australian universities specifically targeted Torres Strait Islanders and Aboriginal students through a targeted recruitment campaign (Brennan, 2017; Schubert & Counihan, 2017). Other higher education systems would have different needs concerning the diversification of their international student body, e.g. South African universities would need to diversify their student body away from a pure SADC focus. The model presented in Figure 1 (Appendix1) can assist universities in the development of a strategic digital marketing and recruitment plan linked to their specific strategic intent.

### International Student Recruitment Plan

HEIs' management and International Offices can no longer rely on a localised recruitment plan to recruit international students. The study has illustrated that a "one-size-fits-all" recruitment plan no longer delivers the international student cohort the university would like. Universities need to invest in a separate international digital student recruitment plan, which targets different types of international students.

*Figure 1. University of Choice model*

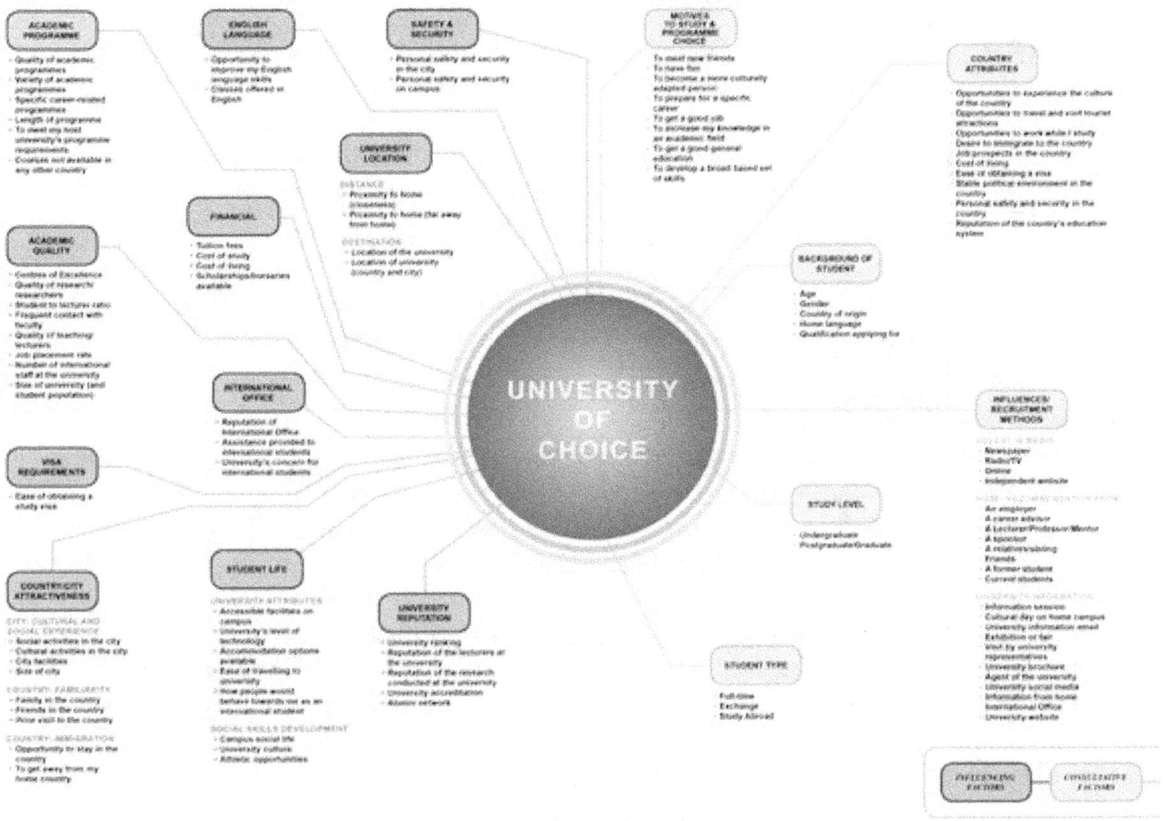


These types of students can be segmented on student type, e.g. full-time and study abroad/exchange as well as based on country. By using the strategic model, the university can develop relevant content and use marketing tools, which will deliver the most return on investment.

As much as a university cannot rely on a "one-size-fits-all" recruitment plan, HEIs cannot meet all the information and other needs of international students. HEIs must determine what sets them apart from other universities in terms of why an international student would opt to study with them instead of another university in their home country or a foreign country. For example, when asked why they opted to study at the NMU in South Africa, the majority of the respondents (68%, n=208) indicated the *location of the university* influenced their decision. Destination and location factors combined with other important factors, for example, safety and security, can be used to develop a more efficient and effective recruitment plan. Due to the highly competitive environment, once the HEI determines its competitive advantage, their unique offering to international students must be the basis from which all recruitment is driven.

Figure 2 illustrates the operationalisation of the Proposed Strategic Model: University of Choice. *Developing a Targeted International Student Recruitment Plan* concludes with the general themes identified by the study. The six steps outlined can be used by all types and sizes of universities as basis for establishing a targeted international student recruitment strategy.

*Figure 2. Developing a targeted international student recruitment plan*

**Step 1** focuses on the intent of the university and the country as a whole. A university must invest in an internationalisation strategy, which will guide the recruitment of international students as well as the internationalisation activities of the staff and students of the university. The strategy must be based in the country's internationalisation policy or framework. For instance, South Africa's Draft Policy Framework for the Internationalisation of Higher Education (DHET, 2017). Furthermore, the strategy must work parallel to the university's local student recruitment strategy in terms of brand cohesiveness and messages regarding the university's key differentiators. Lastly, the university's policies regarding student recruitment must be clear on the percentage of international students it would like to accommodate on campus. For instance, NMU's policy clearly states that international students will only encompass 10% of the student body. Furthermore, NMU has a clearly defined Africa-centric internationalisation strategy in place.

**Step 2** identifies the various target markets of the university. Based on the university's internationalisation strategy, the international office should determine the following target markets:

i. **Maintenance Market.** The maintenance markets for the full-time and study abroad and exchange student markets must be determined. These are international students from certain countries or regions, who make up the majority of the international student cohort. For instance, for NMU these are students from SADC (full-time students) and Germany (study abroad/exchange students). The international office must further determine what percentage of the recruitment budget will be allocated to the maintenance market.
ii. **Growth Market.** The growth markets for the full-time and study abroad and exchange student markets must be determined. Furthermore, the international office must determine what percentage of the recruitment budget will be allocated to the growth markets. The international office must also determine how it will reach these markets. As this is a growth market, the office would need to understand how the students obtain their decision-making information. Should the office invest in personal visits to the country or employ the services of an agent?
iii. **Exploratory Market.** The exploratory market for the full-time and study abroad and exchange student markets must be determined. These markets are based on student mobility trends, as well as the university's internationalisation agenda. Furthermore, the international office must determine what percentage of the recruitment budget will be allocated to the exploratory market. For these markets the international office would invest in digital recruitment tools to determine interest. For instance, social media channels such as Facebook and Instagram can be used to create targeted digital marketing and recruitment campaigns.

**Step 3** is the understanding of the university's various target markets. To understand a target market, market research must be conducted. The questionnaire developed as part of this study can be used by all international offices to gather information on their target markets. The questionnaire can be amended by the university's international office if it would like to determine specific wants and needs of the target market. Furthermore, the questionnaire can also incorporate questions regarding current world events that can influence a student's decision-making, e.g. COVID-19 pandemic. Once the questionnaire has been completed by the various target markets, the international office must invest in analyses of the data and the interpretation of the data.

**Step 4** can only commence once the factors deemed influential in the various target markets' decision-making process are determined. The factors found influential must then be categorised according to the types of factors determined by the model (Figure 1). These types of factors are consultative in nature or influence the target market's decision. The consultative factors must further be divided into (i) study level and student type, (ii) motives to study, programme choice, background of student and country attributes and (iii) recruitment tools. Recruitment tools would encompass the level of importance of the various recruitment tools at the disposal of the international office, the target market's preferred way of receiving information, which tools are deemed to influence their decision and which of the tools are deemed more consultative in nature.

The respondents of this study (n=306) indicated that only five of the 23 marketing and recruitment options presented to them were important. These options were *recommendation from a student* (60%, n=183), *university website* (52%, n=159), *information from your International Office* (51%, n=155) and *friends' recommendation* (50%, 154). *Word-of-mouth* is important in the decision-making process of a prospective international student. For example, a university can ask current and previous international students to make a video of their study experience. To ensure the maximum benefit, the international office can include a snippet of the student speaking in his/her own language as well as English in the video and include where the student is from. The study found that certain influential factors are universal. These factors were *academic programme, academic quality, visa requirements, country/city attractiveness, English language, financial, International Office, student life, safety & security, university location* and *university reputation*. Although these are universal factors influencing a student's decision-making process, the level of influence differs. The level of influence for each target market would be the determining factor in deciding which factor to incorporate in the recruitment message.

**Step 5** is the implementation phase where the international office develops targeted messages, supported by relevant brand visuals, to recruit students from the target market. The office can also decide to use a universal factor, identified by the research, to recruit students. For instance, when asked why they opted to study with NMU in South Africa, the majority of the respondents (68%, n=208) indicated the *location of the university* influenced their decision. Destination and location factors combined with other important factors, for example, safety and security, can be used to develop a recruitment message and appropriate visuals. As the respondents indicated that *university website* (52%, n=159) was a consultative factor, the university marketing department can use striking visuals of its location and campus and a message centred on safety on campus and surroundings on its website. As both country/city attractiveness and safety and security are universal factors, marketing should meet the information need of a general international student.

**Step 6** illustrates how interconnected the recruitment process is. The marketing and recruitment of students cannot be viewed as separate from the experience a student has before he/she applies, during his/her application process and once the student has been accepted. International office staff and other staff dealing with international students must be knowledgeable, answer queries within a respectable timeframe and nurture the application throughout the application process until a decision is made regarding the application. Furthermore, information relevant to international students must continuously be updated on the website and brochures. Social media channels can then be used to inform prospective international students where to find the information.

## FUTURE RESEARCH DIRECTIONS

The study was limited to international students studying at one university in South Africa. This cohort represents a moderate percentage of stakeholders in the South Africa higher education sector. Further research that includes a larger group of current international students studying at other universities as well as from other types of South African universities (Universities of Technology) is suggested.

The findings and discussions of this research study present new opportunities for future research in the South African and African higher education sector. As per the literature reviewed, there is a lack of IoHE knowledge and opinions from the Global South. This research provides the basis for a more extensive study across African borders to identify the factors which influence international students' university of choice in Africa.

From the study, the way an international student is treated was identified as an influencing factor. Research, especially among the African international student cohort, is suggested in determining the effects of xenophobia on the decision-making process of a prospective international student. Furthermore, research is suggested, which investigates if the international student's experience matches his/her perception. This is due to the increase of Word-Of-Mouth influence on an international student's decision-making process.

At the time of writing the chapter, the COVID-19 virus outbreak has affected the higher education sector, worldwide. According to the Institute of International Education (Dennis, 2020), three-quarters of colleges and universities in the United States of America have reported the negative impact of COVID-19 on recruitment. University recruitment and admission practices pertaining to local students and especially international students will have to be revisited. It is suggested that research be conducted on the effect of COVID-19 on international student recruitment as well as the mobility of students across borders.

## CONCLUSION

This chapter has illustrated how a focus on the factors, which influence the university of choice decisions of an international student, can assist in their decision-making process. The identified factors that influence a student's university of choice are beneficial to various stakeholders in the higher education sector, e.g. the prospective student (information to make an informed decision) and the university (recruiting targeted international students). By investing in a targeted marketing and recruitment plan based on factors deemed influential in their decision-making process, the university illustrates their intent and commitment to a long-term relationship between the HEI and the prospective student to a registered student.

The factors which influence university of choice are fluid and can change as the global landscape changes. A comparative analysis of the factors which influence international students' university of choice is suggested between countries on different continents. A strategic university of choice model based on the factors which influence a student to study in a developed country versus the factors which influence a student to study in a developing country can lead to the recruitment of a truly diverse international student body. This would further add to the body of knowledge on stakeholder theory based in the higher education sector.

An important consideration for university management on the stakeholder theory is the requirement to classify the most important stakeholders, including students. A competitive advantage is gained by the institution by involving the stakeholders, specifically students, as strategic resources in institutional decisions, including recruitment strategies. HEIs that take their stakeholders' interests seriously are regarded as more successful than institutions that do not (Caballero et al., 2015). The MET is used in this research on criteria considered important by international student's making university of choice decision (Sorrells & Cole, 2011; Sánchez, 2012). Students opt to study at a specific university of their choice with a certain end-goal in mind. This research added to the body of knowledge regarding Means-End Theory as it relates to the HE context and student decision making.

The chapter has confirmed that the main factors identified by international students studying in South Africa, equated to the main factors identified by other international studies on the university of choice factors. However, the degree of importance differs. Furthermore, the discussions in the study confirmed that some factors are more consultative than influential (e.g. recruitment methods) in the decision-making process. The regular review of the strategic model and the subsequent factors, which influence the University of Choice of students is encouraged to provide up-to-date and relevant information to HEIs for marketing and recruitment purposes. The strategic model can also not be used without the relevant global context being taken into consideration. Current economic, political and social world events must be taken into account when updating the strategic model. With COVID-19 driving the delivery platform to online, a number of physical factors, such as location, might become less important in the future. Future research will re-evaluate the model, taking factors brought about due to the COVID-19 pandemic into consideration.

## REFERENCES

Adams, T., & De Wit, H. (2011). Global competition in higher education: a comparative study of policies, rationales and practices in Australia and Europe. In H. De Wit (Ed.), *Trends, issues and challenges in internationalisation of higher education*. Centre for Applied Research on Economics & Management.

Altbach, P. G., & De Wit, H. (2017). *The new nationalism and internationalisation of HE*. Retrieved from https://www.universityworldnews.com/post.php? story=20170914073027157

Bendor-Samuel, J. T. (2019). *Atlantic Languages*. Retrieved from https://www.britannica.com/topic/African-Atlantic-languages

Bezuidenhout, G., & De Jager, J. (2014). Customer satisfaction at private higher education institutions in South Africa: An importance-performance analysis. *Journal of Contemporary Management*, *11*, 206–229.

Boshoff, H., & Quinlan, O. (2016). Student protests demand change to the underlying fault lines in Higher Education. *Study South Africa*, *1*, 30–34.

Brennan, B. (2017). *Universities set goals to attract more Indigenous students in Australian-first*. Retrieved from https://www.abc.net.au/news/2017-03-01/universitiesaustralia-indigenous-strategy/8313116

Bruhn, E. (2017). Towards a Framework for Virtual Internationalization. *International Journal of E-Learning & Distance Education*, *32*(1), 1–9. https://files.eric.ed.gov/fulltext/EJ1159898.pdf

Caballero, G., Vázquez, X. H., & Quintás, M. A. (2015). Improving Employability through Stakeholders in European Higher Education: The Case of Spain. *Long Range Planning*, *48*(6), 398–411. doi:10.1016/j.lrp.2015.09.005

CBIE. (2014). *CBIE Research in Brief*. Retrieved from https://files.eric.ed.gov/fulltext/ED566119.pdf

Chapleo, C., & O'Sullivan, H. (2017). Contemporary thought in higher education marketing. *Journal of Marketing for Higher Education*, *27*(2), 159–161. doi:10.1080/08841241.2017.1406255

Chapman, D. W. (1981). A model of student college choice. *The Journal of Higher Education*, *52*(5), 490–505. doi:10.2307/1981837

Costa, A. I. A., Dekker, M., & Jongen, W. M. F. (2004). An overview of means-end theory: Potential application in consumer-oriented food product design. *Trends in Food Science & Technology*, *15*(7-8), 403–415. doi:10.1016/j.tifs.2004.02.005

De Wit, H., & Hunter, F. (2015). Understanding internationalisation of higher education in the European context. In H. de Wit, F. Hunter, L. Howard, & E. Egron-Polak (Eds.), *Internationalization of Higher Education* (pp. 41–58). European Parliament, Committee on Culture and Education.

Dearden, J. A., Greal, R., & Lilien, G. L. (2019). Strategic Manipulation of University Rankings, the Prestige Effect, and Student University Choice. *JMR, Journal of Marketing Research*, *56*(4), 691–707. doi:10.1177/0022243719831258

Dennis, M. (2020). *How will higher education have changed after COVID-19?* Retrieved from: https://www.universityworldnews.com/post.php?story=20200324065639773

DHET. (2017). Draft Policy Framework for the Internationalisation of Higher Education in South Africa. Department of Higher Education and Training.

EDUCBA. (2019). *Globalization vs. Internationalization.* Retrieved from https://www.educba.com/globalization-vs-internationalization/

Fleming, C. (2017). *3 Reasons Schools Need Market Research for Student Recruitment.* Retrieved from https://www.ama.org/resources/Best-Practices/Pages/3-Reasons-Schools-Need-Market-Research.aspx

Gaulee, U., Sharma, S., & Bista, K. (2020). Rethinking Education in a Changing World: Emerging Issues and Critical Insights. In U. Gaulee, S. Sharma, & K. Bista (Eds.), *Rethinking Education Across Borders* (pp. 3–17). Springer. doi:10.1007/978-981-15-2399-1_1

Guilbault, M. (2016). Students as customers in higher education: Reframing the debate. *Journal of Marketing for Higher Education*, *26*(2), 13–142. doi:10.1080/08841241.2016.1245234

Günay, D., Asunakutlu, T., & Yildiz, O. (Eds.). (2021). *University-industry Collaboration Strategies in the Digital Era.* IGI Global. doi:10.4018/978-1-7998-3901-9

Hanover Research. (2014). *Trends in Higher Education Marketing, Recruitment and Technology.* Retrieved from http://www.hanoverresearch.com/media/Trends-in-Higher-Education-Marketing-Recruitment-and-Technology-2.pdf

Hearps, R. (2016). *Global trends and disruptors in international student referrals.* Retrieved from http://www.icef.com/wp-content/uploads/seminarprogramme/2016/anza__prov_ag__1450__Rod-Hearps__Global-Trends-and-Disruptors-in-International-Student-Mobility---Where-are-International-Students-Going-and-Why.pdf

Hemsley-Brown, J. V., & Oplatka, I. (2006). Universities in a competitive global marketplace: A systematic review of the literature on higher education marketing. *International Journal of Public Sector Management*, *19*(4), 316–338. doi:10.1108/09513550610669176

ICEF Monitor. (2012). *Student safety: its impact on recruitment and study abroad choices.* Retrieved from https://monitor.icef.com/2012/11/student-safety-its-impact-on-recruitment-and-study-abroad-choices/

ICEF Monitor. (2015). *Four trends that are shaping the future of global student mobility.* Retrieved from https://monitor.icef.com/2015/09/four-trends-that-are-shaping-the-future-of-global-student-mobility/

Jooste, C. (2020). *A Strategic Model to Promote University Of Choice Decisions Among International Students Studying in South Africa.* Doctorate in Business Administration, Business School, Nelson Mandela University.

Jooste, C., Cullen, M., & Calitz, A. (2020). *The Factors that Influence South African Students' University of Choice Decisions*. DigiTAL 2020 online International Online Conference, Durban, South Africa.

Koenings, F., Di Meo, G., & Uebelmesser, S. (2020). University rankings as information source: Do they play a different role for domestic and international students? *Applied Economics*, *52*(59), 1–16. doi:10.1080/00036846.2020.1795075

Lääts, K., Kask, K., Täks, V., Alexandr, T., Tomáš, L., & Kleinheyer, B. (2019). *White paper on digital transformation of universities' internationalization process*. Retrieved from https://www.chedteb.eu/media/attachments/2019/08/25/white_paper_on_digitalisation_universities.pdf

Lee, J. J., & Sehoole, C. (2015). *Regional, continental, and global mobility to an emerging economy: the case of South Africa*. Retrieved from https://repository.up.ac.za/bitstream/handle/ 2263/44053/Lee_Regional_2015.pdf?sequence=1&isAllowed=y

Maringe, F. (2006). University and course choice: Implications for positioning, recruitment and marketing. *International Journal of Educational Management*, *20*(6), 466–479. doi:10.1108/09513540610683711

Mosneaga, A., & Agergaard, J. (2012). Agents of internationalisation? Danish universities' practices for attracting international students. *Globalisation, Societies and Education*, *10*(4), 519–538. doi:10.1080/14767724.2012.690309

Moulton, W. G., & Buccini, A. F. (2019). *Germanic Languages*. Retrieved from https://www.britannica.com/topic/Germanic-languages/The-emergence-of-Germanic-languages

Rumbley, L. E. (2019). *Digitalisation and Internationalisation*. Retrieved from https://www.eaie.org/blog/spring-forum-digitalisation.html

Rumbley, L. E., & Altbach, P. G. (2016). The local and the global in Higher Education Internationalization. In E. Jones, R. Coelen, J. Beelen, & H. De Wit (Eds.), *Global Perspectives on Higher Education: Global and Local Internationalization* (pp. 7–13). Sense Publishers. doi:10.1007/978-94-6300-301-8_2

Sánchez, J. S. (2012). Factors influencing a student's decision to pursue a communications degree in Spain. *Intangible Capital*, *8*(1), 43–60.

Schubert, M., & Counihan, B. (2017). *Universities unveil indigenous participation targets*. Retrieved from https://www.universitiesaustralia.edu.au/Media-and-Events/media-releases/Universities-unveil-indigenous-participation-targets#.W1SsBNIzbIU

Selten, F., Neylon, C., Huang, C.-K., & Groth, P. (2020). A longitudinal analysis of university rankings. *Quantitative Science Studies*, *1*(3), 1109–1135. doi:10.1162/qss_a_00052

Sheppard, P., & Smith, R. (2016). What students want: Using a choice modelling approach to estimate student demand. *Journal of Higher Education Policy and Management*, *38*(2), 140–149. doi:10.1080/1360080X.2016.1150236

Sorrells, A., & Cole, H. (2011). *Undergraduate College Choice Survey: Executive Report and Recommendations*. Office of the Dean of Students, DoS Research Institute, The University of Texas at Austin.

Teichler, U. (2009). Internationalisation of higher education: European experiences. *Asia Pacific Education Review*, *10*(1), 93–106. doi:10.100712564-009-9002-7

Vidal, J., & Ferreira, C. (2020). Universities under Pressure: The Impact of International University Rankings. *Journal of New Approaches in Education Research*, *9*(2), 181–193. doi:10.7821/naer.2020.7.475

Wiese, M., Jordaan, Y., & Van Heerden, C. H. (2010). Differences in the usefulness of communication channels, as experienced by gender and ethnic groups during their university selection process. *Communicatio*, *36*(1), 112–129. doi:10.1080/02500160903525064

Yeravdekar, V. R., & Tiwari, G. (2014). Internationalization of Higher Education and its Impact on Enhancing Corporate Competitiveness and Comparative Skill Formation. *Procedia: Social and Behavioral Sciences*, *157*, 203–209. doi:10.1016/j.sbspro.2014.11.023

Yildiz, O. (2021). Changing Paradigms in the Digital Age and Entrepreneurial Universities. In *University-Industry Collaboration Strategies in the Digital Era*. IGI Global. doi:10.4018/978-1-7998-3901-9.ch001

## ADDITIONAL READING

Ammigan, R., & Jones, E. (2018). Improving the Student Experience: Learning from a Comparative Study of International Student Satisfaction. *Journal of Studies in International Education*, *22*(4), 1–19. doi:10.1177/1028315318773137

Beelen, J., & Jones, E. (2015). Redefining internationalization at home. In A. Curai, L. Matei, R. Pricopie, J. Salmi, & P. Scott (Eds.), *The European higher education area: Between critical reflections and future policies* (pp. 67–80). Springer. doi:10.1007/978-3-319-20877-0_5

Brandenburg, U., & De Wit, H. (2011). The end of internationalization. *Industry and Higher Education*, *62*, 15–16.

De Jager, J., & Du Plooy, T. (2010). Information Sources used to select a Higher Education Institution: Evidence from South African students. *Business Education & Accreditation*, *2*(1), 61–75.

De Wit, H. (2016). Misconceptions about (the end of) internationalisation. In E. Jones, R. Coelen, J. Beelen, & H. De Wit (Eds.), *Global Perspectives on Higher Education: Global and Local Internationalization* (pp. 15–20). Sense Publishers. doi:10.1007/978-94-6300-301-8_3

De Wit, H., Hunter, F., Howard, L., & Egron-Polak, E. (2015). *Internationalisation of Higher Education*. European Union.

Egron-Polak, E., & Marmolejo, F. (2017). Higher Education Internationalization: Adjusting to New Landscapes. In H. De Wit, J. Gacel-Ávila, E. Jones, & N. Jooste (Eds.), *The Globalization of Internationalization: Emerging Voices and Perspectives* (pp. 7–17). Routledge.

Hudzik, J. K. (2015). *Comprehensive Internationalization: Institutional pathways to success*. Routledge.

Yildiz, O. (Ed.). (2021). *Recent Developments in Individual and Organizational Adoption of ICTs*. IGI Global., doi:10.4018/978-1-7998-3045-0

## KEY TERMS AND DEFINITIONS

**Globalisation:** The altering or disregarding of national borders and economic systems to form one global economy. This global economic integration of many national economies includes free trade and free capital mobility as well as easy or uncontrolled migration (Teichler, 2009).

**Higher Education Institution:** In the context of this study will refer to accredited public (government funded) institutions who offer tertiary qualifications to prospective students.

**Higher Education Sector:** In the South African context will represent those institutions that deliver tertiary programmes linked to specific qualifications delivered at a National Qualifications Strategic Model Level 5 and higher.

**International Education:** In the context of this study will refer to international academic and social elements being incorporated in academic programmes and activities.

**International Student:** A person who has physically crossed an international border between two countries to participate in educational activities in a destination country, where the destination country is different from his or her country of origin. It is a student with a study visa who can be registered as a full-time, part-time, or occasional student (study abroad/exchange or short-stay students).

**Internationalisation:** The intentional process of integrating an international, intercultural or global dimension into the purpose, functions and delivery of higher education, in order to enhance the quality of education and research for all students and staff and to make a meaningful contribution to society (De Wit & Hunter, 2015).

**Student:** Any individual registered for tertiary study at an institution of higher learning.

**University:** An accredited public institution that conducts research, has postgraduate offerings and provides tertiary education to individuals who have graduated from high school, who wish to obtain a degree or diploma.

# Compilation of References


AACSB. (2018). *2013 Eligibility procedures and accreditation standards for business accreditation*. https://www.aacsb.edu/accreditation/standards/business

AACSB. (n.d.). *Who we are*. https://www.aacsb.edu/about

Abolhassan, F. (2017). Pursuing digital transformation driven by the Cloud. In F. Abolhassan (Ed.), *The drivers of digital transformation: Why there's no way around the cloud*. Springer Nature. doi:10.1007/978-3-319-31824-0_1

ACBSP. (n.d.a). *Who we are*. https://www.acbsp.org/page/about-who-we-are

ACBSP. (n.d.b). *Accreditation standards*. https://www.acbsp.org/page/accreditation-standards

ACBSP. (n.d.c). *ACBSP accreditation overview*. https://acbsp.org/page/accreditation-overview

Acemoglu, D., & Restrepo, P. (2017). *Robots and Jobs: Evidence from US Labor Markets*. NBER Working Paper No. 23285. National Bureau of Economic Research.

Adamides, G., & Stylianou, A. (2013). ICT and Mobile Phone Use for Agricultural Knowledge Sharing by Cypriot Farmers. *AGRIS On-Line Papers in Economics and Informatics*, *5*(2), 8.

Adams-Prassl, A., Boneva, T., Rauh, C., & Golin, M. (2020). Inequality in the Impact of the Coronavirus Shock: Evidence from Real-Time Surveys. IZA DP No. 13183, IZA Institute of Labor Economics.

Adams, T., & De Wit, H. (2011). Global competition in higher education: a comparative study of policies, rationales and practices in Australia and Europe. In H. De Wit (Ed.), *Trends, issues and challenges in internationalisation of higher education*. Centre for Applied Research on Economics & Management.

Adebiyi. (2020). *Machine Learning-Based Predictive Farmland Optimization and Crop Monitoring System*. https://www.hindawi.com/journals/scientifica/2020/9428281/

Adendorff, R., & Smuts, H. (2019). Critical success factors for cloud computing adoption in South Africa *Twenty-fifth Americas Conference on Information Systems*, Cancun, Mexico.

Adi, S. (2021). Psychological Effect of Brand Image and Brand Reputation on Sustainable Firm Performance in Indonesian Logistic Companies. *Ilkogretim Online*, *20*(4), 820–831. doi:10.17051/ilkonline.2021.04.89

AHPGS. (2019a). *Handbook for program accreditation*. https://ahpgs.de/wp-content/uploads/2020/01/Handbook_for_Programme_Accreditation_AHPGS_January_2020-2.pdf

AHPGS. (2019b). *Handbook for institutional audit*. https://ahpgs.de/wp-content/uploads/2020/01/Handbook_for_Institutional_Audit_January-2020.pdf

AHPGS. (n.d.). *The accreditation agency*. https://ahpgs.de/en/about-us/

Akhtar, M., & Kröner-Herwig, B. (2015). Acculturative stress among international students in context of socio-demographic variables and coping styles. *Current Psychology, 34*, 803–815. doi:10.1007/s12144-015-9303-4

Ali, M. B., Wood-Harper, T., & Ramlogan, R. (2020, March 31-April 1). *Challnges of value creation through cloud SaaS: Business/It alignment in service oriented industries* 25th UK Academy for Information Systems International Conference, Oxford, UK.

Ali, A. Q., Sultan, A. B., & Gani, A. A. A. (2019). A Systematic mapping study on the customization solutions of software as a service spplications. *IEEE Access: Practical Innovations, Open Solutions, 7*, 88196–88217. doi:10.1109/ACCESS.2019.2925499

Alkhateeb, F. M., Arkle, S., McDonough, S. L. K., & Latif, D. A. (2018). Review of national and international accreditation of pharmacy programs in the Gulf Cooperation Council Countries. *American Journal of Pharmaceutical Education, 82*(10), 1162–1175. doi:10.5688/ajpe5980 PMID:30643306

Alma Mater Europaea – European Centre Maribor. (2021). *Accreditation.* https://en.almamater.si/accreditation-s88

Alnumay, W. S. (2020). A brief study on software as a service in cloud computing paradigm. *Journal of Engineering and Applied Sciences (Asian Research Publishing Network), 7*(1), 1–15. doi:10.5455/jeas.2020050101

Alphin, H. C. (2014). Global accreditation for a knowledge-oriented community: Foundational change breeds global access to educational and economic opportunity. In S. Mukerji & P. Tripathi (Eds.), *Handbook of Research on Transnational Higher Education* (pp. 303–328). IGI Global. doi:10.4018/978-1-4666-4458-8.ch016

Altay, I. F. (2005). Developing Cultural Awareness. *Journal of Language and Linguistic Studies., 2*, 171–182.

Altbach, P. G., & De Wit, H. (2017). *The new nationalism and internationalisation of HE.* Retrieved from https://www.universityworldnews.com/post.php? story=20170914073027157

Altbach, Ph. G. (2013). The imperial tongue: English as the dominating academic language. In Ph. G. Altbach (Ed.), *The international imperative in higher education* (pp. 1–6). Sense Publishers.

Altbach, Ph. G. (2015). Academic colonialism in action: American accreditation of foreign universities. *Industry and Higher Education, 32*, 5–7.

Altbach, Ph. G., & Knight, J. (2007). The internationalization of higher education: Motivations and realities. *Journal of Studies in International Education, 11*(3/4), 290–305. doi:10.1177/1028315307303542

Alt, R., & Zimmerman, H. (2001). Preface: Introduction to special section business models. *Electronic Markets, 11*(1), 3–9.

Altshuler, L., Sussman, N. M., & Kachur, E. (2003). Assessing changes in intercultural sensitivity among physician trainees using the intercultural development inventory. *International Journal of Intercultural Relations, 27*(4), 387–401. doi:10.1016/S0147-1767(03)00029-4

AMBA. (2016). *MBA accreditation criteria.* https://www.mbaworld.com/accreditation/become-an-accredited-business-school

AMBA. (2019). *AMBA-accredited business schools.* https://www.associationofmbas.com/business-schools/accreditation/accredited-schools/

Ammigan, R. (2019). Institutional satisfaction and recommendation: What really matters to international students. *Journal of International Students, 9*(1), 262–281. doi:10.32674/jis.v9i1.260

Andersen, T. J. (2001). Information technology, strategic decision making approaches and organizational performance in different industrial settings. *The Journal of Strategic Information Systems, 10*(2), 101–119. doi:10.1016/S0963-8687(01)00043-9

Anderson, G. (1990). *Fundamentals of Educational Research.* The Felmer Press. doi:10.4324/9780203978221

Ángel José Lorente, P., Ángel Hernández, G., & Julián Chaparro, P. (2021). Modelling e-mail marketing effectiveness – An approach based on the theory of hierarchy-of-effects. *Management Letters. Cuadernos de Gestión, 21*(1), 19–27. doi:10.5295/cdg.191094ah

Angel Wong An, K., & Rashad, Y. (2015). The Review of Content Marketing as a New Trend in Marketing Practices. *International Journal of Management, Accounting & Economics, 2*(9), 1055–1064.

Angove, M. (2019). Work-Based Learning and Innovation: A Study of International Commerce Degree Students. In *Innovation and Social Capital in Organizational Ecosystems* (pp. 173–193). IGI Global. doi:10.4018/978-1-5225-7721-8.ch009

Annttiroiko, A.-V. (2008). A brief introduction to the field of e-government. *Electronic Government: Concepts, Methodologies, Tools, and Applications, 1.*

Appel, G., Grewal, L., Hadi, R., & Stephen, A. T. (2020). The future of social media in marketing. *Journal of the Academy of Marketing Science, 48*(1), 79–95. doi:10.100711747-019-00695-1 PMID:32431463

Arik, B. T., & Arik, E. (2014). The role and status of English in Turkish higher education. *English Today, 30*(4), 5–10. doi:10.1017/S0266078414000339

Armenia, S., Casalino, N., Gnan, L., & Flamini, G. (2021). A systems approach to the digital transformation of public administration. *Prospettive In Organizzazıone, 14*, 1–20.

Arun Kumar, R. (n.d.). Grading by Machine Vision and Fuzzy Logic. *Int. J. Comp. Tech. Appl., 2*(5), 1709-1716.

ASIIN. (2021a). *ASIIN - Global leader in quality assurance in higher education.* https://www.asiin.de/en/home.html

ASIIN. (2021b). *Accreditation degree programmes.* https://www.asiin.de/en/quality-management/accreditation-degree-programmes.html

Aspen Institute. (2019). *What is Social, Emotional, and Academic Development?* Retrieved at https://www.aspeninstitute.org/publications/pursuing-social-and-emotional-development-through-a-racial-equity-lens-a-call-to-action/

Ates, M., Ravet, S., Ahmat, A. M., & Fayolle, I. (2011). An identity-centric internet: identity in the cloud, identity as a service and other delights. *Sixth International Conference on Availability, Reliability and Security*, Vienna, Austria. 10.1109/ARES.2011.85

Atiku, S. O. (2021). Human Capacity Building Through University-Industry Collaboration. In *University-Industry Collaboration Strategies in the Digital Era* (pp. 321–336). IGI Global.

Austrian Federal Ministry of Education, Science and Research. (2020). *National mobility and internationalisation strategy for higher education 2020 – 2030.* Austrian Federal Ministry of Education, Science and Research.

Awuor, F., Kimeli, K., Rabah, K., & Rambim, D. (2013). *ICT Solution Architecture for Agriculture.* IST.

Balcazar, F. E., Suarez-Balcazar, Y., & Taylor-Ritzler, T. (2009). Cultural competence: Development of a conceptual framework. *Disability and Rehabilitation, 31*(14), 1153–1160. doi:10.1080/09638280902773752 PMID:19802931

Ball, S. J. (1998). Big Policies/ Small World: An introduction to international perspectives in education policy. *Comparative Education, 34*(2), 119–130. doi:10.1080/03050069828225

Baloutsos, S., Karagiannaki, A., & Mourtos, I. (2020). Business model gneration for industry 4.0: A "lean startup" approach. *The International Technology Management Review*, *9*(1), 34–45. doi:10.2991/itmr.k.200630.001

Balta, Y., & Türel, K. Y. (2013). Çevrimiçi uzaktan eğitimde kullanılan farklı ölçme değerlendirme yaklaşımlarına ilişkin bir inceleme. *Turkish Studies-International Periodical For The Languages. Literature and History of Turkish or Turkic*, *8*(3), 37–45.

Barak, M., Watted, A., & Haick, H. (2016). Motivation to learn in massive open online courses: Examining aspects of language and social engagement. *Computers & Education*, *94*, 49–60. doi:10.1016/j.compedu.2015.11.010

Barker and Mengistae. (2005, June). *Raising Productivity in Africa's Modern Wage enterprises to Foster Job Growth for Youth*. Author.

Barr, N. (2005). Financing Higher Education. *Finance & Development*, *42*(2).

Bartholomew, K. W. (2018). Digital marketing teaching strategies with google analytics and related tools: Tutorial presentation. *Journal of Computing Sciences in Colleges*, *34*(2), 56–57.

Başlıgil, H. (2005). The fuzzy analytic hierarchy process for software selection problems. *Sigma, 2005/3*(3), 24-33.

Beerkens, H. J. J. G. (2004). *Global opportunities and institutional embeddedness: Higher education consortia in Europe and South East Asia*. [Doctoral dissertation]. University of Twente/CHEPS.

Bélanger, F., & Carter, L. (2008). Trust and risk in e-government adoption. *The Journal of Strategic Information Systems*, *17*(2), 165–176. doi:10.1016/j.jsis.2007.12.002

Belfield, B., & Klapp, L. (2015). The economic value of social and emotional learning. New York, NY: Center for Benefit-Cost Studies in Education: Teachers College, Columbia University.

Benavides, L. M. C., Arias, J. A. T., Serna, M. D. A., Bedoya, J. W. B., & Burgos, D. (2020). Digital transformation in Higher Education Institutions: A systematic literature review. *Sensors (Basel)*, *20*(11), 3291. doi:10.339020113291 PMID:32526998

Bendor-Samuel, J. T. (2019). *Atlantic Languages*. Retrieved from https://www.britannica.com/topic/African-Atlantic-languages

Benjamin, M., Earnest, K., Gruenewald, D., & Arthur, G. (2007). The first few weeks of the first year. *New Directions for Student Services*, *2007*(117), 13–24. doi:10.1002s.229

Berlingieri, G., Blanchenay, P., Calligaris, S., & Criscuolo, C. (2017). Firm-level productivity differences: Insights from the OECD's multiprod project. *International Productivity Monitor*, *32*, 97–115.

Bernotas, M., Laurutis, R., & Slotkienė, A. (2005). Issues on forming metadata of editorial system's document management. *Information Technology and Control*, *34*(4).

Berry, J. W. (2003). Conceptual approaches to acculturation. In K. M. Chun., P. Balls-Organista, & G. Marin (Eds.), Acculturation: Advances in theory, measurement, and applied research (pp. 17-38). Washington, DC: American Psychological Association. doi:10.1037/10472-004

Berry, J. W. (2006). *Stress perspectives on acculturation. The Cambridge Handbook of Acculturation Psychology*. University Press.

Bezuidenhout, G., & De Jager, J. (2014). Customer satisfaction at private higher education institutions in South Africa: An importance-performance analysis. *Journal of Contemporary Management*, *11*, 206–229.

Bista, K., & Foster, C. (Eds.). (2016). *Global perspectives and local challenges surrounding international student mobility*. IGI Global. doi:10.4018/978-1-4666-9746-1

Black, J. S., & Mendenhall, M. E. (1990). Cross-Cultural effectiveness: A review and theoretical framework for future research. *Academy of Management Review*, *15*(1), 113–136. doi:10.5465/amr.1990.11591834

BMIT. (2020). *BMIT 2020 Tech Trends* [Market research report]. Retrieved 14/11/2020, from https://www.bmit.africa/bmit-2020-tech-trends

Bologna Declaration. (1999). https://www.ehea.info/media.ehea.info/file/Ministerial_conferences/02/8/1999_Bologna_Declaration_English_553028.pdf

Bologna Declaration. (1999). *The European higher education area*. Joint declaration of the European Ministers of Education convened in Bologna on the 19th of June 1999.

Bonardi, E. (2021). Marketing automation: The next generation of applications for real estate. *Journal of Property Management*, *86*(1), 20–21.

Boshoff, H., & Quinlan, O. (2016). Student protests demand change to the underlying fault lines in Higher Education. *Study South Africa*, *1*, 30–34.

Bound, J., Braga, B., Khanna, G., & Turner, S. (2021). The globalization of postsecondary education: The role of international students in the US higher education system. *The Journal of Economic Perspectives*, *35*(1), 163–184. doi:10.1257/jep.35.1.163

Bouwman, H., de Reuver, M., Solaimani, S., Daas, D., Haaker, T., & Janssen, W. (2012). *Business models tooling and a research agenda* 25th Bled eConference, Bled, Slovenia.

Bouwman, H., Heikkilä, J., Heikkilä, M., Leopold, C., & Haaker, T. (2018). Achieving agility using business model stress testing. *Electronic Markets*, *28*(2), 149–162. doi:10.100712525-016-0243-0

Bowen, G. A. (2009). Document analysis as a qualitative research method. *Qualitative Research Journal*, *9*(2), 27–40. doi:10.3316/QRJ0902027

Boyaci, A. (2011). Erasmus exchange students' comparative views on classroom management in Turkey and in their country (Anadolu University case). *Education in Science*, *36*(159), 270–282.

Boyacioglu, C., & Yıldız, O. (2021). The Impact of Data Protection Regulations on Start-Up Enterprises. In *Recent Developments in Individual and Organizational Adoption of ICTs* (pp. 120–133). IGI Global. doi:10.4018/978-1-7998-3045-0.ch007

Bozkurt, A. (2020). Koronavirüs (Covid-19) pandemi süreci ve pandemi sonrası dünyada eğitime yönelik değerlendirmeler: Yeni normal ve yeni eğitim paradigması. *Açıköğretim Uygulamaları ve Araştırmaları Dergisi*, *6*(3), 112–142.

Brahimi, T., Sarirete, A., & Khalifa, S. (2018). Impact of accreditation on engineering education. In M. Lytras, L. Daniela, & A. Visvizi (Eds.), *Enhancing knowledge discovery and innovation in the digital era* (pp. 91–106). IGI Global. doi:10.4018/978-1-5225-4191-2.ch005

Brennan, B. (2017). *Universities set goals to attract more Indigenous students in Australian-first.* Retrieved from https://www.abc.net.au/news/2017-03-01/universitiesaustralia-indigenous-strategy/8313116

Brink, K. E., & Smith, C. A. (2012). A comparison of AACSB, ACBSP, and IACBE accredited U.S. business programs: An institutional resource perspective. *Business Education & Accreditation*, *4*(2), 1–15.

Bruhn, E. (2017). Towards a Framework for Virtual Internationalization. *International Journal of E-Learning & Distance Education, 32*(1), 1–9. https://files.eric.ed.gov/fulltext/EJ1159898.pdf

Bruno de, L., & George Leal, J. (2021). Digital Transformation for Businesses: Adapt or Die! Reflections on How to Rethink Your Business in the Digital Transformation Context. In A. Pedro Fernandes, P. Cláudio Roberto Magalhães, & J. George Leal (Eds.), Handbook of Research on Digital Transformation and Challenges to Data Security and Privacy (pp. 252-268). IGI Global. doi:10.4018/978-1-7998-4201-9.ch015

Brynjolfsson, E., & McAfee, A. (2014). *The Second Machine Age: Work, Progress, and Prosperity in a Time of Brilliant Technologies*. WW Norton & Company.

Brynjolfsson, E., Rock, D., & Syverson, C. (2019). *1. Artificial Intelligence and the Modern Productivity Paradox: A Clash of Expectations and Statistics*. University of Chicago Press.

Caballero, G., Vázquez, X. H., & Quintás, M. A. (2015). Improving Employability through Stakeholders in European Higher Education: The Case of Spain. *Long Range Planning, 48*(6), 398–411. doi:10.1016/j.lrp.2015.09.005

Carrington Crisp. (2013). *A change of direction? Tomorrow's Masters.* Executive summary 2013. https://www.carringtoncrisp.com/images/PDFs/Tomorrows_Masters_(Exec_Summary).pdf

Casalino, N., Rubichi, V., Gasparri, C., & Pizzolo, G. (2017). Organization of Processes Digitization and E-Invoicing Services for an Effective Digital Transformation of Public Sector. *DigitCult–Scientific Journal on Digital Cultures, 2*(1), 53–62.

CBIE. (2014). *CBIE Research in Brief.* Retrieved from https://files.eric.ed.gov/fulltext/ED566119.pdf

Cebeci, U. (2009). Fuzzy AHP-based decision support system for selecting ERP systems in textile industry by using balanced scorecard. *Expert Systems with Applications, 36*(5), 8900–8909. doi:10.1016/j.eswa.2008.11.046

CEEMAN. (n.d.a). *About us.* http://www.ceeman.org/about-us

CEEMAN. (n.d.b). *Benefits of CEEMAN IQA accreditation.* http://www.ceeman.org/accreditation/benefits-of-ceeman-iqa-accreditation

Center for EU Education and Youth Programmes. (2009). *2009 yılı hayatboyu öğrenme programı (LLP) ve gençlik programı uygulama raporu* [Lifelong learning program (LLP) and youth program implementation report in 2009]. https://www.ua.gov.tr/media/eylif3cm/35_reduced-uygulama-raporu_bask%C4%B1-min.pdf

Chaisit, J., Pansuwan, L., & Isaranontakul, P. (2020). The Development of Digital Marketing Strategies and Distribution Channels for Community Products Using E-Commerce in The Lower Northern Region of Thailand. *Proceedings of the 2020 International Conference on Management of e-Commerce and e-Government.* 10.1145/3409891.3409903

Chan, C. M. L., & Pan, S. L. (2008). User engagement in e-government systems implementation: A comparative case study of two Singaporean e-government initiatives. *The Journal of Strategic Information Systems, 17*(2), 124–139. doi:10.1016/j.jsis.2007.12.003

Chand, R. (2019). *102 Annual Conference Indian Economic Association (IEA) Transforming Agriculture for Challenges of 21st Century*. Academic Press.

Chang, V., Wills, G., & De Reuver, M. (2010). *A Review of Cloud business models and sustainability.* In the third International Conference on Cloud Computing, Miami, FL.

Chang, D.-Y. (1996). Applications of the extent analysis method on fuzzy AHP. *European Journal of Operational Research, 95*(3), 649–655. doi:10.1016/0377-2217(95)00300-2

Chang, V., Bacigalupo, D., Wills, G., & De Roure, D. (2010). A Categorisation of Cloud Computing Business Models. *International Conference on Cluster, Cloud, and Grid Computing.*

Chan, J. O. (2020). Digital transformation in the era of big data and Cloud Computing. *International Journal of Intelligent Information Systems, 9*(3), 16–23. doi:10.11648/j.ijiis.20200903.11

Chapleo, C., & O'Sullivan, H. (2017). Contemporary thought in higher education marketing. *Journal of Marketing for Higher Education, 27*(2), 159–161. doi:10.1080/08841241.2017.1406255

Chapman, D. W. (1981). A model of student college choice. *The Journal of Higher Education, 52*(5), 490–505. doi:10.2307/1981837

Chapman, S. A., Goodman, S., Jawitz, J., & Deacon, A. (2016). A strategy for monitoring and evaluating massive open online courses. *Evaluation and Program Planning, 57*, 55–63. doi:10.1016/j.evalprogplan.2016.04.006 PMID:27213994

Chen, C. P. (1999). Common stressors among international college students: Research and counseling implications. *Journal of College Counseling, 2*(1), 49–65. doi:10.1002/j.2161-1882.1999.tb00142.x

Cheng, C.-H. (1999). Evaluating weapon systems using ranking fuzzy numbers. *Fuzzy Sets and Systems, 107*(1), 25–35. doi:10.1016/S0165-0114(97)00348-5

Chen, Z. (2000). International students' preparation for and adaptation to the American higher education system: A study of cross-cultural communication. *World Communication, 29*(2), 25–48.

Chesbrough, H. (2007). Business model innovation:Its not just about technology anymore. *Strategy and Leadership, 35*(6), 12–17. doi:10.1108/10878570710833714

Chesbrough, H., & Rosenbloom, R. S. (2002). The role of the business model in capturing value from innovation: Evidence from Xerox Corporation's technology spin-off companies. *Industrial and Corporate Change, 11*(3), 529–555. doi:10.1093/icc/11.3.529

Chun, S. H. (2020). Cloud services and pricing Strategies for sustainable business models: Analytical and numerical approaches. *Sustainability, 12*(1), 49. doi:10.3390u12010049

Cloete, N. (2005). Transformation Tensions in Higher Education: Equity, Efficiency, and Development. *Social Research, 72*(3), 693–722.

Clohessy, T., Acton, T., & Morgan, L. (2018). Contemporary digital business model decision making: A cloud computing supply-side perspective. *International Journal of Networking and Virtual Organisations, 19*(1), 1–20. doi:10.1504/IJNVO.2018.093923

Clohessy, T., Acton, T., Morgan, L., & Conboy, K. (2016). The times they are a-chchanging for ICT service provision. *Twenty-fourth European Conference on Information Systems (ECIS)*, Istanbul, Turkey.

Cluley, R., Green, W., & Owen, R. (2020). The changing role of the marketing researcher in the age of digital technology: Practitioner perspectives on the digitization of marketing research. *International Journal of Market Research, 62*(1), 27–42. doi:10.1177/1470785319865129

CMEPIUS. (n.d.a). *Basic info.* https://eng.cmepius.si/about-us/basic-info/

CMEPIUS. (n.d.b). *Mednarodno sodelovanje v številkah 2007–2020* [International cooperation in numbers 2007 –2020]. http://statistike.cmepius.si/

Cohen, L., Manion, L., & Morrison, K. (2007). *Research methods in Education.* Routledge. doi:10.4324/9780203029053

Coleman, J. A. (2006). English-medium teaching in European higher education. *Language Teaching*, *39*(1), 1–14. doi:10.1017/S026144480600320X

Collaborative for Academic, Social, and Emotional Learning (CASEL). (2017). *Making the Case for SEL* (PowerPoint). Retrieved at https://docs.google.com/presentation/d/1Tb9WundNcsURexo2RTvVGVIVlzD_q9i6Vv4jcNtqZjI/edit#slide=id.p4

Commonwealth Secretariat. (2020). *Commonwealth FinTech Toolkit Helping Governments to Leverage Financial Innovation.* https://www.thecommonwealth.io/wp- content/uploads/2020/10/Commonwealth-Fintech-Toolkit.pdf

Cordella, A., & Iannacci, F. (2010). Information systems in the public sector: The e-Government enactment framework. *The Journal of Strategic Information Systems*, *19*(1), 52–66. doi:10.1016/j.jsis.2010.01.001

Costa, A. I. A., Dekker, M., & Jongen, W. M. F. (2004). An overview of means-end theory: Potential application in consumer-oriented food product design. *Trends in Food Science & Technology*, *15*(7-8), 403–415. doi:10.1016/j.tifs.2004.02.005

Costoiu, M., Isopescu, R., Plesu, V., Arsene, I., Alesincu, S., & Iancu, P. (2009). New developments for electronic document management in University Politehnica of Bucharest. *Source: PRES*, *9*, 309–314.

Cots, J. M., Lasagabaster, D., & Garrett, P. (2012). Multilingual policies and practices of universities in three bilingual regions in Europe. *International Journal of the Sociology of Language*, *216*(216), 7–32. doi:10.1515/ijsl-2012-0037

Council of Higher Education. (2017). *Yükseköğretimde uluslararasılaşma strateji belgesi 2018-2022* [Internationalization in higher education strategy document]. https://www.yok.gov.tr/Documents/AnaSayfa/Yuksekogretimde_Uluslararasilasma_Strateji_Belgesi_2018_2022.pdf

Council of Higher Education. (2019). *Study in Turkey*. https://www.studyinturkey.gov.tr/

Coursera. (2021a). *Global Skills Index Report*. https://www.coursera.org/skills-reports/global

Coursera. (2021b). *Transform your workforce with the skills of the future*. https://www.coursera.org/skills-reports/global

Court of Audit of the Republic of Slovenia (2016). *Revizijsko poročilo: Postopki evalviranja, akreditiranja ter podeljevanja koncesij v višjem in visokem šolstvu* [Audit report: Procedures for evaluation, accreditation and granting concessions in higher vocational and higher education]. Court of Audit of the Republic of Slovenia.

Cruise, A. (2020). South Africa to lead cloud adoption race on the continent. *Hi tech security solutions*. http://www.securitysa.com/10256r

Çubukçu, C., & Aktürk, C. (2020). Digital transformation to university 4.0: A roadmap. *Uludağ University Journal of The Faculty of Engineering*, *25*(3), 1391–1408. doi:10.17482/uumfd.702617

Cultural Intelligence Center. (2018). *CQ Assessment*. Retrieved at https://culturalq.com/products-services/assessments/cq-assessments/

Cultural Intelligence Center. (2018a). *Academic Construct Validity*. Retrieved at https://culturalq.com/wp-content/uploads/2018/01/Academic-Construct-Validity_v.1.18.pdf

Cunningham, W., & Villasenor, P. (2016). Employer voices, employer demands, and implications for public skills development policy. Washington, DC: World Bank; Cary, NC: Oxford University Press. doi:10.1093/wbro/lkv019

Curaj, A., Matei, L., Pricopie, R., Salmi, J., & Scott, P. (Eds.). (2015). *The European higher education area Between critical reflections and future policies*. Springer. doi:10.1007/978-3-319-20877-0

de Wit, H. (2002). *Internationalisation of higher education in the United States of America and Europe*. Greenwood Press.

de Wit, H., Gacel-Ávila, J., Jones, E., & Jooste, N. (Eds.). (2017). *The globalization of internationalization: Emerging voices and perspectives*. Routledge. doi:10.4324/9781315657547

De Wit, H., & Hunter, F. (2015). Understanding internationalisation of higher education in the European context. In H. de Wit, F. Hunter, L. Howard, & E. Egron-Polak (Eds.), *Internationalization of Higher Education* (pp. 41–58). European Parliament, Committee on Culture and Education.

de Wit, H., Hunter, F., Howard, L., & Egron-Polak, E. (2015). *Internationalisation of higher education*. European Parliament, Directorate-General for Internal Policies.

De Wit, H., Hunter, F., Howard, L., & Egron-Polak, E. (2015). Internationalisation of higher education: A study for the European Parliament. *European Union*.

Dearden, J. A., Greal, R., & Lilien, G. L. (2019). Strategic Manipulation of University Rankings, the Prestige Effect, and Student University Choice. *JMR, Journal of Marketing Research*, *56*(4), 691–707. doi:10.1177/0022243719831258

Deardorff, D. K. (2004). *The identification and assessment of intercultural competence as a student outcome of internationalization at institutions of higher education in the United States*. Dissertation: North Carolina State University. Retrieved from https://repository.lib.ncsu.edu/ir/bitstream/1840.16/5733/1/etd.pdf

Dekaney, E. M. (2008). Students' pre-departure expectations and post-sojourn observations in a short-term international program abroad on the culture, music, and art of Brazil. *International Education*, *37*(2), 17–29.

Demir, A. H. E., Bayram, A. E., & Kocaoğlu, S. A. B. (2010). Mernis Projesi ve Adrese Dayalı Nüfus Kayıt Sistemi Çevresinde 7201 Sayılı Tebligat Kanunu ve Bu Kanuna Dayalı Çıkarılan Tebligat Tüzüğünde Yapılması Gerekli Değişiklik Önerisi. *Ankara Barosu Dergisi*, (3).

Dennis, M. (2020). *How will higher education have changed after COVID-19?* Retrieved from: https://www.universityworldnews.com/post.php?story=20200324065639773

Dhawan, S. (2020). Online learning: A panacea in the time of COVID-19 crisis. *Journal of Educational Technology Systems*, *49*(1), 5–22. doi:10.1177/0047239520934018

DHET. (2017). Draft Policy Framework for the Internationalisation of Higher Education in South Africa. Department of Higher Education and Training.

Dikmen, S., & Bahçeci, F. (2020). Covid-19 pandemisi sürecinde yükseköğretim kurumlarının uzaktan eğitime yönelik stratejileri: Fırat Üniversitesi örneği. *Turkish Journal of Educational Studies*, *7*(2), 78–98. doi:10.33907/turkjes.721685

Dinev, T., Hu, Q., & Yayla, A. (2008). Is There an On-line Advertisers' Dilemma? A Study of Click Fraud in the Pay-Per-Click Model. *International Journal of Electronic Commerce*, *13*(2), 29–59. doi:10.2753/JEC1086-4415130202

DOBA Faculty. (2021). *Quality assurance*. https://www.dobabusiness-school.eu/why-doba/quality-assurance

Doiz, A., Lasagabaster, D., & Sierra, J. (2013). Globalisation, internationalisation, multilingualism and linguistic strains in higher education. *Studies in Higher Education*, *38*(9), 1407–1421. doi:10.1080/03075079.2011.642349

Doiz, A., Lasagabaster, D., & Sierra, J. M. (2011). Internationalisation, multilingualism and English-medium instruction: The teachers' perspective. *World Englishes*, *30*(3), 345–359. doi:10.1111/j.1467-971X.2011.01718.x

Dombrowski, U., Krenkel, P., & Wullbrandt, J. (2018). Strategic Positioning of Production within the Generic Competitive Strategies. *Procedia CIRP*, *72*, 1196–1201. doi:10.1016/j.procir.2018.03.007

Dornberg, J. H., & Lohmüller, L. (2013). *Optimizing the selection process of document-management systems International Conference on Advanced ICT*, Hainan, China.

Doverton, D. C. V. (2001). Techniques of document management: A review of text retrieval and related technologies. *The Journal of Documentation, 57*(2), 192–217. doi:10.1108/EUM0000000007082

Driessen, C., & Heutinck, L. F. M. (2014). Cows desiring to be milked? Milking robots and the co-evolution of ethics and technology on Dutch dairy farms. *Agriculture and Human Values, 32*(1), 3–20. doi:10.100710460-014-9515-5

Du Plessis, J. J., & Mwalemba, G. (2016). Adoption of emerging technologies into ERP Systems Landscape. A south African Study. *2016 IEEE International Conference on Emerging Technologies and Innovative Business Practices for the Transformation of Societies (EmergiTech).* 10.1109/EmergiTech.2016.7737373

Du, F., Malik, S., Koh, E., & Theocharous, G. (2018). *Interactive Campaign Planning for Marketing Analysts.* Paper presented at the Extended Abstracts of the 2018 CHI Conference on Human Factors in Computing Systems, Montreal, Canada. 10.1145/3170427.3188531

Duin, H., Heindl, M., Marke, E., Suttner, H., Withalm, J., Wolfe, W., & Zand, D. (2010). *Green car environment - A vision of an electric ecosystem in automotive IEEE International Technology Management Conference (ICE)*, Lugano, Switzerland.

Ebinger, S. E. (2011). *International students' perceptions of university assistance with their social adjustment* (Doctoral dissertation).

ECBE. (2019a). *The accreditation process.* https://www.ecbe.eu/index.php/accreditation/accreditation-process

ECBE. (2019b). *Welcome to European Council for Business Education.* https://www.ecbe.eu/

ECBE. (2019c). *Members of ECBE.* https://www.ecbe.eu/index.php/members/members-of-ecbe

ECBE. (2019d). *Benefits of accreditation.* https://www.ecbe.eu/index.php/accreditation

EDUCBA. (2019). *Globalization vs. Internationalization.* Retrieved from https://www.educba.com/globalization-vs-internationalization/

El Alami, A., Sadok, H., & Elhaoud, N. (2015). *Cloud computing & the organizational performance different approach of assessment International Conference on Cloud Technologies and Applications (CloudTech)*, Marrakesh, Morocco.

Elsayed, A. M. (2017). Web content strategy in higher education institutions: The case of King Abdulaziz University. *Information Development, 33*(5), 479–494. doi:10.1177/0266666916671387

Elturki, E., Liu, Y., Hjeltness, J., & Hellmann, K. (2019). Needs, expectations, and experiences of international students in pathway program in the united states. *Journal of International Students, 9*(1), 192–210. doi:10.32674/jis.v9i1.274

ENQA, EUA, ESU, & EURASHE. (2015). *Standards and guidelines for quality assurance in the European Higher Education Area (ESG).* https://www.enqa.eu/wp-content/uploads/2015/11/ESG_2015.pdf

EQAR. (2014). *Recognising International Quality Assurance Activity in the European Higher Education Area (RIQAA): Final project report.* European Quality Assurance Register for Higher Education.

EQAR. (n.d.a). *ASIIN - ASIIN e.V.* https://www.eqar.eu/register/agencies/agency/?id=19&cn-reloaded=1

EQAR. (n.d.b). *Slovenia.* https://www.eqar.eu/kb/country-information/country/?id=157

EQUIS. (2020a). *2019 EQUIS standards and criteria.* https://efmdglobal.org/accreditations/business-schools/equis/equis-guides-documents/

EQUIS. (2020b). *About us.* https://efmdglobal.org/about-efmd-global/

Eraslan, A. (2009). Finlandiya'nın PISA'daki Başarısının Nedenleri: Türkiye için Alınacak Dersler. *Necatibey Eğitim Fakültesi Elektronik Fen ve Matematik Eğitimi Dergisi, 3*(2), 238–248.

Erginer, A. (2006). *Avrupa Birliği Eğitim Sistemleri ve Türkiye Eğitim Sistemiyle Karşılaştırmalar*. PEGEM Akademi Yayıncılık.

EUA. (2013). *Internationalisation in European higher education: European policies, institutional strategies and EUA support*. European University Association.

EUA. (n.d.). *IEP – Institutional Evaluation Programme*. https://www.iep-qaa.org/

European Commission. (2004). *Promoting language learning and linguistic diversity: An action plan 2004–2006*. European Commission.

European Commission. (2013). *Communication from the Commission to the European Parliament, the council, the European economic and social committee and the committee of the regions: European higher education in the world*. European Commission.

European Commission. (2013). *European higher education in the world: Communication from the Commission to the European Parliament, the Council, the European economic and social committee and the Committee of the regions*. https://eur-lex.europa.eu/legal-content/EN/TXT/PDF/?uri=CELEX:52013DC0499&from=NL

European Commission. (2014). *Assessing the Implications of Climate Change Adaptation on Employment in the EU* [Final Report & Annexes]. https://ec.europa.eu/clima/sites/clima/files/adaptation/what/docs/climate_change_employment_eu_en.pdf

European Commission. (2018). *Erasmus+ 2017 in numbers*. https://ec.europa.eu/programmes/erasmus-plus/resources/documents/erasmus-annual-report-factsheets-turkey_en

European Commission. (2019). *Erasmus+ country factsheets 2017*. https://ec.europa.eu/programmes/erasmus-plus/about/factsheets#fsTitle

European Commission. (2019b). *Erasmus+ 2018 in numbers*. https://ec.europa.eu/programmes/erasmus-plus/resources/documents/turkey-erasmus-2018-numbers_en

European Commission. (2020a). *Turkey/Mobility and internationalisation*. https://eacea.ec.europa.eu/national-policies/eurydice/content/mobility-and-internationalisation-85_en

European Commission. (2020b). *Erasmus+ 2019 in numbers*. https://ec.europa.eu/assets/eac/factsheets/factsheet-tr-2019_en.html

European University Association (EUA). (2020). *Learning & teaching paper: Internationalisation in learning and teaching*. European University Association.

Eurydice. (2021). *Mobility in higher education (Slovenia)*. https://eacea.ec.europa.eu/national-policies/eurydice/content/mobility-higher-education-68_en

Faasen, J., Seymour, L. F., & Schuler, J. (2013). SaaS ERP adoption intent: Explaining the South African perspective. Academic Press.

Faculty of Economics and Business UM. (n.d.). *International accreditations of study programmes FEB AACSB, ECBE and ACBSP*. https://www.epf.um.si/en/about-faculty/introduction/international-accreditations-of-study-programmes/

Faculty of Logistics UM. (2019). *Accreditations*. https://fl.um.si/en/akreditacije/

Faculty of Management UP. (2015, June 24). *Mednarodna akreditacija FIBAA za magistrski program management* [International FIBAA accreditation for the master's program management]. https://www.fm-kp.si/novice/mednarodna_akreditacija_fibaa_za_magistrski_program_management

Faculty of Organizational Sciences UM. (2020, February 11). *ECBE akreditacija študijskih programov FOV* [ECBE accreditation of study programs FOS]. https://fov.um.si/sl/studij/ecbe-akreditacija-studijskih-programov-fov

Fang, Z., Chen, J., Yi, M., Wu, Z., & Qian, H. (2010). Cloud computing business model based on value net theory. *IEEE International Conference on E-Business Engineering.*

Fennimore, S. A. (2017). *Automated Weed Control: New Technology to Solve an Old Problem in Vegetable Crops.* Conference presentation at ASA Section: Agronomic Production Systems.

Fenton-Smith, B., Humphreys, P., & Walkinshaw, I. (2017). *English medium instruction in higher education in Asia-Pacific.* Springer. doi:10.1007/978-3-319-51976-0

Firdhous, M. (2014). A Comprehensive taxonomy for the infrastructure as a Service in Cloud Computing. *Fourth International Conference on Advances in Computing and Communications.*

Fitzgerald, B. K., & Sigelman, M. (2018). *The new foundational skills of the digital economy: Developing the professionals of the future.* Burning Glass Technologies. Retrieved from www.burning-glass.com

Fleming, C. (2017). *3 Reasons Schools Need Market Research for Student Recruitment.* Retrieved from https://www.ama.org/resources/Best-Practices/Pages/3-Reasons-Schools-Need-Market-Research.aspx

Floerecke, S., & Lehner, F. (2018). Success driving business model characteristics of IaaS and PaaS providers. *Computer Networks & Communications: An International Journal, 2*(4), 1–22.

Floerecke, S., & Lehner, F. (2019). The Unequal Battle for Market Shares in the Infrastructure-as-a-Service Segment: Success-Driving Business Model Characteristics of Regional Providers in Competition with the Hyperscalers. *HMD, 56*(6), 1334–1354. doi:10.136540702-019-00549-y

Frey, C. B., & Osborne, M. A., (2017). The Future of Employment: How Susceptible are Jobs to Computerisation? *Technological Forecasting and Social Change, 114*, 254–280.

Frey, B. (2018). *The SAGE encyclopedia of educational research, measurement, and evaluation* (Vol. 1–4). Sage. doi:10.4135/9781506326139

Fulbright Scholar Program. (2018). *About Fulbright.* Retrieved from https://www.cies.org/about-us/about-senator-j-william-fulbright

Fulbright Scholars Program. (2020). *About Fulbright.* Retrieved from https://www.cies.org/about-us/about-senator-j-william-fulbright

Future of Jobs Report. (2020). *World Economic Forum.* Retrieved from https://www.weforum.org/ agenda/2020/10/top-10-work-skills-of-tomorrow-how-long-it-takes-to-learn-them/

García-Llorente, M., Rubio-Olivar, R., & Gutierrez-Briceño, I. (2018). Farming for Life Quality and Sustainability: A Literature Review of Green Care Research Trends in Europe. *International Journal of Environmental Research and Public Health, 15*(6), 1282. Advance online publication. doi:10.3390/ijerph15061282 PMID:29914199

Gardner, S. K. (2007). I heard it through the grapevine: Doctoral student socialization in chemistry and history. *Higher Education, 54*(5), 723–740. doi:10.100710734-006-9020-x

Gaulee, U., Sharma, S., & Bista, K. (2020). Rethinking Education in a Changing World: Emerging Issues and Critical Insights. In U. Gaulee, S. Sharma, & K. Bista (Eds.), *Rethinking Education Across Borders* (pp. 3–17). Springer. doi:10.1007/978-981-15-2399-1_1

Gaur, A., Gaud, S., & Jain, A. (2017). Advance computing paradigm with the perspective of cloud computing-An analytical study. *International Journal of Advanced Networking and Applications, 8*(6), 3257–3265.

Ghazizadeh, E., Cusack, B. H. D., & Shahzad, A. (2020). *Cloud surfing: A general comparison of cloud identity guidelines.* Americas Conference on Information Systems (AMCIS), Virtual Conference.

Gilani, S. M. M., Ahmed, J., & Abbas, M. A. (2009). Electronic document management: A paperless university model. *Computer Science and Information Technology, 2009. ICCSIT 2009. 2nd IEEE International Conference on.*

Gillwald, A., Moyo, M., & Stork, C. (2012). *Understanding what is happening in ICT in South Africa a supply and demand side analysis of the ICT sector.* Retrieved 20/02/2016, from https://www.researchictafrica.net/publications/Evidence_for_ICT_Policy_Action/Policy_Paper_7_-_Understanding_what_is_happening_in_ICT_in_South_Africa.pdf

Ginsburg, M., & Kambil, A. (1999). Annotate: A web-based knowledge management support system for document collections. *Systems Sciences, 1999. HICSS-32. Proceedings of the 32nd Annual Hawaii International Conference on.*

González, C. R., Mesanza, R. B., & Mariel, P. (2011). The determinants of international student mobility flows: An empirical study on the Erasmus programme. *Higher Education, 62*(4), 413–430. doi:10.100710734-010-9396-5

Goomaa, I., Abd-Elrahma, E., & Ksentini, A. (2019). Virtual identity performance evaluations of anonymous authentication in IDaaS framework. *IEEE Access: Practical Innovations, Open Solutions, 7*, 34541–34554. doi:10.1109/ACCESS.2019.2904854

Goran, S., Igor, C.-F., Stevan, G., Goran, S., Milan, S., & Miroslav, Z. (2017). Multilayer document model for semantic document management services. *The Journal of Documentation, 73*(5), 803–824. doi:10.1108/JD-07-2016-0095

Gordon, R. (2012). *Is U.S. Economic Growth Over? Faltering Innovation Confronts the Six Headwinds.* Available from: https://www.nber.org/papers/w18315

Guilbault, M. (2016). Students as customers in higher education: Reframing the debate. *Journal of Marketing for Higher Education, 26*(2), 13–142. doi:10.1080/08841241.2016.1245234

Güllüpınar, F., Kuzu, A., Dursun, Ö. Ö., Kurt, A. A., & Gültekin, M. (2013). Milli Eğitimde Teknoloji Kullanımı ve Sonuçları: Velilerin Bakış Açısından Fatih Projesi'nin Pilot Uygulamasının Değerlendirilmesi. *SDÜ Fen Edebiyat Fakültesi Sosyal Bilimler Dergisi*, (30), 195–216.

Gunay, A. (2021). New features of higher education competitiveness in terms of university-industry collaborations. In *University-Industry Collaboration Strategies in the Digital Era* (pp. 22–39). IGI Global. doi:10.4018/978-1-7998-3901-9.ch002

Günay, D., Asunakutlu, T., & Yildiz, O. (2021). *University-industry Collaboration Strategies in the Digital Era.* IGI Global.

Gündüz, M., Alakbarov, N., & Demirci, A. (2020). Improving the Communication Skills of International Students: Case Study of Usak University. In *Academic Language and Learning Support Services in Higher Education* (pp. 140–162). IGI Global. doi:10.4018/978-1-7998-2878-5.ch006

Gupta & Vashisht, S. (2010). A nascent study in cloud pricing. *Amity Journal of Computational Sciences, 3*(2), 28-32.

Gürbüz, R., & Güleç, İ. (2016). Türkiye'de eğitim gören yabancı öğrencilerin Türkçeye ilişkin görüşleri: Sakarya Üniversitesi örneği. *Sakarya University Journal of Education, 6*(2), 141–153. doi:10.19126uje.18712

Haaker, T., Bouwman, H., Janssen, W., & de Reuver, M. (2017). Business model stress testing: A practical approach to test the robustness of a business model. *Futures, 89*, 14–25. doi:10.1016/j.futures.2017.04.003

Habermann, C. (2020). *Study on the impact of ASIIN's programme accreditation in the field of engineering and management.* ASIIN. https://www.asiin.de/files/content/dokumente/Study_on_the_Impact_of_ASIIN_-_FA_06_Engineering_and_Management.pdf

Haliloğlu, E. Y. (2021). Efficiency Assessment of University-Industry Collaboration. In *University-Industry Collaboration Strategies in the Digital Era* (pp. 155–175). IGI Global.

Hall. (2007). Challenges to Strengthening Agricultural Innovation Systems: Where Do We Go From Here? The Commonwealth Scientific and Industrial Research Organization.

Hanover Research. (2014). *Trends in Higher Education Marketing, Recruitment and Technology.* Retrieved from http://www.hanoverresearch.com/media/Trends-in-Higher-Education-Marketing-Recruitment-and-Technology-2.pdf

Hansen, H. R., Shneyderman, Y., McNamara, G. S., & Grace, L. (2018). Assessing acculturative stress of international students at a U.S. community college. *Journal of International Students, 8*, 215–232. doi:10.32674/jis.v8i1.161

Harcleroad, F. F., & Eaton, J. S. (2005). The hidden hand: External constituencies and their impact. In Ph. G. Altbach, R. O. Berdahl, & P. J. Gumport (Eds.), *American higher education in the twenty-first century: Social, political, and economic challenges* (2nd ed., pp. 253–283). The John Hopkins University Press.

Harris, S., Owen, J., Bloor, M., & Hogg, I. (1997). Engineering document management strategy: Analysis of requirements, choice of direction and system implementation. *Proceedings of the Institution of Mechanical Engineers. Part B, Journal of Engineering Manufacture, 211*(5), 385–405. doi:10.1243/0954405971516365

Haskel, J., & Westlake, S. (2017). *Capitalism Without Capital: The Rise of the Intangible Economy*. Princeton University Press. doi:10.2307/j.ctvc77hhj

Hauptman Komotar, M. (2018a). *Internacionalizacija in zagotavljanje kakovosti v visokem šolstvu v Sloveniji in na Nizozemskem* [Internationalization and quality assurance in higher education in Slovenia and the Netherlands] [Doctoral dissertation, University of Ljubljana]. Repository of University of Ljubljana.

Hauptman Komotar, M. (2018b). The evolutionary dynamics of quality assurance systems in European higher education: The view from Slovenia. *Quality in Higher Education, 24*(3), 203–220. doi:10.1080/13538322.2018.1553274

Hauptman Komotar, M. (2019). Comprehensive internationalisation of Slovenian higher education? The rhetoric and realities. *Higher Education, 77*(5), 871–887. doi:10.100710734-018-0306-6

Hauptman Komotar, M. (2021). Global university rankings in European higher education policy and practice: Institutional and national responses from Slovenia and the Netherlands. In D. Günay, T. Asunakutlu, & O. Yildiz (Eds.), *University-industry collaboration strategies in the digital era* (pp. 62–83). IGI Global. doi:10.4018/978-1-7998-3901-9.ch004

Hearps, R. (2016). *Global trends and disruptors in international student referrals.* Retrieved from http://www.icef.com/wp-content/uploads/seminarprogramme/2016/anza__prov_ag__1450__Rod- Hearps__Global-Trends-and-Disruptors-in-International-Student-Mobility---Where-are-International-Students-Going-and-Why.pdf

Hechanova-Alampay, R., Beehr, T. A., Christiansen, N. D., & Van Horn, R. K. (2002). Adjustment and strain among domestic and international student sojourners: A longitudinal study. *School Psychology International, 23*(4), 458–474. doi:10.1177/0143034302234007

Heinicke, A., Bröhl, C., Dokas, I., Walbaum, K., Bützler, J., & Schlick, C. (2015). Development of usability-criteria for the selection process of document management systems. In J. Abascal, S. Barbosa, M. Fetter, T. Gross, P. Palanque, & M. Winckler (Eds.), *Human-Computer Interaction – INTERACT 2015* (Vol. 9299, pp. 514–517). Springer International Publishing. doi:10.1007/978-3-319-22723-8_51

Hemsley-Brown, J. V., & Oplatka, I. (2006). Universities in a competitive global marketplace: A systematic review of the literature on higher education marketing. *International Journal of Public Sector Management, 19*(4), 316–338. doi:10.1108/09513550610669176

Hénard, F., Diamond, L., & Roseveare, D. (2012). *Approaches to internationalisation and their implications for strategic management and institutional practice*. OECD.

Higher Education Council of Turkey. (2020a). https://www.yok.gov.tr/Sayfalar/Haberler/2020/coronavirus_bilgilendirme_1.aspx

Higher Education Council of Turkey. (2020b). https://yokdersleri.yok.gov.tr/

Higher Education Council of Turkey. (2021). https://www.yok.gov.tr/ogrenci/yurt-disinda-kabul-edilecek-ogrenci-kontenjanlari

Hinz & Sulser. (2019). *Agricultural Development and Land Use Change in India: A Scenario Analysis of Trade-Offs Between UN Sustainable Development Goals (SDGs).* https://agupubs.onlinelibrary.wiley.com/doi/pdf/10.1029/2019EF001287

Hofstede, G. (2001). *Cultural consequences. Comparing values, behaviors, institutions, and organizations across nations* (2nd ed.). Sage.

Holmen, A. (2015). Linguistic diversity among students in higher education: A resource in a multilingual language strategy? In A. H. Fabricius & B. Preisler (Eds.), *Transcultural interaction and linguistic diversity in higher education: The student experience* (pp. 116–141). Palgrave. doi:10.1057/9781137397478_6

Hottges, T. (2017). Foreword. In F. Abolhassan (Ed.), *The drivers of digital transformation: Why there's no way around the cloud*. Springer Nature.

Hou, A., Morse, R., Ince, M., Chen, H.-J., Chiang, C.-L., & Chan, Y. (2015). Is the Asian quality assurance system for higher education going glonacal? Assessing the impact of three types of program accreditation on Taiwanese universities. *Studies in Higher Education, 40*(1), 83–105. doi:10.1080/03075079.2013.818638

Ho, W., Xu, X., & Dey, P. K. (2010). Multi-criteria decision making approaches for supplier evaluation and selection: A literature review. *European Journal of Operational Research, 202*(1), 16–24. doi:10.1016/j.ejor.2009.05.009

Hser, M. (2005). Campus internationalization: A study of American universities' internationalization efforts. *International Education, 35*(1), 35–48.

Huang, F. (2014). The internationalisation of the academic profession. In F. Huang, M. J. Finkelstein, & M. Rostan (Eds.), *The internationalization of the academy: Changes, realities and prospects* (pp. 1–21). Springer. doi:10.1007/978-94-007-7278-6_1

Hughes, R. (2011). Strategies for managing and leading an academic staff in multiple countries. *New Directions for Higher Education, 155*(155), 19–28. doi:10.1002/he.441

Hung, N. T. (2021). Higher education in business: A model for international students' choice. *Business Process Management Journal*. Advance online publication. doi:10.1108/BPMJ-11-2020-0516

Hung, S.-Y., Tang, K.-Z., Chang, C.-M., & Ke, C.-D. (2009). User acceptance of intergovernmental services: An example of electronic document management system. *Government Information Quarterly*, *26*(2), 387–397. doi:10.1016/j.giq.2008.07.003

Hunt, S. C. (2015). Research on the value of AACSB business accreditation in selected areas: A review and synthesis. *American Journal of Business Education*, *8*(1), 23–30. doi:10.19030/ajbe.v8i1.9014

Ibrahimi, A. (2017). Cloud computing: Pricing model. *International Journal of Advanced Computer Science and Applications*, *8*(6), 434–441. doi:10.14569/IJACSA.2017.080658

ICEF Monitor. (2012). *Student safety: its impact on recruitment and study abroad choices.* Retrieved from https://monitor.icef.com/2012/11/student-safety-its-impact-on-recruitment-and-study-abroad-choices/

ICEF Monitor. (2015). *Four trends that are shaping the future of global student mobility.* Retrieved from https://monitor.icef.com/2015/09/four-trends-that-are-shaping-the-future-of-global-student-mobility/

ICEF Monitor. (2019). *International students generate global economic impact of US$300 billion.* https://monitor.icef.com/2019/08/international-students-generate-global-economic-impact-of-us300-billion/

IECD. (n.d.). *About the school.* https://www.iedc.si/about-iedc/about-the-school

Indu, I., Anand, P. M. R., & Bhaskar, V. (2018). Identity and access management in cloud environment: Mechanisms and challenges. *Engineering Science and Technology, an International Journal, 21*(4), 574-588.

Institute of International Education. (2015). *Open Doors Data.* https://www.iie.org/Who-We-Are/News-and-Events/Press-Center/Press-Releases/2015/2015-11-16-Open-Doors-Data

Institute of International Education. (2019). *Open Doors 2019: Fast facts: United States.* Institute of International Education. Retrieved from https://www.iie.org/Research-and-Publications/Open-Doors/Data/Fast-Facts

Irani, Z., Love, P. E. D., & Jones, S. (2008). Learning lessons from evaluating eGovernment: Reflective case experiences that support transformational government. *The Journal of Strategic Information Systems*, *17*(2), 155–164. doi:10.1016/j.jsis.2007.12.005

Ismael, A., & Okumus, I. (2017). Design and Implementation of an Electronic Document Management System. *Mehmet Akif Ersoy Üniversitesi Uygulamalı Bilimler Dergisi*, *1*(1), 9–17. doi:10.31200/makuubd.321093

Jackson, M., Ray, S., & Bybell, D. (2013). International students in the U. S.: Social and psychological adjustment. *Journal of International Students*, *3*(1), 17–28. doi:10.32674/jis.v3i1.515

Jacob, M., & Meek, V. L. (2013). Scientific mobility and international research networks: Trends and policy tools for promoting research excellence and capacity building. *Studies in Higher Education*, *38*(3), 331–344. doi:10.1080/03075079.2013.773789

Jagers, R. J., Rivas-Drake, D., & Williams, B. (2019). Transformative Social and Emotional Learning (SEL): Toward SEL in service of educational equity and excellence. *Educational Psychologist*, *54*(3), 162–184. doi:10.1080/00461520.2019.1623032

Jaka, N., & van den Berg, G. (2020). *Learnings from a Cloud Migration Project at a South African Retailer. African Conference on Information Systems and Technology*, Addis Ababa, Ethiopia.

Janice, J. N.-C., & Frank, L.-C. (2021). Marketing communication objectives through digital content marketing on social media. *Fórum Empresarial*, 57-82. doi:10.33801/fe.v25i1.18514

Jenkins, J. (2013). *English as a lingua franca in the international university: The politics of academic English language policy*. Routledge. doi:10.4324/9780203798157

Johansson, B., & Muhic, M. (2017). Relativism in the cloud: Cloud sourcing in virtue of IS development outsourcing - A literature review. *International Journal of Information Systems and Project Management*, *5*(4), 55–65.

Johnson, M. W., Christensen, M. C., & Kagermann, H. (2008). Reinventing your business model. *Harvard Business Review*, 59–67.

Jones, E., & Reffenrath, T. (2018, August 21). Internationalisation at home in practice. *EAIE Blog*. https://www.eaie.org/blog/internationalisation-at-home-practice.html

Jones, D., Crowley, D. M., & Greenberg, M. T. (2017). *Improving social emotional skills in childhood enhances long-term well-being and economic outcomes*. Edna Bennet Pierce Prevention Research Center, Pennsylvania State University.

Jones, E., Leask, B., Brandenburg, U., & de Wit, H. (2021). Global social responsibility and the internationalisation of higher education for society. *Journal of Studies in International Education*, *25*(4), 330–347. doi:10.1177/10283153211031679

Jones, S. (2012). eGovernment document management system: A case analysis of risk and reward. *International Journal of Information Management*, *32*(4), 396–400. doi:10.1016/j.ijinfomgt.2012.04.002

Jones, S., & Khan, J. (2017). *The evidence base for how we learn: Supporting students' social, emotional, and academic development*. Aspen Institute. Retrieved from http://nationathope.org/wp-content/uploads/final_cds-evidence-base.pdf

Jooste, C., Cullen, M., & Calitz, A. (2020). *The Factors that Influence South African Students' University of Choice Decisions*. DigiTAL 2020 online International Online Conference, Durban, South Africa.

Jooste, C. (2020). *A Strategic Model to Promote University Of Choice Decisions Among International Students Studying in South Africa*. Doctorate in Business Administration, Business School, Nelson Mandela University.

Juliandri, A. M. (2012). Positioning cloud computing in machine to machine business models. *International Conference on Cloud Computing and Social Networking (ICCCSN).*

Jyoti, B., Chandel, N., & Agrawal, K. (2020). *Application of Robotics in Agriculture: An Indian Perspective*. Academic Press.

Kaaki, F., Rayner, C., & Alshamrani, M. (2013). Female users' acceptance of the electronic document management system (EDMS). *Modelling Symposium (EMS), 2013 European.*

Kahraman, C., Cebeci, U., & Ulukan, Z. (2003). Multi-criteria supplier selection using fuzzy AHP. *Logistics Information Management*, *16*(6), 382–394. doi:10.1108/09576050310503367

Karadağ, E., & Yücel, C. (2020). Yeni tip Koronavirüs pandemisi döneminde üniversitelerde uzaktan eğitim: Lisans öğrencileri kapsamında bir değerlendirme çalışması. *Yükseköğretim Dergisi*, *10*(2), 181–192. doi:10.2399/yod.20.730688

Karikari, A., Zhu, L., & Dara, R. (2018). Blockchain: The next step in the development of The Internet of Things. 9th Annual Information Technology, *Electronics and Mobile Communication Conference (IEMCON)*, Vancouver; Canada.

Kate. (2020). *How Agriculture Affects Our Daily Life*. https://makebakegrow.com/2020/01/08/how-agriculture-affects-our-daily-lives/

Kautz, Diris, Bas ter Weel, & Borghans. (2014). Fostering and measuring skills: Improving cognitive and non-cognitive skills to promote lifetime success. Paris, France: Organization for Economic Cooperation and Development.

Kegel, K. (2009). Homesickness in international college students. In G. R. Walz, J. C. Bleuer, & R. K. Yep (Eds.), *Compelling counseling interventions: VISTAS 2009* (pp. 67–76). American Counseling Association.

Kelly, P., & Moogan, Y. (2012). Culture shock and higher education performance: Implications for teaching. *Higher Education Quarterly*, *66*(1), 24–46. doi:10.1111/j.1468-2273.2011.00505.x

Kenebayeva, A. S. (2019). Internationalization of higher education in Kazakhstan: National capacity-building initiatives. In F. Silman, F. Altinay Aksal, & Z. Altinay Gazi (Eds.), *Policies and initiatives for the internationalization of higher education* (pp. 153–174). IGI Global. doi:10.4018/978-1-5225-5231-4.ch009

Kerr, D. B., & Madden-Dent, T. (2019). Cultural Transition and Adjustment of International East Asian Undergraduate Students. In S. E. Brock & P. J. McAliney (Eds.), *Discourses on Business Education at the College Level: On the Boundaries of Content and Praxis*. Touro University Press Books. doi:10.1515/9781644691205-009

Keynes, J. M. (2010). Economic Possibilities for our Grandchildren. In *Essays in Persuasion* (pp. 321–332). Palgrave Macmillan. doi:10.1007/978-1-349-59072-8_25

Khoshlessan, R., & Das, K. P. (2019). Analyzing international students' study anxiety in higher education. *Journal of International Students*, *7*(2), 311-328.

Kim, B. S. K., & Abreu, J. M. (2001). Acculturation measurement: Theory, current instruments, and future directions. In J. G. Ponterotto, J. M. Casa, L. A. Suzuki, & C. M. Alexander (Eds.), *Handbook of multicultural counseling*. Sage.

Kim, Y. Y. (2001). *Becoming intercultural: An integrative theory of communication and cross-cultural adaptation*. Sage.

Kiplie, F. H., Yatin, S. F. M., Angutim, M., Hanani, N., & Hamid, A. (2018). System development for document management system. *International Journal of Academic Research in Business & Social Sciences*, *8*(9). Advance online publication. doi:10.6007/IJARBSS/v8-i9/4652

Kırkgöz, Y. (2009). Globalization and English language policy in Turkey. *Educational Policy*, *23*(5), 663–684. doi:10.1177/0895904808316319

Kirkpatrick, A. (2011). English as a medium of instruction in Asian education (from primary to tertiary): Implications for local languages and local scholarship. *Applied Linguistics Review*, *2*(2011), 99–120. doi:10.1515/9783110239331.99

Kıroğlu, K., Kesten, A., & Elma, C. (2010). Türkiye'de Öğrenim Gören Yabancı Uyruklu Lisans Öğrencilerinin Sosyo-Kültürel ve Ekonomik Sorunları. *Mersin Üniversitesi Eğitim Fakültesi Dergisi*, *6*(2), 26–39.

Klapp, A., Bowden, B., Belfield, C., Levin, H., Shand, R., & Zander, S. (2017). A benefit-cost analysis of a long-term intervention on social and emotional learning in compulsory school. *The International Journal of Emotional Education*, (9), 3–19.

Klischewski, R. (2003). Towards an ontology for e-document management in public administration-the case of Schleswig-Holstein. *System Sciences, 2003. Proceedings of the 36th Annual Hawaii International Conference on.*

Klischewski, R. (2006). Ontologies for e-document management in public administration. *Business Process Management Journal*, *12*(1), 34–47. doi:10.1108/14637150610643742

Kluckhohn, C. (1951). *The study of culture. The Policy Sciences*. Stanford University Press.

Knight, J. (1994). Internationalization: Elements and Checkpoints. Research Monograph No. 7. Ottawa: Canadian Bureau for International Education.

Knight, J. (2008). *Higher education in turmoil: The changing world of internationalisation*. Sense Publishers. doi:10.1163/9789087905224

Knight, J. (2013). The changing landscape of higher education internationalisation – for better or worse? *Perspectives: Policy and Practice in Higher Education, 17*(3), 84–90. doi:10.1080/13603108.2012.753957

Knowles, R. (1995). Electronic document management systems: How to select and implement the right documentation management system for your organisation. *The Electronic Library, 13*(6), 527–532. doi:10.1108/eb045423

Koenings, F., Di Meo, G., & Uebelmesser, S. (2020). University rankings as information source: Do they play a different role for domestic and international students? *Applied Economics, 52*(59), 1–16. doi:10.1080/00036846.2020.1795075

Kong, B.-Y., Hwang, B.-K., & Cho, S.-H. (2002). Design and development of XML document management system for Cyber University. *Journal of Digital Contents Society, 3*(1), 37–46.

Kostopoulos, A., Sfakianakis, E., Chochliouros, I., Pettersson, J. S., Krenn, S., Tesfay, W. M. A., & Horandner, F. (2017). Towards the adoption of secure cloud identity services. *12th International Conference on Availability, Reliability and Security, Reggio Calabria*, Italy. 10.1145/3098954.3104061

Kristjansdottir, E. S. (2003). *Invisibility dreaded and desired: Phenomenological inquiry of sojourners' cross-cultural adaptation* (Dissertation). Arizona State University, UMI Dissertations Publishing.

Krueger, M. W. a. D. (2014). Analysis of Cloud Business Models for the Industrial B2B Market. *IT Convergence Practice (INPRA), 2*(2).

Krumeich, J., Burkhart, T., Werth, D., & Loos, P. (2012). Towards a component based description of business models: A state of the art analysis. *Americas Conference on Information Systems*, Seattle, WA.

Krumeich, J., Werth, D., & Loos, P. (2013). Interdependencies between business model components – A literature analysis. *Proceedings of the Nineteenth Americas Conference on Information Systems.*

Külcü, Ö., Çakmak, T., & Özel, N. (2013). Kurumsal bilgi sistemleri içerisinde belge yönetimi: Türkiye'deki kamu üniversitelerinde gerçekleştirilen uygulamalara yönelik bir durum analizi. *Information World/Bilgi Dunyasi, 14*(2).

Lääts, K., Kask, K., Täks, V., Alexandr, T., Tomáš, L., & Kleinheyer, B. (2019). *White paper on digital transformation of universities' internationalization process.* Retrieved from https://www.chedteb.eu/ media/attachments/2019/08/25/white_paper_on_digitalisation_universities.pdf

Labella-Fernández, A., Serrano-Arcos, M. M., & Payán-Sánchez, B. (2021). Firm Growth as a Driver of Sustainable Product Innovation: Mediation and Moderation Analysis. Evidence from Manufacturing Firms. *International Journal of Environmental Research and Public Health, 18*(5), 2588. Advance online publication. doi:10.3390/ijerph18052588 PMID:33807696

Labes, S. N. H., & Zarnekow, R. (2017). Successful business model types of cloud providers. *Business & Information Systems Engineering, 59*(4), 223–233. doi:10.100712599-016-0455-z

Lakka, S., Michalakelis, C., Stamati, T., & Anagnostopoulos, D. (2015). *A framework for the classification of Could Computing business models. PCI '15: 19th Panhellenic Conference on Informatics*, Athens, Greece. 10.1145/2801948.2802028

Lanzolla, G., & Markides, C. C. (2020). A Business Model View of Strategy. *Journal of Management Studies.*

Lasagabaster, D. (2015). Language policy and language choice at European Universities: Is there really a 'choice'? *European Journal of Applied Linguistics, 3*(2), 255–276. doi:10.1515/eujal-2014-0024

Leandro, M. A. P., Nascimento, T. J., dos Santos, D. R., Westphall, C. M., & Westphal, C. B. l. (2012). Multi-tenancy authorization system with federated identity for cloud-based environments using shibboleth. *Proceedings of the Eleventh International Conference on Networks (ICN).*

Lee, J. J., & Sehoole, C. (2015). *Regional, continental, and global mobility to an emerging economy: the case of South Africa.* Retrieved from https://repository.up.ac.za/bitstream/handle/ 2263/44053/Lee_Regional_2015.pdf?sequence=1&isAllowed=y

Leong, F. T. L., & Chou, E. L. (1996). Counseling international students. In P. Pedersen (Ed.), *Counseling across cultures* (4th ed., pp. 210–242). Sage.

Leong, F. T. L., Mallinckrodt, B., & Kralj, M. M. (1990). Cross-cultural variations in stress and adjustment among Asian and Caucasian graduate students. *Journal of Multicultural Counseling and Development, 18*(1), 19–28. doi:10.1002/j.2161-1912.1990.tb00433.x

Leuven Communiqué. (2009). http://www.ehea.info/Upload/document/ministerial_declarations/Leuven_Louvain_la_Neuve_Communique_April_2009_595061.pdf

Lindström, J. (2012). Different languages, one mission? Outcomes of language policies in a multilingual university context. *International Journal of the Sociology of Language, 216*(216), 33–54. doi:10.1515/ijsl-2012-0038

Lindstrom, J., Hermanson, A., Blomstedt, F., & Kyosti, P. (2018). A multi-usable cloud service platform: A case study on improved development pace and efficiency. *Applied Sciences (Basel, Switzerland), 8*(2), 316. doi:10.3390/app8020316

Liu, X., Wei Shi, S., Teixeira, T., & Wedel, M. (2018). Video Content Marketing: The Making of Clips. *Journal of Marketing, 82*(4), 86–101. doi:10.1509/jm.16.0048

Llurda, E., Cots, J. M., & Armengol, L. (2014). Views on multilingualism and internationalisation in higher education: Administrative staff in the spotlight. *Journal of Multilingual and Multicultural Development, 35*(4), 376–391. doi:10.1080/01434632.2013.874435

López, I. D., & Corrales, J. C. (2018). A smart farming approach in automatic detection of favorable conditions for planting and crop production in the upper basin of Cauca River. *Adv. Intell. Syst. Comput., 687*, 223–233. doi:10.1007/978-3-319-70187-5_17

Losha, F., Strang, K. D., & Vajjhala, R. (2017). Assessing the risk of leveraging technology in small businesses entering the European Union. *International Journal of Risk and Contingency Management, 6*(4), 99–122. doi:10.4018/IJRCM.2017100104

Lottes, P., Khanna, R., Pfeifer, J., Siewart, R., & Stachniss, C. (2017). UAV-based crop and weed classification for smart farming. *Proceedings – IEE International Conference on Robotics and Automation*, 3024–3031. 10.1109/ICRA.2017.7989347

Lowrie, A., & Wilmott, H. (2009). Accreditation sickness in the consumption of business education: The vacuum in AACSB standard setting. *Management Learning, 40*(4), 411–420. doi:10.1177/1350507609335851

Luftman, J. (2015). Strategic alignment maturity. In J. V. Brocke & M. Rosemann (Eds.), *Handbook on business process management 2: Strategic alignment, governance, people and culture* (pp. 5–43). Springer. doi:10.1007/978-3-642-45103-4_1

Luoma, E., Ronkko, M., & Tyrvainen, P. (2012). Current software-as-a-Service Business models: Evidence from Finland. *International Conference of Software Business*, Berlin, Germany. 10.1007/978-3-642-30746-1_15

Lustig, M. W., & Koester, J. (2003). *Intercultural competence: Interpersonal communication across cultures* (4th ed.). Pearson Education, Inc.

Luu, V. (2016). *The 10 skills you'll need by 2020 (And beyond).* CareerFAQS. Retrieved from https://www.careerfaqs.com.au/news/news-and-views/the-10-skills-you-ll-need-by-2020-and-beyond

Luxon, T., & Peelo, M. (2009). Internationalisation: Its implications for curriculum design and course development in UK higher education. *Innovations in Education and Teaching International*, *46*(1), 51–60. doi:10.1080/14703290802646172

Macaro, E., Curle, S., Pun, J., An, J., & Dearden, J. (2018). A systematic review of English medium instruction in higher education. *Language Teaching*, *51*(1), 36–76. doi:10.1017/S0261444817000350

Madden-Dent, T. (2021). Advancing equity through culturally responsive social-emotional education: Addressing international student integration. In *Advances in Motivation and Achievement. Motivating the SEL Field Forward Through Equity*. Emerald Publishing Limited. Retrieved at https://www.emerald.com/insight/publication/issn/0749-7423 doi:10.1108/S0749-7423202221

Madden-Dent, T., Jackson, I., & Cason, J. (2021). Culturally-responsive social emotional academic development. In *Leading Schools with Social Emotional Academic Development (SEAD)*. IGI Global Publication. Retrieved at https://www.igi-global.com/book/leading-schools-social-emotional-academic/256645

Madden-Dent, T., Wood, D., & Roskina, K. (2019). A Survey of International Student Services at 200 U.S. Universities and Colleges. *Journal of International Students, 9*(4), 346-362. Retrieved at https://www.ojed.org/index.php/jis/article/view/346/830

Madden-Dent, T. (2014). *A phenomenological study of cultural transition and adjustment of Asian undergraduate international students using different cross-cultural treatments. ProQuest.* UMI Dissertations Publishing.

Madden-Dent, T., & Laden, R. (2016). *Pre-departure cultural preparation for international students. In Global Perspectives and Local Challenges Surrounding International Student Mobility*. IGI Global Publication.

Madisha, M., & Van Belle, J. P. (2012). Factors Influencing SaaS adoption by small South African organisations. *Conference on World Wide Web Applications*, Durban, South Africa.

Magoules, F., Pan, J., & Teng, F. (2012). *Cloud Computing data-Intensive computing and scheduling*. CRC Press.

Mahant, Shukla, Dixit, & Patel. (2012). Uses of ICT in Agriculture. *International Journal of Advanced Computer Research, 2*(3).

Maldonado, C. (2019). *Integrating workforce development practices in higher education*. Workforce Development Center, University of Nevada.

Manguic, D. M. (2012). Cloud Identity and Access Management–A model proposal. Proceedings of the *7th International Conference Accounting and management information systems AMIS*.

Mardani, A., Jusoh, A., & Zavadskas, E. K. (2015). Fuzzy multiple criteria decision-making techniques and applications–Two decades review from 1994 to 2014. *Expert Systems with Applications*, *42*(8), 4126–4148. doi:10.1016/j.eswa.2015.01.003

Marginson, S., & van der Wende, M. (2009). The new global landscape of nations and institutions. In Higher Education to 2030, Volume 2: Globalisation (pp. 17–62). OECD. doi:10.1787/9789264075375-3-en

Maringe, F. (2006). University and course choice: Implications for positioning, recruitment and marketing. *International Journal of Educational Management*, *20*(6), 466–479. doi:10.1108/09513540610683711

Mariussen, A. (2011). Rethinking Marketing Performance Measurement: Justification and Operationalisation of an Alternative Approach to Affiliate Marketing Performance Measurement in Tourism. *Ereview of Tourism Research*, *9*(3), 65–87.

Mark, C. (2018, April 30). *Why is MBA accreditation important?* https://www.businessbecause.com/news/admissions-stories/5174/why-mba-accreditation-important

Marston, S., Li, Z., Bandyopadhyay, S., Zhang, J., & Ghalsasi, A. (2011). Cloud computing— The business perspective. *Decision Support Systems*, *51*(1), 176–189.

Martirosyan, N. M., Bustamante, R. M., & Saxon, D. P. (2019). Academic and social support services for international students: Current practices. *Journal of International Students*, *9*(1), 172–191. doi:10.32674/jis.v9i1.275

Masenya, T. M. (2020). Cloud Computing as a Strategy for Preservation of Digital Resources in Academic Libraries in South Africa. In Research Anthology on Collaboration, and Resource Management for the Sustainability of Libraries. IGI Global. doi:10.4018/978-1-7998-2527-2.ch006

Maserumule, M. D. (2019). The adoption of cloud-based Software as a Service (SaaS): a descriptive and empirical study of South African SMEs [Research Report]. University of the Witwatersrand, Johannesburg, South Africa.

Masiyev, K. H., Qasymov, I., Bakhishova, V., & Bahri, M. (2012). Cloud computing for business. *6th International Conference on Application of Information and Communication Technologies (AICT)*, Tbilisi, Georgia.

Matei, L., & Iwinska, J. (2015). National strategies and practices in internationalization of higher education: Lessons from a cross-country comparison. In *Higher education reforms in Romania: Between the Bologna Process and national challenges* (pp. 205–226). Springer. doi:10.1007/978-3-319-08054-3_11

Mazrekaj, A., Shabani, I., & Sejdiu, B. (2016). Pricing schemes in cloud computing: An vverview. *International Journal of Advanced Computer Science and Applications*, *7*(2), 80–86. doi:10.14569/IJACSA.2016.070211

Mazumdar, A., & Alharahsheh, H. (2019). Insights of Trends and Developments in Cloud Computing. *South Asian Research Journal of Engineering and Technology*, *3*(1), 98–107. doi:10.36346arjet.2019.v01i03.003

Mazzarol, T., Savery, L. K., & Kemp, S. (Eds.). (1996). *International students who choose not to study in Australia: An examination of Taiwan and Indonesia*. AEIF Policy, Research and Analysis Section.

McCowan, T. (2014). *Can higher education solve Africa's job crisis: Understanding Graduate employability in Sub-Saharan Africa*. Policy Brief for British Council.

McGowan, M. A., Andrews, D., & Millot, V. (2017). *The Walking Dead: Zombie Firms and Productivity Performance in OECD Countries*. OECD Economics Department Working Papers, No. 1372.

McMullen, G. (2014). The value and attributes of an effective preparatory English program: Perceptions of Saudi university students. *English Language Teaching*, *7*(7), 131–140. doi:10.5539/elt.v7n7p131

Méda, D., & Vendramin, P. (2013). *Réinventer le Travail*. PUF. doi:10.3917/puf.meda.2013.01

Medina-López-Portillo, A. (2004). Intercultural learning assessment: The link between program duration and the development of intercultural sensitivity. *Frontiers: The Interdisciplinary Journal of Study Abroad*, *X*(1), 179–199. doi:10.36366/frontiers.v10i1.141

Mell, P., & Grance, T. (2011). *The NIST Definition of Cloud Computing*. Retrieved 10/08/2017, from https://csrc.nist.gov/publications/detail/sp/800-145/final

Mertens, Vangeyte, Van Weyenberg, Von Haselberg, Holpp, Doerfler, & Thysen. (2012). Web-Based Research Mapping and Analysis: ICT-AGRI's Meta Knowledge Base Centralizes ICT and Robotics Development in Agriculture and Related Environmental Issues. *Proceedings of the 9th International Conference on Education and Information Systems, Technologies and Applications: EISTA 2011*.

Meyer, J. W., Boli, J., Thomas, G. M., & Ramirez, F. O. (1997). World society and the nation state. *American Journal of Sociology*, *103*(1), 144–181. doi:10.1086/231174

Meyer, S., Gekeler, P., Manger, S., & Urank, D. (2013). Plurilingualism, multilingualism and internationalisation in the European Higher Education Area: Challenges and perspectives at a Swiss university. *Language Learning in Higher Education*, *2*(2), 405–425. doi:10.1515/cercles-2012-0022

Michael, L., & Maximilian, H. (2014). Introduction of electronic documents: How business process simulation can help. *Business Process Management Journal*, *20*(6), 950–970. doi:10.1108/BPMJ-05-2013-0062

Middlehurst, R. (2008). Changing Patterns of Internationalisation: Implications for Higher Education. In K. Clarke (Ed.), *Quality in Partnership: 25 Years of the Council of Validating Universities* (pp. 83–105). Open University Press.

Miemoukanda, M. (2020). *South Africa Public Cloud Market 2019 Analysis and 2020–2024 Forecast*. Retrieved 18/11/2020, from https://www.idc.com/getdoc.jsp?containerId=META46871520

Ministry of Education, Science, and Sport. (2016a). *Strategy for the internationalisation of Slovenian higher education 2016-2020*. https://eng.cmepius.si/wp-content/uploads/2015/08/Strategija-internacionalizacije-slovenskega-visokega-solstva_ENG_2016%E2%80%932020_WEB.pdf

Ministry of Education, Science, and Sport. (2016b). *Pregled stanja v slovenskem visokem šolstvu na področju internacionalizacije* [An overview of the situation in Slovenian higher education in the field of internationalization]. http://mizs.arhiv-spletisc.gov.si/si/delovna_podrocja/direktorat_za_visoko_solstvo/sektor_za_visoko_solstvo/internacionalizacija_vs/

Ministry of Education, Science, and Sport. (2017). *Action plan strategy for the internationalisation of Slovenian higher education 2016–2018: Collected objectives, measures, indicators, responsibilities with a time plan*. https://eng.cmepius.si/wp-content/uploads/2015/08/Akcijski-nacrt-2016-2018_ANG_WEB.pdf

Ministry of Education, Science, and Sport. (2019). *Akcijski načrt za obdobje do leta 2020 - Uresničevanje akcijskega načrta* [Action plan for the period until 2020 - Implementation of the action plan]. https://www.gov.si/teme/internacionalizacija-visokega-solstva/

Ministry of Education, Science, Culture, and Sport. (2012*)*. Javni razpis za vzpostavitev sistema zagotavljanja kakovosti na visokošolskih zavodih v Republiki Sloveniji v letih 2012–2015 [Call for tender for establishing a quality assurance system in higher education in the Republic of Slovenia in 2012–2015]. *Uradni list RS, 77*.

Ministry of Education, Youth, and Sports. (2020). *Strategy for the internationalisation of higher education for the period from 2021*. https://www.msmt.cz/areas-of-work/tertiary-education/strategic-plan-of-the-ministry-for-higher-education-for-the

Ministry of Higher Education, Science, and Technology. (2011). *Nacionalni program visokega šolstva 2011–2020 ter Raziskovalna in inovacijska strategija Slovenije 2011–2020* [The national higher education program 2011–2020 and the research and innovation strategy of Slovenia 2011–2020]. http://www.drznaslovenija.mvzt.gov.si/

Mitchell, C., Sehgal, S., Mathur, H., & Chopra, P. (2020). *Indian Farming's Next Big Moment*. Bain & Company, Bain Capability Centre and CIIE.

Mohiuddin. (2015). Agricultural Robotics and Its Scope in India. *International Journal of Engineering Research & Technology*, *4*(7).

Mohlameane, M., & Ruxwana, N. (2020). Exploring the impact of cloud computing on existing South African regulatory frameworks. *South African Journal of Information Management*, *22*(1), 1–9. doi:10.4102ajim.v22i1.1132

Mok, K. H., Xiong, W., Ke, G., & Cheung, J. O. W. (2021). Impact of COVID-19 pandemic on international higher education and student mobility: Student perspectives from mainland China and Hong Kong. *International Journal of Educational Research*, *105*, 101718. doi:10.1016/j.ijer.2020.101718

Mokwena, S., & Hlebela, C. (2018). Factors affecting the adoption of software as a service in South African small medium enterprises. *2018 Open Innovations Conference*, Johannesburg, South Africa. 10.1109/OI.2018.8535714

Mori, S. C. (2000). Addressing the mental health concerns of international students. *Journal of Counseling and Development, 78*(2), 137–144. doi:10.1002/j.1556-6676.2000.tb02571.x

Morris, M., Schindehutte, M., & Allen, J. (2005). The entrepreneur's business model: Towards a unified perspective. *Journal of Business Research, 58*(6), 726–735. doi:10.1016/j.jbusres.2003.11.001

Mosneaga, A., & Agergaard, J. (2012). Agents of internationalisation? Danish universities' practices for attracting international students. *Globalisation, Societies and Education, 10*(4), 519–538. doi:10.1080/14767724.2012.690309

Moulton, W. G., & Buccini, A. F. (2019). *Germanic Languages*. Retrieved from https://www.britannica.com/topic/Germanic-languages/The-emergence-of-Germanic-languages

Mvelase, P., Dlamini, Z., Macleod, D., Dlodlo, N., & Sithole, H. (2014). A business model for a South African government public cloud platform. *IST-Africa 2014 Conference Proceedings.*

Nachinaab J.O., Nelly, E., Kumah, M., & Alexander, Y. (2019). Parents' Socio-Economic Status As Determinants Of Young Adults' Educational Attainment In Ayeduase, Kumasi. *International Journal of Innovative Research and Advanced Studies, 6*(2).

NAFSA. (2013). *The economic benefits of international students to the U.S. economy for the 2012-2013 academic year: A statistical analysis.* NAFSA: Association of International Educators annual Economic Impact Statement. Retrieved from https://www.iie.org/Research-and-Publications/Open-Doors/Data/Economic-Impact-of-International-Students

NAFSA. (2018). *Economic benefits of international students.* Association of International Educators. Retrieved at https://www.nafsa.org/isev/reports/state?state=NV&year=2018

National Association of Colleges and Employers. (2019). *Career readiness for the new college graduate: A definition of competencies* (revised). Retrieved from https://www.naceweb.org/career-readiness/competencies/career-readiness-defined/

National Network of Business and Industry Associations. (2014). *Common employability skills: A foundation for success in the workplace: The skills all employees need, no matter where they work.* National Network of Business and Industry Associations. Retrieved at http://businessroundtable.org/sites/default/files/Common%20Employability_asingle_fm.pdf

Neill, J. (2008). *The expatriate venture: What role does cross-cultural training play and what theories guide research in the field?* Schmidt Labor Research Center Seminar Research Series. University of Rhode Island.

Nguyen, B. H., & Phuong, P. N. (2021). The Effect of the Covid-19 Pandemic Risk Perception On Students' behavioural Intention Towards Returning Home For Studying. *UED Journal of Social Sciences. Humanities and Education, 11*(1), 122–136. doi:10.47393/jshe.v11i1.964

Niemelä, H., Okkola, T., Nurkka, A., Kuisma, M., & Tuunila, R. (2014). Is an accreditation seal worth the effort? Observations of programme accreditations in Lappeenranta University of Technology, Finland. *Quality Assurance in Education, 22*(3), 226–239. doi:10.1108/QAE-01-2013-0007

Nijman, A. (2011). A proposal and selection of a document management system for staatsolie suriname. Delft University of Technology.

Ntshoe, I. M. (2003). The Political Economy of Access and Equitable Allocation of Resources to Higher Education. *International Journal of Educational Development, 23*(4), 381–398. doi:10.1016/S0738-0593(02)00070-6

Nunez, D., & Agudo, I. (2014). BlindIdM: A privacy preserving approach for identity management as a service. *International Journal of Information Security*, *13*(2), 199–215. doi:10.100710207-014-0230-4

Obukhov, A., Krasnyanskiy, M., & Nikolyukin, M. (2020). Algorithm of adaptation of electronic document management system based on machine learning technology. *Progress in Artificial Intelligence*, *9*(4), 287–303. doi:10.100713748-020-00214-2

OECD (2017b). *OECD Economic Outlook*. OECD Publishing. doi:10.1787/eco_outlook-v2017-2-en

OECD Publishing. https://www.oecd-ilibrary.org/docserver/9789264279179- en.pdf?expires=1632734967&id=id&accname=ocid43023557&checksum=FE8146CB4D1EF B6A1FB3CC236D85F05F

OECD. (2015a). *The Future of Productivity*. OECD Publishing. doi:10.1787/9789264248533-en

OECD. (2017a). *OECD Science, Technology, and Industry Scoreboard 2017: The Digital Transformation*. OECD Publishing. doi:10.1787/9789264268821-en

OECD. (2018). *Broadband Portal database*. Available from: www.oecd.org/sti/broadband/oecdbroadbandportal.htm

OECD. (2018). *Education at a glance 2018: OECD indicators*. OECD Publishing.

OECD. (2018). *Transformative technologies and jobs of the future. Background report for the Canadian G7 Innovation Ministers' Meeting*. https://www.oecd.org/innovation/transformative-technologies-and-jobs-of-the-future.pdf

OECD. (2019). *Education at a Glance 2019: OECD Indicators*. OECD Publishing.

OECD. (2019). *Productivity Growth in the Digital Age*. https://www.oecd.org/going- digital/productivity-growth-in-the-digital-age.pdf

OECD. (2020). *Education at a Glance 2020*. https://www.oecd-ilibrary.org/education/education-at-a-glance-2020_69096873-en

OECD. (2020). *Education at a Glance 2020: OECD Indicators*. OECD Publishing.

Önaçan, M. B. K., Medeni, T. D., & Özkanlı, Ö. (2012). Elektronik belge yönetim sistemi (EBYS)'nin faydaları ve kurum bünyesinde EBYS yapılandırmaya yönelik bir yol haritası. *Journal of Turkish Court of Accounts/Sayistay Dergisi*, (85).

Organization for Economic Co-operation and Development. (2017). International productivity monitor: CSLS-OECD special issue from the first OECD global forum on productivity.

O'Shaughnessy, N. J. (1996). Michael Porter's 'Competitive Advantage' revisited. *Management Decision*, *34*(6), 12.

Osterwalder, A. (2004). The business model ontology a proposition in a design science approach. Academic Press.

Osterwalder, A., & Pigneur, Y. (2002). *An e-Business model ontology for modelling e-Business*. 15th Bled Electronic Commerce Conference e-Reality: Constructing the e-Economy, Bled, Slovenia.

Osterwalder, A., & Pigneur, Y. (2010). *Business model generation*. John Wiley & Sons.

Osterwalder, A., Pigneur, Y., & Tucci, L. C. (2005). Clarifying business models: Origins, present, and future of the concept. *Communications of the Association for Information Systems*, *16*, 1–25. doi:10.17705/1CAIS.01601

Outlook, J. (2016). *The attributes employers want to see on new college graduates' resumes*. National Association of Colleges and Employers. Retrieved from https://www.naceweb.org/career-development/trends-and-predictions/job-outlook-2016-attributes-employers-want-to-see-on-new-college-graduates-resumes/

Özdemirci, F. (2007). Üniversitelerde belge yönetimi ve arşivler. *Türk Kütüphaneciliği, 21*(2), 218–229.

Özer, M. (2016). The internationalization of higher education in Turkey: Realities, motivations and opportunities. *Insight Turkey, 18*(4), 53–63.

Özoğlu, M., Gür, B. S., & Coşkun, İ. (2015). Factors influencing international students' choice to study in Turkey and challenges they experience in Turkey. *Research in Comparative and International Education, 10*(2), 223–237. doi:10.1177/1745499915571718

Özyürek, R. (2009). Türk Devlet ve Topluluklarından Türkiye Üniversitelerine Gelen Türk Soylu Yabancı Uyruklu Öğrencilerin Türkçe Öğrenimlerinde Karşılaştıkları Sorunlar. *Turkish Studies, 4*(3), 1819–1862.

Paramonova, I. E. (2016). Electronic document-management systems: A classification and new opportunities for a scientific technical library. *Scientific and Technical Information Processing, 43*(3), 136–143. doi:10.3103/S0147688216030047

Paris Communiqué. (2018). http://www.ehea.info/media.ehea.info/file/BFUG_Meeting/48/8/BFUG_BG_SR_61_4_FinalDraftCommunique_947488.pdf

Pateli, A. G., & Giaglis, G. M. (2004). A research framework for analysing e-business models. *European Journal of Information Systems, 13*(4), 302–314. doi:10.1057/palgrave.ejis.3000513

Pawar, S. K. (2017). International student mobility in Indian higher education. In H. Alphin Jr, R. Chan, & J. Lavine (Eds.), *The future of accessibility in international higher education* (pp. 51–68). IGI Global. doi:10.4018/978-1-5225-2560-8.ch004

Pega, F., Náfrádi, B., Momen, N. C., Ujita, Y., Streicher, K. N., Prüss-Üstün, A. M., Descatha, A., Driscoll, T., Fischer, F. M., Godderis, L., Kiiver, H. M., Li, J., Magnusson Hanson, L. L., Rugulies, R., Sørensen, K., & Woodruff, T. J. (2021). Global, regional, and national burdens of ischemic heart disease and stroke attributable to exposure to long working hours for 194 countries, 2000–2016: A systematic analysis from the WHO/ILO Joint Estimates of the Work-related Burden of Disease and Injury. *Environment International, 154*, 106595. https://doi.org/10.1016/j.envint.2021.106595

Petrovic, O., Kittl, C., & Teksen, R. D. (2001). Developing business models for ebusiness *International Conference of Electronic Commerce*, Vienna. Austria.

Phillipson, R. (2009). English in higher education: Panacea or pandemic? *ANGLES on the English-Speaking World, 9*, 29–57.

Pieter Van Oudenhoven, J., & Van der Zee, K. I. (2002). Predicting multicultural effectiveness of international students: The Multicultural Personality Questionnaire. *International Journal of Intercultural Relations, 26*(6), 679–694. doi:10.1016/S0147-1767(02)00041-X

Pilhofer, K. (2010). *Cultural knowledge: An ethical deconstruction of the concept as a foundation for respect for cultural differences from a post-colonial and Levinasian perspective*. Copenhagen Business School. Retrieved from http://studenttheses.cbs.dk/bitstream/handle/10417/1677/katharina_pilhofer.pdf?sequence=1

Pitts, M. J. (2009). Identity and the role of expectations, stress, and talk in short-term student sojourner adjustment: An application of the integrative theory of communication and cross-cultural adaptation. *International Journal of Intercultural Relations, 33*(6), 450–462. doi:10.1016/j.ijintrel.2009.07.002

Poyrazli, S., Kavanaugh, P. R., Baker, A., & Al-Timimi, N. (2004). Social support and demographic correlates of acculturative stress in international students. *Journal of College Counseling, 7*(1), 73–82. doi:10.1002/j.2161-1882.2004.tb00261.x

Public Fund. (2021). *Letno poročilo 2019* [Annual Report 2019]. https://www.srips-rs.si/storage/app/media/dokumenti/LP_in_PFN/Letno%20poro%C4%8Dilo%202019.pdf

Ratcheva, V., Leopold, T. A., & Zahidi, S. (2020). *Jobs of Tomorrow: Mapping Opportunity in the New Economy*. World Economic Forum.

Republic of Slovenia (2016). Zakon o spremembah in dopolnitvah zakona o visokem šolstvu (ZViS-K) [Act amending the higher education act (HEA-K)]. *Uradni list RS, 77.*

Republic of Slovenia. (2012). *Zakon o visokem šolstvu* [Higher education act]. Uradni list RS [Official gazette RS], no. 32/12.

Republic of Slovenia. (2016). *Zakon o spremembah in dopolnitvah Zakona o visokem šolstvu (ZViS-K)* [Act amending the higher education act (HEA-K)]. *Uradni list RS, 75*(16).

Rew, L., Becker, H., Cookston, J., Khosropour, S., & Martinez, S. (2003). Measuring cultural awareness in nursing students. *The Journal of Nursing Education, 42*(6), 248–257. doi:10.3928/0148-4834-20030601-07 PMID:12814215

Richardson, J. (2008). The business model: An integrative framework for strategy execution. *Strategic Change, 17*(5-6), 133–144. doi:10.1002/jsc.821

Risager, K. (2012). Language hierarchies at the international university. *International Journal of the Sociology of Language, 216*, 11–130.

Rome Ministerial Communiqué. (2020). https://www.eqar.eu/assets/uploads/2020/11/Rome_Ministerial_Communique.pdf

Rose, J., & Smith, K. (2020). *Embedding culturally responsive practices in Tier I. Center on PBIS.* Positive Behavioral Interventions & Supports. Retrieved at www.pbis.org

Rozsnyai, C. (2003). Quality assurance before and after 'Bologna' in the Central and Eastern region of the European higher education area with the focus on Hungary, the Czech Republic and Poland. *European Journal of Education, 38*(3), 271–284. doi:10.1111/1467-3435.00146

Rui, C. (2006). Design and implementation of document management system. *Modern Electronics Technique, 15*, 33.

Rumbley, L. E. (2019). *Digitalisation and Internationalisation.* Retrieved from https://www.eaie.org/blog/spring-forum-digitalisation.html

Rumbley, L. E., & Altbach, P. G. (2016). The local and the global in Higher Education Internationalization. In E. Jones, R. Coelen, J. Beelen, & H. De Wit (Eds.), *Global Perspectives on Higher Education: Global and Local Internationalization* (pp. 7–13). Sense Publishers. doi:10.1007/978-94-6300-301-8_2

Sahin, M. (2008). Cross-cultural experience in preservice teacher education. *Teaching and Teacher Education, 24*(7), 1777–1790. doi:10.1016/j.tate.2008.02.006

Samovar, L. A., Porter, R. E., & McDaniel, E. R. (2011). *Intercultural communication: A reader* (13th ed.). Wadsworth, Cengage Learning.

Samuel, P., Subbaiyan, S., Balusamy, B., Doraikannan, S., & Gandomi, A. H. (2021). A Technical Survey on Intelligent Optimization Grouping Algorithms for Finite State Automata in Deep Packet Inspection. *Archives of Computational Methods in Engineering, 28*(3), 1371–1396. doi:10.100711831-020-09419-z

Sanchez, J. I., Spector, P. E., & Cooper, C. L. (2000). Adapting to a boundaryless world: A developmental expatriate model. *The Academy of Management Executive, 14*(2), 96–106. doi:10.5465/ame.2000.3819309

Sánchez, J. S. (2012). Factors influencing a student's decision to pursue a communications degree in Spain. *Intangible Capital, 8*(1), 43–60.

Sánchez-Martinez, D., Marín-López, I., & Jiménez-García, T. (2008). *Electronic document management in the University of Murcia*. Academic Press.

Sandeepa & Sarala. (n.d.). Opportunities and Challenges of Agripreuership in India-Some Reviews. *Palarch's Journal of Archaeology of Egypt/Egyptology, 17*(7).

Sandhu, D., & Asrabadi, B. (1994). Development of an acculturative stress scale for international students: Preliminary findings. *Psychological Reports, 75*(1), 435–448. doi:10.2466/pr0.1994.75.1.435 PMID:7809315

Saraswathi, & Kaushik. (2018). Use Cases and Challenges in Smart Farming System on the Verge of Cloud and Internet of Things (IoT). *American Journal of Computer Science and Information Technology, 6*(3), S1.

Schaffer, N., Drieschner, C., & Krcmar, H. (2020). *An Analysis of Business Model Component Interrelations.* Twenty-Fourth Pacific Asia Conference on Information Systems, Dubai, UAE.

Schay, W. M. (2018). *Adoption of ERP software as a service by franchisees in South Africa* [Research report]. Academic Press.

School of Economics and Business UL. (n.d.). *Awards of excellence*. http://www.ef.uni-lj.si/awards_of_excellence

Schubert, M., & Counihan, B. (2017). *Universities unveil indigenous participation targets.* Retrieved from https://www.universitiesaustralia.edu.au/Media-and-Events/media-releases/Universities-unveil-indigenous-participation-targets#.W1SsBNIzbIU

Schwarz, S., & Westerheijden, D. F. (Eds.). (2004). *Accreditation and evaluation in the European higher education area.* Kluwer Academic Publishers. doi:10.1007/978-1-4020-2797-0

Selmer, J. (2001). Coping and adjustment of Western expatriate managers in Hong Kong. *Scandinavian Journal of Management, 17*(2), 167–185. doi:10.1016/S0956-5221(99)00040-8

Selten, F., Neylon, C., Huang, C.-K., & Groth, P. (2020). A longitudinal analysis of university rankings. *Quantitative Science Studies, 1*(3), 1109–1135. doi:10.1162/qss_a_00052

Şen, C. G., Baraçlı, H., & Şen, S. (2009). A literature review and classification of enterprise software selection approaches. *International Journal of Information Technology & Decision Making, 08*(02), 217–238. doi:10.1142/S0219622009003351

Seres, L., Pavlicevic, V., & Tumbas, P. (2018). *Digital transformation in Higher Education competing on analytics*. 12th International Technology, *Education and Development Conference*, Valencia, Spain.

Sewell, W. H., & Davidson, O. M. (1956). The adjustment of Scandinavian students. *The Journal of Social Issues, 12*(1), 9–19. doi:10.1111/j.1540-4560.1956.tb00351.x

Shadowen, N. L., Williamson, A. A., Guerra, N. G., Ammigan, R., & Drexler, M. L. (2019). Prevalence and correlates of depressive symptoms among international students: Implications for university support offices. *Journal of International Students, 9*, 129–148.

Shah, K. (2021). *The future of Indian agriculture lies with 'atmanirbhar' farmers*. https://www.downtoearth.org.in/blog/agriculture/the-future-of-indian-agriculture-lies-with-atmanirbhar-farmers-75228

Shah, H. (1991). Communication and cross-cultural adaptation patterns among Asian Indians. *International Journal of Intercultural Relations, 15*, 311–321.

Sharmaa, D. H., Dhoteb, C. A., & Poteyc, M. M. (2016). Identity and cacess management as security-as-a-service from Clouds. *Procedia Computer Science, 79*, 170–174. doi:10.1016/j.procs.2016.03.117

Shavit, Y., Arum, R., & Gamoran, A. (Eds.). (2007). *Stratification in Higher Education: A Comparative Study*. Stanford University Press. http://report.post2015hlp.org/digital-report-executive-summary.html

Shemshadsara, Z. G. (2012). Developing cultural awareness in foreign language teaching. *English Language Teaching*, *5*(3), 95–99.

Sheppard, P., & Smith, R. (2016). What students want: Using a choice modelling approach to estimate student demand. *Journal of Higher Education Policy and Management*, *38*(2), 140–149. doi:10.1080/1360080X.2016.1150236

Sherry, C., Bhat, R., Beaver, B., & Ling, A. (2004). Students as customer: The expectations and perceptions of local and international students. In *Transforming Knowledge into Wisdom. Proceedings of the 27th HERDSA Annual Conference*. Retrieved from https://www.herdsa.org.au/wp-content/uploads/conference/2004/papers/sherry.pdf

Shim, I., & Paprock, K. E. (2002). A study focusing on American expatriates' learning in host countries. *International Journal of Training and Development*, *6*(1), 13–24. doi:10.1111/1468-2419.00146

Shohamy, E. (2007). Reinterpreting globalisation in multilingual contexts. *International Multilingual Research Journal*, *1*(2), 127–133. doi:10.1080/19313150701495421

Şimşek, B., & Bakır, S. (2016). Uluslararası Öğrenci Hareketliliği ve Atatürk Üniversitesi'nin Uluslararasılaşma Süreci. *Atatürk Üniversitesi Türkiyat Araştırmaları Enstitüsü Dergisi*, (55), 509–542.

Singh, M. K. M. (2021). A Synergized Education 4.0 Ecosystem Sustainably Aligned With Industry 4.0. In University-Industry Collaboration Strategies in the Digital Era (pp. 283– 299). IGI Global.

Sinha, M., Healey, J., & Sengupta, T. (2020). *Designing with AI for Digital Marketing*. Paper Presented at the Adjunct Publication of the 28th ACM Conference on User Modeling, Adaptation and Personalization, Genoa, Italy. 10.1145/3386392.3397600

Skikne, C. (2019). *AACSB accredited business schools—Key advantages*. https://www.businessbecause.com/news/mba-degree/6342/aacsb-accredited-business-schools

Smith, R. A., & Khawaja, N. G. (2011). A review of the acculturation experiences of international students. *International Journal of Intercultural Relations*, *35*(6), 699–713. doi:10.1016/j.ijintrel.2011.08.004

Soderqvist, M. (2002). *Internationalisation and Its Management at Higher Education Institutions: Applying Conceptual, Content, and Discourse Analysis*. Helsinki School of Economics.

Soliman, S., Anchor, J., & Taylor, D. (2019). The international strategies of universities: Deliberate or emergent? *Studies in Higher Education*, *44*(8), 1413–1424. doi:10.1080/03075079.2018.1445985

Soni, M., Naamjoshi, J., & Pillai, S. (2017). Robustness and oppurtuneness based approach for cloud deployment model selection. *International Conference on Advances in Computing, Communications and Informatics (ICACCI)*, Mysore, India.

Sorbonne Declaration. (1998). http://ehea.info/media.ehea.info/file/1998_Sorbonne/61/2/1998_Sorbonne_Declaration_English_552612.pdf

Sorrells, A., & Cole, H. (2011). *Undergraduate College Choice Survey: Executive Report and Recommendations*. Office of the Dean of Students, DoS Research Institute, The University of Texas at Austin.

SORS. (2017). *Student enrolment in tertiary education, Slovenia, academic year 2016/2017*. https://www.stat.si/StatWeb/en/News/Index/6665

SORS. (2018). *Student enrolment in tertiary education, Slovenia, academic year 2017/2018*. https://www.stat.si/StatWeb/news/Index/7433

SORS. (2019). *Student enrolment in tertiary education, Slovenia, academic year 2018/2019*. https://www.stat.si/StatWeb/en/News/Index/8148

SORS. (2020). *Student enrolment in tertiary education, Slovenia, academic year 2019/2020*. https://www.stat.si/StatWeb/en/News/Index/8802

SORS. (2021a). *Student enrolment in tertiary education, Slovenia, academic year 2020/2021*. https://www.stat.si/StatWeb/en/News/Index/9537

SORS. (2021b). *Foreign and mobile students in tertiary education by type of education, group of countries, sex and type of mobility, Slovenia, annually*. https://pxweb.stat.si/SiStatData/pxweb/en/Data/Data/0955066S.px/

SORS. (2021c). *Population*. https://www.stat.si/StatWeb/en/Field/Index/17

Spolsky, B. (2004). *Language policy*. Cambridge University Press.

Spradley, J. P. (1980). *Participant observation*. Harcourt Brace Jovanovich College Publishers.

Sprague, R. H. Jr. (1995). Electronic document management: Challenges and opportunities for information systems managers. *Management Information Systems Quarterly*, *19*(1), 29–49. doi:10.2307/249710

SQAA. (2017). *Strateški razvoj Nacionalne agencije Republike Slovenije za kakovost v visokem šolstvu, NAKVIS, za obdobje 2017–2020* [Strategic development of the Slovenian Quality Assurance Agency for Higher Education of the Republic of Slovenia, SQAA, for the period 2017-2020]. https://www.nakvis.si/wp-content/uploads/2018/11/Strategija-agencije-2017-2020.pdf

SQAA. (2019). *Regulations*. https://www.nakvis.si/accreditations-and-evaluations/regulation-and-legislation/?lang=en

SQAA. (2021). *Public Records*. https://www.nakvis.si/accreditations-and-evaluations/public-records/?lang=en

Stähler, P. (2002). *Business models as a unit of analysis for strategizing*. Retrieved 10/05/2014, from http://www.hec.unil.ch/aosterwa/Documents/workshop/Draft_Staehler.pdf

Stier, J. (2006). Internationalisation, intercultural communication and intercultural competence. *Journal of Intercultural Communication*, *11*(1), 1–12.

Strang, K. D., Bitrus, S. N., & Vajjhala, N. R. (2019). Factors impacting farm management decision making software adoption. *International Journal of Sustainable Agricultural Management and Informatics*, *5*(1), 15–24.

Subashini, S., & Kavitha, V. (2010). A survey on security issues in service delivery models of cloud computing. *Journal of Network and Computer Applications*, *31*, 1–11.

Sullivan, C., & Kashubeck-West, S. (2015). The interplay of international students' acculturative stress, social support, and acculturation modes. *Journal of International Students*, *5*(1), 1–11. doi:10.32674/jis.v5i1.438

Sun, M. (2018). *The Impacts of the Fourth Industrial Revolution on Jobs and the Future of the Third Sector*.

Sunyaev, A. (2020). Cloud Computing. In Internet Computing. Springer.

Suresh, V., Raju, P. S. G., Sri, A. J., Nikhil, S. A. S. R., & Naresh, B. (2017). Sensor cloud to monitor cold chain logistics using Internet of Things (IoT). *International Journal of Innovative Science and Research Technology*, *2*(6).

Susanto, G., & Rahayu, E. Y. (2020). The Emotional Geography of International Students in Online Bahasa Indonesia Learning during the COVID-19 Pandemic. *Journal of International Students*, *10*(S3), 161–179. doi:10.32674/jis.v10iS3.3205

Swagler, M. A., & Ellis, M. V. (2003). Crossing the distance: Adjustment of Taiwanese graduate students in the United States. *Journal of Counseling Psychology, 50*(4), 420–437. doi:10.1037/0022-0167.50.4.420

Swain-Bradway, J., Lindstrom Johnson, S., Bradshaw, C., & McIntosh, K. (2017). *What are the economic costs of implementing SWPBIS in comparison to the benefits from reducing suspensions?* Technical Brief from Center for Positive Behavioral Interventions and Supports. https://assets-global.website-files.com/5d3725188825e071f1670246/5d76c00cb9339d5f3f267ee7_economiccostsswpbis.pdf

Takeaki, W. (2017). Capability-based cost leadership strategy of Japanese firms. *Annals of Business Administrative Science, 17*(1), 1–10. doi:10.7880/abas.0171018a

Taran, Y., Rene, C. G., & Boer, H. (2015). *Managing business model innovation risks - lessons for theory and practice.* 16th International CINet conference on Pursuing Innovation Leadership, Stockholm, Sweden.

Taylor, J. C. (2001). Fifth generation distance education. *Instrumentation Science & Technology, 4*(1), 1–14.

Teece, D. J. (2010). Business models, business strategy and innovation. *Long Range Planning, 43*(2-3), 172–194. doi:10.1016/j.lrp.2009.07.003

Teichler, U. (2009). Internationalisation of higher education: European experiences. *Asia Pacific Education Review, 10*(1), 93–106. doi:10.100712564-009-9002-7

Teichler, U. (2010). Internationalising higher education: Debates and changes in Europe. In D. Mattheou (Ed.), *Changing educational landscapes* (pp. 263–283). Springer. doi:10.1007/978-90-481-8534-4_15

Teichler, U. (2017). Internationalisation trends in higher education and the changing role of international student mobility. *Journal of International Mobility, 1*(1), 177–216. doi:10.3917/jim.005.0179

Teräs, M., Suoranta, J., Teräs, H., & Curcher, M. (2020). Post-Covid-19 education and education technology ‘solutionism’: A seller’s market. *Postdigital Science and Education, 2*(3), 863–878. doi:10.100742438-020-00164-x

Tochkov, K., Levine, L., & Sanaka, A. (2010). Variation in the prediction of cross-cultural adjustment by Asian-Indian students in the United States. *College Student Journal, 44*(3), 677–689.

Today, M. B. A. (n.d.). *The triple accredited business schools (AACSB, AMBA, EQUIS).* https://www.mba.today/guide/triple-accreditation-business-schools

Tomasz, B. (2020). Problem Solving and Innovation on the Farm- A How-To Manual. Academic Press.

Toprak, T. E. (2019). Internationalization, mobility and englishization in higher education across OECD countries. *Journal of University Research, 2*(1), 12–17.

Toprak, T. E. (2019). Internationalization, mobility and Englishization in higher education across OECD countries. *Journal of University Research, 2*(1), 12–17.

Traiandis, H. C., Brislin, R., & Hui, C. H. (1988). Cross-cultural training across the individualism-collectivism divide. *International Journal of Intercultural Relations, 12*(3), 269–289. doi:10.1016/0147-1767(88)90019-3

Training Management Corporation©. (2020). *Cultural Orientations Indicator®.* Retrieved from http://www.tmcorp.com

Trompenaars, F. (1993). *Riding the waves of culture: Understanding cultural diversity in business.* Economist Books.

Turkish National Agency. (2021). *Turkish National Agency official homepage.* https://www.ua.gov.tr/en

UIS. (2021). *Global flow of tertiary-level students.* http://uis.unesco.org/en/uis-student-flow

Ülper, H. (2020). Yabancı Öğrencilerin Türkçe Söyleyiş Akıcılıklarına İlişkin Algılarını Etkileyen Etmenler. *Başkent University Journal of Education*, *7*(2), 328–338.

Uluuysal, B., Demiral, S., Kurt, A. A., & Şahin, Y. L. (2014). Bir Öğretmenin Teknoloji Entegrasyonu Yolculuğu. *Turkish Online Journal of Qualitative Inquiry*, *5*(4).

UNESCO Institute for Statistics (UIS). (2009). *Comparing Education Statistics Across the World.* Montreal: UIS.

UNESCO Institute of Statistics. (2010). *Trends in Tertiary Education in Sub-Saharan Africa.* Fact Sheet No. 10. UNESCO.

UNESCO. (2020). *Startling digital divides in distance learning emerge.* https://en.unesco.org/news/startling-digital-divides-distance-learning-emerge

United Nations Educational, Scientific and Cultural Organization (UNESCO) Secretariat. (1998). Women in Higher Education and Research in Africa. In *UNESCO World Conference on Higher Education.* Paris: UNESCO.

University of Ljubljana. (2013). *Strategy.* https://www.uni-lj.si/university/strategy/

University of Ljubljana. (2014). *Strategy for the internationalisation of the University of Ljubljana 2014 – 2020.* https://www.uni-lj.si/study/news/strategy-internationalisation

University of Ljubljana. (2014). *Strategy for the internationalisation of the University of Ljubljana 2014– 2020.* https://www.uni-lj.si/study/news/strategy-internationalisation

University of Ljubljana. (n.d.). *International evaluations and accreditations.* https://kakovost.uni-lj.si/mednarodne-evalvacije-in-akreditacije/?lang=en

University of Maribor. (2013). *Development strategy of the University of Maribor 2013–2020: Create your future!* https://www.um.si/en/research/human_resources/Documents/Development%20Strategy%20of%20the%20University%20of%20Maribor%202013%202020.pdf

University of Maribor. (2013). *Internationalisation strategy "Internationalisation as Quality Development of the University of Maribor 2013-2020".* https://www.um.si/en/quality/re-accreditation/Documents/INTERNATIONALISATION%20STRATEGY.pdf

University of Nova Gorica. (n.d.). *International assessments and rankings of University of Nova Gorica.* http://www.ung.si/en/about/quality-assurance/international-assessments/

University of Primorska. (2020). *Internal acts of the UP.* https://www.upr.si/en/university/regulations/internal-acts-of-the-up/

*University-Industry Collaboration Strategies in the Digital Era*, 1–21.

Unterhalter, E., & Oketch, M. (2017). *Higher education has considerable potential for benefitting all segments of society. Seminar.* UCL Institute of Education.

Urgel, J. (2007). EQUIS accreditation: Value and benefits for international business schools. *Journal of Management Development*, *26*(1), 73–83. doi:10.1108/02621710710721698

Vajjhala, N. R. (2015). Constructivist Grounded Theory Applied to a Culture Study. In K. D. Strang (Ed.), *Palgrave Handbook of Research Design in Business and Management* (pp. 447–464). Palgrave Macmillan. doi:10.1057/9781137484956_23

Vajjhala, N. R., & Strang, K. D. (2014). Collaboration strategies for a transition economy: Measuring culture in Albania. *International Journal of Cross Cultural Management*, *21*(1), 78–103. doi:10.1108/CCM-02-2013-0023

Vajjhala, N. R., & Strang, K. D. (2018). Sociotechnical challenges of transition economy SMEs during EU integration. In A. M. Dima (Ed.), *Doing Business in Europe - Economic Integration Processes, Policies, and the Business Environment* (pp. 295–313). Springer. doi:10.1007/978-3-319-72239-9_14

van der Voet, E., van Oers, L., & Nikolic, I. (2004). Dematerialization: Not Just a Matter of Weight. *Journal of Industrial Ecology*, *8*(4), 121–137. doi:10.1162/1088198043630432

Van der Walt, C. (2013). *Multilingual higher education: Beyond English medium orientations*. Multilingual Matters. doi:10.21832/9781847699206

Van der Wende, M. C. (1999). Quality assurance of internationalisation and internationalisation of quality assurance. In J. Knight & H. de Wit (Eds.), *Quality and internationalisation in higher education* (pp. 225–240). IMHE/OECD.

Van Laarhoven, P., & Pedrycz, W. (1983). A fuzzy extension of Saaty's priority theory. *Fuzzy Sets and Systems*, *11*(1), 199–227. doi:10.1016/S0165-0114(83)80082-7

Vande Berg, M., Connor-Linton, J., & Paige, R. M. (2009). The Georgetown Consortium Project: Interventions for Student Learning Abroad. *Frontiers: The Interdisciplinary Journal of Study Abroad*, *18*(1), 1–75. doi:10.36366/frontiers.v18i1.251

Vaudour, F., & Heinze, A. (2020). Software as a service: Lessons from the video game industry. *Global Business and Organizational Excellence*, *39*(2), 31–40. doi:10.1002/joe.21982

Vidal, J., & Ferreira, C. (2020). Universities under Pressure: The Impact of International University Rankings. *Journal of New Approaches in Education Research*, *9*(2), 181–193. doi:10.7821/naer.2020.7.475

Vo, T. H., Fuhrmann, W., & Fischer-Hellmann, K. P. (2018). Privacy-preserving user identity in Identity-as-a-Service. *21st Conference on Innovation in Clouds, Internet and Networks and Workshops (ICIN).*

Vroeijenstijn, A. I. (1999). The international dimension in quality assessment and quality assurance. *Assessment & Evaluation in Higher Education*, *24*(2), 237–247. doi:10.1080/0260293990240211

Wächter, B. (2003). An introduction: Internationalisation at home in context. *Journal of Studies in International Education*, *7*(1), 5–11. doi:10.1177/1028315302250176

Wächter, B., & Maiworm, F. (2008). *English-taught programmes in European higher education: The picture in 2007.* Lemmens.

Wächter, B., & Maiworm, F. (2014). *English-taught programmes in European higher education: The state of play in 2014*. Lemmens.

Wang, Y. (2004). Pursuing cross-cultural graduate education: A multifaceted investigation. *International Education,* 52-75.

Wang, P. (2021). Connecting the parts with the whole: Toward an information ecology theory of digital innovation ecosystems. *Management Information Systems Quarterly*, *45*(1).

Wanot, M. (2018, June 20). Advantages of attending an EQUIS accredited business school. *EFMD Global*. https://blog.efmdglobal.org/2018/06/20/advantages-of-attending-an-equis-accredited-business-school/

Ward, C. (2001). *The impact of international students on domestic student and host institutions.* New Zealand Ministry of Education. Retrieved from https://www.educationcounts.govt.nz/publications/international/the_impact_of_international_students_on_domestic_students_and_host_institutions

Ward, C., & Kennedy, C. (1994). Acculturation strategies, psychological adjustment, and sociocultural competence during cross-cultural transitions. *International Journal of Intercultural Relations*, *18*(3), 329–343. doi:10.1016/0147-1767(94)90036-1

Weber, M. (1990). *The Protestant Ethic* (Vol. G). Allen and Unwin Ltd.

Wehling, S. (2008). Cross-cultural competency through service-learning. *Journal of Community Practice, 16*(3), 293–315. doi:10.1080/10705420802255080

Weinhardt, C., Anandasivam, W. A., Blau, B., Borissov, N., Meinl, T., Michalk, W. B., & Stober, J. (2009). Cloud Computing – A classification, business models, and research directions. *Business & Information Systems Engineering, 1*(5), 391–399. doi:10.100712599-009-0071-2

Weng, F., Cheong, F., & Cheong, C. (2010). The combined effect of self-efficacy and academic integration on higher education students studying IT majors in Taiwan. *Education and Information Technologies, 15*(4), 333–353. doi:10.100710639-009-9115-y

Wertenbroch, K. (2021). Marketing Automation: Marketing Utopia or Marketing Dystopia? *NIM Marketing Intelligence Review, 13*(1), 18–23. doi:10.2478/nimmir-2021-0003

Wiese, M., Jordaan, Y., & Van Heerden, C. H. (2010). Differences in the usefulness of communication channels, as experienced by gender and ethnic groups during their university selection process. *Communicatio, 36*(1), 112–129. doi:10.1080/02500160903525064

Wilkins, S., & Huisman, J. (2015). Factors affecting university image formation among prospective higher education students: The case of international branch campuses. *Studies in Higher Education, 40*(7), 1256–1272. doi:10.1080/03075079.2014.881347

Windisch, L., Schwinn, A., & Faix, W. G. (2021). Leadership. Personality. Education: The Innovation-Promoting Triad in University-Industry Collaboration–Real-World Projects Foster Students' Innovative Capability. *University-Industry Collaboration Strategies in the Digital Era*, 337–365.

Wiranota, H., & Wijaya, T. T. (2021, March). The international students' perception towards online learning using the tencent meeting during covid-19 outbreak. Journal of Physics: Conference Series. doi:10.1088/1742-6596/1823/1/012011

Wohl, A. F. (2012). *Citizenship and social activism: A mixed method case study to understand cultural competence in students of a service-learning based course* (Thesis). North Dakota State University.

Wong, C. K., & Blissett, S. (2007). Assessing performance in the area of cultural competence: An analysis of reflective writing. *Journal, Physical Therapy Education, 21*(1), 40–47. doi:10.1097/00001416-200701000-00006

Working Group on Mobility. (2012). *Mobility for better learning: Mobility strategy 2020 for the European Higher Education Area (EHEA).* https://www.ehea.info/cid101043/ministerial-conference-bucharest-2012.html

World Bank. (2014). *Africa's Pulse: An analysis of issues shaping Africa's economic future.* https://data.worldbank.org/indicator/NY.GDP.MKTP.KD.ZG?order=wbapi_data_value_2012+wbapi_data_value+wbapi_data_value-last&sort=desc

World Bank. (2014). *Youth employment in Sub-Saharan Africa: Africa Development Forum.* World Bank.

World Economic Form. (2021). *2030Vision—Partnering together to scale technologies for the global goals.* 2030Vision. https://www.weforum.org/projects/frontier-2030

World Economic Forum. (2020a). *Forecasts for Labour Market Evolution in 2020-2025* (The Future of Jobs Report 2020). World Economic Forum Geneva. http://www3.weforum.org/docs/WEF_Future_of_Jobs_2020.pdf

World Economic Forum. (2020b). *The Future of Jobs Report 2020.* World Economic Forum Geneva. http://www3.weforum.org/docs/WEF_Future_of_Jobs_2020.pdf

Xiang, Y., Rieger, S., & Richter, H. (2010). *Introducing a dynamic federation model for RESTful cloud storage.* First International Conference on Cloud Computing, GRIDs, and Virtualization, Lisbon, Portugal.

Xiao, X., Sarker, S., Wright, R. T., Sarker, S., & Mariadoss, B. J. (2020). Commitment and replacement of existing SaaS delivered applications: A mixed method investigation. *MIS Quarterly, 44*(4), 1811-1857.

Xiao, X., & Hedman, J. (2019). How a software vendor weathered the stormy journey to the cloud. *MIS Quarterly Executive, 18*(1), 37–50. doi:10.17705/2msqe.00007

Yabanova, U., & Özerbas, D. H. (2020). International Student Selection Process in Turkey: Characteristics, Challenges and Opportunities. *International Journal of Progressive Education, 16*(2), 137–156. doi:10.29329/ijpe.2020.241.10

Yager, R. R. (1978). Fuzzy decision making including unequal objectives. *Fuzzy Sets and Systems, 1*(2), 87–95. doi:10.1016/0165-0114(78)90010-6

Yaldır, A., & Özgür Polat, L. (2016). Çok Kriterli Karar Verme Teknikleri İle Elektronik Belge Yönetim Sistemi Seçimi-Electronic Document Management System Selection With Multi-Criteria Decision Making Techniques. *Mehmet Akif Ersoy Üniversitesi Sosyal Bilimler Enstitüsü Dergisi, 8*(14), 88–108. doi:10.20875b.56729

Yeh, C. J., & Inose, M. (2003). International students' reported English fluency, social support satisfaction, and social connectedness as predictors of acculturative stress. *Counselling Psychology Quarterly, 16*(1), 15–28. doi:10.1080/0951507031000114058

Yelapure, S. J. (2012). Literature Review on Expert System in Agriculture. *International Journal of Computer Science and Information Technologies, 3*(5), 5086–5089.

Yemini, M. (2015). Internationalisation discourse hits the tipping point: A new definition is needed. *Perspectives: Policy and Practice in Higher Education, 19*(1), 19–22.

Yeravdekar, V. R., & Tiwari, G. (2014). Internationalization of Higher Education and its Impact on Enhancing Corporate Competitiveness and Comparative Skill Formation. *Procedia: Social and Behavioral Sciences, 157*, 203–209. doi:10.1016/j.sbspro.2014.11.023

Yildiz, O. (2021). Changing Paradigms in the Digital Age and Entrepreneurial Universities. *University-Industry Collaboration Strategies in the Digital Era*, 1-21. https://www.researchgate.net/publication/348767321_Changing_Paradigms_in_the_Digital_Age_and_Entrepreneurial_Universities/citations

Yildiz, O. (2021a). Changing Paradigms in the Digital Age and Entrepreneurial Universities.

Yildiz, O. (2021b). *Recent Developments in Individual and Organizational Adoption of ICTs.* IGI Global. http://doi:10.4018/978-1-7998-3045-0

Yildiz, O. (2021). Changing Paradigms in the Digital Age and Entrepreneurial Universities. In G. Durmuş, A. Tuncer, & Y. Orkun (Eds.), *University-Industry Collaboration Strategies in the Digital Era* (pp. 1–21). IGI Global. doi:10.4018/978-1-7998-3901-9.ch001

Yildiz, O., Ersoy, A. S., & Yıldırım, İ. S. (2021). The Impact of Information and Communication Systems on Organizations. In *Recent Developments in Individual and Organizational Adoption of ICTs* (pp. 1–25). IGI Global.

Ying, Y., & Liese, L. H. (1990). Initial adaptation of Taiwan foreign students to the United States: The impact of prearrival variables. *American Journal of Community Psychology, 18*(6), 825–845. doi:10.1007/BF00938066

Ying, Y., & Liese, L. H. (1991). Emotional well-being of Taiwan students in the U.S: An examination of pre-to post-arrival differential. *International Journal of Intercultural Relations, 15*(3), 345–366. doi:10.1016/0147-1767(91)90007-4

Ying, Y., & Liese, L. H. (1994). Initial adjustment of Taiwanese students to the United States: The impact of post arrival variables. *Journal of Cross-Cultural Psychology*, *25*(4), 466–477. doi:10.1177/0022022194254003

Yoder, N., Atwell, M. N., Godek, D., Dusenbury, L., Bridgeland, J. M., & Weissberg, R. (2020). *Preparing youth for the workforce of tomorrow: Cultivating the social and emotional skills employers demand*. CASEL Publication. Retrieved at https://casel.org/collaborative-state-initiative/

YongvongphaiboonP.ChantamasM. (2021). Influence of digital marketing communication and performance effectiveness between b2b companies and clients in Thailand. *Influencia de comunicacion del marketing digital y la eficacia del rendimiento entre empresas b2b y clientes en Tailandia, 26*, 171-182. doi:10.5281/zenodo.4678872

Yoon, E., Lee, R. M., & Goh, M. (2008). Acculturation, social connectedness, and subjective wellbeing. *Cultural Diversity & Ethnic Minority Psychology*, *14*(3), 246–255. doi:10.1037/1099-9809.14.3.246 PMID:18624589

Yorgancı, S. (2015). Web Tabanlı Uzaktan Eğitim Yönteminin Öğrencilerin Matematik Başarılarına Etkileri. *Kastamonu Eğitim Dergisi*, *23*(3), 1401–1420.

Zahay, D. (2021). Advancing research in digital and social media marketing. *Journal of Marketing Theory and Practice*, *29*(1), 125–139. doi:10.1080/10696679.2021.1882865

Zahidi, S. (2020). *The Jobs of Tomorrow*. International Monetary Fund. https://www.imf.org/external/pubs/ft/fandd/2020/12/WEF-future-of-jobs-report-2020- zahidi.htm

Zantout, H., & Marir, F. (1999). Document management systems from current capabilities towards intelligent information retrieval: An overview. *International Journal of Information Management*, *19*(6), 471–484. doi:10.1016/S0268-4012(99)00043-2

Zhang, Q., He, Y. J., Zhu, Y. H., Pan, M. M., Wu, J. Q., Zhang, X., ... Qu, F. (2020). The evaluation of online course of Traditional Chinese Medicine for Medical Bachelor, Bachelor of Surgery international students during the COVID-19 epidemic period. *Integrative Medicine Research*, *9*(3), 14–14. doi:10.1016/j.imr.2020.100449 PMID:32632357

Zhang, Z., & Kenny, R. (2010). Learning in an online distance education course: Experiences of three international students. *The International Review of Research in Open and Distributed Learning*, *11*(1), 17–36. doi:10.19173/irrodl.v11i1.775

Zhou, Y., Frey, C., & Bang, H. (2011). Understanding of international graduate students' academic adaptation to a U.S. graduate school. *International Education*, *41*(1), 76–94.

Zhu, Y. (2008). From cultural adaptation to cross-cultural discursive competence. *Discourse & Communication*, *2*(2), 185–204. doi:10.1177/1750481307088483

# About the Contributors

**Orkun Yildiz** earned his Postdoctorate Degree in technology management from the Hamburg University of Technology in Germany, his PhD in business sciences (major MIS) from Gazi University, his Master's in business administration from Suleyman Demirel University, and his Bachelor's degree from business administration from Suleyman Demirel University in Turkey. He is interested in academic topics such as business models, digital transformation, human-computer interaction, innovation, and technology management. He has been on the editorial board of various academic journals in the field of management information systems (MIS). These journals are Organizational and End-user Computing (SSCI), Journal of Global Information Systems (SSCI), The Service Industries Journal (SSCI), Neural Computing and Applications Journal (SSCI-E), Australasian Journal of Information Systems (ESCI), Journal of Hospitality and Technology (ESCI), International Journal of e-business (ESCI), International Journal of e-adoption (Scopus), International Journal of Innovation and Technology (Scopus), Theoretical Economics Letters (EconLit), and Journal of Management & Production. Additionally, he has served as a referee on the conferences such as the European Conference of Information Systems (ECIS) 2018 (Portsmouth, UK). Currently, he works as an assistant professor in the MIS department at Izmir Democracy University (Turkey), where he teaches MIS related courses and conducts research.

* * *

**Andre P. Calitz** is a Distinguished Professor in the Department of Computing Sciences at the Nelson Mandela University (NMU) and is a Research Supervisor in the NMU Business School. He has two doctorates, a PhD in Computer Science and a Doctorate in Business Administration (DBA). He is a rated NRF researcher and has published extensively in international journals and conferences. He received the 2016 and 2018 NMU Research Excellence Award. He is a Fellow of the Institute of IT Professionals of South Africa and President of the Southern African Computer Lecturer's Association.

**Roy Alexander Carr-Hill** has taught in Sussex University (1971-74), Universidade Eduardo Mondlane, Mozambique (1978-81) and the Institute of Education (1993-onging); worked on social indicators at the OECD Paris (1974-77); and since 1981 has been a researcher at the MRC Medical Sociology Unit Aberdeen (1981-84); Centre for Health Economics (1984-2011), School of Political and Social Sciences, Hull (1990-93). He has worked in 35 developing countries as a consultant for several of the bilateral and multilateral agencies on a wide variety of evaluation and review consultancies, spanning, education, health and justice. He is currently 20% at IoE and researches on accountability, adult literacy, rationality of drop-out, exploitation of women teachers, interplay between education and extremism; and is currently writing book on understanding social data.

**Margaret D. Cullen** is a Professor at the Nelson Mandela University Business School in Port Elizabeth, South Africa. She heads up the Strategic Focus Area of Entrepreneurship, Design Thinking, and Innovation. She has authored and co-authored several research articles, book chapters and presented at numerous international academic conferences. She consults in the areas of happiness, experiential marketing, strategy, family business and entrepreneurship. Professor Cullen is currently focusing on research in Happiness.

**Edna Mngusughun Denga** is a graduate student at the American University of Nigeria.

**Ömer Güleç** received the B.Sc. degree in Electrical and Electronics Engineering, M.Sc. degree in Computer Engineering and Ph.D. degree in Electrical and Electronics Engineering from Pamukkale University, Denizli, Turkey. Currently he is an Assistant Professor with the Department of Management Information Systems, Pamukkale University. His research interests include algorithms, wireless sensor networks, Internet of things (IoT) and distributed systems.

**Carlien Jooste** obtained her Doctorate in Business Administration from the Nelson Mandela University Business School, South Africa in 2020. She has co-authored several research articles, book chapters and presented papers at international conferences on topics relating to student's university choice decisions, student recruitment and internationalisation of higher education. Presently she is the manager of the Nelson Mandela University Graduate School of Business' Relationship and Admissions Office.

**Sunil Hanmant Khilari** is a Mentor for MCA students for creating learning environments for the subjects, 'Data Science", "Information Security and Audit and Software Testing and Quality Assurance". Sharing and transferring his industry and academic experience for the betterment of student community. Published patent on "Green Calc-Com" in the Government of India –IPR Gazette. And two copyrights and one trademark granted. Constantly focusing to implement IT good Practices as per ITIL for the bridging the gap between Academic and Industry.

**Maruša Hauptman Komotar** is a postdoctoral researcher at the Institute for Social Sciences Research at Alma Mater Europaea - Faculty of Humanities, Institutum Studiorum Humanitatis, Ljubljana, Slovenia. In 2018, she completed her doctoral studies in Education Sciences at the University of Ljubljana, Faculty of Education, and in 2020, she received a recognition award for best doctoral dissertation in the field of education research from the Educational Research Institute and the Slovenian Educational Research Association. Her research interests focus on comparative higher education policy analysis in the European Higher Education Area in terms of quality assurance, internationalisation and globalisation of higher education, as well as on their impact on the formation of academic cultures in (Slovenian) higher education. She has written book chapters and published articles in major journals in the field, including Higher Education, European Educational Research Journal, European Journal of Higher Education, European Journal of Education, Quality in Higher Education, and Quality Assurance in Education. For more information, see Maruša's ORCID, Publons and LinkedIn page.

**Tara Madden-Dent** is a Culturally Responsive Social, Emotional, and Academic Development (SEAD) Specialist. She previously taught at the University of Nevada, Reno while finishing her Ph.D. in Educational Leadership and researching evidence-based practices to strengthen cultural and social-emotional competencies in youth and adults. Afterwards, Dr. Madden-Dent taught and conducted research in China, Japan, Poland, and South Korea before guiding the development of a Global Programs Department at Sierra Nevada University. Later, as a SEAD Specialist, consulting for the Nevada Department of Education, Dr. Madden-Dent helped develop its first SEAD Endorsement for Teacher Licensure, and the nation's first-ever SEAD Center, an interactive virtual support system and professional learning platform for educators. Her most current course offerings, training and consulting menu, and publications for researchers, faculty, and practitioners can be found at https://taramaddendentphd.academia.edu/.

**Ignitia Motjolopane** is a Senior lecturer with over 20 years work experience in research, information systems development and management. She offers experience in innovation management, lecturing and supporting postgraduate research supervision. She has published peer reviewed papers in business-IT alignment, e-commerce, Massive online courses (Moocs), e-learning, knowledge sharing. Her current research focuses on business model innovation.

**Archana Nandanan Nair** has 10 years of experience as a university approved faculty at post-graduation level.

**Leyla Özgür Polat** is a Lecturer in IT Department of Pamukkale University, Turkey. She holds an MSc degree in Industrial Engineering and a PhD degree in the Department of Industrial Engineering at Pamukkale University. Her research interests include decision making techniques, green supply chain management, mathematical modelling, optimization, and information systems.

**Sandip Rakshit** is an academician of versatile talents, involved in the education field with a teaching, consulting and research experience of more than 20 years. Prof. Rakshit has delivered more than 50 keynote addresses, invited seminars, and media briefings in Various IEEE, ACM, AIS, ISACA, Springer, Elsevier, Emeralds Conferences and has been actively involved in organizing more than 50 national and international conferences in various capacities. He has also conducted more than 50 MDP for Top Corporates and ARMY Officers in India and other Countries. Dr. Rakshit also served as IEEE GOLD (Kolkata Section) Chairman for 2012 & 2013 two consecutive years and Current Vice chair ACM Yola Professional Chapter.

**Gamze Sart** earned her PhD in education sciences from Boğaziçi University and in anthropology from Istanbul University, Istanbul, USA. Her Master Science in adult education from Boğaziçi University and master's degree in applied clinical psychology from Istanbul Commerce University – Istanbul, Turkey. Also, her bachelor's in political science and international relations from Boğaziçi University in Istanbul, Turkey. She is an assoc. professor in guidance and psychological counseling, education sciences. Her research interest covers areas like digitalization, higher education policies, organizational psychology. Published many articles in journals and conferences and authored books in her research interests. Assoc. Prof. Dr. Sart worked as a mentor of TUBITAK, Other Public Institution, TUBITAK, University Industry Cooperation Unit Presidency, E-co Consulting, as a board member of Commercial Institution Private, and Aba Academic Scientific Research Organization Education Consultancy Corp.

**Tshinakaho Relebogile Seaba** is acquired his Doctor of Computing in Informatics qualification with the Tshwane University of Technology in 2019. He has 13 years of experience in both IT Practice and research during which he produced peer reviewed research outputs. His research interests include Business Analytics, ICT for Development as well as alignment of Business and IT.

**Chandrani Singh** has Currently working as Director-MCA and Placement Head – MCA (SMI) at Sinhgad Institute of Management Vadgaon, Pune. Co-Founder Director of iTeknika Services and Solutions Pvt Ltd, Pune. Have strong Industry Liaison and HR Connect with around 250 + HRs across India and have placed around 5000 MCA and Engineering students mainly from the state of Maharashtra in MNC's and SME's in last five years. Have been instrumental in human resource provisioning (fresh graduates and postgraduates) to the IT and Manufacturing Industries and also supported them by providing software as a service to the recruitment vertical of the IT and Manufacturing Industries (Companies like Saama Technologies, Raja Softare, LiveHealth, SmarterHi, Arxxus, Exadatum, Universal Tools, SSM Infotech etc. The software has been used by thirty companies and institutions till date. Have been instrumental in liasioning with Barclays, Tata Consultancy Services, Persistent Systems Pvt Ltd, Cognizant Technology Solutions in providing the students an exposure into the industry best practices and Organizational work culture. Have been instrumental in creating an alliance with Quickheal Technologies to impart cyber security awareness to school students of Pune and suburban areas of Maharashtra. Have played a strategic role in Tata Consultancy Services-Sinhgad Institute digital assessment alliance.

**Narasimha Rao Vajjhala** is the Chair of the Department of Telecommunication and Network Engineering at the Faculty of Engineering and Architecture at the University of New York Tirana, Albania. He is a senior member of ACM and IEEE. He has over 18 years of experience in teaching mainly programming and database-related courses at both graduate and undergraduate levels in Europe and Africa. He has also worked as a consultant in technology firms in Europe and has experience participating in an EU-funded project. He has supervised several undergraduate senior design projects and graduate theses. He has completed a Doctorate in Information Systems and Technology (United States); holds a Master of Science in Computer Science and Applications (India), and a Master of Business Administration with a specialization in Information Systems (Switzerland), and an undergraduate degree in Computer Science (India). He has several professional certifications, including Project Management Professional (PMP), Certified Ethical Hacker (CEH), Microsoft Certified Solution Developer (MCSD) among others.

**Tugba Elif Toprak Yildiz** is an assistant professor at Faculty of Science and Letters, Izmir Democracy University, Turkey. Dr. Tugba Elif Toprak-Yildiz is interested in exploring the possible relationships between language policies, multilingualism, and English-medium instruction with the internationalisation processes of European higher education institutions.

# Index

www.ingramcontent.com/pod-product-compliance
Lightning Source LLC
LaVergne TN
LVHW062140300926
849161LV00010B/2585
* 9 7 8 1 7 9 9 8 8 1 6 9 8 *